A DREA
RED MA

A DREAM OF RED MANSIONS

Volume I

TSAO HSUEH–CHIN
and KAO HGO

FOREIGN   LANGUAGES   PRESS   BEIJING

First Edition 1978
Third Printing 1995

Translated by
YANG HSIEN-YI and GLADYS YANG

Illustrated by
TAI TUN-PANG

ISBN 7-119-01643-1
© Foreign Languages Press, Beijing, 1978

Published by Foreign Languages Press
24 Baiwanzhuang Road, Beijing 100037, China

Distributed by China International Book Trading Corporation
35 Chegongzhuang Xilu, Beijing 100044, China
P.O. Box 399, Beijing, China

Printed in the People's Republic of China

Publisher's Note

A Dream of Red Mansions (*Hung Lou Meng*, sometimes translated as *The Dream of the Red Chamber*), the great classical Chinese novel written in the mid-eighteenth century during the reign of Emperor Chien-lung of the Ching Dynasty, has been widely popular throughout the last two hundred years and more.

It was no accident that such a work should appear during the Chien-lung era (1736-95). It was the product of class contradictions and class struggles in that period of Chinese feudalism.

The Ching Dynasty (1644-1911) was the last feudal dynasty in China. Although it saw a period of relative stability, feudal society was already on the decline and all the contradictions inherent in it were sharpening.

The entire state apparatus of this dynasty in the main took over the form of the feudal autocracy of the Ming Dynasty (1368-1644), the political power remaining in the hands of the feudal landlord class. In that sense it was a continuation and development of the feudal political power of the Ming autocracy.

At the start of the Ching Dynasty, the social economy was gravely disrupted by years of warfare; but from the eighteenth century onwards the measures taken by the ruling class to restore production led to a certain rehabilitation and development. By the last decades of the reign of Emperor Kang-hsi (1662-1722) agriculture had not only recovered but was fairly thriving, while the last years of his reign and the reigns of Yung-cheng (1723-35) and Chien-lung witnessed fresh progress not only in agriculture but also in mining, the textile industry, ceramics, printing and other fields, the textile industry actually surpassing the heights it had reached in the sixteenth century. During this period commerce and foreign trade expanded too and the embryos of capitalism, based on trade and handicrafts, recovered from the restrictions imposed on them in the first days of the dynasty.

The Kang-hsi, Yung-cheng and Chien-lung eras were described by the feudal ruling class and its official historians as a "Golden Age," but the development of the economy failed to improve the life of the labouring people. The Ching rulers extorted untold wealth from them and squandered it on luxuries; but while nobles, big landowners, rich merchants and local gentry battened on their blood, the toilers themselves lived in wretched misery. Peasants who had owned land in the early Ching period were gradually deprived of it by nobles and big landlords so that they became utterly destitute. The political oppression and economic exploitation of the peasants by the Ching ruling class further aggravated the principal contradiction in feudal society — that between the landlord class and the peasantry — with the result that the latter fought back to resist taxation and win land to till.

Early in the Ching Dynasty there appeared some progressive thinkers with rudimentary ideas of democracy, which represented a progressive trend. This proved so influential that the rulers resorted to savage suppressive measures. From the start of the dynasty and all through the Kang-hsi, Yung-cheng and Chien-lung eras, the authorities carried out a literary inquisition, persecuting and executing feudal intellectuals with progressive ideas; at the same time, on the pretext of compiling an Imperial Library they screened and censored earlier works which opposed feudal rule, and continued the Ming examination system in an attempt to deceive and befuddle the people. Although all these policies failed to wipe out progressive ideas and crush the people's resistance, they had an adverse effect on the newly emerging democratic ideas.

Furthermore, within the ruling class itself contradictions and struggles over the redistribution of wealth and power between different political forces and factions were growing ever more acute. Thus the Chien-lung era was the turning point towards the decline of the Ching Dynasty. Crisis-riven feudalism was already on its last legs. The whole fabric of Chinese feudal society was tottering on the verge of final collapse.

This was the period in which Tsao Hsueh-chin the author of *A Dream of Red Mansions* lived.

Tsao Hsueh-chin's family were Hans, but they had later become Manchu bannermen. One of his ancestors came south of the Great Wall with the Ching rulers. Subsequently his great-grandfather, grandfather, father and uncle all held one of the posts administering the affairs of the imperial household — Textile Commissioner of Chiangning Prefecture (present-day Nanking and six contiguous counties including Liuho, Kaochun, Chiangpu and others); and his great-grandmother nursed Emperor Kang-hsi. Later, her son, Hsueh-chin's grandfather, accompanied the emperor in his studies. This shows the Tsao family's relationship with the Ching imperial house in general, and with Emperor Kang-hsi in particular.

Towards the end of the reign of Kang-hsi and the beginning of that of Yung-cheng, however, a fierce struggle for the claim to the throne within the ruling class led to a conflict among members of the imperial house. In the fifth year of Yung-cheng (1727) the Tsao family, so favoured by the previous emperor, were charged with the crime of embezzling public funds, their estates were confiscated and they fell into disgrace. After this they moved from the south to Peking; later Tsao Hsueh-chin lived in the western suburb of the city. He was then so poor that his family sometimes had nothing more substantial to eat than porridge. It was in these poverty-stricken circumstances that he started writing his novel. Then the death of his beloved son overwhelmed him with sorrow and he fell ill. Unable to afford good medical treatment, he died in the twenty-eighth year of Chien-lung (1763) without having finished his novel.

The various contradictions in moribund feudal society and the calamities befalling his own family due to struggles within the ruling class opened Tsao Hsueh-chin's eyes to many significant social phenomena which he described most vividly in his book.

A Dream of Red Mansions is a book about political struggle, a political-historical novel. The cruel penalties for
"subversive" writing forced the author to express his ideas in
a veiled, indirect manner. Thus at the start of the book he
says that he "tried to hide the true facts of his experience" by
writing "fiction in rustic language." In other words, he could
not openly present the true facts of the contemporary political
struggle. But although he claimed that his book "did not touch
at all on current events" and that on the contrary "the main
theme was love," this great realist writer in fact mounted a
bitter attack on the evils of real politics. On the surface this
novel deals largely with the love between Pao-yu and Tai-yu;
but actually, through this story as well as many other episodes
in the book, the author penetratingly exposes the evils of the
feudal system and the crimes of the feudal ruling class. It
also describes the sufferings and revolt of the labouring masses,
truthfully reflecting the social contradictions in the last period
of feudalism as well as the actual political struggles of the
time.

Chapter Four gives us the main outline of the novel. In
this chapter the author draws back the curtains of the stage on
class struggle. The "officials' protective charm" mentioned
in this chapter lists the four notable families of Chinling
(present-day Nanking), the rich and powerful Chias, Shihs,
Wangs and Hsuehs.

As Chairman Mao has pointed out: **"The patriarchal-
feudal class of local tyrants, evil gentry and lawless landlords has formed the basis of autocratic government for
thousands of years."**[1] In feudal society the "notable families,"
the cells of the patriarchal-feudal system, were the main props
of its autocratic rule. The emperor was the highest represent-
ative of their interests while the various grades of local government were the instruments to enforce their control. The
four great houses of Chia, Shih, Wang and Hsueh described

---

[1] Mao Tsetung, "Report on an Investigation of the Peasant Movement
in Hunan," *Selected Works*, Foreign Languages Press, Peking, 1967, Vol.
I, p. 27.

in this novel were typical basic political units of feudal society. Such families were linked with the court above and the local officials below to form a network of control with the feudal autocratic state power as its centre. The reactionary rule of these four big families epitomizes the dark rule of feudal society as a whole, just as their decline reflects the inevitable doom of the entire feudal system.

This novel describes the savage political oppression of the labouring masses by these four great families. Outside the Chia mansions, they use their powerful connections to influence local officials to hound people to death. As for the Chia mansions themselves, they are permeated with the darkness and cruelty of feudal rule; many bondmaids no better off than slaves are one by one trampled underfoot and done to death. These magnificent houses described as "a place where flowers and willows flourish, the home of pleasure and luxury," are nothing but a slaughter-house.

This novel also describes the ruthless economic exploitation of the labouring masses by these great families of high officials, big landlords, rich imperial purveyors and big usurers. They build up their fortunes by robbing other people and annexing their property; then by means of exorbitant land rent, high interest and their connection with local officials they insatiably suck the blood of the poor. Their splendid mansions, glittering wealth and wanton luxury are all built on the bleached bones of the working people.

The book also depicts the inevitable doom of these families, riven as they are by fierce struggles among themselves and in society. Outside their walls, drought, flood and crop failure drive the famished peasants to seize land by armed revolt; so their rule is tottering. Within their walls, their own slaves rebel against them, giving their masters and mistresses no rest. The ruling class itself is split into contending factions, the appearance of such rebels as Pao-yu and Tai-yu revealing the violent hammering at feudal orthodoxy by early democratic thinking which reflects the growth of the seeds of capitalism.

All this exposes the corrupt and reactionary nature of the superstructure in the last period of Chinese feudal society.

Chapter Four of this book not only sums up the main content but also the artistic composition. The author has constructed the plot according to the requirements of the theme expressing political struggle. The prosperity and decline of the four big families, especially the Chias, form the main thread running through the whole novel. Around this unfold three sets of closely interconnected contradictions: those between the feudal ruling class and the ruled, those between feudal orthodoxy and the rebels, and those within the ruling class itself. The complex development of these three sets of contradictions throughout the story results finally in the utter bankruptcy of the Chia family. Thus the whole vast, complex artistic structure of the novel is most carefully integrated, fully projecting the theme of political struggle.

The novel not only has a profound ideological content and progressive political tendency, but an art form so brilliantly integrated with these that readers are fascinated and moved by it. With superb artistry the author presents a panoramic genre-painting, a whole gallery of highly individual yet typical characters. Through detailed descriptions of their daily life he succeeds in depicting their different idiosyncrasies, thoughts and feelings. In the use of dialogue too he shows outstanding skill, putting such distinctive speech into each character's mouth that the reader feels as if he can see and hear the speaker. Thus Lu Hsun observed: "The appearance of this novel marked a break with traditional ideas and methods of writing."[1] The novel's political theme revealing class struggle and its telling indictment of the feudal ruling class and feudal system, as well as its mode of artistic expression, did indeed break with earlier traditions, turning over a new page in classical Chinese literature.

Chairman Mao has pointed out: **"To study the development of this old culture, to reject its feudal dross and**

---

[1] Lu Hsun, "The Historical Development of Chinese Fiction," *Collected Works*, Chinese edition, Vol. 8.

assimilate its democratic essence is a necessary condition for developing our new national culture and increasing our national self-confidence, but we should never swallow anything and everything uncritically. It is imperative to separate the fine old culture of the people which had a more or less democratic and revolutionary character from all the decadence of the old feudal ruling class."[1] This is also the attitude we should take towards this novel which belongs to China's fine literary heritage. The ideological value of this work lies in the fact that it deals with political struggle, that by presenting the prosperity and decline of the four typical noble families it truthfully lays bare the corruption and decadence of the feudal ruling class and points out its inevitable doom, and that it gives praise to the revolts of the slaves in Grand View Garden and the unorthodox characters of Pao-yu and Tai-yu.

Regarding the novel's objective artistic effect, it undoubtedly exposes and attacks the feudal system from various angles; hence its main ideological tendency is good. This does not mean, however, that the work contains no feudal dross and the author's own world outlook no feudal ideas. For after all Tsao Hsueh-chin was born in a declining noble family more than two hundred years ago, and this novel was written in the feudal period. His pessimism and fatalistic, nihilistic ideas, his view of life as a tragedy and all on earth as vanity, as well as his feudal approach to certain matters show the clear brandmark of the author's class origin and times on his world outlook and his novel.

Tsao Hsueh-chin did not finish his monumental work. Only eighty chapters written by him are extant in manuscript form with comments by Chih-yen Chai. He wrote more than this but unfortunately the manuscripts of the later chapters were lost. The last forty chapters in the present novel were the work of Kao Ngo, who lived after Tsao Hsueh-chin and carried out

---

[1] Mao Tsetung, "On New Democracy," *Selected Works*, FLP, Peking, 1967, Vol. II, p. 381.

his plan of making the love story between Pao-yu and Tai-yu end in tragedy; and in this respect his forty chapters have great artistic impact. After Kao Ngo's completion of the novel, this book originally known as *The Tale of the Stone* in eighty manuscript chapters was printed in movable type in 1791 as a complete novel in 120 chapters and renamed *A Dream of Red Mansions*. The printing of this edition increased the circulation of the book and helped to preserve the original eighty-chapter version. Kao Ngo while completing the novel made certain revisions in the original text and in his later forty chapters he sometimes went counter to Tsao Hsueh-chin's original intention and fell far short of Tsao Hsueh-chin in his portrayal of life and artistic attainment, due to his distinctive feudal outlook and inferior talent.

The last two hundred years have seen heated controversies regarding the estimation of this book. Prior to the May 4th Movement of 1919, there were numerous critics of the novel who are now known as the "old Red-ologists." Their views might diverge, but all alike made idealistic interpretations or distortions of the book according to the class interests and political needs of landlord-bourgeois scholars. After the May 4th Movement there appeared a group of "new Red-ologists" headed by the reactionary writer Hu Shih. Their "researches" into this novel had a reactionary political motivation. For that period saw the upsurge of a revolutionary mass movement against imperialism and feudalism; so Hu Shih and his followers preached reactionary pragmatism and idealism and through their "researches" opposed the spread of Marxism in China. Lu Hsun, great writer, thinker and revolutionary, fought staunchly against these "new Red-ologists."

After the establishment of New China, the controversy over this novel took a new form under new historical conditions. In 1954, a mass movement led by our great leader Chairman Mao himself to criticize the reactionary ideas of Hu Shih in the study of this book spread throughout the country. Chairman Mao pointed out that this was **"the first serious attack in over thirty years on the erroneous views of a so-called**

authoritative writer in the field of study" of this novel. This struggle thoroughly debunked the subjective idealism of the Hu Shih school and dealt a heavy blow at the bourgeoisie.

So the controversy over this novel has been very fierce and sharp. This was the case in the past, and the struggle will continue in future too.

The numerous editions of this novel can be divided into two main groups: those based on the early manuscript copies of the eighty-chapter version, and those based on the later 120-chapter printed edition. Our first eighty chapters have been translated from the photostat edition published by the People's Literature Publishing House, Peking, in September 1973 according to a lithographic edition printed by the Yu-cheng Press, Shanghai, in about 1911. This Yu-cheng edition had been made from a manuscript copy kept by Chi Liao-sheng of the Chienlung era. The last forty chapters are based on the 120-chapter edition reprinted by the People's Literature Publishing House, Peking, in 1959 from the movable-type edition of 1792. The Chi Liao-sheng manuscript of the first eighty chapters is one of the earliest copies extant. In our translation certain minor errors and omissions made by the man who copied the original manuscript have been corrected according to other versions.

The translation will appear in three volumes of forty chapters each.

CONTENTS

CHAPTER 1

Chen Shih-yin in a Dream Sees the Jade of Spiritual Understanding
Chia Yu-tsun in His Obscurity Is Charmed by a Maid

This is the opening chapter of the novel. In writing this story of the Stone the author wanted to record certain of his past dreams and illusions, but he tried to hide the true facts of his experience by using the allegory of the jade of "Spiritual Understanding." Hence his recourse to names like Chen Shih-yin.[1] But what are the events recorded in this book, and who are the characters? About this he said:

"In this busy, dusty world, having accomplished nothing, I suddenly recalled all the girls I had known, considering each in turn, and it dawned on me that all of them surpassed me in behaviour and understanding; that I, shameful to say, for all my masculine dignity, fell short of the gentler sex. But since this could never be remedied, it was no use regretting it. There was really nothing to be done.

"I decided then to make known to all how I, though dressed in silks and delicately nurtured thanks to the Imperial favour and my ancestors' virtue, had nevertheless ignored the kindly guidance of my elders as well as the good advice of teachers and friends, with the result that I had wasted half my life and not acquired a single skill. But no matter how unforgivable my crimes, I must not let all the lovely girls I have known pass into oblivion through my wickedness or my desire to hide my shortcomings.

"Though my home is now a thatched cottage with matting windows, earthen stove and rope-bed, this shall not stop me

---

[1] Homophone for "true facts concealed."

1

from laying bare my heart. Indeed, the morning breeze, the dew of night, the willows by my steps and the flowers in my courtyard inspire me to wield my brush. Though I have little learning or literary talent, what does it matter if I tell a tale in rustic language to leave a record of all those lovely girls. This should divert readers too and help distract them from their cares. That is why I use the other name Chia Yu-tsun."[1]

*

Do you know, Worthy Readers, where this book comes from? The answer may sound fantastic, yet carefully considered is of great interest. Let me explain, so that there will be no doubt left in your minds.

When the goddess Nu Wa melted down rocks to repair the sky, at Baseless Cliff in the Great Waste Mountain she made thirty-six thousand five hundred and one blocks of stone, each a hundred and twenty feet high and two hundred and forty feet square. She used only thirty-six thousand five hundred of these and threw the remaining block down at the foot of Blue Ridge[2] Peak. Strange to relate, this block of stone after tempering had acquired spiritual understanding. Because all its fellow blocks had been chosen to mend the sky and it alone rejected, it lamented day and night in distress and shame.

One day as the Stone was brooding over its fate, it saw approaching from the distance a Buddhist monk and Taoist priest, both of striking demeanour and distinguished appearance. They came up to the Stone and sat down to chat.

When they saw the pure translucent Stone which had shrunk to the size of a fan-pendant, the monk took it up on the palm of his hand and said to it with a smile:

"You look like a precious object, but you still lack real value. I must engrave some characters on you so that people can see at a glance that you're something special. Then we can take you to some civilized and prosperous realm, to a cultured family of official status, a place where flowers and willows

---

[1] Homophone for "fiction in rustic language."

[2] Homophone for "roots of love."

flourish, the home of pleasure and luxury where you can settle down in comfort."

The Stone was overjoyed.

"May I trouble you to enlighten me," it said, "as to what wonderful merits you will bestow on me? And where do you mean to take me?"

"Don't ask." The monk smiled. "You'll find out all in good time."

With that he tucked the Stone into his sleeve and hurried off with the Taoist. But where they went no one knows.

After no one knows how many generations or aeons, a Taoist known as Reverend Void, searching for the Way and immortality, came to Great Waste Mountain, Baseless Cliff and the foot of Blue Ridge Peak. His eye fell on the inscription on a large stone which was still discernible and he read it through. It was an account of the Stone's rejection for repairing heaven, its transformation and conveyance to the world of men by the Buddhist of Infinite Space and the Taoist of Boundless Time, and the joys and sorrows, partings and encounters, warm and cold treatment from others it had experienced there. On its back was a Buddhist verse:

> Unfit to mend the azure sky,
> I passed some years on earth to no avail;
> My life in both worlds is recorded here;
> Whom can I ask to pass on this romantic tale?

There followed the name of the region where the Stone fell, the place of its incarnation, and the story of its adventures — including trivial family affairs and light verses written to amuse idle hours. The dynasty, year and country's name were, however, obliterated.

The Reverend Void said to the Stone: "Brother Stone, you seem to think that your tale recorded here is interesting enough to merit publication. In my view, in the first place, there is no way of finding out the dynasty and the year; in the second, there is nothing here about worthy and loyal ministers and how they regulated the government and public morality. There are merely some girls remarkable only for their passion or folly, or else for their small gifts and trifling virtues which cannot even compare with those of such talented ladies as Pan Chao or Tsai Yen.[1] Even if I were to transcribe it, it would hardly arouse much interest."

"How can you be so dense, master?" protested the Stone with a smile. "If there's no way of finding out the date, you can easily ascribe this tale to some time in the Han or Tang Dynasty. But since all novels do that, I think my way of dispensing with this convention and just dealing with my own adventures and feelings is more original. Why insist on a certain dynasty or definite date? Besides, most common people of the market-place much prefer light literature to improving books. The trouble is that so many romances contain slanderous anecdotes about sovereigns and ministers or cast aspersions upon other men's wives and daughters so that they are packed with sex and violence. Even worse are those writers of the breeze-and-moonlight school, who corrupt the young with pornography and filth. As for books of the beauty-and-talented-scholar type, a thousand are written to a single pattern and none escapes bordering on indecency. They are filled with allusions to handsome, talented young men and beautiful, refined girls in history; but in order to insert a couple of his own love poems, the author invents stereotyped heroes and heroines with the inevitable low character to make trouble between them like a clown in a play, and makes even the slave girls talk pedantic nonsense. So all these novels are full of contradictions and absurdly unnatural.

"Much better are the girls I have known myself during my young days. I wouldn't presume to rank them as superior to all the characters of earlier works, yet their stories may serve to dispel boredom and care while the few doggerels I have inserted may raise a laugh and add zest to wine. As for the scenes of sad partings and happy meetings, prosperity and

---

[1] Two ladies in the Han Dynasty noted for their scholarship.

decline, these are all true to fact and not altered in the slightest to cause a sensation or depart from the truth.

"At present the daily concern of the poor is food and clothing, while the rich are never satisfied. All their leisure is taken up with amorous adventures, material acquisition or trouble-making. What time do they have to read political and moral treatises? I neither want people to marvel at this story of mine, nor do I insist that they should read it for pleasure; I only hope they may find distraction here when they are sated with food and wine or searching for some escape from worldly cares. By glancing over it in place of other vain pursuits, they may save their energies and prolong their lives, sparing themselves the harm of quarrels and arguments, or the trouble of chasing after what is illusory.

"Besides, this story offers readers something new, unlike those hackneyed and stale hodge-podges of sudden partings and encounters which teem with talented scholars and lovely girls — Tsao Tzu-chien, Cho Wen-chun, Hung-niang, Hsiao-yu[1] and the like. What do you say, master?"

The Reverend Void thought it over, then carefully re-read *The Tale of the Stone*. He found in it both condemnation of treachery and criticism of flattery and evil, but it was clearly not written to pass censure on the times. Moreover it surpassed other books in its voluminous accounts of benevolent princes, good ministers, kind fathers and filial sons, and all matters pertaining to proper human relations, as well as eulogies of virtuous deeds. Although the main theme was love, it was simply a true record of events, superior to those sham meretricious works devoted to licentious assignations and dissolute escapades. Since it did not touch at all on current events he copied it out from beginning to end and took it away to find a publisher.

---

[1] Tsao Tzu-chien (192-232), Tsao Tsao's younger son, entitled Prince of Chen, a noted poet of Wei of the Three Kingdoms Period; Cho Wen-chun, the widow who married the scholar Ssuma Hsiang-ju in the second century B.C.; Hung-niang, the maid and go-between in the Yuan drama *The Western Chamber*; Huo Hsiao-yu, the heroine of a Tang romance.

Since all manifestations are born of nothingness and in turn give rise to passion, by describing passion for what is manifest we comprehend nothingness. So the Taoist changed his name to the Passionate Monk and changed the title of the book from *The Tale of the Stone* to the *Record of the Passionate Monk*.

Kung Mei-hsi of eastern Lu[1] suggested the title *Precious Mirror of Love*. Later Tsao Hsueh-chin in his Mourning-the-Red Studio pored over the book for ten years and re-wrote it five times. He divided it into chapters, furnished headings for each, and renamed it *The Twelve Beauties of Chinling*. He also inscribed on it this verse:

> Pages full of fantastic talk
> Penned with bitter tears;
> All men call the author mad,
> None his message hears.

Now that the origin of the story is clear, let us see what was recorded on the Stone.

Long ago the earth dipped downwards in the southeast, and in that southeast part was a city named Kusu;[2] and the quarter around Chang-men Gate of Kusu was one of the most fashionable centres of wealth and nobility in the world of men. Outside this Chang-men Gate was a certain Ten-*li* Street, off which ran the Lane of Humanity and Purity; and in this lane stood an old temple, which being built in such a narrow space was known from its shape as Gourd Temple. Beside this temple lived a gentleman named Chen Fei, whose courtesy name was Shih-yin. His wife, née Feng, was a worthy virtuous woman with a strong sense of propriety and right. Although neither very rich nor noble, their family was highly regarded in that locality.

Chen Shih-yin had a quiet disposition. Instead of hankering after wealth or rank, he was quite happy tending flowers, growing bamboos, sipping wine or writing poems — spending his time very much like an immortal. One thing alone was

---

[1] Present-day Shantung.

[2] Present-day Soochow.

lacking: he was now over fifty but had no son, only a three-year-old daughter named Ying-lien.

One long hot summer day as Shih-yin was sitting idly in his study, the book slipped from his hand and, leaning his head on the desk, he fell asleep.

In dream he travelled to an unknown place, where he suddenly noticed a monk and a Taoist approaching, talking together. He heard the Taoist ask:

"Where do you mean to take that stupid object?"

"Don't worry," replied the monk. "A love drama is about to be enacted, but not all its actors have yet been incarnated. I'm going to slip this silly thing in among them to give it the experience it wants."

"So another batch of amorous sinners are bent on making trouble by reincarnation," commented the Taoist. "Where will this drama take place?"

"It's an amusing story." The monk smiled. "You've never heard anything like it. In the west, on the bank of the Sacred River, beside the Stone of Three Incarnations there grew a Vermilion Pearl Plant which was watered every day with sweet dew by the attendant Shen Ying in the Palace of Red Jade. As the months and years went by and the Vermilion Pearl Plant imbibed the essences of heaven and earth and the nourishment of rain and dew, it cast off its plant nature and took human form, albeit only that of a girl. All day long she roamed beyond the Sphere of Parting Sorrow, staying her hunger with the fruit Secret Love and quenching her thirst at the Sea of Brimming Grief. But her heart was heavy because she had not repaid the care lavished on her.

"Just then, as it happened, Shen Ying was seized with a longing to assume human form and visit the world of men, taking advantage of the present enlightened and peaceful reign. He made his request to the Goddess of Disenchantment, who saw that this was a chance for Vermilion Pearl to repay her debt of gratitude.

" 'He gave me sweet dew,' said Vermilion Pearl, 'but I've no water to repay his kindness. If he's going down to the world of men, I would like to go too so that if I repay him with as many tears as I can shed in a lifetime I may be able to clear this debt.'

"This induced many other amorous spirits who had not atoned for their sins to accompany them and take part in this drama."

"That certainly is odd," remarked the Taoist. "I've never heard of repayment with tears before. I imagine this story should have more fine points than the usual run of breeze-and-moonlight tales."

"The old romances give us only outlines of their characters' lives with a number of poems about them," said the monk. "We're never told the details of their intimate family life or daily meals. Besides, most breeze-and-moonlight tales deal with secret assignations and elopements, and have never really expressed the true love between a young man and a girl. I'm sure when these spirits go down to earth, we'll see lovers and lechers, worthy people, simpletons and scoundrels unlike those in earlier romances."

"Why don't you and I take this chance to go too and win over a few of them? That would be a worthy deed."

"Exactly what I was thinking. But first we must take this stupid object to the palace of the Goddess of Disenchantment and clear all the formalities. After all these romantic souls have gone down we can follow. So far only half of them have descended to earth."

"In that case I'm ready to go with you," said the Taoist.

Chen Shih-yin had heard every word of their conversation but did not know what was meant by the "stupid object." He could not resist accosting them with a bow.

"Greetings, immortal masters!" he said with a smile.

When they had returned his greeting he continued: "Rare indeed is the opportunity to listen to such a discussion of cause and effects as I have just heard. But I am too dull to grasp it. If you would kindly elucidate to enlighten me, I promise to listen most attentively. For profiting by your wisdom may prove my salvation."

"This is a mystery which we cannot divulge." The two immortals smiled. "When the time comes, think of us. Then you may be able to escape from the fiery pit."

Shih-yin could hardly press them. "I mustn't probe into a mystery," he said, "but could you show me that object you mentioned just now?"

"If you want to know, you are destined in your life to meet with it," said the monk.

With that he produced a beautiful piece of translucent jade and handed it to Shih-yin. On the obverse were carved the words Precious Jade of Spiritual Understanding. Before Shih-yin could look carefully at the columns of smaller characters on the reverse the monk snatched it away from him, saying:

"We've reached the Land of Illusion."

He passed with the Taoist through a large stone archway on which was inscribed: Illusory Land of Great Void. A couplet on the two pillars read:

When false is taken for true, true becomes false;
If non-being turns into being, being becomes non-being.

Shih-yin was starting after the two immortals when he heard a fearful crash, as if mountains had collapsed and the earth split asunder. With a cry he woke up and stared about him. There was the fiery sun still blazing down on the rustling plantain leaves. Already half of his dream had slipped his mind.

The nurse came up then with Ying-lien in her arms, and it struck Shih-yin that his daughter was growing prettier and more lovable every day. He picked her up and played with her for a while, then took her to the gate to watch a religious procession pass by. He was just about to go in again when a monk and a Taoist priest drew near, laughing and gibbering like two maniacs. The monk was barefooted, his head scabby; the priest, lame with tangled, tousled hair. When they reached Shih-yin's gate and saw the child in his arms, the monk burst into lamentations.

"Why are you carrying that ill-fated creature, sir?" he asked. "She will bring nothing but trouble to her parents."

Shih-yin thought the man was raving and paid no attention. "Give her to me!" cried the monk. "Give her to me!"

Losing patience, Shih-yin clasped his daughter more tightly and was turning to re-enter the house when the monk pointed at him and let out a roar of laughter. He then declaimed:

> "Fool, to care for this tender child:
> An image in the mirror, snow melting away.
> Beware what will follow the Lantern Feast,
> The vanishing like smoke when the fire burns out."

Shih-yin, hearing this clearly, wondered what it meant. Before he could ask, the Taoist told the monk:

"This is where our paths divide. Each must go about his own business. Three aeons from now I shall wait for you at Mount Peimang, and together we can go to the Land of Illusion to have this affair expunged from the register."

"Very good," said the monk.

Then both vanished without a trace.

Shih-yin realized then that these were no ordinary men and regretted not having questioned them. His rueful reflections were cut short by the arrival of a poor scholar who lived next door in Gourd Temple. His name was Chia Hua,[1] his courtesy name Shih-fei, and his pen-name Yu-tsun. A native of Huchow, he was the last of a line of scholars and officials. His parents had exhausted the family property and died leaving him alone in the world. Since nothing was to be gained by staying at home, he had set out for the capital in the hope of securing a position and restoring the family fortunes. But by the time he had reached here a couple of years ago his money had run out and he had gone to live in the temple where he made a precarious living by working as a scrivener. For this reason Shih-yin saw a good deal of him.

Having greeted Shih-yin, Yu-tsun asked, "What are you watching from your gate, sir? Is there any news in town?"

"Nothing," was the reply. "My little girl was crying, so I brought her out to play. You couldn't have arrived at a bet-

---

[1] Homophone for "false talk."

ter moment, as I was feeling thoroughly bored. Come in and help me while away the long summer day."

He told a servant to take his daughter inside, and led Yu-tsun into his study, where a boy served tea. They had not exchanged many remarks when a servant hurried in to announce the arrival of a certain Mr. Yen.

Then Shih-yin excused himself, saying, "Forgive my rudeness. Do you mind waiting here for a few minutes?"

"Don't stand on ceremony, sir," said Yu-tsun, rising. "I am a regular guest here, I don't mind waiting."

So after Shih-yin went to the front room Yu-tsun passed the time by leafing through some books, until he heard a young woman coughing outside. He slipped over to the window and looked out. It was a maid picking flowers. She had uncommon features, bright eyes and graceful eyebrows, and although no great beauty she possessed considerable charm. Yu-tsun stared at her, spell-bound.

Just as she was leaving with her flowers, the girl abruptly looked up and caught sight of him. His clothes were shabby yet he was powerfully built with an open face, firm lips, eyebrows like scimitars, eyes like stars, a straight nose and rounded cheeks. She turned away thinking to herself, "He's a fine-looking man for all his tattered clothes. This must be the Chia Yu-tsun my master keeps talking about, whom he'd gladly help if only he had the chance. Yes, I'm sure it's him, our family has no other friends who are poor. No wonder my master also says he's a man who won't remain long in this plight." She could not resist looking back a couple of times.

Yu-tsun seeing this was overjoyed, thinking that she must have taken a fancy to him. He decided that she had good judgement and was one of the few who could appreciate him in his obscurity.

Presently the boy came back and let Yu-tsun know that the guest was staying to a meal. Since this made it out of the question to wait any longer, Yu-tsun went through a passage to the side gate and left. And after the departure of Mr. Yen, Shih-yin did not trouble to invite him back.

In time the Mid-Autumn Festival came round. After the family meal, Shih-yin had another table laid in his study and strolled over in the moonlight to the temple to invite Yu-tsun over.

Ever since the Chens' maid had looked back that day, Yu-tsun flattered himself that she was well-disposed to him and thought of her constantly. As he gazed at the full moon, his thoughts turned to her again and he declaimed this verse:

> "Not yet divined the fate in store for me,
> Good reason have I for anxiety,
> And so my brows are knit despondently;
> But she, as she went off, looked back at me.
> My shadow in the wind is all I see,
> Will she by moonlight keep me company?
> If sensibility were in its power
> The moon should first light up the fair one's bower."

Having recited this, Yu-tsun rumpled his hair and sighed as he reflected how far he was from realizing his ambitions. He chanted the couplet:

> "The jade in the box hopes to fetch a good price,
> The pin in the casket longs to soar on high."

He was overheard by Shih-yin, who arrived just then.

"I see you have high ambitions, Brother Yu-tsun!" he joked.

"Not in the least," replied Yu-tsun, somewhat embarrassed. "I was merely reciting some lines by a former poet. I don't aspire so high. To what do I owe the pleasure of this visit?"

"Tonight is mid-autumn, commonly known as the Festival of Reunion. It occurred to me that you might be feeling lonely in this temple, brother. I've prepared a little wine in my humble place and wonder if you'd condescend to share it?"

Yu-tsun needed no urging.

"You lavish too much kindness on me, sir," he said. "Nothing would please me better."

They went to the court in front of Shih-yin's study. Soon they had finished their tea and sat down to a collation of choice wine and delicacies. At first they sipped slowly, but their spirits rose as they talked and they began to drink more recklessly. The sound of flutes and strings could be heard from all the houses in the neighbourhood; everywhere was singing; and overhead the bright moon shone in full splendour. The two men became very merry and drained cup after cup.

Yu-tsun, eight-tenths drunk, could not suppress his elation. He improvised a quatrain to the moon and declaimed it:

> "On the fifteenth the moon is full,
> Bathing jade balustrades with her pure light;
> As her bright orb sails up the sky
> All men on earth gaze upwards at the sight."

"Excellent!" cried Shih-yin. "I've always maintained that you were cut out for great things. These lines foretell rapid advancement. Very soon you will be treading upon the clouds. Let me congratulate you."

He filled another large cup. Yu-tsun tossed it off and then sighed.

"Don't think this is just drunken talk," he said. "I'm sure I could acquit myself quite creditably in the examinations; but I have no money in my wallet for travelling expenses and the capital is far away. I can't raise enough as a scrivener...."

"Why didn't you say so before?" interposed Shih-yin. "I've often wondered about this, but since you never mentioned it I didn't like to broach the subject. If that's how things are, dull as I am at least I know what's due to a friend. Luckily the Metropolitan Examinations are coming up next year. You must go as fast as you can to the capital and prove your learning in the Spring Test. I shall count it a privilege to take care of the travelling expenses and other business for you."

He sent his boy in to fetch fifty taels of silver and two suits of winter clothes.

"The nineteenth is a good day for travelling," he continued. "You can hire a boat then and start your journey westward. How good it will be to meet again next winter after you have soared up to dizzy heights."

Yu-tsun accepted the silver and clothes with no more than perfunctory thanks, then said no more of the matter but went on feasting and talking. They did not part until the third watch, when Shih-yin saw his friend off and returned to his room to sleep until the sun was high in the sky. Then, remembering the previous night's business, he decided to write Yu-tsun two letters of introduction to certain officials in the capital who might put him up.

But the servant sent to ask his friend over brought back word, "The monk says that Mr. Chia left for the capital at the fifth watch this morning. He asked the monk to tell you that scholars are not superstitious about lucky or unlucky days but like to act according to reason; so he had no time to say goodbye in person."

This Shih-yin had to accept.

Uneventful days pass quickly. In a flash the merry Festival of Lanterns came round and Shih-yin told his servant Huo Chi to take Ying-lien out to see the fireworks and ornamental lanterns. Towards midnight Huo Chi set the little girl down on a doorstep while he stepped round the corner to urinate. When he came back she had gone. He made a frantic search for her all night. And at dawn, not daring to face his master without her, he ran away to another district.

Shih-yin and his wife were naturally alarmed when their daughter failed to come home. They sent search parties out, but all returned without any word of her. She was the middle-aged couple's only child, and her loss nearly drove them distracted. They wept day and night and were tempted to take their own lives. After a month's grief Shih-yin fell ill, and then his wife. Every day they sent for doctors.

Then, on the fifteenth day of the third month, a fire broke out in Gourd Temple — the monk preparing the sacrifice carelessly let a pan of oil catch fire and soon the window paper was alight. Since most of the nearby buildings had bamboo walls and were probably doomed to destruction, the flames spread from house to house until the whole street was ablaze like a flaming mountain. Soldiers and civilians tried to put out the fire, but it was beyond control. The conflagration raged for a whole night and destroyed none knew how many houses before it burned itself out. The Chens' home, being next to the temple, was reduced to a pile of rubble. Although they and their few servants were lucky enough to escape with their lives, poor Shih-yin could do nothing but stamp his feet and sigh.

He and his wife decided then to go and live on their farm. But the last few years' harvests had been ruined by flood and drought and the countryside was overrun by bandits who seized fields and land, giving the people no peace. The punitive expeditions by government troops only made matters worse. Finding it impossible to settle there, Shih-yin had to mortgage his land and take his wife and two maids to find refuge with his father-in-law Feng Su.

Now this Feng Su, a native of Tajuchou, although only a farmer was quite comfortably off. He was not pleased by the arrival of his daughter and son-in-law in this sorry state. Fortunately Shih-yin had some money left from the mortgage of his land, and he asked Feng Su to invest this for him in some estate on which he could live in future. His father-in-law tricked him, however, by pocketing half the sum and buying him some poor fields and a ramshackle cottage. As a scholar, Shih-yin had no knowledge of business or farming. He struggled along for a year or two, losing money all the time, while Feng ·Su kept admonishing him to his face and complaining to all and sundry behind his back of his incompetence, idleness and extravagance.

To the shock Shih-yin had suffered the previous year and the toll taken by his subsequent misfortunes was now added the bitter realization that he had misplaced his trust. Ageing and a prey to poverty and ill health, he began to look like a man with one foot in the grave.

He made the effort one day to find some distraction by taking a walk in the street, leaning on his cane. Suddenly a Taoist limped towards him, a seeming maniac in hemp sandals and tattered clothes, who as he came chanted:

"All men long to be immortals
Yet to riches and rank each aspires;
The great ones of old, where are they now?
Their graves are a mass of briars.

All men long to be immortals,
Yet silver and gold they prize
And grub for money all their lives
Till death seals up their eyes.

All men long to be immortals
Yet dote on the wives they've wed,
Who swear to love their husband evermore
But remarry as soon as he's dead.

All men long to be immortals
Yet with getting sons won't have done.
Although fond parents are legion,
Who ever saw a really filial son?"

At the close of this song Shih-yin stepped forward.

"What was that you just chanted?" he asked. "I had the impression that it was about the vanity of all things."

"If you gathered that, you have some understanding," the Taoist remarked. "You should know that all good things in this world must end, and to make an end is good, for there is nothing good which does not end. My song is called *All Good Things Must End*."

Shih-yin with his innate intelligence at once grasped the other's meaning. Putting on a smile he said, "Wait a minute. Will you let me expound this song of yours?"

"By all means do," said the Taoist.

Shih-yin then declaimed:

"Mean huts and empty halls
Where emblems of nobility once hung;
Dead weeds and withered trees,
Where men have once danced and sung.

Carved beams are swathed in cobwebs
But briar-choked casements screened again with gauze;
While yet the rouge is fresh, the powder fragrant,
The hair at the temples turns hoary — for what cause?

Yesterday, yellow clay received white bones;
Today, red lanterns light the love-birds' nest;
While men with gold and silver by the chest
Turn beggars, scorned by all and dispossessed.

A life cut short one moment makes one sigh,
Who would have known it's her turn next to die?
No matter with what pains he schools his sons,
Who knows if they will turn to brigandry?

A pampered girl brought up in luxury
May slip into a quarter of ill fame;
Resentment at a low official rank
May lead to fetters and a felon's shame.

In ragged coat one shivered yesterday,
Today a purple robe he frowns upon;
All's strife and tumult on the stage,
As one man ends his song the next comes on.

To take strange parts as home
Is folly past compare;
And all our labour in the end
Is making clothes for someone else to wear."

The lame, eccentric Taoist clapped his hands. "You have hit the nail on the head," he cried.

"Let's go," was Shih-yin's brief reply.

He transferred the sack from the Taoist's shoulder to his own, and then, without even calling in at his home, he strode off with the priest.

This caused a sensation in the neighbourhood and word of it soon reached Shih-yin's wife, who gave way to a storm of weeping. After consultation with her father she had a thorough search made, but there was no news of her husband. She had perforce to go back and live with her parents. Luckily she still had her two maids, and the three of them by sewing day and night helped to defray Feng Su's expenses. For his part, grumble as he might, he had to lump it.

One day the elder of the two maids was buying some thread at the gate when she heard men shouting to clear the street, and people said the new prefect had arrived to take up office. She hid in the doorway to watch. First soldiers and runners marched past two by two. Then came a large sedan-chair in which was seated an official in a black gauze cap and red robe. The maid stared in surprise and thought: His face looks familiar. Have I seen him somewhere before? But once back in the house she thought no more of the matter.

That evening, just as they were going to bed, there came a loud knocking on the gate and a clamour of voices. Messengers from the yamen ordered Feng Su to appear for questioning by the prefect. His jaw dropped and he gaped in consternation. Did this mean fresh calamity?

To find out, read the next chapter.

CHAPTER 2

Lady Chia Dies in the City of Yangchow
Leng Tzu-hsing Describes the Jung Mansion

A verse says:

> Who can guess the outcome of a game of chess?
> Incense burned out, tea drunk — it's still in doubt.
> To interpret the signs of prosperity or decline
> An impartial onlooker must be sought out.

Hearing the hubbub at his gate, Feng Su hurried out to see what the messengers wanted.

"Ask Mr. Chen to come out," they bawled. "Be quick about it."

"My name is Feng, not Chen," he answered with an ingratiating smile. "My son-in-law's name is Chen, but he left home a year or two ago to become a priest. Is he the man you want?"

"How would we know? We're here on the prefect's orders. If you're his father-in-law, you must come and clear this up with His Honour to save us another trip."

Giving Feng Su no chance to protest they dragged him off, while his whole household trembled, not knowing what this portended.

Towards the end of the second watch he returned in the highest of spirits. Asked what had happened, he told them: "This new prefect, Chia Hua, is a native of Huchow and an old friend of my son-in-law. When he passed our gate and saw our Chiao-hsin buying thread, he supposed that Shih-yin had moved his household here. He seemed very upset when I explained all that had happened. He asked after my granddaughter too and I told him she was lost on the Feast of Lanterns. 'Never mind,' said His Honour. 'I'll have a search made and I'm certain we shall find her.' At the end of our conversation, as I was leaving, he gave me two taels of silver."

Chen's wife was very moved by this. And so the night passed.

Early the next morning a messenger arrived from Chia Yu-tsun with two packets of silver and four lengths of brocade for Mrs. Chen as a token of gratitude. There was also a confidential letter for Feng Su asking him to persuade Mrs. Chen to let the prefect have Chiao-hsin as his secondary wife. Feng Su could hardly contain himself for joy. Eager to please the prefect, he prevailed on his daughter to agree and that very same night put Chiao-hsin in a small sedan-chair and escorted her to the yamen.

We need not dwell on Yu-tsun's satisfaction. He gave Feng Su a hundred pieces of silver and sent Mrs. Chen many gifts, urging her to take good care of her health while he ascertained her daughter's whereabouts. Feng Su went home, and there we can leave him.

Now Chiao-hsin was the maid who had looked back at Yu-tsun that year in Kusu, little dreaming that one casual glance could have such an extraordinary outcome. And so doubly kind was fate that within a year of marriage she bore a son; while after another half year Yu-tsun's wife contracted a disease and died, and then he made Chiao-hsin his wife, further improving her position.

> A single chance hiatus
> Raised her status.

Yu-tsun, after receiving Shih-yin's gift of silver that year, had left on the sixteenth for the capital. He did so well in the examinations that he became a Palace Graduate and was given a provincial appointment. He had now been promoted to this prefectship.

But although a capable administrator Yu-tsun was grasping and ruthless, while his arrogance and insolence to his superiors made them view him with disfavour. In less than two years they found a chance to impeach him. He was accused of "ingrained duplicity, tampering with the rites and, under a show of probity, conspiring with his ferocious underlings to foment trouble in his district and make life intolerable for the local people."

The Emperor, much incensed, sanctioned his dismissal. The arrival of this edict rejoiced the hearts of all officials in the Prefecture. But Yu-tsun, although mortified and enraged, betrayed no indignation and went about looking as cheerful as before. After handing over his affairs he gathered together the capital accumulated during his years in office and moved his household back to his native place. Having settled them there he set off, "the wind on his back, moonlight in his sleeves," to see the famous sights of the empire.

One day his travels again took him to Yangchow, where he learned that the Salt Commissioner that year was Lin Hai — his courtesy name was Lin Ju-hai — who had come third in a previous Imperial examination and recently been promoted to the Censorate. A native of Kusu, he had now been selected by the Emperor as a Commissioner of the Salt Inspectorate. He had been little more than a month in this present post.

One of Lin Ju-hai's ancestors five generations earlier had been ennobled as a marquis. The rank had been conferred for three generations; then, as the benevolence of the present gracious Emperor far exceeded that of his noble predecessors, he had as a special favour extended it for one more generation, so that Lin Ju-hai's father had inherited the title as well. He himself, however, had made his career through the examinations, for his family was cultured as well as noble. Unfortunately it was not prolific, although several branches existed, and Lin Ju-hai had cousins but no brothers or sisters. Now he was in his forties and his only son had died at the age of three the previous year. He had several concubines but fate had not granted him another son, and he could not remedy this. By his wife, née Chia, he had a daughter Tai-yu just five years old. Both parents loved her dearly. And because she was as intelligent as she was pretty, they decided to give her a good education to make up for their lack of a son and help them forget their loss.

It so happened that Yu-tsun had caught a chill which laid him up in his inn for a month and more. Exhausted by his illness, and short of funds, he was searching for somewhere to recuperate. Fortunately he had two old friends here who knew that the Salt Commissioner was looking for a tutor. Upon their recommendation Yu-tsun was given the post, which provided the security he needed. He was lucky, too, to have as pupil only one small girl accompanied by two maids. Since the child was so delicate, her lessons were irregular and this meant that his duties were light.

In a twinkling another year went by and then his pupil's mother unexpectedly fell ill and died. The little girl attended her during her illness and then went into strict mourning. Yu-tsun considered resigning, but Lin Ju-hai kept him on so as not to interrupt his daughter's education during the period of mourning. Recently, grief had brought about a relapse in the delicate child's health, and for days at a time she had to abandon her studies. Then Yu-tsun, finding time hang heavy on his hands, used to take a walk after his meals when the weather was fine.

One day he strolled to the outskirts of the city to enjoy the countryside. He came to luxuriant woods and bamboo groves set among hills and interlaced by streams, with a temple half hidden among the foliage. The entrance was in ruins, the walls were crumbling. A placard above the gate bore the inscription: Temple of Perspicacity. And flanking the gate were two mouldering boards with the couplet:

> Though plenty was left after death, he forgot
>   to hold his hand back;
> Only at the end of the road does one think of
>   turning on to the right track.

"Trite as the language is, this couplet has deep significance," thought Yu-tsun. "I've never come across anything like it in all the famous temples I've visited. There may be a story behind it of someone who has tasted the bitterness of life, some repentant sinner. I'll go in and ask."

But inside he found only a doddering old monk cooking gruel. Not very impressed, Yu-tsun casually asked him a few questions. The man proved to be deaf as well as dim-witted, for his mumbled answers were quite irrelevant.

Yu-tsun went out again in disgust and decided to improve the occasion by drinking a few cups in a village tavern. He had scarcely set foot inside the door when one of the men who was drinking there rose to his feet and accosted him with a laugh.

"Fancy meeting you here!"

It was Leng Tzu-hsing, a curio-dealer whom he had met in the capital. As Yu-tsun admired his enterprise and ability while Tzu-hsing was eager to cultivate one of the literati, they had hit it off well together and become good friends.

"When did you arrive, brother?" asked Yu-tsun cheerfully. "I'd no idea you were in these parts. What a coincidence, meeting you here."

"I went home at the end of last year and stopped here on my way back to the capital to look up an old friend. He was good enough to ask me to stay, and since I've no urgent business I'm breaking my journey for a couple of days. I shall go on about the middle of the month. My friend's busy today, so I came out for a stroll and stopped here to rest. I'd no idea I'd run into you like this."

He made Yu-tsun sit down at his table and ordered more food and wine. Drinking slowly, they spoke of all they had done since parting.

"Is there any news from the capital?" asked Yu-tsun.

"Nothing much," replied Tzu-hsing. "But something rather curious has happened in the house of one of your noble kinsmen."

"I've no kinsmen in the capital. Who do you mean?"

"You have the same surname even if you don't belong to the same clan."

Yu-tsun asked to whom he alluded.

"The Chia family of the Jung Mansion. You needn't be ashamed of the connection."

"Oh, that family." Yu-tsun laughed. "To tell the truth, our clan is a very large one. Since the time of Chia Fu of the Eastern Han Dynasty its branches have multiplied until now you find Chias in every province. Impossible to keep track of them all. The Jung branch and mine are, however, on the same clan register, but they're so grand that we've never claimed relationship and are gradually drifting further and further apart."

"Don't talk like that, friend. Both the Ning and Jung branches have declined." Tzu-hsing sighed. "They're not what they used to be."

"How is that possible? They used to be enormous households."

"I know. It's a long story."

"Last year when I was in Chinling,"[1] said Yu-tsun, "on my way to visit the Six Dynasty ruins I went to the Stone City[2] and passed the gates of their old mansions. Practically the whole north side of the street is taken up by their houses, the Ning Mansion on the east and the Jung Mansion adjoining it on the west. True, there wasn't much coming and going outside their gates, but over the wall I caught glimpses of most imposing halls and pavilions, while the trees and rockeries of the gardens behind had a flourishing, opulent look. There was nothing to suggest a house in decline."

"For a Palace Graduate you're not very smart." Tzu-hsing chuckled. "A centipede dies but never falls down, as the old saying goes. Although they're not as prosperous as before, they're still a cut above ordinary official families. Their households are increasing and their commitments are growing all the time, while masters and servants alike are so used to lording it in luxury that not one of them thinks ahead. They squander money every day and are quite incapable of economizing. Outwardly they may look as grand as ever, but their purses are nearly empty. That's not their worst trouble,

---

[1] Present-day Nanking.

[2] The northwestern section of Nanking.

though. Who would've thought that each new generation of this noble and scholarly clan is inferior to the last."

"Surely," countered Yu-tsun in surprise, "a family so cultured and versed in etiquette knows the importance of a good upbringing? I can't vouch for our other branches, but I've always heard that these two houses take great pains over the education of their sons."

"It's these two houses I'm talking about," rejoined Tzu-hsing regretfully. "Just hear me out. The Duke of Ningkuo and the Duke of Jungkuo were brothers by the same mother. The Duke of Ningkuo, the elder, had four sons and after his death the oldest of these, Chia Tai-hua, succeeded to the title. The elder of his two sons, Chia Fu, died at the age of eight or nine, leaving the younger, Chia Ching, to inherit the title. But he's so wrapped up in Taoism that he takes no interest in anything but distilling elixirs. Luckily when he was younger he had a son Chia Chen, to whom he's relinquished the title so that he can give all his mind to becoming an immortal; and instead of going back to his native place he's hobnobbing with Taoist priests outside the city. Chia Chen has a son called Jung just turned sixteen. Chia Ching washes his hands of all mundane matters, and Chia Chen has never studied but lives for pleasure. He's turning the Ning Mansion upside down, yet no one dares to restrain him.

"Now for the Jung Mansion, where that curious business I just mentioned took place. After the death of the Duke of Jungkuo, his elder son Chia Tai-shan succeeded to the title and married a daughter of Marquis Shih of Chinling, by whom he had two sons, Chia Sheh and Chia Cheng. Chia Tai-shan has been dead for many years but his wife, Lady Dowager Shih, is still alive. Their elder son Chia Sheh inherited the title. The younger, Chia Cheng, was so fond of studying as a child that he was his grandfather's favourite and he hoped to make a career for himself through the examinations. When Chia Tai-shan died, however, he left a valedictory memorial, and the Emperor out of regard for his former minister not only conferred the title on his elder son but asked what other sons there were, granted Chia Cheng an audience, and as an additional favour gave him the rank of Assistant Secretary with instructions to familiarize himself with affairs in one of the ministries. He has now risen to the rank of Under-Secretary.

"Chia Cheng's wife, Lady Wang, bore him a son called Chia Chu who passed the district examination at fourteen, married before he was twenty and had a son, but then fell ill and died. His second child was a daughter, born strangely enough on the first day of the year. But stranger still was the birth later of a son who came into the world with a piece of clear, brilliantly coloured jade in his mouth. There are even inscriptions on the jade. Isn't that extraordinary?"

"It certainly is. The boy should have a remarkable future."

"That's what everyone says." Tzu-hsing smiled cynically. "And for that reason his grandmother dotes on him. On his first birthday Chia Cheng tested his disposition by setting all sorts of different objects before him to see which he would select. Believe it or not, ignoring everything else he reached out for the rouge, powder-boxes, hair ornaments and bangles! His father was furious and swore he'd grow up to be a dissolute rake. Because of this he's not too fond of the boy, but the child's still his grandmother's darling. He's seven or eight now and remarkably mischievous, yet so clever you won't find his equal in a hundred. And he says the strangest things for a child. 'Girls are made of water, men of mud,' he declares. 'I feel clean and refreshed when I'm with girls but find men dirty and stinking.' Isn't that absurd? He's bound later on to run after women like the very devil."

"That doesn't follow," put in Yu-tsun, grown suddenly grave. "You don't know how he's come into the world. I suspect his father is making a mistake as well if he thinks the boy depraved. To understand him you'd need to be widely read and experienced, able to recognize the nature of things, grasp the Way and comprehend the Mystery."

He spoke so seriously that Tzu-hsing asked him to expand on this.

"All men, apart from the very good and the very bad, are much alike," said Yu-tsun. "The very good are born at a propitious time when the world is well governed, the very bad in times of calamity when danger threatens. Examples of the first are Yao, Shun, Yu and Tang, King Wen and King Wu, Duke Chou and Duke Shao, Confucius and Mencius, Tung Chung-shu, Han Yu, Chou Tun-yi, the Cheng brothers, Chang Chai and Chu Hsi.[1] Examples of the second are Kung Kung, Chieh, Chou, Chin Shih Huang, Wang Mang, Tsao Tsao, Huan Wen, An Lu-shan and Chin Kuai.[2]

"The good bring order to the world, the bad plunge it into confusion. The good embody pure intelligence, the true essence of heaven and earth; the bad, cruelty and perversity, the evil essence.

"This is a prosperous, long-enduring reign when the world is at peace and there are many people in the court and in the countryside who are endowed with the good essences. The over-abundance of this good essence, having nowhere to go, is transformed into sweet dew and gentle breezes and scattered throughout the Four Seas.

"But because there is no place under the clear sky and bright sun for the essence of cruelty and perversity, it congeals in

---

[1] Yao and Shun were legendary sage kings of ancient China; Yu, founder of the Hsia Dynasty (21st-16th century B.C.), was the legendary pacifier of flood; Tang founded the Shang Dynasty (16th-11th century B.C.); King Wen and King Wu founded the Western Chou Dynasty (11th century-771 B.C.); Duke Chou and Duke Shao were early Chou statesmen; Tung Chung-shu (179-104 B.C.) was a Confucian philosopher of the Han Dynasty; Han Yu (768-824) a Confucian writer of the Tang Dynasty; Chou Tun-yi, Cheng Hao, Cheng Yi and Chu Hsi were neo-Confucianists of the Northern Sung Dynasty (960-1127); and Chang Chai (1020-77) was a Northern Sung philosopher with some materialist ideas.

[2] Kung Kung, a legendary figure, was considered a rebel by China's feudal rulers; Chieh and Chou were the last rulers of the Hsia and Shang dynasties; Chin Shih Huang (259-210 B.C.) was the founder and First Emperor of the Chin Dynasty; Wang Mang usurped power towards the end of the Western Han Dynasty; Tsao Tsao (155-220) was a poet, statesman and military strategist of the Three Kingdoms Period; Huan Wen (312-373) was an eastern Tsin general; An Lu-shan was a rebel general in the Tang Dynasty, and Chin Kuai was a corrupt prime minister in the Southern Sung Dynasty (1127-1279).

deep caverns and in the bowels of the earth. If wafted by winds or pressed upon by clouds, it is thrown into agitation and traces of it may escape. And should these meet the pure essence, good refuses to yield to evil while evil envies good — neither can prevail over the other. This is like wind, rain, lightning and thunder which cannot vanish into thin air or give way but must battle until they are spent. So in order to find some outlet these essences permeate human beings, who come into the world embodying both. Such people fall short of sages or perfect men, but neither are they out-and-out villains.

"The pure intelligence with which they are endowed sets them above their myriad fellow creatures, but their perversity and unnatural behaviour sink them lower than other men too. Born into rich and noble families, such people will become romantic eccentrics; born into poor but cultured families, they will become high-minded scholars or recluses. Even if born into luckless and humble homes, they will never grow up into yamen runners or servants at the beck and call of the vulgar — they'll turn out celebrated actors or courtesans. People of this type in the past were Hsu Yu, Tao Chien, Yuan Chi, Chi Kang and Liu Ling, the two families of Wang and Hsieh, Ku Kai-chih, Chen Shu-pao, the Tang emperor Ming-huang, the Sung emperor Hui-tsung, Wen Ting-yun, Mi Fei, Shih Yen-nien, Liu Yung and Chin Kuan.[1] More recent examples are Ni Tsan, Tang Yin and Chu Yun-ming.[2] Then there are others like

---

[1] Hsu Yu, an ancient legendary hermit; Tao Chien (365-427), an Eastern Tsin poet who gave up an official career to live in retirement; Yuan Chi, Chi Kang and Liu Ling, third century poets and eccentrics; the Wang and Hsieh families, nobles of the Eastern Tsin Dynasty (317-420); Ku Kai-chih, a famous Eastern Tsin painter; Chen Shu-pao, last ruler of the Chen Dynasty (557-589); Ming-huang (685-762); Hui-tsung (1082-1135), a Northern Sung emperor, painter and calligrapher; Wen Ting-yun, a romantic poet of the late Tang Dynasty; Mi Fei (1051-1107), a Sung Dynasty painter; Shih Yen-nien, a Sung Dynasty poet; Liu Yung, a Sung poet; Chin Kuan, a Sung poet, author of many love poems.

[2] Ni Tsan, a Yuan scholar and painter; Tang Yin, a Ming painter and poet, celebrated especially for his paintings of beautiful women; Chu Yun-ming, a Ming scholar and calligrapher.

Li Kuei-nien, Huang Fan-cho, Ching Hsin-mo, Cho Wen-chun, Hung-fo, Hsüeh Tao, Tsui Ying-ying and Chao-yun.[1] All of these, in their different fields, were essentially the same."

"You're saying that such people may become princes or thieves, depending on whether they're successful or not."

"Exactly. You don't know yet that since my dismissal I've spent two years travelling through different provinces and come across one or two remarkable children. Hence my guess that this Pao-yu you mentioned belongs to the same category. Let me give you an example no further away than Chinling. You know Mr. Chen, who was principal of the Chinling Provincial College?"

"Who doesn't know him? The Chen and Chia families are interrelated and on a very friendly footing. I've done business with the Chens a number of times."

"Last year when I was in Chinling," said Yu-tsun, "someone recommended me to the Chens as a resident tutor. I was surprised to find their household so grand, yet it combined wealth with propriety. Posts like that are not easy to come by. But although my pupil was a beginner, he was harder to teach than a candidate for the Provincial Examination. Here's an example of the absurd things he'd say: 'I must have two girls as company while I study, or I can't learn characters — my brain gets muddled.' He told his pages, 'The word "girl" is so honourable and pure, not even the supreme Buddhist and Taoist titles can compare with it. You with your filthy mouths and stinking tongues must never violate it. Before you utter this word, mind you rinse your mouths with clear water or fragrant tea. If you don't, your teeth will grow crooked and rip through your cheeks.'

"He had a fearful temper and could be incredibly stubborn and obstreperous; but as soon as classes were over and he

---

[1] Li Kuei-nien, a Tang musician; Huang Fan-cho, a Tang actor; Ching Hsin-mo, a tenth-century actor; Hung-fo, the beautiful servant girl who married Li Ching, a duke in the early Tang Dynasty; Hsueh Tao, a Tang poetess; Tsui Ying-ying, heroine of *The Western Chamber*; Chao-yun, concubine of the Sung poet Su Tung-po.

joined the girls he became a different person — amiable, sensible and gentle. More than once, because of this, his father thrashed him within an inch of his life, but still that didn't change him. When the pain became too much for him, he would start yelling, 'Sister! Little Sister!' Once the girls in the inner chambers teased him saying, 'Why do you call us when you're being beaten? Do you want us to beg you off? For shame!' You should have heard his answer. He said, 'The first time I called I didn't know it would ease the pain. But then I discovered that it worked like magic. So when the pain's worst, I keep on calling "Sister."' Have you ever heard anything so ludicrous?

"His grandmother indulged him so unwisely that she was often rude to his tutor or blamed her son. That's why I resigned from that post. A boy like that is bound to lose the property he inherits and won't benefit by the advice of teachers and friends. The pity is, all the girls in his family are admirable."

"The three girls in the Chia family aren't bad either," rejoined Tzu-hsing. "Chia Cheng's elder daughter Yuan-chun was chosen to be a Lady-Clerk in the palace of the heir apparent because of her goodness, filial piety and talents. The second, Ying-chun, is Chia Sheh's daughter by a concubine. The third, Tan-chun, is Chia Cheng's daughter by a concubine. The fourth, Hsi-chun, is the younger sister of Chia Chen of the Ning Mansion. The Lady Dowager is so attached to these grand-daughters that she makes them study in the Jung Mansion near her, and I hear good reports of them all."

"I prefer the Chen family's way of giving their daughters the same sort of names as boys instead of choosing flowery names meaning Spring, Red, Fragrant, or Jade," remarked Yu-tsun. "How could the Chia family sink to such vulgarity?"

"You don't understand," said Tzu-hsing. "They named the eldest girl Yuan-chun[1] because she was born on New Year's

---

[1] Cardinal Spring.

Day, and so the others have *chun* in their names too.   But all
the girls of the last generation had names like those of boys.
For proof, look at the wife of your respected employer Mr. Lin,
the sister of Chia Sheh and Chia Cheng in the Jung Mansion.
Her name, before she married, was Chia Min.[1]   If you don't
believe me, check up when you go back."

Yu-tsun pounded the table with a laugh.   "No wonder my
pupil always pronounces *min* as *mi* and writes it with one
or two strokes missing.[2]   That puzzled me, but now you've
explained the reason.   And no wonder she talks and behaves
so differently from the general run of young ladies nowadays.
I suspected she must have had an unusual mother.   If she's
a grand-daughter of the Jung family that explains it.   What
a pity that her mother died last month."

"She was the youngest of four sisters, but now she's gone
too."   Tzu-hsing sighed.   "Not one of those sisters is left.
It will be interesting to see what husbands they find for the
younger generation."

"Yes.   Just now you spoke of Chia Cheng's son born with
jade in his mouth, and mentioned a young grandson left by
his elder son.   What about the venerable Chia Sheh?   Has
he no sons?"

"After the birth of this son with the jade Chia Cheng had
another by his concubine, but I know nothing about him.   So
he has two sons and a grandson.   However, there's no saying
how they'll turn out.   Chia Sheh has two sons as well.   Chia
Lien, the elder, is over twenty now.   Two years ago he married
a relative, the niece of Chia Cheng's wife Lady Wang.   This
Chia Lien, who has bought the rank of a sub-prefect, takes no
interest in books but is a smooth man of the world; so he lives
with his uncle Chia Cheng and helps him to manage his
domestic affairs.   Since his marriage he's been thrown into
the shade by his wife, who is praised by everybody high and
low.   I hear she's extremely good-looking and a clever talker,

---

[1] *Min* has the same radical as *Sheh* and *Cheng*.

[2] A parent's name was taboo and had to be used in an altered form.

so resourceful and astute that not a man in ten thousand is a match for her."

"That bears out what I was saying. These people we've been discussing are probably all pervaded by mixed essences of both good and evil. They are people of similar ways."

"Never mind about good and evil," protested Tzu-hsing. "We've been doing nothing but reckoning accounts for others. You must drink another cup."

"I've been talking so hard, I'm already slightly tipsy."

"Gossip goes well with wine. Why not drink some more?"

Yu-tsun looked out of the window. "It's growing late. They'll soon be closing the city gates. Let's stroll back and continue our conversation in town."

With that they paid the bill. They were on the point of leaving when a voice from behind called out:

"Congratulations, Brother Yu-tsun! What are you doing here in the wilds of the country?"

Yu-tsun turned to look. But to know who it was, you must read the chapter which follows.

CHAPTER 3

Lin Ju-hai Recommends a Tutor to His Brother-in-Law
The Lady Dowager Sends for Her Motherless Grand-Daughter

To continue. Yu-tsun turned and saw that it was Chang Ju-kuei, a native of this place and his former colleague who had also been dismissed from his post for the same reason as himself, and had returned home to Yangchow. Now there was word from the capital that a request for the reinstatement of former officials had been sanctioned, and he was busily pulling strings to find some opening. He congratulated Yu-tsun the instant he saw him and lost no time, once greetings had been exchanged, in telling him the good news. Yu-tsun was naturally overjoyed, but after some hurried remarks each went his own way.

Leng Tzu-hsing, who had heard everything, at once proposed asking Lin Ju-hai to enlist the support of Chia Cheng in the capital. Accepting his advice, Yu-tsun went back alone to verify the report from the *Court Gazette.*

The next day he laid his case before Lin Ju-hai.

"What a lucky coincidence!" exclaimed Ju-hai. "Since my wife's death my mother-in-law in the capital has been worried because my daughter has no one to bring her up. She has sent two boats with male and female attendants to fetch the child, but I delayed her departure while she was unwell. I was wondering how to repay you for your goodness in teaching her: now this gives me a chance to show my appreciation. Set your mind at rest. I foresaw this possibility and have written a letter to my brother-in-law urging him to do all he can for you as a small return for what I owe you. You mustn't

33

worry either about any expenses that may be incurred — I've made that point clear to my brother-in-law."

Yu-tsun bowed with profuse thanks and asked: "May I know your respected brother-in-law's position? I fear I am too uncouth to intrude on him."

Ju-hai smiled. "My humble kinsmen belong to your honourable clan. They're the grandsons of the Duke of Jungkuo. My elder brother-in-law Chia Sheh, whose courtesy name is En-hou, is a hereditary general of the first rank. My second, Chia Cheng, whose courtesy name is Tsun-chou, is an undersecretary in the Board of Works. He is an unassuming, generous man who takes after his grandfather. That is why I am writing to him on your behalf. If he were some purse-proud, frivolous official, I'd be dishonouring your high principles, brother, and I myself would disdain to do such a thing."

This confirmed what Tzu-hsing had said the previous day, and once more Yu-tsun expressed his thanks.

"I've chosen the second day of next month for my daughter's departure for the capital," continued Ju-hai. "It would suit both parties, surely, if you were to travel together?"

Yu-tsun promptly agreed with the greatest satisfaction, and took the gifts and travelling expenses which Ju-hai had prepared.

His pupil Tai-yu, who had just got over her illness, could hardly bear to leave her father, but she had to comply with the wishes of her grandmother.

"I am nearly fifty and don't intend to marry again," Ju-hai told her. "You're young and delicate, with no mother to take care of you, no sisters or brothers to look after you. If you go to stay with your grandmother and uncles' girls, that will take a great load off my mind. How can you refuse?"

So parting from him in a flood of tears, she embarked with her nurse and some elderly maid-servants from the Jung Mansion, followed by Yu-tsun and two pages in another junk.

In due course they reached the capital and entered the city. Yu-tsun spruced himself up and went with his pages to the gate of the Jung Mansion, where he handed in his visiting-card on which he had styled himself Chia Cheng's "nephew."

Chia Cheng, who had received his brother-in-law's letter, lost no time in asking him in. Yu-tsun cut an impressive figure and was by no means vulgar in his conversation. Since Chia Cheng was well-disposed to scholars and, like his grandfather before him, delighted in honouring worthy men of letters and helping those in distress, and since moreover his brother-in-law had recommended Yu-tsun, he treated him uncommonly well and did all in his power to help him. The same day that he presented a petition to the throne Yu-tsun was rehabilitated and ordered to await an appointment. In less than two months he was sent to Chinling to fill the vacated post of prefect of Yingtien.[1] Taking leave of Chia Cheng he chose a day to proceed to his new post. But no more of this.

To return to Tai-yu. When she disembarked, a sedan-chair from the Jung Mansion and carts for her luggage were waiting in readiness. She had heard a great deal from her mother about the magnificence of her grandmother's home; and during the last few days she had been impressed by the food, costumes and behaviour of the relatively low-ranking attendants escorting her. She must watch her step in her new home, she decided, be on guard every moment and weigh every word, so as not to be laughed at for any foolish blunder. As she was carried into the city she peeped out through the gauze window of the chair at the bustle in the streets and the crowds of people, the like of which she had never seen before.

After what seemed a long time they came to a street with two huge stone lions crouching on the north side, flanking a great triple gate with beast-head knockers, in front of which ten or more men in smart livery were sitting. The central gate was shut, but people were passing in and out of the smaller side gates. On a board above the main gate was written in large characters: Ningkuo Mansion Built at Imperial Command.

Tai-yu realized that this must be where the elder branch of her grandmother's family lived.

---

[1] Another name for Nanking.

A little further to the west they came to another imposing triple gate. This was the Jung Mansion. Instead of going through the main gate, they entered by the smaller one on the west. The bearers carried the chair a bow-shot further, then set it down at a turning and withdrew. The maid-servants behind Tai-yu had now alighted and were proceeding on foot. Three or four smartly dressed lads of seventeen or eighteen picked up the chair and, followed by the maids, carried it to a gate decorated with overhanging flowery patterns carved in wood. There the bearers withdrew, the maids raised the curtain of the chair, helped Tai-yu out and supported her through the gate.

Inside, verandahs on both sides led to a three-roomed entrance hall in the middle of which stood a screen of marble in a red sandalwood frame. The hall gave access to the large court of the main building. In front were five rooms with carved beams and painted pillars, and on either side were rooms with covered passageways. Cages of brilliantly coloured parrots, thrushes and other birds hung under the eaves of the verandahs.

Several maids dressed in red and green rose from the terrace and hurried to greet them with smiles.

"The old lady was just talking about you," they cried. "And here you are."

Three or four of them ran to raise the door curtain, and a voice could be heard announcing, "Miss Lin is here."

As Tai-yu entered, a silver-haired old lady supported by two maids advanced to meet her. She knew that this must be her grandmother, but before she could kowtow the old lady threw both arms around her.

"Dear heart! Flesh of my child!" she cried, and burst out sobbing.

All the attendants covered their faces and wept, and Tai-yu herself could not keep back her tears. When at last the others prevailed on her to stop, Tai-yu made her kowtow to her grandmother. This was the Lady Dowager from the Shih family mentioned by Leng Tzu-hsing, the mother of Chia Sheh and Chia Cheng, who now introduced the family one by one.

"This," she said, "is your elder uncle's wife. This is your second uncle's wife. This is the wife of your late Cousin Chu."

Tai-yu greeted each in turn.

"Fetch the girls," her grandmother said. "They can be excused their lessons today in honour of our guest from far away."

Two maids went to carry out her orders. And presently the three young ladies appeared, escorted by three nurses and five or six maids.

The first was somewhat plump and of medium height. Her cheeks were the texture of newly ripened lichees, her nose as sleek as goose fat. Gentle and demure, she looked very approachable.

The second had sloping shoulders and a slender waist. She was tall and slim, with an oval face, well-defined eyebrows and lovely dancing eyes. She seemed elegant and quick-witted with an air of distinction. To look at her was to forget everything vulgar.

The third was not yet fully grown and still had the face of a child.

All three were dressed in similar tunics and skirts with the same bracelets and head ornaments.

Tai-yu hastily rose to greet these cousins, and after the introductions they took seats while the maids served tea. All the talk now was of Tai-yu's mother. How had she fallen ill? What medicine had the doctors prescribed? How had the funeral and mourning ceremonies been conducted? Inevitably, the Lady Dowager was most painfully affected.

"Of all my children I loved your mother best," she told Tai-yu. "Now she has gone before me, and I didn't even have one last glimpse of her face. The sight of you makes me feel my heart will break!" Again she took Tai-yu in her arms and wept. The others were hard put to it to comfort her.

All present had been struck by Tai-yu's good breeding. For in spite of her tender years and evident delicate health, she had an air of natural distinction. Observing how frail she looked, they asked what medicine or treatment she had been having.

"I've always been like this," Tai-yu said with a smile. "I've been taking medicine ever since I was weaned. Many well-known doctors have examined me, but none of their prescriptions was any use. The year I was three, I remember being told, a scabby monk came to our house and wanted to take me away to be a nun. My parents wouldn't hear of it. The monk said, 'If you can't bear to part with her she'll probably never get well. The only other remedy is to keep her from hearing weeping and from seeing any relatives apart from her father and mother. That's her only hope of having a quiet life.' No one paid any attention, of course, to such crazy talk. Now I'm still taking ginseng pills."

"That's good," approved the Lady Dowager. "We're having pills made, and I'll see they make some for you."

Just then they heard peals of laughter from the back courtyard and a voice cried:

"I'm late in greeting our guest from afar!"

Tai-yu thought with surprise, "The people here are so respectful and solemn, they all seem to be holding their breath. Who can this be, so boisterous and pert?"

While she was still wondering, through the back door trooped some matrons and maids surrounding a young woman. Unlike the girls, she was richly dressed and resplendent as a fairy.

Her gold-filigree tiara was set with jewels and pearls. Her hair-clasps, in the form of five phoenixes facing the sun, had pendants of pearls. Her necklet, of red gold, was in the form of a coiled dragon studded with gems. She had double red jade pendants with pea-green tassels attached to her skirt.

Her close-fitting red satin jacket was embroidered with gold butterflies and flowers. Her turquoise cape, lined with white squirrel, was inset with designs in coloured silk. Her skirt of kingfisher-blue crepe was patterned with flowers.

She had the almond-shaped eyes of a phoenix, slanting eyebrows as long and drooping as willow leaves. Her figure was slender and her manner vivacious. The springtime charm of

her powdered face gave no hint of her latent formidability. And before her crimson lips parted, her laughter rang out.

Tai-yu rose quickly to greet her.

"You don't know her yet." The Lady Dowager chuckled. "She's the terror of this house. In the south they'd call her Hot Pepper. Just call her Fiery Phoenix."

Tai-yu was at a loss how to address her when her cousins came to her rescue. "This is Cousin Lien's wife," they told her.

Though Tai-yu had never met her, she knew from her mother that Chia Lien, the son of her first uncle Chia Sheh, had married the niece of Lady Wang, her second uncle's wife. She had been educated like a boy and given the school-room name Hsi-feng.[1] Tai-yu lost no time in greeting her with a smile as "cousin."

Hsi-feng took her hand and carefully inspected her from head to foot, then led her back to her seat by the Lady Dowager.

"Well," she cried with a laugh, "this is the first time I've set eyes on such a ravishing beauty. Her whole air is so distinguished! She doesn't take after her father, son-in-law of our Old Ancestress, but looks more like a Chia. No wonder our Old Ancestress couldn't put you out of her mind and was for ever talking or thinking about you. But poor ill-fated little cousin, losing your mother so young!" With that she dabbed her eyes with a handkerchief.

"I've only just dried my tears. Do you want to start me off again?" said the old lady playfully. "Your young cousin's had a long journey and she's delicate. We've just got her to stop crying. So don't reopen that subject."

Hsi-feng switched at once from grief to merriment. "Of course," she cried. "I was so carried away by joy and sorrow at sight of my little cousin, I forgot our Old Ancestress. I deserve to be caned." Taking Tai-yu's hand again, she asked, "How old are you, cousin? Have you started your schooling yet? What medicine are you taking? You mustn't be home-

---

[1] Splendid Phoenix.

sick here. If you fancy anything special to eat or play with, don't hesitate to tell me. If the maids or old nurses aren't good to you, just let me know."

She turned then to the servants. "Have Miss Lin's luggage and things been brought in? How many attendants did she bring? Hurry up and clear out a couple of rooms where they can rest."

Meanwhile refreshments had been served. And as Hsi-feng handed round the tea and sweetmeats, Lady Wang asked whether she had distributed the monthly allowance.

"It's finished," was Hsi-feng's answer. "Just now I took some people to the upstairs storeroom at the back to look for some brocade. But though we searched for a long time we couldn't find any of the sort you described to us yesterday, madam. Could your memory have played you a trick?"

"It doesn't matter if there's none of that sort," said Lady Wang. "Just choose two lengths to make your little cousin some clothes. This evening don't forget to send for them."

"I've already done that," replied Hsi-feng. "Knowing my cousin would be here any day, I got everything ready. The material's waiting in your place for your inspection. If you pass it, madam, it can be sent over."

Lady Wang smiled and nodded her approval.

Now the refreshments were cleared away and the Lady Dowager ordered two nurses to take Tai-yu to see her two uncles.

At once Chia Sheh's wife, Lady Hsing, rose to her feet and suggested, "Won't it be simpler if I take my niece?"

"Very well," agreed the Lady Dowager. "And there's no need for you to come back afterwards."

Lady Hsing assented and then told Tai-yu to take her leave of Lady Wang, after which the rest saw them to the entrance hall. Outside the ornamental gate pages were waiting beside a blue lacquered carriage with kingfisher-blue curtains, into which Lady Hsing and her niece entered. Maids let down the curtains and told the bearers to start. They bore the carriage to an open space and harnessed a docile mule to it.

They left by the west side gate, proceeded east past the main entrance of the Jung Mansion, entered a large black-lacquered gate and drew up in front of a ceremonial gate.

When the pages had withdrawn, the curtains were raised, and Lady Hsing led Tai-yu into the courtyard. It seemed to her that these buildings and grounds must be part of the Jung Mansion garden; for when they had passed three ceremonial gates she saw that the halls, side chambers and covered corridors although on a smaller scale were finely constructed. They had not the stately splendour of the other mansion, yet nothing was lacking in the way of trees, plants or artificial rockeries.

As they entered the central hall they were greeted by a crowd of heavily made-up and richly dressed concubines and maids. Lady Hsing invited Tai-yu to be seated while she sent a servant to the library to ask her husband to join them.

After a while the servant came back to report, "The master says he hasn't been feeling too well the last few days, and meeting the young lady would only upset them both. He isn't up to it for the time being. Miss Lin mustn't mope or be homesick here but feel at home with the old lady and her aunts. Her cousins may be silly creatures, but they'll be company for her and help to amuse her. If anyone is unkind to her, she must say so and not treat us as strangers."

Tai-yu had risen to her feet to listen to this message. Shortly after this she rose again to take her leave. Lady Hsing insisted that she stay for the evening meal.

"Thank you very much, aunt, you're too kind," said Tai-yu. "Really I shouldn't decline. But it might look rude if I delayed in calling on my second uncle. Please excuse me and let me stay another time."

"You're quite right," said Lady Hsing. She told a few elderly maids to escort her niece back in the same carriage, whereupon Tai-yu took her leave. Her aunt saw her to the ceremonial gate and after giving the maids some further instructions waited to see them off.

Back in the Jung Mansion, Tai-yu alighted again. The nurses led her eastwards, round a corner, through an entrance hall into a hall facing south, then passed through a ceremonial gate into a large courtyard. The northern building had five large apartments and wings on either side. This was the hub of the whole estate, more imposing by far than the Lady Dowager's quarters.

Tai-yu realized that this was the main inner suite, for a broad raised avenue led straight to its gate. Once inside the hall she looked up and her eye was caught by a great blue tablet with nine gold dragons on it, on which was written in characters large as peck measures:

Hall of Glorious Felicity.

Smaller characters at the end recorded the date on which the Emperor had conferred this tablet upon Chia Yuan, the Duke of Jungkuo, and it bore the Imperial seal.

On the large red sandalwood table carved with dragons an old bronze tripod, green with patina, stood about three feet high. On the wall hung a large scroll-picture of black dragons riding the waves. This was flanked by a bronze wine vessel inlaid with gold and a crystal bowl. By the walls were a row of sixteen cedar-wood armchairs; and above these hung two panels of ebony with the following couplet inset in silver:

> Pearls on the dais outshine the sun and moon;
> Insignia of honour in the hall blaze like
>   iridescent clouds.

Small characters below recorded that this had been written by the Prince of Tungan, who signed his name Mu Shih and styled himself a fellow provincial and old family friend.

Since Lady Wang seldom sat in this main hall but used three rooms on the east side for relaxation, the nurses led Tai-yu there.

The large *kang* by the window was covered with a scarlet foreign rug. In the middle were red back-rests and turquoise bolsters, both with dragon-design medallions, and a long greenish yellow mattress also with dragon medallions. At each side stood a low table of foreign lacquer in the shape of plum-blossom. On the left-hand table were a tripod, spoons, chop-sticks and an incense container; on the right one, a slender-waisted porcelain vase from the Juchow Kiln containing flowers then in season, as well as tea-bowls and a spittoon. Below the *kang* facing the west wall were four armchairs, their covers of bright red dotted with pink flowers, and with four foot-stools beneath them. On either side were two tables set out with teacups and vases of flowers. The rest of the room need not be described in detail.

The nurses urged Tai-yu to sit on the *kang*, on the edge of which were two brocade cushions. But feeling that this would be presumptuous, she sat instead on one of the chairs on the east side. The maids in attendance served tea, and as she sipped it she studied them, observing that their make-up, clothes and deportment were quite different from those in other families. Before she had finished her tea in came a maid wearing a red silk coat and a blue satin sleeveless jacket with silk borders. With a smile this girl announced:

"Her Ladyship asks Miss Lin to go in and take a seat over there."

At once the nurses conducted Tai-yu along the eastern cor-ridor to a small three-roomed suite facing south. On the *kang* under the window was a low table laden with books and a tea-service. Against the east wall were a none too new blue satin back-rest and a bolster.

Lady Wang was sitting in the lower place by the west wall on a none too new blue satin cover with a back-rest and a bolster. She invited her niece to take the seat on the east. But guessing that this was Chia Cheng's place, Tai-yu chose one of the three chairs next to the *kang*, which had black-dotted antimacassars, looking none too new. Not until she had been pressed several times did she take a seat by her aunt.

"Your uncle's observing a fast today," said Lady Wang. "You'll see him some other time. But there's one thing I want to tell you. Your three cousins are excellent girls, and I'm sure you'll find them easy to get on with during lessons, or when you're learning embroidery or playing together. Just one thing worries me: that's my dreadful son, the bane of my life, who torments us all in this house like a real devil. He's gone to a temple today in fulfilment of a vow, but you'll see what he's like when he comes back this evening. Just pay no attention to him. None of your cousins dare to provoke him."

Tai-yu's mother had often spoken of this nephew born with a piece of jade in his mouth, his wild ways, aversion to study and delight in playing about in the women's apartments. Apparently he was so spoiled by his grandmother that no one could control him. She knew Lady Wang must be referring to him.

"Does aunt mean my elder cousin with the jade in his mouth?" she asked with a smile. "Mother often spoke of him. I know he's a year older than me, his name is Pao-yu, and for all his pranks he's very good to his girl cousins. But how can I provoke him? I'll be spending all my time with the other girls in a different part of the house while our boy cousins are in the outer courtyards."

"You don't understand," replied Lady Wang with a laugh. "He's not like other boys. Because the old lady's always doted on him, he's used to being spoilt with the girls. If they ignore him he keeps fairly quiet though he feels bored. He can always work off his temper by scolding some of his pages. But if the girls give him the least encouragement, he's so elated he gets up to all kinds of mischief. That's why you mustn't pay any attention to him. One moment he's all honey-sweet; the next, he's rude and recalcitrant; and in another minute he's raving like a lunatic. You can't take him seriously."

As Tai-yu promised to remember this, a maid announced that dinner was to be served in the Lady Dowager's apartments. Lady Wang at once led her niece out of the back door, going west along a corridor and through a side gate to a broad road running from north to south. On the south side was a dainty three-roomed annex facing north; on the north a big screen wall painted white, behind which was a small door leading to an apartment.

"That's where your cousin Hsi-feng lives." Lady Wang pointed out the place. "So next time you know where to find her. If you want anything just let her know."

By the gate several young pages, their hair in tufts, stood at attention. Lady Wang led Tai-yu through an entrance hall running from east to west into the Lady Dowager's back courtyard. Stepping through the back door, they found quite a crowd assembled who, as soon as they saw Lady Wang, set tables and chairs ready. Chia Chu's widow, Li Wan, served the rice while Hsi-feng put out the chopsticks and Lady Wang served the soup.

The Lady Dowager was seated alone on a couch at the head of the table with two empty chairs on each side. Hsi-feng took Tai-yu by the hand to make her sit in the first place on the left, but she persistently declined the honour.

"Your aunt and sisters-in-law don't dine here," said her grandmother with a smile. "Besides, you're a guest today. So do take that seat."

With a murmured apology, Tai-yu obeyed. The Lady Dowager told Lady Wang to sit down; then Ying-chun and the two other girls asked leave to be seated, Ying-chun first on the right, Tan-chun second on the left, and Hsi-chun second on the right. Maids held ready dusters, bowls for rinsing the mouth and napkins, while Li Wan and Hsi-feng standing behind the diners plied them with food.

Although the outer room swarmed with nurses and maids, not so much as a cough was heard. The meal was eaten in silence. And immediately after, tea was brought in on small trays. Now Lin Ju-hai had taught his daughter the virtue of moderation and the harm caused to the digestive system by drinking tea directly after a meal. But many customs here were different from those in her home. She would have to adapt herself to these new ways. As she took the tea, however, the rinse-bowls were proffered again, and seeing the others rinse their mouths she followed suit. After they had washed their hands tea was served once more, this time for drinking.

"You others may go," said the Lady Dowager now. "I want to have a chat with my grand-daughter."

Lady Wang promptly rose and after a few remarks led the way out, followed by Li Wan and Hsi-feng. Then her grandmother asked Tai-yu what books she had studied.

"I've just finished the *Four Books*,"[1] said Tai-yu. "But I'm very ignorant." Then she inquired what the other girls were reading.

"They only know a very few characters, not enough to read any books."

The words were hardly out of her mouth when they heard footsteps in the courtyard and a maid came in to announce, "Pao-yu is here."

Tai-yu was wondering what sort of graceless scamp or little dunce Pao-yu was and feeling reluctant to meet such a stupid creature when, even as the maid announced him, in he walked.

He had on a golden coronet studded with jewels and a golden chaplet in the form of two dragons fighting for a pearl. His red archer's jacket, embroidered with golden butterflies and flowers, was tied with a coloured tasselled palace sash. Over this he wore a turquoise fringed coat of Japanese satin with a raised pattern of flowers in eight bunches. His court boots were of black satin with white soles.

His face was as radiant as the mid-autumn moon, his complexion fresh as spring flowers at dawn. The hair above his temples was as sharply outlined as if cut with a knife. His eyebrows were as black as if painted with ink, his cheeks as red as peach-blossom, his eyes bright as autumn ripples. Even when angry he seemed to smile, and there was warmth in his glance even when he frowned.

Round his neck he had a golden torque in the likeness of a dragon, and a silk cord of five colours, on which hung a beautiful piece of jade.

His appearance took Tai-yu by surprise. "How very strange!" she thought. "It's as if I'd seen him somewhere before. He looks so familiar."

---

[1] Confucian classics.

Pao-yu paid his respects to the Lady Dowager and upon her instructions went to see his mother.

He returned before long, having changed his clothes. His short hair in small plaits tied with red silk was drawn up on the crown of his head and braided into one thick queue as black and glossy as lacquer, sporting four large pearls attached to golden pendants in the form of the eight precious things. His coat of a flower pattern on a bright red ground was not new, and he still wore the torque, the precious jade, a lock-shaped amulet containing his Buddhistic name, and a lucky charm. Below could be glimpsed light green flowered satin trousers, black-dotted stockings with brocade borders, and thick-soled scarlet shoes.

His face looked as fair as if powdered, his lips red as rouge. His glance was full of affection, his speech interspersed with smiles. But his natural charm appeared most in his brows, for his eyes sparkled with a world of feeling. However, winning as his appearance was, it was difficult to tell what lay beneath.

Someone subsequently gave an admirable picture of Pao-yu in these two verses written to the melody of *The Moon over the West River*:

> Absurdly he courts care and melancholy
> And raves like any madman in his folly;
> For though endowed with handsome looks is he,
> His heart is lawless and refractory.
>
> Too dense by far to understand his duty,
> Too stubborn to apply himself to study,
> Foolhardy in his eccentricity,
> He's deaf to all reproach and obloquy.
>
> Left cold by riches and nobility,
> Unfit to bear the stings of poverty,
> He wastes his time and his ability,
> Failing his country and his family.
>
> First in this world for uselessness is he,
> Second to none in his deficiency.
> Young fops and lordlings all, be warned by me:
> Don't imitate this youth's perversity!

With a smile at Pao-yu, the Lady Dowager scolded, "Fancy changing your clothes before greeting our visitor. Hurry up now and pay your respects to your cousin."

Of course, Pao-yu had seen this new cousin earlier on and guessed that she was the daughter of his Aunt Lin. He made haste to bow and, having greeted her, took a seat. Looking at Tai-yu closely, he found her different from other girls.

Her dusky arched eyebrows were knitted and yet not frowning, her speaking eyes held both merriment and sorrow; her very frailty had charm. Her eyes sparkled with tears, her breath was soft and faint. In repose she was like a lovely flower mirrored in the water; in motion, a pliant willow swaying in the wind. She looked more sensitive than Pi Kan,[1] more delicate than Hsi Shih.[2]

"I've met this cousin before," he declared at the end of his scrutiny.

"You're talking nonsense again," said his grandmother, laughing. "How could you possibly have met her?"

"Well, even if I haven't, her face looks familiar. I feel we're old friends meeting again after a long separation."

"So much the better." The Lady Dowager laughed. "That means you're bound to be good friends."

Pao-yu went over to sit beside Tai-yu and once more gazed fixedly at her.

"Have you done much reading, cousin?" he asked.

"No," said Tai-yu. "I've only studied for a couple of years and learned a few characters."

"What's your name?"

She told him.

"And your courtesy name?"

"I have none."

"I'll give you one then," he proposed with a chuckle. "What could be better than Pin-pin?"[3]

---

[1] A prince noted for his great intelligence at the end of the Shang Dynasty.

[2] A famous beauty of the ancient Kingdom of Yueh.

[3] Knitted Brows.

"Where's that from?" put in Tan-chun.

"*The Compendium of Men and Objects Old and New* says that in the west is a stone called *tai* which can be used instead of graphite for painting eyebrows. As Cousin Lin's eyebrows look half knit, what could be more apt than these two characters?"

"You're making that up, I'm afraid," teased Tan-chun.

"Most works, apart from the *Four Books*, are made up; am I the only one who makes things up?" he retorted with a grin. Then, to the mystification of them all, he asked Tai-yu if she had any jade.

Imagining that he had his own jade in mind, she answered, "No, I haven't. I suppose it's too rare for everybody to have."

This instantly threw Pao-yu into one of his frenzies. Tearing off the jade he flung it on the ground.

"What's rare about it?" he stormed. "It can't even tell good people from bad. What spiritual understanding has it got? I don't want this nuisance either."

In consternation all the maids rushed forward to pick up the jade while the Lady Dowager in desperation took Pao-yu in her arms.

"You wicked monster!" she scolded. "Storm at people if you're in a passion. But why should you throw away that precious thing your life depends on?"

His face stained with tears, Pao-yu sobbed, "None of the girls here has one, only me. What's the fun of that? Even this newly arrived cousin who's lovely as a fairy hasn't got one either. That shows it's no good."

"She did have one once," said the old lady to soothe him. "But when your aunt was dying and was unwilling to leave her, the best she could do was to take the jade with her instead. That was like burying the living with the dead and showed your cousin's filial piety. It meant, too, that now your aunt's spirit can still see your cousin. That's why she said she had none, not wanting to boast about it. How can you compare with her? Now put it carefully on again lest your mother hears about this."

She took the jade from one of the maids and put it on him herself. And Pao-yu, convinced by her tale, let the matter drop.

Just then a nurse came in to ask about Tai-yu's quarters.

"Move Pao-yu into the inner apartment of my suite," said his grandmother. "Miss Lin can stay for the time being in his Green Gauze Lodge. Once spring comes, we'll make different arrangements."

"Dear Ancestress!" coaxed Pao-yu. "Let me stay outside Green Gauze Lodge. I'll do very well on that bed in the outer room. Why should I move over and disturb you?"

After a moment's reflection the Lady Dowager agreed to this. Each would be attended by a nurse and a maid, while other attendants were on night duty outside. Hsi-feng had already sent round a flowered lavender curtain, satin quilts and embroidered mattresses.

Tai-yu had brought with her only Nanny Wang, her old wet-nurse, and ten-year-old Hsueh-yen, who had also attended her since she was a child. Since the Lady Dowager considered Hsueh-yen too young and childish and Nanny Wang too old to be of much service, she gave Tai-yu one of her own personal attendants, a maid of the second grade called Ying-ko. Like Ying-chun and the other young ladies, in addition to her own wet-nurse Tai-yu was given four other nurses as chaperones, two personal maids to attend to her toilet and five or six girls to sweep the rooms and run errands.

Nanny Wang and Ying-ko accompanied Tai-yu now to Green Gauze Lodge, while Pao-yu's wet-nurse, Nanny Li, and his chief maid Hsi-jen made ready the big bed for him in its outer room.

Hsi-jen, whose original name was Chen-chu, had been one of the Lady Dowager's maids. The old lady so doted on her grandson that she wanted to make sure he was well looked after and for this reason she gave him her favourite, Hsi-jen, a good, conscientious girl. Pao-yu knew that her surname was

Hua[1] and remembered a line of poetry which ran, "the fragrance of flowers assails men." So he asked his grandmother's permission to change her name to Hsi-jen.[2]

Hsi-jen's strong point was devotion. Looking after the Lady Dowager she thought of no one but the Lady Dowager, and after being assigned to Pao-yu she thought only of Pao-yu. What worried her, though, was that he was too headstrong to listen to her advice.

That night after Pao-yu and Nanny Li were asleep, Hsi-jen noticed that Tai-yu and Ying-ko were still up in the inner room. She tiptoed in there in her night clothes and asked:

"Why aren't you sleeping yet, miss?"

"Please sit down, sister," invited Tai-yu with a smile.

Hsi-jen sat on the edge of the bed.

"Miss Lin has been in tears all this time, she's so upset," said Ying-ko. "The very day of her arrival, she says, she's made our young master fly into a tantrum. If he'd smashed his jade she would have felt to blame. I've been trying to comfort her."

"Don't take it to heart," said Hsi-jen. "I'm afraid you'll see him carrying on even more absurdly later. If you let yourself be upset by his behaviour you'll never have a moment's peace. Don't be so sensitive."

"I'll remember what you've said," promised Tai-yu. "But can you tell me where that jade of his came from, and what the inscription on it is?"

Hsi-jen told her, "Not a soul in the whole family knows where it comes from. It was found in his mouth, so we hear, when he was born, with a hole for a cord already made in it. Let me fetch it here to show you."

But Tai-yu would not hear of this as it was now late. "I can look at it tomorrow," she said.

After a little more chat they went to bed.

The next morning, after paying her respects to the Lady Dowager, Tai-yu went to Lady Wang's apartments. She found her and Hsi-feng discussing a letter from Chinling. With them

---

[1] Flower.
[2] Literally "assails men."

were two maid-servants who had brought a message from the house of Lady Wang's brother.

Tai-yu did not understand what was going on, but Tan-chun and the others knew that they were discussing Hsueh Pan, the son of Aunt Hsueh in Chinling. Presuming on his powerful connections, he had had a man beaten to death and was now to be tried in the Yingtien prefectural court. Lady Wang's brother Wang Tzu-teng, having been informed of this, had sent these messengers to the Jung Mansion to urge them to invite the Hsueh family to the capital. But more of this in the next chapter.

CHAPTER 4

An Ill-Fated Girl Meets an Ill-Fated Man
A Confounded Monk Ends a Confounded Case

To resume. Tai-yu and the other girls found Lady Wang discussing family affairs with messengers sent by her brother, and heard that her sister's son was involved in a murder case. Since she was so occupied, the girls called on Li Wan.

Li Wan was the widow of Chia Chu who had died young, but luckily she had a son, Chia Lan, just five and already in school. Her father, Li Shou-chung, a notable of Chinling, had served as a Libationer in the Imperial College. All the sons and daughters of his clan had been devoted to the study of the classics. When he became head of the family, however, in the belief that "an unaccomplished woman is a virtuous woman," instead of making his daughter study hard he simply had her taught enough to read a few books such as the *Four Books for Girls, Biographies of Martyred Women,* and *Lives of Exemplary Ladies* so that she might remember the deeds of worthy women of earlier dynasties while devoting her main attention to weaving and household tasks. That was why he gave her the name Li Wan[1] and the courtesy name Kung-tsai.[2]

So this young widow living in the lap of luxury was no better off than withered wood or cold ashes, taking no interest in the outside world. Apart from waiting on her elders and looking after her son, all she did was to accompany the girls at their embroidery or reading.

---

[1] Plain Silk.

[2] Palace Seamstress.

Though Tai-yu was only a guest here, with cousins like these to keep her company she felt completely at home, except for worrying sometimes about her father.

But to return to Chia Yu-tsun. No sooner had he taken up his post as prefect of Yingtien than a charge of murder was brought to his court. It was a case of two parties claiming to have purchased the same slave girl, neither willing to give way, and in consequence one of them had been beaten to death. Yu-tsun summoned the plaintiff for questioning.

"The murdered man was my master," the plaintiff testified. "He bought a slave girl not knowing that she'd been kidnapped and paid for her in silver. Our master said he'd take her home three days later because that would be a lucky day. Then the kidnapper sold her on the sly to the Hsueh family. When we found this out, we went to him to demand the girl. But the Hsuehs lord it in Chinling with their money and powerful backing. A pack of their thugs beat my master to death, after which the murderers, master and men, disappeared without a trace, leaving here only a few people who weren't involved. I lodged a charge a year ago, but nothing came of it. I beg Your Honour to arrest the criminals, punish the evil-doers and help the widow and orphan. Then both the living and the dead will be everlastingly grateful!"

"This is a scandal!" fumed Yu-tsun. "How can men commit a murder and go scot-free?"

He was about to order his runners to arrest the criminals' relatives for interrogation, in order to find out the murderers' whereabouts and issue warrants for their arrest, when an attendant standing by his table shot him a warning glance. Then Yu-tsun refrained and left the court in some bewilderment.

Back in his private office he dismissed everyone but the attendant, who went down on one knee in salute, then said with a smile:

"Your Honour has risen steadily in the official world. After eight or nine years, do you still remember me?"

"Your face looks very familiar, but I can't place you."

The attendant smiled. "High officials have short memories," he said. "So you've forgotten the spot you started from, Your Honour, and what happened in Gourd Temple?"

At this disconcerting remark, the past came back to Yu-tsun like the crash of a thunder-bolt. Now this attendant had been a novice in Gourd Temple. When the fire left him stranded he decided that work in a yamen would be easier and, having had enough of monastic austerity, instead of going to another temple he had taken advantage of his youth to grow his hair again and get this post. No wonder Yu-tsun had failed to recognize him.

Now, taking his hand, the prefect observed with a smile: "So we are old acquaintances."

He invited him to take a seat, but the attendant declined the honour.

"We were friends in the days when I was hard up," said Yu-tsun. "Besides, this is my private office. As we are going to have a good talk, how can you remain standing all the time?"

Then, deferentially, the attendant perched sideways on the edge of a chair. And Yu-tsun asked why he had stopped him from issuing the warrants.

"Now that Your Honour's come to this post," said the attendant, "surely you've copied out the Officials' Protective Charm for this province?"

"Officials' Protective Charm? What do you mean?"

"Don't tell me you've never heard of it? In that case you won't keep your job long. All local officials nowadays keep a secret list of the most powerful, wealthy and high-ranking families in their province. Each province has such a list. Because if unknowingly you offend one of these families, you may lose not only your post but your life as well. That's why it's called a Protective Charm. This Hsueh family mentioned just now is one Your Honour can't afford to offend. There's nothing difficult about this case, but out of deference to them it was never settled by your predecessor."

With that he took a hand-written copy of the Officials' Protective Charm from his pocket and handed it to Yu-tsun. It was a doggerel catalogue of the most notable families in that district with notes on their ancestry, ranks and family branches. It started off:

> The Chinling Chias,
> If truth be told,
> Have halls of jade,
> Stables of gold.

>> *Twenty branches descended from the Duke of Ningkuo and the Duke of Jungkuo. Apart from eight branches in the capital, there are twelve branches in their ancestral district.*

> Vast O Fang Palace,
> Fit for a king,
> Isn't fine enough
> For the Shihs of Chinling.

>> *Twenty branches descended from Marquis Shih of Paoling, Prime Minister. Ten in the capital, ten in the ancestral district.*

> If the Dragon King wants
> A white jade bed,
> He applies to the Wangs
> Of Chinling, it's said.

>> *Twelve branches descended from Earl Wang the High Marshal. Two in the capital, the rest in the ancestral district.*

> The Hsuehs in their affluence
> Are so rich and grand,
> Gold is like iron to them
> And pearls like sand.

>> *Eight branches descended from Lord Hsueh, Imperial Secretary. Now in charge of the Treasury.*

Before Yu-tsun could finish reading the list, a chime sounded at the gate and a certain Mr. Wang was announced. Putting on his official robes and cap again, he went to receive the caller, coming back in the time it takes for a meal to ask for more information.

"These four families are all closely connected," said the attendant. "Injure one and you injure them all, honour one and

you honour them all. They help each other and cover up for each other. This Hsueh charged with murder is one of the Hsuehs on that list. Not only can he count on the support of those three other families, he has plenty of influential friends and relatives both in the capital and in the provinces. So whom is Your Honour going to arrest?"

"If that's so, how are we to settle the case?" asked Yu-tsun. "I take it you know the murderer's hiding-place?"

"I won't keep it from Your Honour." The attendant grinned. "I know not only where the murderer has gone, I know the kidnapper who sold the girl, and I knew the poor devil who bought her. Let me put all the facts before you.

"The man who was killed, Feng Yuan, was the son of one of the minor local gentry. Both his parents died when he was young and he had no brothers; he lived as best he could on his small property. Up to the age of eighteen or nineteen he was a confirmed queer and took no interest in women. But then, no doubt as retribution for entanglements in a former life, he ran into this kidnapper and no sooner set eyes on this girl than he fell for her and made up his mind to buy her for his concubine. He swore to have no more to do with men and to take no other wife. That was why he insisted on her coming to him three days later. Who was to know that the kidnapper would sell her on the sly to the Hsuehs, meaning to abscond with the payment from both parties? Before he could get away with this, they nabbed him and beat him within an inch of his life. Both refused to take back their money — both wanted the girl. Then young Hsueh, who will never give an inch to anyone, ordered his men to beat Feng Yuan into a pulp. Three days after being carried home he died.

"Young Hsueh had already fixed on a day to set off for the capital. But happening to see this girl two days before leaving he decided to buy her and take her along, not knowing the trouble that would come of it. Then, having killed a man and carried off a girl, he set off with his household as if nothing had happened, leaving his clansmen and servants here to settle the business. A trifling matter like taking a man's life wouldn't frighten him away. So much for him. But do you know who the girl is?"

"How could I know?"

"She's by way of being Your Honour's benefactress." The attendant sniggered. "She's Ying-lien, the daughter of Mr. Chen who lived next to Gourd Temple."

"Well!" exclaimed Yu-tsun in astonishment. "So that's who she is! I heard that she was kidnapped when she was five. Why didn't they sell her before?"

"Kidnappers of this type make a point of stealing small girls. They bring them up somewhere out of the way until they're eleven or twelve, then take them elsewhere to sell according to their looks. We used to play with Ying-lien every day. Although seven or eight years have passed and she's now a good-looking girl of twelve or thirteen, her features haven't changed and anyone who knew her can easily recognize her. Besides, she had a red birthmark the size of a grain of rice between her eyebrows, which makes me quite sure it's her.

"As the kidnapper happened to rent rooms from me, one day when he was away I asked her outright. She'd been beaten so much she was afraid to talk; she just insisted that he was her father, selling her to clear his debts. When I tried repeatedly to wheedle it out of her, she burst into tears and said she didn't remember a thing about her childhood. So there's no doubt. It's her, all right.

"The day that young Feng met her and paid down his silver, the kidnapper got drunk. Then Ying-lien sighed, 'At last my trials are over!' She started worrying again, though, when she heard Feng wouldn't be fetching her for three days. I was so sorry for her that as soon as the kidnapper went out I sent my wife to cheer her up.

"My wife told her: 'Mr. Feng's insistence on waiting for a lucky day is proof that he won't be treating you like a servant. Besides, he's a very fine gentleman, quite well-to-do, who never could abide women in the past, yet now he's paid a fancy price for you. That all goes to show you're quite safe. Just be patient for two or three days. You've no reason to worry.'

"She perked up a bit then, believing that she'd soon have a place where she belonged. But this world is full of disappointments: the very next day she was sold to the Hsuehs. Any other family wouldn't have been so bad; but this young Hsueh, otherwise known as the Stupid Tyrant, is the most vicious ruffian alive, who throws money about like dirt. He started a big fight and then dragged her off by force more dead than alive. What's become of her since, I don't know.

"Feng Yuan dreamed of happiness, but instead of finding it he lost his life. Wretched luck, wasn't it?"

"This was retribution, no accident," replied Yu-tsun with a sigh. "Otherwise, why should Feng Yuan have taken a fancy to Ying-lien and no one else? As for her, after being knocked about all those years by the kidnapper she at last saw a way out with a man who loved her, and if she'd married him all would have been well; but then this had to happen! Of course, Hsueh's family is richer than Feng's, but a profligate like Hsueh Pan is sure to have troops of maids and concubines and to be thoroughly debauched — he could never be as true to one girl as Feng Yuan. So this romance was an empty dream, a chance encounter between an ill-fated young couple. Well, enough of that. What's the best way to settle this case?"

"Your Honour used to be shrewd enough in the past," said the attendant with a smile. "What's made you so short of ideas today? I heard that your appointment was due to the good offices of the Chias and Wangs, and this Hsueh is related to the Chias by marriage. So why not sail with the stream and do them a good turn, settling this case in such a way that you can face them in future?"

"There's much in what you say. But a man's life is involved. Moreover, I've been re-instated by the Emperor's favour and am in fact beginning a new life. I should be doing my utmost to show my gratitude. How can I flout the law for private considerations? I really can't bring myself to do such a thing."

The attendant sneered: "Your Honour is right, of course. But that won't get you anywhere in the world today. Remember the old sayings: 'A gentleman adapts himself to cir-

cumstances' and 'The superior man is one who pursues good
fortune and avoids disaster.' If you do as you just said, not
only will you be unable to repay the Emperor's trust, you may
endanger your own life into the bargain. Better think it over
carefully."

Yu-tsun lowered his head. After a long silence he asked:
"What do *you* suggest?"

"I've thought of a very good plan," said the attendant. "It's
this. When Your Honour tries the case tomorrow, make a
great show of sending out writs and issuing warrants. Of
course the murderer won't be forthcoming and the plaintiff will
press his case; then you can arrest some of Hsueh's clansmen
and servants for interrogation. Behind the scenes I'll fix things
so that they report Hsueh Pan's 'death by sudden illness,' and
we'll get his clan and the local authorities to testify to this.

"Then Your Honour can claim to be able to consult spirits
through the planchette. Have one set up in the court and invite both military and civilians to come and watch. You can
say: The spirit declares that Hsueh Pan and Feng Yuan were
enemies in a former existence who were fated to clash in order
to settle scores; that, hounded by Feng Yuan's ghost, Hsueh
Pan has perished of some mysterious disease; that since this
trouble was caused by the man who kidnapped the girl with
such-and-such a name, he must be dealt with according to the
law, but no one else is involved . . . and so on and so forth.

"I'll see to it that the kidnapper makes a full confession,
and when the spirit's message confirms this, people will be
convinced.

"The Hsuehs are rolling in money. You can make them
pay a thousand or five hundred taels for Feng Yuan's funeral
expenses. His relatives are insignificant people, and all they're
out for is money. So the silver will shut their mouths.

"What does Your Honour think of this scheme of mine?"

"Impossible." Yu-tsun laughed. "I shall have to think this
over carefully in order to suppress idle talk."

Their consultation lasted late into the afternoon.

The next day a number of suspects were summoned to court and Yu-tsun cross-examined them carefully. He found that the Feng family was indeed a small one and just out for more money for the funeral, but the case had been confused and left unsettled because of the stubborn Hsuehs' powerful connections.

So Yu-tsun twisted the law to suit his own purpose and passed arbitrary judgement. The Fengs received a large sum for funeral expenses and made no further objections.

Once the case was settled Yu-tsun lost no time in writing to Chia Cheng and Wang Tzu-teng, Commander-in-Chief of the Metropolitan Garrison, to inform them that the charge against their worthy nephew was dropped and they need not worry about it any longer. All this was due to the attendant who had been a novice in Gourd Temple, but Yu-tsun, dismayed by the thought that this man might disclose certain facts about the days when he was poor and humble, later found some fault with him and had him exiled to a distant region.

Let us return now to young Hsueh, who had bought Ying-lien and had Feng Yuan beaten to death. He came of a scholarly Chinling family, but having lost his father while still a child he was thoroughly spoiled by his mother as the only son and heir, with the result that he grew up good for nothing. For they were millionaires, in receipt of an income from the State Treasury as Purveyors for the Imperial Household.

Young Hsueh's name was Pan, his courtesy name Wen-chi, and since the age of five or six he had shown himself extravagant in his habits and insolent in his speech. At school he merely learned a few characters, spending all his time on cockfights, riding or pleasure trips. Although a Court Purveyor, he knew nothing of business or worldly affairs but prevailed on his grandfather's old connections to find him a well-paid sinecure in the Board of Revenue and left all business to his agents and old family servants.

His widowed mother, née Wang, was the younger sister of Wang Tzu-teng, Commander-in-Chief of the Metropolitan Garrison, and the sister of Lady Wang, wife of Chia Cheng of the Jung Mansion. She was about forty years of age and

Hsueh Pan was her only son. But she also had a daughter two years younger whose infant name was Pao-chai, a beautiful, dainty girl of great natural refinement. While her father was still alive he made her study, and she turned out ten times better than her brother. However, after her father's death it was so clear that Hsueh Pan would prove no comfort to their mother that Pao-chai gave up her studies and devoted herself to needlework and the household management, so as to share her mother's burden and cares.

Recently, to honour culture, encourage propriety and search out talent, in addition to selecting consorts and ladies-in-waiting the Emperor in his infinite goodness had made the Board compile a list of the daughters of ministers and noted families from whom to choose virtuous and gifted companions for the princesses in their studies.

Moreover, since the death of Hsueh Pan's father, all the managers and assistants in the Purveyor's offices of different provinces had taken advantage of his youth and inexperience to start swindling, and even the business in the various family shops in the capital was gradually falling off.

Thus Hsueh Pan, who had long heard of the splendours of the capital, now had three pretexts for a visit to it: First, to escort his sister there for the selection; secondly, to see his relatives; and thirdly, to clear his accounts and decide on further outlay. His real reason, of course, was to see the sights of the great metropolis.

He had long since packed his luggage and valuables and prepared local specialities of every kind as gifts for relatives and friends. An auspicious day for departure had just been chosen when he met the kidnapper who was selling Ying-lien and, struck by her good looks, promptly purchased her. When Feng Yuan demanded her back, Hsueh Pan relying on his powerful position ordered his bullies to beat the young man to death. Then entrusting the family affairs to some clansmen and old servants, he left with his mother and sister. To him a murder charge was just a trifle which could easily be settled with some filthy lucre.

After some days on the road they were approaching the capital when word came of the promotion of his uncle Wang Tzu-teng to the post of Commander-in-Chief of Nine Provinces with orders to inspect the borders.

Hsueh Pan told himself gleefully, "I was just thinking what a bore it would be to have an uncle cramping my style in the capital. Now he's been upgraded and is leaving. It shows Heaven is kind."

He suggested to his mother, "Although we have some houses in the capital, none of us has lived there for ten years or more and the caretakers may have rented them out. Let's send someone on ahead to have one cleaned up."

"Why go to such trouble?" she asked. "When we arrive, we should first call on relatives and friends. We can stay with your uncle or aunt. Both of them have plenty of space. Wouldn't it be simpler to put up there first and take our time over opening up other houses?"

"But uncle's just been promoted and is going to the provinces, so his place is bound to be upside down. If we descend on him like a swarm of bees, it will look most inconsiderate."

"Your uncle may be leaving for his new post, but there's still your aunt's house. They've written year after year inviting us to visit the capital. Now that we're here and your uncle's getting ready to leave, your Aunt Chia is sure to press us to stay there. It will appear very strange to them if we're in such a rush to open up one of our own houses.

"I know what you're after. You're afraid of being under restraint if you stay with your uncle or aunt. You'd prefer to be on your own, free to do as you please. In that case, go and find yourself some lodgings. I've been parted all these years from your aunt and we old sisters want to spend a little time together. I shall take your sister there with me. Have you any objection to that?"

Realizing that he could not talk his mother round, Hsueh Pan had perforce to order his servants to make straight for the Jung Mansion.

Meanwhile Lady Wang, who had learned with relief of the dismissal thanks to Yu-tsun of the charge against Hsueh Pan, had been dismayed again by her brother's promotion to a frontier post, for this confronted her with the lonely prospect of having none of her own family to visit. But a few days later a servant suddenly announced that her sister had brought her son and daughter and whole household to the capital, and they were just alighting outside the gate.

In her joy, Lady Wang hurried out to the reception hall with her daughter and daughter-in-law to greet the whole party and conduct them inside. We need not dwell on the mingled delight and sorrow of these two sisters meeting again in the evening of life or all their tears, laughter and reminiscences.

Lady Wang took them in to pay their respects to the Lady Dowager, and they distributed the gifts they had brought. When the entire family had been introduced, a feast of welcome was spread for the travellers. And after Hsueh Pan had paid his respects to Chia Cheng, Chia Lien took him over to call on Chia Sheh and Chia Chen.

Then Chia Cheng sent a message to his wife saying, "My sister-in-law has seen many springs and autumns, and my nephew is young and inexperienced. He may get into some scrapes if they live outside. The ten rooms and more in Pear Fragrance Court in the northeast corner of our grounds are empty. Let us have them swept clean and ask your sister and her children to stay there."

Before Lady Wang could extend this invitation, the Lady Dowager also sent to urge, "Do invite your sister to stay here, so that we can all be close together."

Aunt Hsueh was only too glad to comply so as to have some check on her son, who was likely to get up to fresh mischief if they lived outside. She promptly accepted with thanks and in private intimated to Lady Wang that, if she was to make a long stay, she must be allowed to defray all her household's daily expenses. Lady Wang knew that this presented no difficulty for the Hsueh family, and therefore agreed. So Aunt Hsueh and her children moved into Pear Fragrance Court.

This court where the Duke of Jungkuo had spent his declining years was small but charming, its dozen or so rooms including a reception hall in front and the usual sleeping quarters and offices behind. It had its own entrance to the street which the Hsueh household used, while a passage from a southwest gate led to the east courtyard of Lady Wang's main apartment. Every day after lunch or in the evening, Aunt Hsueh would walk over to chat with the Lady Dowager or to talk over the old days with her sister.

Pao-chai spent her time with Tai-yu, Ying-chun and the other girls, very happy to read, play chess or sew with them.

Only Hsueh Pan at first disliked this arrangement, for fear that his uncle would control him so strictly that he would not be his own master. He had to comply for the time being, however, because his mother had made up her mind to it and the Chia family pressed them so hard to stay. None the less, he sent servants to make ready one of his own houses for when he decided to move.

To his relief, after less than a month he found himself on familiar terms with half the Chia sons and nephews, and all the rich young men of fashion among them enjoyed his company. One day they would meet to drink, the next to look at flowers, and soon they included him in gambling parties or visits to the courtesans' quarters, with the result that Hsueh Pan rapidly became even ten times worse than before.

Although Chia Cheng was known for his fine method of schooling his sons and disciplining his household, the family was too large for him to see to everything. Moreover the head of the clan was Chia Chen, who as the eldest grandson of the Duke of Ningkuo had inherited the title and was responsible for all clan affairs.

Besides, Chia Cheng, occupied as he was by public and private business, was too easy-going to take mundane matters seriously, preferring to give all his leisure to reading and chess.

Since Pear Fragrance Court was two courtyards away from his quarters and had its own entrance to the street through which people could pass as they pleased, the young men caroused and enjoyed themselves just as they chose. For these reasons, before very long Hsueh Pan gave up all thought of moving.

To know what followed, turn to the next chapter.

CHAPTER 5

The Spiritual Stone Is Too Bemused to Grasp
the Fairy's Riddles
The Goddess of Disenchantment in Her Kindness
Secretly Expounds on Love

Drowsy in spring beneath embroidered quilts,
In a trance with a goddess he leaves the world
of men.
Who is this now entering the Land of Dreams?
The most unregenerate lover since time began.

The fourth chapter told briefly how the Hsuehs came to stay in the Jung Mansion, but now let us return to Tai-yu.

Since her coming to the Jung Mansion, the Lady Dowager had been lavishing affection on her, treating her in every respect just like Pao-yu so that Ying-chun, Tan-chun and Hsi-chun, the Chia girls, all had to take a back seat. And Pao-yu and Tai-yu had drawn closer to each other than all the others. By day they strolled or sat together; at night they went to bed in the same apartment. On all matters, indeed, they were in complete accord.

But now Pao-chai had suddenly appeared on the scene. Although only slightly older, she was such a proper young lady and so charming that most people considered Tai-yu inferior to her. In the eyes of the world, of course, everyone has some merits. In the case of Tai-yu and Pao-chai, one was lovely as a flower, the other graceful as a willow, but each charming in her own way, according to her distinctive temperament.

Besides, Pao-chai's generous, tactful and accommodating ways contrasted strongly with Tai-yu's stand-offish reserve and won the hearts of her subordinates, so that nearly all the maids liked to chat with her. Because of this, Tai-yu began to feel some twinges of jealousy. But of this Pao-chai was completely unaware.

Pao-yu was still only a boy and a very absurd and wilful one at that, who treated his brothers, sisters and cousins alike, making no difference between close and distant kinsmen. Because he and Tai-yu both lived in the Lady Dowager's quarters, he was closer to her than to the other girls, and being closer had grown more intimate; but precisely because of this he sometimes offended her by being too demanding and thoughtless.

Today the two of them had fallen out for some reason and Tai-yu, alone in her room, was again shedding tears. Sorry for his tactlessness, Pao-yu went in to make it up and little by little contrived to comfort her.

As the plum blossom was now in full bloom in the Ning Mansion's garden, Chia Chen's wife Madam Yu invited the Lady Dowager, Lady Hsing, Lady Wang and the others to a party to enjoy the flowers. She brought Chia Jung and his wife with her to deliver the invitations in person, and so the Lady Dowager and the rest went over after breakfast. They strolled round the Garden of Concentrated Fragrance and were served first with tea then wine; but it was simply an informal gathering of the womenfolk of both houses for a family feast, with nothing of special interest to record.

Soon Pao-yu was tired and wanted to have a nap. The Lady Dowager ordered his attendants to take good care of him and bring him back after a rest.

At once Chia Jung's wife Chin Ko-ching said with a smile: "We have a room ready here for Uncle Pao-yu. The Old Ancestress can set her mind at rest and leave him safely to me." She told his nurses and maids to follow her with their young master.

The Lady Dowager had every confidence in this lovely slender young woman who with her gentle, amiable behaviour was her favourite of all the great-grandsons' wives of the Jung and Ning branches. She was therefore sure Pao-yu would be in good hands.

Ko-ching led the party to an inner room, where Pao-yu noticed a fine painting of "The Scholar Working by Torch-light."[1] Without even seeing who the artist was, he took a dislike to the picture. Then he read the couplet flanking it:

> A grasp of mundane affairs is genuine knowledge,
> Understanding of worldly wisdom is true learning.

These two lines disgusted him with the place for all its refinement and luxury, and he begged to go somewhere else.

"If this isn't good enough, where can we take you?" asked his hostess with a laugh. "Well, come along to my room."

Pao-yu nodded and smiled but one of his nurses protested: "It's not proper for an uncle to sleep in his nephew's room."

"Good gracious!" Ko-ching smiled. "I won't mind his being offended if I say he's still a baby. At his age such taboos don't apply. Didn't you see my brother who came last month? He's the same age as Uncle Pao-yu, but if they stood side by side I'm sure he'd be the taller."

"Why haven't I met him?" asked Pao-yu. "Do bring him in and let me have a look at him."

The women burst out laughing. "He's miles away, how can we bring him? You'll meet him some other time."

Now, having reached the young matron's room, they were met at the threshold by a subtle perfume which misted over Pao-yu's eyes and melted his bones.

"How good it smells here!" he cried.

Entering, he saw on the wall a picture by Tang Yin[2] of a lady sleeping under the blossom of a crab-apple tree in spring. On the two scrolls flanking it, Chin Kuan[3] the Sung scholar had written:

> Coolness wraps her dream, for spring is chill;
> A fragrance assails men, the aroma of wine.

---

[1] A Han Dynasty scholar, Liu Hsiang, was said to have been studying late one night when a god came with a torch to teach him the classics.

[2] See Note 2 on p. 28.

[3] See Note 1 on p. 28.

On the dressing-table was a rare mirror from Wu Tse-tien's[1] Hall of Mirrors. In the gold tray by it, on which Chao Fei-yen[2] once danced, was the quince thrown in fun by An Lu-shan[3] at Lady Yang,[4] which had wounded her breast. At one end of the room stood the couch on which Princess Shou-yang[5] had slept in the Hanchang Palace, and over it hung the curtains strung from pearls by Princess Tung-chang.[6]

"It's nice in here," exclaimed Pao-yu repeatedly in his delight.

"This room of mine is probably fit for a god," rejoined Ko-ching with a smile.

With her own hands she spread a gauze coverlet washed by Hsi Shih[7] and arranged the bridal pillow carried by Hung-niang.[8] Then the nurses and attendants made Pao-yu lie down and slipped out leaving only four maids — Hsi-jen, Mei-jen, Ching-wen and Sheh-yueh — to keep him company. Ko-ching told them to wait on the verandah and watch the kittens and puppies playing there.

Pao-yu fell asleep as soon as he closed his eyes and dreamed that Ko-ching was before him. Absent-mindedly he followed her a long way to some crimson balustrades and white marble steps among green trees and clear streams, in a place seldom trodden by the foot of man, unreached by swirling dust.

In his dream he thought happily, "This is a pleasant spot. If only I could spend my whole life here! For that I'd gladly give up my home where my parents and teachers keep caning me every day."

His fancy was running away with him when he heard someone singing a song on the other side of a hill:

---

[1] A Tang empress.

[2] A Han emperor's favourite, a light dancer, hence her name "Fei-yen," meaning "Flying Swallow."

[3] See Note 2 on p. 27.

[4] The favourite of the Tang emperor Ming-huang.

[5] The beautiful daughter of Emperor Wu of the Sung Kingdom (420-479), the Northern and Southern Dynasties.

[6] A Tang princess.

[7] See Note 2 on p. 48.

[8] See Note 1 on p. 5.

> Gone with the clouds spring's dream,
> Flowers drift away on the stream.
> Young lovers all, be warned by me,
> Cease courting needless misery.

Pao-yu realized that the voice was a girl's and before the song had ended he saw the singer come round the hill and approach him. With her graceful gait and air she was truly no mortal being. Here is as proof her description:

> Leaving the willow bank, she comes just now through the flowers. Her approach startles birds in the trees in the court, and soon her shadow falls across the verandah. Her fairy sleeves, fluttering, give off a heady fragrance of musk and orchid. With each rustle of her lotus garments, her jade pendants tinkle.
>
> Her dimpled smile is peach-blossom in spring, her blue-black hair a cluster of clouds. Her lips are cherries and sweet the breath from her pomegranate teeth.
>
> The curve of her slender waist is snow whirled by the wind. Dazzling her pearls and emeralds and gosling-gold the painted design on her forehead.
>
> She slips in and out of the flowers, now vexed, now radiant, and floats over the lake as if on wings.
>
> Her mothlike eyebrows are knit yet there lurks a smile, and no sound issues from her lips parted as if to speak as she glides swiftly on lotus feet and, pausing, seems poised for flight.
>
> Her flawless complexion is pure as ice, smooth as jade. Magnificent her costume with splendid designs. Sweet her face, compact of fragrance, carved in jade; and she bears herself like a phoenix or dragon in flight.
>
> Her whiteness? Spring plum-blossom glimpsed through snow. Her purity? Autumn orchids coated with frost. Her tranquillity? A pine in a lonely valley. Her beauty? Sunset mirrored in a limpid pool. Her grace? A dragon breasting a winding stream. Her spirit? Moonlight on a frosty river.
>
> She would put Hsi Shih to shame and make Wang Chiang[1] blush. Where was this wonder born, whence does she come?
>
> Verily she has no peer in fairyland, no equal in the purple courts of heaven.
>
> Who can she be, this beauty?

Overjoyed by the apparition of this fairy, Pao-yu made haste to greet her with a bow.

"Sister Fairy," he begged with a smile, "do tell me where you are from and whither you are going. I have lost my way. May I beg you to be my guide?"

---

[1] A famous beauty in the Han Dynasty.

"My home is above the Sphere of Parting Sorrow in the Sea of Brimming Grief," she answered with a smile. "I am the Goddess of Disenchantment from the Grotto of Emanating Fragrance on the Mountain of Expanding Spring in the Illusory Land of Great Void. I preside over romances and unrequited love on earth, the grief of women and the passion of men in the mundane world. The reincarnations of some former lovers have recently gathered here, and so I have come to look for a chance to mete out love and longing. It is no accident that we have met.

"My realm is not far from here. All I can offer you is a cup of fairy tea plucked by my own hands, a pitcher of fine wine of my own brewing, some accomplished singers and dancers, and twelve new fairy songs called 'A Dream of Red Mansions.' But won't you come with me?"

Forgetting Ko-ching in his delight, Pao-yu followed the goddess to a stone archway inscribed: Illusory Land of Great Void. On either pillar was this couplet:

> When false is taken for true, true becomes false;
> If non-being turns into being, being becomes non-being.

Beyond this archway was a palace gateway with the inscription in large characters: Sea of Grief and Heaven of Love. The bold couplet flanking this read:

> Firm as earth and lofty as heaven, passion from
>   time immemorial knows no end;
> Pity silly lads and plaintive maids hard put to
>   it to requite debts of breeze and moonlight.

"Well, well," thought Pao-yu, "I wonder what's meant by 'passion from time immemorial' and 'debts of breeze and moonlight.' From now on I'd like to have a taste of these things."

Little did he know that by thinking in this way he had summoned an evil spirit into his inmost heart.

He followed the goddess through the second gate past two matching halls on both sides, each with its tablet and couplet. He had no time to read them all but noticed the names: Board of Infatuation, Board of Jealousy, Board of Morning Tears,

Board of Night Sighs, Board of Spring Longing and Board of Autumn Sorrows.

"May I trouble you, goddess, to show me over these different boards?" he asked.

"They contain the records of the past and future of girls from all over the world," she told him. "These may not be divulged in advance to you with your human eyes and mortal frame."

But Pao-yu would not take no for an answer and at last she yielded to his importunity.

"Very well then," she conceded. "You may go in here and have a look round."

Pao-yu was overjoyed. He looked up and saw on the tablet the name Board of the Ill-Fated. This was flanked by the couplet:

> They brought on themselves spring grief and
> autumn anguish;
> Wasted, their beauty fair as flowers and moon.

Grasping the meaning of this and strangely stirred, Pao-yu entered and saw more than ten large cabinets, sealed and labelled with the names of different localities. Having no interest in other provinces, he was eager to find his native place and soon discovered one cabinet labelled *First Register of Twelve Beauties of Chinling*. When he asked what this meant, Disenchantment told him:

"That is a record of the twelve foremost beauties in your honourable province. That's why it's called the First Register."

"I've always heard that Chinling's a very large place," replied Pao-yu. "Why are there only twelve girls? In our family alone just now, if you count the servants, we must have several hundreds."

"True, there are many girls in your honourable province. Only those of the first grade are registered here. The next two cabinets contain records of those in the second and third grade. As for the rest, they are too mediocre for their lives to be worth recording."

Pao-yu looked at the next two cabinets and saw written on them: *Second Register of Twelve Beauties of Chinling* and *Third Register of Twelve Beauties of Chinling*. He opened the door of this last, took out the register and turned to the first page. This was covered by a painting in ink, not of any figures or landscape but of black clouds and heavy mist. Beside this were the lines:

> A clear moon is rarely met with,
> Bright clouds are easily scattered;
> Her heart is loftier than the sky,
> But her person is of low degree.
> Her charm and wit give rise to jealousy,
> Her early death is caused by calumny,
> In vain her loving master's grief must be.

On the next page Pao-yu saw painted a bunch of flowers and a tattered mat, with the legend:

> Nothing avail her gentleness and compliance,
> Osmanthus and orchid with her fragrance vie;
> But this prize is borne off by an actor,
> And luck passes the young master by.

Unable to make anything of this, he put the album down, opened the door of another cabinet and took out the *Second Register*. This opened at a picture of fragrant osmanthus above withered lotus in a dried-up pond. By this was written:

> Sweet is she as the lotus in flower,
> Yet none so sorely oppressed;
> After the growth of a lonely tree in two soils
> Her sweet soul will be dispatched to its final rest.

Still baffled, Pao-yu put this volume aside and took out the *First Register*. The first page had a painting of two withered trees on which hung a jade belt, while at the foot of a snow-drift lay a broken golden hairpin. Four lines of verse read:

> Alas for her wifely virtue,
> Her wit to sing of willow-down, poor maid!
> Buried in snow the broken golden hairpin
> And hanging in the wood the belt of jade.

Pao-yu could make nothing of this either. He knew the goddess would not enlighten him, yet he could not bring him-

self to put the book down.   So he turned to a painting of a
bow from which was suspended a citron.   This bore the legend:

> For twenty years she arbitrates
> Where pomegranates blaze by palace gates.
> How can the late spring equal the spring's start?
> When Hare and Tiger meet,[1]
> From this Great Dream of life she must depart.

On the next page was a picture of two people flying a kite,
while in a large boat out at sea sat a girl, weeping, covering
her face with her hands.   With this were the lines:

> So talented and high-minded,
> She is born too late for luck to come her way.
> Through tears she watches the stream
> On the Clear and Bright Day;[2]
> A thousand *li* the east wind blows,
> But her home in her dreams is far away.

Next came a painting of drifting clouds and flowing water
with the legend:

> Nought avail her rank and riches,
> While yet in swaddling clothes an orphan lone;
> In a flash she mourns the setting sun,
> The river Hsiang runs dry, the clouds over Chu
>   have flown.

Next was depicted a fine piece of jade dropped in the mud,
with the verse:

> Chastity is her wish,
> Seclusion her desire;
> Alas, though fine as gold or jade
> She sinks at last in the mire.

There followed a sketch of a savage wolf pursuing a lovely
girl to devour her.   The verdict read:

> For husband she will have a mountain wolf,
> His object gained he ruthlessly berates her;
> Fair bloom, sweet willow in a golden bower,
> Too soon a rude awakening awaits her.

---

[1] "Tiger" and "Hare" are the third and fourth years in the twelve-year
cycle.

[2] The festival, usually on the 5th of April, when the Chinese visited
their family graves.

Next was depicted a seated girl reading a sutra alone in an old temple. This had the legend:

> She sees through the transience of spring,
> Dark Buddhist robes replace her garments fine;
> Pity this child of a wealthy noble house
> Who now sleeps alone by the dimly lit old shrine.

Next came a female phoenix perched on an iceberg, with the verdict:

> This bird appears when the world falls on evil times;
> None but admires her talents and her skill;
> First she complies, then commands, then is dismissed,
> Departing in tears to Chinling more wretched still.

After this was a lonely village with a pretty girl spinning in a humble cottage. The inscription read:

> When fortune frowns, nobility means nothing;
> When a house is ruined, kinsmen turn unkind.
> Because of help given by chance to Granny Liu,
> In time of need she is lucky a friend to find.

After this was painted a pot of orchids in bloom beside a beauty in ceremonial dress. The legend ran:

> Peach and plum in spring winds finish seeding,
> Who can bloom like the orchid at last?
> Pure as ice and water she arouses envy,
> Vain the groundless taunts that are cast.

Next came a picture of a beautiful woman hanging herself on a tower, with the verdict:

> Love boundless as sea and sky is but illusion;
> When lovers meet, lust must be king.
> Say not all evil comes from the Jung Mansion,
> Truly, disaster originates from the Ning.

Pao-yu would have read on, but the goddess knowing his high natural endowments and quick intelligence feared the secrets of Heaven might be divulged. She closed the book therefore and said to him with a smile:

"Why not come with me to enjoy the strange sights here instead of puzzling your head over these silly riddles?"

As if in a daze he left the registers and followed her past pearl portières and embroidered curtains, painted pillars and carved beams. Words fail to describe those brilliant vermilion rooms, floors paved with gold, windows bright as snow and palaces of jade, to say nothing of the delectable fairy flowers, rare plants and fragrant herbs.

As Pao-yu was feasting his eyes on these marvellous sights Disenchantment called with a laugh: "Come out quickly and welcome our honoured guest."

At once out came several fairies, lotus sleeves swaying, feathery garments fluttering, lovely as spring blossom, entrancing as the autumn moon. At sight of Pao-yu they reproached the goddess:

"So this is your guest! Why should we hurry out to meet *him*? You told us that today, at this hour, the spirit of Sister Vermilion Pearl would be coming to revisit her old haunts. That's why we've been waiting all this time. Why bring this filthy creature here instead to pollute this domain of immaculate maidens?"

Pao-yu started at that and wished he could slip away, feeling intolerably gross and filthy, but Disenchantment took him by the hand.

"You don't understand," she explained to the fairies. "I did set off to the Jung Mansion today to fetch Vermilion Pearl, but as I was passing the Ning Mansion I met the spirits of the Duke of Ningkuo and the Duke of Jungkuo who told me, 'Since the start of this dynasty, for some generations, our family has enjoyed a fine reputation as well as riches and rank. But after a hundred years our good fortune is at an end, gone beyond recall. Although we have many descendants, the only one fit to continue our work is our great-grandson Pao-yu. Even though he is headstrong and eccentric, lacking in intelligence, we nonetheless had certain hopes of him. However, our family's luck has run out and there seemed to be no one to show him the right way. How fortunate we are to have met you, goddess. We beg you to warn him of the dangers of lusting after women, so that he may escape from their snares and set his feet on the right path. Then we two brothers will be happy.'

"Sympathizing with their request, I fetched him here. To begin with I made him look at the three registers of the girls in his own household. When he failed to understand, I brought him here to taste the illusion of carnal delight so that later he may perchance awaken to the truth."

With that she led Pao-yu inside. A subtle perfume hung in the air and he could not help asking what incense was being burned.

"You don't have this scent in the dusty world so you wouldn't know it," Disenchantment told him, smiling. "This is made from the essences of the different exotic young plants which grow in all famous mountain resorts. Distilled with the resin of every precious tree, its name is Marrow of Manifold Fragrance."

As Pao-yu marvelled at this they took seats and young maids served tea with such a pure scent, exquisite flavour and refreshing quality that again he asked its name.

"This tea grows in the Grotto of Emanating Fragrance on the Mountain of Expanding Spring," Disenchantment told him. "Infused with the night dew from fairy flowers and spiritual leaves, its name is Thousand Red Flowers in One Cavern."

Nodding in appreciation Pao-yu looked round him. He saw jasper lutes, rare bronze tripods, ancient paintings, new volumes of verse — nothing was lacking. But what delighted him most was the rouge by the window and the spilt powder left from a lady's toilet. On the wall hung this couplet:

> Spiritual, secluded retreat,
> Celestial world of sweet longing.

Lost in admiration of everything about him, he asked the fairies' names. They were introduced by their different appellations as Fairy of Amorous Dreams, Great Mistress of Passion, Golden Maid Bringing Grief, and Saint of Transmitted Sorrow.

Presently little maids brought in tables and chairs and set out wine and refreshments. Verily, glass vessels overflowed with nectar and amber cups brimmed with ambrosia. No need to dwell on the sumptuousness of that feast. He could not resist inquiring, though, what gave the wine its remarkably pure bouquet.

"This wine is made from the stamens of a hundred flowers and the sap of ten thousand trees mixed with the marrow of unicorns and fermented with phoenix milk," the goddess told him. "We call it Ten Thousand Beauties in One Cup."

As Pao-yu sipped it, twelve dancing girls stepped forward to ask what they should perform.

"The twelve new songs called 'A Dream of Red Mansions,'" ordered Disenchantment.

The dancers assented. Lightly striking their sandalwood castanets and softly plucking their silver lyres, they began:

> At the dawn of creation....

But the goddess interrupted them to tell Pao-yu, "This is not like your romantic dramas in the dusty world in which there are always the fixed parts of scholars, girls, warriors, old men and clowns, and the set nine tunes of the south or north. These songs of ours lament one person or event in an impromptu fashion and are easily set to wind or stringed accompaniments. But no outsider can appreciate their subtle qualities, and I doubt whether you will really understand their meaning. Unless you first read the text, they will seem to you as tasteless as chewed wax."

With that she turned and ordered a maid to bring the words of the "Dream of Red Mansions" songs. She handed the manuscript to Pao-yu, who followed the text as he listened.

FIRST SONG:
PROLOGUE TO THE DREAM OF RED MANSIONS
> At the dawn of creation
> Who sowed the seeds of love?
> From the strong passion of breeze and moonlight
>   they came.
> So in this world of sweet longing
> On a day of distress, in an hour of loneliness,
> Fain would I impart my senseless grief

By singing this *Dream of Red Mansions*
To mourn the Gold and the Jade.

SECOND SONG:
A LIFE MISSPENT

Well-matched, all say, the gold and the jade;
I alone recall the pledge between plant and stone.
Vainly facing the hermit in sparkling snow-clad hills
I forget not the fairy in lone woods beyond the
    world.
I sigh, learning that no man's happiness is complete:
Even a pair thought well-matched
May find disappointment.

THIRD SONG:
VAIN LONGING

One is an immortal flower of fairyland,
The other fair flawless jade,
And were it not predestined
Why should they meet again in this existence?
Yet, if predestined,
Why does their love come to nothing?
One sighs to no purpose,
The other yearns in vain;
One is the moon reflected in the water,
The other but a flower in the mirror.
How many tears can well from her eyes?
Can they flow on from autumn till winter,
From spring till summer?

Pao-yu could see no merit in these disjointed and cryptic
songs, but the plaintive music intoxicated his senses. So
without probing into the meaning or asking where the songs
came from, he listened for a while to pass the time. The
singers went on:

FOURTH SONG:
THE TRANSIENCE OF LIFE

At the height of honour and splendour
Death comes for her;
Open-eyed, she has to leave everything behind
As her gentle soul passes away.
So far her home beyond the distant mountains
That in a dream she finds and tells her parents:
"Your child has gone now to the Yellow Spring;
You must find a retreat before it is too late."

FIFTH SONG:
SEPARATION FROM DEAR ONES

Three thousand *li* she must sail through wind
    and rain,
Giving up her home and her own flesh and blood;
But afraid to distress their declining years with tears
She tells her parents: "Don't grieve for your child.
From of old good luck and bad have been predestined,
Partings and reunions are decreed by fate;
Although from now on we shall dwell far apart,
Let us still live at peace;
Don't worry over your unworthy daughter."

SIXTH SONG:
SORROW   AMIDST   JOY

She is still in her cradle when her parents die,
Although living in luxury who will dote on her?
Happily she is born too courageous and open-hearted
Ever to take a love affair to heart.
Like bright moon and fresh breeze in a hall of jade
She is matched with a talented and handsome
    husband;
May she live with him for long years
To make up for her wretched childhood!
But over the Kaotang Tower the clouds disperse,
The river Hsiang runs dry.
This is the common fate of mortal men,
Useless it is to repine.

SEVENTH SONG:
SPURNED BY THE WORLD

By nature fair as an orchid,
With talents to match an immortal,
Yet so eccentric that all marvel at her.
To her, rich food stinks,
Silken raiment is vulgar and loathsome;
She knows not that superiority fosters hatred,
For the world despises too much purity.
By the dim light of an old shrine she will fade away,
Her powder and red chamber, her youth and beauty
    wasted,
To end, despite herself, defiled on the dusty road —
Even as flawless white jade dropped in the mud.
In vain young scions of noble houses will sigh for her.

EIGHTH SONG:
UNION OF ENEMIES

A mountain wolf, a savage ruthless beast,
Mindless of past obligations

Gives himself up to pride, luxury and license,
Holding cheap the charms of a noble family's
        daughter,
Trampling on the precious child of a ducal mansion.
Alas, in less than a year her sweet soul fades away.

NINTH SONG:
PERCEPTION OF THE TRANSIENCE OF FLOWERS

She will see through the three Springs[1]
And set no store
By the red of peach-blossom, the green of willows,
Stamping out the fire of youthful splendour
To savour the limpid peace of a clear sky.
Though the peach runs riot against the sky,
Though the clouds teem with apricot blossom,
Who has seen any flower that can win safely
        through autumn?
Even now mourners are lamenting by groves of
        poplars,
Ghosts are wailing below green maples,
And the weeds above their graves stretch to the
        skyline.
Truly, changes in fortune are the cause of men's toil,
Spring blooming and autumn withering the fate of
        flowers.
Who can escape the gate of birth, the fate of death?
Yet in the west, they say, grows the *sal* tree[2]
Which bears the fruit of immortality.

TENTH SONG:
RUINED BY CUNNING

Too much cunning in plotting and scheming
Is the cause of her own undoing;
While yet living her heart is broken
And after death all her subtlety comes to nothing.
A rich house, all its members at peace,
Is ruined at last and scattered;
In vain her anxious thought for half a lifetime,
For like a disturbing dream at dead of night,
Like the thunderous collapse of a great mansion,
Or the flickering of a lamp that gutters out,
Mirth is suddenly changed to sorrow.
Ah, nothing is certain in the world of men.

---

[1] A pun meaning the three months of Spring and the three elder Chia
girls. All the Chia girls had the character *chun* or spring in their names.

[2] It was said that Sakyamuni attained Buddhahood in a grove of *sal* trees.

ELEVENTH SONG:
A LITTLE ACT OF KINDNESS

Thanks to one small act of kindness
She meets by chance a grateful friend;
Fortunate that her mother
Has done some unnoticed good.
Men should rescue the distressed and aid the poor,
Be not like her heartless uncle or treacherous cousin
Who for love of money forget their own flesh and
    blood.
Truly, rewards and punishments
Are meted out by Heaven.

TWELFTH SONG:
SPLENDOUR COMES TOO LATE

Love is only a reflection in a mirror,
Worse still, rank and fame are nothing but a dream,
So quickly youth and beauty fade away.
Say no more of embroidered curtains and love-bird
    quilts,
Nor can a pearl tiara and phoenix jacket
Stave off for long Death's summons.
Though it is said that old age should be free
    from want,
This depends on the unknown merits laid by for
    one's children.
Jubilant in official headdress
And glittering with a gold seal of high office,
A man may be awe-inspiring and exalted,
But the gloomy way to the Yellow Spring is near.
What remains of the generals and statesmen of old?
Nothing but an empty name admired by posterity.

THIRTEENTH SONG:
GOOD THINGS COME TO AN END

Fragrant dust falls from painted beams at the close
    of spring;
By nature passionate and fair as the moon,
The true root is she of the family's destruction.
The decline of the old tradition starts with Ching,
The chief blame for the House's ruin rests with Ning.
All their sins come about through Love.

EPILOGUE:
THE BIRDS SCATTER TO THE WOOD

An official household declines,
Rich nobles' wealth is spent.
She who did good escapes the jaws of death,
The heartless meet with certain retribution.

Those who took a life have paid with their own lives,
The tears one owed have all been requited in kind.
Not light the retribution for sins against others;
All are predestined, partings and reunions.
Seek the cause of untimely death in a past existence,
Lucky she who enjoys rank and riches in old age;
Those who see through the world escape from the
    world,
While foolish lovers forfeit their lives for nothing.
When the food is gone the birds return to the wood;
All that's left is emptiness and a great void.

After this they would have gone on to sing the second series, but the Goddess of Disenchantment saw that Pao-yu was utterly bored.

"Silly boy!" she sighed. "You still don't understand."

Pao-yu asked the fairies then not to sing any more, explaining that he was drunk and would like to sleep off the effects of the wine.

Disenchantment ordered the feast to be cleared away and escorted him into a scented chamber hung with silk, more luxuriously furnished than any he had seen in his life. More amazing still, he saw there a girl whose charm reminded him of Pao-chai, her grace of Tai-yu. He was puzzling over this when Disenchantment said:

"In your dusty world, countless green-windowed chambers and embroidered boudoirs of rich and noble families are desecrated by amorous men and loose women. Worse still, all dissolute wretches since ancient times have drawn a distinction between love of beauty and carnal desire, between love and lust, so as to gloss over their immorality. Love of beauty leads to lust, and desire even more so. Thus every sexual transport of cloud and rain is the inevitable climax of love of beauty and desire.

"And what I like about you is that you are the most lustful man ever to have lived in this world since time immemorial."

"You must be mistaken, goddess," protested the frightened Pao-yu. "My parents are always scolding me because I'm too lazy to study. How dare I risk being called 'lustful' as well? Besides, I'm still young and hardly know what that word means."

"Don't worry," said Disenchantment. "In principle all lust is the same, but it has different connotations. For instance, there are profligates in the world who delight only in physical beauty, singing, dancing, endless merriment and constant rain-and-cloud games. They would like to possess all the beauties in the world to gratify their momentary desires. These are coarse creatures steeped in fleshly lust.

"In your case, you were born with a passionate nature which we call 'lust of the mind.' This can be grasped by the mind but not expressed, apprehended intuitively but not described in words. Whereas this makes you a welcome companion to women, in the eyes of the world it is bound to make you appear strange and unnatural, an object of mockery and scorn.

"After meeting your worthy ancestors the Duke of Ningkuo and the Duke of Jungkuo today and hearing their heartfelt request, I could not bear to let you be condemned by the world for the greater glory of women. So I brought you here to entertain you with divine wine and fairy tea, then tried to awaken you with subtle songs. And now I am going to match you with my younger sister Chien-mei,[1] whose childhood name is Ko-ching, and this very night at the auspicious hour you must consummate your union. This is simply to let you know that after you have proved for yourself the illusory nature of pleasures in fairyland you should realize the vanity of love in your dusty world. From this day on you must understand this and mend your ways, giving your minds to the teachings of Confucius and Mencius and devoting yourself to the betterment of society."

With that she initiated him into the secrets of sex. Then, pushing him forward, she closed the door and left.

Pao-yu in a daze did all the goddess had told him. We can draw a veil over his first act of love.

---

[1] "Combining the best," i.e., the best features of Pao-chai and Tai-yu.

The next day, he and Ko-ching had become so attached and exchanged so many endearments that they could not bear to part. Hand in hand they walked out for a stroll.

Suddenly they found themselves in a thorny thicket infested with wolves and tigers. In front a black torrent barred their way and there was no bridge across. They were in a quandary when Disenchantment overtook them.

"Stop! Stop!" she cried. "Turn back before it's too late."

Standing petrified Pao-yu asked, "What is this place?"

"The Ford of Infatuation," Disenchantment told him. "It's a hundred thousand feet deep and a thousand *li* wide, and there is no boat to ferry you across. Nothing but a wooden raft steered by Master Wood and punted by Acolyte Ashes, who accept no payment in silver or gold but ferry over those who are fated to cross. You strolled here by accident. If you had fallen in, then all my well-meant advice to you would have been wasted."

Even as she spoke there came a crash like thunder from the Ford of Infatuation as hordes of monsters and river devils rushed towards Pao-yu to drag him in. Cold sweat poured off him like rain. And in his terror he shouted:

"Ko-ching! Save me!"

Hsi-jen hurried in with the other maids in dismay to take him in her arms.

"Don't be afraid, Pao-yu," cried the girls. "We're here."

Chin Ko-ching was on the verandah telling the maids to watch the kittens and puppies at their play, when she heard Pao-yu call her childhood name in his dream.

"No one here knows my childhood name," she thought in surprise. "How is it that he called it out in his dream?"

Truly:

> Strange encounters take place in a secret dream,
> For he is the most passionate lover of all time.

CHAPTER 6

Pao-yu Has His First Taste of Love
Granny Liu Pays Her First Visit
to the Jung Mansion

The theme:

> She knocks one day at the gate of the rich,
> And the rich themselves talk of want;
> Their gift is not a thousand pieces of gold
> But more than her own flesh and blood could give.

Chin Ko-ching was amazed to hear Pao-yu call her child-hood name in his dream, but she could hardly question him. As for Pao-yu, he felt as bemused as if he had lost his wits. Attendants promptly brought him a longan decoction and after sipping a couple of mouthfuls he got up to adjust his clothes.

As Hsi-jen reached out to fasten his trousers for him, she touched his thigh and found it cold and sticky. She drew back in alarm and asked what was the matter. Flushing crimson, Pao-yu simply squeezed her hand.

Now Hsi-jen was an intelligent girl, and being a couple of years older than Pao-yu she already knew the facts of life. She guessed from the state he was in what must have happened and blushing herself helped him to tidy his clothes without any further questions.

They went then to where the Lady Dowager was and after a hasty meal returned to his room, where in the absence of the other maids and nurses Hsi-jen fetched him a change of clothes.

"Don't tell anyone, please, dear sister," begged Pao-yu sheepishly.

With an embarrassed smile she asked, "What did you dream about to dirty yourself like that?"

"It's a long story," answered Pao-yu, then told her his dream in full, concluding with his initiation by Disenchantment into the "sport of cloud and rain." Hsi-jen, hearing this, covered her face and doubled up in a fit of giggles.

Since Pao-yu had long been attracted by Hsi-jen's gentle, coquettish ways, he urged her to carry out the instructions with him; and as she knew that the Lady Dowager had given her to Pao-yu she felt this would not be an undue liberty. So they tried it out secretly together, and luckily they were not discovered. From that hour Pao-yu treated Hsi-jen with special consideration and she served him even more faithfully than before.

Now although the Jung Mansion was not unduly large, masters and servants together numbered three or four hundred. And although it had not too much business, a score of things had to be seen to every day — easier to unravel a skein of tangled hemp than to recount them! Just as I was wondering with which event or person to begin, suddenly from a thousand *li* away came a humble individual as insignificant as a mustard-seed, who being remotely connected with the Jung House was that day paying them a visit. Let me take her family, then, as a starting point.

Do you know the name of this family and its remote connection with the Jung Mansion? If you think this too trivial or vulgar, Gentle Readers, you had better put this book down and choose one more to your liking. If you fancy this senseless story will serve to while away the time, then let me, the stupid Stone, tell it you in detail.

The surname of these humble folk I have just mentioned was Wang. They were local people whose grandfather while a petty official in the capital had come to know Hsi-feng's grandfather, Lady Wang's father. Eager to attach himself to the powerful Wangs, he "joined family" with them, calling himself Wang's nephew. At that time only Lady Wang and her elder brother, Hsi-feng's father, both of whom had accompanied their father to the capital, were aware of this remote "clansman." The rest of the Wangs knew nothing about these connections.

The grandfather had died leaving a son Wang Cheng who, since the family was then in a poor way, moved back to their native village outside the capital. Recently Wang Cheng too had fallen ill and died, leaving a son Kou-erh, who had married a girl from a family called Liu by whom he had a son called Pan-erh and a daughter called Ching-erh. Their family of four lived on the land.

As Kou-erh was busy during the day and his wife had the housework to see to, there was nobody to mind the children until he fetched his mother-in-law Granny Liu to live with them. An old widow who had been through much and was supporting herself as best she could on two *mu* of poor land because she had no son, she was only too glad to be taken in and cared for by her son-in-law. She did her best to make herself useful to him and her daughter.

Autumn had ended, the cold was setting in, and because they had made no provision for the winter Kou-erh drank a few cups to drown his cares then started venting his spleen on his family. His wife was afraid to talk back, but Granny Liu was not going to stand for this.

"You mustn't mind me butting in, son-in-law," she said. "We villagers are simple honest folk who eat according to the size of our bowl. Your trouble is that your father gave you such a soft time of it when you were young that you're a bad manager. When you have money you never look ahead; when you've none you fly into a temper. That's no way for a grown man to behave. We may be living outside the capital but we're still at the feet of the Emperor. And 'Changan's streets are strewn with money' — for those who know how to lay hands on it. What's the use of flying into a huff at home?"

"It's easy for you to jabber away on the *kang*," Kou-erh retorted. "Do you want me to go out and steal? To rob someone?"

"Who's asking you to rob anyone? But let's put our heads together and think of something. Do you expect silver coins to come rolling in of themselves?"

"Would I have waited all this time if there was some way out?" Kou-erh snorted. "I've no relatives who live on rent, no friends in official posts — what can I do? Even if I had, they'd most likely cold-shoulder us."

"Don't be so sure," said Granny Liu. "Man proposes, Heaven disposes. Work out a plan, trust to Buddha, and something may come of it for all you know.

"As a matter of fact, I've thought of a chance for you. In the old days you joined families with the Wangs of Chinling, and twenty years back they treated you not badly. Since then of course you've been too pig-headed to go near them, so that now you've drifted apart.

"I recollect calling on them once with my daughter. Their second young lady was really open-handed, so pleasant and free from airs. She's now the wife of the second Lord Chia of the Jung Mansion. I hear she's grown even more charitable and is always setting aside rice and money to give alms to Buddhists and Taoists. Her brother has been promoted to some post at the frontier, but I'm sure this Lady Wang would remember us. Why not go and try your luck? She may do something for us for old times' sake. If she's at all willing to help, one hair from her body would be thicker than our waist."

"Mother's right," put in her daughter. "But how could frights like us go to their gate? Most likely their gatekeepers would refuse to announce us. Why ask for a slap on the face?"

But Kou-erh had an eye to the main chance. Attracted by this suggestion, he laughed at his wife's objection and proposed:

"Since this is your idea, mother, and you've called on the lady before, why not go there tomorrow and see how the wind blows?"

"Aiya! 'The threshold of a noble house is deeper than the sea.' And who am I? The servants there don't know me, it's no use my going."

"That's no problem. I'll tell you what to do. Take young Pan-erh with you and ask for their steward Chou Jui. If you see him, we stand a chance. This Chou Jui had dealings with my old man and used to be on the best of terms with us."

"I know him too. But how will they receive me after all this time? Still, you're a man and too much of a fright to go, and my daughter's too young to make a show of herself. I'm old enough not to mind risking a snub. If I have any luck we'll all share it. And even if I don't bring back any silver the trip won't be wasted — I'll have seen a little high life."

They all laughed at that, and that same evening the matter was settled.

The next day Granny Liu got up before dawn to wash and comb her hair and to coach Pan-erh. Being an ignorant child of five or six, he was so delighted at the prospect of a trip to the city that he agreed to everything he was told.

In town they asked their way to Jung Ning Street. But Granny Liu was too overawed by the crowd of sedan-chairs and horses there to venture near the stone lions which flanked the Jung Mansion's main gate. Having dusted off her clothes and given Pan-erh fresh instructions, she timidly approached the side entrance where some arrogant, corpulent servants were sunning themselves on long benches, engaged in a lively discussion.

Granny Liu edged forward and said, "Greetings, gentlemen."

The men surveyed her from head to foot before condescending to ask where she had come from.

"I've come to see Mr. Chou who came with Lady Wang when she was married," she told them with a smile. "May I trouble one of you gentlemen to fetch him out for me?"

The men ignored her for a while, but finally one of them said, "Wait over there by that corner. One of his family may come out by and by."

An older man interposed, "Why make a fool of her and waste her time?" He told Granny Liu, "Old Chou has gone

south but his wife is at home. His house is at the back. Go
round to the back gate and ask for her there."

Having thanked him, Granny Liu took Pan-erh round to
the back gate. Several pedlars had put down their wares
there and about two dozen rowdy servant boys had crowded
round those selling snacks and toys.

The old woman caught hold of one of these youngsters and
asked, "Can you tell me, brother, if Mrs. Chou is at home?"

"Which Mrs. Chou?" he retorted. "We have three Mrs.
Chous and two Granny Chous. What's her job?"

"She's the wife of Chou Jui who came with Lady Wang."

"That's easy then. Come with me."

He scampered ahead of her through the back gate and
pointed out a compound. "That's where she lives." Then
he called, "Auntie Chou! Here's a granny asking for you."

Mrs. Chou hurried out to see who it was while Granny Liu
hastened forward crying, "Sister Chou! How are you?"

It took the other some time to recognize her. Then she
answered with a smile, "Why, it's Granny Liu! I declare,
after all these years I hardly knew you. Come on in and sit
down."

Smiling as she walked in, Granny Liu remarked, "The
higher the rank, the worse the memory. How could you remember us?"

Once indoors, Mrs. Chou told a maid to pour tea. Then
looking at Pan-erh she exclaimed, "What a big boy he is!"
After a short exchange of polite inquiries, she asked Granny
Liu whether she just happened to be passing or had come with
any special object.

"I came specially to see you, sister, and also to inquire after
Her Ladyship's health. If you could take me to see her, that
would be nice. If you can't, I'll just trouble you to pass on
my respects."

This gave Mrs. Chou a shrewd idea of the reason for her
visit. Since Kou-erh had helped her husband to purchase some
land, she could hardly refuse Granny Liu's appeal for help.

Besides, she was eager to show that she was someone of consequence in this household.

"Don't worry, granny," she replied with a smile. "You've come all this way in good earnest and of course I'll help you to see the real Buddha. Strictly speaking, it's not my job to announce visitors. We all have different duties here. My husband, for instance, just sees to collecting rents in spring and autumn or escorting the young gentlemen in his spare time, while all I do is accompany the ladies on their outings. But since you're related to Her Ladyship and have come to me for help as if I were someone, I'll make an exception and take in a message for you.

"I must tell you, though, that things have changed here in the last five years. Her Ladyship doesn't handle much business any more but leaves everything to the second master's wife. And who do you think she is? My lady's own niece, the daughter of her elder brother and the one whose childhood name was 'Master Feng.'"

"You don't say!" cried Granny Liu. "No wonder I predicted great things for her. In that case I must see her today."

"Of course. Nowadays Her Ladyship can't be troubled with much business, so whenever possible she leaves it to the young mistress to entertain visitors. Even if you don't see Her Ladyship you must see her, or your visit will have been wasted."

"Buddha be praised! I'm most grateful for your help, sister."

"Don't say that. 'He who helps others helps himself.' All I need do is say one word — no trouble at all." She sent her little maid in to see if the Lady Dowager's meal had been served.

"This young mistress Feng can't be more than twenty," remarked Granny Liu as the two of them went on chatting. "Fancy her being able to run a great household like this!"

"You don't know the half of it, my dear granny. Young as she is, she handles things much better than anyone else. She's grown up a beauty too. Clever isn't the word for her!

As for talking, ten eloquent men are no match for her. You'll see for yourself by and by. If she has a fault, it's that she's rather hard on those below her."

At this point the maid came back to report, "The old lady's finished her meal. The second mistress is with Lady Wang."

At once Mrs. Chou urged Granny Liu to hurry. "Come on! Our chance is while she has her own meal. Let's go and wait for her. Later on such a crowd will be going there on business, we'll hardly get a look in. And after her nap there'll be even less chance to see her."

They both got down from the *kang* and brushed their clothes. After some last-minute instructions to her grandson, Granny Liu followed Mrs. Chou by winding ways to Chia Lien's quarters, then waited in a covered passageway while Mrs. Chou went past the spirit screen into the court and, before Hsi-feng's return, explained who Granny Liu was to her trusted maid Ping-erh, who had come here as part of Hsi-feng's dowry and then become Chia Lien's concubine.

"She's come all this way today to pay her respects. In the old days Her Ladyship always used to see her, so I'm sure she'll receive her: that's why I've brought her in. When your mistress comes I'll tell her the whole story. I don't think she'll blame me for taking too much on myself."

Ping-erh decided to invite them in to sit down and accordingly Mrs. Chou went out to fetch them. As they mounted the steps to the main reception room, a young maid raised a red wool portière and a waft of perfume greeted them as they entered. Granny Liu did not know what it was but felt she was walking on air. And she was so dazzled by everything in the room that her head began to swim. She could only nod, smack her lips and cry "Gracious Buddha!"

Ping-erh was standing by the *kang* in the east room, the bedroom of Chia Lien's daughter. Casting two searching glances at Granny Liu she greeted her rather curtly and bade her be seated.

Ping-erh's silk dress, her gold and silver trinkets, and her face which was pretty as a flower made Granny Liu mistake her for her mistress. But before she could greet her as "my lady" she heard the girl and Mrs. Chou address each other as equals and realized that this was just one of the more favoured maids.

Granny Liu and Pan-erh were given seats on the *kang*, while Ping-erh and Mrs. Chou sat face to face on the edge. Maids brought tea and as she sipped it the old woman heard a steady *tock-tock-tock* like the sound made by a flour-bolting machine. Staring about her she saw a box-like object attached to one of the pillars in the room, with a weight of sorts swinging to and fro below it.

"Whatever can that be?" she wondered. "What's it doing?"

The next instant she started at a loud *dong!* like the sound of a bronze bell or copper chimes repeated eight or nine times. Before she could clear up this mystery, a flock of maids ran in crying:

"The mistress is coming!"

Ping-erh and Mrs. Chou stood up at once, telling Granny Liu to wait till she was sent for. They left her straining her ears, with bated breath, as she waited there in silence.

In the distance laughter rang out. Ten to twenty serving women swished through the hall to another inner room, while two or three bearing lacquered boxes came to this side to wait. When the order was given to serve the meal, all left but a few who handed round the dishes. A long silence followed. Then two women brought in a low table covered with scarcely touched dishes of fish and meat which they set down on the *kang*. At once Pan-erh set up a clamour for some meat, but his grandmother slapped him and told him to keep away.

Next Mrs. Chou came to beckon them with a smile. Granny Liu at once lifted her grandson off the *kang* and led him into the hall. After some whispered advice from Mrs. Chou she followed her slowly into Hsi-feng's room.

A soft scarlet flowered portière hung from brass hooks over the door, and the *kang* below the south window was spread with a scarlet rug. Against the wooden partition on the east were a back-rest and bolster of brocade with chain designs next to a glossy satin mattress with a golden centre. Beside them stood a silver spittoon.

Hsi-feng had on the dark sable hood with a pearl-studded band which she wore at home. She was also wearing a peach-red flowered jacket, a turquoise cape lined with grey squirrel and a skirt of crimson foreign crêpe lined with snow-weasel fur. Dazzlingly rouged and powdered she sat erect, stirring the ashes of her hand-stove with a tiny brass poker. Ping-erh stood by the *kang* with a small covered cup on a little lacquered tray, but Hsi-feng ignored the tea and kept her head lowered as she stirred the ashes.

"Why haven't you brought her in yet?" she finally asked.

Then, raising her head to take the tea, she saw Mrs. Chou with her two charges before her. She made a motion as if to rise and greeted them with a radiant smile, scolding Mrs. Chou for not speaking up before.

Granny Liu had already curtseyed several times to Hsi-feng, who now hastily said:

"Help her up, Sister Chou, she mustn't curtsey to me. Ask her to be seated. I'm too young to remember what our relationship is, so I don't know what to call her."

"This is the old lady I was just telling you about," said Mrs. Chou.

Hsi-feng nodded.

By now Granny Liu had seated herself on the edge of the *kang*, and Pan-erh took refuge behind her. Coaxed to come forward and bow, he would not budge.

"When relatives don't call on each other they drift apart," observed Hsi-feng with a smile. "People who know us would say you're neglecting us. Petty-minded people who don't know us so well might imagine we look down on everyone else."

"Gracious Buddha!" exclaimed Granny Liu. "We're too hard up to gad about. And even if Your Ladyship didn't slap our faces for coming, your stewards might take us for tramps."

"That's no way to talk!" Hsi-feng laughed. "We're simply poor officials trying to live up to our grandfather's reputation. This household is nothing but an empty husk left over from the past. As the saying goes: 'The Emperor himself has poor relations.' How much more so in our case?"

She asked Mrs. Chou if she had notified Lady Wang.

"I was waiting for madam's instructions," was the reply.

"Go and see how busy she is. If she has visitors, never mind. But if she's free, let her know and see what she says."

After Mrs. Chou left on this errand, Hsi-feng told the maids to give Pan-erh some sweetmeats. She was asking Granny Liu questions when Ping-erh announced the arrival of a number of servants to report on affairs in their charge.

"I have a guest. They can come back this evening," said Hsi-feng. "Only bring in anyone whose business won't wait."

Ping-erh went out, reappearing to say, "They've nothing pressing so I sent them away."

As Hsi-feng nodded, Mrs. Chou came back.

"Her Ladyship isn't free today," she said. "She hopes you'll entertain them and thank them for coming. If they just dropped in for a call, well and good. If they have any business they should tell you, madam."

"I've no special business," put in Granny Liu. "I just came to call on Her Ladyship and Madam Lien, seeing as how we're related."

"If you've nothing special, all right," said Mrs. Chou. "If you have, telling our second mistress is just the same as telling Her Ladyship."

She winked at Granny Liu, who took the hint. Although her face burned with shame, she forced herself to pocket her pride and explain her reason for coming.

"By rights, I shouldn't bring this up at our first meeting, madam. But as I've come all this way to ask your help, I'd better speak up. . . ."

Just then pages by the second gate called out, "The young master from the East Mansion is here."

Cutting Granny Liu short Hsi-feng asked, "Where is Master Jung?"

Booted footsteps sounded and in walked a handsome youth of seventeen or eighteen. Slender and graceful in light furs, he wore a jewelled girdle, fine clothes and a gorgeous hat. Granny Liu didn't know whether to sit or stand and longed for some hiding-place.

"Sit down," said Hsi-feng with a twinkle. "It's only my nephew."

Granny Liu perched gingerly on the edge of the *kang*.

Chia Jung announced cheerfully, "My father's sent me to ask a favour, aunt. He's expecting an important guest tomorrow, and he'd like to borrow that glass screen for the *kang* that our Grand-Aunt Wang gave you. He'll return it promptly."

"You're too late," replied Hsi-feng. "I gave it to somebody only yesterday."

Chuckling, Chia Jung half knelt by the foot of the *kang*. "If you won't lend it, aunt, I'll be given another sound thrashing for not asking properly. Have pity on your nephew!"

"You seem to imagine all the Wangs' things are special. Haven't you plenty of stuff of your own over there?"

"Nothing half as good." He laughed. "Please, aunt, be kind!"

"Then look out for your skin if you chip it!"

She ordered Ping-erh to fetch the keys to the upstairs rooms and find trustworthy people to deliver the screen.

"I've brought men to carry it." Chia Jung's face lit up, his eyes twinkled. "I'll see that they're careful."

He had barely left when she suddenly called him back.

Servants outside echoed, "Master Jung, you're asked to go back."

The young man hurried in again and stood at attention to hear his aunt's instructions. Hsi-feng sipped her tea slowly and thoughtfully for a while, then said with a laugh:

"Never mind. Come back again after supper. I've company now and don't feel in the mood to tell you at the moment."

So Chia Jung slowly withdrew.

Granny Liu felt easy enough at last to say, "The reason I brought your nephew here today is that his parents haven't a bite to eat. And winter's coming on, making things worse. So I brought your nephew here to ask for your help." She nudged Pan-erh. "Well, what did your dad tell you? What did he send us here for? Was it just to eat sweets?"

Hsi-feng smiled at this blunt way of talking. "Don't say any more. I understand." She asked Mrs. Chou, "Has granny eaten yet?"

"We set out first thing in such a rush, we'd no time to eat anything," said Granny Liu.

At once Hsi-feng ordered a meal for the visitors. Mrs. Chou passed on the order and a table was set for them in the east room.

"Sister Chou, see that they have all they want," said Hsi-feng. "I can't keep them company."

When Mrs. Chou had taken them to the east room, Hsi-feng called her back to hear what Lady Wang had said.

"Her Ladyship says they don't really belong to our family," Mrs. Chou told her. "They joined families because they have the same surname and their grandfather was an official in the same place as our old master. We haven't seen much of them these last few years, but whenever they came we didn't let them go away empty-handed. Since they mean well, coming to see us, we shouldn't slight them. If they need help, madam should use her own discretion."

"I was thinking, if we were really relatives it was funny I didn't know the first thing about them."

As Hsi-feng was speaking Granny Liu came back from her meal with Pan-erh, loud in her thanks.

"Sit down now and listen to me, dear old lady," said Hsi-feng cheerfully. "I know what you were hinting at just now. We shouldn't wait for relatives to come to our door before we take care of them. But we've plenty of troublesome business here, and now that Her Ladyship's growing old she sometimes forgets things. Besides, when I took charge recently I didn't really know all our family connections. Then again, although we look prosperous you must realize that a big household has big difficulties of its own, though few may believe it. But since you've come so far today and this is the first time you've asked me for help, I can't send you away empty-handed. Luckily Her Ladyship gave me twenty taels of silver yesterday to make clothes for the maids, and I haven't yet touched it. If you don't think it too little, take that to be going on with."

Talk of difficulties had dashed all Granny Liu's hopes and set her heart palpitating. The promise of twenty taels put her in a flutter of joy.

"Ah," she cried, "I know what difficulties are. But 'A starved camel is bigger than a horse.' No matter how, 'A hair from your body is thicker than our waist.' "

Mrs. Chou kept signalling to her not to talk in this crude way, but Hsi-feng merely laughed and seemed not to mind. She sent Ping-erh for the package of silver and a string of cash and presented these to the old woman.

"Here's twenty taels to make the child some winter clothes. If you refuse it, I shall think you're offended. With the cash you can hire a cart. When you've time, drop in again as relatives should. It's growing late, I won't keep you for no purpose. Give my compliments to everyone at home to whom I should be remembered."

She stood up and Granny Liu, having thanked her profusely, took the silver and cash and followed Mrs. Chou towards the servants' quarters.

"Gracious me!" exclaimed Mrs. Chou. "What possessed you when you saw her to keep on about 'your nephew'? At the risk of offending you I must say this: Even if he were a real nephew you should have glossed it over. Master Jung, now, he's her honest-to-goodness nephew — where would she get a nephew like Pan-erh?"

"My dear sister!" Granny Liu beamed. "I was struck all of a heap at sight of her and didn't know what I was saying."

Chatting together they reached Chou Jui's house and sat down for a few moments. Granny Liu wanted to leave a piece of silver to buy sweets for Mrs. Chou's children, but this Mrs. Chou most resolutely declined — such small sums meant nothing to her. Then with boundless thanks Granny Liu left by the back gate.

To know what followed, you must read the next chapter. Truly:

> In affluence, charity is freely dispensed,
> One deeply grateful is better than kinsmen or
>   friends.

CHAPTER 7

Madam Yu Invites Hsi-feng Alone
At a Feast in the Ning Mansion Pao-yu
First Meets Chin Chung

The theme:

> Twelve maids pretty as flowers,
> But who is it that loves them?
> Do you ask the name of the one he meets?
> It is Chin whose home is south of the Yangtze River.

After seeing off Granny Liu, Mrs. Chou went to report to Lady Wang. On being told by her maids that their mistress had gone to chat with Aunt Hsueh, she made her way through the east side gate and the east courtyard to Pear Fragrance Court. On the verandah steps there, Lady Wang's maid Chin-chuan was playing with a girl who had just let her hair grow. Realizing that Mrs. Chou had come on business, Chin-chuan nodded towards the door.

Mrs. Chou softly raised the portière and went in. Lady Wang and her sister were having a good long gossip on domestic matters, and not wanting to disturb them she went into the inner room where Pao-chai in a house dress, her hair pinned into a loose knot, was copying an embroidery pattern with her maid Ying-erh at the low table on the *kang*. She put down her brush and turned with a smile to offer the visitor a seat.

"How are you, miss?" asked Mrs. Chou, sitting on the edge of the *kang*. "I haven't seen you over on our side for several days. Did Pao-yu do something to annoy you?"

"What an idea! I've been staying in for a couple of days because an old ailment's been troubling me again."

"Why, miss, what is it? Better send for a doctor at once to make out a prescription. A few doses should set you right once and for all. It's no joke being an invalid at your age."

"Don't talk to me about medicine!" Pao-chai laughed. "Goodness knows how much silver we've squandered on doctors and medicines to cure this illness of mine. The most famous physicians and the most fabulous drugs were of no use at all. In the end, luckily, there came a tonsured monk who claimed to specialize in mysterious diseases. We called him in and he diagnosed my trouble as a choleric humour I'd brought from the womb, but which thanks to my good constitution wasn't too serious. No ordinary pills bring any relief, but he gave us an exotic prescription from across the seas, together with a packet of aromatic powder he'd procured as adjuvant goodness knows where. He prescribed one pill each time an attack comes on. And strange to say that's done me good."

"What is this prescription from across the seas? If you'll tell me, miss, we'll keep it in mind and recommend it to others with the same trouble. That would be a good deed."

"Well, better not ask. But if you must know, it's the most troublesome prescription." Pao-chai laughed. "There aren't too many ingredients and they're easily obtainable, but each has to be gathered at just the right time. You have to take twelve ounces of the stamens of white peonies that bloom in the spring, twelve ounces of the stamens of white lotus that blooms in the summer, twelve ounces of the stamens of white hibiscus that blooms in the autumn, and twelve ounces of the stamens of white plum that blooms in the winter. These four kinds of stamens must be dried in the sun on the following vernal equinox, then mixed well with the powder. Then you must take twelve drams of rain that fell on the day Rain Begins. . . ."[1]

"Aiya!" broke in Mrs. Chou. "That would take three years. And what if it doesn't rain on the day Rain Begins?"

[1] About February 20.

"Exactly. You can't always count on it. If it doesn't, you just have to wait. You also have to collect twelve drams of dew on the day White Dew,[1] twelve drams of frost on the day Frost Falls,[2] and twelve drams of snow on the day Slight Snow.[3] These liquids are mixed with the other ingredients, then twelve drams of honey and twelve of white sugar are added to make pills the size of longans. These must be kept in an old porcelain jar and buried beneath the roots of flowers. When the illness comes on, this jar can be dug up and one pill taken with twelve candareens of a phellodendron concoction."

"Gracious Buddha!" Mrs. Chou chuckled. "How terribly chancy! You might wait ten years without such a run of luck."

"Well, we were lucky enough to collect all the ingredients and have them carefully made up within two years of the monk's telling us. We brought the pills up from the south. They're buried under one of the pear trees now."

"Has this medicine any name?"

"Yes, the scabby monk told us they're called Cold Fragrance Pills."

Mrs. Chou nodded. "What are the symptoms of this illness of yours, miss?"

"Nothing serious. Slight fits of coughing and shortness of breath. But one pill clears it up."

Before they could say more, Lady Wang asked who was there. Mrs. Chou hurried out and seized this chance to tell her about Granny Liu. It seemed Lady Wang had no further instructions for her, and she was on the point of leaving when Aunt Hsueh stopped her.

"Wait a minute," she said with a smile. "I've something for you to take back."

She called for Hsiang-ling and the portière clacked as in came the girl who had been playing with Chin-chuan.

"Did you call, madam?" she asked.

---

[1] About September 8.

[2] About October 23.

[3] About November 22.

"Bring me that box of flowers," ordered Aunt Hsueh.

Hsiang-ling accordingly fetched a brocade box.

"These are twelve sprays of gauze flowers of the new sort made in the Palace," explained Aunt Hsueh. "I remembered them yesterday, and thought it a pity to leave them tucked away when the girls might like to wear them. I meant to send them over yesterday, but forgot. You may as well take them now that you're here. Give two each to your three young ladies. Of the six left, give a couple to Miss Lin and the other four to Master Feng."

"It's kind of you to think of them," remarked Lady Wang. "But why not keep them for Pao-chai?"

"You don't know what an odd girl she is, sister. She dislikes wearing flowers or make-up."

Going out with the box, Mrs. Chou found Chin-chuan still sunning herself on the steps. "Tell me," she said, "isn't Hsiang-ling the girl there was all that talk about? The one bought just before they came to the capital, who was at the bottom of that manslaughter case?"

"That's right," said Chin-chuan.

Just then Hsiang-ling came over, smiling. Mrs. Chou took her hand and studied her intently, then turned to Chin-chuan again:

"She's a handsome girl. Reminds me of Master Jung's wife in our East Mansion."

"That's what I say," agreed Chin-chuan.

Mrs. Chou asked Hsiang-ling how old she had been when sold, where her parents were, her age now and her native place. But the girl simply shook her head and said she could not remember, so that their hearts bled for her.

Then Mrs. Chou took the flowers to the back of Lady Wang's principal apartment. Recently the Lady Dowager had found it inconvenient to have all her grand-daughters crowded together in her compound. Keeping just Pao-yu and Tai-yu for company, she had sent Ying-chun, Tan-chun and Hsi-chun to live in three small suites behind Lady Wang's quarters, under the care of Li Wan. Hence Mrs. Chou stopped here first as it was on her way, and found a few maids waiting in the hall for when they should be wanted.

Ying-chun's maid Ssu-chi and Tan-chun's maid Tai-shu raised the portière at that moment and stepped out, each carrying a cup and saucer. This meant that their young mistresses must be together, so Mrs. Chou went in and discovered Ying-chun and Tan-chun playing draughts by the window. She presented the flowers, explaining where they came from. The two girls stopped their game to bow their thanks, then ordered their maids to put the gifts away.

As Mrs. Chou handed over the flowers she remarked, "The fourth young lady isn't here. Is she with the old lady, I wonder?"

"Isn't she there in the next room?" the maids said.

Mrs. Chou walked into the adjoining room and found Hsi-chun laughing and chatting with Chih-neng, a young nun from the Water Moon Convent. Hsi-chun asked Mrs. Chou her business. The box was opened and the gift explained.

"I was just telling Chih-neng that I'd shave my head some day and become a nun too, and now you turn up with flowers." Hsi-chun smiled. "Where shall I wear them if my head is shaved?"

Amid the banter that followed, Hsi-chun told her maid Ju-hua to put the present away.

Then Mrs. Chou asked Chih-neng, "When did you arrive? And where's that bald-headed, crotchety abbess of yours?"

"We came here first thing this morning. After calling on Lady Wang the abbess went to Mr. Yu's mansion, telling me to wait for her here."

"Have you received the monthly allowance and donation for incense due on the fifteenth?"

Chih-neng shook her head. "I don't know."

Hsi-chun asked who was in charge of the monthly donations for different temples.

"Yu Hsin," was Mrs. Chou's answer.

"So that's it." Hsi-chun giggled. "As soon as the abbess arrived, Yu Hsin's wife hurried over and whispered with her for a while. That must be why."

After chatting for a time with the nun, Mrs. Chou went on to Hsi-feng's quarters. She walked through the passage, past Li Wan's back window, and skirting the west wall entered Hsi-feng's compound by the west side-gate. In the main hall outside the bedroom door sat Feng-erh, who hastily motioned her to the east room. Taking the hint, Mrs. Chou tiptoed in and found a nurse patting Hsi-feng's daughter to sleep.

"Is your mistress having a nap?" whispered Mrs. Chou. "It's time somebody woke her."

As the nurse shook her head, from Hsi-feng's room came the sound of laughter and Chia Lien's voice. The door opened and out stepped Ping-erh with a large copper basin which she told Feng-erh to fill with water and take in. Then Ping-erh came over and asked Mrs. Chou, "What brings you here again, auntie?"

Mrs. Chou stood up and explained her errand, handing over the box. Ping-erh took out four sprays and went off with them, returning presently with two which she ordered Tsai-ming to take to Master Jung's wife in the Ning Mansion. After this she asked Mrs. Chou to convey Hsi-feng's thanks to Aunt Hsueh.

Only then did Mrs. Chou make her way to the Lady Dowager's compound. In the entrance hall she ran into her own daughter, dressed in her best, come from her mother-in-law's house.

"What are *you* doing here?" asked Mrs. Chou.

"Have you been keeping well, ma?" Her daughter beamed. "I waited and waited at home but you didn't come. What's been keeping you all this time? When I got tired of waiting I went on my own to pay my respects to the old lady, and I was just going to see Lady Wang. Aren't you through yet with your business? What's that in your hand?"

"Ai! Granny Liu would choose today to call, and I put myself out running here and there for her. Then Madam

Hsueh spotted me and asked me to deliver these flowers to the young ladies. I'm not through with it yet. But you must want something of me, coming at this time."

"You've guessed right, ma. The fact is, your son-in-law had a cup too much the other day and a row started. Someone, I don't know why, has spread ugly rumours and says he's got a shady past. A charge has been lodged against him at the yamen to have him sent back to his native place. I came to ask your advice. Who can we get to help us out?"

"I thought as much," said her mother. "A fuss about nothing. You go home while I deliver these flowers to Miss Lin. Her Ladyship and Madam Lien aren't free just now, so go back and wait for me. Why get so excited?"

"Well, be as quick as you can, ma," urged her daughter walking off.

"Of course. You young people lack experience, that's why you're so worked up."

Tai-yu was not in her room but Mrs. Chou found her in Pao-yu's, trying to unravel the nine-ring puzzle with him.

Mrs. Chou greeted her with a smile as she entered and said, "Madam Hsueh asked me to bring you these flowers to wear."

"What flowers?" demanded Pao-yu. "Let me see them."

He reached for the box and, opening it, saw the two sprigs of gauze flowers from the Palace.

Tai-yu glanced briefly at them in Pao-yu's hand. "Am I the only one getting these?" she asked. "Or have the other girls been given some too?"

"Each of the young ladies has some. These two are for you, miss."

"I might have known." Tai-yu smiled bitterly. "I wouldn't get mine till the others had taken their pick."

Mrs. Chou had nothing to say to this, but Pao-yu put in, "What were you doing over there, Sister Chou?"

"I had a message for Her Ladyship, who's there. And Madam Hsueh asked me to bring back these flowers."

"What's Pao-chai doing at home? Why hasn't she been here for the last few days?"

"She's not very well."

At once Pao-yu told his maids, "One of you go and see her. Tell her Miss Lin and I sent you to ask how our aunt and cousin are. Find out what's wrong with her and what medicine she's taking. I ought to go myself, but say I'm just back from school and have caught a chill as well. I'll call some other time."

As Chien-hsueh offered to go, Mrs. Chou left.

Now Mrs. Chou's son-in-law was none other than Chia Yu-tsun's good friend Leng Tzu-hsing. Finding himself involved in a lawsuit arising from the sale of some curios, he had sent his wife to ask for help. With full confidence in her master's power, Mrs. Chou did not take this to heart. In fact she settled the matter that same evening by applying to Hsi-feng.

When the lamps were lit and Hsi-feng had disrobed, she went to see Lady Wang.

"I've taken charge of those things the Chens sent today," she announced. "As for our presents to them, I have sent them back by their boats which have come for the New Year provisions."

When Lady Wang nodded, Hsi-feng went on, "I've prepared our birthday presents for the Earl of Linan's mother. Who should deliver them, madam?"

"Any four women you see are free. Why consult me about such trifles?"

With a smile Hsi-feng went on, "Today Brother Chen's wife invited me to spend tomorrow with them. I haven't anything special to do that I know of."

"Even if you had, it wouldn't matter. She usually asks us all, which can't be much fun for you. Since she hasn't invited us this time, only you, she obviously wants you to have a little fun, so don't disappoint her. Even if you had business you ought to go."

Hsi-feng had just agreed when Li Wan, Ying-chun, Tan-chun and the other girls came in to say goodnight, after which all retired to their own rooms.

The next day after Hsi-feng had finished her toilet she went to tell Lady Wang that she was off. She then went to the Lady Dowager; and when Pao-yu heard where she was going he insisted on going too. Hsi-feng had to agree and wait until he had changed. Then the two of them drove quickly to the Ning Mansion.

Chia Chen's wife Madam Yu and Chia Jung's wife Chin Ko-ching had gathered a troop of concubines and maids to welcome them at the ceremonial gate. Having greeted Hsi-feng in her usual teasing fashion, Madam Yu led Pao-yu to a seat in the drawing room.

When Ko-ching had served tea Hsi-feng asked, "Well, what did you invite me for today? If you've something good for me, hand it over quickly. I've other things to attend to."

Before Madam Yu or Ko-ching could reply, a concubine retorted laughingly, "In that case you shouldn't have come. Now that you're here, madam, you can't have it all your own way."

Chia Jung entered then to pay his respects, and Pao-yu asked if Chia Chen were at home.

"He's gone out of town to inquire after his father's health," said Madam Yu. "But you must find it dull sitting here. Why not go out for a stroll?"

"As it happens," put in Ko-ching, "my brother whom Uncle Pao was so eager to meet last time is here today. He's probably in the library. Why don't you go and have a look, uncle?"

But as Pao-yu slipped down from the *kang* Madam Yu and Hsi-feng interposed, "Steady on. What's the hurry?" They ordered some maids to go with him. "Don't let him get into any trouble," they warned. "The old lady isn't here to keep an eye on him today."

"Why not ask young Master Chin in here?" suggested Hsi-feng. "Then I can see him too. Or am I forbidden to see him?"

"You'd much better not," retorted Madam Yu. "He's not like our boys with their rough, rowdy ways. Other people's sons behave in a more civilized fashion. How could he face a terror like you? You'd be a laughing-stock."

"I'm the one who laughs at others." Hsi-feng smiled. "How can a boy laugh at *me*?"

"It's not that, aunt," said Chia Jung. "He's shy and hasn't seen much of the world. You'd have no patience with him."

"Even if he's a monster, I insist on seeing him. Don't talk like a fool! Fetch him in at once or I'll give you a good slap."

"How dare I disobey?" Chia Jung chuckled. "I'll bring him in at once."

With that, he fetched in a lad more slightly built than Pao-yu yet even more handsome, with fine features, a fair complexion, red lips, a graceful figure and pleasing manners, but as bashful as a girl. He bowed shyly to Hsi-feng and inquired almost inaudibly after her health.

Hsi-feng nudged Pao-yu delightedly and cried, "Now you must take a back seat." She leaned forward to take the young stranger's hand and made him sit down beside her, then began questioning him about his age and the books he was studying. She learned that his school name was Chin Chung.

Since this was Hsi-feng's first meeting with Chin Chung but she hadn't prepared the usual gifts, some of her maids had hurried back to consult Ping-erh. And Ping-erh, knowing how intimate her mistress was with Chin Ko-ching, decided that she would want to give the boy something handsome. So she handed them a length of silk and two small gold medallions inscribed with the wish that the owner would win first place in the Palace Examination. When these were brought Hsi-feng protested that the gift was too poor, while Ko-ching and the others thanked her profusely.

After lunch Madam Yu, Hsi-feng and Ko-ching sat down to a game of cards, leaving the two boys to amuse themselves as they pleased.

At sight of Chin Chung, Pao-yu had felt quite eclipsed. He lapsed into a spell of stupefaction, and then gave way to foolish fancies again. "Imagine there being such people in the world!" he thought. "Why, compared with him I'm no better than a filthy pig or mangy dog. Why did I have to be born into this noble family? If I were the son of a poor scholar or some minor official, I might have made friends with him long ago and life would have been worth living. Although my status is higher, I'm just a stump of rotten wood swathed in silks and satins, just a cess-pool or gutter filled with choice wines and meats. Riches and rank are anathema to me."

In Chin Chung's eyes, Pao-yu's striking appearance and in-genuous behaviour were a fine foil to his rich costume, pretty maids and handsome pages. He for his part reflected, "No wonder everyone is so fond of Pao-yu. Why did I have to be born into a poor family, unable to have him as an intimate friend? What a barrier there is between wealth and poverty. This is one of the greatest curses of this life."

Thus both were lost in equally foolish reflections until Pao-yu abruptly asked Chin Chung what he was reading and, the latter answering frankly, they embarked on an animated con-versation which soon made them feel even more drawn to each other. Then tea and refreshments were served.

"We two shan't be drinking any wine," said Pao-yu. "Why not put a plate or two of these things on that small *kang* in the inner room and let us sit there where we won't disturb you?"

So they went inside to have their tea. And Ko-ching, after serving Hsi-feng with wine and refreshments, slipped in to tell Pao-yu:

"Your nephew's young, Uncle Pao. If he says anything he shouldn't, please overlook it for my sake. He's a stubborn boy for all his shyness and likes to have his own way."

"Just leave us," Pao-yu laughed. "We're all right."

Having urged her brother to behave himself, Ko-ching re-turned to Hsi-feng.

Presently Hsi-feng and Madam Yu sent to remind Pao-yu, if he wanted anything to eat from their room, just to ask for it. Pao-yu agreed but he had no interest in food, so eager was he to learn more about how his new friend lived.

"My tutor died last year," confided Chin Chung. "My father's old and unwell, with so much to keep him busy that he hasn't had time to find me another yet. At present I'm just going over old lessons at home. In any case, in studying you need one or two congenial companions to talk things over with from time to time, to get the best out of it."

"Just what I think," broke in Pao-yu. "We have a school for members of our clan who can't engage a tutor, and some other relatives attend it too. My tutor went home last year, so I'm at a loose end myself for the time being. My father wanted to send me to this school to go over the old lessons until my tutor returns next year, when I can go on studying alone at home. But my grandmother was against it, for fear so many boys would get up to mischief; and as I've been unwell for a few days the matter's been dropped for a while.

"If, as you say, your worthy father is concerned over this, why not tell him about it when you go home today, and come and study in our school? I'll be your schoolfellow, and we can help each other. What could be better?"

"The other day when my father brought up the question of a tutor he spoke highly of this free school here," replied Chin Chung eagerly. "He meant to come and talk it over with Lord Chen, but didn't like to trouble him about such a trifle when everyone here is so busy. If you think, Uncle Pao, I could grind your ink or wash the inkstone for you, let's try to fix it as soon as possible. Then neither of us need waste our time, we'd have plenty of chances to talk, our parents' minds would be set at rest, and we could become real friends. Wouldn't that be fine?"

"Don't worry," said Pao-yu. "Let's go and tell your brother-in-law and sister, as well as Sister Hsi-feng. You can speak to your father when you get home, and I'll tell my grandmother. There's no reason why it shouldn't be arranged quickly."

By the time this was settled, lamps were being lit and they went out to watch the game. When the score was reckoned, Ko-ching and Madam Yu had lost again and it was agreed that they should stand treat to a meal and an opera show in two days' time. Then they chatted a while.

After dinner, because it was dark, Madam Yu suggested that they send two men-servants to see Chin Chung home, and maids went out with these orders. When some time later the boy took his leave, she asked who was to accompany him.

"Chiao Ta," said the maids. "But he's roaring drunk and using foul language again."

"But why send him?" protested Madam Yu and Ko-ching. "We've all those young fellows who could go. Why pick Chiao Ta?"

"I've always said you're too soft with your servants," was Hsi-feng's comment. "Fancy letting them have their own way like this!"

"You know Chiao Ta, surely?" Madam Yu sighed. "Not even the master can control him, let alone your Cousin Chen. He went out with our great-grandfather on three or four expeditions when he was young, and saved his master's life by carrying him off a battlefield heaped with corpses. He went hungry himself but stole food for his master; and after two days without water, when he got half a bowl he gave it to his master and drank horse urine himself. Because of these services, he was treated with special consideration in our great-grandfather's time and nobody likes to interfere with him now. But since growing old he has no regard for appearances. He does nothing but drink and when he's drunk he abuses everyone. Time and again I've told the stewards to write him off and not give him any jobs. Yet he's being sent again today."

"Of course I know Chiao Ta, but you ought to be able to handle him," scoffed Hsi-feng. "Pack him off to some distant farm and have done with it." She asked if her carriage was ready.

"Ready waiting, madam," said the attendants.

Hsi-feng rose to take her leave and led Pao-yu out. Madam Yu and the others escorted them to the main hall, where by the bright light of lanterns they saw attendants waiting in the court. Because Chia Chen was out — though he could have done nothing even if at home — Chiao Ta was fairly letting himself

go. Roaring drunk, he lashed out at the head steward Lai Erh's injustice, calling him a cowardly bully.

"You give all the soft jobs to others, but when it comes to seeing someone home late at night in the dark you send me. Black-hearted son of a turtle! A fine steward you are! I can lift my leg up higher than your head. Twenty years ago I'd nothing but contempt for this household, not to mention you bastards, you crew of turtle-eggs."

He was cursing away full blast as Chia Jung saw Hsi-feng in her carriage out, and ignored all the servants' shouts to him to be quiet. Chia Jung could hardly let this pass. He swore at Chiao Ta and told men to tie him up.

"We'll ask him tomorrow, when he's sobered up, what he means by this disgraceful behaviour," he blustered.

Chiao Ta had a low opinion, of course, of Chia Jung. He bore down on him bellowing still more angrily:

"Don't try to lord it over Chiao Ta, young Brother Jung! Not to speak of the likes of you, not even your dad or grand-dad dare stand up to Chiao Ta. If not for me, and me alone, you'd have no official posts, fancy titles or riches. It was your great-granddad who built up this estate, and nine times I snatched him back from the jaws of death. Now instead of showing yourselves properly grateful, you try to lord it over me. Shut up, and I'll overlook it. Say one word more, and I'll bury a white blade in you and pull it out red!"

"Why don't you get rid of this lawless wretch?" asked Hsi-feng from her carriage. "He's nothing but a source of trouble. If this came to the ears of our relatives and friends, how they'd laugh at the lack of rules and order here."

As Chia Jung agreed to this, some servants overpowered Chiao Ta and dragged him off towards the stables, for this time he had really gone too far. Then he let loose a flood of abuse in which even Chia Chen was included.

"Let me go to the Ancestral Temple and weep for my old master," he fumed. "Little did he expect to beget such degen-erates, a houseful of rutting dogs and bitches in heat, day in and day out scratching in the ashes[1] and carrying on with younger brothers-in-law. Don't think you can fool me. I only tried to hide the broken arm in your sleeve. . . ."

These obscenities frightened the servants half out of their wits. Hurriedly trussing him up, they stuffed his mouth with mud and horse-dung.

Hsi-feng and Chia Jung pretended not to have heard, whereas Pao-yu in the carriage was rather entertained by this drunken outburst.

"Did you hear that, sister?" he asked. "What's meant by 'scratching in the ashes'?"

"Don't talk nonsense," snapped Hsi-feng, glowering. "What's come over you? You not only listen to drunken raving but have to ask questions too. Just wait until we get back and I tell your mother — you'll pay for this with a thrashing."

"Dear sister," apologized Pao-yu fearfully, "I promise not to do it again."

"That's more like it, brother. The important thing, once we're home, is to talk to the old lady about sending you and your nephew Chin Chung to school."

They were back now in the Jung Mansion. To know what followed, turn to the next chapter.

> Good looks pave the way to friendship,
> A mutual attraction starts boys studying.

---

[1] A slang term for adultery between a man and his daughter-in-law.

Nanny Li Makes a Nuisance of Herself by
Warning Against Drinking
Pao-yu Breaks a Teacup and
Flies into a Temper

After Hsi-feng and Pao-yu reached home and had paid their greetings, Pao-yu told the Lady Dowager of Chin Chung's eagerness to attend their clan school, and the incentive it would be for him to have a friend and companion in his studies. He painted a glowing picture of the other boy's admirable character and lovable qualities.

Hsi-feng backed him up, adding, "In a day or two Chin Chung will be coming to pay his respects to our Old Ancestress." She then took advantage of the old lady's pleasure at this news to invite her to the opera in two days' time.

In spite of her age, the Lady Dowager looked forward to any excitement. When the day arrived and Madam Yu came to invite her, she took Lady Wang, Tai-yu, Pao-yu and others along to watch the performances.

At noon the old lady went home for her siesta. And Lady Wang, who liked peace and quiet, returned too after her mother-in-law's departure. Then Hsi-feng moved into the seat of honour and enjoyed herself to the full until the evening.

After Pao-yu had seen his grandmother back for her nap, he would have returned to see the show if not for his reluctance to disturb Ko-ching and the rest. Remembering that he had not gone in person to ask after Pao-chai's recent indisposition, he decided to pay her a visit. He feared that if he went past the main apartment something might happen to hold him up, while

117

he dreaded still more the thought of meeting his father. So he decided to go the long way round.

His nurses and maids were waiting to take off his ceremonial clothes, but he went out again without changing. They followed him through the second gate under the impression that he was going back to the other mansion, instead of which he turned northeast round the back of the hall.

There, however, he ran into two of his father's protégés, Chan Kuang and Shan Pin-jen, who hurried forward smiling. One threw an arm round him, the other took his hand.

"Little Bodhisattva!" they cried. "We so rarely see you, this is a delightful surprise."

Having paid their respects, asked after his health and chatted for a while, they were moving on when his nurse inquired if they were going to see the master.

They nodded. "His Lordship is sleeping now in his Mengpo Studio. Don't worry," they assured Pao-yu, moving on.

These words made Pao-yu laugh in spite of himself. He then turned north and hurried towards Pear Fragrance Court. Just then the chief treasurer Wu Hsin-teng and the manager of the granaries Tai Liang emerged from the counting-house with five other stewards. They hurried forward at sight of Pao-yu and stood at respectful attention. One of them, Chien Hua, who had not seen Pao-yu for some time, stepped forward and fell on one knee. Smiling slightly, Pao-yu quickly helped him up, while one of the other men said cheerfully:

"The other day we saw some inscriptions written by you, young master. Your calligraphy's even better than before. When will you give us a few samples to put on our walls?"

"Where did you see them?" asked Pao-yu.

"In several places," they answered. "People admire them so much they asked us to get them some."

"They're not worth having," protested Pao-yu, laughing. "But you can ask my pages for some if you want."

The whole party waited until he had walked on before going their different ways. But enough of this digression.

On reaching Pear Fragrance Court, Pao-yu went first to see Aunt Hsueh, whom he found distributing sewing to her maids. He paid his respects to his aunt, who caught him in her arms and hugged him.

"How good of you to come, dear boy, on a cold day like this." She beamed. "But get up here quickly on the warm *kang*." She ordered hot tea to be served.

"Is Cousin Pan at home?" asked Pao-yu.

"Ah, he's like a horse without a halter," she sighed. "He's for ever rushing about outside. Not a day does he spend at home."

"Is Pao-chai better?"

"Yes, thank you. It was thoughtful of you to send over to ask how she was the other day. She's in her room now. Why not go in and see her? It's warmer there. Go and keep her company and I'll join you as soon as I'm through here."

Pao-yu promptly slipped off the *kang* and went to his cousin's door, before which hung a somewhat worn red silk portière. Lifting this he stepped inside.

Pao-chai was sewing on the *kang*. Her glossy black hair was knotted on top of her head. She was wearing a honey-coloured padded jacket, a rose-red sleeveless jacket lined with brown- and snow-weasel fur, and a skirt of leek-yellow silk. There was nothing ostentatious about her costume, which was none too new. Her lips needed no rouge, her blue-black eyebrows no brush; her face seemed a silver disk, her eyes almonds swimming in water. Some might think her reticence a cloak for stupidity; but circumspect as she was she prided herself on her simplicity.

As Pao-yu observed her he asked, "Are you better now, cousin?"

Pao-chai looked up and rose swiftly to her feet, saying, "Ever so much better, thank you for your kind concern."

She made him sit on the edge of the *kang* and told Ying-erh to pour tea. As she asked after the old lady and her aunts and cousins, she took in Pao-yu's costume.

He was wearing a golden filigree coronet studded with gems, a gold chaplet in the form of two dragons fighting for a pearl, a yellowish green archer's jacket embroidered with serpents and lined with white fox-fur, and a sash embroidered with many-coloured butterflies. From his neck hung a longevity locket, a talisman inscribed with his name, and the precious jade found in his mouth at the time of his birth.

"I've heard so much about that jade of yours but I've never seen it," said Pao-chai edging forward. "Do let me have a good look at it today."

Pao-yu leaned forward too, and taking the stone from his neck laid it in her hand. She held it on her palm. It was the size of a sparrow's egg, iridescent as clouds at sunrise, smooth as junket, and covered with coloured lines. This was the form taken by the stupid Stone from the foot of Blue Ridge Peak in Great Waste Mountain. A later poet wrote these mocking lines:

> Fantastic, Nu Wa's smelting of the stone,
> Now comes fresh fantasy from the Great Waste;
> The Stone's true sphere and spirit lost,
> It takes a new form stinking and debased.
> Know that when fortune frowns, pure gold is dulled,
> And jade, in evil times, will cease to shine;
> Heaped high the white bones of the nameless dead,
> Who in their day were lords and ladies fine.

The stupid Stone had also recorded its transformation and below we shall reproduce the seal characters engraved on it by the scabby monk.

As the jade was small enough to be held in the mouth of a new-born child, if we were to reproduce the real size of the characters they would be so minute that our readers would find them a troublesome strain on their eyes. We are therefore enlarging them to scale to enable readers to study them by lamplight or even in their cups. This point is made clear so that nobody may sneer, "How big a mouth could an infant in the womb have, to hold this clumsy object!"

The obverse side read:

> Precious Jade of Spiritual Understanding
> Never Lose, Never Forget,
> Eternal Life, Lasting Prosperity.

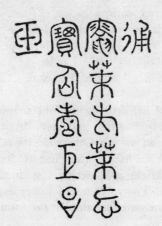

The reverse side:

1. Expels Evil Spirits.
2. Cures Mysterious Diseases.
3. Foretells Happiness and Misfortune.

After examining both sides Pao-chai turned the jade over to study the face more closely and read the inscription aloud, not once but twice. Then she turned to ask Ying-erh:

"Why are you standing gaping there instead of getting us tea?"

Ying-erh answered with a giggle, "Those two lines seem to match the words on your locket, miss."

"Why, cousin," cried Pao-yu eagerly, "does that locket of yours have an inscription too? Do let me see it."

"Don't listen to her," replied Pao-chai. "There aren't any characters on it."

"I let you see mine, dear cousin," he countered coaxingly.

Cornered like this, Pao-chai answered, "As it happens, there is a lucky inscription on it. Otherwise I wouldn't wear such a clumsy thing all the time." She unbuttoned her red jacket and drew out a bright gold necklace studded with glittering pearls and jewels. Pao-yu took the locket eagerly and found two inscriptions, one on either side, in the form of eight minute characters.

Never Leave, Never Abandon,   Fresh Youth, Eternally Lasting.

Pao-yu read this twice, then twice repeated his own.

"Why, cousin, this inscription of yours matches mine exactly," he declared laughingly.

"It was given her by a scabby monk," explained Ying-erh. "He said it must be engraved on something made of gold."

Before she could say more Pao-chai called her to task for not bringing them some tea. Then she asked Pao-yu where he had come from. He was now close enough to her to catch whiffs of some cool, sweet fragrance which he could not identify.

"What incense do you use to scent your clothes with?" he asked. "I've never smelt this perfume before."

"I don't like incense perfumes. They just make good clothes reek of smoke."

"What is that perfume, then?"

Pao-chai thought for a moment. "I know. It must be the pill I took this morning."

"What pills smell so good? Won't you give me one to try?"

"Don't be silly!" She laughed. "You don't take medicine for the fun of it."

Just then a servant outside announced, "Miss Lin is here." And in came Tai-yu.

"Ah!" she exclaimed at sight of Pao-yu. "I've chosen a bad time to come."

Pao-yu rose with a smile to offer her a seat while Pao-chai asked cheerfully, "What do you mean?"

"If I'd known he was here, I wouldn't have come."

"That's more puzzling than ever," said Pao-chai.

"Either everybody comes at once or no one comes," explained Tai-yu mischievously. "If he came one day and I the next, spacing out our visits, you'd have callers every day and would find it neither too lonely nor too distracting. What's so puzzling about that, cousin?"

Pao-yu saw that she was wearing a crimson camlet cloak which buttoned in front. "Is it snowing outside?" he asked.

"It's been hailing for some time," replied the maids.

"Have they brought my cape?"

"Wasn't I right?" cried Tai-yu. "As soon as I come, he must go."

"When did I say a word about going? I just want to be prepared."

"It's snowing and it's getting late now," put in Nanny Li. "Just amuse yourself here with your cousins. Your aunt's prepared refreshments in the other room. I'll send a maid for your cape and tell your pages not to wait."

As Pao-yu agreed to this, his nurse went out and sent the pages away.

Meanwhile Aunt Hsueh had tea and other good things ready for them. When Pao-yu spoke highly of the goose feet and duck tongues served a couple of days before by Madam Yu, she produced some of her own, pickled with distiller's grain, for him to try.

"These taste even better with wine," he hinted, smiling.

His aunt promptly sent for the best wine in the house.

"No wine, please, Madam Hsueh," protested Nanny Li.

"Just one cup, dear nanny," begged Pao-yu.

"No you don't! If the Lady Dowager or Lady Wang were here I wouldn't mind your drinking a whole jarful. But I haven't forgotten the way they scolded me for two days on end just because some irresponsible fool who wanted to get on the right side of you gave you a sip of wine behind my back. You've no idea what a rascal he is, Madam Hsueh. And drinking brings out all the worst in him. On days when the old lady's in a good humour she lets him drink all he wants, but on other days she won't let him touch a drop. And I'm always the one that gets into trouble."

"Don't worry, poor old thing," said Aunt Hsueh, laughing. "Go and have a drink yourself. I'll see that he doesn't drink too much. If the old lady says anything, I'll take the blame." She ordered her maids, "Take the nurses along to drink a few cups now to keep out the cold." So Nanny Li had to join the other servants to enjoy her drink.

As soon as she had gone Pao-yu said, "Don't bother to heat it. I prefer cold wine."

"That won't do," said his aunt. "Cold wine will make your hand shake when you write."

"Brother Pao," put in Pao-chai teasingly, "you've the chance every day to acquire miscellaneous knowledge. How come you don't realize how heating wine is? Drunk hot, its fumes dissipate quickly; drunk cold, it stays in your system and absorbs heat from your vital organs. That's bad for you. So do stop drinking cold wine."

Since this made sense, Pao-yu put down the wine and asked to have it warmed. Tai-yu had been smiling rather cryptically as she cracked melon-seeds. Now her maid Hsueh-yen brought in her little hand-stove.

"Who told you to bring this?" demanded Tai-yu. "Many thanks. Think I was freezing to death here?"

"Tzu-chuan was afraid you might be cold, miss, so she asked me to bring it over."

Nursing the stove in her arms Tai-yu retorted, "So you do whatever *she* asks, but let whatever *I* say go in one ear and out the other. You jump to obey her instructions faster than if they were an Imperial edict."

Although Pao-yu knew these remarks were aimed at him, his only reply was to chuckle. And Pao-chai, aware that this was Tai-yu's way, paid no attention either. Aunt Hsueh, however, protested:

"You've always been delicate and unable to stand the cold. Why should you be displeased when they're so thoughtful?"

"You don't understand, aunt," replied Tai-yu with a smile. "It doesn't matter here, but people anywhere else might well take offence. Sending a hand-stove over from my quarters as if my hosts didn't possess such a thing! Instead of calling my maids too fussy, people would imagine I always behave in this outrageous fashion."

"You take such things too seriously," said Aunt Hsueh. "Such an idea would never have entered my head."

By now Pao-yu had already drunk three cups, and Nanny Li came in again to remonstrate. But he was enjoying himself so much talking and laughing with his cousins, he refused to stop. "Dear nanny," he coaxed, "just two more cups — that's all."

"You'd better look out," she warned. "Lord Cheng's at home today, and he may want to examine you on your lessons."

With a sinking heart, Pao-yu slowly put his cup down and hung his head.

"Don't be such a spoil-sport," protested Tai-yu. "If uncle sends for you, cousin, we can say Aunt Hsueh is keeping you. This nanny of yours has been drinking and is working off the effects of the wine on us." She nudged Pao-yu to embolden him and whispered, "Never mind the old thing. Why shouldn't we enjoy ourselves?"

"Now, Miss Lin, don't egg him on," cried Nanny Li. "You're the only one whose advice he might listen to."

"Why should I egg him on?" Tai-yu gave a little snort. "I can't be bothered with offering him advice either. You're too pernickety, nanny. The old lady often gives him wine, so why shouldn't he have a drop more here with his aunt? Are you suggesting that auntie's an outsider and he shouldn't behave like that here?"

Amused yet vexed, Nanny Li expostulated, "Really, every word Miss Lin says cuts sharper than a knife. How can you suggest such a thing?"

Even Pao-chai couldn't suppress a smile. She pinched Tai-yu's cheek and cried, "What a tongue the girl has! One doesn't know whether to be cross or laugh."

"Don't be afraid, my child," said Aunt Hsueh. "I've nothing good to offer you, but I'll feel bad if you get a fright which gives you indigestion. Just drink as much as you want, I'll answer for it. You needn't leave till after supper. And if you do get tipsy you can sleep here." She ordered more wine to be heated, saying, "I'll drink a few cups with you and then we'll have our rice."

Pao-yu's spirits rose again at this.

His nurse told the maids, "Stay here and keep an eye on him. I'm going home to change, then I'll come back." She urged Aunt Hsueh on the sly: "Madam, don't let him have it all his own way or drink too much."

When she had gone the two or three other elderly servants who were left, not being over-conscientious, slipped out to enjoy themselves. There remained only two maids eager to please Pao-yu. But by dint of much coaxing and teasing, Aunt Hsueh kept him from drinking too many cups before the wine was whisked away. Then Pao-yu had two bowls of soup made from pickled bamboo-shoots and duck-skin and half a bowl of green-rice porridge. By this time Pao-chai and Tai-yu had finished too and all of them drank some strong tea, after which Aunt Hsueh felt easier in her mind.

Now Hsueh-yen and three other maids came back from their own meal to wait on them, and Tai-yu asked Pao-yu:

"Are you ready to go?"

He glanced at her sidewise from under drooping eyelids. "I'll go whenever you do."

Tai-yu promptly rose to her feet. "We've been here nearly all day, it's time we left. They may be wondering where we are."

As they took their leave their wraps were brought, and Pao-yu bent his head for a maid to help him on with his hood. She shook out the crimson hood and started slipping it over his head.

"Stop, stop! Not so roughly, you silly thing," he protested, stopping her. "Have you never seen anyone put on a hood before? Better let me do it myself."

"What a commotion!" Tai-yu stood up on the *kang*. "Come here. Let me see to it."

Pao-yu went up to Tai-yu, who put her hand gently over his coronet and placed the edge of the hood on his chaplet. Then she made the red velvet pompon, the size of a walnut, bob up in front.

"That's better," she said, surveying her handiwork. "Now you can put on your cloak."

As Pao-yu did so his aunt remarked, "None of the nurses who came with you is here. Why not wait a bit?"

"Why should we wait for them?" he asked. "We've the maids to go with us. We shall be all right."

To be on the safe side, however, Aunt Hsueh told two older servants to accompany them. Then Pao-yu and Tai-yu thanked their hostess and made their way to the Lady Dowager's quarters.

The Lady Dowager had not yet dined but was very pleased when she learned where they had been. Observing that Pao-yu had been drinking, she packed him straight off to rest, forbidding him to leave his room again that evening. As she gave orders for him to be well looked after, she wondered who was attending him and asked:

"Where's Nanny Li?"

The maids dared not disclose that she had gone home. "She was here a moment ago," they said. "She must have gone out on some business."

Swaying a little, Pao-yu called over his shoulder, "She has a better time of it than our old lady. Why ask for her? I wish she'd leave me in peace to live a little longer."

While saying this he reached his apartment, where his eye fell on the brush and ink on the desk.

Ching-wen greeted him with a smile, exclaiming, "A fine one you are! You made me grind that ink for you this morning because you were feeling good; but you only wrote three characters, then threw down your brush and marched off. You've kept us waiting for you the whole day. You must set to work quickly now and use up this ink."

Reminded of that morning's happenings, Pao-yu asked, "Where are the three characters I wrote?"

"This fellow's drunk!" Ching-wen laughed. "Just before you went over to the other house you told me to have them pasted above the door, yet now you ask where they are. Not trusting anyone else to do a good job, I got up on a ladder to paste them up myself. My hands are still numb with cold."

"I forgot." Pao-yu grinned. "Let me warm your hands for you." He took Ching-wen's hands in his while they both looked up at the inscription over the lintel.

Just then Tai-yu came in and he asked her, "Tell me honestly, dear cousin, which of these three characters is the best written?"

Tai-yu raised her head and read the inscription: Red Rue Studio.

"They're all good. I didn't know you were such a calligrapher. You must write an inscription for me some time too."

"You're making fun of me again." Pao-yu chuckled. "Where's Hsi-jen?" he asked Ching-wen.

Ching-wen tilted her head towards the *kang* in the inner room, where Pao-yu saw Hsi-jen lying, fully dressed.

"That's good," he said. "But it's rather early to sleep. At breakfast in the other house this morning there was a plate of beancurd dumplings. Knowing you'd like them, I asked Madam Yu to let me have them for supper, and they were sent over. Did you get them all right?"

"Don't ask!" answered Ching-wen. "I knew at once they were meant for me, but as I'd just finished my breakfast I left them here. Then Nanny Li came and saw them. 'Pao-yu won't be wanting these,' she said. 'I'll take them for my grandson.' She got somebody to send them home for her."

At this point Chien-hsueh brought in tea and Pao-yu said, "Do have some tea, Cousin Lin."

The maids burst out giggling. "She's gone long ago, yet you offer her tea."

After drinking half a cup himself he remembered something else and asked Chien-hsueh, "Why did you bring me *this* tea? This morning we brewed some maple-dew tea, and I told you its flavour doesn't really come out until after three or four steepings."

"I did save that other tea," she replied. "But Nanny Li insisted on trying it and she drank it all."

This was too much for Pao-yu. He dashed the cup to pieces on the floor, spattering the maid's skirt with tea. Then springing to his feet he stormed:

"Is she your grandmother, that all of you treat her so respectfully? Just because she suckled me for a few days when I was small, she carries on as if she were more important than our own ancestors. I don't need a wet-nurse any more, why should I keep an ancestress like this? Send her packing and we'll all have some peace and quiet."

He wanted to go straight to his grandmother to have the old woman dismissed.

Now Hsi-jen had only been shamming sleep, in the hope that Pao-yu would come in to tease her. She hadn't troubled to get up when he asked about the dumplings; but now that he had smashed a cup and flown into a passion she jumped up and came out to smooth things over, just as a maid arrived from his grandmother to ask the reason for the noise.

"I'd just poured out some tea," said Hsi-jen. "I slipped because of snow on my shoes and the cup was smashed."

Then she turned to calm Pao-yu. "So you've decided to dismiss her. Good. We'd all like to leave. Why not take this chance to get rid of the lot of us? That would suit us, and you'd get better attendants too."

Thus silenced, Pao-yu let them help him to the *kang* and take off his clothes. He was still mumbling to himself but could hardly keep his eyes open, so they put him straight to bed. Hsi-jen took the precious jade off his neck, wrapped it up in her own handkerchief and tucked it under his mattress, so that it should not be cold to the touch when he put it on the next day.

Pao-yu fell asleep as soon as his head touched the pillow. Meantime Nanny Li had come in. Hearing that he was drunk she dared not risk further trouble, and having quietly made sure that he was asleep she left easier in her mind.

Upon waking the next morning, Pao-yu was told that Chia Jung from the other mansion had brought Chin Chung over to pay his respects. He hastened to greet his new friend and presented him to the Lady Dowager, who was delighted by his handsome looks and pleasing manner. Convinced that he would make an excellent schoolmate for Pao-yu, she kept him to tea and a meal, then ordered servants to take him to meet Lady Wang and the rest of the family.

Chin Ko-ching was a general favourite, and they liked her brother for himself as well. All gave him presents on parting. The Lady Dowager's gift was a purse containing a small golden effigy of the God of Learning symbolizing literary talent and harmony.

"You live so far away," she said, "in hot or cold weather you may find the journey too much. You are welcome to stay here and must make yourself at home. Stay with your Uncle Pao-yu, and don't get into mischief with those lazy young rascals."

Chin Chung agreed readily, then went home to report what had happened. His father Chin Yeh, a secretary in the Board of Works, was nearly seventy and had lost his wife early. Having no children of his own he had adopted a son and daughter from an orphanage, but the boy had died leaving only the little girl, Ko-ching. She grew up to be a graceful, charming young woman. Because Chin was remotely connected with the Chia family, they arranged a match and she became Chia Jung's wife.

Chin Chung was born when his father was over fifty. His tutor had died the previous year and Chin Yeh had not yet found another; thus the boy had been revising his lessons at home. His father was thinking of approaching the Chias about sending his son to their school in order not to waste the boy's time, when as luck would have it Chin Chung met Pao-yu.

The old man was also overjoyed to learn that the school was now run by Chia Tai-ju, a venerable Confucian scholar under whose instruction Chin Chung was bound to make progress and might even win a name for himself.

Chin Yeh was a poor official, but the whole Chia household, high and low alike, thought so much of riches and rank that in the interest of his son's career he had to pinch and scrape to get together twenty-four taels of silver as a handsome entrance gift. Then he took Chin Chung to pay his respects to Chia Tai-ju, after which they waited for Pao-yu to fix a day on which both boys could enter school.

Truly:

> If one knew that in time to come there would be
> trouble,
> Who would send his son to study today?

CHAPTER 9

Devoted Friends Join the Clan School
Mud-Slinging Boys Brawl
in the Classroom

Chin Yeh and his son did not have long to wait for a message from the Chia family telling them the date on which to start school, for Pao-yu was so eager to be with Chin Chung he could think of nothing else. He sent a servant with a note asking his friend to come to his house in two days' time, in the morning, to go to school together.

On the day appointed, while Pao-yu was still asleep, Hsi-jen made a neat package of his books and writing materials, then sat down dejectedly on the edge of the *kang*. When he woke, she helped him with his toilet.

"Why are you looking so unhappy, dear sister?" he asked gently. "Are you upset because you'll all feel lonely while I'm at school?"

"What an idea!" She smiled. "There's nothing like study, if you don't want to be a failure in life and get nowhere. Just remember to keep your mind on your books in class, and out of class to think of the people at home. Don't get into mischief with the other boys. It would be no joke if you were caught by the master. I know they say you should give your whole heart to study, but don't overdo it or you'll bite off more than you can chew and your health will suffer. At least that's my idea. Do think it over."

Pao-yu agreed with all she said.

"I've packed your fur coats and given them to the pages," Hsi-jen continued. "If you find the school cold, mind you put more on, because we shan't be there to look after you. I've given them charcoal for your hand-stove and foot-stove too. Mind those lazy scamps keep them filled. If you don't keep them up to scratch they won't lift a finger but leave you to freeze."

"Don't worry," Pao-yu assured her. "I know how to take care of myself outside. And you mustn't stay here moping either, but drop in from time to time to chat with Cousin Tai-yu."

By now he was dressed and she urged him to pay his respects to his grandmother and parents. After some brief instructions to Ching-wen and Sheh-yueh, he took his leave of the Lady Dowager, who naturally had some advice for him too. He went next to his mother and then to his father's study.

Chia Cheng happened to have come home early today. He was talking with some secretaries and protégés when Pao-yu went in to pay his respects and announce his departure to school.

"Don't make me die of shame with this talk about school." His father laughed scornfully. "All you're fit for, in my opinion, is to go on fooling about. Your presence here contaminates this place and contaminates my door."

"Your Lordship is too hard on him," protested his companions, who had risen. "A few years at school and your worthy son is sure to show his mettle and make a name. He's not a child any more. It's nearly time for breakfast, he should be off." With that, two of the older men led Pao-yu out.

Chia Cheng asked who was accompanying his son, and three or four sturdy fellows who had been waiting outside came in and fell on one knee to pay their respects.

Recognizing Li Kuei, the son of Pao-yu's old wet-nurse, Chia Cheng demanded, "What has he learned all the time you've attended him at his lessons? Nothing but a pack of nonsense and some clever tricks. As soon as I have leisure I'll flay you alive and then settle accounts with that young reprobate."

In consternation Li Kuei fell on both knees, snatched off his cap and thumped his head on the ground submissively.

"I wouldn't dare tell a lie, sir," he exclaimed. "The young master has studied three volumes of the *Book of Songs,* down to '*Yu-yu* cry the deer, lotus leaves and duckweed.'"

This unintentional travesty of the original line set the whole room in a roar of laughter. Even Chia Cheng himself could not help smiling.

"Even if he studied another thirty volumes, it would just be fooling people," he retorted. "Give my compliments to the school principal, and tell him from me that such works as the *Book of Songs* and classical essays are a waste of time. He'd far better expound the *Four Books* and make his pupils learn them by heart."

Li Kuei promised to do this and then withdrew, seeing that his master had no further orders.

All this time Pao-yu had been waiting with bated breath in the courtyard. He hurried away as soon as he saw them emerging from the house.

Li Kuei and the others, dusting off their clothes, asked, "Did you hear that? He's going to flay us alive. Other people's slaves get some reflected credit from their masters. All we get for waiting on you is beatings and abuse. Do have a little pity on us in future."

"Cheer up, good brothers," replied Pao-yu with a smile. "I'll give you a treat tomorrow."

"Who are we to expect treats, little ancestor? Just listen to our advice once in a while."

By now they were back at the Lady Dowager's quarters. She was chatting with Chin Chung, who had been there for some time. The two boys exchanged greetings, then took their leave of her.

Pao-yu, remembering that he had not said goodbye to Tai-yu, hurried to her room. She was sitting before her mirror by the window and smiled when he told her that he was off to school.

"Good," she said. "So you're going to 'pluck fragrant osmanthus in the palace of the moon.' I'm sorry I can't see you off."

"Don't have supper till I'm back, dear cousin," he begged. "And wait for me to mix your rouge."

After chatting for a while he turned to leave.

"'Aren't you going to say goodbye to Pao-chai?" Tai-yu called after him.

With no answer but a smile he left with Chin Chung.

Now this Chia family school, which was only a *li* away, had been set up several generations earlier so that members of the clan who could not afford to engage a tutor would have somewhere to educate their sons. It was supported by those with official positions, who contributed according to the size of their stipends, and an elderly man of good reputation in the clan was elected to take charge of the boys' instruction.

When Pao-yu and Chin Chung had been introduced to the other students, they embarked on their studies. From this day onward the two of them became inseparable, going to school and leaving it together. And thanks to the Lady Dowager's partiality, Chin Chung often stayed for a few days with the Chia family. Indeed, she treated him like one of her own grandsons, giving him clothes, shoes and other necessities when she saw that his family was hard up. In less than a month he was on good terms with everyone in the Jung Mansion.

Since Pao-yu always followed his own bent regardless of what was due to his position, in his usual unconventional way he privately urged Chin Chung: "We're the same age, and schoolmates too. Let's forget that we're uncle and nephew and just be brothers and friends."

At first Chin Chung would not agree to this, but since Pao-yu kept calling him "brother" or using his courtesy name, he started doing the same.

Now although all the pupils in this school were members of the Chia clan or relations by marriage, as the proverb so aptly says, "A dragon begets nine offspring, each one different." And inevitably among so many boys there were low types too, snakes mixed up with dragons.

These two new arrivals were both remarkably handsome. Chin Chung was bashful and gentle, so shy that he blushed like a girl before he spoke, while Pao-yu was naturally self-effacing and modest, considerate to others and pleasant in his speech. And they were on such intimate terms, it was no wonder that their schoolmates suspected the worst. They began to talk about the pair behind their backs, spreading ugly rumours inside the school and out.

Now Hsueh Pan had not been long in the Jung Mansion before he learned of this school, and the thought of all the boys there appealed to his baser instincts. So he enrolled as a student. But he was like the fisherman who fishes for three days and then suns his net for two. The fee he paid Chia Tai-ju was thrown away, for he had no intention of really studying, his sole aim being to find some 'sweet-hearts' there. In fact, tempted by his money and other gifts several boys did fall into his clutches, but we need not dwell on this.

Chief among these were two amorous youths whose real names have not been ascertained, nor the branches of the family to which they belonged. But on account of their good looks and charm they were nicknamed Sweetie and Lovely. Although the object of general admiration, so that others also had designs on them, they were left unmolested for fear of Hsueh Pan.

Pao-yu and Chin Chung were naturally attracted by these boys too, but knowing them to be Hsueh Pan's friends they did not venture to make any overtures. Sweetie and Lovely were equally drawn to them. But not one of the four spoke of what was in his heart. Every day from four different seats four pairs of eyes kept meeting, and while trying to escape detection they contrived by hints and allusions to reveal their thoughts. However, some sly rascals discovered their secret and began to raise their eyebrows, wink, and cough or clear their throats behind their backs.

This had been going on for some time when one day, as luck would have it, Chia Tai-ju went home early on business, giving the boys a seven-character line to be matched with another and promising them a new lesson in the classics the next day. He left his eldest grandson Chia Jui in charge. Chin Chung took advantage of the fact that nowadays Hsueh Pan had virtually stopped coming even to roll-call to make eyes at Sweetie and secretly signal to him. Having asked to be excused, they went out to the back courtyard for a quiet chat.

"Do your parents mind what friends you make?" asked Chin Chung.

The words were barely out of his mouth when a cough behind them made both boys look round in dismay. It was their schoolmate Chin Jung. Sweetie was a hot-tempered lad. In embarrassment and annoyance he demanded:

"What are you coughing for? Can't we talk if we want to?"

"If you can talk, why can't I cough?" Chin Jung sniggered. "But why not talk openly instead of in this hole-and-corner fashion? I've caught you at last. There's no use denying it. Let me have a go first, and I'll keep quiet about it. Otherwise I'll rouse the whole school."

Flushing crimson the two boys demanded indignantly, "What have you caught us at?"

"I've caught you red-handed!" Clapping and grinning, he yelled, "Fine pancakes for sale. Come on, fellows, and buy one."

The two friends rushed furiously in to complain to Chia Jui of Chin Jung's uncalled-for insult.

Now Chia Jui was an unscrupulous, grasping scoundrel who used his position in the school to fleece the boys. In return for money and good meals from Hsueh Pan, he had not checked his disgraceful behaviour but actually abetted him in order to curry favour.

But Hsueh Pan was as fickle as water-weed which drifts east today, west tomorrow. Having recently acquired new friends he had dropped Sweetie and Lovely, to say nothing of Chin Jung whom they had replaced; and now that they were discarded, Chia Jui had nobody to put in a good word for him. Instead of blaming Hsueh Pan's fickleness, he bore his favourites a grudge for this. And because he, Chin Jung and the rest all had this grievance against the two boys, when Chin Chung and Sweetie came in with their complaint it only increased his annoyance. Not daring to reprove Chin Chung he made a scapegoat of Sweetie, abusing him roundly for being a trouble-maker.

After this rebuff, Sweetie and Chin Chung returned sullenly to their seats while Chin Jung triumphantly wagged his head and smacked his lips as he poured out more abuse. This was too much for Lovely, and they started bickering from their respective places.

"I saw them just now as plain as day in the back yard," insisted Chin Jung. "They were discussing where and how to meet."

He held forth wildly regardless of who might hear, although one of his listeners was already enraged. And who do you think this was? It was Chia Chiang, a direct descendant of the Duke of Ningkuo, who had been brought up by Chia Chen after the untimely death of his own parents. He was now sixteen and even more handsome and engaging than Chia Jung, from whom he was virtually inseparable.

Now "the more people, the more talk," and the disgruntled servants in the Ning Mansion were good for nothing but slandering their masters. When their dirty talk reached Chia Chen's ears, to avoid coming under suspicion himself he had given Chia Chiang his own establishment outside the Ning Mansion and told him to live on his own.

Chia Chiang was as intelligent as he was handsome, but he attended the school only as a blind for his visits to cock-fights, dog-races and brothels. None of his clansmen dared to cross him, however, because he was a favourite with Chia Chen and had Chia Jung to stand by him. Naturally, intimate as he was with them, he was not going to let anyone bully Chin Chung with impunity! His first impulse was to take his side openly, but on second thought he decided, "Chin Jung, Chia Jui and that lot are thick with Uncle Hsueh, who has always been on good terms with me. If I side against them and they tell Old Hsueh, that will spoil our friendly relations. If I do nothing, though, they'll just spread these tiresome rumours. I must find some way of stopping their mouths without any loss of face."

He left the room on the customary excuse and quietly got hold of Ming-yen, one of Pao-yu's pages, to work on his feelings with his account of the matter.

Ming-yen was Pao-yu's most serviceable page but he was young and inexperienced. Chia Chiang told him that the insults to Chin Chung reflected on his master, and if Chin Jung were allowed to get away with this he would take even greater liberties the next time.

Ming-yen always liked to throw his weight about, and with this encouragement from Chia Chiang he rushed in to beard Chin Jung. Not addressing him as a servant should, he cried, "Hey, you fellow Chin! Who do you think you are?"

At this point Chia Chiang stamped the dust off his boots, straightened his clothes and looking at the height of the sun remarked, "It's time I was off." He asked Chia Jui's permission to leave early to deal with some business, and Chia Jui dared not stop him.

By now Ming-yen had grabbed hold of Chin Jung. "What we do is no business of yours," he yelled. "If you've any guts, come and take on your Master Ming."

The whole roomful of boys was dumbfounded.

"How dare you, Ming-yen!" bellowed Chia Jui.

Livid with anger Chin Jung bawled, "The rebel! How dare a slave run wild like this? I'll have a word with your master." Tearing himself loose he rounded on Pao-yu and Chin Chung.

Wham! A square inkstone hurled by some unknown assailant whizzed past Chin Jung's head to crash on to the next desk, one occupied by Chia Lan and Chia Chun.

Chia Chun was a great-great-grandson of the Duke of Jung-kuo, and the only son of his mother who had been widowed early. He sat at the same desk as Chia Lan because they were firm friends. This hot-tempered, fearless little scamp had watched indifferently while one of Chin Jung's friends hurled an inkstone at Ming-yen; but when the stone landed smack in front of him, smashing his water-bottle and spattering his books with ink, this was more than he could stand.

"You gaolbirds!" he swore. "If you want a fight, you can have it." He grabbed his own inkstone ready to let it fly.

Timid Chia Lan intervened, saying this was none of their business. But Chia Chun paid no attention. Since his inkstone was pinned down he caught up his satchel and hurled it at the offender. Being small and weak, he missed his target. The satchel landed with a tremendous crash in front of Pao-yu and Chin Chung, scattering books, paper, brushes and ink over their desk and smashing Pao-yu's teacup so that tea poured all over it too.

Chia Chun launched himself at the boy who had thrown the inkstone, while Chin Jung caught up a bamboo pole and played havoc with it in that narrow crowded room.

Ming-yen was the first to be hit. "What are you waiting for?" he roared to Pao-yu's other pages Chu-yao, Sao-hung and Mo-yu, all of whom were ready for mischief.

"Sons of bitches!" they shouted. "They're using weapons now."

In they charged, Mo-yu armed with a door bar, the other two brandishing whips.

Chia Jui tried desperately to hold back or persuade the contendants in turn. But no one listened to him, the place was a bedlam. Some boys threw themselves eagerly into the scrimmage, punching those who could not hit back, the more timid shrank aside, others stood on their desks clapping and laughing wildly as they urged the combatants on. The school was like a seething cauldron.

Li Kuei and the servants outside hearing this uproar hurried in to stop the fight. When they asked how it had started, everyone answered at once, each blaming another. With an oath Li Kuei drove Ming-yen and the pages out.

Chin Chung had been hit on the head and bruised by Chin Jung's pole, and Pao-yu was rubbing the place with his coat lapel. Now that order had been restored he told Li Kuei:

"Collect my books and bring round my horse. I'm going to report this to the principal. They insulted us gratuitously, but when we complained quite properly to Mr. Chia Jui he laid the blame on us. He let them abuse us and actually encouraged them to beat us. Ming-yen seeing us bullied naturally took our side, but then they ganged up to beat him. They've even broken open Chin Chung's head. How can we go on studying here after this?"

Li Kuei begged him not to be hasty. "It would look very inconsiderate to disturb the principal over such a little thing when he's busy. Trouble should be settled on the spot, I say. There's no need to go and disturb the old gentleman. It's Mr. Chia Jui who's to blame. You're in charge here, sir, in the old gentleman's absence. If anyone misbehaves, you should punish him. How could you let them get so out of hand?"

"I did tell them to stop," said Chia Jui. "But no one paid any attention."

"You mustn't mind if I speak frankly, sir," rejoined Li Kuei. "It's because your own conduct leaves much to be desired that these boys don't obey you. So if this business comes to the principal's ears, it will go hard with you. Hurry up and think of a way to hush it up."

"I won't have it hushed up," declared Pao-yu. "I'm going to report it."

"I'm not coming here any more," sobbed Chin Chung, "if Chin Jung is allowed to stay."

"What an idea!" cried Pao-yu. "Why should *we* have to keep away because *they* come? I'm going to tell everyone and have him expelled." He asked Li Kuei to which branch of the family Chin Jung was related.

Li Kuei thought for a moment, then said, "Better not ask. If I tell you, it will only cause bad feeling among relatives."

"He's the nephew of Mrs. Chia Huang of the East Lane," called Ming-yen through the window. "I don't know how he had the nerve to beard us. Mrs. Chia Huang is his aunt on the father's side. She's a sponger who sucks up to people and goes down on her knees to Madam Lien for things to pawn. How can we respect a 'mistress' like that?"

"Shut up, you dirty bugger. Don't talk such rot," roared Li Kuei.

"So that's who he is!" said Pao-yu scornfully. "Cousin Chia Huang's nephew. I shall go and see her about this."

He ordered Ming-yen to come in and wrap up his books.

The page did so, saying exultantly, "Why go yourself, sir? Let me go and tell her the old lady wants her. I'll hire a carriage to bring her, and you can question her in the Lady Dowager's presence. Wouldn't that save trouble?"

"Do you want to die?" shouted Li Kuei. "Just wait, I'll give you such a thrashing when we get back. Then I'll tell our master and mistress that you were the one who put Pao-yu up to this. I've had trouble enough getting him halfway calmed down, and here you go again. You started this rumpus, but instead of trying to smooth things over you're adding fuel to the fire."

Ming-yen dared say no more then. And Chia Jui, afraid of being incriminated if this went any further, had to pocket his grievance and ask Chin Chung and Pao-yu to forget it.

After holding out for some time Pao-yu said, "All right, I won't tell if Chin Jung apologizes."

At first Chin Jung refused. But Chia Jui put pressure on him, and Li Kuei and the others joined in.

"You started this," Li Kuei pointed out. "It's up to you to end it."

Under pressure from all sides, Chin Jung bowed to Chin Chung. But Pao-yu would not be satisfied with anything less than a full kowtow.

Chia Jui, anxious to smooth things over, urged Chin Jung softly, "Remember the proverb 'A murderer can only lose his head.' Since you began this you must humble yourself a little. Once you've kowtowed, that will be the end of it."

So at last Chin Jung stepped forward and kowtowed to Chin Chung.

To know what followed, read the next chapter.

CHAPTER 10

Widow Chin Pockets Her Pride Because
of Self-Interest
Dr. Chang Diagnoses Ko-ching's Illness

With heavy pressure on him and orders from Chia Jui to apologize, Chin Jung had to appease Pao-yu by kowtowing to Chin Chung. Then school was dismissed and he went home, where the more he brooded the angrier he grew.

"That flunkey Chin Chung is only Chia Jung's brother-in-law, not a son or grandson of the Chia family," he fumed. "He's only in the school on sufferance, just as I am. But on the strength of his friendship with Pao-yu he looks down on everyone else. If he at least behaved decently no one would mind; but the two of them must think the rest of us are blind, the way they carry on. Well, I caught him today making up to someone else, so I needn't be afraid even if the whole thing comes out."

"What scrape are you in now?" asked his mother, née Hu, when she heard this muttering. "I had to rope in your aunt and put her to no end of trouble to beg Madam Hsi-feng in the West Mansion to get you this place in the family school. Where would we be if not for their help? We couldn't afford a tutor. Besides, you get free meals there, don't you? That's meant a great saving on your board these last two years. It's fitted you out in all those smart clothes you're so fond of. It was through the school, too, that you met Mr. Hsueh who's helped us this last year or so to the tune of seventy or eighty taels of silver at least. If you're expelled because of this row, don't expect me to find another school like this. I can tell you, that would be harder than climbing up to heaven. Just amuse

143

yourself quietly now before going to bed. That would be much better."

Chin Jung had to swallow his anger and hold his tongue, and very soon he turned in. The next day he went back to school as if nothing had happened.

Now Chin Jung's paternal aunt had married Chia Huang of that generation of the family which used the "jade" (*yu*) radical in personal names. Needless to say, not all members of the clan were as wealthy as those in the Ning and Jung Mansions. Chia Huang and his wife had very slender means and were only able to live as they did by keeping on good terms with both households and by making up to Hsi-feng and Madam Yu, who often helped them out.

Since today was fine and she had nothing to do, Chia Huang's wife, née Chin, accompanied by a woman-servant, came over by carriage to see her widowed sister-in-law and nephew.

In the course of conversation Chin Jung's mother described the quarrel in the school the previous day, giving a detailed account of the whole affair. Aunt Huang immediately flew into a passion.

"Our boy Jung is just as much a relative of the Chia family as that young fool Chin Chung," she cried. "How can some people suck up like that to the rich? Especially when they behave so disgracefully. As for Pao-yu, he's no call to make such a favourite of him. I'm going to the East Mansion to see Madam Yu, then I'll tell Chin Chung's sister about this and see what she has to say."

"I should never have told you, sister." Chin Jung's mother was frantic. "For goodness' sake don't say anything to them. Never mind who's right and who's wrong. If trouble came of it my boy would lose his place. And apart from the fact that we couldn't afford a tutor we'd have to spend a lot more on his food and clothes."

"Never mind that!" retorted Aunt Huang. "Let me tell them the facts and we'll see what they have to say."

Ignoring the widow's protests, she called for her carriage and drove to the Ning Mansion, alighting at the small gate on the east side and going in on foot to see Madam Yu.

Not daring to vent her anger, she made polite conversation for a while, then asked, "Why don't I see Madam Jung today?"

"I don't know what the matter is," said Madam Yu. "But she's missed her periods for two months and more, yet the doctors say she's not expecting. She's too tired to move or talk by the afternoon nowadays, and she has dizzy spells. I told her, 'Don't trouble to pay your respects here mornings and evenings, just have a good rest. If relatives call, I'll receive them. And if the old folk wonder at your absence, I'll make apologies for you.' I told Jung not to let anyone tire or annoy her, so that she can rest quietly until she's better. 'If she fancies anything to eat, come to me for it,' I said. 'If we don't have it you can ask Hsi-feng. If anything were to happen to her, you'd never find another wife with her good looks and sweet temper, not if you were to search around with a lantern.' She's quite won the hearts of the old folk and all our relations. So I've been most dreadfully worried the last few days.

"But then her brother had to come and see her this morning. He's too young to know any better, but when he saw she was ill he shouldn't have troubled her with his affairs, not to say a trifle like this. Even if he was treated unfairly, he shouldn't have told her. They had a fight, you know, in school yesterday. Some other boy bullied him and there was dirty talk — he repeated it all to her. You know how she is. For all she's so pleasant and so capable, she's sensitive and takes everything to heart. She'll brood over the least little thing for days on end. It's this habit of worrying that's made her ill. When she heard today that someone had picked on her brother, it upset her and made her angry. Angry with those dirty dogs who cause trouble and gossip; upset because Chin Chung doesn't study hard or give his mind to his books, and that's how this trouble started. Because of this, she wouldn't touch any breakfast.

"When word of this reached me I went over to soothe her. I gave her brother a talking-to, then packed him off to Pao-yu in the other mansion. I didn't come back till I'd seen her take half a bowl of bird's-nest soup. You can't imagine how worried I am, sister. We haven't got any good doctors nowadays, either. This illness is keeping me on tenterhooks. Do you know of any good doctor?"

Aunt Huang's furious determination while with her sister-in-law to have it out with Ko-ching had, during this recital, been scared away into the Sea of Java.

"We've been hoping to hear of some good doctors, but so far we don't know of any," she replied. "But judging by what you tell me, this may still mean she's pregnant. Don't let anyone give her the wrong medicine, though. That could be dangerous."

"Just what I think," agreed Madam Yu.

At this point Chia Chen came in. Seeing Chia Huang's wife he inquired, "Is this Mrs. Huang?"

She stepped forward to greet him, and before returning to his room he urged his wife to keep her to a meal.

Aunt Huang had come there to complain about Chin Chung's treatment of her nephew, but after hearing of Ko-ching's illness she hadn't the courage to mention this, much less to complain. Moreover Chia Chen's and Madam Yu's kind reception had transformed her indignation into pleasure. She chatted a little longer, then took her leave.

Once she had gone, Chia Chen came in and sat down.

"What business brought her here today?" he asked.

"She didn't seem to have any," replied his wife. "She looked rather put out when she arrived but she calmed down little by little as I told her about our daughter-in-law's illness. Because of that she couldn't very well stop to a meal, as you suggested. She left quite soon without making any requests.

"But to get back to our daughter-in-law, you really must find a good doctor for her without any more delay. These that have been attending her are useless. They just listen to what we tell them and then dress it up in high-sounding language. They go to a lot of trouble, to be sure, three or four of them coming several times a day to feel her pulse in turn. After consulting together they write their prescriptions, but the medicine hasn't done her the least bit of good. In fact, it's bad for a patient to have to change her clothes four or five times a day and sit up to see the doctor."

"Why should the silly child keep changing?" asked Chia Chen. "If she caught cold that would be even worse. This will never do. The finest clothes are nothing compared with her health. She can wear new ones every day if it comes to that.

"What I was going to tell you is that Feng Tzu-ying called just now. He asked why I looked so worried. I told him I was upset because our daughter-in-law isn't well but we can't find a good doctor to tell whether she's ill or pregnant, and whether there's any danger or not. Well, Feng knows a doctor named Chang Yu-shih who was his childhood tutor, a very learned man with a comprehensive knowledge of medicine, and an excellent diagnostician. He's come to the capital this year to purchase an official rank for his son, and he's staying with Feng. Fate may have meant him to cure our daughter-in-law. You never can tell. I've sent a servant with my card to invite him. It may be too late today, but I'm sure he'll come to-morrow. Especially as Feng Tzu-ying promised to ask him as soon as he reached home. Let's wait, then, till this Dr. Chang has seen her."

Madam Yu cheered up at this. "And how are we to celebrate your father's birthday the day after tomorrow?"

"I've just been to pay my respects to him," answered Chia Chen. "I invited him here to receive congratulations from the whole family, but he said, 'I'm used to a peaceful life and don't want to be disturbed by all the commotion in your house. Of course, you're inviting me to go and have everyone kowtow to me because it's my birthday, but it would be a hundred times more to my liking if you had my annotated *Rewards and*

Punishments[1] neatly copied out and printed. Suppose you entertain the two families for me at home the day after tomorrow instead of having them come here. Don't send me any presents either. In fact, there's no need for you to come yourself the day after tomorrow. You can kowtow to me now, if that will make you feel better. If you bring a great crowd to disturb me on my birthday, I shall be very displeased.'

"Since he made such a point of this, I shan't venture to go again. You had better order Lai Sheng to arrange for the two days' banqueting. It must be handsomely done. You can go to the West Mansion to deliver invitations in person to the old lady, Lady Hsing, Lady Wang and Hsi-feng."

As he was saying this, Chia Jung came in to pay his respects, and Madam Yu told him what her husband had said.

"Your father has heard today of a good doctor," she added. "We've sent to ask him round and he should be coming tomorrow. You'll have to tell him all your wife's symptoms."

Her son assented and had just withdrawn when he met the page sent to invite Dr. Chang.

"I've been to Mr. Feng's house with His Lordship's card," said the page. "The doctor said Mr. Feng had just told him about it, but he was so exhausted after a whole round of visits that even if he came now he couldn't take the pulse. He'll come tomorrow after a good night's rest. He added, 'I know very little about medicine and really shouldn't presume to take up this responsibility, but since Mr. Feng has done me the honour of recommending me to your master I mustn't decline. Go and give your master this message. As for His Lordship's card, I really can't presume to keep it.' So I've brought it back. Will you please pass on this message for me, sir?"

Chia Jung went back to tell his parents this, after which he sent for Lai Sheng to instruct him to prepare the two days' feast. And the steward went off to make his preparations.

The next day at noon the doctor was announced. Chia Chen conducted him into the reception hall and made him take a

---

[1] A Taoist tract on divine retribution.

seat. When they had drunk tea he broached the subject, saying, "Yesterday I was overwhelmed with admiration by all Mr. Feng told me of your character, learning and profound knowledge of medicine, sir."

"I am simply an ignorant layman," replied Dr. Chang. "But when I heard yesterday from Mr. Feng that Your Lordship's family is considerate to ordinary scholars and had condescended to send for me, how could I disobey your orders? I am ashamed, though, that I have no real learning."

"You are too modest, sir. May I trouble you to have a look at my daughter-in-law? I am relying on your superior knowledge to relieve our anxiety."

Chia Jung accompanied the doctor to Ko-ching's bedside.

"Is this your worthy wife?" asked Dr. Chang.

"Yes, sir," said Chia Jung. "Do sit down! Would you like me to describe her symptoms to you before you take the pulse?"

"May I suggest that I take her pulse before you enlighten me?" countered the doctor. "This is my first visit to your honourable mansion, and being quite unqualified I would not have come but for Mr. Feng's insistence. Let me take her pulse, and you may gauge the correctness of my diagnosis before you describe her condition recently. Then we can devise an efficacious prescription and submit it to the discretion of His Lordship."

"I see you are an authority," replied Chia Jung. "I am only sorry we did not meet earlier. Do examine her and let us know if she can be cured, to spare my father further anxiety."

Some maids rested Chin Ko-ching's arm on a pillow and raised her sleeve to expose the wrist. The doctor first took the pulse of the right wrist, feeling it carefully for a considerable time before he turned to the left wrist.

This done, he proposed, "Shall we go and sit outside?"

Chia Jung conducted him to another room, where they seated themselves on the *kang*. A serving woman brought in tea, and when they had drunk it Chia Jung asked:

"Judging by her pulse, doctor, is there any cure for her?"

"Your honourable wife's left distal pulse is deep and agitated, the median pulse deep and faint," replied the doctor. "The right distal pulse is faint and feeble, the median pulse slight and lacking in energy.

"A deep and agitated left distal pulse indicates a febrile condition arising from the weak action of the heart; the deep and faint median pulse is due to anemia caused by a sluggish liver. A faint and feeble distal pulse on the right wrist comes of debility of the lungs; a slight and listless median pulse indicates a wood element in the liver too strong for the earth element in the spleen.

"The fire produced by the weak action of the heart results in irregular menses and insomnia. A deficiency of blood and sluggish condition of the liver produce pain in the ribs, delayed menses and heartburn. Debility of the lungs leads to giddiness, perspiration in the early hours of the morning, and a feeling like sea-sickness. And the predominance of the wood element in the liver over the earth element in the spleen causes loss of appetite, general lassitude and soreness of the limbs. These are the symptoms I would expect from my reading of the lady's pulse. I cannot agree with the view that this pulse indicates a pregnancy."

An old woman who had been attending Ko-ching exclaimed, "That's exactly how it is. This doctor must have second sight: there's no need for us to tell him anything. Quite a few of our household physicians have seen her, but not one of them came so close to the truth. One says it's a pregnancy, another that it's an illness; this one declares it's of no consequence, that one that there'll be a crisis at the winter solstice. They can't make up their minds. Please tell us just what to do, sir."

"Those gentlemen have delayed your lady's recovery," said the doctor. "If she had taken the right medicine when she first missed her menses, she'd have been quite well by now. Since she's had no effective treatment, this trouble is only to be expected. I would rate her chances of recovery at three out of ten. If she sleeps well tonight after taking my medicine, that will about double her chances.

"Judging by her pulse, your lady is highly strung and unusually intelligent. Because of this she is easily upset and prone to worry, which has affected her spleen. The element of wood in the liver has produced hot humours which have upset her menstruation. Am I right in assuming that your lady's periods always tended to be irregular and several days late?"

"Yes, to be sure," said the woman. "Never early but two or three days later than normal, sometimes as much as ten days behind time."

"Quite so," observed the doctor. "There's the cause of her illness. If she'd taken a tonic to regulate her menses, this could have been avoided. This is clearly a case of enervation caused by too little water and too much wood. We'll see how she responds to medicine."

Thereupon he wrote out and gave Chia Jung the following prescription:

DECOCTION TO IMPROVE THE RESPIRATION, FORTIFY
THE BLOOD AND TRANQUILLIZE THE LIVER

Ginseng	.2 oz
Atractylis (clay baked)	.2 oz
Pachyma cocos	.3 oz
Prepared Ti root	.4 oz
Aralia edulis (cooked in wine)	.2 oz
White peony (cooked)	.2 oz
Szechuan selinum	.15 oz
Sophora tomentosa	.3 oz
Cyperus rotundus (processed)	.2 oz
Gentian soaked in vinegar	.08 oz
Dioscorea from the Huai region (cooked)	.2 oz
Genuine Tung-ngo glue (prepared with powdered oyster-shell)	.2 oz
Carydalis ambigua (cooked in wine)	.15 oz
Dried liquorice	.08 oz

Adjuvant: Seven Fukien lotus-seeds with the pits extracted and two large red dates.

"Excellent," remarked Chia Jung after reading this. "Can you tell me, doctor, if her life is in any danger?"

"A man of your intelligence must know that at this stage it is impossible to predict how long the illness may last. We must see how she responds to this treatment. In my humble opinion, there is no danger this winter and if she gets through the spring equinox we may expect a cure."

Chia Jung was too sensible to press the matter. After seeing the doctor out he showed his father the prescription and diagnosis and told his parents all that had been said.

"No other doctor has been so definite," observed Madam Yu to her husband. "His prescription must be good."

"He is not a professional doctor," replied Chia Chen. "He doesn't practise medicine for a living and only came as a favour to our friend Feng Tzu-ying. With his help, there's hope that our daughter-in-law may be cured. I see his prescription calls for ginseng. You can use that catty of a superior quality we bought the other day."

Chia Jung withdrew to see about buying the medicine, which was then prepared and given to his wife. To know the effect of the treatment, read the next chapter.

CHAPTER 11

Chia Ching's Birthday Is Celebrated
in the Ning Mansion
Chia Jui Meets and Lusts
After Hsi-feng

Chia Ching's birthday had now arrived. Chia Chen had six large hampers filled with choice delicacies and rare fruit and sent Chia Jung with some servants to deliver them.

"Make sure your grandfather's agreeable before you pay your respects," he cautioned his son. "Tell him that in compliance with his wishes I've not ventured to go, but I am assembling the whole family here to honour him."

After Chia Jung had left the guests began to arrive. First Chia Lien and Chia Chiang. Observing the seating arrangements, they asked what entertainment was to be offered.

"His Lordship originally planned to invite the old master, so he didn't prepare any theatricals," said the servants. "But the day before yesterday, when he heard that the old gentleman wouldn't be coming, he got us to hire some young actors and musicians. They're getting ready now on the stage in the garden."

Next to arrive were Lady Hsing, Lady Wang, Hsi-feng and Pao-yu. They were welcomed in by Chia Chen and Madam Yu, whose mother had already come. After greetings had been exchanged they were urged to be seated. Chia Chen and his wife handed round tea.

"The Lady Dowager is our Old Ancestress," said Chia Chen with a smile. "My father is only her nephew, and we wouldn't have presumed to invite her on his birthday if not for the fact that the weather is refreshingly cool now and all the chrysanthemums in our garden are at their best. We thought it might prove a pleasant distraction for her to watch all her children and grandchildren enjoying themselves. She hasn't favoured us with her presence, however."

"Up to yesterday she meant to come," explained Hsi-feng before Lady Wang could get a word in. "But yesterday evening she saw Pao-yu eating some peaches and she couldn't resist eating nearly a whole peach. She had to get up twice just before dawn, which left her tired out this morning. She asked me to tell you that she couldn't come, but she hopes you'll send her a few delicacies if you have some that are easy to digest."

"That explains it," said Chia Chen. "The old lady is so fond of lively parties, I was sure there must be some reason for her absence."

Lady Wang remarked, "The other day Hsi-feng told me that Jung's wife is indisposed. What's wrong with her?"

"It's a very puzzling illness," replied Madam Yu. "At the Mid-Autumn Festival last month she enjoyed herself half the night with the old lady and you, and came home none the worse. But for a fortnight since the twentieth of last month she's grown weaker and weaker every day and lost all her appetite. And she hasn't had a period for two months."

"Can she be pregnant?" asked Lady Hsing.

Just then the arrival of Chia Sheh, Chia Cheng and the other gentlemen was announced. They were in the reception hall. Chia Chen hurried out.

Madam Yu continued, "Some doctors thought it might mean a happy event. But yesterday she was examined by an excellent physician recommended by Feng Tzu-ying, who once studied with him, and according to him it isn't a pregnancy but a serious illness. He made out a prescription, and today after one dose she feels less dizzy but there hasn't been much other improvement."

"If she weren't quite incapable of any exertion, I know she'd have made an effort to be here today," observed Hsi-feng.

"You saw her here on the third," said Madam Yu. "She forced herself to bear up for several hours, because she's so fond of you she couldn't bear to tear herself away."

Hsi-feng's eyes became moist. After a pause she exclaimed, "Truly, 'Storms gather without warning in nature, and bad luck befalls men overnight.' But life is hardly worth living if such an illness can carry off one so young!"

As she was speaking Chia Jung walked in. Having greeted the visitors he told his mother, "I've just taken the delicacies to my grandfather. I told him my father was waiting on Their Lordships and entertaining the young gentlemen here, and that in compliance with his orders he wouldn't presume to go over. Grandfather was very pleased. He expressed approval and told me to ask you and my father to attend to the elder generation while we entertain the younger. He also wants to have ten thousand copies of his version of *Rewards and Punishments* printed and distributed as quickly as possible. I've already given this message to my father. Now I must hurry and see to the food for all the grand-uncles, uncles and other gentlemen."

"Just a minute, Master Jung," interposed Hsi-feng. "Tell me, how is your wife today?"

"Not well at all." The young man's face clouded. "Do go and see her for yourself, aunt, on your way home." He left without saying any more.

Madam Yu asked Lady Hsing and Lady Wang, "Would you prefer to eat here or in the garden? The actors are preparing out there."

"Why not eat here and then go out?" suggested Lady Wang. "That would be simpler."

Lady Hsing seconded this.

So Madam Yu ordered the meal to be served at once. There was an answering cry in unison outside the door and the maids went to fetch the dishes. Soon the feast was ready. Madam Yu made Lady Hsing, Lady Wang and her mother take the places of honour, while she sat at a side table with Hsi-feng and Pao-yu.

"We came to congratulate the old gentleman on his birthday," remarked Lady Hsing and Lady Wang. "But now it looks, doesn't it, as if we were celebrating our own?"

"The Elder Master is fond of retirement," said Hsi-feng. "He's lived so long as an ascetic, we can already consider him an immortal. So he'll know by divine intuition what you've just said."

This set the whole company laughing. The ladies, having by now finished their meal, rinsed their mouths and washed their hands. Just as they were ready to go into the garden, Chia Jung turned up to tell his mother:

"All my grand-uncles, uncles and cousins have finished their meal. Lord Sheh has some business at home, and Lord Cheng has also left as he doesn't care for theatricals or anything rowdy. Uncle Lien and Cousin Chiang have taken the others over to watch the performance.

"Cards and gifts have been brought from the four princes of Nanan, Tungping, Hsining and Peiching, from Duke Niu of Chenkuo and five other dukes, as well as from Marquis Shih of Chungching and seven other marquises. I've reported this to my father, had the presents put in the counting-house and the catalogues of gifts placed on file, and my father's 'received with thanks' cards handed to the messengers, who were given the usual tips and a meal before they left.

"Won't you ask the ladies to go and sit in the garden now, mother?"

"We've just finished our meal too," said Madam Yu. "We're coming over."

"I'd like to drop in and see Jung's wife first, madam," said Hsi-feng. "May I join you later?"

"A good idea," approved Lady Wang. "We'd all go if not for fear of disturbing her. Tell her we asked after her."

"My daughter-in-law always does as you ask her, dear sister," said Madam Yu. "I'll feel much easier in my mind if you go and cheer her up. But join us in the garden as soon as you can."

Pao-yu asked permission to go with Hsi-feng.

"Go if you want, but don't be long," said his mother. "Remember she's your nephew's wife."

So Madam Yu took Lady Hsing, Lady Wang and her own mother to the Garden of Concentrated Fragrance, while Hsifeng and Pao-yu went with Chia Jung to see Ko-ching.

They entered her room quietly and when she made an effort to rise Hsi-feng protested, "Don't. It would make you dizzy." She hurried forward to clasp Ko-ching's hand, exclaiming, "How thin you've grown, my poor lady, in the few days since last I saw you!"

She sat down on her mattress, while Pao-yu also asked after his niece's health and took a chair opposite.

"Bring in tea at once," called Chia Jung. "My aunt and second uncle had none in the drawing-room."

Holding Hsi-feng's hand, Ko-ching forced a smile.

"Living in a family like this is more than I deserve," she said. "My father-in-law and mother-in-law treat me as their own daughter. And although your nephew's young, we have such a regard for each other that we've never quarrelled. In fact the whole family, old and young, not to mention you, dear aunt — that goes without saying — have been goodness itself to me and shown me nothing but kindness. But now that I've fallen ill all my will power's gone, and I haven't been able to be a good daughter-in-law. I want so much to show how I appreciate your goodness, aunt, but it's no longer in my power now. I doubt if I shall last the year out."

Pao-yu was looking pensively at the picture *Sleeping Under a Crab-Apple Tree in Spring* and Chin Kuan's couplet:

> Coolness wraps her dream, for spring is chill;
> A fragrance assails men, the aroma of wine.

As he raptly recalled his dream here of the Illusory Land of Great Void, Ko-ching's remarks pierced his heart like ten thousand arrows and unknown to himself his tears flowed. Hsifeng, distressed as she was, did not want to upset the patient even more, knowing it would be better to distract and console her.

"You're a regular old woman, Pao-yu," she scolded. "It's not as bad as your niece would have us believe." She turned to Ko-ching. "How can someone your age give way to such foolish fancies just because of a little illness? Do you want to make yourself worse?"

"She'd be all right if only she'd eat," put in Chia Jung.

"Her Ladyship told you not to be too long," Hsi-feng reminded Pao-yu. "Don't hang about here upsetting Ko-ching and making Her Ladyship worry." She then turned to Chia Jung and said, "Take Uncle Pao to rejoin the others while I stay here a little longer."

So Chia Jung led Pao-yu to the Garden of Concentrated Fragrance while Hsi-feng soothed Ko-ching and whispered some well-meant advice into her ear.

When Madam Yu sent a servant for the third time to fetch her she said to Ko-ching, "Take good care of yourself. I'll come back again to see you. The fact that this good doctor has been recommended to us is a sign that you're going to get better. Don't you worry."

"Even if he were an immortal, he could cure a disease but not avert my fate," retorted Ko-ching with a smile. "I know it's only a matter of time now, auntie."

"How can you get better if you keep thinking like that? You must look on the bright side. In any case, I'm told the doctor said that even if you're not cured there's no danger until the spring. It's only the middle of the ninth month now. You've four or five months yet, quite long enough to recover from any illness. It would be another matter if our family couldn't afford ginseng; but your father and mother-in-law can easily give you two catties of ginseng a day, not to mention two drams. Mind you rest well. I'm off now to the garden."

"I'm sorry I can't go with you, dear aunt," said Ko-ching. "Do come back again when you've time and let's have a few more good talks."

Hsi-feng's eyes smarted again at this. "Of course I'll come whenever I'm free," she promised.

Accompanied by her own maids and some from the Ning Mansion, she took a winding path to the side gate of the garden. There a rare sight met her eyes.

Yellow chrysanthemums carpeted the ground,
Green willows covered the slopes;
Small bridges spanned the brooks
And winding pathways led to quiet retreats.
Clear springs welled from the rocks,
Fragrance was wafted from trellises laden with
    flowers,
While russet tree-tops swayed
In scattered copses lovely as a painting.
The autumn wind was chilly
And the song of golden orioles had ceased,
But crickets were still chirping in the warm sunshine.
At the far southeast end
Cottages nestled among the hills;
On the northwest side
Pavilions brooded over the lake water.
Fluting cast a subtle enchantment over men's senses,
And silk-gowned girls strolling through the woods
Added to the charm of the scene.

Hsi-feng was strolling along enjoying this sight when a man appeared without warning from behind an artificial rockery and accosted her with, "Greetings, sister-in-law!"

She stepped back, startled, and asked, "Is it Master Jui?"

"Who else could it be? Don't tell me you don't know me."

"Of course I do, but you took me by surprise."

"We must have been fated to meet, sister-in-law." He was devouring her with his eyes as he spoke. "I slipped away from the banquet just now for a quiet stroll in this secluded spot. And I meet you here! What is this if not fate?"

Hsi-feng had sense enough to see through him. "No wonder Lien always speaks so highly of you," she rejoined with a smile, feigning pleasure. "From seeing you today and hearing you talk, I can see how clever and understanding you are. I've no time to spare now, I must join Her Ladyship. But perhaps we shall meet again some other day."

"I've often wanted to call and pay my respects. But I thought, being young, you might not welcome me."

"What nonsense." She assumed another smile. "Aren't we of the same family?"

Enraptured by this unexpected good fortune, Chia Jui looked ready to make more indecent advances. But Hsi-feng urged him, "You must hurry back before you're missed, or they'll make you drink forfeits."

Half numbed by this tantalizing remark he walked slowly away, looking back at her over his shoulder. Hsi-feng purposely slowed down until he was out of sight.

"You can know a man's face but not his heart," she reflected. "I'll show the beast! If he tries anything like that with me, I'll sooner or later make him die at my hands, to let him know my ability."

Then, rounding a miniature hill, she met several matrons hurrying breathlessly towards her.

"Our mistress sent us to fetch you, madam," they cried. "She was worried because you didn't come."

"Your mistress is devilish impatient!"

Continuing to saunter along, she asked how many items had been performed. The answer was: Eight or nine. They had now reached the back door of the Pavilion of Heavenly Fragrance, where Pao-yu was amusing himself with some maids.

"No silly tricks now, Cousin Pao-yu," she warned him.

"The ladies are all in the gallery," one of the girls told her. "Just up those stairs, madam."

Hsi-feng gathered up her skirts to mount the stairs and found Madam Yu waiting for her on the landing.

"You and your niece are so thick, I thought you'd never tear yourself away," teased Madam Yu. "You'd better move over tomorrow and stay with her. Sit down now and let me give you a toast."

Hsi-feng asked Lady Hsing and Lady Wang's permission to be seated and exchanged a few polite remarks with Madam Yu's mother, then she sat down beside her hostess to sip wine and watch the performance. Madam Yu sent for the list of their repertoire and asked her to choose a few items.

"How can I presume when Their Ladyships are present?" demurred Hsi-feng.

"Old Mrs. Yu has chosen several already," replied Lady Hsing and Lady Wang. "It's your turn to pick a couple of good ones for us."

Hsi-feng rose to signify obedience. Taking the list she read through it and marked *The Resurrection*[1] and *The Rhapsody*.[2] Handing it back she observed, "When they've finished this *Double Promotion*[3] there'll be just time enough for these two."

"Yes," said Lady Wang. "We must let our hosts have some rest soon. Especially as this is a worrying time for them."

"You come over so seldom," protested Madam Yu, "I do hope you'll stay a bit longer. It's early yet."

Hsi-feng stood up to look below and asked, "Where are the gentlemen?"

"They've gone to drink in the Pavilion of Lingering Dawn," replied one of the matrons. "They took the musicians with them."

"Our presence cramps their style," remarked Hsi-feng. "I wonder what they're up to behind our backs?"

"How can you expect everybody to be as proper as you?" said Madam Yu jokingly.

So they laughed and chatted till the plays came to an end, when the wine was taken away and rice brought in. After the meal they returned to the drawing-room for tea, then ordered their carriages and took their leave of old Mrs. Yu. They were seen to their carriages by Madam Yu, attended by all the concubines and maids, and there they found the young men waiting with Chia Chen. The latter urged Lady Hsing and Lady Wang to come back again the next day, but Lady Wang declined. "We've spent the whole day here and we're tired. We shall have to rest tomorrow."

Chia Jui kept his eyes on Hsi-feng as the visitors got into their carriages and drove off.

After Chia Chen and the others had gone indoors, Li Kuei led round Pao-yu's horse and the boy mounted it and followed his mother home. When Chia Chen and all the young men

---

[1] A scene from *The Peony Pavilion*, by the Ming playwright Tang Hsien-tsu.

[2] A scene from *The Palace of Eternal Youth*, by the Ching playwright Hung Sheng.

[3] A popular opera chosen for its auspicious title.

had dined, the party broke up; and there is no need to describe the entertainment they offered all their kinsmen the next day.

Hsi-feng dropped in more often now to see Ko-ching, who seemed slightly better on some days although in general her health did not improve, to the great dismay of her husband and his parents. And Chia Jui, calling several times on Hsi-feng, invariably found she had gone to the Ning Mansion.

The thirtieth day of the eleventh month would be the winter solstice. As it approached, the Lady Dowager, Lady Wang and Hsi-feng sent daily to inquire after Ko-ching and were told each time that she was neither better nor worse.

"It's a hopeful sign," Lady Wang told the Lady Dowager, "if an illness grows no worse at a season like this."

"Yes, of course," replied the old lady. "If anything were to happen to the dear child, I'm sure it would break my heart."

In her distress she sent for Hsi-feng and said, "You and she have always been good friends. Tomorrow's the first of the twelfth month, but the day after that I want you to call on her and see just how she is. If she's any better, come and tell me. That would take a great weight off my mind. And you must have the things she used to like to eat made and sent round."

Hsi-feng promised to do this and after breakfast on the second she went to the Ning Mansion to see Ko-ching. Although the invalid appeared no worse, she had grown very thin and wasted. Hsi-feng sat and chatted with her for some time, assuring her that she had no cause for alarm.

"Whether I'll ever recover or not we'll know when spring comes," said Ko-ching. "Maybe I shall, for the winter solstice has passed and I'm no worse. Please tell the old lady and Lady Wang not to worry. Yesterday I ate two of the yam cakes stuffed with dates that the old lady sent, and I think they did me good."

"We'll send you some more tomorrow," offered Hsi-feng. "Now I must go to see your mother-in-law before hurrying back to tell the old lady how you are."

"Please send my respects to her and Lady Wang."

Promising to do so, Hsi-feng left. She went to sit with Madam Yu who asked, "Tell me frankly, how did you find her?"

Hsi-feng lowered her head for a while. "There seems to be little hope," she said at last. "If I were you I'd make ready the things for the funeral. That may break the bad luck."

"I've had them secretly prepared. But I can't get any good wood for you know what, so I've let that go for the time being."

After drinking some tea and chatting a little longer, Hsi-feng said she must go back to report to the Lady Dowager.

"Don't break it to her yet," said Madam Yu. "We don't want to alarm the old lady."

Hsi-feng agreed to this and took her leave. Home again, she told the Lady Dowager, "Jung's wife sends her respects and kowtows to you. She says she's better and you mustn't worry. When she's a little stronger, she'll come herself to kowtow and pay her respects."

"How did she seem?"

"For the present there's nothing to fear. She's in good spirits."

The Lady Dowager thought this over, then said, "Go and change your clothes now and rest."

Hsi-feng withdrew and reported to Lady Wang before going back to her room. Ping-erh helped her into the informal clothes she had warming by the fire. Then Hsi-feng, taking a seat, asked what had happened during her absence.

"Nothing much." The maid handed her a bowl of tea. "Lai Wang's wife came with the interest on that three hundred taels, which I put away. And Master Jui sent round again to ask if you were in, as he wanted to pay his respects."

"That wretch! He deserves to die." Hsi-feng snorted. "Just see what I do to the beast if he comes!"

"Why does he keep calling?"

Hsi-feng described their meeting and all he had said to her in the Ning Mansion garden during the ninth month.

"A toad hankering for a taste of swan," scoffed Ping-erh. "The beast hasn't a shred of common decency. He deserves a bad end for dreaming of such a thing."

"Let him come," said Hsi-feng. "I know how to deal with him."

What happened to Chia Jui when he came is told in the next chapter.

CHAPTER 12

Hsi-feng Sets a Vicious Trap
for a Lover
Chia Jui Looks into the Wrong Side of
the Precious Mirror of Love

While Hsi-feng was talking to Ping-erh, Chia Jui was announced. She ordered him to be admitted at once.

Overjoyed at being received, he hastened in and greeted her effusively, beaming with smiles. With a show of regard she made him take a seat and offered him tea. The sight of her in informal dress threw him into raptures. Gazing amorously at her he asked:

"Why isn't Second Brother Lien home yet?"

"I wouldn't know," Hsi-feng replied.

"Perhaps he's been caught by someone and can't tear himself away?"

"Perhaps. Men are like that. Bewitched by every pretty face they see."

"Not all of us, sister-in-law. I'm not like that."

"How many are there like you? Not one in ten."

Tweaking his ears and rubbing his cheeks with delight, the young man insinuated, "You must be very bored here day in and day out."

"Yes, indeed. I keep wishing someone would drop in for a chat to cheer me up."

"I have plenty of time. Suppose I were to drop in to amuse you every day?"

"Now you're joking," she replied archly. "You wouldn't want to come and see me."

"I mean every word I say. May a thunderbolt strike me if I don't! I didn't dare come before because I was told you

165

were very strict and took offence at the least little thing. Now I see how charming and how kind you are, you may be sure I'll come, even if it costs me my life."

"You're certainly much more understanding than Chia Jung and his brother. They look so refined one would expect them to be understanding, but they're stupid fools with no insight at all into other people's hearts."

Inflamed by this praise, he edged closer. Staring at the purse hanging from her girdle, he asked if he might look at her rings.

"Take care," she whispered. "What will the maids think?"

He drew back instantly as if obeying an Imperial decree or a mandate from Buddha.

"You had better go now." Hsi-feng smiled.

"Don't be so cruel. Let me stay a little longer."

"This is no place for you during the day with so many people about," she murmured. "Go now but come back again secretly at the first watch. Wait for me in the western entrance hall."

To Chia Jui this was like receiving a pearl of great price. "You're not joking are you?" he demanded. "How can I hide there with people passing back and forth all the time?"

"Don't worry. I'll dismiss all the pages on night duty. Once the gates on both sides are locked, no one can come through."

Hardly able to contain himself for joy, the young man hurried off, convinced he would have his desire and longing for the evening.

That night, sure enough, he groped his way to the Jung Mansion, slipping into the entrance hall just before the gates were bolted. It was pitch dark and not a soul was about. Already the gate to the Lady Dowager's quarters was locked, only the one on the east remaining open.

He waited, listening intently, but no one came. Then with a sudden clatter the east gate was bolted too. Frantic as he was, he dared not make a sound. He crept out to try the gate and found it securely closed. Escape was out of the question, for the walls on either side were too high to climb.

The entrance hall was bare and draughty. As it was the depth of winter the nights were long and an icy north wind chilled him to the bone. He almost froze to death.

At last dawn came and a matron appeared to open the east gate. As she went over to knock on the west gate and was looking the other way, Chia Jui shot out like a streak of smoke, hugging his shoulders. Luckily no one else was up at this early hour. He was able to escape unseen through the postern door.

Chia Jui had been orphaned early and left in the charge of his grandfather Chia Tai-ju, a strict disciplinarian who allowed him no freedom for fear he drink or gamble outside and neglect his studies. Now that he had stayed out all night his grandfather was furious and suspected him of drinking, gambling or whoring, little guessing the truth of the matter.

In a cold sweat with fright, Chia Jui tried to lie his way out.

"I went to my uncle's house, and because it was late he kept me for the night."

"You have never dared leave home before without permission," thundered his grandfather. "You deserve a beating for sneaking off like that. And a worse one for deceiving me."

He gave Chia Jui thirty or forty strokes with a bamboo, would not let him have any food, and made him kneel in the courtyard to study ten days' lessons. This thrashing on an empty stomach and kneeling in the wind to read essays completed the wretched youth's misery after his freezing night.

But still too blinded by infatuation to realize that Hsi-feng was playing with him, he seized his first chance a couple of days later to call. She reproached him for his breach of faith, earnestly as he protested his innocence; and since he had delivered himself into her hands she could not but devise further means to cure him.

"Tonight you can wait for me in another place — that vacant room off the passage behind this apartment. But mind you don't make any mistake this time."

"Do you really mean it?"

"Of course I do. If you don't believe me, don't come."

"I'll come, I'll come, even if I should die for it."

"Now, you'd better go."

Assuming that this time all would go well, Chia Jui went off.

Having got rid of him, Hsi-feng held a council of war and baited her trap while the young man waited at home impatiently, for to his annoyance one of their relatives called and stayed to supper. By the time he left the lamps were being lit, and Chia Jui had to wait for his grandfather to retire before he could slip over to the Jung Mansion and wait in the place appointed. He paced the room frantic as an ant on a hot griddle, but there was no sight or sound of anyone.

"Is she really coming?" he wondered. "Or shall I be left to freeze for another whole night?"

Just then a dark figure appeared. Sure that it was Hsi-feng, he threw caution to the winds and barely had the figure stepped through the door than he flung himself on it like a ravenous tiger, or a cat pouncing on a mouse.

"Dearest!" he cried. "I nearly died of longing."

He carried her to the *kang*, where he showered kisses on her and fumbled with her clothes, pouring out incoherent endearments. Not a sound came from the figure in his arms.

Chia Jui had just pulled down his pants and prepared to set to work when a sudden flash of light made him look up. There stood Chia Chiang, a taper in his hand.

"What's going on in here?" he demanded.

The figure on the *kang* said with a chuckle, "Uncle Jui was trying to bugger me."

When Chia Jui saw that it was Chia Jung, he wished he could sink through the ground. In utter confusion he turned to run away.

"Oh, no you don't!" Chia Chiang grabbed him. "Aunt Hsi-feng has told Lady Wang that without any reason you tried to make love to her. To escape your attentions she played this trick to trap you. Lady Wang's fainted from shock. I was sent here to catch you. I found you on top of him, you can't deny it. So come along with me to Lady Wang!"

Chia Jui nearly gave up the ghost. "Dear nephew," he pleaded, "do tell her you couldn't find me. I'll pay you well for it tomorrow."

"I might do that. Depends how much you're willing to pay. I can't just take your word for it, I must have it down in writing."

"How can I put a thing like this down in writing?"

"That's no problem. Just write that you borrowed so much silver from the bank to pay a gambling debt."

"All right. But I've no paper or brush."

"That's easy." Chia Chiang disappeared for a moment and promptly returned with writing materials, whereupon the two of them forced Chia Jui to write and sign an I.O.U. for fifty taels which Chia Chiang pocketed. When he urged Chia Jung to leave, however, the latter at first absolutely refused and threatened to lay the matter before the whole clan the next morning. Chia Jui kowtowed to him in desperation. However, with Chia Chiang mediating between them, he was forced to write another I.O.U. for fifty taels of silver.

"I'll get the blame if you're seen leaving," said Chia Chiang. "The Lady Dowager's gate is closed, and the Second Master is in the hall looking over the things which have arrived from Chinling, so you can't get out that way. You'll have to go through the back gate. But if anyone meets you I'll be finished too. Let me see if the coast is clear. You can't hide here, they'll be bringing stuff in presently. I'll find you somewhere to wait."

He blew out the light and dragged Chia Jui out to the foot of some steps in the yard.

"Here's a good place," he whispered. "Squat down there until we come back and don't make a sound."

As the two others left, Chia Jui squatted obediently at the foot of the steps. He was thinking over his predicament when he heard a splash above him and a bucket of slops was emptied over his head. A cry of dismay escaped him. But he clapped one hand over his mouth and made not another sound, though covered with filth from head to foot and shivering with cold. Then Chia Chiang hurried over calling:

"Quick! Run for it!"

At this reprieve, Chia Jui bolted through the back door to his home. By now the third watch had sounded, and he had to knock at the gate. The servant who opened it wanted to know how he came to be in such a state.

"I fell into a cesspool in the dark," lied Chia Jui.

Back in his own room he stripped off his clothes and washed. Only then did he realize with rage the trick Hsi-feng had played him, yet the recollection of her charms still made him long to embrace her. There was no sleep for him that night. Afterwards, however, although he still longed for Hsi-feng, he steered clear of the Jung Mansion.

Both Chia Jung and Chia Chiang kept dunning him for payment, so that his fear of being found out by his grandfather and the hopeless passion which consumed him were now aggravated by the burden of debts, while he had to work hard at his lessons every day. The unmarried twenty-year-old, constantly dreaming of Hsi-feng, could not help indulging in "finger-play." All this, combined with the effect of two nights of exposure, soon made him fall ill. Before a year was out he suffered from heartburn, loss of appetite, emissions in his urine and blood in his phlegm; his legs trembled, his eyes smarted; he was feverish at night and exhausted by day. And finally he collapsed in a fit of delirium.

The doctors who were called in dosed him with dozens of catties of cinnamon, aconitum roots, turtle-shell, liriope, polygonatum and so forth — but all to no effect. With the coming of spring he took a turn for the worse.

His grandfather rushed to and fro in search of new physicians, yet they proved useless. And when pure ginseng was prescribed this was beyond Chia Tai-ju's means: he had to ask for help from the Jung Mansion. Lady Wang told Hsi-feng to weigh out two ounces for him.

"All our recent supply was used the other day in the old lady's medicine," said Hsi-feng. "You told me to keep the remaining whole roots for General Yang's wife, and as it happens I sent them round yesterday."

"If we've none, send to your mother-in-law's for some. Or your Cousin Chen's household may let us have what's needed. If you can save the young man's life, that will be a good deed."

But instead of doing as she was told, Hsi-feng scraped together less than an ounce of inferior scraps which she dispatched with the message that this was all Her Ladyship had. To Lady Wang, however, she reported that she had collected two ounces and sent them over.

Chia Jui was so anxious to recover that there was no medicine he would not try, but all the money spent in this way was wasted.

One day a lame Taoist priest came begging for alms and professed to have specialized in curing diseases due to retribution. Chia Jui heard him from his sick-bed. At once, kowtowing on his pillow, he loudly implored his servants to bring the priest in.

When they complied he seized hold of the Taoist and cried: "Save me, Bodhisattva! Save me!"

"No medicine can cure your illness," rejoined the Taoist gravely. "However, I can give you a precious object which will save your life if you look at it every day."

He took from his wallet a mirror polished on both sides and engraved on its handle with the inscription: Precious Mirror of Love.

"This comes from the Hall of the Illusory Spirit in the Land of Great Void," he told Chia Jui. "It was made by the Goddess of Disenchantment to cure illnesses resulting from lust. Since it has the power to preserve men's lives, I brought it to the world for the use of intelligent, handsome, high-minded young gentlemen. But you must only look into the back of the mirror. On no account look into the front — remember that! I shall come back for it in three days' time, by when you should be cured." He strode off then before anyone could stop him.

"This is a strange business," reflected Chia Jui. "Let me try looking at this Taoist's mirror and see what happens." He picked it up and looked into the back. Horrors! A skeleton was standing there! Hastily covering it, he swore, "Confound that Taoist, giving me such a fright! But let me see what's on the other side."

He turned the mirror over and there inside stood Hsi-feng, beckoning to him. In raptures he was wafted as if by magic into the mirror, where he indulged with his beloved in the sport of cloud and rain, after which she saw him out.

He found himself back in his bed and opened his eyes with a cry. The mirror had slipped from his hands and the side with the skeleton was exposed again. Although sweating profusely after his wet dream, the young man was not satisfied. He turned the mirror over again, Hsi-feng beckoned to him as before, and in he went.

But after this had happened four times and he was about to leave her for the fourth time, two men came up, fastened iron chains upon him and proceeded to drag him away. He cried out:

"Let me take the mirror with me!"

These were the last words he uttered.

The attendants had simply observed him look into the mirror, let it fall and then open his eyes and pick it up again. This time, however, when the mirror fell he did not stir. They pressed round and saw that he had breathed his last. The sheet under his thighs was cold and wet.

At once they laid him out and made ready the bier, while his grandparents gave way to uncontrollable grief and cursed the Taoist.

"This devilish mirror!" swore Chia Tai-ju. "It must be destroyed before it does any more harm." He ordered it to be thrown into the fire.

A voice from the mirror cried out: "Who told you to look at the front? It's you who've taken false for true. Why should you burn me?"

That same instant in hustled the lame Taoist, shouting, "I can't let you destroy the Precious Mirror of Love!" Rushing forward he snatched it up, then was off like the wind.

Chia Tai-ju lost no time in preparing for the funeral, notifying all concerned that sutras would be chanted in three days' time and the funeral would take place in seven. The coffin would be left in Iron Threshold Temple until it could be taken to their old home.

All the members of the clan came to offer condolences. Chia Sheh and Chia Cheng of the Jung Mansion contributed twenty taels each towards the expenses, and Chia Chen of the Ning Mansion did the same. Others gave three or five taels according to their means, while the families of Chia Jui's schoolmates collected another twenty or thirty taels. So Chia Tai-ju, although not well-off, was able to conduct the funeral in style.

And then, at the end of winter, a letter came from Lin Ju-hai saying that he was seriously ill and wished to have his daughter sent home. This increased the Lady Dowager's distress, but they had to prepare with all speed for Tai-yu's departure; and although Pao-yu was most upset he could hardly come between her and her father.

The Lady Dowager decided that Chia Lien should accompany her grand-daughter and bring her safely back. We need not dwell on the presents and arrangements for the journey, which naturally left nothing to be desired. A day was quickly chosen on which Chia Lien and Tai-yu took their leave of everyone and, accompanied by attendants, set sail for Yangchow.

For further details, read the next chapter.

CHAPTER 13

Ko-ching Dies and a Captain of the Imperial
Guard Is Appointed
Hsi-feng Helps to Manage Affairs
in the Ning Mansion

Hsi-feng found life excessively dull after her husband's departure with Tai-yu for Yangchow. She passed the evenings as best she could chatting with Ping-erh before retiring listlessly to bed.

One evening, tired of embroidering, she sat nursing her hand-stove by the lamp and told the maid to warm her embroidered quilt early, after which they both went to bed. When the third watch sounded they were still reckoning on their fingers the stage Chia Lien must have reached on his journey. Soon after that, Ping-erh fell fast asleep. And Hsi-feng's eyelids were drooping drowsily when to her astonishment in came Ko-ching.

"How you love to sleep, aunt!" cried Ko-ching playfully. "I'm going home today, yet you won't even see me one stage of the way. But we've always been so close, I couldn't go without coming to say goodbye. Besides, there's something I'd like done which it's no use my entrusting to anyone else."

"Just leave it to me," replied Hsi-feng, rather puzzled.

"You're such an exceptional woman, aunt, that even men in official belts and caps are no match for you. Is it possible you don't know the sayings that 'the moon waxes only to wane, water brims only to overflow,' and 'the higher the climb the harder the fall'? Our house has prospered for nearly a hundred years. If one day it happens that at the height of good fortune the 'tree falls and the monkeys scatter' as the old saying has it, then what will become of our cultured old family?"

Quick to comprehend, Hsi-feng was awe-struck. "Your fears are well-founded," she said. "But how can we prevent such a calamity?"

"Now you're being naive, aunt." Ko-ching laughed caustically. "Fortune follows calamity as disgrace follows honour. This has been so from time immemorial. How can men prevent it? The only thing one can do is to make some provision for lean years in times of plenty. All's well at present except for two things. Take care of them and the future will be secure."

Hsi-feng asked what she had in mind.

"Although seasonal sacrifices are offered at the ancestral tombs there's no fixed source of income for this, and although we have a family school there's no definite fund for it. Of course, while we're still prosperous, we don't lack the wherewithal for sacrifices, but where's it to come from once we fall on hard times?

"I'd like to suggest that while we're still rich and noble we should invest in some farms and estates near our ancestral tombs to provide for sacrifices. The family school should be moved to the same place.

"Let the whole family, old and young alike, draw up rules whereby each branch of the family will take it in turn to manage the land, income and sacrifices for a year. Taking turns will prevent disputes and malpractices like mortgages or sales.

"Then even if the family property were confiscated because of some crime, the estate for ancestral worship would be exempted and in those hard times the young people could go there to study and farm. They'd have something to fall back on, and there would be no break in the sacrifices.

"It would be very short-sighted not to take thought for the future in the belief that our present good fortune will last for ever. Before long something marvellous is going to happen which will really 'pour oil on the flames and add flowers to brocade.' But it will simply be a flash in the pan, a brief moment of bliss. Whatever happens don't forget the proverb,

'Even the grandest feast must have an end.' Take thought for the future before it is too late."

"What marvellous thing is going to happen?" asked Hsi-feng.

"Heaven's secrets mustn't be divulged. But because of the love between us let me give you some parting advice, and do remember it, aunt!" With that she declaimed:

> "After the three months of the spring, all flowers will fade
> And each will have to find his own way out."

Before Hsi-feng could ask more she was woken with a start by four blows on the chime-bar at the second gate. And a servant announced, "Madam Chia Jung of the East Mansion has passed away."

Hsi-feng broke into a cold sweat. When she had recovered from her stupefaction, she dressed quickly and hurried over to Lady Wang.

By that time the whole household was lamenting, distressed by this shocking news. The old people recalled Ko-ching's filial behaviour, the young people her affectionate ways and the children her kindness; while not one of the servants but wept for grief recollecting her compassion for the poor and humble and her loving goodness to old and young alike.

But let us return to Pao-yu, who was so desolate after Tai-yu's departure that he had given up playing with his companions and went disconsolate to bed each night. Roused from sleep by the announcement of Ko-ching's death, he sprang suddenly from his bed. At once he felt a stab of pain in his heart, and with a cry spat out a mouthful of blood.

Hsi-jen and his other maids rushed up to help him back to bed, asking anxiously what was the matter. Should they get the Lady Dowager to send for a doctor?

"There's no need, it's nothing," he said. "A hot humour seized on my heart and stopped the normal flow of blood." He got up again and demanded to be dressed so that he could go to his grandmother and then to the other mansion.

Anxious though Hsi-jen was, she dared not stop him when he was in this mood.

The Lady Dowager however protested, "Just after a death their house is unclean. Besides, at night the wind is high. You may just as well go tomorrow."

When Pao-yu insisted, she ordered a carriage and plenty of attendants for him. They found the gates of the Ning Mansion wide open and brilliantly lit with lanterns on either side. There was an excited coming and going of people and the air was rent by the vociferous wailing from inside the house.

Alighting from his carriage Pao-yu hurried to the room in which Ko-ching lay and having wept there went in to see Madam Yu, who happened to be laid up with another bout of dyspepsia. He then paid his respects to Chia Chen.

By now Chia Tai-ju had arrived with Chia Tai-hsiu, Chia Cheh, Chia Hsiao, Chia Tun, Chia Sheh, Chia Cheng, Chia Tsung, Chia Pien, Chia Huang, Chia Hung, Chia Kuang, Chia Shen, Chia Chiung, Chia Lin, Chia Chiang, Chia Chang, Chia Ling, Chia Yun, Chia Chin, Chia Tsen, Chia Ping, Chia Tsao, Chia Heng, Chia Fen, Chia Fang, Chia Lan, Chia Chun and Chia Chih.

Bathed in tears, Chia Chen was telling Chia Tai-ju and the others, "Everyone in the family, old and young, distant kin or close friends, knows that my daughter-in-law was infinitely superior to my son. Now that she has gone, my branch of the family is fated to die out." With that he broke down again.

The men present tried to console him: "Since she has departed this world it is useless to weep. The main thing now is to decide what must be done."

"What must be done?" Chia Chen clapped his hands. "I'm ready to dispose of all in my possession."

He was interrupted by the arrival of Chin Yeh, Chin Chung and some relatives of Madam Yu as well as her younger sisters. Leaving Chia Chiung, Chia Shen, Chia Lin and Chia Chiang to keep the guests company, Chia Chen sent to invite someone from the Department of Astrology to choose auspicious days.

It was decided that the body should remain in the house for seven times seven or forty-nine days, and mourning should start the third day after her death with the issue of obituary notices. During the forty-nine days a hundred and eight Buddhist monks were to perform the Litany of Great Compassion in the main hall to release the souls of those passed away before and after her and win remission for the sins of the deceased. At an altar erected in the Heavenly Fragrance Pavilion, ninety-nine Taoists of the Perfect Truth Sect should pray for forty-nine days for absolution. The coffin would then be taken to the Garden of Concentrated Fragrance, where another fifty high bonzes and fifty high Taoists would sacrifice before it once every seventh day during the forty-nine days.

Chia Ching alone was untouched by the death of his eldest grandson's wife. Expecting to attain immortality shortly himself, how could he go home to be soiled by mundane dust and squander all the merit he had acquired? So he left all the funeral arrangements to his son.

His father's indifference gave Chia Chen a free hand to indulge his extravagance. He decided that the cedar-boards he had seen would not do for the coffin and was searching for something better when Hsueh Pan called to offer condolences.

"In our timber-yard is some *chiang* wood from the Iron-Net Mountain across the sea," said the young man. "A coffin made of this would last for ten thousand years. My father bought this timber for Prince Yi Chung, but after his disgrace the prince didn't take it. It's still stored with us because no one has ventured to buy it. If you like, I'll have it sent over."

Overjoyed by this news, Chia Chen had the timber fetched without delay. Everyone gathered round and exclaimed in wonder, for the planks for the sides and the base were eight inches thick with a grain like that of the areca palm and the perfume of sandalwood or musk. When tapped they gave off a clear ringing sound like metal or jade.

Chia Chen, his face radiant, inquired the price.

"You couldn't buy this for a thousand taels," replied Hsueh Pan with a smile. "Don't worry about the price. All you need pay for is having it made up."

After copious thanks Chia Chen lost no time in giving directions for the wood to be sawn and varnished.

Chia Cheng objected, "This seems too sumptuous for ordinary people. The best quality cedar-boards would be quite adequate."

But Chia Chen, who would gladly have died in Ko-ching's place, would not listen to this suggestion.

Word was brought that after Ko-ching's death one of her maids, Jui-chu, had dashed out her own brains against a pillar. The whole clan praised this act of rare loyalty and Chia Chen ordered that she be buried with the rites befitting a grandchild, her coffin resting in the Pavilion of Attained Immortality in the Garden of Concentrated Fragrance.

Another maid, Pao-chu, offered to act as Ko-ching's goddaughter and take the chief mourner's part, since her mistress had no child. This pleased Chia Chen so much that he directed that henceforward Pao-chu should be addressed as "miss," as if she were a daughter of the house.

Then Pao-chu mourned like an unmarried daughter, weeping by the coffin as if her heart would break, while all the clansmen and servants observed the etiquette traditionally prescribed for such occasions with unimpeachable propriety.

What distressed Chia Chen now was the fact that his son was only a state scholar. This would not look well in the inscription on the funeral banner and it meant that the retinue would have to be small.

As luck would have it, however, on the fourth day of the first week of mourning servants with sacrificial offerings arrived from the eunuch Tai Chuan, chamberlain of the Palace of Great Splendour, who followed in a great palanquin with an official umbrella and gonging and drumming to offer an oblation.

Chia Chen ushered him eagerly in and offered him tea in the Bee-Teasing Pavilion. He already had a scheme in mind and soon found occasion to express his wish to purchase a rank for his son.

Tai Chuan rejoined with a knowing smile, "To make the funeral more sumptuous, I presume?"

"Your assumption is correct, sir."

"By a fortunate coincidence there happens to be a good post going. There are two vacancies in the corps of three hundred officers of the Imperial Guard. Yesterday the third brother of the Marquis of Hsiangyang sent me 1,500 taels and asked me for one of them; and since we are old friends, as you know, for his grandfather's sake I made no difficulties but agreed out of hand. Who would have expected that Fatty Feng, Military Governor of Yunghsing, wants to buy the other appointment for his son; but I haven't yet had time to give him an answer. If your boy wants it, make haste and write out a statement of his antecedents."

Chia Chen at once sent a servant to pass on these instructions to his secretaries. The man returned presently with a sheet of red paper. After glancing at it Chia Chen handed it to Tai Chuan, who read:

> Chia Jung, twenty, State Scholar of Chiangning District, Chiangning Prefecture, Chiangnan.
> Great-grandfather: Chia Tai-hua, commander-in-chief of the Metropolitan Garrison and a hereditary general of the first class with the appellation Spiritual Might.
> Grandfather: Chia Ching, Metropolitan Scholar of the Yi Mao year.
> Father: Chia Chen, hereditary general of the third rank with the appellation Mighty Intrepidity.

Tai Chuan ordered one of his attendants, "Take this to Old Chao, chief of the Board of Revenue, with my compliments. Ask him to draw up a warrant for an officer of the fifth rank in the Imperial Guard and to fill out a commission according to these particulars. Tomorrow I will weigh out the silver and send it over."

Tai Chuan then took his leave. His host, who could not detain him, saw him out. Before the eunuch mounted his palanquin Chia Chen asked:

"Shall I take the money to the Board or to you, sir?"

"Just weigh out 1,200 taels and send it to my house. If you go to the Board, they'll fleece you."

Chia Chen thanked him warmly and promised, "When the mourning is over I shall bring my worthless son to kowtow his thanks." And so they parted.

Then runners could be heard clearing the way for the wife of Shih Ting, Marquis of Chungching. Lady Wang, Lady Hsing and Hsi-feng welcomed her into the drawing-room. Then sacrificial gifts from the Marquises of Chinhsiang and Chuanning as well as the Earl of Shoushan were displayed before the coffin. Presently these three nobles alighted from their palanquins and Chia Chen ushered them into the main hall.

So relatives and friends past counting came and went. Indeed, for forty-nine days the street outside the Ning Mansion was a sea of mourners in white interspersed by officials in their brilliant robes.

At his father's order Chia Jung changed into court dress the next day to collect his commission, after which the funerary ware in front of the coffin as well as the insignia for the cortège were made to befit an official of the fifth rank. The obituary tablet and notice were inscribed: "Obsequies of Lady Chin, Spouse of the House of Chia, Granted a Rank by Imperial Decree of the Celestial Court."

The street gate in the Garden of Concentrated Fragrance was opened, and on platforms erected at both sides groups of blue-clad musicians played at appropriate times. The retinue stood in pairs in perfect symmetry, and two large vermilion boards set up outside the gate bore the bold gilt inscriptions "Imperial Guard and Defender of the Palace Roads in the Inner Court of the Forbidden City."

Across the road, facing each other, towered two altars for Buddhist and Taoist priests. The announcement on them read,

"Obsequies of Lady Chin of the Chia Family, Consort of the Eldest Great-Grandson of the Hereditary Duke of Ningkuo, Imperial Guard and Defender of the Palace Roads in the Inner Court of the Forbidden City.

"In this land of peace and empire ruled according to the will of Heaven, in the centre of the four continents, we, Chief Buddhist Abbot Wang Hsu, Controller of the School of the

Void and Asceticism, and Chief Taoist Abbot Yeh Sheng, Controller of the Primordial School of the Trinity, having reverently purified ourselves raise our eyes to Heaven and kowtow to Buddha. We humbly invoke all divinities to show their divine compassion and display their spiritual majesty afar in these forty-nine days of grand sacrifice, that the departed may be delivered from sins and absolved from retribution. . . ." There was more in the same vein.

Now all that still troubled Chia Chen was the fact that his wife was ill in bed again, unable to see to things. If any breach of etiquette occurred while so many nobles were calling, the family would be laughed at.

Pao-yu noticed his preoccupation and asked: "Why do you look so anxious, cousin, now that everything's settled so satisfactorily?" When told the reason he said cheerfully, "That's no problem. I'll recommend someone to take charge for you. Let her see to things this month and I guarantee that everything will go smoothly."

"Who do you mean?"

Since there were many friends and relatives present, Pao-yu drew closer and whispered into his ear.

"Excellent!" Chia Chen sprang to his feet, overjoyed. "I must see to it at once." Taking leave of the others he hurried off with Pao-yu to the drawing-room.

As this was not one of the major days on which masses were said, only a few ladies who were close relatives had come. They were being entertained by Lady Hsing, Lady Wang, Hsi-feng and other women of the household when Chia Chen was announced. The ladies uttered cries of astonishment and hurriedly tried to slip into the inner room. Only Hsi-feng stood up composedly.

Chia Chen was not in good health himself at this time and, being weighed down with grief, he limped in with a cane.

"You are not well," said Lady Hsing. "After all your recent exertions you ought to rest. What business brings you here?"

Still clutching his cane, Chia Chen made an effort to kneel to greet and thank his kinswomen. Lady Hsing urged Pao-yu to restrain him and had a chair placed for him, but he would not take it.

Forcing a smile he announced, "Your nephew has come to ask a favour of his aunts and cousin."

"What is it?" inquired Lady Hsing.

"You know how it is, aunt. With my daughter-in-law gone and my wife ill in bed, everything is at sixes and sevens in the inner apartments. If my cousin Hsi-feng would condescend to take charge here for a month, that would set my mind at rest."

"So that's it." Lady Hsing smiled. "Hsi-feng is part of your Aunt Wang's establishment, so you'll have to ask *her* permission."

"She's young and inexperienced in these matters," said Lady Wang. "If she handled things badly people would laugh. You'd better find someone else."

"I can guess your real objection, aunt," he replied. "You're afraid she'd find it too tiring. As for handling things badly, I know that wouldn't be the case. And any little slip would be overlooked. Ever since she was a child at play Cousin Hsi-feng has known her own mind, and by managing the other house since her marriage she's gained experience. I've been thinking this over for some days and there's no one else so competent. If you won't agree for my sake or my wife's, aunt, do it for the one who's dead." His tears flowed again.

Lady Wang's only concern had been lest Hsi-feng, having no experience of funerals, might lay herself open to ridicule by managing badly. The earnestness of Chia Chen's request softened her heart and she eyed Hsi-feng thoughtfully.

Now Hsi-feng loved nothing better than displaying her administrative ability. Although she ran the household competently, as she had never been entrusted with grand affairs like weddings or funerals she was afraid others were not yet fully convinced of her efficiency and she was longing for a chance like this. Chia Chen's request delighted her. Seeing that his eagerness was overcoming Lady Wang's initial reluctance, she said:

"Since my cousin is so earnest and pressing, won't you give your consent, madam?"

"Are you sure you can cope?" whispered Lady Wang.

"I don't see why not. Cousin Chen has seen to all the important outside arrangements, it's just a question of keeping an eye on the domestic side. And in case of doubt, I can consult you."

Since this was reasonable, Lady Wang made no further objection.

"I can't see to everything," Chia Chen said to Hsi-feng. "I must beg you to help us, cousin. Let me express my gratitude now, and when everything's over I shall come round to your side to thank you properly."

He made a low bow and, before she could return it, produced the Ning Mansion tally from his sleeve and asked Pao-yu to hand it to her.

"You will have a free hand, cousin," he promised. "Just use this to requisition whatever you want, there's no need to consult me. I've only two requests to make. First, please don't try to spare me expense, as I want everything done handsomely. And secondly, treat the servants here as you would your own, don't be afraid they may resent it. Apart from these two provisos, nothing else worries me."

Hsi-feng did not venture to take the tally but glanced at Lady Wang.

"Do as your cousin asks," said Lady Wang. "But don't take too much upon yourself. If there are any decisions to make, send to ask him and your sister-in-law what should be done."

Pao-yu had already taken the tally from Chia Chen and forced it on Hsi-feng.

"Would you prefer to stay here or to come over every day?" Chia Chen asked her. "Coming over every day might be rather tiring. Why not let me clear out an apartment for you to stay in. Wouldn't that save you trouble?"

"There's no need," replied Hsi-feng gaily. "They can't do without me over there. I'll come every day."

Chia Chen did not insist but left them after a little further chat.

As soon as the visitors had gone Lady Wang asked Hsi-feng what she proposed to do now.

"Please don't wait for me, madam. I must sort things out before I come home."

So Lady Wang left first with Lady Hsing, while Hsi-feng retired to a small three-roomed annex to reflect as follows:

"First, this household is such a mixed one that things may get lost. Secondly, unless duties are assigned the servants may shirk work. Thirdly, the heavy expenditure may lead to extravagance and faked receipts. Fourthly, if no distinction is made between large tasks and small ones, some will have a harder time than others. Fifthly, these servants are so out of hand that those with any pretensions may defy me, and those with none won't do their best."

These were indeed the five distinguishing features of the Ning Mansion. To know how Hsi-feng coped, read the following chapter.

Truly:

Not one in ten thousand officials can rule the
state,
Yet how splendidly a fair lady can run a household.

CHAPTER 14

Lin Ju-hai Dies in Yangchow
Pao-yu Meets the Prince of Peiching
on the Road

When the news that Hsi-feng was to take charge reached Lai Sheng, chief steward of the Ning Mansion, he summoned all his colleagues.

"Madam Chia Lien of the West Mansion is coming to supervise our household," he told them. "When she asks for things or gives orders, we must be extra careful. Better turn up earlier and leave later every day, working hard this month and resting afterwards, in order not to lose face. You know what a terror she is, sour-faced, hard-hearted and no respecter of persons once she's angry."

They agreed and one remarked with a laugh, "Actually we need her to get this place into shape. Things are too out of hand."

Along came Lai Wang's wife just then with a tally and a receipt for the amount required, to fetch sacrificial paper and paper for supplications and prayers. They made her take a seat and have some tea while someone went for the amount required and carried it for her to the inner gate, where he handed it over to her to take inside.

Then Hsi-feng ordered Tsai-ming to prepare a register and sent for Lai Sheng's wife to bring her a list of the staff. She announced that all the men-servants' wives were to come to her early the next morning for instructions. After checking quickly through the list and asking Lai Sheng's wife a couple of questions, she went home in her carriage.

She was back at half past six the next morning to find all the old serving-women and stewards' wives assembled. They did not venture into the ante-chamber when they saw that she and Lai Sheng's wife were busy assigning tasks, but from outside the window they heard her tell the latter:

"Since I've been put in charge here I daresay I shall make myself unpopular. I'm not as easy-going as your own mistress who lets you do as you please; so don't tell me how things used to be managed here, but just do as I say. The least disobedience will be dealt with publicly, no matter how much face the offender may have."

She made Tsai-ming call the roll and the servants entered one by one for inspection. After this she ordered:

"These twenty, divided into two shifts of ten, will be solely responsible for serving tea to the guests on their arrival and before their departure. They will have no other duties. These twenty, also in two shifts of ten, will see to the family's meals and tea every day. They will have no other duties either. These forty, divided into two shifts, will have the job of burning incense, keeping the lamps filled with oil, hanging up curtains, watching by the coffin, offering sacrificial rice and tea, and mourning with the mourners. Nothing else.

"These four will be responsible for the cups, plates and tea things in the pantry, and will have to replace anything that is missing. These four will take charge of the dinner-sets and wine vessels, and likewise make good any loss. These eight will receive the presents of sacrificial offerings.

"These eight will look after the distribution of lamps, oil, candles and sacrificial paper to various places according to a list which I shall issue. These thirty will take night duty in turns, seeing that the gates are locked and keeping a look-out for fires, as well as sweeping the grounds.

"The rest of you will be assigned to different apartments and must stick to your posts. You will be responsible for everything there, from furniture and antiques to spittoons and dusters and each blade of grass — and will have to make good any loss or damage.

"Lai Sheng's wife will make a general inspection every day and report to me instantly any slackness, gambling, drinking, fighting or quarrelling. If I find you being too soft, I shall make no allowances for you, even though your family has been in service here for three or four generations.

"Now you all have your duties, and if anything goes wrong I shall deal with the group concerned. My own servants have clocks and watches, because everything large or small must be done on time. Well, at least you have clocks here in your master's rooms. I shall call the roll at half past six, you will have your meal at ten, and applications for stores or reports should be handed in punctually before half past eleven. At seven in the evening, after the burning of sacrificial paper, I shall make a tour of inspection, then issue those on night duty with their keys. I shall be back again at half past six the next morning. I needn't remind you that we must all do our best during this period. When it's over, no doubt your master will reward you."

She then ordered the distribution of supplies of tea, oil, candles, feather whisks, brooms and so forth, and had tablecloths, antimacassars, cushions, rugs, spittoons, stools and other furnishings issued. While this was being done, the servants in charge of each place and the articles taken by each were carefully recorded.

Now that all the servants had their respective duties, they were no longer able to pick the easy jobs and leave the hard ones undone. Nor were things mislaid any more on account of confusion. However many guests came and went everything ran smoothly, unlike the previous disorder when a maid serving tea had to fetch in rice as well, or one accompanying the mourners was sent to welcome new arrivals. That day saw the end, too, of disorder, negligence and pilfering. And Hsi-feng was thoroughly gratified by the authority she now wielded.

As Madam Yu was ill and grief had made Chia Chen lose his appetite, Hsi-feng every day sent over from the other mansion some fine congee and delicacies she had prepared especially for them. And Chia Chen also ordered the best food to be served for her alone in her annex every day.

Hsi-feng was not afraid of hard work. She came over punctually every morning at half past six to call the roll and see to any business, sitting alone in her annex and not even joining the other young wives to greet lady guests.

On the thirty-third day Buddhist monks performed the rites to cleave the earth asunder, break open Hell and light the dead down with lanterns to pay homage to the King of Hell; to arrest evil demons; to invoke Prince Ksitigarbha under the ground to raise up the Golden Bridge and lead the way with streamers. Taoists offered prayers and invocations, worshipping the Three Pure Ones and the Jade Emperor. Bonzes chanting sutras burned incense, sacrificed to the hungry ghosts and intoned the *Water Penitential* while thirteen young nuns in red slippers and embroidered robes recited incantations before the coffin to lead the soul on its way. All was bustle and noise.

Knowing that many guests could be expected, Hsi-feng told Ping-erh to wake her at four that day. By the time she had finished her toilet, sipped some milk and sweetened rice congee and rinsed her mouth, it was half past six and Lai Wang's wife was already waiting with the other servants. Hsi-feng left the hall and mounted her carriage, in front of which were two brilliant horn lanterns inscribed with the large characters: "The Jung Mansion."

As she slowly approached the Ning Mansion the lanterns above its main gate and the lamps on both sides shed a light bright as day on the two rows of attendants there in white mourning. At the main entrance her pages withdrew and maid-servants raised the curtain of the carriage. Hsi-feng was helped out by Feng-erh and escorted in by two serving-women with hand-lanterns. All the stewards' wives of the Ning Mansion advanced to greet her.

Hsi-feng walked slowly through the Garden of Concentrated Fragrance to the Pavilion of Attained Immortality, where at the sight of the coffin her tears fell like pearls from a broken string. Pages were waiting respectfully in the court for the burning of the sacrificial paper and now she ordered this to be done and an offering of tea presented. After one beat on the gong the music started. A large arm-chair had been set in front of the shrine and seating herself she gave way to loud lamentations. At once all the others, both men and women, high and low, joined in, until Chia Chen and Madam Yu sent to persuade her to restrain her grief.

Then Lai Wang's wife brought her tea to rinse her mouth, and Hsi-feng rose to take her leave of her kinsmen and proceed to the annex.

All the women-servants were present at the roll-call except for one usher. She came when summoned in great fear and trembling.

"So you're the one." Hsi-feng smiled scornfully. "You must consider yourself above the rest to disobey me like this."

"I've been on time every day before," said the woman. "But when I woke today it was still early, so I went back to sleep. That's why I was a few minutes late. Please overlook it, madam, this once!"

Just then Wang Hsing's wife from the other mansion peeped in. Without dismissing the usher, Hsi-feng asked her what she wanted.

Eager to have her business attended to first, Wang Hsing's wife came forward and presented a request for silk thread to make tassels for the carriages and sedan-chairs. On Hsi-feng's instructions Tsai-ming read out the number of strings of beads and tassels needed for two palanquins and four sedan-chairs as well as four carriages. Finding the figures correct, Hsi-feng told Tsai-ming to register them and gave a Jung Mansion tally to Wang Hsing's wife, who left.

Before Hsi-feng could deal with the offender in came four stewards from the Jung Mansion with indents for stores. Hsi-feng had their orders read out and pointed at two of the four items.

"These figures are wrong. Come back when you've worked them out correctly."

The two stewards whose indents she tossed back withdrew very sheepishly.

Then she noticed Chang Tsai's wife and asked her business. The woman handed her an order form, saying, "The covers for the carriages and sedan-chairs are finished, and I've come for the money for the tailor."

Hsi-feng told Tsai-ming to enter this, and when Wang Hsing's wife had returned the tally and fetched the accountant's receipt for the right sum Chang Tsai's wife was sent to get the money. Another order for wall-paper to paper Pao-yu's outer study was read out and registered. After Chang Tsai's wife had finished her business and returned the tally, the other was sent with it to get wall-paper.

Then at last Hsi-feng turned to deal with the usher.

"If you're late today and I'm late tomorrow, there will soon be nobody here," she said. "I should have liked to let you off, but if I overlook the first offence the others will get out of hand. I shall be obliged to make an example of you."

With a stern look she ordered the woman to be taken out and given twenty strokes with the bamboo. She then threw down the Ning Mansion tally and gave orders that Lai Sheng should dock this usher of a month's wages.

When the others heard this and saw Hsi-feng's angry frown, they dared not show slackness in carrying out her orders. Some hastily dragged out the woman; others passed on the order to Lai Sheng. After the usher had been given twenty strokes she had to return to kowtow to Hsi-feng.

Hsi-feng warned the servants, "Anyone late again tomorrow will get forty strokes, and sixty the day after that. So those who want a beating, just come late." With that she dismissed them.

The people outside the window, hearing this, went off to attend to their tasks. Then a steady stream of domestics from both mansions kept coming to hand in or apply for indents, while the woman who had been beaten also left shamefacedly. After this demonstration of Hsi-feng's severity, the servants of the Ning Mansion worked hard and, to be on the safe side, dared not neglect their duties. But no more of this.

Let us return to Pao-yu. There were so many visitors about that day that, fearing Chin Chung might be slighted, he urged him to go with him to see Hsi-feng.

Chin Chung objected that she would be too busy to welcome visitors and might think them a nuisance.

"Us, a nuisance?" retorted Pao-yu. "Not a bit of it. Come on."

He took Chin Chung to the annex where Hsi-feng was having a meal. At sight of them she smiled. "You do have long legs, don't you? Come and join me."

"We've eaten already," Pao-yu told her.

"Here? Or over in the other house?"

"Why should we eat here with these dolts? We had a meal over there with the old lady." He and Chin Chung sat down.

As soon as the meal was finished, a woman from the Ning Mansion arrived with an indent for incense and lamps.

"I knew it was time for you to come today but thought you'd forgotten," observed Hsi-feng, smiling. "If you had, you'd have had to pay for them yourself. And so much the better for me."

"It quite slipped my mind," replied the maid cheerfully. "I only remembered a moment ago and hurried here just in time."

She took the tally and went off. Soon the tally was returned and the amount entered.

"You use the same tallies in both your mansions," remarked Chin Chung with a smile. "What if someone faked one and ran off with your money?"

"Do you think us such a lawless lot?" Hsi-feng asked, laughing.

"How is it that no one has come from our house to ask for things?" put in Pao-yu.

"When they came you were still fast asleep. But tell me, when are you two going to start your evening lessons?"

"We'd like to start right away. Only we can't because they're so slow getting the study ready."

"If you'll treat me, I'll speed things up."

"How can you? They're doing it in their own good time."

"They need materials for the job. They can't do a thing if I withhold the tally."

Pao-yu cuddled up to her at that and coaxed, "Dear cousin, do give them the tally so that they can get what they need."

"I'm so tired, my bones are aching," protested Hsi-feng. "Must you jostle me like that? Don't worry, they've just taken the wall-paper for your study. You must be crazy if you think they need telling when to ask."

When Pao-yu refused to believe this she made Tsai-ming show him the record. Just then someone announced that Chao-erh was back from Soochow and Hsi-feng promptly ordered him to be brought in. Chao-erh fell on one knee to greet her.

"Why have you come back?" she asked.

"The master sent me, madam. Lord Lin died on the third of the ninth month, at nine in the morning. The master and Miss Lin are escorting his coffin to Soochow and should be home about the end of the year. He sent me to bring the news with his greetings and to ask for the old lady's instructions. I was to see, too, if you were well at home, madam, and to take back some of his fur-lined gowns."

"Have you reported to the other ladies?"

"Yes, madam. Everyone." With that he withdrew.

Hsi-feng turned to Pao-yu with a smile. "Now your cousin Tai-yu can stay with us a good long time."

"Poor thing!" exclaimed Pao-yu. "Think how much she must have been crying the last few days." He knit his brows and sighed.

Hsi-feng was anxious for news of her husband but had not liked to question Chao-erh too closely in the presence of others. Tempted to go home but kept by unfinished business and afraid of making herself look ridiculous, she had to restrain her impatience until the evening, when she summoned Chao-erh to give her all the particulars of their journey. That same night she got Ping-erh to help her select some fur-lined clothes and carefully thought out what else her husband might need. Having packed these things together she handed them to Chao-erh and cautioned him:

"Mind you look after your master properly outside and don't make him angry. Try to keep him from drinking too much, and don't pander to him by finding him loose women — if you do, I'll break your legs when you get back."

By then it was well after the fourth watch and though she went to bed she had lost all desire to sleep. Soon it was dawn. She made a hasty toilet and went over to the Ning Mansion.

Now that the day for the funeral was approaching, Chia Chen drove in person with a geomancer to Iron Threshold Temple to inspect the repository for the coffin and enjoin on Abbot Seh-kung, who was in charge, the need for the finest furnishings and the help of the most noted monks for the coffin's reception.

Seh-kung hastily prepared supper, but Chia Chen had no interest in food. Since it was too late to return to town, however, he put up that night in the guest room, starting back first thing in the morning to arrange for the funeral procession. He sent men ahead to the temple to spend that night in redecorating the repository and in seeing to refreshments and the reception of the funeral party.

Meanwhile Hsi-feng too had made careful preparations, choosing the servants, carriages and sedan-chairs of the Jung Mansion that would accompany Lady Wang to the funeral, and a place in which to stay herself for the occasion.

As the Duke of Shankuo's wife had just died, Lady Hsing and Lady Wang had to send sacrificial gifts and attend her funeral. Then birthday presents had to be sent to the consort of the Prince of Hsian. Then a first son was born to the Duke of Chenkuo and congratulatory gifts had to be sent. Then Hsi-feng had to write a letter home and prepare gifts for her brother Wang Jen to take when he returned south with his family. Then Ying-chun fell ill and every day they had to call in doctors, study their diagnoses, discuss the cause of the illness and decide on prescriptions....

As the day of the funeral approached, a thousand and one affairs kept Hsi-feng so busy that she had no time to eat and was hardly able to have a moment's rest. When she went to the Ning Mansion, servants from the Jung Mansion followed her there; when she returned to the Jung Mansion, servants from the Ning Mansion would come after her. Yet busy as she was, her spirits were high. She shirked not a single task, determined to give no one any grounds for complaint. Indeed, she worked so hard day and night and handled everything so well that not one of the household, high or low, but was impressed.

Now the time had come for the wake. The family's two troupes of actors and some musicians, dancers and acrobats were to perform a long programme of items, and the place was thronged with relatives and friends. As Madam Yu was still keeping to her bed Hsi-feng had to look after them single-handed; for all the other married women in the family were either tongue-tied, flighty, shy of strangers or awed by nobles and officials. None of them could compare with Hsi-feng with her charm, ready tongue and elegance. Having no fear of anyone, she gave whatever orders she pleased and did as she liked, regardless of anyone else.

That night was all brilliance and bustle, needless to say, with the lanterns and torches of the officials and guests coming and going.

When the auspicious hour arrived at dawn, sixty-four bearers in blue bore out the coffin. It was preceded by a great funeral banner bearing the inscription in large characters:

> Spiritual Abode of Lady Chin of the Chia Family, Consort of the Imperial Guard and Defender of the Palace Roads of the Inner Court of the Forbidden City, and Eldest Great-Great-Grandson of the Duke of Ningkuo Enfeoffed with the First Rank by the Heaven-Sent, Splendidly-Established, Long-Enduring Dynasty.

The brand-new funeral paraphernalia was a dazzling sight. And Pao-chu, observing the rites for an unmarried daughter, dashed an earthen basin to pieces when the coffin was lifted to be carried away and lamented bitterly before it.

Among the officials attending the funeral were: Niu Chi-tsung, hereditary earl of the first rank, grandson of Niu Ching, Duke of Chenkuo; Liu Fang, hereditary viscount of the first rank, grandson of Liu Piao, Duke of Likuo; Chen Jui-wen, hereditary general of the third rank, grandson of Chen Yi, Duke of Chikuo; Ma Shang, hereditary general of the third rank, grandson of Ma Kuei, Duke of Chihkuo; and Hou Hsiao-kang, hereditary viscount of the first rank, grandson of Hou Hsiao-ming, Duke of Hsiukuo. Since the Duke of Shankuo's wife had died, his grandson Shih Kuang-chu was in mourning and unable to come. These six families, with those of Ning and Jung, were known as the "Eight Ducal Households."

The other mourners included: the grandson of the Prince of Nanan; the grandson of the Prince of Hsining; Shih Ting, Marquis of Chungching; Chiang Tzu-ning, hereditary baron of the second rank, grandson of the Marquis of Pingyuan; Hsieh Ching, hereditary baron of the second rank, captain of the Metropolitan Garrison, grandson of the Marquis of Tingcheng; Chi Chien-hui, hereditary baron of the second rank, grandson of the Marquis of Hsiangyang; Chiu Liang, garrison commander of five cities, grandson of the Marquis of Chingtien.

Also present were Han Chi, son of the Earl of Chinhsiang; Feng Tzu-ying, son of the General of Divine Valour; Chen Yeh-chun, Wei Jo-lan and countless other sons of nobles.

There were also over a dozen palanquins and thirty to forty sedan-chairs for lady guests. These together with the carriages and sedan-chairs of the Chia family numbered well over a hundred. With the elaborate equipage in front and the performances given on the way, the procession extended a good three or four li.

Before long they reached stands with coloured silk awnings by the roadside where music was played and sacrificial offerings had been set out by different families. The first four belonged to the houses of the Prince of Tungping, the Prince of Nanan, the Prince of Hsining, and the Prince of Peiching.

The original Prince of Peiching had won the highest distinction of these four princes, and therefore his descendants had

inherited his title. The present holder of the title, Shui Yung, was a charming and modest young man of less than twenty with remarkable good looks. When he heard that the eldest great-great-grandson of the Duke of Ningkuo had lost his wife, the thought of their forefathers' friendship, shared dangers and glory as if of one family had made him lay aside all considerations of rank and go in person to express his condolences. Now he had set up a funeral booth by the roadside to offer a libation. He made some of his officers wait there while he went to court at dawn. The audience over, he changed into mourning clothes and came here by palanquin, preceded by sounding gongs and ceremonial umbrellas. He halted his palanquin at the stand and his officers ranged themselves on either side, forbidding soldiers and civilians to pass.

Presently, from the north, the Ning Mansion's magnificent funeral procession bore down on them like a great silver landslide. The runners sent ahead to clear the way had reported the prince's arrival to Chia Chen, who now ordered the procession to halt while he, Chia Sheh and Chia Cheng went to greet the prince according to state ceremonial. The prince bowed affably in return from his palanquin, treating them as old family friends without any affectation.

Chia Chen said, "We are overwhelmed by the favour done us by Your Highness in honouring my daughter-in-law's funeral with your presence."

"That is no way for good friends to talk," protested the prince.

Then he turned and ordered his chief steward to preside at the sacrifice for him and pour a libation. Chia Sheh and the others, having bowed in return, stepped forward to express their gratitude.

The Prince of Peiching was completely unassuming. He asked Chia Cheng, "Which is the young gentleman born with a piece of jade in his mouth? I have long wanted to meet him but have never had the time. I am sure he must be here today. Won't you present him?"

Chia Cheng withdrew at once to fetch Pao-yu. He made him change out of mourning, then took him to meet the prince.

Pao-yu had heard from his family and friends of the Prince of Peiching's fine qualities, his talent, good looks, refinement and unconventionality. He had often wanted to meet him, but his father kept him under such strict control that hitherto he had never had a chance. Of course he was delighted to be sent for. Walking forward, he was struck by the dignity with which the prince was sitting in his palanquin.

To know the sequel, read the chapter which follows.

CHAPTER 15

Hsi-feng Abuses Her Power at
Iron Threshold Temple
Chin Chung Amuses Himself in
Steamed-Bread Convent

Looking up, Pao-yu saw that the Prince of Peiching had on a princely silver-winged cap with white tassels, a white robe embroidered with zigzag wave patterns and five-clawed dragons, and a red leather belt studded with green jade. With his face fair as jade, his eyes bright as stars, he was truly a handsome figure.

Pao-yu started forward to make his obeisance. As the prince from his palanquin raised him up, he noticed that Pao-yu was wearing a silver chaplet in the form of two dragons rising from the sea, an archer's coat embroidered with white serpents, and a silver belt set with pearls. His face seemed a flower in spring, his eyes black as lacquer.

"You live up to your name," remarked the prince. "You are really like precious jade. But where is that gem with which you came into the world?"

Pao-yu hastily took the jade from inside his garments and handed it to the prince, who examined it carefully and read the inscription.

"Does it actually have magic powers?" he asked.

"So they say," answered Chia Cheng. "But it has never yet been put to the test."

The prince was very struck by the jade and, smoothing its silken cord, with his own hands he put it round Pao-yu's neck. Then taking the boy's hand he asked him his age and what he was studying.

The clarity and fluency of Pao-yu's answers made the prince turn to observe to Chia Cheng, "Your son is truly a dragon's colt or young phoenix. May I venture to predict that in time to come this young phoenix may even surpass the old one?"

"My worthless son does not deserve such high praise," rejoined Chia Cheng hurriedly with a courteous smile. "If thanks to the grace of Your Highness such proves the case, that will be our good fortune."

"There is one thing, however," cautioned the prince. "Because your son is so talented his grandmother and mother must have doted on him; but over-indulgence is very bad for young people like ourselves as it makes us neglect our studies. I went astray in this way myself and suspect your honourable son may do the same. If he finds it difficult to study at home, he is very welcome to come as often as he likes to my humble house. For although untalented myself, I am honoured by visits from scholars of note from all parts of the empire when they come to the capital. Hence my poor abode is frequented by eminent men, and conversation with them should improve his knowledge."

Chia Cheng bowed and assented to this without hesitation.

The prince now took a string of beads from his wrist and gave it to Pao-yu saying, "This first meeting of ours is so hurried that I have brought no gift to show my respect, but please accept this string of beads made of the aromatic seeds of some plant which His Majesty gave me the other day."

Pao-yu took it and turned to present it to his father, who together with his son offered formal thanks.

Then Chia Sheh and Chia Chen stepped forward and begged the prince to return, but he demurred: "The deceased has become an immortal and left our dusty world. Although by the favour of the Son of Heaven I have succeeded to this title, how can I precede the carriage of an immortal?"

Seeing that he was adamant, Chia Sheh and the others thanked him and withdrew to stop the music, so as to let the long procession pass on. And thereupon the prince went back. But no more of this.

The whole road hummed with excitement as the great procession passed. By the city gate friends and colleagues of Chia Sheh, Chia Cheng and Chia Chen had set up sacrificial tents and not until each had been thanked in turn did the cortège leave the city and proceed along the highway towards Iron Threshold Temple.

Now Chia Chen and Chia Jung urged their elders to mount their chairs or horses. All of Chia Sheh's generation mounted carriages or chairs while Chia Chen's contemporaries rode on horseback.

Hsi-feng was afraid that Pao-yu, unchecked by his father, might come to some harm through reckless riding in the open country, for he would not listen to anyone else in the household. And if there were any mishap it would be hard to account for it to the old lady. Accordingly she ordered a page to summon him to her carriage, and when perforce he came she told him with a smile:

"Dear cousin, you have your dignity and are as delicate as any girl. Don't copy those apes on horseback. Wouldn't it be better to come and share my carriage?"

Pao-yu hurriedly dismounted to join her. They drove on laughing and chatting until two horsemen galloped up and alighted by the carriage to report, "We have reached a halting place, madam. Will you stop for a rest?"

Having asked to know the wishes of Lady Hsing and Lady Wang, Hsi-feng was told, "Their Ladyships are not stopping, but they want you to suit your convenience."

Thereupon Hsi-feng ordered a halt. Attendants led their carriage northwards away from the cortège and at Pao-yu's orders went to invite Chin Chung, who was riding behind his father's chair, to join them. When Pao-yu's page brought him this invitation and he saw his friend's riderless horse following Hsi-feng's carriage north, Chin Chung knew that Pao-yu must be with her. He promptly overtook them and together they entered the gateway of a farm.

The menfolk here had long since been packed off, but the farmhouse had so few rooms that the womenfolk had nowhere to go to keep out of the way. The sudden appearance in their midst of Hsi-feng, Pao-yu and Chin Chung with their gorgeous clothes and refined looks and manners made these village women stare with admiration.

Once in the thatched house Hsi-feng suggested to Pao-yu that he should amuse himself outside. Taking the hint, he led Chin Chung and the pages off to look around. He had never seen farm implements before and was thoroughly intrigued by the spades, picks, hoes and ploughs, although quite ignorant of their names and uses. When a page who knew informed him he nodded and remarked with a sigh:

"Now I understand the words of the old poet:

> Who knows that each grain of rice we eat
> Is the fruit of intensive toil?"

Strolling into an outhouse, he was still more intrigued by a spinning-wheel on the *kang*. His pages told him this was used to weave yarn. He had just climbed up on the *kang* to turn the wheel for fun when in came a peasant girl of seventeen or eighteen. She ran over crying:

"Don't! You'll break it!"

She was shouted at by his pages, but Pao-yu had already let go of the wheel.

"I've never seen one before," he explained with a smile. "I just wanted to have a try."

"How could you people know how?" said the girl. "Get out of my way and I'll show you."

Chin Chung plucked at Pao-yu's sleeve and whispered, "Isn't she fun?"

Pao-yu gave him a shove. "You rascal. If you talk any more nonsense I'll clout you."

Meanwhile the girl had started spinning. Pao-yu was just about to speak to her when an old woman called, "Come here, quick, Second Daughter!"

At that she went off, much to his disappointment.

Then a messenger summoned them back to Hsi-feng, who had washed and changed to remove the dust of the journey.

She urged the two boys to change, but Pao-yu declined. Their attendants now produced the tea-service and hamper which they had brought for the journey, and after some refreshments they smartened up and mounted their carriage again.

Once outside, Lai Wang presented a packaged gratuity to the peasant family, whose womenfolk came to thank them. Hsi-feng, however, took no notice of them, while Pao-yu looked eagerly for the spinning-girl. But she was not in the group. They had not gone far, though, when he saw her, her little brother in her arms, approaching laughing and chatting with some smaller girls. Pao-yu longed to alight and go with her, but knowing that the others would not agree he could only follow her with his eyes as their carriage drove swiftly off. Soon she was out of sight.

Before very long, they overtook the procession. Ahead of them were temple drums and cymbals, pennants and umbrellas, while monks from Iron Threshold Temple lined the road. Soon they entered the temple, where again Buddhist rites were performed and incense burned, after which the coffin was installed in one of the side-chambers of the inner hall and Pao-chu prepared to keep vigil there that night.

In the outer apartments Chia Chen entertained their male friends and relatives, some of whom stayed for a meal while others took their leave immediately. He tendered them thanks one by one for coming. Then the guests began to take their leave from dukes, marquises, earls, viscounts and barons downwards, and by three o'clock all had dispersed.

The ladies were entertained in the inner apartments by Hsi-feng. They, too, left in order of precedence, and by about two o'clock all had gone except a few close relatives who would remain for the three days' requiems for the dead.

Knowing that Hsi-feng could not return with them, Lady Hsing and Lady Wang proposed to take Pao-yu back with them to the city. But as this was his first visit to the country and he insisted on staying behind with Hsi-feng, his mother had to leave him in her charge.

Now this Iron Threshold Temple had been built in the days of the Dukes of Jungkuo and Ningkuo and still had enough land of its own to provide for incense and lamps and repositories for the coffins of clansmen. Since there was accommodation for both the dead and the living, the mourners escorting coffins had somewhere to stay. However, now that the family had grown the views of the rich members differed from those of the poor. Whereas the latter were content to stay here, those who were wealthy and fond of display maintained that the place was inconvenient and preferred to find accommodation in some nearby village or convent to retire to at the end of the ceremonies.

On this occasion of Chin Ko-ching's funeral most members of the clan stayed at Iron Threshold Temple. Only Hsi-feng, deciding that it would not suit her, had sent a servant to ask Abbess Ching-hsu of Steamed-Bread Convent to clear a few rooms for her. Steamed-Bread Convent was the popular name for Water Moon Convent because of the good steamed bread made here. It stood not far from Iron Threshold Temple.

As soon as the monks had completed their devotions and the evening offering of tea had been made, Chia Chen sent Chia Jung to urge Hsi-feng to rest. Then leaving her sisters-in-law to look after the women guests she took Pao-yu and Chin Chung off to Steamed-Bread Convent. Chin Chung's father, too old and frail to remain himself, had told his son to attend the requiems, and so the boy stayed with Hsi-feng and Pao-yu.

They were met at the convent gate by Abbess Ching-hsu and two novices, Chih-shan and Chih-neng. After an exchange of greetings Hsi-feng retired to a rest room. While she was changing she noticed how tall and pretty Chih-neng had grown.

"Why haven't you and your abbess been to see us lately?" she asked.

"A few days ago a son was born to Mr. Hu," explained the abbess. "His good lady sent us ten taels of silver to get some of our sisters to chant the *Nativity* sutra for three days, so we've been too busy to come and pay our respects."

But let us return to Pao-yu and Chin Chung, who were fooling about in the hall when Chih-neng came in.

"Look who's here," said Pao-yu with a smile.

"What about it?" retorted Chin Chung.

"It's no use play-acting. What were you doing with her on your lap that day in my grandmother's room, when no one else was about? Stop trying to fool me."

"You're just making that up!" protested Chin Chung.

"Well, never mind. Tell her to pour me some tea and I'll let you off."

"Don't be ridiculous. Could she refuse if you ask her yourself? Why should I ask for you?"

"For you she would do it for love, but not for me."

Then Chin Chung said, "Bring me some tea, Chih-neng, will you?"

This young novice had been in and out of the Jung Mansion since childhood. She knew everyone there and had often romped with Pao-yu and Chin Chung; and now that she was old enough to know the meaning of love she had taken a fancy to handsome young Chin Chung, who was attracted in turn by her pretty looks. Although nothing had passed between them, they already had a secret understanding. So now with a radiant glance at him she complied. Soon she was back again with a cup of tea.

"Give it to me!" urged Chin Chung with a smile.

"No, to me!" cried Pao-yu.

Chih-neng laughed mockingly. "Do I have honey on my hands that you squabble even over a cup of tea?"

Pao-yu grabbed hold of the cup and started drinking, and before he could speak again Chih-shan came to fetch Chih-neng to lay the table. Presently she returned to invite them to have some refreshments, but the tea and cakes served in the convent did not tempt them. They sat a while, then escaped as soon as they could to amuse themselves elsewhere.

Hsi-feng retired presently, too, to the rest room accompanied by the abbess. When the older maid-servants saw there was nothing to do they went off to bed themselves, leaving only a few trusted younger maids in attendance.

The abbess seized this chance to say, "There's something I've been meaning to go and ask Her Ladyship, but I'd like to have your advice on it first, madam."

"What is it?" asked Hsi-feng.

"Amida Buddha!" sighed the abbess. "When I became a nun in Shantsai Convent in the county of Changan, one of our benefactors was a very wealthy man called Chang, whose daughter Chin-ko often came to our temple to offer incense. A young Mr. Li, who is brother-in-law to the prefect of Changan, met her there. He fell in love at first sight and sent to ask for her hand; but she was already engaged to the son of the former inspector of Changan. The Changs would have liked to cancel the engagement but were afraid the inspector might object, so they explained to the Lis that she was betrothed. Still young Mr. Li insisted on having her, making things very difficult for the Changs.

"When word of this reached the inspector's family, without even finding out the truth of the matter they came and stormed, 'How many more men will you engage your daughter to?' They refused to take back the betrothal gifts and took the matter to court.

"The girl's family are desperate. They've sent to the capital to enlist help and are quite determined to return the gifts.

"Well, I understand that General Yun the Military Governor of Changan is on friendly terms with your family. If Lady Wang would get His Lordship to write to General Yun, asking him to have a word with the inspector, I'm sure he'd drop the suit. And the Changs would gladly give anything — even their whole fortune — in return for this favour."

"There shouldn't be any great difficulty about this," rejoined Hsi-feng. "But Her Ladyship doesn't trouble herself with such matters."

"In that case, madam, could you attend to it?"

"I'm neither short of money nor do I meddle with affairs of this sort."

The abbess' face fell. After a short pause she observed with a sigh, "Well, the Changs know that I'm appealing to your family. If you do nothing, they won't realize that you can't be troubled and don't want the money — it would look as if you can't even handle such a trifling business."

This put Hsi-feng on her mettle. "You know me," she replied. "I've never believed all that talk about Hell and retribution. I do what I please and am always as good as my word. Let them bring me three thousand taels and I'll see to this for them."

"Very good!" cried the abbess, overjoyed. "That's easy."

"I'm not one of your go-betweens just out for money," said Hsi-feng. "These three thousand taels will just cover the expenses of the servants I send out and reward them for their trouble. I myself don't want a cent. I could lay my hands any moment on *thirty* thousand."

"Of course, madam. Will you do us this favour, then, tomorrow?"

"Can't you see how busy I am, needed right and left? But since I've told you I'll do it, of course I'll settle it for you speedily."

"A little thing like this might throw other people into a fearful flurry, but I know you'd have no trouble handling bigger things than this, madam. As the proverb says, 'The abler a man, the busier he gets.' It's because you're so capable that Her Ladyship leaves everything to you. But you mustn't wear yourself out."

This flattery made Hsi-feng forget her exhaustion and start chatting more cheerfully.

Meanwhile Chin Chung had taken advantage of the darkness and the fact that nobody was about to go in search of Chih-neng. Having found her alone in a back room washing up the tea things, he threw his arms around her and kissed her.

"What are you doing?" The novice stamped her foot in desperation and threatened to call out.

"Darling," he pleaded, "I'm dying of longing for you. If you refuse me again this evening, I'll die here on the spot."

"What are you thinking of? At least wait till I'm clear of this prison and these people."

"That's easy to manage, but 'distant water can't quench a present thirst.'"

With that he blew out the lamp, plunging the room into pitch darkness, and carried her to the *kang*. Chih-neng struggled in vain to free herself but did not like to scream, so she had to let him have his way with her.

He was just getting down to work when someone slipped in and pinned the pair of them down. Since no word was said, they did not know who it was. The two of them were frightened out of their wits until a chuckle revealed that it was Pao-yu.

Chin Chung sprang up swearing, "What are you playing at?"

"Will you do as I say or shall I raise the alarm?"

Chih-neng fled, blushing, under cover of the dark and Pao-yu pulled his friend out.

"Well, do you still deny it?" he demanded.

"Be a good fellow! I'll do whatever you say as long as you don't shout."

"We'll say no more about it just now. I'll settle with you after we go to bed."

Soon it was time to sleep. Hsi-feng had the inner room, the two boys the outer, while the maids slept on the floor or sat up to keep watch. For fear lest the precious jade might disappear while Pao-yu was asleep, Hsi-feng had it fetched and put it under her own pillow.

As for how Pao-yu settled scores with Chin Chung, what the eye does not see can only be surmised, and far be it from us to speculate.

The next morning the Lady Dowager and Lady Wang sent to urge Pao-yu to dress more warmly and to go home if there was nothing to keep him. This was the last thing he wanted. And Chin Chung, infatuated as he was with Chih-neng, made him beg Hsi-feng to stay a little longer.

Though the obsequies were over there remained certain trifles to attend to, so Hsi-feng decided she could spare one more day. In the first place, this would satisfy Chia Chen; in the second, she could attend to the abbess' business; in the third, the Lady Dowager would be pleased to know that Pao-yu was enjoying himself.

"My own business here is finished," she told him with these considerations in mind. "If you want to amuse yourself here a little longer, I suppose I'll have to put up with it. But we must leave tomorrow at the latest."

"Just one day, dear, kind cousin. We'll leave tomorrow."

So they arranged to spend another night there.

Hsi-feng sent someone secretly to explain the abbess' business to Lai Wang. He grasped at once what was wanted and hurried into town to get the chief secretary to write a letter in Chia Lien's name, and set off with it that same night for Changan County. Since Changan was only a hundred *li* away, within two days the matter was settled. Military Governor Yun Kuang had long wanted to please the Chia family and was only too glad to agree to this trifling request. Lai Wang brought back a letter from him to this effect.

Meanwhile Hsi-feng, after one more day in the convent, had said goodbye to the abbess, telling her to come for news in three days' time.

Chin Chung and Chih-neng could hardly bear to part and bid each other a sad farewell after arranging to meet again in secret.

Hsi-feng went to take a last look at Iron Threshold Temple, where Pao-chu insisted on remaining. Chia Chen later was obliged to send maids there to keep her company.

To know the sequel, read the next chapter.

CHAPTER 16

Yuan-chun Is Selected as Imperial Consort in Phoenix Palace
Chin Chung Dying Before His Time Sets Off for the Nether Regions

Before long Pao-yu's outer study was ready. He had agreed with Chin Chung to start evening lessons together; but Chin Chung had a weak constitution, and a cold he had caught in the country following his secret affair with Chih-neng had upset him; thus on his return to town he developed a cough and lost his appetite completely. Too weak to go out, he had to rest at home. Although Pao-yu was very disappointed, he could do nothing but wait for his friend's recovery.

Meanwhile Hsi-feng had received Yun Kuang's reply, and the abbess had informed the Changs that their problem was solved. So the inspector had to swallow his anger and take back the betrothal gifts.

But though Chang and his wife were snobbish and mercenary, they had a principled and feeling daughter. When Chin-ko learned that her engagement had been broken she found a rope and quietly hanged herself; and the inspector's son was so much in love that he drowned himself when he heard of her suicide, showing that he was worthy of his good fiancée.

Thus the Chang and Li families were unlucky enough to lose both girl and money. Only Hsi-feng was the gainer by three thousand taels, quite unknown to Lady Wang and the rest of the household. This emboldened her from that time on to undertake countless similar transactions but we need not recount these here.

Now it was Chia Cheng's birthday and both households had gathered to congratulate him. At the height of the festivities the gateman suddenly rushed in to announce:

"His Excellency Hsia, Chief Eunuch of the Six Palaces, has come with a Decree from the Emperor!"

This startled Chia Sheh, Chia Cheng and the rest, who did not know what it could mean. They at once called a halt to the theatricals and had the feast cleared away. A table was set out with incense. Then, throwing open the central gate they knelt down to receive the Decree.

Soon Hsia Shou-chung the Chief Eunuch arrived on horse-back, followed by a considerable retinue of eunuchs. He was not carrying an Imperial Edict, however. Having alighted in front of the main hall, he mounted the steps with a beaming smile and, facing south, announced:

"By special order of the Emperor, Chia Cheng is to present himself at once for an audience in the Hall of Respectful Approach." This said, without even taking a sip of tea, he re-mounted his horse and rode off.

Chia Sheh and the others could not guess what this portend-ed. Chia Cheng lost no time in putting on his court robes and going to the Palace, leaving the whole family in dire suspense. The Lady Dowager sent one mounted messenger after another in search of news; but it was four hours before Lai Ta and a few other stewards came panting through the inner gate, crying:

"Good news! His Lordship asks the old lady to go at once to the Palace with the other ladies to thank His Majesty."

The Lady Dowager had been waiting anxiously in the cor-ridor outside the great hall with Lady Hsing, Lady Wang, Madam Yu, Li Wan, Hsi-feng and the Chia girls, as well as Aunt Hsueh. On hearing this, they called Lai Ta over and demanded more details.

"We had to wait in the outer court," Lai Ta told them. "So we had no idea what was going on inside. But then Chief Eunuch Hsia came out. He congratulated us on the promotion of our eldest young lady. She's to be Chief Secretary of the Phoenix Palace with the title of Worthy and Virtuous Consort.

And then His Lordship came out and confirmed this. Now he has gone to the East Palace and he begs Your Ladyship and the other ladies to go at once to offer thanks."

They were all so relieved that their faces shone with delight as each dressed in the ceremonial robes appropriate to her rank. And presently four large sedan-chairs, with the Lady Dowager's at the head, followed by Lady Hsing's, Lady Wang's and Madam Yu's, were making their way to the Palace. They were escorted by Chia Sheh and Chia Chen, also in court robes, as well as Chia Jung and Chia Chiang.

Then high and low alike in both mansions were filled with joy. Their faces radiant with pride, they broke into a tumult of talk and laughter.

Now, a few days previously, Chih-neng had stolen away from Water Moon Convent and come to town to look for Chin Chung in his home. She had been caught by his father, who drove her away and gave his son a beating. The old man's rage had brought on an attack of his chronic disorder, and within a few days he was dead. Chin Chung had never been strong nor had he fully recovered from his illness when he received this beating. His father's death filled him with such remorse that his condition was now serious.

All this was preying so much on Pao-yu's mind that the honour conferred on Yuan-chun failed to raise his spirits. He alone remained utterly indifferent to the trip made by the Lady Dowager and the rest to offer thanks for the Imperial favour, the visits of congratulations paid by relatives and friends, the excitement which filled both mansions. The general delight left him completely unmoved, just as if these things had never happened. His apathy made everyone declare that he was growing more and more eccentric.

Luckily a messenger arrived at this time from Chia Lien to announce that he and Tai-yu were on their way back and would be home the following day. A little cheered, Pao-yu questioned the man and learned that Chia Yu-tsun was also coming to the capital to pay homage. For thanks to Wang Tzu-teng's recommendations he had been summoned to wait for a metropolitan appointment; and being a distant cousin of Chia Lien's and Tai-yu's former tutor, he was travelling with them. Lin Ju-hai had been buried in the ancestral graveyard and, his obsequies completed, Chia Lien was able to start back for the capital. Normally, the trip would have taken them till the beginning of the next month; however, the good news about Yuan-chun had made Chia Lien decide to hurry back posthaste. The journey had been smooth and uneventful.

Pao-yu was only eager to know that Tai-yu was all right, taking no interest in the rest of this news. He could hardly contain himself until their arrival was announced just after noon the next day. But the joy of their reunion was tempered by grief. After a storm of weeping they exchanged condolences and congratulations.

Pao-yu observed that Tai-yu was looking even more ethereal. She had brought back a whole library of books, and lost no time in tidying her bedroom and setting out her things. She presented some brushes and stationery to Pao-chai, Ying-chun, Pao-yu and others. But when he produced the precious scented beads given him by the Prince of Peiching and offered them to her, Tai-yu protested:

"I don't want them. They've been handled by some stinking man."

She tossed the beads back and Pao-yu had to take them.

But let us return to Chia Lien. After he had greeted the rest of the family he went to his own quarters; and busy as Hsi-feng was, with not a moment to herself, she set everything aside to welcome her husband back from his long journey.

Once they were alone she said jokingly, "Congratulations, Your Excellency, kinsman of the Imperial House! Your Excellency must have had a tiring journey. Your handmaid, hearing yesterday that your exalted carriage would return today, prepared some watery wine by way of welcome. Will the Imperial Kinsman deign to accept it?"

"You honour me too much," Chia Lien replied with a chuckle. "I am quite overwhelmed."

When Ping-erh and the other maids had paid their respects and served tea, Chia Lien asked his wife what had happened during his absence and thanked her for looking after things so well.

"I'm incapable of running things," she sighed. "I'm too ignorant, blunt and tactless, always getting hold of the wrong end of the stick. And I'm so soft-hearted, anyone can get round me. Besides, lack of experience makes me nervous. When Her Ladyship is the least displeased I'm too frightened to sleep a wink. Time and again I've begged to be relieved of such a responsibility, but instead of agreeing she accuses me of being lazy and unwilling to learn. She doesn't realize what a cold sweat I'm in, terrified of saying one word out of turn or taking one false step.

"And you know how difficult our old stewardesses are, laughing at the least mistake and 'accusing the elm while pointing at the mulberry tree' if one shows the least bias. Talk about 'sitting on a hill to watch tigers fight,' 'murdering with a borrowed sword,' 'borrowing wind to fan the fire,' 'watching people drown from a dry bank' and 'not troubling to right an oil bottle that's been knocked over' — they're all old hands at such tricks. On top of that, I'm too young to carry much weight; so naturally they pay no attention to me.

"As if that weren't bad enough, when Jung's wife suddenly died Cousin Chen repeatedly begged Her Ladyship on his knees to let me help them out for a few days. I declined over and over again, but as she insisted I had to have a try. As usual I made a shocking mess of things — even worse than here. I'm sure Cousin Chen is still regretting his rashness. When you see him tomorrow, do apologize for me. Tell him he should never have entrusted such a task to someone so young and inexperienced."

Just then they heard voices outside and Hsi-feng asked who was there. Ping-erh came in and said, "Madam Hsueh sent Hsiang-ling over to ask me something. I've given her an answer and sent her back."

"That reminds me," said Chia Lien. "When I called on Aunt Hsueh just now, I ran into a very handsome young woman whom I didn't think belonged to our household and wondered who she could be. In the course of conversation I learned she's the girl they bought just before coming to the capital. Her name's Hsiang-ling. She belongs to that imbecile Hsueh now, and since he made her his concubine and her face has been slicked she's grown even lovelier. She's too good for that silly fool."

"Well!" exclaimed Hsi-feng. "I should have thought you'd have seen enough of the world now that you're back from a trip to Soochow and Hangchow, but you're never satisfied. If you love her, that's simple: I'll exchange our Ping-erh for her — how about that? Hsueh Pan is another of those greedy-guts who keep 'one eye on the bowl and the other on the pan.' Look how he plagued his mother for a whole year just to get hold of Hsiang-ling. It's because Aunt Hsueh saw she's not only pretty but really well-behaved, being even gentler and quieter than most young ladies, that she went to all the trouble of inviting guests to a feast to make her his concubine in proper style. Yet in less than a fortnight he's treating her like dirt. It's really too bad. . . ."

At this point a page from the inner gate reported that Chia Cheng was waiting for Chia Lien in the big library. The young man hastily straightened his clothes and went out.

Then Hsi-feng asked Ping-erh, "What on earth did Aunt Hsueh send Hsiang-ling along for just now?"

"It wasn't Hsiang-ling," said Ping-erh, giggling. "I made that up. Really, madam, that wife of Lai Wang's is losing all the little sense she had." She drew nearer and lowered her voice. "She wouldn't come earlier or later but had to choose this very moment, when the master's just got home, to bring you the interest on that money. It's lucky I met her in the hall or she'd have come in and blurted everything out. If our master had asked what it was, of course you'd have to tell him — you wouldn't want to deceive him. And being what he is, ready to snatch money from a pan of scalding oil, he'd start spending

even more recklessly if he knew that you had private savings.
So I took it from her double-quick and gave her a piece of my
mind, not knowing you'd hear. That's why, in front of the
master, I said it was Hsiang-ling."

Hsi-feng laughed. "I was wondering why Aunt Hsueh should
suddenly send a concubine here when she knew that your
master was back. So it was just one of your tricks."

Just then Chia Lien returned. Hsi-feng called for wine and
dishes, and husband and wife took their seats opposite each
other. Although Hsi-feng was a good drinker she didn't venture to drink much today. She was sipping her wine to keep
him company when Chia Lien's old wet-nurse Nanny Chao
came in. The young couple promptly invited her to join them
on the *kang*. Nanny Chao resolutely declined this honour.
But Ping-erh and the others had already set a small table and
stool beside the *kang,* and when the nurse had sat down Chia
Lien gave her two dishes from their own table.

"Nanny can't chew those, they're too hard for her teeth,"
said Hsi-feng. She turned to Ping-erh. "That bowl of fresh
pork stewed with ham I remarked was so tender this morning
would be just the thing for her. Take it and get them to heat
it up quickly, will you?" She urged the nurse, "Nanny, try this
Hui Fountain wine your boy brought back."

"I will," said the nurse. "But you must take a cup too.
Don't be afraid! The thing is not to drink too much. I didn't
come all this way for wine or food, though, but on some serious
business. I hope you'll lay it to heart, madam, and help me.
Our Master Lien is good at making promises, but when the
time comes he forgets all about them. Yes, I nursed and brought
you up, and now that I'm old all I have are my two sons. If
you'd do them a favour no one could say a word; yet I've
begged you again and again and you've always agreed, but
to this very day not a thing have you done. Now this wonderful stroke of luck has come out of the blue, you'll be needing
extra hands. So I've come to ask your help, madam. If I
relied on our Master Lien alone, I'd probably have starved to
death by now."

Hsi-feng laughed. "Just leave his two foster-brothers to me, nanny," she said. "You who nursed your boy from babyhood know what he's like. He goes out of his way to help complete strangers, people nowhere near as deserving as his two foster-brothers. Who could possibly object if he did something for them? But he just favours outsiders. Well, perhaps I shouldn't say that. The people we consider outsiders are 'in' with him, I suppose."

That raised a general laugh. Nanny Chao chortled as if she would never stop. "Amida Buddha!" she cackled. "So here comes an impartial judge. Our master wouldn't be so cruel as to treat us as outsiders; but he's so kind-hearted he can't say 'no' to other people's requests."

"Oh yes, he's very soft and generous to those 'in' with him. It's only to us womenfolk that he's adamant."

"You've been so good, madam, and made me so happy that I'll have another cup of that excellent wine. Now that I've got you to look after us, I needn't worry any more."

Chia Lien, rather put out, smiled sheepishly. "Stop talking nonsense and let's start on the rice," he said. "I still have to go and see Cousin Chen on some business."

"Yes, we mustn't delay you," said his wife. "What did your uncle want you for just now?"

"It was about this Imperial visitation."

"Has permission been granted then?" she asked eagerly.

"Not quite, but ten to one it will be."

"What a great act of Imperial kindness!" She beamed. "I never heard of such a thing in any book or opera about the old days."

"That's right," chimed in the nurse. "But I'm growing so stupid in my old age that although I've heard high and low talk of nothing else for days, I can't make head or tail of it all. Just what is this Imperial visitation?"

Chia Lien explained. "Our present Emperor is concerned for all his subjects. No duty is higher than filial piety, and he knows that all, irrespective of rank, have the same family feeling. Though he himself waits day and night upon his Imperial parents, he considers this too little to express all his filial devotion; and he realizes that the secondary consorts and ladies-in-waiting in the Palace who have been away from their parents for many years must naturally be longing to see them again, for it's only right for children to miss their parents. But if the parents at home fall ill or even die of longing for their daughters, this must impair the harmony ordained by Heaven. So he requested Their Most High Majesties to allow the female relatives of the court ladies to visit them in the Palace on the days ending in two and six each month.

"His Majesty's parents were delighted by the Emperor's piety, humanity and manifestion of Heaven's will on earth. In their infinite wisdom the two venerable sages moreover decreed that, since court etiquette might prevent the mothers of the Palace ladies from gratifying all the wishes of their hearts during such visits, they should be granted an even greater favour. Then in a special Edict it was decreed that, apart from the favour of these visits on certain days of the month, all those court ladies with adequate accommodation at home for the reception of an Imperial retinue might ask for a Palace carriage to visit their families. In this way they can show their affection and enjoy a reunion with their dear ones.

"All were so grateful for this Decree, they leapt for joy. The father of the Imperial Lady of Honour Chou has already started building a separate court for her visit home; and Wu Tien-yu, father of the Imperial Concubine Wu, is looking for a site outside the city. Doesn't this show that the thing is practically certain?"

"Amida Buddha! So that's it!" cried Nanny Chao. "I suppose our family will be preparing, too, for a visit from our eldest young mistress?"

"Of course," said Chia Lien. "What else do you think we're all so busy about?"

"If it's really true, I shall have a chance to see some great doings," exulted Hsi-feng. "I've often wished that I'd been born twenty or thirty years earlier, so that the old folk wouldn't be despising me now for having seen so little of the world.

Their descriptions of how our first Emperor toured the country like the sage king Shun of old are better than anything in history, but alas! I was born too late — I missed seeing it."

"Ah, such a thing only happens once in a thousand years," declared Nanny Chao. "I was just old enough then to remember things. In those days our Chia family was in charge of making ocean-going ships and repairing the sea-wall round Soochow and Yangchow. To prepare for that Imperial visit, we spent money just like pouring out sea-water. . . ."

"Our Wang family did the same," put in Hsi-feng. "At that time my grandfather was in sole charge of all the foreign tribute, and whenever envoys came from abroad to pay homage it was our family who entertained them. All the goods brought by foreign ships to Kwangtung, Fukien, Yunnan and Chekiang passed through our hands."

"Who doesn't know that!" said Nanny Chao. "There's still a rhyme:

> When the Dragon King wants
> A white jade bed,
> He asks the Wangs
> Of Chinling, it's said.

That's your family, madam. And the Chens south of the Yangtze, oh, how rich and great they were! That family alone entertained the Emperor four times. No one who was told such a thing, if he hadn't seen it with his own eyes, could believe it. Don't talk about silver treated like dirt, every precious thing you could name was heaped up like hills, no one bothering to check the wicked waste."

"So my grandfather and grand-uncles often said, and of course I believe it. What amazes me is how one family could have so much wealth."

"Why, madam, the truth is they were just spending the Emperor's money on the Emperor. Otherwise who would waste so much on empty show?"

Just then Lady Wang sent to inquire if Hsi-feng had finished her meal, and realizing that she was wanted she hastily ate half a bowl of rice and rinsed her mouth. She was starting out

when some pages from the inner gate reported the arrival of
Chia Jung and Chia Chiang, whereupon Chia Lien rinsed his
mouth and Ping-erh brought him a basin to wash his hands.
As soon as the young men came in he asked what they wanted,
and Hsi-feng stayed to hear Chia Jung's reply:

"My father sent me to tell you, uncle, that the old gentlemen have settled on a plan. We've measured the distance
from the east wall through the garden of the East Mansion to
the north, and it comes to three *li* and a half, enough to build
a separate court for the visit. Someone has been commissioned
to draw a plan which should be ready tomorrow. Since you
must be tired after your journey, please don't think of coming
over. If you've any proposals, you can make them first thing
tomorrow."

"Kindly thank your father for his consideration," replied
Chia Lien. "I shall do as he says and not call on him now.
This is the best possible scheme, the easiest and the simplest
to carry out. Any other site would entail more work without
such good results. Tell him when you get back that I thoroughly approve, and if the old gentlemen have second thoughts I
hope he will dissuade them from looking for another site. When
I come tomorrow to pay my respects we can talk it over in
detail."

Chia Jung agreed at once to pass on this message.

Chia Chiang now stepped forward to announce, "My uncle
has given me the job of going to Soochow with Lai Ta's two
sons and the two secretaries Shan Ping-jen and Pu Ku-hsiu.
We're to hire instructors, buy girl actresses and musical instruments and costumes there. He told me to let you know."

Chia Lien looked quizzically at the young man and asked,
"Are you sure you're up to it? This may not be a big job, but
there should be plenty of perks — if you know the ropes."

"I shall have to learn," was Chia Chiang's cheerful reply.

Chia Jung, standing in the shadow, quietly plucked Hsi-
feng's lapel. Taking the hint she said to her husband, "Don't
worry. Your cousin knows best whom to send. Why should
you be afraid Chiang isn't up to it? Is everyone born capable?

The boy's grown up now. He's old enough to have seen a pig run, even if he hasn't yet tasted pork himself. Cousin Chen is sending him as a supervisor, not to do all the bargaining and accounting himself. I think it's an excellent choice."

"Of course I wasn't querying that," protested Chia Lien. "I only wanted to offer some advice." He asked Chia Chiang, "Where is the money for this coming from?"

"We've just been discussing that. Old Lai sees no need to take silver with us from here. The Chens down south have fifty thousand taels of ours. Tomorrow a draft can be written for us to take. We shall first draw thirty thousand, leaving twenty thousand to buy ornamental lanterns, candles, streamers, bamboo curtains and hangings of every kind."

Chia Lien nodded his approval. "Very good."

"Well, if that's settled," interposed Hsi-feng, "I have two good men you can take along to help you."

"What a coincidence!" Chia Chiang forced a smile. "I was just going to ask you to recommend a couple of people, aunt." He inquired their names.

Hsi-feng asked Nanny Chao, who had been listening as if in a dream. When Ping-erh nudged her she woke up and answered quickly, "One of them is called Chao Tien-liang, the other Chao Tien-tung."

"Don't forget," Hsi-feng cautioned Chia Chiang. "Now I must get back to my duties." With that she left.

Chia Jung slipped out after her and whispered, "If there's anything you want, aunt, make out a list and I'll give it to Chiang to see to."

"Don't talk rubbish!" Hsi-feng snorted. "I've so many things already, I've nowhere to put them. I don't care for your sneaky way of doing things." And so she went off.

Meanwhile Chia Chiang was telling Chia Lien, "If you want anything, uncle, I'll be happy to get it for you."

"Don't look so pleased," replied Chia Lien mockingly. "So this trick is the first thing you learn when you start handling business. If I need anything, of course I'll write. There's no time for it at present."

With that he saw the young men out. Then several servants came to make reports, after which Chia Lien felt so tired that he sent orders to the inner gate to admit no one else: all business must wait until the next day. Hsi-feng did not get to bed until the third watch, but no more need be said about that night.

The next morning, after calling on Chia Sheh and Chia Cheng, Chia Lien went to the Ning Mansion. With some old stewards, secretaries and friends he inspected the grounds of both mansions, drew plans for the palaces for the Imperial visit and estimated the number of workmen required.

Before long all the craftsmen and workmen were assembled, and endless loads of supplies were brought to the site: gold, silver, copper and tin, as well as earth, timber, bricks and tiles. First they pulled down the walls and pavilions of the Garden of Concentrated Fragrance in the Ning Mansion to connect it with the large eastern court of the Jung Mansion; and all the servants' quarters there were demolished.

Formerly a small alley had separated the two houses, but since this was private property and not a public thoroughfare the grounds of both could now be thrown into one.

As a stream already ran from the northern corner of the Garden of Concentrated Fragrance, there was no need to bring in another. And though there were not enough rocks or trees, the bamboos, trees and rockeries as well as the pavilions and balustrades in the original garden of the Jung Mansion where Chia Sheh lived were brought over. The proximity of the two mansions made amalgamation easy, in addition to saving much labour and expense. On the whole, not too many new features had to be added.

The whole was designed by an old landscape gardener known as Gardener Yeh.

As Chia Cheng was unaccustomed to practical business he left it to Chia Sheh, Chia Chen, Chia Lien, Lai Ta, Lai Sheng, Lin Chih-hsiao, Wu Hsin-teng, Chan Kuang and Cheng Jih-hsing. Artificial mountains and lakes were made, pavilions constructed, and bamboos and flowers planted, according to the plan of the gardener. All Chia Cheng did on his return from court was to make a tour of inspection and discuss the most important problems with Chia Sheh and the rest.

As for Chia Sheh, he took his ease at home. If any minor points had to be settled, Chia Chen and the others would explain them to him or send him a written report, while he passed on his instructions through Chia Lien and Lai Ta.

Chia Jung's task was to supervise the making of the gold and silver utensils. As for Chia Chiang, he had already left for Soochow. Chia Chen, Lai Ta and the rest were in charge of the workmen, keeping a register and superintending operations. Impossible to describe in full all that bustle and commotion!

Owing to this all-engrossing business, Chia Cheng had stopped asking Pao-yu about his studies and the boy was having an easy time. The only thing that worried him and spoiled his pleasure was Chin Chung's illness, now growing daily worse.

One morning, he had just washed and dressed and was thinking to ask his grandmother's permission to pay another visit to his friend, when Ming-yen peeped round the spirit screen by the inner gate. Pao-yu hurried over to him.

"What is it?"

"Master Chin Chung. He's dying!"

Pao-yu was staggered.

"He was clear-headed when I saw him only yesterday," he cried. "How can he be dying?"

"I don't know. That's what an old fellow from his home just told me."

At once Pao-yu went to tell the Lady Dowager, who instructed some trustworthy men to accompany him. "You may call to show your friendship for your schoolmate," she told him. "But mind you don't stay too long."

Pao-yu hastily changed his clothes, then paced up and down frantically, calling for his carriage. When at last it arrived he scrambled in and drove off, escorted by Li Kuei, Ming-yen and others.

Finding the gate of Chin Chung's house deserted, they swarmed into the inner apartments, to the consternation of

Chin Chung's two aunts and cousins who quickly made themselves scarce.

Chin Chung had already lost consciousness several times and been lifted on to a trestle-bed to die. At this sight Pao-yu burst out sobbing.

"Don't take on like that," urged Li Kuei. "You know how delicate Master Chin is. They've moved him for the time being to somewhere more comfortable than the hard *kang*. Going on in this way, little master, will only make him worse."

At that Pao-yu restrained himself and approached his friend. Chin Chung lying back on his pillow was as pale as wax; his eyes were closed and his breath was coming in gasps.

"Dear brother!" Pao-yu cried. "It's me — Pao-yu!"

He called several times but Chin Chung made no reply. Still Pao-yu went on calling: "Pao-yu's here!"

Chin Chung was at his last gasp. His spirit, which had already left its body, saw that ghostly guards had come with a warrant and chains to drag him off. He was unwilling to leave, for there was no one to manage the household's affairs and his father had left three or four thousand taels of savings. He was longing, too, for news of Chih-neng. But hard as he pleaded the ghosts were adamant.

"You're an educated young fellow," they scoffed. "Don't you know the saying, 'If the King of Hell summons you at the third watch, who dares keep you till the fifth?' We shades are strictly impartial, not like you mortals with all your soft-heartedness and favouritism."

As they were shouting at him, Chin Chung's spirit heard Pao-yu call.

"Have pity, divine messengers," he begged. "Let me go back to say one word to my good friend. Then I'll come with you."

"What good friend is this?" asked the ghosts.

"The grandson of the Duke of Jungkuo. His name is Pao-yu."

The ghost in command gave a howl of dismay, then swore at his followers. "I told you to let him go back for a while, but you wouldn't. Now he's produced this favourite of fortune, what are we to do?"

The ghosts, flustered by their officer's alarm, protested, "You were thundering mad yourself just now, but the name Pao-yu seems to have terrified you. Why should we shades be afraid of a mortal like him? What can he do for us?"

Their officer swore, "That's rubbish! You know the proverb, 'The empire's officials control all in the empire.' That's how it is in the nether regions too — the same for spirits as for mortals. It'll do no harm to show some consideration."

Hearing this, the ghosts had to let Chin Chung's soul return to its body.

The dying boy gave an indistinct cry and, opening his eyes, saw Pao-yu by his side.

"Why didn't you come earlier?" he asked faintly. "If you'd left it any longer, I shouldn't have seen you."

Pao-yu clasped his friend's hands and asked through tears, "What last message have you for me?"

"Just this. When you and I first met, we thought ourselves above the common herd. Now I know how wrong we were. You should set your mind on making a name through the examinations, on winning distinction, in future. . . ."

With that he gave a long sigh and breathed his last.

For what followed, read the next chapter.

CHAPTER 17

Literary Talent Is Tested by Composing
Inscriptions in Grand View Garden
Those Losing Their Way at Happy Red Court
Explore a Secluded Retreat

Pao-yu wept over Chin Chung's death as if he would never stop; and it was some time before Li Kuei and the rest could prevail on him to leave off. Even after his return he could not overcome his grief. The Lady Dowager gave the Chin family several dozen taels of silver in addition to funeral gifts; Pao-yu went to offer his condolences and, seven days later, the funeral and burial took place. No need to record it in detail. Pao-yu mourned for his friend and missed him every day, but there was no help for it.

Some time later Chia Chen came to report to Chia Cheng that the work on the new garden had been completed and Chia Sheh had inspected it.

"All is ready for you to look over, sir," he announced. "If there is anything unsuitable, we can have it changed before the inscriptions for different places are chosen."

Chia Cheng reflected for a while, then said, "The inscriptions *do* present a problem. By rights, we should ask the Imperial Consort to do us the honour of composing them, but she can hardly do this without having seen the place. On the other hand, if we leave the chief sights and pavilions without a single name or couplet until her visit, the garden, however lovely with its flowers and willows, rocks and streams, cannot fully reveal its charm."

"You are absolutely right, sir," agreed his cultured companions.

"I have an idea," said one. "The inscriptions for different places can't be dispensed with, but neither can they be fixed in advance. Why not briefly prepare some tentative couplets and names to suit each place? We can have them painted on lanterns in the shape of plaques and scrolls for the time being. Then, when Her Highness favours us with a visit, we can ask her to decide on permanent names. Wouldn't this be a way out of the dilemma?"

"A sound idea," agreed Chia Cheng. "Let us have a look round then today and think up some inscriptions. If suitable, they can be used; if unsuitable, we can ask Chia Yu-tsun over to help."

"Your suggestions are bound to be excellent, sir," they countered. "Why need we call in Yu-tsun?"

"Frankly, I was never a good hand even in my young days at writing verse about nature — flowers, birds and scenery. Now that I'm old and burdened with official duties I've quite lost the light touch required for belles-lettres. Any efforts of mine would undoubtedly be so clumsy and pedantic that they would fail to bring out the garden's beauty — they might even have the opposite effect."

"Have no fears about that," his secretaries assured him. "We can put our wits together. If each of us uses his ingenuity and we then choose the best suggestions, discarding the rest, we should be able to manage."

"Very well. Luckily it's a fine day for a stroll."

Chia Cheng rose to his feet and set off at the head of the party, while Chia Chen went on in advance to let everyone in the garden know they were coming.

It so happened that Pao-yu had just arrived in the garden. For he was still grieving so much over Chin Chung's death that the Lady Dowager often told his servants to take him there to distract him.

Chia Chen, coming upon him, warned him jokingly, "You'd better clear out! Lord Cheng is on his way here."

Pao-yu rushed out like a streak of smoke, with his nurse and pages behind him. But just round the corner he ran into

Chia Cheng's party. Since escape was impossible, Pao-yu stepped to one side.

Now Chia Cheng had recently heard Pao-yu's tutor speak highly of his skill in composing couplets, remarking that the boy, though not studious, showed considerable originality. Having happened upon him like this, Chia Cheng ordered his son to accompany them. Pao-yu had to comply, not knowing what his father wanted.

At the entrance to the garden, they found Chia Chen with a group of stewards lined up in wait.

"Close the gate," said Chia Cheng. "Let us see what it looks like from outside before we go in."

Chia Chen had the gate closed and Chia Cheng inspected the gatehouse, a building in five sections with an arched roof of semi-circular tiles. The lintels and lattices, finely carved with ingenious designs, were neither painted nor gilded; the walls were of polished bricks of a uniform colour, and the white marble steps were carved with passion-flowers. The garden's spotless whitewashed wall stretching to left and right had, at its base, a mosaic of striped "tiger-skin" stones. The absence of vulgar ostentation pleased him.

He had the gate opened then and they went in, only to find their view screened by a green hill. At this sight his secretaries cried out in approval.

"If not for this hill," observed Chia Cheng, "one would see the whole garden as soon as one entered, and how tame that would be."

"Exactly," agreed the rest. "Only a bold landscape gardener could have conceived this."

On the miniature mountain they saw rugged white rocks resembling monsters and beasts, some recumbent, some rampant, dappled with moss or hung about with creepers, a narrow zigzag path just discernible between them.

"We'll follow this path," decided Chia Cheng. "Coming back we can find our way out at the other side. That should take us over the whole grounds."

He made Chia Chen lead the way and, leaning on Pao-yu's shoulder, followed him up through the boulders. Suddenly raising his head, he saw a white rock polished as smooth as a mirror, obviously intended for the first inscription.

"See, gentlemen!" he called over his shoulder, smiling. "What would be a suitable name for this spot?"

"Heaped Verdure," said one.

"Embroidery Ridge," said another.

"The Censer."[1]

"A Miniature Chungnan."[2]

Dozens of different suggestions were made, all of them stereotyped clichés; for Chia Cheng's secretaries were well aware that he meant to test his son's ability. Pao-yu understood this too.

Now his father called on him to propose a name.

Pao-yu replied, "I've heard that the ancients said, 'An old quotation beats an original saying; to recut an old text is better than to engrave a new one.' As this is not the main prominence or one of the chief sights, it only needs an inscription because it is the first step leading to the rest. So why not use that line from an old poem:

> A winding path leads to a secluded retreat.

A name like that would be more dignified."

"Excellent!" cried the secretaries.

"Our young master is far more brilliant and talented than dull pedants like ourselves."

"You mustn't flatter the boy," protested Chia Cheng with a smile. "He's simply making a ridiculous parade of his very limited knowledge. We can think of a better name later."

They walked on through a tunnel into a ravine green with magnificent trees and ablaze with rare flowers. A clear stream welling up where the trees were thickest wound its way through clefts in the rocks.

---

[1] The Censer Peak of Mount Lushan in Kiangsi Province.

[2] The scenic Chungnan Mountain in Shensi Province.

Some paces further north, on both sides of a level clearing, rose towering pavilions whose carved rafters and splendid balustrades were half hidden by the trees on the slopes. Looking downwards, they saw a crystal stream cascading as white as snow and stone 'steps going down through the mist to a pool. This was enclosed by marble balustrades and spanned by a stone bridge ornamented with the heads of beasts with gaping jaws. On the bridge was a little pavilion in which the whole party sat down.

"What would you call this, gentlemen?" asked Chia Cheng.

One volunteered, "Ouyang Hsiu's[1] *Pavilion of the Old Drunkard* has the line, 'A winged pavilion hovers above.' Why not call this Winged Pavilion?"

"A delightful name," rejoined Chia Cheng. "But as this pavilion is built over the pool there should be some allusion to the water. Ouyang Hsiu also speaks of a fountain 'spilling between two peaks.' Could we not use that word 'spilling'?"

"Capital!" cried one gentleman. " 'Spilling Jade' would be an excellent name."

Chia Cheng tugging thoughtfully at his beard turned with a smile to ask Pao-yu for his suggestion.

"I agree with what you just said, sir," replied his son. "But if we go into this a little deeper, although 'spilling' was an apt epithet for Ouyang Hsiu's fountain, which was called the Brewer's Spring, it would be unsuitable here. Then again, as this is designed as a residence for the Imperial Consort we should use more courtly language instead of coarse, inelegant expressions like this. Could you not think of something more subtle?"

"Do you hear that, gentlemen?" Chia Cheng chuckled. "When we suggest something original he is all in.favour of an old quotation; but now that we are using an old quotation he finds it too coarse. Well, what do *you* propose?"

"Wouldn't 'Seeping Fragrance' be more original and tasteful than 'Spilling Jade'?"

---

[1] A Sung Dynasty writer.

Chia Cheng stroked his beard again and nodded in silence while the others, eager to please him, hastened to commend Pao-yu's remarkable talent.

"The selection of two words for the tablet is easy," said his father. "Go on and make a seven-character couplet."

Pao-yu rose to his feet and glanced round for inspiration. Then he declaimed:

> "Willows on the dyke lend their verdancy
>   to three punts;
> Flowers on the further shore spare a
>   breath of fragrance."

His father nodded with a faint smile amid another chorus of approval.

They left the pavilion then, crossed the bridge and strolled on, admiring each rock, each height, each flower and each tree on the way, until they found themselves before the whitewashed enclosing walls of a fine lodge nestling in a dense glade of fresh green bamboos. With cries of admiration they walked in.

From the gate porch a zigzag covered walk with a cobbled path below and parallel to it wound up to a little cottage of three rooms, with the cottage door in the middle one and furniture made to fit the measurements of the rooms. Another small door in the inner room opened on to the back garden with its large pear-tree, broad-leafed plantain and two tiny side courts. Through a foot-wide opening below the back wall flowed a brook which wound past the steps and the lodge to the front court before meandering out through the bamboos.

"This is pleasant. If one could study at this window on a moonlit night one would not have lived in vain," observed Chia Cheng. He glanced at Pao-yu, who hung his head in confusion while the others quickly changed the subject, one of them suggesting:

"We need a four-character inscription here."

"What four characters?" asked Chia Cheng.

"Shades of the River Chi?"[1]

---

[1] According to the *Book of Songs,* the area around the River Chi, in the northern part of present-day Honan, abounded with bamboo in ancient time.

"Too commonplace."

"Traces of the Sui Garden?"[1]

"That is equally hackneyed."

Chia Chen proposed, "Let Cousin Pao make a suggestion."

"Before he makes any suggestion," objected Chia Cheng, "the impudent fellow criticizes other people's."

"But his comments are correct. How can you blame him?"

"Don't pander to him like that." He turned to his son. "We're putting up with your wild talk today, so let's have your criticisms first before we hear your own proposals. Were either of these gentlemen's suggestions appropriate?"

"I didn't think so, sir."

His father smiled sardonically. "Why not?"

"Since this will be the first place where our Imperial visitor stops, we should pay some tribute to Her Highness here. If we want a four-character inscription there are plenty of old ones ready at hand, why need we compose anything new?"

"Aren't 'The River Chi' and 'The Sui Garden' both classical allusions?"

"Yes, but they sound too stiff. I propose 'Where the Phoenix Alights.'"

The rest were loud in their praise and Chia Cheng nodded.

"You young rascal," he said, "with your pitiful smattering of knowledge. All right, now let's hear your couplet."

Pao-yu declaimed:

> "Still green the smoke from tea brewed in a
>   rare tripod;
> Yet cold the fingers from chess played by
>   quiet window."

Chia Cheng shook his head. "No better either!"

He was leading the party on when a thought struck him and turning to Chia Chen he said, "All these compounds and lodges are furnished with tables and chairs, but what about curtains, blinds, knick-knacks, curios and so forth? Have appropriate ones for each place been prepared?"

---

[1] Garden of Prince Hsiao of Liang in the Han Dynasty.

"We have got in a large stock of ornaments which will be properly set out in due course," replied Chia Chen. "As for the curtains and blinds, Cousin Lien told me yesterday that they are not all ready yet. We took exact measurements from the building plans for each place when the work started, and sent out our designs to be made up. By yesterday about half of them were finished."

Since he was clearly ignorant of the details, Chia Cheng sent for Chia Lien and asked him, "What are the different items? How many are ready and how many are not?"

Chia Lien promptly pulled out a list from the leg of one boot. After referring to it he replied, "Of the one hundred and twenty satin curtains embroidered with dragons and brocade hangings large and small with different designs and colours, eighty were ready yesterday and forty are still to come. Two hundred blinds were delivered yesterday. Beside these, there are two hundred portières of crimson felt, two hundred of red lacquered bamboo with gold flecks, two hundred of black lacquered bamboo, and two hundred woven with coloured silks. Half of each kind is ready, the rest will be finished by the end of autumn. Then there are chair-covers, table-drapes, valances and stool-covers — one thousand two hundred of each — which we already have."

As they walked on talking, their eyes fell on some green hills barring their way. Skirting these they caught sight of brown adobe walls with paddy-stalk copings and hundreds of apricot-trees, their blossoms bright as spurting flames or sunlit clouds. Inside this enclosure stood several thatched cottages. Outside grew saplings of mulberry, elm, hibiscus and silkworm-thorn trees, whose branches had been intertwined to form a double green hedge. Beyond this hedge, at the foot of the slope, was a rustic well complete with windlass and well-sweep. Below, neat plots of fine vegetables and rape-flowers stretched as far as eye could see.

"I see the point of this place," declared Chia Cheng. "Although artificially made, the sight of it tempts one to retire to the country. Let us go in and rest a while."

Just as they were on the point of entering the wicker gate they saw a stone by the pathway which was obviously intended for an inscription.

"That's the finishing touch," they cried, chuckling. "A plaque over the gate would have spoilt the rustic flavour, but this stone here adds to the charm. It would take one of Fan Cheng-ta's poems[1] on country life to do justice to this place."

"What shall we call it then, gentlemen?"

"As your worthy son just remarked, 'An old quotation beats an original saying.' The ancients have already supplied the most fitting name — Apricot Village."

Chia Cheng turned with a smile to Chia Chen, saying, "That reminds me. This place is perfect in every other respect, but it still lacks a tavern-sign. You must have one made tomorrow. Nothing too grand. Just a tavern-sign of the sort used in country places. Let it be hung on a bamboo pole from a tree-top."

Chia Chen readily agreed to this, then suggested, "Other birds would be out of place here, but we ought to have some geese, ducks, hens and so on."

When this proposal had met with general approval, Chia Cheng observed, "'Apricot Village' is first-rate, but since it is the name of a real place we should have to get official permission to use it."

"True," agreed the others. "We shall have to think of something else. What shall it be?"

Without giving them time to think or waiting to be asked by his father, Pao-yu blurted out, "An old poem has the line, 'Above flowering apricot hangs a tavern-sign.' Why not call this 'Approach to Apricot Tavern'?"

"'Approach' is superb," they cried. "It suggests the idea of Apricot Village too."

"'Apricot Village' would be too vulgar a name." Pao-yu smiled scornfully. "But an old poet wrote 'A wicker gate by a stream sweet with paddy.' How about 'Paddy-Sweet Cottage'?"

---

[1] Fang Cheng-ta, a Sung Dynasty poet, is famous for his poems on country life.

Again the secretaries clapped in approbation but his father sternly silenced him. "Ignorant cub! How many ancient writers have you read and how many old poems have you memorized that you dare show off in front of your elders? I put up with your nonsense just now to test you in fun — don't take it seriously."

With that he led the party into one of the cottages. It was quite free of ostentation, having papered windows and a wooden couch. Secretly pleased, he glanced at his son and asked, "Well, what do you think of *this* place?"

The secretaries nudged the boy to induce him to express approval. But ignoring them he answered, "It can't compare with 'Where the Phoenix Alights.'"

"Ignorant dolt!" Chia Cheng sighed. "All you care for are red pavilions and painted beams. With your perverse taste for luxury, how can you appreciate the natural beauty of such a quiet retreat? This comes of neglecting your studies."

"Yes sir," replied Pao-yu promptly. "But the ancients were always using the term 'natural.' I wonder what they really meant by it?"

Afraid his pig-headedness would lead to trouble, the others hastily put in, "You understand everything else so well, why ask about the term 'natural'? It means coming from nature, not due to human effort."

"There you are! A farm here is obviously artificial and out of place with no villages in the distance, no fields near by, no mountain ranges behind, no source for the stream at hand, above, no pagoda from any half hidden temple, below, no bridge leading to a market. Perched here in isolation, it is nothing like as fine a sight as those other places which were less far-fetched. The bamboos and streams there didn't look so artificial. What the ancients called 'a natural picture' means precisely that when you insist on an unsuitable site and hills where no hills should be, however skilfully you go about it the result is bound to jar...."

"Clear off!" thundered Chia Cheng. "Stop. Come back. Make up another couplet. If it's no good I'll slap your face on both accounts."

Pao-yu had to comply. He declaimed:

> "The green tide fills the creek where clothes
>   are washed;
> Clouds of fragrance surround the girls plucking
>   water-cress."

"Worse and worse," growled Chia Cheng, shaking his head as he led the company out.

The path now curved around a slope, past flowers and willows, rocks and springs, a trellis of yellow roses, an arbour of white ones, a tree-peony pavilion, a white peony plot, a court of rambler roses and a bank of plantains. Suddenly they heard the plash of a spring gushing from a cave overhung by vines, and saw fallen blossoms floating on the water below. As they cried out in delight, Chia Cheng asked them to suggest another inscription.

"What more apt than 'The Spring of Wuling'?" said one.

"Too hackneyed. Besides, it's also the name of a real place," objected Chia Cheng with a smile.

"Then how about 'The Refuge of a Man of Chin'?"[1]

"Even more impossible," cried Pao-yu. "How can we use something that implies taking refuge in time of trouble? I suggest 'Smartweed Bank and Flowery Harbour.'"

"That makes even less sense," scoffed his father. He strolled to the water's edge and asked Chia Chen, "Do you have any boats here?"

"There will be four punts for lotus-gathering and one pleasure boat, but they aren't ready yet."

"What a pity we can't cross."

"We can make a detour by the path over the hills," said Chia Chen, and proceeded to lead the way.

---

[1] Both "The Spring of Wuling" and "The Refuge of a Man of Chin" refer to the imaginary land beyond the peach-blossom stream at Wuling described by the Tsin poet Tao Yuan-ming.

The others followed, clinging to creepers and trees as they clambered up. There were more fallen blossoms now on the stream, which appeared more translucent than ever as it swirled down its circuitous course. It was flanked by weeping willows and peach and apricot trees which screened the sun, and there was not a mote of dust in the air.

Presently, in the shade of the willows, they glimpsed an arched wooden bridge with scarlet railings. Once over this a choice of paths lay before them; but their attention was caught by an airy house of smooth brick with spotless tiles and an ornamental wall on one of the lesser slopes of the main hill.

"That building seems very out of place here," remarked Chia Cheng.

But stepping over the threshold he was confronted by tall weathered rocks of every description which hid the house from sight. In place of trees and flowers there was a profusion of rare creepers, vines and trailers, which festooned the artificial mountains, grew through the rocks, hung from the eaves, twined round the pillars and carpeted the steps. Some seemed like floating green belts or golden bands; others had berries red as cinnabar and flowers like golden osmanthus which gave off a penetrating scent, unlike the scent of ordinary flowers.

"This is charming!" Chia Cheng could not help exclaiming. "But what are all these plants?"

"Climbing fig and wistaria?" someone suggested.

"But they don't have such a strange fragrance, do they?"

"They certainly don't," interposed Pao-yu. "There *are* climbing fig and wistaria here, but the fragrance comes from alpinia and snakeroot. That one over there is iris, I fancy, and here we have dolichos, dwarf-mallow and glyrcyrrhia. That crimson plant is purple rue, of course; the green, angelica. A lot of these rare plants are mentioned in the *Li Sao* and *Wen Hsuan*,[1] plants with names like *huona, chiangtan, tsulun*

---

[1] *Li Sao,* long narrative poem by the Chu poet Chu Yuan in the fourth century B.C.; *Wen Hsuan,* an anthology of literature compiled by a prince of Liang in the sixth century.

and *chiangtzu; shihfan, shuisung* and *fuliu; luyi, tanchiao, miwu* and *fenglien.* But after all these centuries scholars can no longer identify these plants, for which new names have been found. . . ."

"Who asked *your* opinion?" roared his father.

Pao-yu stepped back nervously and said no more.

Covered corridors ran along both sides of this court and Chia Cheng led his party down one of these to a cool five-section gallery with roofed verandahs on four sides, green windows and painted walls, more elegant than any they had yet seen.

"One could brew tea here and play the lyre without having to burn rare incense." He sighed appreciatively. "This is certainly unexpected. We need a good inscription, gentlemen, to do it justice."

"What could be apter than 'Wind in the Orchids and Dew on Angelicas'?" one ventured.

"I suppose we have no other choice. Now what about a couplet?"

"I have thought of one," said another. "The rest of you must correct it.

> Fragrance of musk-orchids fills the court at dusk,
> Scent of alpinia floats to the moonlit island."

"Very good," they commented. "Only the reference to 'dusk' seems inappropriate."

He quoted the old poem then with the line, "The alpinia in the court weeps in the dusk."

"Too sad, too sad," they protested.

"Here's one for your consideration," said another.

> "Along three paths white angelica scents the breeze,
> In the court a bright moon shines on golden orchids."

Chia Cheng thoughtfully tugged at his beard and seemed about to propose a couplet himself when, raising his head, he caught sight of Pao-yu, now afraid to open his mouth.

"Well?" he said sternly. "When it's time to speak you say nothing. Are you waiting to be begged for the favour of your instruction?"

"We have no musk, moon or islands here," said Pao-yu. "If you want allusive couplets of that kind, we can easily compose hundreds."

"Who is putting pressure on you to use those words?"

"Well then, I suggest 'Pure Scent of Alpinia and Iris.' And for the couplet:

> Singing on cardamons makes lovely poetry;
> Sleeping beneath roses induces sweet dreams."

Chia Cheng laughed. "You got that from the line 'Write on plantain leaves and green is the writing.' This is mere plagiarism."

"There's nothing wrong with plagiarism provided it's well done," countered the others. "Even Li Po copied from *Yellow Crane Pavilion*[1] when he wrote his *Phoenix Tower*. If you consider this couplet carefully, sir, it is livelier and more poetical than the original. It even looks as if the other line plagiarizes this by our young master."

"Preposterous!" Chia Cheng smiled.

From there they went on some way until ahead of them loomed towering pavilions enclosed by magnificent buildings, all of them connected by winding passageways. Green pines brushed the eaves, white balustrades skirted the steps, the animal designs glittered like gold and the dragon-heads blazed with colour.

"This must be the main reception palace," observed Chia Cheng. "Its one fault is that it is too luxurious."

"Unavoidably so," they reasoned. "Although Her Royal Highness prizes frugality, this is no more than is due to her present exalted rank."

They were now at the foot of a marble arch finely carved with rampant dragons and coiling serpents.

"What should be inscribed here?" asked Chia Cheng.

---

[1] A poem by Tsui Hao, another Tang poet.

" 'The Fairy Land of Penglai'?"

He shook his head and said nothing.

As for Pao-yu, he felt strangely stirred by this sight, as if he had seen a place of this kind before — though just when he could not remember. Called upon to compose an inscription, he was too preoccupied to think of anything else. The others, not knowing this, imagined that his wits were wandering and he was exhausted after his long ordeal. Fearing that if he were pressed too hard the consequences might be serious, they urged his father to give him a day's grace.

Chia Cheng, aware that his mother might well be anxious, said with an ironic smile, "So sometimes you are at a loss too, you young rascal. Very well, I'll give you until tomorrow. But if no inscription is ready then, so much the worse for you. This is the most important place, so mind you do your best."

They continued with the tour of inspection and had covered little more than half the grounds when a servant reported that someone had arrived with a message from Yu-tsun.

"We can't see the rest of the places," said Chia Cheng. "But by going out the other way we can at least get a general idea, even if we don't see them all."

He led the way to a large bridge above a crystal curtain of cascading water. This was the sluice admitting water from outside. Chia Cheng asked for a name for it.

"Since this is the source of the River of Seeping Fragrance it could be called 'Seeping Fragrance Lock,' " Pao-yu suggested.

"Rubbish," said his father. "We just won't have 'Seeping Fragrance.' "

On they went past quiet lodges and thatched huts, stone walls and pergolas of flowers, a temple secluded in the hills and a convent half hidden among the trees, long covered walks, meandering grottoes, square mansions and round kiosks, none of which they had time to enter. However, it was so long since their last rest that all were footsore and weary by the time they saw another lodge in front, and Chia Cheng said, "Here we must rest a little."

He led the way in past some double-flowering peach in blossom and through a moon-gate made of bamboo over which climbed flowering plants. Whitewashed walls and green willows confronted them then. Along the walls ran covered corridors, and the rockery in the centre of the courtyard was flanked on one side by plantains, on the other by a red multi-petalled crab-apple tree, its branches trained in the shape of an umbrella, with green trailing tendrils and petals red as cinnabar.

"What superb blossoms!" they exclaimed. "We have never seen such a splendid one before."

"This is a foreign variety called 'Maiden Apple,'" Chia Cheng told them. "Tradition has it that it comes from the Land of Maidens, and that it blossoms profusely in that country; but that is nothing but an old wives' tale."

"If so, how did the name come to be handed down?" they wondered.

"Quite likely the name 'Maiden' was given by some poet," said Pao-yu, "because this flower is as red as rouged cheeks and as frail as a delicate girl. Then some vulgar character made up that story and ignorant people believed it."

"A most plausible explanation," said the others.

They sat down on some benches in the corridor and Chia Cheng at once asked for another inscription.

"'Plantains and Storks'?" one proposed.

"Or 'Towering Splendour and Shimmering Radiance.'"

Chia Cheng and the rest approved, as indeed did Pao-yu, adding, "It's a pity, though...." Asked to explain himself, he said, "Plantain and crab-apple blossom suggest both red and green. It's a pity to refer to one and not the other."

"What do you suggest then?" demanded his father.

"Something like 'Red Fragrance and Green Jade' would bring out the charm of both, I think."

"Too feeble!" Chia Cheng shook his head.

He led the way into the building. It was unusually set out with no clear-cut divisions between the different rooms. There were only partitions formed of shelves for books, bronze tripods, stationery, flower vases and miniature gardens, some round, some square, some shaped like sunflowers, plantain leaves or intersecting arcs. They were beautifully carved with the motifs "clouds and a hundred bats" or the "three companions of winter" — pine, plum and bamboo — as well as landscapes and figures, birds and flowers, scrollwork, imitation curios and symbols of good fortune or long life. All executed by the finest craftsmen, they were brilliantly coloured and inlaid with gold or precious stones. The effect was splendid, the workmanship exquisite. Here a strip of coloured gauze concealed a small window, there a gorgeous curtain hid a door. There were also niches on the walls to fit antiques, lyres, swords, vases or other ornaments, which hung level with the surface of the wall. Their amazement and admiration for the craftsmen's ingenuity knew no bounds.

After passing two partitions Chia Cheng and his party lost their way. To their left they saw a door, to their right a window; but when they went forward their passage was blocked by a bookshelf. Turning back they glimpsed the way through another window; but on reaching the door they suddenly saw a party just like their own confronting them — they were looking at a big mirror. Passing round this they came to more doorways.

"Follow me, sir," urged Chia Chen with a smile. "Let me take you to the back courtyard and show you a short cut."

He conducted them past two gauze screens out into a courtyard filled with rose trellises. Skirting round the fence, Pao-yu saw a clear stream in front.

All exclaimed in astonishment, "Where does this water come from?"

Chia Chen pointed to a spot in the distance.

"It flows from that lock we saw through the ravine, then from the northeast valley to the little farm, where some is diverted southwest. Here both streams converge to flow out underneath the wall."

"Miraculous!" they marvelled.

Now another hill barred their way and they no longer had any sense of direction; but Chia Chen laughingly made them follow him, and as soon as they rounded the foot of the hill they found themselves on a smooth highway not far from the main entrance.

"How diverting," they said. "Really most ingenious."

And so they left the garden.

Pao-yu was longing to get back to the girls, but receiving no dismissal from his father he had to follow him to the library. Now Chia Cheng suddenly remembered his presence.

"Why are you still here?" he demanded. "Haven't you had enough of wandering around? The old lady will be worrying about you. She's wasting her love on you. Off you go, quick."

Then at last Pao-yu could withdraw. What followed is recorded in the next chapter.

CHAPTER 18

Yuan-chun Visits Her Parents
on the Feast of Lanterns
Tai-yu Helps Her True Love
by Passing Him a Poem

As soon as Pao-yu was out of the courtyard, the pages who attended Chia Cheng stepped forward to throw their arms around his waist.

They said, "It's lucky for you that the master was in such a good mood today. The old lady sent several times to ask how things were, and you should thank us for telling her he looked pleased. Otherwise she'd have sent for you and you wouldn't have had this chance to shine. Everybody said your poems were the best. Today's your lucky day, so give us a tip."

"You shall each have a string of cash," he promised them.

"Who hasn't seen a string of cash?" cried one. "Give me your pouch."

Swarming round without so much as a "by your leave," they stripped him of his scented pouch, fan-sheath and other pendants.

"Now let's see him back!" they cried.

With one of them carrying him, the others in a troop escorted him along to the outer courtyard of the Lady Dowager's apartments.

Since she had sent several times to see how her grandson was faring, she was naturally pleased when her nannies and maids brought him in, none the worse for his experience.

When presently Hsi-jen handed him tea she noticed that not one of his pendants was left. "So those shameless wretches have taken all your things again," she remarked with a smile.

Tai-yu came over to see if this was true.   Sure enough, all his trinkets had gone.

"So you've given them that pouch I made you too!" she remarked.   "All right, that's the last thing you'll ever get from me."

Going crossly back to her own room, she took her scissors and started cutting up the sachet she had been making for him at Pao-yu's own request.

Pao-yu, seeing that she was angry, knew that something was up and hurried after her.   Too late.   Although the sachet had not been finished, the embroidery on it was very fine and she had put a lot of work into it, so he was annoyed to see it spoilt for no reason.   Quickly undoing his collar, he pulled out the pouch he was wearing over his red tunic.

"Look, what's this?" he asked, showing it to her.   "When have I ever given anything of yours to someone else?"

Realizing that he treasured her gift so much that he had kept it safely hidden away, Tai-yu repented of her hastiness and hung her head in silence.

"You didn't have to cut it up," went on Pao-yu reproachfully. "I know you don't like giving me anything, so I'll let you have this one back too, how about that?"   Tossing it into her lap, he turned to go.

Choking with anger Tai-yu burst into tears.   She picked up the pouch meaning to cut it to pieces as well.   But he rushed back to stop her, begging, "Dear cousin, spare it!"

She threw down the scissors to brush away her tears.

"You don't have to treat me like that, kind one moment and cruel the next.   If it's a quarrel you want, we'd better have nothing more to do with each other.   Why carry on like this?"

She flung herself tearfully down on her bed with her face towards the wall, wiping her streaming eyes.   In desperation, Pao-yu leant over her begging, "Dear cousin, dear, *kind* cousin, do forgive me!"

Meanwhile the Lady Dowager had been asking where Pao-yu was.   Hearing that he was with Tai-yu she said, "That's good. Let them amuse themselves together for a while. He deserves a little relaxation after being kept so long under check by his father. Just see that they don't quarrel. You mustn't upset him." And to this the servants agreed.

Unable to shake Pao-yu off, Tai-yu got up. "Since you won't give me any peace, I'm going to leave you," she declared.

As she started out he said with a smile, "Wherever you go, I'll go with you." He was fastening on the pouch again as he spoke.

Tai-yu snatched at it, scolding, "First you say you don't want it, and now you're putting it on again. I really blush for you." She started to giggle.

"Dear cousin, do make me another sachet tomorrow."

"We'll have to see how I feel."

They went together then to Lady Wang's quarters where they happened to find Pao-chai. Everyone was in a state of great excitement, as the twelve young actresses bought by Chia Chiang in Soochow had just arrived, together with the instructors he had hired and the costumes for the operas they would perform.

Aunt Hsueh had moved to quiet, secluded quarters in the northeast part of the grounds, and Pear Fragrance Court had been made ready for the rehearsals. Some family maids who had once trained as opera-singers themselves but were now hoary dames were sent to look after the little actresses, while Chia Chiang was put in charge of their daily expenses and the provision of everything they required.

Just at this time, Lin Chih-hsiao's wife came to report, "The twenty-four little nuns — twelve Buddhist and twelve Taoist — whom I selected and purchased have now arrived, and their twenty-four new habits are ready. There's another girl, too, who has entered holy orders without shaving her head. She comes from a Soochow family of scholars and officials. She was delicate as a child, and although they bought many substitute novices for her it was no use — her health didn't improve until she joined the Buddhist order herself. That's how she became a lay sister. She's eighteen this year and her name in religion is Miao-yu. Her parents are dead now and she only has two old nurses and one maid to look after her. She's widely read and well-versed in the sutras, besides being very good-looking. She came to the capital last year, having heard there were relics of Kuanyin here and canons inscribed on pattra leaves. She's been living in the Sakyamuni Convent outside the West Gate. Her tutor was an excellent diviner, but she passed away last winter. Miao-yu had meant to escort the coffin back to her native place; but as her tutor lay dying she told the girl not to go back home but to wait quietly where she was for something fortune had in store for her. So she didn't accompany the coffin back."

"In that case, why not ask her here?" put in Lady Wang.

"She'd refuse," objected Lin Chih-hsiao's wife. "She'd be afraid of being looked down on in a noble household."

"A young lady from an official family is bound to be rather proud," agreed Lady Wang. "Why not send her a written invitation?"

Lin Chih-hsiao's wife agreed and left. One of the secretaries was instructed to make out an invitation, and the following day servants were sent with a carriage and sedan-chair to fetch Miao-yu. As to what followed, we can leave that till later.

A servant came just then to request Hsi-feng to open the storeroom and issue the gauze and silk needed by the workmen for screens. Another asked her to store away the gold and silver utensils. Meanwhile Lady Wang and her maids were busy too.

So Pao-chai suggested, "Let's not stay here where we're only in the way. Let's go and find Tan-chun."

She took Pao-yu and Tai-yu to the rooms of Ying-chun and others to while away the time.

For Lady Wang and her helpers the days passed in a flurry of preparations until, towards the end of the tenth month, all was ready. The stewards had handed in their accounts; antiques and precious objects had been set out; the pleasure grounds were well-stocked with cranes, peacocks, deer, rabbits, chicken and geese to be reared in appropriate places; Chia Chiang had twenty operas ready; and the little Buddhist and Taoist nuns had memorized various sutras and incantations.

Then Chia Cheng, able at last to breathe more freely, invited the Lady Dowager to make a final inspection of the Garden and see that all was in order with nothing overlooked. This done, he chose an auspicious date and wrote a memorial, and the very same day that it was presented the Son of Heaven acceded to his request. The Imperial Consort would be permitted to visit her parents for the Feast of Lanterns on the fifteenth of the first month the following year. This threw the whole household into such a commotion that, hard at work day and night, they scarcely had time to celebrate the New Year.

In a twinkling the Feast of Lanterns would arrive. On the eighth of the first month eunuchs came from the Palace to inspect the general layout of the Garden and the apartments where the Imperial Consort would change her clothes, sit with her family, receive their homage, feast them and retire to rest. The eunuch in charge of security also posted many younger eunuchs as guards by the screened and curtained entrances to the retiring rooms. Detailed instructions were given to all members of the household as to where they should withdraw, where they should kneel, serve food or make announcements — all the exact etiquette to be observed. Outside, officers from the Board of Works and the Chief of the Metropolitan Police had the streets swept and cleared of loiterers. Chia Sheh superintended the craftsmen making ornamental lanterns and fireworks, and by the fourteenth everything was ready. But no one, high or low, slept a wink that night.

Before dawn the next day all those with official ranks from the Lady Dowager downwards put on full ceremonial dress. Everywhere in the Garden were hangings and screens brilliantly embroidered with dancing dragons and flying phoenixes; gold and silver glittered, pearls and precious stones shimmered; richly blended incense burnt in the bronze tripods, and fresh flowers filled the vases. Not a cough broke the solemn silence.

Chia Sheh and the other men waited outside in the west street entrance, the Lady Dowager and the women outside

the main gate, the ends of the street and the alleys leading to
it all having been screened off.

They were growing tired of waiting when a eunuch rode up
on a big horse. The Lady Dowager welcomed him in and asked for news.

"It will be a long time yet," the eunuch told her. "Her
Highness is to dine at one, pray to Buddha in the Palace of the
Precious Spirit at half past two, and at five go to feast in the
Palace of Great Splendour and look at the display of lanterns
before asking leave from the Emperor. She can hardly set out
until seven."

This being the case, Hsi-feng suggested that the Lady
Dowager and Lady Wang should go inside to rest and come
back later.

So the Lady Dowager and others retired, leaving Hsi-feng
in charge. She ordered the stewards to conduct the eunuchs
to where refreshments were waiting. Then she had loads of
candles carried in for all the lanterns.

It was not until the candles had been lit that a clatter of
hooves was heard in the street. The next moment up panted
ten or more eunuchs, clapping their hands as they ran. At this
signal the other eunuchs said, "Her Highness is coming!" They
all rushed to their posts.

For a long time they waited in silence, Chia Sheh and the
young men of the family by the entrance of the west street,
the Lady Dowager and the women in front of the main gate.

Then two eunuchs wearing scarlet uniforms rode slowly up
to the entrance of the west street. Dismounting, they led their
horses behind the screens, then stood to attention, their faces
turned towards the west. After some time another pair appeared, then another, until there were ten pairs lined up and
soft music could be heard in the distance.

And now a long procession approached: several pairs of
eunuchs carrying dragon banners, others with phoenix fans,
pheasant plumes and ceremonial insignia, as well as gold cen-
sers burning Imperial incense. Next came a curved-handled
yellow umbrella on which were embroidered seven phoenixes,

and under this a head-dress, robe, girdle and slippers. After this came attendant eunuchs bearing a rosary, embroidered handkerchiefs, a rinse-bowl, fly-whisks and the like.

Last of all, borne slowly forward by eight eunuchs, came a gold-topped palanquin embroidered with phoenixes.

All present, including the Lady Dowager, hastily fell to their knees by the side of the road. Eunuchs rushed over to help up the old lady as well as Lady Hsing and Lady Wang.

The palanquin was carried through the main gate to the entrance of the courtyard on the east, where a eunuch holding a whisk knelt down and invited the Imperial Consort to dismount and change her clothes. Then the palanquin was borne inside and the eunuchs withdrew, leaving Yuan-chun's ladies-in-waiting to help her alight.

She observed that the courtyard was brightly lit with ornamental lanterns of every kind, all exquisitely made of finest gauze. The highest, a rectangular lantern, bore the inscription: Fraught with Favour, Basking in Kindness.

Yuan-chun entered the robing room and changed, then remounted her palanquin which was carried into the Garden. She found it wreathed with the perfumed smoke of incense, splendid with flowers, brilliant with countless lanterns, melodious with strains of soft music. Words fail to describe that scene of peaceful magnificence and noble refinement.

Here, Readers, recalling the scene of desolation at the foot of Blue Ridge Peak in the Great Waste Mountain, I cannot but thank the scabby Buddhist and lame Taoist for bringing me to this place. For how otherwise could I have seen such a sight? I was tempted to write a lantern-poem or a eulogy on family reunion to pay tribute to it, but feared slipping into the vulgar vein of other books. Besides, even writing an ode or eulogy could not do justice to the scene's enchantment. If, on the other hand, I omit to write one my worthy readers can imagine its magnificence for themselves. So I had better save both time and paper and return from this digression to our story.

Now, as she gazed from her palanquin at the dazzling display both within and without the Garden, the Imperial Consort sighed softly:

"This is too extravagant!"

Then a eunuch with a whisk knelt down by the palanquin and invited her to proceed by boat. As she alighted she saw before her a clear waterway winding like a dragon. From the marble balustrades on either bank lanterns of crystal and glass of every description shed a silvery light, clear as snow. The wintry boughs of the willows and apricot trees above them were festooned with artificial flowers and leaves made of rice-paper and silk, and from every tree hung lanterns. Lovely too on the water were the lotus flowers, duckweed and water-fowl made out of shells and feathers. Lanterns high and low seemed trying to outshine each other. It was truly a world of crystal and precious stones! The boats were magnificent too, with lanterns, rare miniature gardens, pearl portières, embroidered curtains, rudders of cassia and oars of aromatic wood, which we need not describe in detail.

By now they had reached a marble landing-stage. The lantern-sign above it bore the words, "Smartweed Bank and Flowery Harbour."

Regarding this name, Reader, and others such as "Where the Phoenix Alights" from the last chapter in which Chia Cheng tested Pao-yu's literary talent, you may wonder to find them actually used as inscriptions. For the Chias, after all, were a scholarly family all of whose friends and protégés were men of parts. Moreover they could easily find well-known writers to compose inscriptions. Why then make shift with phrases tossed off by a boy? Were they like newly rich upstarts who throw money about like dirt and, having painted their mansion crimson, put up huge inscriptions such as "Green willows with golden locks before the gate, Blue hills like embroidered screens behind the house," fancying these the height of elegance? Could that be the way of the Chia family described in this *Tale of the Stone?* This is surely a contradiction? Let me, stupid as I am, explain this to you.

The Imperial Consort, before she entered the Palace, had been brought up from childhood by the Lady Dowager. And after Pao-yu was born, as Yuan-chun was his elder sister and Pao-yu her younger brother, bearing in mind that their mother had given birth to him late in life, she loved him more than her other brothers and lavished all her care on him. They both stayed with their grandmother and were inseparable. Even before Pao-yu started school, when he was hardly four years old, she taught him to recite several texts and to recognize several thousand characters. She was more like a mother to him than an elder sister. After she entered the Palace she often wrote letters home reminding her parents to educate him well, for unless strictly disciplined he would not amount to much, but if treated too sternly he might also give them cause for anxiety. Her loving concern for him had never ceased.

Chia Cheng, earlier on, had scarcely believed the tutor's report that Pao-yu had a flair for literary composition. As the Garden happened then to be ready for inspection, he had called on his son for inscriptions in order to test him. And although Pao-yu's childish efforts were far from inspired, at least they were passable. The family could easily enough have enlisted the help of famous scholars; but it seemed to them that a special interest attached to names chosen by a member of the house. Besides, when the Imperial Consort learned that these were the work of her beloved younger brother, she would feel that he had not fallen short of her hopes. For these reasons Pao-yu's inscriptions were adopted. Not all had been chosen that day; some he supplied later. But enough of this.

When the Imperial Consort saw this name, she commented with a smile: "Just 'Flowery Harbour' would do. Why 'Smart-weed Bank' too?"

As soon as the eunuch in attendance heard this, he hastily disembarked and went ashore to report to Chia Cheng, who immediately had the alteration made.

Meanwhile the boat had reached the further shore and again Yuan-chun mounted her palanquin. Before her now there towered the beautiful hall of an imposing palace. The marble archway in front of it bore the inscription: "Precious Realm for the Immortal." At once she ordered this to be changed to "House of Reunion."

As she entered this temporary palace, she saw torches in the courtyard flaring to the sky, powdered incense strewing the ground, flaming trees, jasper flowers, gilded windows and jade balustrades, to say nothing of screens as fine as the shrimp's antennae, carpets of otter-skin, musk burning in tripods, and fans made from pheasant plumage. Truly this was:

> An abode with golden gates and jade doors fit
>   for immortals,
> Its cassia and orchid chambers a worthy setting
>   for the Imperial Consort.

After glancing around she asked, "Why has this place no name?"

The eunuch attendant fell on his knees. "Because this is the main palace," he replied, "no subject outside the Court dared suggest a name."

The Imperial Consort nodded and said nothing.

Another eunuch, the Master of Ceremonies, knelt and begged her to sit in a chair of state to receive the obeisances of her family. On both sides of the steps music was played as two eunuchs ushered in Chia Sheh and the men of the family to range themselves below the dais; but when a lady-in-waiting relayed the Imperial Consort's command to dispense with this ceremony they withdrew. Then the Lady Dowager of the Jung Mansion and the female relatives were led up the east flight of steps to the dais, but they too were exempted from the ceremony and shown out.

After tea had been served three times, Yuan-chun descended from the throne and the music ceased while she went into a side chamber to change her clothes. Meanwhile a carriage had been prepared to drive her out of the Garden to visit her parents.

First she went to the Lady Dowager's reception room to pay her respects as a grand-daughter of the house; but before she could do so her grandmother and the others knelt to prevent her. The Imperial Consort's eyes were full of tears as her family drew near to greet her. As she clasped the hands of her grandmother and mother, the hearts of all three were too full to speak — they could do nothing but sob. Lady Hsing, Li Wan, Hsi-feng, Yuan-chun's half sister Tan-chun and her cousins Ying-chun and Hsi-chun also stood beside them weeping silently. But at last the Imperial Consort mastered her grief and forced a smile as she tried to comfort them.

"Since you sent me away to that forbidden place, it hasn't been easy getting this chance today to come home and see you all again," she said. "But instead of chatting and laughing, here we are crying! Soon I shall have to leave you, and there is no knowing when I can come back again." At this she broke down afresh.

Lady Hsing and the others did their best to console her and the Lady Dowager asked her to take a seat, after which she exchanged courtesies with each in turn and more tears were shed. Next the stewards and attendants of both mansions paid their respects outside the door, and so did their wives and the maids.

This ceremony at an end, Yuan-chun asked why Aunt Hsueh, Pao-chai and Tai-yu were missing.

Lady Wang explained that they were afraid to presume, not being members of the Chia family and having no official status.

The Imperial Consort asked them to be invited in at once, and they were about to pay homage according to Palace etiquette when she exempted them too and chatted with them.

Next Pao-chin and the other maids whom Yuan-chun had taken with her to the Palace kowtowed to the Lady Dowager, who hastily stopped them and sent them off to have some refreshments in another room. The senior eunuchs and ladies-in-waiting were also entertained by members of the staff of both mansions, leaving only three or four young eunuchs in attendance.

When the ladies of the family had spoken with feeling about their separation and all that had happened since, Chia Cheng from outside the door-curtain asked after the health of his daughter, and she in turn paid her respects.

With tears she told him, "Simple farmers who live on pickles and dress in homespun at least know the joys of family life together. What pleasure can I take in high rank and luxury when we are separated like this?"

With tears too he replied, "Your subject, poor and obscure, little dreamed that our flock of common pigeons and crows would ever be blessed with a phoenix. Thanks to the Imperial favour and the virtue of our ancestors, your Noble Highness embodies the finest essences of nature and the accumulated merit of our forbears — such fortune has attended my wife and myself.

"His Majesty, who manifests the great virtue of all creation, has shown us such extraordinary and hitherto unknown favour that even if we dashed out our brains we could not repay one-thousandth part of our debt of gratitude. All I can do is to exert myself day and night, loyally carry out my official duties, and pray that our sovereign may live ten thousand years as desired by all under heaven.

"Your Noble Highness must not grieve your precious heart in concern for your ageing parents. We beg you to take better care of your own health. Be cautious, circumspect, diligent and respectful. Honour the Emperor and serve him well, so as to prove yourself not ungrateful for His Majesty's bountiful goodness and great kindness."

Then it was Yuan-chun's turn to urge her father to devote himself to affairs of state, look after his health and dismiss all anxiety regarding her.

After this Chia Cheng informed her, "All the inscriptions on the pavilions and lodges in the Garden were composed by Pao-yu. If you find one or two of the buildings not too tame, please condescend to re-name them yourself, that would make us extremely happy."

The news that Pao-yu was already able to compose inscriptions made her exclaim with delight, "So he's making progress!"

When Chia Cheng had withdrawn, the Imperial Consort observed that Pao-chai and Tai-yu stood out from their girl cousins, being truly fairer than flowers or finest jade. Then she inquired why Pao-yu had not come to greet her. The Lady Dowager explained that, unless specially summoned, as a young man without official rank he dared not presume.

At once the Imperial Consort sent for him and a young eunuch ushered him in to pay homage according to Palace etiquette. His sister called him to her and took his hand. Drawing him close to her bosom, she stroked his neck and commented with a smile, "How you have grown!" But even as she spoke her tears fell like rain.

Madam Yu and Hsi-feng stepped forward then to announce, "The banquet is ready. We beg Your Highness to favour us with your presence." Then she rose and told Pao-yu to lead the way.

Accompanied by all the rest she walked into the Garden, where the magnificent sights were lit up by lanterns. Past "Where the Phoenix Alights," "Crimson Fragrance and Green Jade," "Approach to Apricot Tavern" and "Pure Scent of Alpinia and Iris" they strolled, mounting pavilions, crossing streams, climbing miniature hills and enjoying the view from various different points. All the buildings were distinctively furnished, and each corner had such fresh, unusual features that Yuan-chun was lavish with her praise and approval. But she cautioned them:

"You mustn't be so extravagant in future. This is far too much!"

When they reached the main reception palace she desired them to dispense with ceremony and take their seats. It was a sumptuous banquet. The Lady Dowager and the rest sat at tables on either side, while Madam Yu, Li Wan and Hsi-feng passed round dishes and poured the wine. Meanwhile Yuan-chun asked for writing-brush and inkstone and with her own hand wrote names for the spots she liked best. For the main reception palace she wrote the inscription: Recalling Imperial Favour, Mindful of Duty. And the couplet:

> Compassion vast as the universe extends to old and young,
> Grace unknown before honours every state and land.

The pleasure grounds were named the Grand View Garden.
"Where the Phoenix Alights" was renamed "Bamboo
Lodge," "Crimson Fragrance and Green Jade" was changed
to "Happy Red and Delightful Green" and also called Happy
Red Court. The name "Pure Scent of Alpinia and Iris" was
altered to "Alpinia Park," the "Approach to Apricot Tavern"
became "Hemp Washing Cottage." The main pavilion became
"Grand View Pavilion," its eastern wing "Variegated Splendour Tower," that on the west "Fragrant Tower." Other
names given were "Smartweed Breeze Cot," "Lotus Fragrance
Anchorage," "Purple Caltrop Isle" and "Watercress Isle."
She composed a dozen or so other inscriptions too such as
"Pear Blossom in Spring Rain," "Plane Trees in Autumn Wind"
and "Artemisia in Evening Snow." The rest of the inscriptions
cannot all be recorded here. The other former inscriptions at
her order remained unaltered.

Then the Imperial Consort wrote this verse:

> Enfolding hills and streams laid out with skill —
> What labour went to build this pleasure ground!
> For these, the finest sights of earth and heaven,
> No fitter name than "Grand View" can be found.

With a smile she showed this to the girls and said, "I have
never had a ready wit or any skill in versifying, as all of you
know, but tonight I had to try my hand at a verse in honour
of these pleasure grounds. Some day when I have more time,
I promise to write a *Description of Grand View Garden* and
a panegyric called *The Family Reunion* to commemorate this
occasion.

"Now I want each of you to write an inscription and a
poem to go with it. Do your best, and don't feel restricted by
my lame attempt. It was such a delightful surprise to me to
find that Pao-yu can compose inscriptions and poems. The
Bamboo Lodge and Alpinia Park are the places I like best, and
after them Happy Red Court and Hemp-Washing Cottage. We
must have four poems specially written for these. Although

Pao-yu's couplets composed earlier are charming, I want him now in my presence to write four *lu-shih*[1] in five-character lines on each of these places. That will repay the efforts I made to teach him when he was a little boy."

Pao-yu had to agree and went off to rack his brains.

Of Ying-chun, Tan-chun and Hsi-chun, Tan-chun was the cleverest, but she realized that she was no match for Pao-chai and Tai-yu. Still she had to write something, as the others were doing. Li Wan, too, contrived to compose a verse of sorts.

The Imperial Consort looked first at the girls' attempts. Here is what they had written:

REFRESHING THE HEART

Landscapes strange and rare here we find:
Bashfully, at the word of command, I take up my pen;
Who dreamed of such loveliness in the world of men?
A stroll through these grounds refreshes heart and
    mind.

Ying-chun

ALL THINGS VIE IN SPLENDOUR

This garden laid out with consummate art —
I blush, with my poor skill, its fame to render.
Past telling are the marvels in this place
For here, indeed, all things compete in splendour.

Tan-chun

REFINEMENT IN CREATION

This landscape stretches to infinity,
Its high pavilions soaring to the sky;
Laid out in radiance of the moon and sun,
Nature itself is by these scenes outdone.

Hsi-chun

FAIR AND FINE

Bright hills and crystal water intertwine,
No fairy isle is half as fair or fine.
Green fans of singers mid sweet herbs are lost,
Plum-petals by red skirts of dancers tossed.
Rare verses should record this golden hour —
Our joy at the nymph's descent from jasper tower.

---

[1] A kind of poem consisting of eight lines with five or seven characters in each line.

Once she has visited these lovely grounds
No mortal foot may overstep their bounds.

Li Wan

CONCENTRATED SPLENDOUR,
BESTOWED FELICITY

West of the Palace in this pleasure ground
Sunlight, auspicious clouds, rare sights abound;
High willows orioles from the vale invite,
Tall bamboos tempt the phoenix to alight.
This night's royal tour gives rise to poetry,
Her visit fosters filial piety.
Such wisdom flows from her immortal brush,
Too awed to pen more lines I can but blush.

Hsueh Pao-chai

A FAIRYLAND FAR FROM THE WORLD OF MEN

Who knows where this illustrious garden lies?
Far from the dusty world this paradise.
Here streams and mountains lend their fair delight
Enhanced by many a novel scene and sight.
Scents heady as the wine from Golden Dell[1]
Bind all in these jade halls with flowery spell;
Blessed by Imperial favour, we would fain
Welcome the royal visitant again.

Lin Tai-yu

Yuan-chun praised all these verses, then remarked with a smile, "Cousin Pao-chai's and Cousin Tai-yu's are specially good. We others are no match for them."

Now Tai-yu had intended to outshine them all that night by a great display of her brilliance; but when the Imperial Consort asked them each for merely one inscription and one poem, she knew it would be presumptuous to write more and simply dashed off a verse for the occasion.

Meanwhile Pao-yu was far from finished with his verses. Having written on Bamboo Lodge and Alpinia Park, he was now tackling Happy Red Court. His draft contained the line:

The green jade leaves in spring are yet furled tight.

Pao-chai, glancing at it while no one else was looking, nudged him surreptitiously.

---

[1] A celebrated garden in Honan owned by Shih Chung (249-300).

"She didn't like 'Red Fragrance and Green Jade,'" she whispered. "That's why she changed it to 'Happy Red and Delightful Green.' If you use 'green jade' again, won't that look as if you're challenging her judgement? Besides, there are plenty of allusions to plantain leaves you could use. Better find another phrase."

Pao-yu mopped his perspiring forehead. "I can't for the moment think of *any*," he said.

Pao-chai smiled. "Just change 'green jade' into 'green wax.'"

"Is there such an allusion?"

With a mocking smile and a smack of the lips she nodded. "If you're in such a state tonight, by the time you sit for the Palace Examination I dare say you'll even forget the first primer you ever read. Have you forgotten the opening line of that poem on the plantain by the Tang poet Chien Yi, 'Smokeless the cold candles, the green wax is dry'?"

Pao-yu felt as if a veil had been lifted from his eyes. "How stupid of me!" he chuckled. "Fancy forgetting a ready-made phrase like that. You're really my 'one-word-teacher.' From now on I shall have to address you as 'master,' not as 'sister' any more."

Suppressing a smile Pao-chai replied, "Hurry up and finish instead of talking such nonsense. Who are you calling 'sister'? That's your sister sitting up there in the golden robes. Why call *me* your sister?" Afraid to delay him by chatting, she slipped away.

Pao-yu persevered until three poems were done and Tai-yu, depressed at having no chance to shine, came up to his desk where he was struggling alone, meaning to help him out by writing a couple of poems for him.

Asked if he had finished, Pao-yu said, "I've only done three. All left now is *Approach to Apricot Tavern*."

"Well then, let me do that for you, while you copy out the other three."

After thinking for a moment with lowered head, she scribbled the poem out on a slip of paper, screwed it into a ball and tossed it to Pao-yu. When he smoothed it out he found it ten times better than his own attempts. He was overjoyed. Having hurriedly copied it out with care he presented all four poems to Yuan-chun.

This is what she read:

WHERE THE PHOENIX ALIGHTS

The fruit fresh formed on jade stalks rare
Makes for the phoenix fitting fare;
So green each stem they seem to drip
With coolness seeping from each verdant tip.
Bursting through stones, they change the water's
    track;
Piercing through screens, hold tripod's incense back;
Let none disturb these chequered shades,
That sweetly she may dream till daylight fades.

PURE SCENT OF ALPINIA AND IRIS

Alpinia fills the courtyard free from dust,
By climbing fig its fragrance reinforced;
Softly they heighten the fresh green of spring,
Gently they trail their perfume, ring on ring.
A light mist hides the winding path from view,
From covered walks drips chill and verdant dew.
But who will celebrate the pool in song?
Lost in a dream, at peace, the poet sleeps long.

HAPPY RED AND DELIGHTFUL GREEN

In quiet court long days pass tranquilly;
A charming match, plantain and apple-tree;
The green wax leaves in spring are yet furled tight,
The blossom decked in red keeps watch at night;
With crimson sleeves one sweeps the balustrade,
One, misty green, is by the rocks arrayed.
Facing each other in the soft east wind
They surely bring their mistress peace of mind!

APPROACH TO APRICOT TAVERN

A grove of apricots, a tavern-sign,
And a hillside hamlet beyond:
Elms, mulberries, swallows on rafters,
And geese on the caltrop pond.
In the fields spring leeks are green;
All round, the paddy flowers scent the breeze;
None goes hungry in these good times,
Ploughman and weaver alike can take their ease.

Yuan-chun, delighted with these poems, exclaimed, "He has certainly made great progress!"

Having pointed out that the last poem was the best, she changed the name "Hemp-Washing Cottage" into "Paddy-Sweet Cottage." She then made Tan-chun copy out all eleven poems on ornamental paper, and a eunuch delivered them to Chia Cheng and the other men waiting outside, who praised them highly. Chia Cheng also presented a panegyric of his own composition entitled *The Visitation*.

Yuan-chun had junket, ham and other delicacies presented to Pao-yu and Chia Lan, who was too young to do more than pay his respects after his mother and uncles, for which reason he has not been previously mentioned.

Chia Huan had not yet recovered from an illness contracted over New Year and was still convalescing in his own apartments; this is why no mention has been made of him either.

All this time Chia Chiang was waiting impatiently down below with his twelve young actresses. But now a eunuch ran down to him, exclaiming, "They have finished their poems. Give me your programme, quick!"

Chia Chiang lost no time in handing him a programme with a brocade cover and a list of the stage names of the twelve players. Presently four pieces were chosen: "The Sumptuous Banquet,"[1] "The Double Seventh Festival,"[2] "Meeting the Immortals"[3] and "The Departure of the Soul."[4]

Chia Chiang put on the first item without delay. All his players sang bewitchingly and danced divinely; thus although this was merely a stage performance they conveyed genuine grief and joy.

No sooner had they finished than a eunuch appeared backstage with a golden tray of cakes and sweetmeats, and asked which of the actresses was Ling-kuan. Realizing that this was a present for her, Chia Chiang accepted it gladly and made her kowtow her thanks.

---

[1] From *A Handful of Snow* by the Ming playwright Li Yu.

[2] From *The Palace of Eternal Youth* by the early Ching playwright Hung Sheng.

[3] From *The Dream at Hantan* by the Ming playwright Tang Hsien-tsu.

[4] From *The Peony Pavilion* by Tang Hsien-tsu.

The eunuch announced, "The Imperial Consort says that Ling-kuan is superb. She is to play in two more pieces of her own choice."

Chia Chiang hastily agreed and suggested "A Visit to the Garden" and "The Dream."[1] But since neither formed part of her repertoire, Ling-kuan insisted on "The Pledge" and "The Quarrel"[2] instead. And Chia Chiang had to let her have her way.

The Imperial Consort was so enchanted that she gave special instructions that this girl must be well treated and carefully trained. She gave Ling-kuan an extra reward of two rolls of Imperial satin, two embroidered pouches, some gold and silver trinkets and various delicacies.

Then they left the banqueting hall to visit the places Yuan-chun had not yet seen, among them a Buddhist convent set among hills, where she washed her hands before going in to burn incense and worship Buddha. She chose as inscription for this convent the words, "Ship of Mercy on the Sea of Suffering." And here she gave additional gifts to the Buddhist nuns and Taoist priestesses.

Soon a eunuch knelt to report that the list of gifts was ready for her approval. She read it through, found it satisfactory, and gave orders that the presents should be distributed. This was done by the eunuchs.

The Lady Dowager received two ju-yi[3] sceptres, one of gold, the other of jade; a staff made of aloeswood; a chaplet of sandal-wood beads; four lengths of Imperial satin with designs signi-fying wealth, nobility and eternal youth; four lengths of silk with designs signifying good fortune and long life; ten bars of gold with designs signifying "May Your Wishes Come True," and ten silver bars with fish and other designs to symbolize felicity and abundance.

---

[1] Two more scenes from *The Peony Pavilion*.

[2] Scenes from *The Hairpin and the Bracelet* by a Ming playwright by the pseudonym of Master of the Moon Pavilion.

[3] Meaning "as you wish."

Lady Hsing and Lady Wang received the same gifts with the exception of the sceptres, staff and chaplet.

Chia Ching, Chia Sheh and Chia Cheng each received two new books of His Majesty's own composition, two cases of rare ink-sticks, four goblets, two of gold and two of silver, and lengths of satin identical with those described above.

Pao-chai, Tai-yu and the other girls each received one new book, a rare mirror and two pairs of gold and silver trinkets of a new design.

Pao-yu received the same.

Chia Lan received one gold and one silver necklet, a pair of gold and a pair of silver medallions.

To Madam Yu, Li Wan and Hsi-feng were given two gold and two silver medallions and four lengths of silk.

In addition, twenty-four lengths of satin and a hundred strings of newly minted cash were allotted to the women-servants and maids in attendance on the Lady Dowager, Lady Wang and the girls.

Chia Chen, Chia Lien, Chia Huan and Chia Jung each received one length of satin and a pair of gold medallions.

A hundred rolls of variegated satin, a thousand taels of gold and silver, with various delicacies and wine from the Palace were given to those in both mansions responsible for the construction and maintenance of the Garden, the furnishing and upkeep of the various houses in the Garden, the theatre management and the preparation of lanterns. Five hundred strings of newly minted cash were also given as largesse to the cooks, actresses and jugglers.

It was nearly three in the morning by the time all had expressed their thanks, and the eunuch in charge announced that it was time to leave. At once Yuan-chun's eyes filled with tears again, but forcing a smile she clasped the hands of her grandmother and mother and could not bring herself to let them go.

"Don't worry about me," she begged them. "Just take good care of yourselves. Thanks to the Emperor's kindness you can now come to the Palace once a month to see me, so we shall have many chances to meet again. There is no need to be upset.

If next year by Imperial grace I'm allowed another visit home, you must promise not to be so extravagant."

The Lady Dowager and other women were sobbing too bitterly to make any reply. But although Yuan-chun could hardly bear to leave, she could not disobey the Imperial regulations and had no alternative but to re-enter her palanquin which carried her away. The whole household did their best to console the Lady Dowager and Lady Wang as they helped them out of the Garden. But more of this in the next chapter.

CHAPTER 19

An Eloquent Maid Offers Earnest Advice
One Fine Night
A Sweet Girl Shows Deep Feeling
One Quiet Day

The day after her return to the Palace the Imperial Consort appeared before the Emperor to thank him for his kindness, and so pleased him with an account of her visit home that he sent rich gifts of satin, gold and silver from his privy store to Chia Cheng and other fathers of visiting ladies. But no more of this.

The inmates of the Jung and Ning Mansions were completely worn out after their recent exertions, and it took several days to remove and store away all the decorations and other movables from the Garden. The heaviest responsibility devolved upon Hsi-feng, who, unlike the others, had not a moment's respite; but she was always so eager to shine, so anxious to give no one a handle against her, that she strove to carry out her many tasks as if they were nothing. Pao-yu, on the other hand, was the one with the least to do and the most leisure.

One morning Hsi-jen's mother came and asked the Lady Dowager's permission to take her daughter home to tea and keep her until the evening. So Pao-yu was left to amuse himself with the other maids at dice or draughts. He was feeling rather bored when a girl announced that a message had come from Chia Chen inviting him over to the Ning Mansion to watch some operas and see their New Year lanterns. While Pao-yu was changing his clothes before setting out, a gift of sweetened junket arrived from the Imperial Consort. Remembering how Hsi-jen had enjoyed this delicacy the last time they had some, he asked them to keep it for her. Then, having taken his leave of the Lady Dowager, he went over to the other mansion.

He was rather taken aback to find them performing operas like *Master Ting Finds His Father, Huang Po-yang Deploys Ghosts in a Battle, Monkey Plays Havoc in Heaven* and *The Patriarch Chiang Kills Generals and Deifies Them*. In all these, especially the two last, gods, ghosts, monsters and ogres took the stage among waving pennants, temple processions, invocations to Buddha and offerings of incense, while the din of gonging, drumming and shouting carried to the street outside. The passers-by commented appreciatively that no other family but the Chias could afford to put on such a lively entertainment. Only Pao-yu, disgusted by such rowdy, showy proceedings, soon slipped away to amuse himself elsewhere.

First he went to the inner rooms to chat with Madam Yu and tease the maids and concubines there. And when he strolled out of the inner gate they did not see him off, assuming that he was going back to watch the performance. The menfolk — Chia Chen, Chia Lien, Hsueh Pan and the rest — were having such a good time gaming and drinking that they did not worry about his absence either, taking it for granted that he had gone inside. As for the servants who had come with him, the older ones, not expecting him to leave before dusk, sneaked off to gamble, drink New Year tea with relatives and friends or visit some brothel or tavern, intending to be back by dark. The younger ones, for their part, squeezed into the theatre to watch the fun.

When Pao-yu found himself alone he thought, "There's a marvellously lifelike painting of a beauty in the small study here. In all this excitement today she must be lonely. I'd better go and cheer her up." He made his way towards the study.

As he neared the window he heard a moaning inside which pulled him up with a start. Could the beauty in the picture have come to life? Screwing up his courage, he made a hole in the window-paper with his tongue and peeped through. No, the painted beauty had not come to life, but his page Ming-yen was holding down a girl and indulging in the game taught Pao-yu by the Goddess of Disenchantment.

"Heavens above!"

As Pao-yu charged into the room, the trembling lovers quickly broke apart. And when Ming-yen saw who it was, he fell on his knees to beg for mercy.

"A fine way to carry on in broad daylight!" cried Pao-yu. "Do you want Lord Chia Chen to kill you?" Meanwhile he was sizing up the maid, no beauty but a girl with a fair complexion and a certain charm. Red to the ears with shame, she hung her head in silence.

"Are you going to stand there all day?" He stamped his foot.

Coming to her senses, she dashed out like the wind. He rushed after her, shouting:

"Don't be afraid! I shan't tell anyone."

"Holy ancestors!" swore Ming-yen behind him. "Aren't you telling everyone now?"

"How old is that girl?"

"Sixteen or seventeen, I suppose, at most."

"If you didn't even ask her age that shows how little you care for her. She's wasted on you, poor thing. What's her name?"

"That's quite a story," replied Ming-yen with a guffaw. "It's really a case of truth being stranger than fiction. She says that just before she was born her mother dreamed that she had a length of brocade with coloured designs of the lucky swastika. So she called her daughter Swastika."

"That *is* strange," agreed Pao-yu, chuckling. "Her good fortune may be coming later on." He looked thoughtful.

Ming-yen asked, "Why aren't you watching those grand operas, Second Master?"

"I did watch for a while, then got so bored that I came out to wander around. That's how I discovered the two of you. Well, what shall we do now?"

"No one knows where we are." Ming-yen grinned and stepped closer. "If we slip out of town to amuse ourselves and come back later, they won't be any the wiser."

"That won't do," replied Pao-yu. "We might get kidnapped. Besides, if they did find out what a row there'd be! We'd better

go somewhere within easy distance so that it wouldn't take long to come back."

"Yes, but where? That's the question."

"Why not call on Hsi-jen? Let's see what she's up to at home."

"A fine idea. I'd forgotten her house." Ming-yen chuckled. "But what if they find out and give me a beating for leading you astray?"

"Leave it to me," said Pao-yu.

Then Ming-yen brought round his horse, and they left by the back gate.

Luckily, Hsi-jen's home was only a few hundred yards away, so that in no time at all they reached its gate. Ming-yen went in first to call her brother Hua Tzu-fang.

Mrs. Hua, having fetched Hsi-jen home, was enjoying tea and sweetmeats with her daughter and a few nieces when they heard shouts of "Brother Hua!" And Hua Tzu-fang was considerably taken aback when he hurried out and found master and servant there. Helping Pao-yu to alight, he called out from the yard:

"Here's the young master!"

This came as a greater surprise to Hsi-jen than to any of the rest. Running out to meet Pao-yu she caught his arm and asked, "How did you come here?"

"I was rather bored," he told her with a laugh. "I just came to see what you're doing."

Reassured, she gave a cry of exasperation. "So you're up to mischief again. Why should you come *here*?" She turned to Ming-yen. "Who else is with you?"

"No-one." Ming-yen grinned. "Nobody knows we're here."

This worried Hsi-jen again and she protested, "You're quite impossible. What if you ran into someone? What if Lord Cheng saw you? The streets are jammed with people and carriages, and if your horse bolted you could quite easily have an accident. This is no joke. You two really have a nerve. You're the one to blame, Ming-yen, and when I get back I shall tell the nurses to give you a good hiding."

Ming-yen pulled a face. "Why shove the blame on to me? The young master cursed me and beat me to make me bring him. I told him not to come. Well, we'd better go back."

"Never mind," interposed Tzu-fang quickly. "Since you're here, there's no point in complaining. It's just that our shabby place is so cramped and dirty, we don't know where to ask the young master to sit."

By now Hsi-jen's mother had come out to greet him too, and Hsi-jen led Pao-yu in. He saw four or five girls inside, who lowered their heads and blushed at his entry. Afraid that the young gentleman might feel cold, Tzu-fang and his mother made him sit on the *kang* and hastily set out fresh sweetmeats and brewed some choice tea.

"You're just wasting your time. I know him." Hsi-jen smiled. "It's no use putting out those sweetmeats. He can't eat just anything."

She fetched her own cushion and plumped it on the *kang* for Pao-yu to sit on, then put her own foot-stove under his feet. Next she took two slabs of perfumed incense shaped like plum-blossom from her pouch, slipped them into her hand-stove, put its lid on again and placed it in Pao-yu's lap. This done, she poured him some tea in her own cup.

Meanwhile her mother and brother had carefully set out a whole table of titbits — none of them things he could eat, as Hsi-jen well knew.

"Since you've come, you mustn't go away without tasting something," she said gaily. "At least try something to show you've been to our house." She picked up a few pine kernels, blew off the skins, and gave them to Pao-yu on a handkerchief.

He noticed that her eyes were red and there were traces of tears on her powdered cheeks. "Why have you been crying?" he whispered.

"Who's been crying?" she retorted cheerfully. "I've just been rubbing my eyes." In this way she glossed the matter over.

Hsi-jen saw that Pao-yu was wearing his red archer's tunic embroidered with golden dragons and lined with fox-fur under a fringed bluish-grey sable coat. "Surely you didn't change into these new clothes just to come here?" she said. "Did no one ask where you were going?"

"No, I changed to go to Cousin Chen's to watch some operas.

She nodded. "Well, after a short rest you'd better go back. This is no place for you."

"I wish you'd come home now," coaxed Pao-yu. "I've kept something good for you."

"Hush!" she whispered. "What will the others think if they hear?" She reached out to take the magic jade from his neck and turning to her cousins said with a smile, "Look! Here's the wonderful thing that you've heard so much about. You've always wanted to see this rarity. Now's your chance for a really good look. There's nothing so very special about it, is there?"

After passing the jade around for their inspection she fastened it on Pao-yu's neck again, then asked her brother to hire a sedan-chair or a small carriage and escort Pao-yu home.

"I can see him back quite safely on horseback," said Tzu-fang.

"That's not the point. I'm afraid of his meeting someone."

Then Tzu-fang hurried out to hire a sedan-chair, and not daring to detain Pao-yu they saw him out. Hsi-jen gave Ming-yen some sweetmeats and money to buy firecrackers, warning him that he must keep this visit secret if he wanted to steer clear of trouble. She saw Pao-yu out of the gate, watched him get into the chair and lowered its curtains. Her brother and Ming-yen followed behind with the horse.

When they reached the street where the Ning Mansion stood, Ming-yen ordered the chair to stop and told Tzu-fang, "We must look in here for a while before going home, if we don't want people to suspect anything."

Since this made good sense, Tzu-fang handed Pao-yu out and helped him to mount his horse, while the boy apologized for troubling him. Then they slipped through the back gate, and there we will leave them.

During Pao-yu's absence, the maids in his apartments had amused themselves as they pleased at draughts, dice and cards, until the floor was strewn with melon-seed shells. Nanny Li chose this moment to hobble along with her cane to call on Pao-yu and see how he was. She shook her head over the way the maids were carrying on behind his back.

"Since I've moved out and don't come so often, you've grown quite out of hand," she scolded. "The other nurses don't dare take you to task either. As for Pao-yu, he's like a ten-foot lampstand that sheds light on others but none on itself. He complains that other people are dirty, yet leaves you to turn his own rooms topsyturvy. Disgraceful, I call it."

The maids knew quite well that Pao-yu would not mind, and since Nanny Li had retired and left the house she had no further authority over them. They went on amusing themselves and simply ignored her. Asked how much Pao-yu ate at each meal and what time he went to bed, they just answered at random.

"What an old pest she is!" one muttered.

"Is that a bowl of junket?" asked Nanny Li. "Why didn't you send it over to me? I'd better eat it here right now." She picked up a spoon and started eating it.

"You leave that alone!" cried one girl. "That's for Hsi-jen. He'll be annoyed when he comes back, and unless you own up you'll get all of us into trouble."

"I can't believe it of him." Nanny Li was both indignant and embarrassed. "What is this, after all, but a bowl of milk? He shouldn't begrudge me that — or more costly things either. Does he think more of Hsi-jen than of me? Has he forgotten who brought him up? It's my milk from my own heart's blood that he was raised on, so why should he be angry if I have a bowl of his milk? I declare I will, just to see what he'll do. You seem to think the world of Hsi-jen, but who is she? A low-class girl. I should know, I trained the creature." With that, in a huff, she finished off the junket.

"They've no manners," said another maid soothingly. "I don't wonder you're cross, granny. Pao-yu often sends you presents. This isn't going to upset him."

"You don't have to humour me in that sly way," Nanny Li snorted. "Do you think I don't know how Chien-hsueh was dismissed, all because of a cup of tea? I'll come back tomorrow to hear what my punishment's to be." She went off then in a temper.

Presently Pao-yu came home and sent someone to fetch Hsi-jen. He saw Ching-wen lying motionless on her bed.

"Is she ill?" he asked. "Or did she lose some game?"

"She was winning," Chiu-wen told him. "But then Grandame Li came along and raised such a rumpus that she lost the game. She went to bed to sulk."

"You mustn't take Nanny Li so seriously." Pao-yu smiled. "Just leave her alone."

He turned then to welcome Hsi-jen who had only just come in. After asking where he had dined and what time he had reached home, she gave the girls greetings from her mother and cousins. When she had changed out of her visiting clothes, Pao-yu called for the junket.

"Granny Li ate the lot," his maids reported.

Before he could make any comment Hsi-jen interposed with a smile, "So that's what you kept for me — thank you. The other day I enjoyed it, but it gave me a bad stomachache afterwards until I'd brought it all up. So it's just as well she's had it. Otherwise it would have been wasted. What I'd fancy now are some dried chestnuts. Will you peel a few for me while I make your bed?"

Taking this for the truth, Pao-yu thought no more of the matter but started peeling chestnuts by the lamp. And since the others had left he asked with a smile, "Who was that girl in red this afternoon?"

"My mother's sister's child."

Pao-yu heaved a couple of admiring sighs.

"Why are you sighing?" asked Hsi-jen. "I know how your mind works. You think she isn't good enough to wear red."

"What an idea! If a girl like that isn't good enough to wear red, who is? I found her so charming, I thought how nice it would be if we could get her here to live with us."

"Nice, you call it?" Hsi-jen snorted. "Nice to be a slave here?"

"Don't be so touchy," he retorted with a smile. "Living in our house doesn't have to mean being a slave. Couldn't she be our relative?"

"We're too far beneath you for that."

When Pao-yu went on peeling the chestnuts in silence, Hsi-jen laughed. "Why don't you say anything? Have I offended you? All right, tomorrow you can buy her for a few taels of silver."

"How do you expect anyone to answer you?" Pao-yu grinned. "All I meant was that she looks just the person to live in a mansion like this, much more so than some of us clods who were born here."

"She may not have your luck but she's her parents' darling, the apple of their eye. She's just turned seventeen and all her dowry is ready. She'll be married next year."

The word "married" made Pao-yu exclaim in dismay and feel put out.

Hsi-jen observed with a sigh, "These last few years, since I came here, I haven't seen much of my cousins. Soon I'll be going home, but they'll all be gone."

Shocked by the implication of this, he dropped the chestnuts.

"What do you mean — going home?"

"Today I heard my mother discussing it with my. brother. They told me to be patient for one more year and then they'd buy me out of service."

"Why should they do that?" Pao-yu was flabbergasted.

"What a strange question! I wasn't born a slave in your family. I have my own people outside. What future is there for me if I stay on here alone?"

"Suppose I won't let you go?"

"That wouldn't be right. Why, even in the Palace they make it a rule to choose new girls every few years. They can't keep them for ever either, so how can you?"

He decided upon reflection that she was right. None the less he objected, 'Suppose, though, the old lady won't let you go?"

"Why shouldn't she? If I were somebody special or had so won the hearts of the old lady and Lady Wang that they couldn't do without me, they might give my people a few extra taels so as to keep me. But I'm no one out of the usual: there are plenty much better than me. When I came here as a child I was with the old lady; then I waited on Miss Shih for a couple of years, and now I've been waiting on you for quite a time. If my people come to redeem me, your family is bound to let me go. They may even be generous enough not to ask for any money. If you say I look after you well, there's no merit in that — it's my job. And my place will be taken by someone else just as good. I'm not indispensable."

By now it did indeed sound to Pao-yu as if she had every reason to leave and none at all to stay. Yet in desperation he argued, "Well, but if I insist the old lady will speak to your mother and pay her so much that she won't like to take you away."

"Of course my mother wouldn't dare refuse. Even if you didn't talk nicely to her or pay her a cent, so long as you insisted on my staying how could she stand out? But your family has never thrown its weight about like that in the past. This isn't like offering ten times the usual price for something you happen to like, when the owner finds it worth his while to sell. If you kept me for no reason, it would do you no good and would break up my family. The old lady and Lady Wang wouldn't dream of such a thing."

Pao-yu remained sunk in thought for several minutes.

"So this means you'll be going for certain?"

"Yes."

"How can she be so heartless?" he wondered,

Aloud, he said with a sigh, "If I'd known that you'd be going, I shouldn't have taken you on in the first place. I shall be left all alone here, a poor forsaken ghost." And he retired sulkily to bed.

Now it so happened that when Hsi-jen went home and heard her mother and brother talk of buying her out, she had assured them that Pao-yu would never let her go so long as he lived.

"When you had nothing to eat and your only way of raising a little money was by selling me, I couldn't stop you," she said. "What girl can see her parents starve to death? I was lucky to be sold to this family, where I'm fed and clothed like a daughter of the house, not beaten all day long and scolded all night. Besides, even though father's dead, you've got the family back on its feet and are as well-off again as you ever were. If you were still hard up, there might be some reason for re-deeming me and re-selling me at a profit. But since there's no need, why do it? Just pretend I'm dead and stop thinking of buying me back."

She wept and stormed until her mother and brother realized that she was adamant and would never leave. In any case she had been sold for life and although they thought the Chia family might be generous enough to let her go without asking for any money, they also knew that the servants there were not ill-used but shown more kindness than severity. Indeed, the girls who were personal attendants of members of the family, old or young, were generally treated more handsomely than servants in other jobs. In fact, they were even better off than daughters of ordinary humble households. So Mrs. Hua and her son did not press the point.

Pao-yu's unexpected visit and the apparent intimacy between maid and master opened their eyes to the true situation, leaving them much reassured. In fact, this was something they had not even hoped for. So they abandoned all thought of buying her freedom.

As for Hsi-jen, these years had shown her that Pao-yu was no ordinary youth but more high-spirited and wilful than other boys, with some indescribably perverse streaks in his character. Of late he had been so indulged by his grandmother that his parents were unable to control him strictly and he had now become so reckless and headstrong that he was losing patience with all conventions. She had long wanted to speak to him about this, but was convinced he would not listen to her.

Luckily, by throwing dust in his eyes today, she was able to sound him out and get him into a chastened mood for a good lecture. His silent retreat to bed indicated how upset he was and how wounded.

As for the chestnuts, she had pretended to hanker after them to make him forget the junket, for fear of a repetition of that incident involving maple-dew tea which had landed Chien-hsueh in trouble.

Now she gave the chestnuts to the other maids and, coming back, nudged Pao-yu gently. She found his face wet with tears.

"Why take on like this?" she coaxed. "If you really want me here, of course I won't go."

Sensing something behind this, Pao-yu quickly rejoined, "Go on. Just tell me what else I must do to keep you. *I* don't know how to persuade you."

"We needn't talk now of how well we get on together. If you want to keep me that's beside the point. I've two or three things to ask you. If you agree to them, I'll take it that you really and truly want me to stay. Then not even a knife at my throat could make me leave you."

Pao-yu's face lit up. "Well, what are your conditions? I agree to them all, dear sister, good kind sister. I'd agree to three hundred conditions, let alone three. I only beseech you all to stay and watch over me until the day that I turn into floating ashes — no, not ashes. Ashes have a trace of form and consciousness. Stay until I've turned into a puff of smoke and been scattered by the wind. Then you'll no longer be able to watch over me, and I shall no longer be able to care about you — you can let me go, and I'll have to let you go wherever you please as well."

"Steady on!" Hsi-jen frantically clapped her hand over his mouth. "This is just what I wanted to warn you against, yet here you go, talking more wildly than ever."

"All right," agreed Pao-yu promptly. "I promise not to."

"This is the first fault you must correct."

"Done. If I ever talk that way again, you can pinch my lips. What else?"

"The second thing is this. Whether you like studying or not, in front of the old master and other people stop running it down and making sarcastic remarks about it. At least pretend to like studying, so as not to provoke your father and give him a chance to speak well of you to his friends. After all, he thinks: The men of our family have been scholars for generations, but this son of mine has let me down — he doesn't care for books. As if this wasn't bad enough, you keep saying crazy things in public as well as in private, sneering at those who study hard so as to get on and calling them career-grubbers. You also say that, apart from that classic on 'manifesting bright virtue,'[1] all the rest are trash produced by fools of old who didn't understand the Sage. No wonder your father gets so angry with you that he keeps punishing you. What sort of impression does that make on people?"

"All right." Pao-yu laughed. "That was just wild talk when I was too young to know any better. I don't say such things nowadays. What else?"

"You must stop abusing Buddhist monks and Taoist priests and playing about with girls' cosmetics and powder. Most important of all, you must stop kissing the rouge on girls' lips and running after everything in red."

"I promise, I promise. What else is there? Tell me, quick!"

"That's all. Just be a bit more careful about things in general instead of getting carried away by all your whims and fancies. If you'll do all I've asked, I promise never to leave you, not

---

[1] The Confucian classic *The Great Learning* says: "The way to great learning is manifesting bright virtue."

even if they send a big sedan-chair with eight bearers to fetch me away."

Pao-yu chuckled. "If you stay here long enough, you'll have your sedan-chair and eight bearers some day."

"I don't covet such luck." She smiled disdainfully. "If I'm not entitled to it what's the good of riding on one?"

At this point Chiu-wen appeared and said, "It's nearly the third watch: time you were in bed. Just now the old lady sent round a nurse to ask, and I told her you were asleep."

Pao-yu asked her to hand him a watch and saw it was twelve o'clock. He washed and rinsed his mouth all over again, then undressed and lay down to sleep.

When Hsi-jen got up first thing the next morning she felt heavy and out of sorts. Her head ached, her eyes were swollen, her limbs were burning like fire. She tried to carry on as usual at first but soon had to give up and lie down, fully dressed, on the *kang*. Pao-yu at once informed the Lady Dowager, and a doctor was sent to examine her.

"It's nothing but a cold," said the doctor. "She will be all right after a couple of doses of medicine to relieve the congestion."

The doctor left after making out the prescription. The medicine was brought and decocted, and Hsi-jen drank it. Pao-yu left her well covered so as to induce perspiration and went off to see Tai-yu.

Tai-yu was having a siesta, and since all her maids had gone out on their own business the place was unusually quiet. Pao-yu raised the embroidered curtain and walked into the inner room, where he found her sleeping.

"Dear cousin!" he called, shaking her gently. "How can you sleep just after a meal?"

When Tai-yu woke and saw who it was, she said, "Why don't you go for a stroll? I haven't recovered yet from all that excitement the other night. I'm still aching from head to foot."

"A few aches are nothing, but if you go on sleeping you'll really fall ill. Let me amuse you to keep you awake and then you'll be all right."

"I'm not sleepy." She closed her eyes. "All I want is a little rest. Run away and play for a while. You can come back later."

"Where can I go?" He nudged her again. "I find everyone else so boring."

Tai-yu could not suppress a laugh. "All right, if stay you must, go and sit down properly over there and we'll talk."

"I want to curl up too." Seeing that there was no extra pillow, he added, "Why don't we share that pillow of yours?"

"What nonsense! Aren't there pillows in the outer room? Just help yourself to one."

Pao-yu went out to have a look, coming back to say, "I don't want any of them. Who knows what dirty old woman has been using them?"

Tai-yu opened her eyes at this and sat up, laughing.

"You really are the bane of my life! All right, have this." She pushed her pillow towards him and fetched herself another. Then they lay down facing each other. Observing on his left cheek a bloodstain the size of a button, she leaned over to look at it carefully and laid one finger on it.

"Whose nails was it this time?"

Pao-yu drew back, grinning. "That's not a scratch. I may have splashed myself with the lip-salve I've just been mixing for the girls."

As he searched for a handkerchief, Tai-yu rubbed the place clean with her own, scolding as she did so, "Isn't that just like you? And you have to leave traces too. Even if uncle doesn't see it, that's the sort of thing people love to gossip about and some may tell on you in order to win favour; and if such stories reach his ears it'll mean trouble for all of us."

Pao-yu was not listening, however, so intent was he on the fragrance emanating from Tai-yu's sleeve, which he found intoxicating — it seemed to melt the marrow of his bones. He caught hold of her sleeve to see what she had hidden inside.

"Who wears anything fragrant in mid-winter?" she asked.

"Where does that scent come from then?"

"How do I know? Unless it's some fragrance from my wardrobe that's clung to my gown."

Pao-yu shook his head. "I doubt it. It's a very unusual scent. Not the kind you would get from perfumed pastilles, scent-balls or sachets."

"Do I have a Buddhist arhat to give me scent?" demanded Tai-yu archly. "Even if I had some rare recipe, I've no kind cousin or brother to concoct it for me with stamens, buds, dew and snow. All I have are common scents."

"Whenever I say one word, off you go!" Pao-yu grinned. "I shall have to teach you a lesson. From now on, I'll show you no mercy."

He rose to his knees, blew on his hands, then stretched them out and started tickling her in the ribs and under her armpits.

Tai-yu had always been ticklish, and this surprise attack set her giggling so much that she very nearly choked.

"Stop it, Pao-yu," she gasped. "Stop, or I'll be angry."

He desisted then, demanding with a smile, "Will you talk that way any more?"

"I dare not." Smoothing her hair she laughed. "You say I've an unusual scent, have you a *warm* scent?"

"A warm scent?" He looked puzzled.

Tai-yu shook her head with a sigh. "How dense you are! You have jade, and someone else has gold to match it. So don't you have a warm scent to match her cold scent?"

Pao-yu caught her meaning then and chuckled. "You were begging for mercy a minute ago, but now you're worse than ever." He reached out again.

"Dear cousin, I promise not to tease," she cried hastily.

"All right, I'll forgive you if you let me smell your sleeve."

With that he covered his face with her sleeve and started sniffing as if he would never stop. She pulled away her arm.

"You ought to go now."

"Go I can't. Let's lie down in a civilized way and chat."

He stretched out again while Tai-yu lay down too, covering her face with her handkerchief and paying no attention to his rambling questions. How old had she been when she came to the capital? What fine sights and monuments had she seen on the way? What places of historical interest were there in Yangchow? What were the local customs and traditions? Tai-yu made no reply, and to keep her awake — for he feared sleep might give her indigestion — Pao-yu played a new trick.

"Aiya!" he exclaimed. "Do you know the extraordinary thing that happened near your yamen in Yangchow?"

Taken in by his straight face and earnest manner, Tai-yu asked to hear about it. Then Pao-yu, suppressing a laugh, started romancing.

"In Yangchow there's a hill called Mount Tai, in the side of which is a cavern called Lin Cavern."

"You're making this up," cried Tai-yu. "I've never heard of such a hill."

"Do you know all the hills and streams in the world? Let me finish my story before you pull it to pieces."

"Go on, then."

Pao-yu went on, "In Lin Cavern lived a number of rat spirits. One year on the seventh day of the twelfth moon, the Rat Patriarch ascended his throne to hold a council. He announced, 'Tomorrow is the Feast of Winter Gruel when all men on earth will be cooking their sweet gruel. Here in our cave we have few fruits or nuts; we must go foraging.' He handed an arrow of command to an able young rat and ordered him to go out and reconnoitre.

"Soon the young rat returned to report, 'I have made a thorough search and inquired far and wide. The best store of grain and dried fruits is to be found in the temple at the foot of this hill.'

" 'How many kinds of grain? How many sorts of dried fruits?'

" 'A whole granary full of rice and beans past counting, and five kinds of dried fruits: dates, chestnuts, peanuts, caltrops and sweet taros.'

"Delighted by this information, the Patriarch promptly detailed rats to go forth. Taking up an arrow of command he asked:

" 'Who will steal rice?'

"One rat took the arrow and went off.

" 'Who will steal beans?' the Patriarch asked, picking up another arrow.

"Another rat accepted the mission.

"One by one they went off until finally there were only sweet taros left to be stolen.

"The Patriarch, holding an arrow, asked, 'Who will go and steal sweet taros?'

"A very small, puny mouse volunteered, 'I'll go!'

"Seeing how small and weak she was, the Patriarch and the rest of the tribe would not hear of her going, for fear she proved unequal to the task.

"But the little mouse insisted, 'Young and weak as I am, I have wonderful magic powers and great eloquence and cunning. I swear to manage better than all the rest.'

"Asked to explain how, she said, 'I shan't steal outright like them, but change myself into a sweet taro and mix in a pile of others to escape detection. Then I shall spirit the taros away one by one, until there are none left. Wouldn't that be more effective than stealing outright?'

" 'It certainly sounds it,' replied the other rats. 'But how do you manage the metamorphosis? Do show us.'

" 'That's easy.' The little mouse laughed. 'Just watch.' She shook herself and changed into a lovely girl with a most bewitching face.

"The other rats laughed. 'You've made a mistake,' they cried. 'You've changed into a young lady, not a sweet taro.'

" 'You ignorant lot!' retorted the little mouse, resuming her original form. 'You only know what sweet taros are, but don't know that the daughter of Salt Commissioner Lin is sweeter than any taro.' "[1]

---

[1] This is an untranslatable pun. The *yu* in Tai-yu's name has the same sound as *yu* meaning "taro."

Tai-yu scrambled over and pinned Pao-yu down. "You scoundrel!" she cried laughing. "I knew you were making fun of me."

She pinched Pao-yu until he begged for mecry. "Dear cousin, let me off. I won't do it again," he pleaded. "It was smelling that sweet scent of yours that reminded me of this allusion."

"You make fun of me and dare pretend it's an allusion. . . ."

Just then in walked Pao-chai with a radiant face. "Who's talking about allusions?" she asked. "I must hear this."

Tai-yu hastily offered her a seat. "Can't you see?" She laughed. "He mocks me, then pretends it's an allusion."

"Cousin Pao, is it? No wonder." Pao-chai smiled. "He knows so many allusions. The only trouble is that he forgets them just when he needs them most. If his memory is so good today, why didn't he remember that allusion about the plantain the other night? He actually forgot the most obvious one. Everyone else was freezing, but he was so frantic that he was perspiring. So now his memory has come back again."

"Amida Buddha!" cried Tai-yu laughing outright. "She's my good sister after all. You've met your match now. This just shows that no one can escape retribution."

At that moment the sound of squabbling and angry shouting broke out in Pao-yu's apartments. What it was will be disclosed in the next chapter.

CHAPTER 20

Hsi-feng Reproves a Jealous Woman
Tai-yu Mocks a Prattling Girl

Pao-yu, as we saw, was in Tai-yu's room telling her the story about the rat spirits when Pao-chai burst in and teased him for forgetting the "green wax" allusion on the night of the Feast of Lanterns. Pao-yu felt relieved as they laughed and made fun of each other, for he had feared that sleeping after lunch might give Tai-yu indigestion or insomnia that night, and so injure her health. Luckily Pao-chai's arrival and the lively conversation that followed it had woken Tai-yu up.

Just then, a commotion broke out in Pao-yu's apartments and the three of them pricked up their ears.

"It's your nanny scolding Hsi-jen," announced Tai-yu. "There's nothing wrong with Hsi-jen, yet your nanny is for ever nagging at her. Old age has befuddled her."

Pao-yu wanted to rush straight over, but Pao-chai laid a restraining hand on his arm. "Don't quarrel with your nurse now," she warned him. "She's a silly old thing, but you should bear with her."

"I know," said Pao-yu, and dashed off.

Back in his apartments he found Nanny Li leaning on her cane in the middle of his room and roundly abusing Hsi-jen.

"Ungrateful slut!" she scolded. "You owe your position to me, yet there you lie giving yourself such airs on the *kang,* and won't even look at me when I come in. All you think about is making up to Pao-yu, so that he pays no attention to *me* but does everything *you* say. A slave girl bought for a few taels of stinking silver, you've turned everything here topsyturvy. If you don't behave, you'll be dragged out and married off. We'll see whether you can still bewitch Pao-yu then."

Imagining that Nanny Li was angry with her for lying in bed, Hsi-jen at first explained, "I'm ill and just starting to perspire, so I'd covered up my head and didn't see you, granny."

But when the old woman accused her of vamping Pao-yu and threatened to have her married off, the injustice of these taunts reduced her to tears.

Pao-yu overheard this tirade, but there was not much he could do except explain that Hsi-jen was unwell and had just taken medicine.

"If you don't believe me," he added, "ask any of the maids."

This only added fuel to the fire.

"That's right. Stick up for those vixens of yours. Who am I, after all?" his nurse stormed. "Which of them am I supposed to ask? They'll all take your side. They're all under Hsi-jen's thumb. I know everything that goes on here. I'm going to have this out with you in the presence of the old lady and Lady Wang. I suckled you, I raised you; but now that you don't need my milk any more, you push me aside and let your maids insult me." She was weeping with rage.

By this time Tai-yu and Pao-chai had come over too and they set to work to soothe her.

"Make some allowances for them, nanny," they urged. "Let it blow over."

The old woman seized on them to pour out her complaints: Chien-hsueh's dismissal for drinking a cup of tea, and the business of the junket the previous day.... It was hard to make head or tail of her maundering.

Hsi-feng happened just then to be in the Lady Dowager's apartments totting up the scores after a game. When she heard angry voices she knew that Nanny Li was on the rampage again, working off on Pao-yu's maids her annoyance over her gambling losses today. She hurried across and pulled the nurse aside.

"Don't be angry, nanny dear," she said with a smile. "It's just after the festival and the old lady's had a happy day. At your age you ought to stop other people from brawling. Don't forget yourself and start a rumpus here which may upset the old lady. Tell me who's been annoying you and I'll have her beaten for you. Now I've a broiled pheasant in my room, piping hot. Come along and have a drink with me, quick!"

With these words she tugged the nurse out, calling over her shoulder to her maid, "Feng-erh, bring Nanny Li's cane for her, and a handkerchief to dry her tears."

Unable to hold her ground Nanny Li was borne off, lamenting as she went, "I'm old enough to die and have done with it. But I'd sooner forget myself and lose face making a scene like this than put up with the insolence of that dirty bitch."

Pao-chai and Tai-yu in the background had been watching how Hsi-feng handled the situation. Now they laughed and clapped their hands.

"How lucky that this hurricane sprang up and carried the old creature off!"

Pao-yu nodded and sighed. "Goodness only knows how this started. She keeps picking on people who can't defend themselves. I suppose one of the other girls annoyed her yesterday, and she tried to settle scores like this. . . ."

The words were scarcely out of his mouth when Ching-wen gave a laugh.

"We're not off our heads," she said. "Why should we annoy her? And even if we had, we'd have taken the blame ourselves, not shift it to somebody else."

Hsi-jen caught hold of Pao-yu's hand and sobbed, "First you offend your old nurse because of me, and now because of me you're offending everyone here. Haven't I enough to put up with, without dragging them in as well?"

Because she was ill and upset Pao-yu had to be patient. He urged her to lie down again and perspire. She was burning with fever and stretching out beside her he tried to soothe her.

"Just think of your health. Don't upset yourself over such trifles."

Hsi-jen smiled bitterly.

"If I got upset easily, how could I stay a single minute in this room? But when it goes on like this day after day, what do you expect us to do? I'm always urging you to stop offending people on our account. You're just out to stick up for us on the spur of the moment, but *they* remember it, and the next chance they have at the very least they say something unpleasant. Think how difficult you make it for us all." She could not help crying as she spoke, but for fear of upsetting Pao-yu she fought back her tears.

Presently the odd-job woman brought in the second dose of medicine. Pao-yu would not let Hsi-jen get up since she seemed on the point of perspiring. Instead he carried the medicine to her and raised her on the pillow to drink it. Then he told some of the younger maids to prepare his *kang*.

"Whether you mean to eat there or not, you'd better go and sit with the old lady and Lady Wang for a while," suggested Hsi-jen. "Then keep the young ladies company for a bit before coming back. I shall be all right after a quiet nap here."

Hearing this, Pao-yu removed her hairpins and bracelets for her and settled her for the night before going to dine in the Lady Dowager's quarters.

After dinner his grandmother felt disposed to play cards with some of the old stewardesses. Pao-yu, still worried about Hsi-jen, went back to find her dozing. It was still early for him to go to bed, but Ching-wen, Yi-hsien, Chiu-wen and Pi-hen had gone off to have some fun with Yuan-yang and Hu-po, leaving only Sheh-yueh playing solitaire by the lamp in the outer room.

With a smile Pao-yu asked, "Why didn't you go with the others?"

"I haven't any money."

"There's a pile stacked under the bed. Isn't that enough for you to lose?"

"If we all went off to play, who'd mind this place, with her lying ill here too? There are lamps above and stoves below everywhere. Those old women deserve a rest after waiting on you all day, and the girls ought to have some fun too after a day's work. So I let them all go while I keep an eye on things here."

Why, she's another Hsi-jen, thought Pao-yu and smiled.

"I'll be here," he told her. "Don't worry. You can go."

"If you're here there's even less reason for me to go. Why don't we both sit here and talk?"

"Just the two of us sounds rather dull. What can we do? I know! You were saying this morning that your head felt itchy. Since we've nothing to do, let me comb your hair for you."

"If you like."

Sheh-yueh fetched her dressing-case and mirror, then pulled out her hairpins and let down her hair. Pao-yu had just started combing it with a fine comb when Ching-wen hurried in to fetch some money. She laughed mockingly at the sight of them.

"Fancy! You haven't yet drunk the bridal cup but already you're doing her hair."

Pao-yu grinned.

"Come, I'll comb yours too if you like."

"I'm not destined for such good fortune."

Ching-wen went off with the money, slamming the portière behind her.

Pao-yu was standing just behind Sheh-yueh, who was seated in front of the mirror. They exchanged glances in it and Pao-yu smiled.

"She's got the sharpest tongue of you all," he remarked.

Sheh-yueh wagged a warning finger, but it was too late. With another clack of the portière, Ching-wen ran in again.

"Just what did you mean by that? We must have this out."

"Run along!" Sheh-yueh giggled. "Why take it up?"

"You're covering up for him again. I know all your sly tricks. We must have this out after I've won back my money."

With that she went straight out.

When Pao-yu had finished combing Sheh-yueh's hair he asked her to help him quietly to bed without disturbing Hsi-jen.

The rest of the night passed without incident.

The next morning Hsi-jen was better, having perspired, and after taking some gruel she lay back to rest. After breakfast Pao-yu felt easy enough in his mind to go and call on Aunt Hsueh.

Because it was the first month when the schools were on holiday and needlework was taboo for the womenfolk, everyone was free. And Chia Huan, going there to play, had found Pao-chai, Hsiang-ling and Ying-erh enjoying a game of dice. He asked to join in.

Pao-chai, who always treated Chia Huan exactly like Pao-yu, made him sit down beside them. They were staking ten cash on each throw, and Chia Huan gloated when he won the first round; but then he lost several times running and started to fret.

The next time it came to his turn he stood to win if he threw more than six, while Ying-erh needed only three to win. Chia Huan shook the two dice from the pot as hard as he could. One turned up five, the other rolled over and over. Ying-erh clapped her hands and cried, "One!" while Chia Huan, his eyes glued to the dice, yelled at random, "Six, seven, eight!" Finally, however, the dice came to rest at one. In exasperation he snatched up both dice and grabbed the stakes, insisting that he had thrown six.

"Anyone could see it was one," protested Ying-erh.

Observing how upset Chia Huan was, Pao-chai shot her a reproving glance.

"You're getting above yourself," she said. "Is it likely that one of the young masters would cheat you? Hurry up and put down your stake."

The unfairness of this made Ying-erh fume, but she dared not answer back. As she slapped down some cash she muttered under her breath: "Fancy a young gentleman cheating! Even *I* wouldn't make such a fuss over a few cash. Last time we played with Pao-yu he lost a whole packet, yet *he* didn't mind. Even when the girls grabbed all he had left, he only laughed."

She would have gone on in this vein, but Pao-chai told her sharply to hold her tongue.

"How can I compare with Pao-yu?" whined Chia Huan. "You keep in with him because you're afraid of him, but you bully me because I'm a concubine's son." He started to snivel.

"Don't talk like that, dear cousin, or people will laugh at you," Pao-chai advised him.

She was scolding Ying-erh again when Pao-yu walked in and, seeing this state of affairs, asked them what had happened. Chia Huan lacked the courage to tell him.

Pao-chai knew the Chia family's rule: a younger brother must show respect to an elder. What she did not realize was that Pao-yu did not want anyone to be afraid of him. He reasoned: We all have our parents to train us. Why should I butt in and strain relations with the younger ones? As I'm the wife's son and he's a concubine's son, people will gossip even if I do nothing, much more so if I now try to control him.

He had an even more fantastic idea — do you know what it was, Reader? As a result of being brought up among girls — his sisters Yuan-chun and Tan-chun, his cousins Ying-chun and Hsi-chun of the Chia house, and his distaff-cousins Shih Hsiang-yun, Lin Tai-yu and Hsueh Pao-chai — he had come to the conclusion that while human beings were the highest form of creation, the finest essences of Nature were embodied in girls, men being nothing but the dregs and scum. To him, therefore, all men were filthy clods who might just as well not have existed. Only deference to Confucius, the greatest sage of all time who taught that fathers, uncles and brothers should be respected, made him keep on a fairly good footing with his brothers and boy cousins. It never entered his head that he as a man should set the younger boys a good example. This is why Chia Huan and the others were not afraid of him, only yielding to him to some extent for fear of the Lady Dowager.

To prevent Pao-yu from scolding Chia Huan, which would only have made matters worse, Pao-chai covered up for him as best she could.

"The first month is no time for snivelling," said Pao-yu. "If you don't like it here, find somewhere else to play. All that studying every day seems to have made you even more muddle-headed. Suppose you find one thing no good and another good, just drop the first and go for the second. Can you improve on something you dislike by sticking to it and crying over it? You came here to have a good time. Since you don't feel happy, go somewhere else to enjoy yourself. Why vex yourself so? Better take yourself off, quick."

Chia Huan went back to his mother, the concubine Chao.

At sight of his dejected face she asked, "Who's been treating you as a doormat this time?" When he did not answer, she repeated the question.

"I was playing with Cousin Pao-chai. Ying-erh was mean to me and cheated me. Then Brother Pao-yu turned me out."

His mother spat in disgust.

"Shameless little brat! Who told you to put yourself forward? Is there nowhere else for you to play? Why go looking for trouble?"

Hsi-feng, who was passing outside, overheard this exchange and called back through the window:

"What's this rumpus in the middle of the first month? Huan's only a child. If he makes some small mistake you can set him right. Why carry on at him like that? No matter where he goes, the master and Her Ladyship are there to keep him in order. Imagine spitting at him! He's one of the young masters, and if he does misbehave there are people to correct him — what business is it of yours? Come on, Brother Huan, come out and play with me."

Chia Huan stood in even greater awe of Hsi-feng than of Lady Wang. He made haste, therefore, to obey and his mother dared raise no objection.

"You're too spineless," Hsi-feng scolded. "I've told you time and again that you're free to eat or drink whatever you like and to play with any of the girls or boys. But instead of doing as I say, you let other people warp your mind and teach you these sneaky ways. You've no self-respect but *will* lower yourself. You behave spitefully yourself and then complain that everybody else is unfair! How much did you lose to make you take on like this?"

"A couple of hundred cash," he told her meekly.

"All this fuss over a couple of hundred cash! And you one of the young masters!" She turned to Feng-erh. "Go and fetch a string of cash. Then take him to the back where the girls are playing. If you do anything so mean and sneaky again, Huan, first I'll give you a good spanking and then send someone to tell your teacher about it — he'll flay you alive for it. Your total lack of self-respect has got Cousin Lien gnashing his teeth. He'd have ripped out your guts before now if I hadn't stopped him. Now be off with you!"

"Yes," said Chia Huan and trotted off with Feng-erh, taking the string of cash. He then joined Ying-chun and the others at their game. And there we can leave him.

Let us return to Pao-yu. He was joking with Pao-chai when someone announced, "Miss Shih has arrived."

He started up at once to go and see her.

"Wait," said Pao-chai. "Let's go together."

She got down from the *kang* and went with Pao-yu to the Lady Dowager's apartments, where they found Shih Hsiang-yun laughing and chattering away. After they had greeted each other, Tai-yu, who was also there, asked Pao-yu where he had been.

"With Cousin Pao-chai."

"I thought so," said Tai-yu tartly. "Thank goodness there was someone to keep you there, or you'd have flown here long ago."

"Are you the only one I'm allowed to play with or to amuse?" he answered with a smile. "I happen to drop in on her once and you make such an issue of it."

"Nonsense. What do I care if you go to see her or not? I've never asked you to amuse me either. You can leave me alone in future."

With that she retired angrily to her room.

Pao-yu promptly followed her there.

"Why lose your temper for no reason at all?" he protested. "Even if I said something wrong, you might at least sit there and chat with the others for a bit, instead of sulking alone."

"What I do is none of your business."

"Of course not, but I can't bear to see you ruining your health."

"If I ruin my health and die, that's *my* affair. Nothing to do with you."

"Why talk about 'dying' or 'living' just after the New Year?"

"I shall, so there! I'm ready to die any minute. If you're so afraid of death, you can live to be a hundred — how about that?"

"If you just carry on like this all the time I'm not afraid." He smiled. "Death would be better."

"Exactly!" she retorted swiftly. "If you carry on like this it would be better for me to die."

"I meant better for *me* to be dead. How you twist my words!"

As they were bickering, Pao-chai slipped in.

"Cousin Shih is waiting for you."

She propelled Pao-yu out.

More wretched than ever, Tai-yu sat down by her window and shed tears of rage.

But in less time than it takes to drink two cups of tea Pao-yu was back again. The sight of him made her sob convulsively. He knew it would be hard to pacify her and was prepared to coax her with all sorts of blandishments and kind words. But she forestalled him by asking:

"What have you come back for? You've got a new play-mate now, someone better than I am at reading, writing and versifying, better at talking and laughing with you too. Someone who dragged you away for fear you might lose your temper. So why come back? Why not leave me to die in peace?"

Pao-yu stepped to her side and said softly, "Someone of your intelligence should know that distant relatives can't come between close ones, and new friends can't take the place of old. Dense as I am, *I* know that. Look, you're the daughter of my father's sister, while Pao-chai's a cousin on my mother's side — you're more closely related to me than she is. Besides, you came here first, we've eaten at the same table, slept in the same bed and grown up together, while she has only recently arrived. How could I be less close to you because of her?"

"Do I want you to be less close to *her*? What do you take me for? It's just that my feelings are hurt."

"And it's *your* feelings that concern me. Do you only know your own heart and not mine?"

Tai-yu lowered her head and was silent. After a pause she said:

"You blame other people for finding fault with you, without realizing how provoking you can be. Take today, for example. Why leave off your fox-fur cape when it's turned so cold?"

Pao-yu laughed.

"I was wearing it till you grew angry. Then I got so hot and bothered that I took it off."

"Well," she sighed, "if you catch cold there'll be the devil to pay."

They were interrupted by Hsiang-yun's arrival.

"Why, *Ai* Brother and Sister Lin!" she cried cheerfully. "You can be together every day, but it's rarely I have a chance to visit you; yet you pay no attention to poor little me."

"The lisper loves to rattle away," said Tai-yu with a laugh. "Fancy saying *ai* instead of *erh*[1] like that. I suppose, when we start dicing, you'll be shouting one, love, three, four, five...."

"If you copy her long enough, you'll soon be talking the same way," Pao-yu teased.

"How you do pick on one!" cried Hsiang-yun. "Always finding fault! Even if you *are* better than all the rest of us, there's no need to go making fun of everyone else. But I know someone you'd never dare find fault with. If you do, I'll really respect you."

"Who's that?" Tai-yu promptly asked.

"Dare you pick fault with Cousin Pao-chai? If so, good for you. I may not be up to you, but you've met your match in *her*."

---

[1] *Erh* means "two" or "second" and *ai* "love."

"Oh, *her*." Tai-yu snorted. "I wondered whom you meant. How could I ever presume to find fault with her?"

Pao-yu tried to stop them, but Hsiang-yun rattled on:

"Naturally I'll never come up to you in this lifetime. I just pray that you'll marry a husband who talks like me, so that you hear nothing but 'love' the whole day long. Amida Buddha! May I live to see that day!"

That set everyone laughing, and Hsiang-yun turned and ran out.

To know the sequel, you must read the next chapter.

CHAPTER 21

Prudent Hsi-jen Gently Takes
Pao-yu to Task
Pretty Ping-erh Quietly Comes to
Chia Lien's Rescue

As Hsiang-yun ran out of the room to escape Tai-yu, Pao-yu called after her, "Mind you don't fall! She can't catch you." He barred Tai-yu's way at the door and urged with a chuckle, "Do let her off this time!"

"I'll kill myself first," she cried, tugging at his arm.

Seeing Pao-yu blocking the doorway and Tai-yu unable to get past, Hsiang-yun stopped and called with a laugh, "Let me off, dear cousin, please! Just this once!"

Pao-chai who had come up behind her chimed in, "Do make it up, both of you, for Pao-yu's sake."

"Not I!" cried Tai-yu. "Are you all ganging up to make fun of me?"

"Who dares make fun of you?" countered Pao-yu. "She wouldn't if you hadn't teased her first."

The four of them were still at loggerheads when a summons to dinner arrived and they went through the dusk to the Lady Dowager's quarters where Lady Wang, Li Wan, Hsi-feng and the three Chia girls had already assembled. After dinner they chatted for a while before retiring for the night, and Hsiang-yun went back to Tai-yu's rooms, with Pao-yu escorting them there. It was after the second watch and Hsi-jen had to hurry him several times before he would return to his own room to sleep.

As soon as it was light next morning he scrambled into his clothes and hurried over in his slippers to Tai-yu's quarters. Tzu-chuan and Tsui-lu were nowhere to be seen, and his two cousins were still sleeping. Tai-yu lay peacefully with closed eyes, snugly wrapped in an apricot-red silk quilt, while Hsiang-yun's black hair had tumbled all over the pillow, her quilt bare-ly reached her shoulders, and she had flung one white arm adorned with two gold bracelets outside the covers.

"She fidgets even in her sleep," he sighed. "If there's a draught she'll be complaining of a stiff neck again." He gently pulled up the covers.

Tai-yu, awake now, had sensed someone's presence and guessed that it was Pao-yu. Looking round to make sure she asked:

"What are *you* doing here so early?"

"Early? Get up and see what time it is."

"You'd better go outside if you want us to get up."

Pao-yu withdrew to the sitting-room while Tai-yu roused Hsiang-yun. As soon as they were up and dressed he rejoined them and sat by the dressing-table watching as Tzu-chuan and Hsueh-yen helped them with their toilet. When Hsiang-yun finished washing, Tsui-lu picked up the basin to empty it.

"Wait!" cried Pao-yu. "I may as well wash here to save the trouble of going back to my room."

He went over and leant down to wash his face but declined Tzu-chuan's offer of soap, explaining, "There's plenty in here, I don't need any more." After dabbling for a while he asked for a towel.

"Still up to your old tricks," teased Tsui-lu. "Will you never grow up?"

Ignoring this, Pao-yu called for salt to brush his teeth and rinse his mouth. This done, he saw that Hsiang-yun had finish-ed doing her hair, so he went over and begged her:

"Good cousin, do my hair for me, will you?"

"I can't," she said.

"Dear cousin, you did before," he coaxed with a smile.

"Well, now I've forgotten how to."

"I'm not going out today anyway, and I'm not going to wear a cap," he persisted. "Just plait it anyhow."

He coaxed and wheedled her with endless terms of endear-
ment until Hsiang-yun took hold of his head and combed his
hair. Since he wore no cap at home, she simply plaited the
short hairs round his head and looped them together on top in
one big queue tied with a crimson braid. This braid was
decorated with four pearls and had a golden pendant at the
end.

"There are only three of these pearls left," she commented.
"This fourth one doesn't belong to the set. I remember they
used to match. Why is one missing?"

"I lost it."

"You must have dropped it when you were out. How lucky
for whoever picked it up!"

Tai-yu washing her hands near by smiled ironically. "Who
knows whether it was lost or given to someone to be mounted
in a trinket?"

Instead of answering, Pao-yu started playing with the toilet
articles on the dressing-table by the mirror, absent-mindedly
picking up some rouge. He was wondering if he could taste
it without Hsiang-yun noticing when she reached out from behind him and, holding his queue with one hand, with the other
knocked the rouge out of his grasp.

"Are you never going to change your silly ways?" she
demanded.

Just then Hsi-jen entered the room, but withdrew on seeing
that Pao-yu had obviously finished his toilet. She went back
and was attending to her own when in came Pao-chai and asked her where he was.

"He's hardly ever at home nowadays," replied Hsi-jen
bitterly.

Pao-chai understood.

The maid went on with a sigh, "It's all right to be fond of
cousins, but still there's a limit. They shouldn't play about
together day and night. But it's no use *our* talking, we just
waste our breath."

Why, thought Pao-chai, judging by what she says this maid
shows excellent sense.

She sat down on the *kang* to ask Hsi-jen her age and where she came from, carefully sounding her out on various subjects and receiving a most favourable impression. But soon Pao-yu returned, and then she took her leave.

"You two seemed to be having a good chat," said Pao-yu to Hsi-jen. "Why did Cousin Pao-chai leave when I came in?"

Hsi-jen did not answer till he repeated the question.

"Why ask *me*?" she retorted then. "Do I know what goes on between you?"

Pao-yu saw she was not her usual self. "What's made you so cross?" he asked gently.

"Who am I to be cross?" Hsi-jen smiled sarcastically. "But you'd better keep away from here. There are others who'll look after you, so don't bother me. I shall go back to wait on the old lady." She lay down on the *kang* and closed her eyes.

In dismay Pao-yu hurried to her side to soothe her, but she kept her eyes shut and paid no attention to him. He was puzzling over this when in came Sheh-yueh.

"What's the matter with her?" he asked.

"How should I know? Better ask yourself."

This took Pao-yu so aback that he said nothing. Then, sitting up, he sighed, "All right. If you're going to ignore me I'll go to sleep too."

He left the *kang* and went over to his own bed. When he had been quiet for some time and his regular breathing made Hsi-jen sure he was sleeping, she got up to put a cape over him. The next moment she heard a soft thud. With closed eyes, still shamming sleep, he had thrown it off. Hsi-jen smiled knowingly and nodded.

"You needn't lose your temper. From now on I'll play dumb and not say one word against you — how about that?"

This goaded Pao-yu into sitting up.

"What have I done now?" he demanded. "Why do you keep on at me? I don't mind your scolding, but you didn't scold just now. When I came in you ignored me and lay down in a huff — I've no idea why. Now you accuse me of temper, but I haven't heard you say anything against me yet."

"You know perfectly well without my telling you."

This tiff was cut short by a summons from the Lady Dowager. Pao-yu joined her for a meal and managed to swallow half a bowl of rice before going back to his quarters. He found Hsi-jen asleep on the *kang* in the outer room with Sheh-yueh playing solitaire beside her. Knowing that the two girls were good friends he ignored her too and raising the door curtain went into his bedroom. When Sheh-yueh followed him he pushed her out.

"I wouldn't think of troubling you."

She withdrew with a smile and sent in two younger maids. Pao-yu curled up with a book until, wanting some tea, he raised his head and saw the two girls standing there. The elder of the two had a certain delicate charm.

"What is your name?" he asked.

"Hui-hsiang."

"Who gave you that name?"

"My name used to be Yun-hsiang, but Sister Hua changed it to Hui-hsiang."

"You should be called Hui-chi,[1] not Hui-hsiang.[2] How many girls are there in your family?"

"Four."

"And where do you come?"

"I'm the youngest."

"Then we'll call you Ssu-erh, Number Four, and drop this business of fragrance and of orchids. Which of *you* can compare with such flowers? It's an insult to *them*, calling you by their lovely names."

Thereupon he ordered tea. Hsi-jen and Sheh-yueh, listening outside, compressed their lips to check their laughter.

That whole day Pao-yu stayed indoors moping, not playing about with the girls of the house or his maids, just reading or writing to while away the time. And instead of calling for any other attendants he gave all his orders to Ssu-erh, who

[1] Bad Luck.
[2] Orchid.

being a clever minx made full use of this chance and put herself out to please him.

After dinner, flushed by a few cups of wine, Pao-yu would normally have amused himself with Hsi-jen and the others; but this evening he sat all alone, disconsolate, by the lamp. Although tempted to join the girls, he was afraid that would make them gloat and give him even more talkings-to in future, while if he threw his weight about as the young master that would be too unkind.

"I'll pretend they're dead," he resolved, "and I have to fend for myself. That'll leave me free to amuse myself as I please."

Then he read the chapter "The House-Breaker" in *Chuang-tzu* till he came to the following passage:

> "Do away with sages and wise men, and great robbers will disappear. Destroy jade and pearls, and no petty thieves will arise. Burn tallies and smash seals, and the people will revert to their natural simplicity. Break measures and scales, and they will no longer quarrel. Abolish all the sacred laws of the world and the people will discuss things freely.
>
> "Confuse the musical scales, break harps and lutes, stop the ears of good musicians, and all men under heaven will learn to hear for themselves. Dispense with ornaments and coloured patterns, glue up the eyes of the keen-sighted, and all men under heaven will learn to see for themselves. Destroy quadrants and yard-measures, throw away compasses and squares, cut off the fingers of deft artisans, and all men under heaven will learn skill for themselves."

Pao-yu was so delighted with this passage that, stimulated as he was by wine, he picked up his brush and continued in the same vein:

> "Burn the flower (Hsi-jen), get rid of the musk (Sheh-yueh), and those in the inner apartments will keep their advice to themselves. Spoil the beauty of the precious trinket (Pao-chai), dull the intelligence of the black jade (Tai-yu), do away with affection, and in the inner chambers fair and foul will then be on an equal footing. Advice kept to oneself does away with the danger of discord; beauty marred obviates affection; intelligence dulled cuts out admiration for talents. For trinket, jade, flower and musk are

alike spreading nets and laying traps to ensnare and bewitch all
men under heaven. . . ."

This written he threw down his brush and went to bed, falling into a dreamless sleep as soon as his head touched the
pillow.

He did not awake till the morning, when he turned and saw
Hsi-jen lying fully dressed on the cover at his side. Yesterday's
grievance forgotten, he nudged her gently.

"Get up and sleep properly. You'll catch cold like that."

Now the wild way Pao-yu played around with his cousins
at all hours of the day and night had convinced Hsi-jen that
he would be impervious to advice, and so she had decided to
teach him a lesson by disclosing her own feelings, expecting
that he would soon get over it. When he sulked for a whole
day it was her turn to be at a loss, and she passed a sleepless
night. Seeing that he was obviously feeling better today, she
deliberately ignored him. When he tried to take off her jacket,
undoing a button, she pushed his hand away and buttoned it
up again.

Pao-yu caught hold of her hand then and asked softly:

"What's really the matter?"

He had to repeat his question several times before Hsi-jen
opened her eyes.

"Nothing," she said. "If you're awake, go over there to
wash before it's too late."

"Where am I to go?"

"How should I know?" Hsi-jen snorted. "Go wherever you
like. We may as well part company from now on, to stop
people laughing at our rows and rumpuses. Besides, if you
get tired of them over there you've a Ssu-erh and Wu-erh here
to look after you. The rest of us are just a disgrace to our
lovely names."

Pao-yu chuckled. "So you still remember that?"

"I'll remember it if I live to be a hundred. I'm not like *you*,
letting what I say go in at one ear and out at the other, forgetting what's said at night by the next morning."

Touched by the cloud on her pretty face, Pao-yu took a jade hairpin from beside the pillow and threw it on the floor, breaking it in two.

"May the same thing happen to me if I don't listen to you in future," he cried.

"What a way to talk! First thing in the morning too." Hsi-jen hastily picked up the pieces. "It doesn't really matter whether you listen to me or not, but why carry on like that?"

"You don't know how bad I feel."

"So you can feel bad too?" She smiled. "Then how do you think I feel? Hurry up and get dressed now."

They both got up then and began their toilet.

Pao-yu had gone to pay his respects to his grandmother when Tai-yu came to his room. Finding him out, she looked through the books on his desk and discovered the passage in *Chuang-tzu* which he had been reading the previous evening. Amused as well as provoked by the lines he had added, she picked up a brush and appended a quatrain herself:

> Who can the scurrile writer be
> Who makes of *Chuang-tzu* such a travesty
> And, blind to his own incapacity,
> Heaps such abuse on others?

This done, she went to pay her respects to the Lady Dowager and then Lady Wang.

It so happened that Hsi-feng's daughter Ta-chieh was ill, so the household was upside down. A doctor had just been summoned and after examining the child he announced:

"I am happy to inform Her Ladyship and Madam Lien that the little girl's fever is simply due to smallpox."

At once Lady Wang and Hsi-feng sent to ask whether the small patient was in any danger.

The answer was: "Although this is a serious illness, it is taking its natural course. There is no need to worry. But you must prepare loranthus and *sanguis caudae* or hog-tail's blood."

Hsi-feng lost no time in having a room cleared out for sacrifice to the Goddess of Smallpox. At the same time she directed that no fried food should be served in her quarters, ordered

Ping-erh to take some bedding and clothes to a different room for Chia Lien, and issued red cloth to her nurses, maids and other attendants for clothes. Clean rooms were also prepared for the two doctors who would take it in turn to attend the child and make out prescriptions for her, remaining there in residence for twelve days.

So Chia Lien had to move to his study in the outer compound, while Hsi-feng and Ping-erh joined Lady Wang in daily sacrifice to the Goddess of Smallpox.

Chia Lien was the sort of man who once away from his wife was bound to get into mischief. Two nights alone were more than he could bear: he vented his ardour on his handsome page boys.

Now in the Jung Mansion was a rascally drunkard of a cook by the name of To Kuan, a man so useless and cowardly that he was commonly known as To the Muddy Worm. While he was young his parents had found him a wife who was now just about twenty, and whose good looks were the admiration of all. But she was a flighty creature who loved nothing better than to have affairs. The Muddy Worm made no objection, for provided he had wine, meat and money himself he cared for nothing else. So most of the men in the Ning and Jung Mansions had had their fling with her. And because she was such a remarkably good-looking wanton, everyone called her "Miss To."

Chia Lien was now inflamed by his banishment from his own bedroom. He used to eye Miss To avidly but had so far taken no steps to get her for fear of his wife at home and his fancy boys outside.

Miss To for her part had been hankering after Chia Lien too, waiting eagerly for her chance. As soon as she heard that he had moved to the study she kept strolling past to flaunt her charms, and Chia Lien rose to the bait like a famished rat. He consulted his trusted pages, who agreed to arrange a secret assignation for him, for not only did he promise them rich rewards — they were all on intimate terms themselves with Miss To. So the matter was settled at once.

At the second watch that night, when the household had retired and the Muddy Worm lay on his *kang* in a drunken stupor, Chia Lien slipped into her room. The mere sight of her threw him into such a frenzy that with no preliminary professions of love he flung off his clothes and set to work.

Now this woman was so curiously constituted that the touch of a man seemed to melt her very bones, so that he felt as if bedded in cotton-wool, while in her wanton tricks and amorous cries she outdid any prostitute. No man but was driven to utter frenzy by her. Chia Lien only wished he could melt into her body!

To inflame him further, the woman under him teased, "Your daughter has smallpox and they're sacrificing in your home to the goddess. You ought to lead a clean life for a couple of days, not dirty yourself for me. Hurry up and get out of here."

"You're my goddess," he panted, going all out. "What do I care for any other goddess?"

The more wanton the woman, the more debauched Chia Lien revealed himself. At the end of this bout they vowed to be true to each other and could hardly bear to part. From that day they became sworn lovers.

But Ta-chieh's illness spent its course, her pustules gradually healed. After twelve days they "saw off" the goddess and the whole family sacrificed to Heaven and their ancestors, made offerings, burnt incense, exchanged congratulations and distributed largesse. When these ceremonies were at an end, Chia Lien returned to his old quarters and Hsi-feng. As the proverb says, "Reunion after long separation is better than a wedding night." We need not dwell on the transports of their love.

The next morning when Hsi-feng had gone to pay her respects to the senior ladies, Ping-erh brought back the clothes and bedding Chia Lien had used outside. To her surprise a long strand of hair fell out of the pillow-case. The knowing maid quickly tucked it in her sleeve and went into Chia Lien's room, where she showed him the hair with a smile.

"What's this?" she demanded.

As Chia Lien tried to grab it, Ping-erh turned to fly. He caught hold of her and threw her on to the *kang*, then tried to snatch the hair from her.

"You vixen! Give it to me, or I'll break your arm."

"You heartless brute!" she giggled. "I was kind enough to keep this between ourselves, yet you start manhandling me. Wait till she comes back and I tell her. You won't half catch it!"

At once Chia Lien begged with a smile, "Give it me, there's a good girl, and I won't use force."

Just at that moment they heard Hsi-feng's voice. Ping-erh had barely regained her feet when Hsi-feng came in and told her: "Get the patterns out of that box for the mistress, quick."

As the maid was doing this, the sight of Chia Lien reminded Hsi-feng of something else.

"Have you brought back all the things he used outside?"

"Yes, madam."

"Anything missing?"

"No. I was worried too that there might be, but I've checked carefully and there's nothing missing."

"Is anything there that shouldn't be?"

Ping-erh laughed.

"Isn't it enough that nothing's missing? What else could be there?"

"Who knows what dirty business he's been up to this last fortnight." Hsi-feng smiled coldly. "One of his little friends might have left something: a ring or sash or pouch. Or even some locks of hair or finger-nails, for all we know. They're all souvenirs."

Chia Lien turned pale at this. Behind his wife's back he sawed at his throat to warn Ping-erh not to speak. She pretended not to see him, however, and laughed.

"Fancy, exactly the same idea occurred to me, madam. That's why I searched carefully. But there wasn't a sign of any monkey business. If you don't believe me, madam, look for yourself. I haven't put the things away yet."

"Silly girl! If he had anything of the sort, would he let us find it?"

She went off again with the patterns.

Pointing at her own nose, Ping-erh shook her head and laughed.

"How are you going to thank me for that?"

Chia Lien, beaming, rushed to embrace her, pouring out an incoherent flood of endearments.

Dangling the hair in front of him, she teased, "I'll have this hold over you for the rest of my life. If you're nice to me, well and good. If not, I'll let the cat out of the bag."

"Keep it safely then. Don't, for goodness' sake, let her find out."

As he spoke, catching her off guard, he snatched the hair.

"I don't trust you with it," he chortled. "I'd better burn it and be done with it." He stuffed the hair into his boot.

"You beast!" she cried through clenched teeth. "As soon as the river's crossed you pull down the bridge. Don't ever expect me to lie for you again."

Inflamed by her charming show of temper, Chia Lien threw his arms round her and tried to make love to her. But Ping-erh slipped from his grasp and ran out of the room, leaving him doubled up in frustration.

"Little flirt!" he swore. "You get a man all worked up then run away."

From outside the window Ping-erh laughed. "If I'm a flirt that's my business. Who told you to get so worked up? If I let you have your way and she got to know, I'd be the one to suffer."

"Don't be afraid of her. One of these days when I really lose my temper, I'm going to give that vinegary bitch a good beating to show her who's master here. She spies on me as if I were a thief. It's all right for her to talk to other men, but she won't let me say a word to another woman. If I do, she suspects the worst. Yet she carries on as she pleases, chattering and laughing with any younger brother-in-law or nephew, old or young, quite regardless of my feelings. I'll forbid her to see anyone in future."

"She's right to be jealous of you, but you're wrong to be jealous of her," retorted Ping-erh. "She's done nothing that's improper. But you, you're up to no good. Even *I* wouldn't trust you."

"The two of you are in league. All *you* two do is right, all I do is wrong. Sooner or later I'll settle scores with you both."

While he was fuming Hsi-feng came back to the courtyard, and seeing Ping-erh at the window demanded:

"Why not talk inside? Why run out here to shout through the window? What's the idea?"

"That's right!" Chia Lien called from the room. "The way she acts, you'd think there was a tiger here waiting to eat her."

"Why should I stay there alone with him?" asked Ping-erh.

"All the better, surely." Hsi-feng smiled.

"Is that remark aimed at me?"

"Who else?" Hsi-feng laughed.

"Don't make me say things you'll be sorry for!"

Instead of raising the door curtain for her mistress Ping-erh swept in ahead of her, swishing the curtain behind her, and passed through the hall into the other room.

Hsi-feng raised the curtain herself and walked in remarking, "The girl must be out of her mind, trying to get the upper hand of *me*. You'd better watch out, little bitch!"

Chia Lien had fallen back laughing on the *kang*.

"I never knew Ping-erh had it in her," he crowed, clapping his hands. "She's gone up in my estimation."

"It's you who've spoilt her. I hold you responsible."

"When you two fall out, why put the blame on me? I'd better make myself scarce."

"Where are you going?"

"I'll be back presently."

"Wait," said Hsi-feng. "There's something I want to discuss with you."

To know what it was, read the next chapter.

Truly:

> Virtuous maids have always harboured grief,
> And charming wives since of old have known jealousy.

CHAPTER 22

A Song Awakens Pao-yu to Esoteric Truths
Lantern-Riddles Grieve Chia Cheng with
Their Ill Omens

Hearing that Hsi-feng wanted to consult him about something, Chia Lien stopped to ask what it was.

"It's Pao-chai's birthday on the twenty-first," she said. "What do you intend to do about it?"

"Why ask me that?" he retorted. "You've handled plenty of big birthday celebrations. Why can't you cope with this?"

"For big birthdays there are definite rules but this is neither big nor small, that's why I wanted your advice."

He lowered his head to think before answering.

"You're losing your grip," he said after a pause. "There's a precedent in Tai-yu's birthday. Just celebrate this the same way."

"As if that hadn't occurred to me too!" Hsi-feng smiled mockingly. "But yesterday the old lady told me she'd been asking everybody's age and learned that Pao-chai would be fifteen this year, and although that's not a round number it means she's reached marriageable age. If the old lady wants to celebrate her birthday specially, it'll have to be different from Tai-yu's in the past."

"In that case, have things on a more lavish scale."

"That's what I thought, but I wanted to sound you out so as not to be blamed for doing something extra on my own initiative without consulting you."

"Well, well! Why this sudden show of consideration? Me blame *you*? I'm quite satisfied if you don't find fault with me."

With that he left, but where he went does not concern us.

Let us return now to Hsiang-yun. After spending several
days in the Jung Mansion it was time for her to go home, but
the Lady Dowager urged her to wait until after Pao-chai's
birthday and the performance of operas. So Hsiang-yun, having
to stay on, sent home for two pieces of her embroidery as a
birthday-present for her cousin.

The fact was that the Lady Dowager had taken a fancy to
Pao-chai since her arrival on account of her steady, amiable
behaviour. And as this would be her first birthday in their
house, the old lady summoned Hsi-feng and gave her twenty
taels of silver from her own coffer for a feast and an opera.

Hsi-feng teased, "When an Old Ancestress wants to celebrate
some grandchild's birthday, no matter how grandly, who are
we to protest? So there's to be a feast and opera too, is there?
Well, if you want it to be lively you'll have to pay for it yourself instead of trying to play host with a mouldy twenty taels.
I suppose you expect me to make up the rest? If you really
couldn't afford it, all right. But your cases are bursting with
gold and silver ingots of every shape and size — the bottoms
of the chests are dropping out, they're so full. Yet you're still
squeezing *us*. Look, aren't all of us your children? Is Pao-
yu the only one who'll carry you as an immortal on his head
to Mount Wutai,[1] that you keep everything for him? Even if
the rest of us aren't good enough, don't be so hard on us. Is
this enough for a feast or theatricals?"

The whole company burst out laughing.

"Listen to that tongue of hers!" The old lady chuckled.
"I'm not exactly tongue-tied myself but I'm no match for this
monkey. Not even your mother-in-law would think of arguing
with me, but you give me tit for tat."

"My mother-in-law dotes on Pao-yu just as much as you
do," retorted Hsi-feng with a smile. "So I've no one to take
my side. Instead, you make me out a termagant."

That set the old lady crowing with laughter and put her in
the highest of spirits.

---

[1] Mount Wutai was a holy Buddhist mountain.

That night, after the family had gathered to pay their evening respects to the Lady Dowager and then gone on to chat, she asked Pao-chai to name her favourite operas and dishes. Knowing the old lady's partiality for lively shows and sweet, pappy food, Pao-chai gave these as her own preferences, adding even more to the Lady Dowager's pleasure.

The first thing next day she had presents of clothing and trinkets sent to the girl. Lady Wang, Hsi-feng, Tai-yu and the others also sent theirs according to the status of each. But these need not be enumerated in detail.

On the twenty-first a small stage was set up in the Lady Dowager's inner courtyard and a new troupe of young actresses had been hired who were able to perform both *Kunchu* and *Yiyang* operas. Tables were laid in the hall for a family feast, to which no outsiders were asked: apart from Aunt Hsueh, Hsiang-yun and Pao-chai, who were guests, all the rest would be members of the family.

Not seeing Tai-yu that morning, Pao-yu went to look for her and found her curled up on her *kang*.

"Come on to breakfast," he said. "The show will soon be starting. Tell me which opera you'd like and I'll ask for it."

Tai-yu smiled disdainfully.

"If that's how you feel, you'd better hire a special company to play my favourite pieces instead of expecting me to cash in on someone else's birthday."

"That's easy, we'll hire a company next time and let the rest of them cash in on us."

He pulled her up and they went off hand in hand.

After breakfast it was time to choose the plays and the Lady Dowager called on Pao-chai to name her choice. The girl declined the honour at first but finally, to the old lady's delight, named a scene from *Pilgrimage to the West*. Next, Hsi-feng was ordered to take her pick. And knowing the old lady's liking for lively plays, especially comedies and burlesques, she pleased her even more by selecting *Liu Erh Pawns His Clothes*.

Tai-yu, told to choose next, deferred to Aunt Hsueh and Lady Wang.

"I planned today as a treat for you girls," said the Lady Dowager. "So make your choice and never mind your aunts. I didn't lay on this show and feast for them. They're lucky to be here at all, able to watch and eat free of charge, but I won't let them choose any items."

All laughed at that, and then Tai-yu suggested one piece. She was followed by Pao-yu, Hsiang-yun, the three Chia girls and Li Wan, and their choices were put on in turn.

When the feast was ready the Lady Dowager told Pao-chai to select another opera, and she asked for *The Drunken Monk*.

"You always choose something rowdy," objected Pao-yu.

"You've been watching operas all these years for nothing if you don't know how good this is," retorted Pao-chai. "Besides being spectacular it has some magnificent lines."

"I never could stand noisy shows," he persisted.

"If you call this noisy that just shows how little you know about opera," she rejoined. "Come over here and let me explain. This opera has most stirring arias sung in the northern mode *Tien Chiang Chun*, which needless to say is an excellent melody; and the verses set to *Chi Sheng Tsao* are quite superb, did you but know it."

Pao-yu edged closer then and begged her to recite them to him.

Pao-chai declaimed:

> "Dried are the hero's tears,
> My patron's house left behind;
> By grace divine
> Tonsured below the Lotus Throne.
> Not destined to stay,
> I leave the monastery in a flash,
> Naked I go without impediment;
> My sole wish now
> To roam alone in coir cape and bamboo hat,
> And in straw sandals with a broken alms bowl
> To wander where I will."

Pao-yu pounded his lap to the rhythm of the verse and nodded appreciatively, loud in his praise of these words as well as of her erudition.

"Do be quiet and watch," said Tai-yu. "Before we've seen *The Drunken Monk* you're playing *The General Feigns Madness*."

This set Hsiang-yun giggling.

They went on watching operas until dusk. By then the Lady Dowager had taken a special fancy to the girl who played the part of the heroines and the one who took the clown's role. She had them brought to her and on closer inspection found them even sweeter. All marvelled when it was disclosed that the heroine was only eleven, the clown only nine. The old lady rewarded them with some extra delicacies and two additional strings of cash.

"When that child's made up she's the living image of someone here," remarked Hsi-feng. "Have none of you noticed?"

Pao-chai knew whom she meant but she just smiled. Pao-yu too had guessed but did not dare to speak out.

Hsiang-yun, however, blurted out, "I know! She looks just like Cousin Tai-yu."

Too late Pao-yu shot her a warning glance, for by now everyone had noticed the resemblance and laughingly declared that it was most striking. Soon afterwards they scattered.

That evening while undressing, Hsiang-yun ordered Tsui-lu to pack her things.

"What's the hurry?" asked the maid. "We can start packing when it's time to leave."

"We're leaving tomorrow morning. Why should we stay here and put up with dirty looks?"

Pao-yu overheard this exchange and hurried in to take Hsiang-yun by the hand.

"Dear cousin, you've got me wrong," he said. "Tai-yu is so terribly sensitive that the others didn't name her for fear of upsetting her. How could she help being annoyed, the way you blurted it out? I looked at you warningly because I didn't want you to hurt her feelings. It's ungrateful as well as unfair of you to be angry with *me*. If it had been anybody else but you, I wouldn't care how many people she offended."

Hsiang-yun waved him crossly away.

"Don't try to get round me with your flattering talk. I'm not in the same class as your Cousin Tai-yu. It's all right for other people to make fun of her, but I'm not even allowed to mention her. She's a grand young lady, I'm a slave — how dare I offend her?"

"I was only thinking of you, yet now you put me in the wrong." Pao-yu was desperate. "If I meant any harm, may I turn into dust this instant and be trampled on by ten thousand feet!"

"Stop talking such nonsense just after the New Year. Or go and rave if you must to those petty-minded creatures who are so quick to take offence, and who know how to manage you. Don't make me spit at you!"

She flounced off to the Lady Dowager's inner room and threw herself down angrily on a couch.

After this snub Pao-yu went to look for Tai-yu, but scarcely had he set foot in her room than she pushed him out and closed the door in his face. Mystified, he called in a subdued voice through the window:

"Dear cousin!"

But Tai-yu simply ignored him.

He hung his head then in dejected silence. Hsi-jen knew it would be useless to reason with him just then. So he was standing there like a fool when Tai-yu opened the door, thinking him gone. When she saw him still standing there, she hadn't the heart to shut him out again. She turned away and curled up on her bed, while he followed her into the room.

"There's always a reason for everything," he said. "If you'd explain, people wouldn't feel so hurt. What's upset you suddenly?"

"A fine question to ask!" Tai-yu gave a short laugh. "*I* don't know. For you I'm a figure of fun, to be compared with an actress in order to raise a laugh."

"But why be angry with *me*? I didn't make the comparison. I didn't laugh."

"I should hope not, indeed! But what you did was even worse than the others laughing and making comparisons."

Pao-yu did not know how to defend himself and was silent.

"I wouldn't have minded so much if you hadn't made eyes at Hsiang-yun," Tai-yu went on. "Just what did you mean by that? That she'd lower and cheapen herself by joking with me? She's the daughter of a noble house, I'm a nobody. If she were to joke with me and I answered back, that would be degrading for her — was that the idea? That was certainly kind on your part. Too bad she didn't appreciate your thoughtfulness, but flared up all the same. Then you tried to excuse yourself at my expense, calling me 'petty-minded and quick to take offence.' You were afraid she might offend me, were you? But what is it to you if I get angry with her? Or if she offends me?"

Pao-yu realized that she had overheard his conversation with Hsiang-yun. He had intervened in an attempt to prevent bad feeling between them but, having failed, was now held to blame by both sides. This reminded him of the passage in *Chuang-tzu*:

> "The ingenious work hard, the wise are full of care; but those without ability have no ambition. They enjoy their food and wander at will like drifting boats freed from their moorings."

And again:

> "Mountain trees are the first to be felled, clear fountains the first to be consumed."

The more he thought the more depressed he grew.

"If I can't even cope now with just these two, what will it be like in future?" he reflected. At this point it seemed quite useless to attempt to justify himself, so he started back to his room.

Tai-yu realized that he must be very dejected by what had occurred to go off so sulkily without a word. But this only made her angrier than ever.

"Go, then!" she cried. "And don't ever come back! Don't speak to me again!"

Pao-yu paid no attention. Returning to his room, he lay down on his bed staring fixedly before him. Although Hsi-jen knew what had happened, she dared not mention it and tried to distract him with some more cheerful subject.

"Today's plays are bound to lead to others," she prophesied. "Miss Pao-chai is sure to give a return party."

"What do I care whether she does or not?" he snapped back, quite unlike his usual self.

"What do you mean?" asked Hsi-jen. "This is the beginning of a new year when all the ladies and girls are enjoying themselves. Why carry on like this?"

"I don't care whether they're enjoying themselves or not."

"If they are so obliging to each other, shouldn't you be obliging too? Wouldn't that be pleasanter for everyone?"

"For everyone? Let *them* oblige each other while 'naked I go without impediment.'"

Tears ran down his cheeks and, seeing them, she said no more.

Pao-yu, pondering the significance of that line, suddenly burst out sobbing. Getting up, he went to his desk, took up a brush and wrote this verse in the style of a Buddhist *gatha*:

> Should you test me and I test you,
> Should heart and mind be tested too,
> Till there remained no more to test,
> That test would be of all the best.
> When nothing can be called a test,
> My feet will find a place to rest.

For fear that others might not grasp the meaning, he then appended a verse after the melody *Chi Sheng Tsao* and read the whole through again. Then he went to bed, feeling less frustrated, and slept.

Now some time after Pao-yu's abrupt departure Tai-yu came, ostensibly to see Hsi-jen, to find out how things were. Told that he was asleep she was turning to leave when Hsi-jen said with a smile:

"Just a minute, miss! He wrote something you might like to look at."

She quietly fetched and handed Tai-yu the verses Pao-yu had just written, and the girl was both touched and amused to see what he had tossed off in a fit of pique.

"It's just a joke, nothing serious," she told Hsi-jen.

She took it back to her own room and showed it to Hsiang-yun. Next day she showed it to Pao-chai as well. Pao-chai read the second verse. It ran:

> If there's no "I," then neither is there "you,"
> If she misunderstands you then why rue?
> Freely I come and freely too I go,
> Giving myself to neither joy nor woe,
> Close kin or distant — it's the same to me.
> What did it serve, my assiduity?
> Today I see its true futility.

Having read this she read the first verse, then laughed.

"So that's the enlightenment he's attained! This is all my fault for reciting that song to him yesterday. There's nothing so apt to lead people astray as these Taoist teachings and Zen paradoxes. If he really starts taking such nonsense seriously and gets it fixed in his head just because of that song I quoted, I'm the first to blame."

She tore up the verses and told her maids to burn them at once.

"You shouldn't have done that," protested Tai-yu with a smile. "I've some questions to ask him. Come with me, both of you. We'll soon cure him of this nonsense."

So the three girls went together to Pao-yu's rooms. Tai-yu opened the attack by saying:

"Listen, Pao-yu. *Pao* means that which is most precious, and *yu* that which is most solid. But in what way are you precious? In what way are you solid?"

When Pao-yu could not answer, the girls clapped their hands and laughed.

"And this stupid fellow wants to dabble in metaphysics!"

Tai-yu continued, "The last two lines of your verse are all very well —

> When nothing can be called a test
> My feet can find a place to rest.

But it seems to me they still lack a little something. Let me add two more:

> When there's no place for feet to rest,
> That is the purest state and best."

"Yes, that shows *real* understanding," put in Pao-chai. "In the old days when the Sixth Patriarch Hui-neng of the Southern Sect went to Shaochow in search of a teacher, he heard that the Fifth Patriarch Hung-jen was in the monastery on Mount Huangmei, so he took a job as cook there. The Fifth Patriarch, on the look-out for a successor, ordered each of his monks to compose a Buddhist *gatha*. His senior disciple Shen-hsiu recited:

> 'The body is a Bodhi tree,
> The mind a mirror clear;
> Then keep it cleaned and polished —
> Let no dust settle there.'

"Hui-neng heard this as he was hulling rice in the kitchen and commented, 'Very fine, but it needs rounding off.' With that he declaimed:

> 'The Bodhi tree is no tree,
> The mirror no mirror clear;
> Since nothing actually exists,
> Where can any dust appear?'

Then the Fifth Patriarch passed on his robe and alms bowl to him. Your verse amounts to much the same thing. But what about the conundrum you set him just now? He hasn't answered it yet. How can you leave it at that?"

"Failure to answer promptly means defeat," said Tai-yu. "And even if he answered it now it would hardly count. But you mustn't talk about Zen any more. You know even less about it than the two of us yet you dabble in metaphysics."

Pao-yu had in fact fancied that he had already attained enlightenment, but now that he had been floored by Tai-yu, and Pao-chai had quoted Buddhist lore that he had never suspected her of knowing, he thought to himself, "They understand more about these things than I do, yet still they haven't attained full enlightenment. Why should I trouble my head over such matters?" Thereupon he said with a laugh:

"I wasn't dabbling in metaphysics. I just wrote that for fun."

So the four of them made it up.

Just then they were told that the Imperial Consort had sent over a lantern-riddle for everybody to guess, after which they were to make up a riddle apiece and send these to the Palace.

At once the four of them hurried to the Lady Dowager's quarters where they found a young eunuch with a square, flat-topped lantern of red gauze made specially for lantern-riddles. One riddle was already hanging on it. They gathered round to read it and try to guess it, while the eunuch passed on the order:

"When the young ladies have guessed, they are not to tell anyone their answers but write them down privately to be sealed up and taken to the Palace. Her Royal Highness will see which are correct."

Pao-chai stepped forward with the others then to look at the riddle. It was a quite nondescript quatrain, but of course she praised its ingenuity and pretended to be thinking hard although she had guessed it at once. Pao-yu, Tai-yu, Hsiang-yun and Tan-chun had guessed it too and they went off quietly to write down their answers. Then Chia Huan, Chia Lan and others were fetched, and having racked their brains they wrote down their answers. After that each made up a riddle, copied it out neatly and hung it on the lantern for the eunuch to take away.

Towards evening the eunuch returned to announce that the Imperial Consort's riddle had been correctly guessed by all except the Second Young Lady and Third Young Master, and Her Highness had thought of answers to theirs but did not know whether or not they were correct. With that he showed them the answers written down. Some were right, others wrong, but all made haste to say they were correct.

The eunuch then proceeded to give the winners their prizes: a poem-container made in the Palace and a bamboo whisk for cleaning teapots. The only two left out were Ying-chun and Chia Huan, and while she regarded this as a game and did not take it to heart he was most disappointed.

And then the eunuch announced, "Her Highness did not attempt to guess the answer to the Third Young Master's riddle, because it did not seem to her to make sense. She told me to bring it back and ask what it means."

All of them gathered round to read the riddle:

> First Brother has eight corners,
> Second Brother two horns instead;
> Second Brother likes to squat on the roof,
> First Brother just sits on the bed.

A roar of laughter went up, and Chia Huan told the eunuch that the answer was a head-rest and an animal-head tile. The eunuch having noted this down accepted some tea and then left.

The old lady was delighted to know that Yuan-chun was in such good spirits. She ordered a dainty screen-lantern to be made at once and put in the hall so that the girls could make up riddles and paste them on it. Scented tea and sweetmeats were prepared, as well as various little prizes.

Chia Cheng on his return from court found his mother in a cheerful frame of mind, and since this was a festival he came over that evening to join in the fun. He also had refreshments and prizes prepared and coloured lanterns lit in the hall, then invited the old lady in to see them. She sat with Chia Cheng and Pao-yu at the highest table, while below, Lady Wang, Pao-chai, Tai-yu and Hsiang-yun occupied one table and Ying-chun, Tan-chun and Hsi-chun another. The hall was thronged with nurses and maids in attendance. Li Wan and Hsi-feng had a table in the inner room.

When Chia Cheng commented on Chia Lan's absence, a nurse went inside to ask Li Wan the reason. She rose to reply:

"He says he won't come because the master hasn't invited him."

When this was reported to Chia Cheng the others laughed and remarked, "What a queer, stubborn boy."

Chia Cheng promptly sent Chia Huan and two serving-women to fetch him. And the Lady Dowager made him sit next to her and helped him to dainties, while the others chatted and enjoyed themselves.

Normally Pao-yu liked to hold forth at great length but to-day, in his father's presence, he simply answered briefly when spoken to; and Hsiang-yun, although a great chatterbox for a girl, seemed afflicted with dumbness by her uncle too. Tai-yu was too reserved ever to talk much in company, and Pao-chai also behaved in the manner natural to her, choosing her words with care. So there was a constraint about this family party.

The Lady Dowager, knowing that Chia Cheng was the cause, suggested after three rounds of drinks that he should withdraw to rest. Aware that she wanted him out of the way so that the young people might enjoy themselves better, Chia Cheng said with a smile:

"When I heard today that you had prepared all these lantern-riddles, I brought some gifts and delicacies to join in. Won't you spare your son a little of the love you have for your grandchildren?"

The old lady chuckled.

"None of them will laugh and talk with you here, and that's very dull," she said. "Well, if it's riddles you want, I'll give you one. But if you guess wrong you'll have to pay a forfeit."

"Certainly. And if I guess right shall I win a prize?"

"Of course." Then she recited, "The monkey, being light of limb, stands on the topmost branch. It's the name of a fruit."

Chia Cheng knew of course that the answer was lichee,[1] but he deliberately gave wrong answers and had to pay several forfeits before he guessed right and received a prize from his mother. Then he in turn set her a riddle:

> Its body is square,
> Its substance firm and hard;
> Though it cannot speak
> It will assuredly[2] record anything said.
>
> — *A useful object.*

He whispered the answer to Pao-yu, who took the hint and secretly told his grandmother. The old lady thought it over and decided he was right.

"An inkstone," she said.

---

[1] Homophone for "stand on a branch."

[2] Assuredly (*pi*) is a homophone for writing-brush.

"Trust you, mother, to get it right first time." Chia Cheng smiled and turned to order, "Bring in the presents." There was an answering cry from the women below, who brought forward various trays and little boxes. The Lady Dowager, inspecting them one by one, was delighted to find them novelties for the Lantern Festival.

"Pour wine for the master," she ordered.

Pao-yu poured the wine and Ying-chun presented it, after which the old lady said:

"Let me hear you guess some of the riddles the children have put on the screen."

Chia Cheng rose and walked up to the screen. The first riddle he saw was:

> Monsters I can affright and put to flight;
> A roll of silk my form; my thunderous crash
> Strikes dread into the hearts of all,
> Yet when they look around I've turned to ash.

"Isn't this a firecracker?" asked Chia Cheng.

When Pao-yu said that was right, his father read on:

> No end to the labours of men, to heaven's decrees,
> But labour unblessed by Heaven will fruitless be.
> What causes this constant, frenzied activity?
> The uncertainty of mortal destiny.

"An abacus?"

Ying-chun agreed with a smile.

Chia Cheng read the next riddle:

> The children by the steps look up:
> Spring surely has no fitter decoration.
> But when the silk cord breaks it drifts away,
> Blame not the east wind for this separation.

"That sounds like a kite," said Chia Cheng.

When Tan-chun had confirmed this he looked at another riddle:

> A former life's appearance come to nought,
> Deaf to folk-songs the chanting of sutras
>   she now hears:
> Say not this life is sunk in a sea of darkness,
> For in her heart a shining light appears.

"The lamp before a Buddhist shrine?" queried Chia Cheng. "Yes," said Hsi-chun with a smile.

Chia Cheng thought to himself: "Her Royal Highness wrote about a firecracker which disintegrates after a single explosion. Ying-chun's subject, the abacus, is in constant commotion; Tan-chun's kite is something which drifts away with the wind; Hsi-chun's temple lamp is even more lonely and neglected. What ill-omened subjects for all of them to choose so soon after the New Year!"

The more he reflected, the deeper his dismay. But in his mother's presence he dared not disclose it and forced himself to look at the other riddles. Observing that the last was a verse by Pao-chai, he read it.

> Who leaves the levée with smoke-scented sleeves?
> Not destined by the lute or quilt to sit,
> It needs no watchman to announce the dawn,
> No maid at the fifth watch to replenish it.
> Burned with anxiety both day and night,
> Consumed with anguish as time slips away,
> As life speeds past we learn to hold it dear —
> What cares it whether foul or fair the day?

After reading this Chia Cheng reflected with dismay, "The object itself isn't ill-omened,[1] but what inauspicious lines for a young girl to write. It doesn't look as if any of these girls will have good fortune or long life."

Sunk in gloom he looked the picture of grief as he lowered his head in thought.

His mother imagined that he must be tired, and felt his presence was spoiling the young people's enjoyment.

"There's no need for you to guess any more answers," she said. "You'd better go and rest. We shan't sit up much longer either."

Chia Cheng assented with alacrity and forced himself to toast his mother once more before he withdrew. Back in his own apartment, he turned the matter over in his mind with a grievous sense of foreboding and was unable to sleep. But no more of this.

---

[1] The object described in this verse is a joss-stick.

As soon as he had gone the Lady Dowager urged her grandchildren, "Now relax and have some fun!"

Pao-yu had already run up to the screen-lantern and was prancing about like a monkey freed from its chain, pulling different riddles to pieces.

"Why not sit down as you were before," said Pao-chai, "and chat with us in a more civilized way?"

Hsi-feng, who had joined them now, chimed in, "You ought to have the master keeping you by his side all the time. I forgot just now to suggest that you should make up some riddles in his presence. If I had, I'm sure you'd still be in a cold sweat."

Pao-yu made a frantic grab at her and a scrimmage ensued.

After chatting a little with Li Wan and the girls the Lady Dowager began to feel tired, and hearing the fourth watch sounded she ordered the food to be cleared away, telling the servants they could have what was left.

"Let's rest now," she said, rising to her feet. "Tomorrow's still a holiday, and we ought to get up early. We can enjoy ourselves again in the evening."

To know what happened next day, read the chapter which follows.

CHAPTER 23

Lines from "The Western Chamber"
Are Quoted in Fun
A Song from "Peony Pavilion"
Distresses a Tender Heart

After Yuan-chun's return to the Palace from her visit to Grand View Garden she gave instructions that Tan-chun should copy out all the poems written that day for her to arrange in order of merit, because she wished them to be inscribed on the tablets in the Garden as a lasting memorial to that splendid occasion. Chia Cheng accordingly ordered skilled artisans to be found to polish and engrave the stones under the supervision of Chia Chen, assisted by Chia Jung and Chia Ping. As Chia Chiang had his hands full looking after the twelve actresses and their properties, he asked Chia Chang and Chia Ling to supervise the work instead. In due course wax was melted over the tablets and the poems were engraved in vermilion. But no more of this.

The twenty-four young Buddhists and Taoists from the Dharma Convent and Jade Emperor's Temple in the Garden had now been moved out, and Chia Cheng had been thinking of sending them to various temples elsewhere. Word of this reached Chia Chin's mother née Chou who lived in the street behind just as she had decided to look in Chia Cheng's house for some remunerative job, whether big or small, for her son. So she came by sedan-chair to enlist Hsi-feng's help.

As this woman was normally unassuming, Hsi-feng agreed. Having thought out the right approach she told Lady Wang:

"We mustn't send away the little Buddhists and Taoists, because they'll be needed next time Her Highness comes, and it would be hard to get them together again if once they'd been dispersed. My idea is to move them all to our family's Iron Threshold Temple. Then all we need do is to send someone with a few taels of silver every month for their firewood and rice, and they can be fetched back if needed without any trouble."

Lady Wang passed on this proposal to her husband.

"Quite right," he agreed. "I'm glad you reminded me." He sent for Chia Lien.

Chia Lien and Hsi-feng were having their meal together when this summons arrived. Not knowing what he was wanted for, he put down his rice bowl at once and started out.

"Wait a minute and listen to me!" She caught hold of his arm. "If this is some other business, that's not my affair; but if it's about those little novices, you must handle it my way." She told him then exactly what to say.

Chia Lien shook his head, laughing.

"This is none of my business. If you're so clever, go and ask uncle yourself."

Hsi-feng threw back her head and laid down her chopsticks, staring at Chia Lien with an icy smile.

"Do you mean that, or are you joking?"

"Yun, the son of Fifth Sister-in-Law who lives in West Lane, has come several times begging me to find him a job, and I promised him I would if he would wait. Now here's a job at last, but as usual you want to snatch it away."

"Don't worry. Her Highness wants more pines and cypresses planted in the northeast corner of the Garden, as well as more flowers at the foot of the tower. When that job comes up, I promise to let Yun have it."

"All right then," he chuckled. "But why were you so uncooperative last night when all I wanted was to try something different?"

Hsi-feng snorted with laughter and spat at him in mock disgust, then lowered her head and went on with her meal.

Grinning broadly, Chia Lien left. When he found that his uncle had indeed sent for him about the novices, taking his cue from his wife he suggested:

"Chia Chin seems to be shaping well. We might entrust this to him. He can just draw the allowance every month in the usual way."

Since Chia Cheng never took much interest in such matters, he made no objection. As soon as Chia Lien went back to tell Hsi-feng, she sent a maid to notify Chia Chin's mother, and the young man came to thank them both profusely. As a special favour Hsi-feng asked her husband to let him have three months' allowance in advance and made him write a receipt, to which Chia Lien put his signature. He was then given the tally to fetch from the treasury three months' allowance — two or three hundred taels of glittering silver. One piece he picked up casually and gave as a tip to the men who had weighed the silver, "For a cup of tea," as he put it. The rest he told his servant to carry home. On his mother's advice he lost no time in hiring a sturdy donkey for himself and several covered carts. Taking these round to the side gate of the Jung Mansion, he called out the twenty-four little novices and seated them in the carts. Then together they set off for Iron Threshold Temple. And there we leave them.

Now it had occurred to Yuan-chun while she was editing the poems on Grand View Garden that it would be a pity if her father locked up such charming pleasure grounds after her visit in deference to her, so that nobody could go there. The more so when the girls of the family had a taste for poetizing, and if they were to move there the Garden would make a perfect setting for them while its flowers and willows would not lack admirers. Then she reflected that Pao-yu was unlike other boys, having been brought up among girls, so that if he alone were excluded he would feel left out in the cold, and this might distress the Lady Dowager and Lady Wang. She had better give directions for him to move in there too.

Having reached this decision, she sent the eunuch Hsia Chung to the Jung Mansion with the order: "Pao-chai and the other young ladies are to live in the Garden, which is not to be closed. Pao-yu is to move in as well to continue his studies there."

This edict was received by Chia Cheng and Lady Wang. As soon as the eunuch had left, they reported it to the Lady Dowager and sent servants to clean up the Garden and prepare the buildings, hanging up blinds, portières and bed-curtains.

The others took the news fairly calmly, but Pao-yu was beside himself with joy. He was just discussing it with his grandmother, demanding this, that and the other, when a maid announced that his father wanted him. At this bolt from the blue he turned pale, his spirits quite dashed. He clung like a limpet to the Lady Dowager, too terrified to leave her.

"Go, my treasure," she urged him. "I won't let him be hard on you. Besides, it's because you wrote so well that Her Highness has said you should move into the Garden, and I dare say your father only wants to warn you to behave yourself when you're there. Just say 'Yes' to whatever he tells you and you'll be all right."

She called two old nurses and ordered them to take Pao-yu there and see that he was not frightened.

The nurses complied and Pao-yu left with dragging steps. It so happened that Chia Cheng was discussing some business in his wife's room while her maids Chin-chuan, Tsai-yun, Tsai-hsia, Hsiu-luan and Hsiu-feng were standing outside under the eaves. At sight of Pao-yu they smiled knowingly, and Chin-chuan caught hold of his sleeve.

"I've just put some scented rouge on my lips," she whispered. "Do you want to taste it?"

Tsai-yun pushed her away.

"Don't tease him when he's feeling low," she scolded. "Go in quickly, while the master's in a good mood."

Pao-yu sidled fearfully in. His parents were in the inner room. The concubine Chao raised the portière, and with a bow he entered. His father and mother sat facing each other on the *kang* talking, while on a row of chairs below sat Ying-chun, Tan-chun, Hsi-chun and Chia Huan, all of whom except Ying-chun rose to their feet at his entrance.

Chia Cheng glanced up and saw Pao-yu standing before him. The boy's striking charm and air of distinction contrasted so strongly with Chia Huan's vulgar, common appearance that he was reminded of his dead son Chu. He glanced at Lady Wang. She had only this one son left and she doted on him. As for him, his beard was already turning grey. Bearing all this in mind, he forgot his usual aversion to Pao-yu. After a pause he said:

"Her Highness has ordered you to study and practise calligraphy with the girls in the Garden, instead of fooling around outside and neglecting your studies. Mind that you apply yourself there to your lessons. If you go on misbehaving, watch out!"

"Yes, sir," agreed Pao-yu hastily.

Then his mother drew him over to sit beside her while Chia Huan and the other two sat down again. Stroking her son's neck fondly Lady Wang asked:

"Have you finished those pills prescribed for you the other day?"

"All but one."

"You must fetch ten more tomorrow. Get Hsi-jen to see that you take one each evening at bedtime."

"Ever since you ordered it, madam, Hsi-jen has been giving me one every evening."

"Who is Hsi-jen?" demanded Chia Cheng.

"One of the maids," his wife told him.

"A maid can be called anything, I suppose. But who thought up such a suggestive name for her?"

To shield Pao-yu from his father's displeasure Lady Wang said, "It was the old lady's idea."

"Such a name would never occur to the old lady. This must have been Pao-yu's doing."

Since there was no hiding the truth Pao-yu rose to confess: "I remembered that line of an old poem:

> When the fragrance of flowers assails men
> we know the day is warm.

As this maid's surname is Hua (Flower), I called her Hsi-jen."[1]

---

[1] "Assails men."

"You must change it when you go back," put in Lady Wang quickly. Then she turned to her husband. "Don't be angry, sir, over such a little thing."

"It doesn't really matter, there's no need to change it. But this shows that instead of studying properly Pao-yu gives all his time to romantic trash." Then he said sternly to Pao-yu: "What are you standing there for, you unnatural monster?"

"Run along," urged Lady Wang. "The old lady is probably waiting for you for supper."

Pao-yu assented and slowly withdrew. Once outside he grinned and stuck out his tongue at Chin-chuan before hurrying off with the two nurses. He found Hsi-jen leaning in the doorway of the entrance hall. Her face lit up when she saw that he was back safely, and she asked what his father had wanted.

"Nothing much. Just to warn me to be on my best behaviour when I move into the Garden."

Having by now reached the Lady Dowager's room he told her what had happened. Then he asked Tai-yu, who was there, in which part of the Garden she would like to live.

Tai-yu had been thinking this over and she answered: "My choice would be Bamboo Lodge. I love those bamboos half hiding the winding balustrade, and the place is quieter than anywhere else."

"Just what I thought!" Pao-yu clapped his hands. "That's where I want you. With me in Happy Red Court, we shall be close together and beautifully quiet."

At this point Chia Cheng sent a servant to report to the Lady Dowager that the twenty-second of the second month would be an auspicious day for the move into the Garden, and the young people's quarters would be ready by then. Pao-chai was to have Alpinia Park, Tai-yu Bamboo Lodge, Ying-chun the Pavilion of Variegated Splendour, Tan-chun the Studio of Autumn Freshness, Hsi-chun Smartweed Breeze Cot, Li Wan Paddy-Sweet Cottage, and Pao-yu Happy Red Court. Two old nurses and four maids were assigned to each apartment in addition to the occupant's nanny and own attendants, and there were other servants whose sole duty was cleaning and sweeping.   On the twenty-second they all moved in and at once the Garden gay with flowers and willows ruffled by a fragrant breeze from embroidered sashes lost its former air of desolation; but no need to describe this in detail.

Pao-yu found life in the Garden all he could wish.   He asked nothing better than to spend every day with his sisters, cousins and maids, reading, writing, strumming the lute, playing chess, painting, chanting poems, watching the girls embroider their phoenix patterns, enjoying the flowers, softly singing, guessing riddles or playing the guess-fingers game.   In a word, he was blissfully happy.   There he wrote the following verses on the four seasons, which although quite commonplace give some idea of his sentiments and the scenery.

SPRING NIGHT

The walls flaunt hangings bright as sunset clouds
To muffle the frogs' croaking in the lane;
The rain outside the window chills my pillow,
This vision of spring seems like the girl of my
    dreams.
The candle sheds slow tears — for whom?
The blossoms fall as if reproaching me;
My maids are indolent from long indulgence;
Wearied by their laughter and prattle, I snuggle
    down in my quilt.

SUMMER NIGHT

Weary of embroidery, the beauty dreams;
In its golden cage the parrot cries, "Brew tea!"
Bright window, moon like musk-scented palace
    mirror,
Dim the chamber with fumes of sandalwood and
    incense.
Clear dew from the lotus is poured from amber cups,
Cool air from the willows wafts past crystal railings;
In lake pavilions everywhere flutter silken fans,
And the blinds are rolled up on the vermilion tower
As she finishes her evening toilet.

AUTUMN NIGHT

The red pavilion scented with rue is hushed,
Moonlight floods the gauze dyed with madder;
Crows asleep by the well are wet with dew from the
    plane tree,

And storks roost on mossy boulders.
A maid spreads the gold-phoenix quilt,
The girl coming back from the balcony drops her
  trinkets;
Sleepless at night and thirsty after wine
I relight the incense and call for fresh tea.

WINTER NIGHT

Plum-blossom and bamboo dream, the third watch
  has come,
But sleep eludes them under silk eiderdowns.
Only a stork can be seen in the pine-shadowed court,
No oriole sings in the snow which has drifted
  like pear-blossom.
Cold is the green-sleeved girl as she writes a poem,
Tipsy the young lord in gold and sable gown;
Happily the maid knows how to make good tea
And gathers up fresh fallen snow to brew it.

When some toadies learned that these poems were the work
of a son of the Jung Mansion who was only twelve or thirteen,
they copied them out and praised them far and wide, while
young gallants attracted by the romantic images in them inscribed them on their fans or walls and kept chanting and
admiring them. As a result, Pao-yu was flattered to find himself applied to for poems, calligraphy, paintings and inscriptions; and supplying these occupied much of his time every day.

But after a while this quiet life began to pall. Pao-yu became
restless, dissatisfied and bored. Most of the Garden's inmates
were innocent, ingenuous girls who laughed and romped all
day long without any inhibitions, quite unaware of his feelings.
Then, too restless to stay with them he started fooling around
outside, but still went on feeling disgruntled and frustrated.

His page Ming-yen tried to think of some way to distract
him and decided that there was only one thing that might appeal to him as a novelty. He went to a bookshop and bought
his master a pile of novels old and new, tales about imperial
concubines and empresses, as well as romantic librettos. Pao-
yu had never read such works before. He felt he had discovered a treasure-trove.

"Don't take them into the Garden," Ming-yen warned him. "If they were found I'd be in serious trouble."

But how could Pao-yu agree to this? After much hesitation he picked out several volumes written in a more refined style and smuggled these in, keeping them on the canopy over his bed to read when he was alone. The cruder and more indecent he kept hidden in his study outside the Garden.

One day, about the middle of the third month, carrying a copy of *The Western Chamber* he strolled after breakfast across the bridge above Seeping Fragrance Lock. There he sat down on a rock to read under a blossoming peach-tree. He had just reached the line

Red petals fall in drifts

when a gust of wind blew down such a shower of petals that he and his book were covered with them and the ground near by was carpeted with red. Afraid to trample on the flowers if he shook them off, Pao-yu gathered them into the skirt of his gown and carried them to the water's edge where he shook them into the brook. They floated and circled there for a while, then drifted down the River of Seeping Fragrance.

Going back, he found the ground still strewn with blossoms and was wondering how to dispose of these when a voice behind him asked:

"What are you doing here?"

He turned and saw Tai-yu, a hoe over one shoulder, a gauze bag hanging from the hoe, and a broom in her hand.

"You're just in time to sweep up these petals and throw them into the water," cried Pao-yu. "I've just thrown in a pile."

"Not into the water," objected Tai-yu. "It may be clean here, but once it flows out of these grounds people empty all sorts of dirt and filth into it. The flowers would still be spoiled. I've a grave for flowers in that corner over there. I'm sweeping them up and putting them in this silk bag to bury them there. In time they'll turn back into soil. Wouldn't that be cleaner?"

Pao-yu was delighted by this idea.

"Just let me put this book somewhere and I'll help," he offered.

"What book's that?"

He hastily tucked it out of sight.

"Just the *Doctrine of the Mean* and *The Great Learning*."[1]

"You're trying to fool me again. You'd have done better to show me in the first place."

"I don't mind showing *you*, dear cousin, but you mustn't tell anyone else. It's a real masterpiece. You won't be able to give a thought to eating once you start reading it." He passed her the book.

Tai-yu laid down her gardening tools to read, and the more she read the more enthralled she was. In less time than it takes for a meal she had read all the sixteen scenes. The sheer beauty of the language left a sweet taste in her mouth. After finishing reading she sat there entranced, recalling some of the lines.

"Well, don't you think it's wonderful?" he asked.

She smiled.

"It's certainly fascinating."

"I'm the one 'sick with longing,' " he joked. "And yours is the beauty which caused 'cities and kingdoms to fall.' "[2]

Tai-yu flushed to the tips of her ears. Knitting her sulky brows, her eyes flashing with anger beneath half-drooping lids, she pointed a finger at Pao-yu in accusal.

"You really are the limit! Bringing such licentious songs in here and, what's more, insulting me with nasty quotations from them." Her eyes brimmed with tears. "I'm going to tell uncle and aunt."

She turned to go.

In dismay Pao-yu barred her way.

"Forgive me this once, dear cousin! I shouldn't have said that. But if I meant to insult you, I'll fall into the pond tomorrow and let the scabby-headed tortoise swallow me, so that

---

[1] Two of the Confucian *Four Books*.
[2] Lines from *The Western Chamber*.

I change into a big turtle myself. Then when you become a lady of the first rank and go at last to your paradise in the west, I shall bear the stone tablet at your grave on my back for ever."

Tai-yu burst out laughing at this and wiped her eyes.

"You're so easy to scare, yet still you indulge in talking such nonsense," she teased. "Why, you're nothing but 'a flowerless sprout,' 'a lead spearhead that looks like silver.' "

It was Pao-yu's turn to laugh.

"Now listen to *you*! I'll tell on you too."

"You boast that you can 'memorize a passage with one reading.' Why can't I 'learn ten lines at a glance'?"

Laughing he put the book away.

"Never mind that. Let's get on with burying the flowers."

No sooner had they buried the blossom than Hsi-jen appeared.

"So here you are," she said. "I've been looking all over for you. The Elder Master is unwell and all the young ladies have gone to inquire after his health. The old lady wants you to go too. Come back quickly and change."

Then Pao-yu, taking his book, took leave of Tai-yu and went back to his own room with Hsi-jen.

With Pao-yu gone and the other girls all out too, Tai-yu did not know what to do and decided to go back to her own room. As she rounded the corner of Pear Fragrance Court where the twelve actresses were rehearsing, she heard sweet fluting and singing over the wall. Normally the words of operas made little appeal to her, so she did not listen carefully; but now as she proceeded on her way two lines carried to her distinctly:

> What a riot of brilliant purple and tender crimson,
> Among the ruined wells and crumbling walls.

Strangely touched by this, she stopped to listen. The singer went on:

> What an enchanting sight on this fine morning,
> But who is there that takes delight in the spring?

Tai-yu nodded and sighed.

"So there are fine lines in these operas," she thought. "What a pity that people just care for the spectacle without understanding the meaning."

Then, sorry to have missed a stanza through her preoccupation, she listened again and heard:

> For you are as fair as a flower
> And youth is slipping away like flowing water.

Tai-yu's heart missed a beat. And the next line

> Alonc you sit in your secluded chamber

affected her so much that she sank down on a rock to ponder the words.

> For you are as fair as a flower
> And youth is slipping away like flowing water.

They reminded her of a line in an old poem:

> Water flows and flowers fall, knowing no pity....

and the lines from another poem:

> Spring departs with the flowing water and
>   fallen blossom,
> Far, far away as heaven from the world of men.

She compared this with the lines she had just read in *The Western Chamber*:

> Flowers fall, the water flows red,
> Grief is infinite....

As she brooded over the meaning of all these verses, her heart ached and tears coursed down her cheeks. She might have remained there in a quandary had not someone come up behind her all of a sudden and given her a shove in the back. She turned to look.

But to know who it was, you must read the next chapter. Truly:

> She minds not her morning toilet, her embroidery
>   at night;
> Facing the moon, cooling off in the breeze, she
>   feels grief.

CHAPTER 24

The Drunken Diamond Proves Himself
Generous and Gallant
An Ambitious Girl Loses Her Handkerchief
as an Enticement

Tai-yu's heart was touched, her thoughts were in a whirl, when someone came up from behind and shoved her in the back, asking:

"What are you doing here all on your own?"

Startled, she looked round. It was Hsiang-ling.

"You stupid creature to frighten me so," cried Tai-yu. "Where have you sprung from?"

Hsiang-ling giggled.

"I can't find our young lady anywhere. Your Tzu-chuan is looking for you too. She says the Second Mistress has sent you some tea. Let's go back to your place, shall we?"

She took Tai-yu by the hand and they went back to Bamboo Lodge, where they found two small flasks of new tea from the Palace sent over by Hsi-feng. The two girls sat down. If you ask what serious matters they discussed, these were merely the relative merits of different pieces of embroidery and tapestry. They also played a game of chess and read some passages from a book together before Hsiang-ling took her leave.

But let us return to Pao-yu. When Hsi-jen fetched him back he discovered Yuan-yang leaning over the couch in his outer room examining some of Hsi-jen's needlework.

"Where have you been?" she asked him. "The old lady is waiting for you. She wants you to go over to the other house to inquire after the Elder Master's health. You had better change quickly and go."

As Hsi-jen went into the next room to fetch his clothes and boots, Pao-yu sat on the edge of the couch and kicked off his shoes, waiting. He turned and noticed that Yuan-yang was wearing a pink silk jacket, a sleeveless black satin jacket and a white silk sash. Her head, turned away from him, was bent over the needlework, and there was a flowered collar around her neck. Laying his cheek against the nape of her neck he inhaled her scent and could not resist stroking her, for her skin was just as white and smooth as Hsi-jen's. He mischievously nestled close to her.

"Good sister, let me taste the rouge on your lips!"

With this smiling appeal he clung to her like sticky toffee.

"Hsi-jen!" called Yuan-yang. "Come and look at this. All these years you've been with him, yet you still haven't taught him how to behave."

Hsi-jen, walking in with her arms full of clothes, protested to Pao-yu: "I wear out my tongue talking, but you still carry on like this. What's to become of you? If you go on in this way, you'll make it impossible for us to stay here."

She made him change quickly and go with Yuan-yang to the front apartment. After seeing the Lady Dowager he went out to where his pages and horse were waiting; but just as he was about to mount, Chia Lien arrived back from his father's house and, dismounting in front of Pao-yu, exchanged a few words with him. At this point someone else came over to greet Pao-yu too. This was a tall youth in his late teens with an oval face and intelligent, handsome appearance. But familiar though his face was, Pao-yu could not remember his name or which branch of the clan he belonged to.

"Why are you staring at him like that?" asked Chia Lien. "Don't you know Yun, the son of Fifth Sister-in-Law who lives in the back lane?"

"Of course. I can't think how I forgot." Pao-yu asked after Yun's mother and inquired his business.

Indicating Chia Lien, the young man said, "I've come to have a word with Second Uncle."

"You've grown very handsome since I saw you last." Pao-yu grinned. "You could almost be my son."

"For shame!" Chia Lien chortled. "Your son? He's four or five years older than you."

Pao-yu smiled.

"What age *are* you?"

"Eighteen."

Chia Yun had all his wits about him. He seized this chance to add: "As the proverb says, 'A grandfather in the cradle may have a grandson who leans on a stick.' I may be older than you but 'The highest mountain can't shut out the sun.' These last few years since my father died I've had no one to instruct me properly. If you don't think me too stupid to be your adopted son, Uncle Pao, that would be my great good fortune."

"Hear that?" Chia Lien laughed. "It's no joke adopting a son." With that he went inside.

"If you're free tomorrow," said Pao-yu to Yun, "just drop in and see me. Don't learn *their* sneaky ways. I'm busy now but come to my study tomorrow. We can have a good talk and I'll show you round the Garden."

He swung himself into the saddle then and his pages escorted him to Chia Sheh's house, where he found that his uncle had nothing worse than a cold. Having delivered his grandmother's message he paid his own respects. Chia Sheh stood up to reply to the Lady Dowager's inquiries after his health, then ordered a servant to take Pao-yu to his wife.

Pao-yu went to the back, to Lady Hsing's apartment, and when she had risen to convey her respects to his grandmother he bowed on his own account. She made him sit beside her on the *kang* and asked after the rest of the family. While they sipped the tea she had ordered, Chia Tsung came in to greet Pao-yu.

"Did you ever see such a monkey?" asked Lady Hsing. "Is that nanny of yours dead that she doesn't tidy you up? With that grubby face you look a regular dunce, not like the son of a cultured family."

Just then Chia Huan and his nephew Chia Lan arrived together to pay their respects, and Lady Hsing offered them chairs to sit on. But Huan so resented the sight of Pao-yu sharing the same cushion with his aunt, who was fondling him and making much of him, that before long he signalled to Lan that they should leave. Lan had to comply, so they both got up to beg leave. Pao-yu rose to go too, but Lady Hsing stopped him with a smile.

"Just sit where you are. I've something else to say to you."

He had to resume his seat. She then told the two others:

"When you get back, give my regards to your mothers. I'm so dizzy from the rumpus the girls have raised here that I won't keep you to dinner."

The two boys promised to do as she said and left.

"Did all the girls come?" asked Pao-yu. "Where are they now?"

"After sitting here for a while they went off. They're at the back somewhere or other."

"You said you had something to tell me, aunt. What is it?"

"What have I got to say to you! It was only to ask you to stay for dinner with the girls. And I've something amusing to give you to take back."

They chatted until it was time for the meal. A table and chairs were arranged, the table laid, and they had dinner with the girls. Then Pao-yu took his leave of Chia Sheh and went home with his sister and cousins. After bidding goodnight to the Lady Dowager and Lady Wang they dispersed to their own rooms to rest.

But let us return to Chia Yun, who had gone in to see Chia Lien. He asked him:

"Have you any job for me yet?"

"Something did turn up the other day, but your aunt begged me to let Chia Chin have it. However, she said there's soon to be a lot of planting of flowers and trees in the Garden. As soon as that job comes up, she promises you can have it."

After a short silence Chia Yun said: "I'll just have to wait in that case. Please don't tell my aunt that I came today to ask. I'll mention it to her myself next time I see her."

"Why should *I* mention it? What time do I have to gossip? Tomorrow I've got to set off at the fifth watch to make the trip to Hsingyi and back on the same day. Wait until the day after to come back for news — but not before the first watch, I shan't be free till then." With that Chia Lien went inside to change his clothes.

On his way home from the Jung Mansion a scheme occurred to Chia Yun. He called on his maternal uncle Pu Shih-jen,[1] who kept a perfumery from which he had just returned.

"What brings you here at such a late hour?" asked Pu after exchanging greetings with his nephew.

"I've a favour to ask you, uncle. I need some Borneo camphor and musk. Could you possibly let me have four ounces of each on credit? I'll pay you by the Moon Festival without fail."

"Don't talk to me about credit." His uncle smiled coldly. "Some time ago one of my assistants gave goods worth several taels of silver on credit to a relative, who still hasn't paid up. We had to make good the loss between us. So we agreed never again to give credit to relatives or friends under pain of a twenty taels' fine.

"In any case, those spices are in short supply. Even if you brought ready cash, a little shop like ours couldn't let you have so much. We'd have to try to get you some elsewhere. That's one thing.

"In the second place, you're obviously up to no good but want these things to do something foolish with them. Now don't go complaining that your uncle finds fault with you each time we meet! You young people have simply no sense. If you'd just think up some way to earn a few cash to keep yourself well fed and decently dressed, how pleased I should be!"

"You're quite right, uncle," replied Chia Yun amiably.

---

[1] Homophone for "not a human being."

"When my father died I was too small to understand, but later my mother told me how grateful we should be to you for coming over to take things in hand and managing the funeral. And you know better than anyone else, uncle, that I didn't have any property or land left after my father's death which I squandered. Even the cleverest housewife can't cook a meal without rice. What do you expect *me* to do? You're lucky I'm not one of those thick-skinned people, for then I'd keep pestering you for three pecks of rice today, two pecks of beans tomorrow. What could you have done then, uncle?"

"Whatever your uncle has is yours for the asking, my boy. But as I keep telling your aunt, what worries me is that you won't use your head. Your best bet is to go to the big mansion. If you can't get to see the masters, pocket your pride and get on good terms with their stewards, and they may put some business in your way. The other day, out of town, I ran into the fourth son of your third uncle riding on a donkey with five carts behind him, taking forty or fifty novices to your family temple. His head is screwed on the right way, to get such a job."

This lecture was too much for Chia Yun, who rose to leave.

"What's the hurry?" asked his uncle. "Have a bite with us before you go."

"Are you crazy?" put in his wife before he had half finished. "I told you we've no rice left. All I've got for you is half a catty of noodles which I'm cooking for you now. Why pretend to be rich? If he stays he'll only go hungry."

"Just buy another half catty then," said Pu.

"Yin-chieh!" his wife called to her daughter. "Go and ask Mrs. Wang across the road to lend us twenty or thirty cash — we'll pay her back tomorrow."

But by this time Chia Yun, murmuring "Don't trouble," had already made himself scarce.

He left his uncle's house in a temper and was trudging home with lowered head, fuming over such shabby treatment, when he bumped into a drunkard. As Chia Yun started, the fellow swore:

"Are you blind, fuck you, charging into me like that?"

Before Chia Yun could get out of the way, the drunkard grabbed hold of him. Looking closer he saw that it was his neighbour Ni Erh, a rowdy who lived on usury and his winnings in gambling-dens. He was always drinking and getting into fights. Having just collected some interest from one of his creditors, he was lurching drunkenly home when he bumped into Chia Yun. Spoiling for a fight, he raised a menacing fist.

"Hold on, old chap! It's me."

The voice sounded familiar. Peering with bleary eyes, Ni Erh recognized Chia Yun and let go of him. Staggering, he said with a smile:

"So it's Master Chia. Strike me dead! Where are you off to?"

"Don't ask me. I've never been so snubbed in my life!"

"Never mind. Tell me who's been bullying you. I'll settle accounts with him for you. If anyone in the three streets or six lanes near by, no matter who he is, offends a neighbour of the Drunken Diamond, I'll see to it that his relatives are scattered and his home destroyed."

"Take it easy, old chap. Listen to me." Chia Yun described how Pu had cold-shouldered him.

Ni Erh was highly incensed.

"If he weren't your uncle, wouldn't I just blast him! How maddening! Now don't worry. I've a few taels of silver here. If you want to buy something, just take it. On one condition though. All these years we've been neighbours, and everybody knows I'm a money-lender, yet you've never once asked for a loan. I don't know whether you don't want to dirty your hands having any dealings with a racketeer, or whether you're afraid of getting involved, thinking my interest too high. If so, I'm not asking now for *any* interest on this loan. Not for an I.O.U. either. But if you're afraid you'll be lowering yourself, I won't presume to lend it. We can just go our different ways."

With that he produced a packet of silver from his pouch.

Chia Yun thought, "Ni Erh may be a rascal but he's open-handed and has the name of standing up boldly for his friends.

It would be a mistake to annoy him by refusing. I'll take his silver and later pay him back double."

He said, "I know you're a real sport, old chap. I *did* think of approaching you, but was afraid you might ignore someone so useless, as all your friends are such bold and capable people. I thought if I asked for a loan you'd be bound to turn me down. But now since you're so generous I can't refuse. I'll send you an I.O.U. when I get home."

Ni Erh bellowed with laughter.

"How you talk! But I won't hear of it," he declared. "You spoke of 'friends.' Well then, how can I charge you interest? If I did, that wouldn't be the act of a friend. Let's cut the cackle. As you don't look down on me and this is only a paltry sum — a mere fifteen taels thirty cents — take it to buy what you need. If you insist on writing an I.O.U. I won't give you the silver but lend it to others whom I expect to pay interest."

"All right," said Chia Yun, accepting the silver. "I'll not write any I.O.U. So don't blaze up!"

"What you'd just said wasn't right," Ni Erh chuckled. "It's dark now so I won't invite you to have a drink. I have some business to see to. You'd better go back. I'll trouble you to tell my family to lock up early and turn in, as I shan't be home tonight. If they want me for anything urgent, our daughter can come and fetch me tomorrow morning. They'll find me with the horse-dealer, Short-Legged Wang." So saying, he reeled away.

Marvelling at this stroke of luck Chia Yun reflected, "Ni Erh is certainly a character! But what if he's only generous in his cups? Suppose he asks for a hundred per cent interest tomorrow?" This worried him for a while. Then he decided, "Never mind, once that job comes my way I can pay him back double."

He took the silver to a money shop to be weighed and was delighted to find that Ni Erh was honest and it was indeed fifteen taels and 34.2 cents. He first went next-door and gave Ni Erh's message to his wife before going home. His mother, who was rolling thread on the *kang*, asked where he had been all day. For fear of vexing her he made no mention of going to see her brother.

"I was waiting for Uncle Lien in the west mansion," he said. "Have you had your meal?"

"Yes, and I've kept you yours."

She told the maid to fetch it. It was already time to light the lamp, and after supper Chia Yun went straight to bed.

As soon as he was up and dressed the next morning, he went to a large perfumery outside the South Gate and bought camphor and musk, which he took to the Jung Mansion. Having first made sure that Chia Lien had indeed left, he went to the gate of his courtyard at the back. Some pages were sweeping the yard with long-handled brooms. Presently Chou Jui's wife came out.

"Stop sweeping," she told them. "The mistress is coming out."

Chia Yun swiftly stepped forward to ask:

"Where is Second Aunt going?"

"The old lady has sent for her," said Mrs. Chou. "To cut out some clothes, I fancy."

That same moment Hsi-feng emerged with a throng of attendants. Knowing her weakness for flattery and ceremonial, Chia Yun stepped forward respectfully, saluted her with great deference, and inquired after her health.

Hsi-feng hardly glanced at him, however, merely asking as she walked on how his mother was and why she never called.

"She is not too well, aunt," he replied. "She often thinks of you and would like to come, but she can't get away."

Hsi-feng laughed.

"What a liar you are! You wouldn't have said that if I hadn't asked about her."

"May lightning strike me if I dare to lie to my seniors!" protested Chia Yun. "Only last night she was speaking of you, aunt. She said, 'Your aunt's delicate yet look at all she has on her hands. I don't know where she finds the energy to manage everything so well. Anyone less efficient would be quite worn out.' "

Hsi-feng beamed at this and involuntarily halted.

"Why, pray, should you and your mother gossip about me like that behind my back?"

"The fact is that a very good friend of mine, who owns a perfumery, has bought the rank of an assistant sub-prefect and was recently appointed to a post somewhere in Yunnan. Since he is taking the whole family with him, he's decided to close the shop. He's been going through his stock, giving some things away, selling others cheap, and presenting the more valuable stuff to relatives and friends. That's how I acquired some Borneo camphor and musk. My mother and I agreed that if we tried to sell it we wouldn't be able to get the proper price, because who is there willing to spend so much on such things? Even the richest families would only want a few grams at the most. And even if we gave the stuff away, we couldn't think of anyone who deserves to use so much valuable perfume as these — in fact he may sell the stuff to someone else for next to nothing. Then I thought of you, aunt, and remembered the packets of money you've spent in the past on such things. This year, what with the Imperial Consort in the Palace and the Dragon-Boat Festival coming, I'm sure you'll be needing ten times the usual amount. So after thinking it over we decided the most appropriate thing to do was to make a present of it to you, aunt, as a token of esteem. This way it won't be wasted."

He took out a brocade-covered box and respectfully raised it in both hands to present it.

Hsi-feng, as it so happened, needed some festival gifts and had been thinking of buying some spices and aromatic herbs. Gratified and delighted by this unexpected gift and Chia Yun's little speech, she told Feng-erh:

"Take my nephew's present home and give it to Ping-erh."

Then to Chia Yun she said, "I see you have good sense. No wonder your uncle is always telling me how sensibly you talk and what tact you have."

Chia Yun, hearing this, felt he was getting somewhere. He stepped closer.

"Has uncle been talking to you about me then?" he asked significantly.

Hsi-feng was tempted to tell him about the job of supervising tree-planting which they had in mind for him, but was afraid he might take it the wrong way and imagine she was offering it in return for a few aromatics. So she refrained, saying not a word about it. And after a few casual remarks she went on to see the Lady Dowager. Chia Yun had to go home without having broached the subject.

As Pao-yu had invited him the previous day to call on him in his study, after lunch he went back and made his way to Luminous Clouds Studio outside the ceremonial gate leading to the Lady Dowager's apartments. He found Pei-ming having a game of chess with Chu-yao and squabbling over a move. Four other pages, Ying-chuan, Sao-hua, Tiao-yun and Pan-heh, were up on the roof robbing a bird's nest. As Chia Yun entered the courtyard he stamped his foot.

"Up to your monkey-tricks again! Can't you see a visitor's come?"

Hearing this, all the pages scampered off. Chia Yun went into the study and took a seat.

"Has Master Pao been here today?" he asked.

"No, he hasn't. If you want to talk to him, I'll scout round and find out his whereabouts for you." Pei-ming went out.

For the time it takes for a meal Chia Yun inspected the calligraphy, paintings and curios. Then, as Pei-ming had not returned, he looked round for the other pages; but they had all gone off to amuse themselves. He was feeling put out and bored when a sweet voice just outside the door called:

"Brother!"

Looking out he discovered a maid of sixteen or seventeen, a slender, neat, clever-looking girl. She was shrinking back at sight of Chia Yun when Pei-ming returned.

"Good," he said. "I was looking for a messenger."

Chia Yun walked out to question the page, who told him:

"I waited for a long time, but nobody came out. This is one of the girls from Happy Red Court." He turned to her. "Be a good girl and tell him, will you, that the Second Master from the back lane has called."

On learning that Chia Yun belonged to her masters' clan, the maid did not avoid him as she had before but shot him one or two penetrating glances.

"Never mind about the back lane," he joked. "Just tell him Yun has come."

The girl gave a faint smile.

"If you please, sir, I think you'd better go home and come back tomorrow. I'll tell him this evening if I have a chance."

"What do you mean?" asked Pei-ming.

"He missed his nap this afternoon, so he's sure to dine early and won't be coming here this evening. Are you going to make this gentleman wait and go hungry? He'd much better go home now and come back tomorrow. Because even if someone promised to take a message, he mightn't deliver it."

The girl spoke so concisely and prettily that Chia Yun wanted to ask her name. But as she worked for Pao-yu he thought better of it, simply remarking:

"Right you are. I'll come tomorrow."

Pei-ming urged him to have a cup of tea before leaving.

"No thanks," said Chia Yun. "I have some other business." Walking off as he spoke, he looked back at the girl still standing there, and then made his way home.

The next day Chia Yun went back. In front of the main gate he ran into Hsi-feng on her way to the other house to pay her respects. She had just got into her carriage, but at sight of Chia Yun she ordered a servant to stop him and called to him with a smile through the carriage window:

"You've got a nerve, Yun, playing that trick on me! I see now why you gave me that present. You had a favour to ask. Yesterday your uncle told me you'd already approached him."

"Please don't bring that up, aunt," he pleaded, smiling. "I'm sorry I ever asked him. If I'd know how things stood I'd have come to you in the first place, and it would all have been settled long ago. I didn't know it was no use appealing to uncle."

Hsi-feng laughed.

"No wonder! So it was after failing with him that you came to me yesterday."

"That's not fair, aunt. I had no such idea in my mind. If I had, wouldn't I have appealed to you yesterday? But since you know about it now, I'll bypass uncle and beg *you*, aunt, to show me some kindness."

"What a roundabout way of doing things!" She smiled sarcastically. "You make it hard for me. If you'd told me earlier, this little business wouldn't have taken so long. Some trees and flowers are to be planted in the Garden, and I was looking for someone to put in charge. If you'd spoken before, it could have been fixed up some time ago."

"Well, you can put me in charge, aunt."

Hsi-feng thought for a moment.

"I think better not. Suppose we wait until next New Year and give you the bigger job of buying fireworks and lanterns?"

"Let me have this job first, dear aunt. If I do all right in this, you can give me the other later."

"You do look ahead, don't you?" She chuckled. "All right. But I wouldn't have bothered if your uncle hadn't put in a word for you. I shall be back after breakfast, so come about noon for the money and you can start your planting the day after tomorrow."

She ordered the servants to start the carriage and left.

Overjoyed, Chia Yun went to Luminous Clouds Studio and asked for Pao-yu, only to find he had gone out early that morning to call on the Prince of Peiching. He sat quietly there till noon when he heard that Hsi-feng was back, and then wrote a receipt and went to get the tally. He waited outside the courtyard while a servant announced him. Then Tsai-ming came out and took his receipt. When the amount to be drawn and the date had been filled in, the page returned it to him with the tally. He saw to his delight that the sum entered was two hundred taels and went straight to the treasury to get the silver, then home to inform his mother, who rejoiced with him.

At the fifth watch the next morning, he sought out Ni Erh to return his loan, and seeing that he was in funds Ni Erh took the money.

Then Chia Yun took fifty taels to the house of Fang Chun, a gardener who lived outside the West Gate, from whom he bought trees.

To revert now to Pao-yu. His invitation to Chia Yun that day had been no more than a rich lordling's way of talking, and not being seriously meant was soon forgotten. Upon his return from the palace of the Prince of Peiching in the evening, he paid his respects to his grandmother and mother before going back to the Garden, where he took off his formal clothes and waited for his bath.

It so happened that Hsi-jen had been asked over by Pao-chai to help braid some knot-buttons; Chiu-wen and Pi-hen had gone to hurry the servants bringing water; Tan-yun had asked leave for her mother's birthday; and Sheh-yueh was ill at home. The other maids who did the rougher work, not expecting to be summoned, had gone off in search of their friends. Thus for a short while Pao-yu was all alone. And precisely at this moment he wanted some tea. He called several times before two or three old nannies came in. These he hastily waved away saying:

"It's all right. I don't need you."

Then the old women had to withdraw.

As none of the girls were about, Pao-yu fetched a bowl himself and went to get the teapot.

"Don't scald yourself, Master Pao. Let me do that," called a voice from behind. A girl stepped forward and took the bowl from him.

Pao-yu started.

"Where did *you* spring from?" he asked. "What a fright you gave me!"

Handing him the tea she answered: "I was in the back yard. Didn't you hear me come in by the back door, Master Pao?"

Pao-yu sized her up as he sipped his tea. Her clothes were by no means new, but with her fine black hair gathered in a knot, her oval face and her trim, slender figure, she looked altogether a most sweet, pretty girl.

"Do you work here?" he asked with a smile.

"Yes," she answered.

"How is it, in that case, I've never seen you?"

The maid laughed mockingly.

"There are plenty of us you haven't seen. I'm not the only one by any means. How could you know me? I don't fetch and carry for you, or wait on you personally."

"Why not?"

"That's asking! But I've something to report, sir. Yesterday a young gentleman called Yun came to see you. I told Pei-ming to send him away as I thought you were busy, and asked him to come back this morning. But by then you'd already gone to call on the prince."

Just at this moment Chiu-wen and Pi-hen staggered back, laughing and chatting, holding up their skirts, a bucket between them from which the water was splashing. This maid hurried to relieve them of their load.

"You've wet my skirt," Chiu-wen complained to Pi-hen.

"You trod on my shoe!" Pi-hen retorted.

Looking at this girl who had appeared so abruptly, they saw it was Hsiao-hung. Both put down the bucket in surprise and hurried in. They were very put out to find Pao-yu on his own. As soon as they had prepared his bath and helped him undress, they closed the door behind them and went round again to the back to find Hsiao-hung.

"What were you doing in there just now?" they demanded.

"I hadn't been in," she said. "I couldn't find my handkerchief, so I was looking for it at the back when Master Pao called for tea. As none of you sisters was about, I went in to pour it for him. And that's when you turned up."

Chiu-wen spat in her face.

"Shameless slut! I told you to go and hurry them with the water, but you said you were busy and made us go instead. Then you seized this chance to wait on him here yourself. You're making your way up, aren't you? Think we can't keep up with you, eh? Have a look at yourself in a mirror. Are you fit to serve Master Pao tea?"

Pi-hen chimed in: "Tomorrow we'll tell the others that if he wants tea or water or anything, we needn't stir — she'll do it."

"The rest of us may just as well clear off, leaving her on her own here."

They were laying into Hsiao-hung in turn when an old nanny arrived with a message from Hsi-feng.

"Someone's bringing gardeners tomorrow to plant trees, so you must watch out. Don't go sunning your clothes and skirts all over the place. All the artificial hills will be screened off. You're not to go running wild."

"Who'll be in charge of the workmen?" asked Chiu-wen.

"Some Master Yun from the back lane," was the answer.

The name meant nothing to Chiu-wen and Pi-hen, who put some other questions; but Hsiao-hung knew it must be the man she had met the day before in the study outside.

Now Hsiao-hung's family name was Lin and her childhood name was Hung-yu (Red Jade); but because "*yu*" (jade) came in the names Tai-yu and Pao-yu she was called Hsiao-hung instead. Her family had served the Chias for generations, and her father was now in charge of various farms and properties outside. Hsiao-hung was sixteen this year. When first sent into Grand View Garden she had been assigned to Happy Red Court, which was pleasantly quiet at the time. But after the girls and Pao-yu were commanded to move there to live and these rooms were taken by him, simple as Hsiao-hung was, with her good looks she was foolishly eager to climb up in the world. She had long been looking for a chance to attract Pao-yu's attention, but his other attendants were too smart to allow her to put herself forward. Today her opportunity had come, but her hopes had been dashed by the spitefulness of Chiu-wen and Pi-hen. She was feeling most disgruntled when the old nanny mentioned that Chia Yun would be coming, and that put a new idea into her head. She went dejectedly back to her room and lay down to think it over. As she tossed and turned some-one called softly through the window:

"Hsiao-hung! I've found your handkerchief for you."

She ran out to look. It was no other than Chia Yun. With a blush of confusion she asked:

"Where did you find it, sir?"

Chia Yun laughed.

"Come here and I'll tell you."

He grabbed for her. She turned frantically and fled, but stumbled over the threshold and woke with a start. So it was only a dream!

If you want to know the upshot, read the next chapter.

CHAPTER 25

Five Devils Invoked by Sorcery Take Possession
of Pao-yu and Hsi-feng
Two Sages See the Jade of Spiritual Understanding
in the Dream of Red Mansions

Hsiao-hung fell into a doze, her thoughts running on love.
When Chia Yun tried to seize her she turned and fled, but
stumbling over the threshold woke with a start to the realization that it was only a dream. She tossed and turned sleeplessly
until day dawned, when some other maids called her to help
them sweep and fetch water. Without washing her face or putting on any make-up, she casually smoothed her hair in front
of the mirror and hastily rinsed her hands, after which she tied
a sash round her waist and set about her work.

Now Pao-yu had been so struck by Hsiao-hung the previous
day that he would have liked to have her wait on him, but he
feared this might upset Hsi-jen and the others; besides, there
was no saying how the girl would turn out. If she proved satisfactory, well and good; if not, sending her away again would
be awkward. So he got up moodily and sat there brooding, not
even troubling to comb his hair or wash.

Presently the shutters were taken down and through the
gauze window he had a clear view of the maids sweeping the
courtyard. All of them were powdered and rouged, with
flowers or willow shoots in their hair, but he saw no sign of
Hsiao-hung. He slipped on his shoes and strolled out, ostensibly
to look at the flowers, gazing this way and that until he
glimpsed, half-hidden by a crab-apple tree, a figure leaning over
the balustrade in the southwest corner of the covered walk.
He strolled round the tree and looked more closely. Yes, it
was the girl of the day before, apparently lost in thought. He

was wondering whether to accost her when Pi-hen fetched him in again to wash. He had no choice but to go back.

And now Hsiao-hung was aroused from her abstraction by the sight of Hsi-jen beckoning. She went to see what was wanted.

"Our watering-can's broken and hasn't been mended yet," said Hsi-jen. "I want you to go and borrow one of Miss Lin's."

The girl set off on this errand to Bamboo Lodge. As she crossed Green Mist Bridge the sight of the artificial hills screened off reminded her that this was the day for tree-planting. Some distance away a band of men could be seen digging under the supervision of Chia Yun, seated on a nearby boulder. Not having the courage to approach him, she proceeded quietly to Bamboo Lodge, borrowed a watering-can and took it back, then lay down in her room in low spirits. The others, assuming that she was feeling unwell, paid no attention. And the day dragged by, uneventful.

The day after that was the birthday of Wang Tzu-teng's wife, and the Lady Dowager and Lady Wang had been invited to the celebrations. Since her mother-in-law did not go, neither did Lady Wang; but Aunt Hsueh, Hsi-feng, the three Chia girls, Pao-chai and Pao-yu went along, not returning till the evening.

It so happened that when Chia Huan came back from school Lady Wang had told him to copy out for her some incantations invoking the Buddhist guardian deities, the dvarapalas. The boy took a seat on the *kang* in her room, ordered candles to be lighted, and set about writing with a great show of importance. Now he called Tsai-hsia to pour him tea, now told Yu-chuan to trim the wicks of his candles, now complained that Chin-chuan was standing in his light. As all the maids disliked him they took no notice — all except Tsai-hsia who still kept in with him. She poured him some tea and, noticing that Lady Wang was chatting with some other people, she whispered:

"Be quiet. Don't be such a nuisance. You're only making yourself unpopular."

"Don't try to fool me," he retorted. "I can see what's happening. Now you're friendly with Pao-yu, you mean to ignore me."

Tsai-hsia bit her lips and with one finger rapped him on the forehead.

"You ungrateful thing! Like the dog that bit Lu Tung-pin — you bite the hand that feeds you."

Just then Hsi-feng came in to pay her respects, and Lady Wang wanted a detailed account of the party — the other guests, the operas and the feast. Before long Pao-yu, too, arrived. Having greeted his mother and made some polite conversation, he told the maids to help him off with his chaplet, gown and boots, then nestled up to his mother. As she stroked and caressed him he put his arms round her neck and chattered.

"You've had too much to drink again, my son," scolded Lady Wang. "How hot your face is! If you go on tossing about like this, the wine may go up to your head. Why not lie down and rest a while."

She called for a pillow and Pao-yu, lying down behind her, asked Tsai-hsia to come and massage him. But when he joked with her she cold-shouldered him and kept her eyes on Chia Huan. Pao-yu took her hand.

"Do be nice to me, sister!" he begged.

Tsai-hsia snatched her hand away.

"If you do that again, I'll shout," she warned him.

This was overheard by Chia Huan, who had always hated Pao-yu. At the sight of him teasing Tsai-hsia, he felt ready to explode with jealousy. He dared not protest outright, but he had mulled over a plan and now that they were so close he saw his chance to put it into action. He would blind Pao-yu with burning candle-wax! Deliberately knocking over the candlestick, he splashed the hot melted wax on his half-brother's face. Pao-yu's cry of pain made everyone jump for fright. They hastily brought over the standard lamp as well as several lamps from other rooms, and saw with consternation that Pao-yu's face was covered with wax. Frantic and furious,

Lady Wang ordered the servants to wipe it off, and then rounded on Chia Huan.

"What a dunderhead!" scolded Hsi-feng with a smile on her face, as she scrambled on to the *kang* to attend to Pao-yu. "Huan's not fit to mix in decent company. His mother really ought to bring him up better."

This remark was the cue for Lady Wang to stop abusing Chia Huan and to send for the concubine Chao.

"Why don't you teach that spiteful brat of yours to behave himself?" she fumed. "Time and again I've overlooked this sort of thing, but it only makes you worse. Conceited creature!"

Although the concubine was eaten up by jealousy of Hsi-feng and Pao-yu, she dared not show it either. Now that Chia Huan had made such trouble, she had no alternative but to accept these taunts meekly and show concern for Pao-yu. His left cheek was badly blistered, but luckily no damage had been done to his eyes. Lady Wang's heart ached for him even as she wondered how she was to answer for this to her mother-in-law tomorrow. She vented her anger again on the concubine, then went on soothing Pao-yu and dabbing his cheeks with a disinfectant ointment.

"It stings a bit but it's nothing serious," Pao-yu assured her. "Tomorrow if grandmother asks, I'll say I scalded myself."

"She'll scold us all the same for our negligence," retorted Hsi-feng smiling. "There'll be a row anyway, no matter what you say."

Lady Wang then had Pao-yu escorted back to his rooms, where Hsi-jen and the others were horrified by his appearance.

Tai-yu had been lonely all day in Pao-yu's absence, and sent several times that evening to ask whether he was back. When she learned of his accident she hurried over to find him in front of the mirror, his left cheek daubed with ointment. Imagining that the burn was serious, she approached to have a look; but Pao-yu, knowing how fastidious she was, covered his cheek with one hand and waved her away. Tai-yu knew her own weakness; she also knew that Pao-yu was afraid of disgusting her.

"I just wanted to see where the burn is," she said gently. "Why do you have to hide it?"

She then came closer and turned his head to have a look. "Does it hurt much?" she asked.

"Not really. I'll be all right in a couple of days."

After keeping him company for a while she left, feeling rather depressed.

The next day when Pao-yu saw the Lady Dowager, although he took the blame for the burn on himself, sure enough she reprimanded all his attendants.

Another day went by and they had a visit from Priestess Ma, Pao-yu's Buddhist godmother. The sight of him gave her a shock and she asked with concern what had happened. Learning that he had been scalded she nodded and sighed, then passed her fingers over his face with some muttered incantations.

"He'll be all right now," she declared. "This was just a chance misfortune. You don't know, Old Ancestress, all the solemn warnings there are in the Buddhist sutras about the sons born into noble families, who are always dogged by evil spirits who pinch them, nip them, knock their rice-bowls out of their hands, or trip them up on the road. That's why so many sons of great houses die young."

"Is there no way to prevent it?" asked the Lady Dowager anxiously.

"Of course there is. Just do more good deeds on his behalf. The sutras tell us of a great Bodhisattva in the west whose glory illumines all around and whose special charge it is to bring to light the evil spirits in dark places. If faithful believers worship him devoutly, their descendants are assured of peace and health and no evil spirits can get possession of them."

"What offerings does this Bodhisattva require?"

"Nothing of any great value. Apart from incense and candles, a few catties of oil every day for the Big Lamp. For that lamp is a manifestation of the Bodhisattva. It has to be kept burning day and night."

"How much oil does it take to keep it burning for one whole day and night? If you tell me the exact amount, I should like to donate it."

"There's no fixed amount, it's up to the donor. Several of the royal consorts have presented offerings of this kind in our convent. The mother of the Prince of Nanan has made a generous donation, forty-eight catties of oil a day and another catty of lampwicks, so her lamp is almost as large as a water vat. The lady of the Marquis of Chintien comes next with twenty-four catties. Other families give anything from five to three or one — it doesn't matter. Some poor families who can't afford so much may just donate a quarter or half a catty, but we keep a lamp burning for them just the same."

The Lady Dowager nodded thoughtfully.

"Of course, more can be given for parents or elders," continued the priestess. "But if our Old Ancestress gives too much for Pao-yu, it won't be good for the boy and may even spoil his luck. Five catties or seven at the most would be ample."

"Make it five catties a day then," said the Lady Dowager. "You can collect a month's donation at a time."

"May Amida Buddha the Merciful Great Bodhisattva preserve you!" cried the grateful priestess.

The old lady ordered the servants, "In future when Pao-yu goes out give his pages a few strings of cash to distribute as alms to bonzes, Taoists and the poor."

The priestess sat with them there a little longer, then made the rounds of different apartments, coming presently to that of the concubine Chao who, after exchanging greetings, ordered tea. It was clear from a heap of satin remnants on the *kang* that she had been making slippers.

"I could do with some silk for uppers myself," remarked Ma. "Can you spare me a few odd pieces? I don't mind what colour."

"You won't find anything good in that lot," said the concubine with a sigh. "Good things don't come *my* way. That's all there is. But if you don't think them too bad you're welcome to choose a couple."

The priestess picked out several pieces and tucked them in her sleeves.

"The other day," the concubine went on, "I sent over five hundred cash. Did you sacrifice to the God of Medicine for me?"

"Yes, days ago."

"Amida Buddha!" She sighed again. "If I'd only more in hand I'd be giving oftener. I just haven't the means."

"Don't worry. Just hold out till Master Huan grows up and gets an official post. Then you can do all the good works you want."

"Well, well, don't talk about that!" The concubine snorted. "You can see how things are. My son and I are the least and lowest in this household. Of course Pao-yu is the precious dragon of the house. Mind you, he's still just a child with winning ways, so I've nothing to say if his elders dote on him. But I refuse to crawl to *her*." She held up two fingers.

"You mean the second young mistress, Madam Lien?"

The concubine hastily signed to her to be quiet. Having raised the portière to make sure that no one was there, she came back and whispered:

"She's a terror, a real terror! If she doesn't end by shifting all the property here to her mother's house, I'm not a human being!"

The priestess, hearing this, decided to sound her out further.

"You don't have to tell me, it's plain enough," she said. "It's kind of you to put up with it and let her have her own way. That's fine."

"What else can we do, for goodness' sake? Who would have the nerve to say a word against her?"

The priestess gave a short laugh. After a moment's pause she said: "I don't want to talk like a trouble-maker, but I do think if you don't stick up for yourselves you can't very well blame others. Even if you dare not tackle her openly you could have done something in secret, instead of letting things drag on like this."

Sensing something behind this, the concubine brightened up.

"In secret? Do explain how," she cried. "I've thought of that, but there's no one capable of doing it. If you'll show me some way, I'll make it well worth your while."

"Amida Buddha, don't ask me that," protested the priestess, although well aware that they both had the same thing in mind. "What do I know about such matters? No, that would be a sin, a wicked sin."

"Come on, you're always good to those in trouble. Are you going to stand by and watch that woman trample us, mother and child, to death? Or are you afraid I shan't be able to pay you?"

Ma smiled.

"It's right to say that I'm sorry to see you and your son bullied, but it's wrong of you to talk about *paying* me. Why, even if I hoped for some reward, what have you got that could tempt me?"

The concubine felt that Ma was yielding.

"How can a smart woman like you be so dense?" she asked. "If you know some good magic to get rid of those two, the family property's bound to come to my son. When that happens you can have anything you want."

The priestess lowered her head for a while.

"When that happens," she said at last, "and everything's in the bag, unless I've something in writing you'll just ignore me."

"That's no problem," said the concubine. "Though I haven't got much at the moment, I've saved a few taels of silver and I have some clothes and trinkets too. You can take some of them to be going on with. And I can write you a promissory note and, if you like, find a witness too, so that you can be sure I'll pay you in full later on."

"Do you really mean that?"

"How could I lie to you on such a matter?"

The concubine then called in a trusted old servant to whom she whispered certain instructions. The woman went out, returning after a while with a promissory note for five hundred taels. Concubine Chao pressed her fingerprints on this, then opened her chest and took out some loose silver. This she showed to the priestess.

"Take this first to spend on offerings. How's that?"

At the sight of this gleaming pile of silver and the promissory note, the priestess did not scruple to assent with alacrity. First she put away the silver and then the note. Next she rummaged in her waistband for a while and fished out twelve paper figures — two of human beings and ten of devils with white hair and blue faces — which she gave to the concubine.

"Write the eight characters of their horoscopes on these two figures," she whispered. "Then put them, with five devils each, in their beds. That's all you have to do. I shall do my magic at home. It's sure to work. Mind you're very careful, and don't look alarmed."

They were interrupted by the arrival of a maid from Lady Wang.

"So here you are," she said to the concubine. "Her Ladyship's waiting for you."

Then the two women parted company.

But let us return to Tai-yu. Now that Pao-yu's burn kept him indoors, she often dropped in for a chat. Today after lunch she did some reading but soon became bored with the book; then she did a little needlework with Tzu-chuan and Hsueh-yen, but found this even more tedious. So she stood for a while leaning against the doorway in a brown study, before stepping out to look at the bamboo shoots sprouting below the steps. And then, hardly knowing what she did, she stepped out of the courtyard. There was no one in sight in the Garden, nothing to be seen but the brightness of flowers and the shadows of willows, nothing to be heard but birdsong and gurgling streams. And so she made her way to Happy Red Court. Some maids on the terrace there, having just fetched water, were watching the thrushes have their bath. Inside there was laughter and going in she found Li Wan, Hsi-feng and Pao-chai assembled there. At sight of her they smiled.

"Here comes another!"

"Were invitations sent out that you're here in force?" asked Tai-yu jokingly.

"I sent you two canisters of tea the other day," interposed Hsi-feng. "Where were you?"

"Oh, it had slipped my mind. Thank you very much."

"How did you like it?" Hsi-feng asked.

"It's all right but I didn't care for it much," put in Pao-yu. "I don't know how the rest of you found it."

"The flavour was quite delicate, but the colour wasn't too good," remarked Pao-chai.

"That was tribute tea from Siam," Hsi-feng told them. "Personally, I didn't find it as good as the kind we drink every day."

"I liked it," retorted Tai-yu. "Different people have different tastes."

"In that case you can have mine," offered Pao-yu.

"If you really like it I've plenty more," said Hsi-feng.

"Fine. I'll send a maid to fetch it," Tai-yu promised.

"No need," rejoined Hsi-feng. "I'll have it sent round. I was going to send over to you tomorrow anyway to ask a favour."

"Listen to her!" cried Tai-yu. "Just take a little tea from her and she starts ordering you about."

Hsi-feng chuckled.

"Asked a favour, you make such a fuss! Over drinking tea too. 'Drink our family's tea, a daughter-in-law to be'!"

As the whole party burst out laughing, Tai-yu blushed and turned her head away, saying nothing.

Li Wan observed with a smile to Pao-chai, "Our second sister-in-law will have her joke."

"Joke?" Tai-yu spat. "I call it disgustingly vulgar."

"Are you dreaming? What's wrong with being our daughter-in-law?" teased Hsi-feng, then pointed at Pao-yu. "Look, isn't he handsome enough for you? Isn't his status good enough for you? Isn't his family rich enough for you? Who could think it a bad match in any respect?"

Tai-yu rose at once to go.

"You're offended," cried Pao-chai. "Come back, Tai-yu! It'll spoil the fun if you go."

She ran after Tai-yu to stop her. But at the doorway they were intercepted by the concubines Chao and Chou, who had come to inquire after Pao-yu. Li Wan, Pao-chai and Pao-yu invited them to sit down. Hsi-feng, however, went on talking with Tai-yu and ignored them. Pao-chai was just about to speak when a maid sent by Lady Wang announced that Wang Tzu-teng's wife had called and would like to see the young ladies. Li Wan at once urged Hsi-feng and the girls to go over, and the two concubines also took a hasty leave of Pao-yu.

"I can't go out," said Pao-yu. "Whatever happens, don't let my aunt come over here! Do wait a bit, Cousin Lin. I've something to tell you."

Hsi-feng, hearing this, turned to Tai-yu with a smile.

"You'd better stay. You're wanted."

She pushed the girl back into the room and went off with Li Wan.

Pao-yu, left alone with Tai-yu, clasped her sleeve and smiled but could not get a word out. She could not help blushing and tried to break away.

"Aiya!" he cried suddenly. "How my head aches!"

"Serves you right. Buddha be praised."

The next moment he let out a piercing cry.

"I'm dying!"

He leapt several feet into the air, babbling and raving. Tai-yu and the maids rushed in panic to tell the Lady Dowager and Lady Wang; and as Wang Tzu-teng's wife was with them, the whole party hurried over. By now Pao-yu had turned the whole place upside down in search of a sword or stick to kill himself with. His grandmother and mother shook with terror, bursting into loud lamentations for their darling. At once the whole household was thrown into confusion as everyone flocked to the Garden — from Chia Sheh, Lady Hsing, Chia Cheng, Chia Lien, Chia Huan, Chia Jung, Chia Yun, Chia Ping, Aunt Hsueh and Hsueh Pan down to Chou Jui's wife and all the other female servants.

They were all in a great commotion and wondering what to do when in rushed Hsi-feng, brandishing a bright steel sword, with which she was trying to cut down all the chickens, dogs and people in her way. This was even more staggering! Chou Jui's wife, aided by some of the stronger and braver maids, managed to overpower her and disarm her. They then carried her back to her room where Ping-erh and Feng-erh gave way to a storm of weeping.

Even Chia Cheng was quite distracted, trying to attend to both Pao-yu and Hsi-feng at once. The others, it goes without saying, were still more distraught. But of them all Hsueh Pan was the most frantic, being afraid that in the crush his mother might be knocked over, Pao-chai stared at, or Hsiang-ling exposed to indignities — for he knew what libertines Chia Chen and the rest were. Then, his eye suddenly falling on Tai-yu, he was so enraptured by her charms that he almost melted on the spot.

By now proposals of all kinds were being made. Some suggested calling in exorcists to drive out evil spirits; some, getting a witch to lure them out by dancing; others recommended the Taoist Chang from the Jade Emperor's Temple. . . . Pandemonium reigned as they tried all conceivable remedies together with incantations, divination and prayers. But all to no avail. And at sunset Wang Tzu-teng's wife took her leave.

Next day Wang Tzu-teng came in person to make inquiries. This was followed by visits from young Marquis Shih's wife, the brothers and relations of Lady Hsing, and the wives of other family connections. Some brought charm water. Others sent round bonzes and Taoists. Still nothing proved of any use.

Pao-yu and Hsi-feng had fallen into a coma. They lay on their beds burning with fever and babbling deliriously. As the night wore on, because none of the maids or nannies dared go near them, they were carried to Lady Wang's quarters where some pages in the charge of Chia Yun kept watch in turn. The Lady Dowager, Lady Wang, Lady Hsing and Aunt Hsueh, racked by sobs, refused to stir from their side.

Afraid that their mother might fall ill of grief, Chia Sheh and Chia Cheng bestirred themselves so frantically day and night that no one, high or low, had any rest or could offer any advice. Chia Sheh kept summoning more bonzes and Taoists, but because these could do no good Chia Cheng lost patience and tried to dissuade him.

"Their fate rests with Heaven," he said. "Human beings are powerless. Since their disorder is quite unforeseen and no drugs can cure it, it must be the will of Heaven. We shall just have to leave them to their fate."

His counsel fell on deaf ears. Chia Sheh would not relax his exertions. But still there was no improvement.

By the third day the patients were lying at death's door and the whole household despaired. Then, as all hope was relinquished, preparations were started for the funeral. The Lady Dowager, Lady Wang, Chia Lien, Ping-erh and Hsi-jen wept even more bitterly than the rest, unable to take food or sleep. Only the concubine Chao and Chia Huan were secretly exulting.

On the morning of the fourth day Pao-yu opened his eyes.

"I am going to leave you now," he told his weeping grandmother. "You must make haste and get me ready to go."

These words made her feel as if he had wrenched out her heart.

"Don't take it too hard, madam," urged the concubine. "The boy's as good as gone. Better lay him out and let him make an end of his misery. If you insist on holding him back, he'll not be able to breathe his last and will only suffer for it in the next world. . . ."

Before she could finish the old lady spat in her face.

"May your tongue rot, you bitch!" she swore. "Who asked for your opinion? How do *you* know he'll suffer in the next world? Why say he's as good as gone? What good will it do *you* if he dies? You're dreaming! If he does die, I'll make you pay for it. You're the ones to blame for this, forcing the child to study and breaking his spirit so that the sight of his father made him as scared as a mouse chased by a cat. It's you bitches who have hounded him to his death. But don't gloat too soon — you've still me to reckon with."

Quite beside himself to hear her curses and sobs, Chia Cheng hastily ordered his concubine away and tried to calm his mother. But just then a servant came in to announce that the two coffins were ready for his inspection. This added fuel to the fire of the old lady's anger.

"Who ordered coffins?" she screamed. "Fetch the coffin-makers here! Have them beaten to death!"

She was storming fit to convulse heaven and earth when the faint sound of a monk's wooden clapper reached their ears.

"Put your trust in Buddha who absolves sins," the monk chanted. "All those afflicted, distressed, imperilled or possessed by evil spirits, we can cure."

At once the Lady Dowager and Lady Wang asked to have the monk brought in. Though Chia Cheng disapproved, he could not disregard his mother's wishes. He was marvelling, too, that the voice carried so clearly right into the house. So he gave the order to the servants. Then in came a scabby-headed bonze and a lame Taoist. What was he like, this bonze?

> His nose was bulbous and his eyebrows long,
> His two eyes glittered with a starry light;
> Ragged, in shoes of straw, with scabby head,
> This vagrant monk was an obnoxious sight.

As for the Taoist:

> With one leg short and one leg long,
> All soaked with rain and caked with mud was he;
> If asked from whence he came he would reply:
> "West of the Penglai Isles in Weightless Sea."

Chia Cheng asked this pair which monastery they were from.

"There is no need to inquire into that, sir," replied the bonze with a smile. "We hear there is illness in your house and have come to cure it."

"Yes, two members of the family are bewitched. Have you perhaps some miraculous remedy?"

"Why ask us for a remedy?" retorted the Taoist. "You already have in your house a rare treasure capable of curing them."

With a start Chia Cheng grasped the significance of this remark.

"It is true that my son was born with a piece of jade in his mouth," he replied. "And the inscription on it claims that it can ward off evil. But it has proved ineffective."

"You do not understand the miraculous powers of that precious jade, sir. It has not proved efficacious because it is confused by music, beauty, riches and lust for gain. Just bring it to me and I think we can restore its powers by incantation."

Chia Cheng took the jade from Pao-yu's neck and passed it to them. The monk laid it reverently on the palm of one hand.

"Thirteen years have passed in a twinkling since we left you at the foot of Blue Ridge Peak," he said with a sigh. "How quickly time flies in this human world! Yet already you are full of worldly desires. Alas, how much better off you were before!

> Untrammelled by heaven and earth,
> From joy and grief alike your heart was free;
> Then smelting gave you spiritual perception,
> And you came to this world in search of misery.

What a deplorable state you are in now!

> Powder and rouge have dulled your precious lustre;
> Days and nights within silk chambers entrap your heart;
> But you must wake at last from your sweet dream;
> Poor lovers, when all debts are paid, must part."

Having chanted this he rubbed the jade again and muttered some gibberish over it, then handed it back to Chia Cheng.

"Its power has now been restored," he said. "But it must not be profaned. Keep the two patients in one room; hang it over the door of that room, and let no women apart from your wife and mother go inside. In thirty-three days' time, I guarantee they will have recovered completely."

With that he and the Taoist turned and left.

Chia Cheng hurried after them, urging them to sit down and have some tea, for he wanted to offer them some remuneration; but the two men had gone. And when the Lady Dowager sent servants to overtake them, no trace of them could be found.

Then, following the monk's instructions, the jade was hung over the doorway of Lady Wang's bedroom where the two patients were lying; and she herself kept watch there to prevent anyone else from entering. By evening both patients had slowly regained consciousness and said they were hungry. The Lady Dowager and Lady Wang were overjoyed. Some rice gruel was prepared and after eating it they felt better, the evil spirits which had possessed them retreating. At last everyone was able to breathe again. Li Wan, the Chia girls, Pao-chai and Tai-yu were waiting with Ping-erh and Hsi-jen in the outer room when they heard that the patients had come to and eaten some gruel. Before the rest could say anything, Tai-yu exclaimed:

"Buddha be praised!"

Pao-chai turned to look at her and gave a laugh. This passed unnoticed by all but Hsi-chun.

"What are you laughing at, Cousin Pao-chai?" she asked.

"I was thinking how much busier Buddha must be than men are. Apart from expounding the truth and saving all living creatures, he has to preserve the sick and restore them to health, as he has done with Pao-yu and Hsi-feng who are on the mend today. And he'll have to take care of Miss Lin's marriage as well. Just think how busy he must be! Don't you find it amusing?"

Tai-yu flushed and spat in disgust.

"How horrid you all are! I can't think what end you'll come to. Instead of following the example of good people, you're learning from Hsi-feng to make vulgar jokes."

She swept aside the portière and went out.

To learn what followed, turn to the next chapter.

CHAPTER 26

On Wasp-Waist Bridge, Hsiao-hung Hints
at Her Feelings
In Bamboo Lodge, Drowsy in Spring,
Tai-yu Bares Her Heart

After thirty-three days' convalescence, when Pao-yu had completely recovered his strength and the burns on his face had healed, he moved back into the Garden.

During his illness, Chia Yun had taken in pages to watch day and night beside him and had seen so much of Hsiao-hung and the other maids there that they were now on a familiar footing. Hsiao-hung noticed that Chia Yun had a handkerchief very like the one she had lost. She nearly asked him about it, but was too shy. After the visit of the monk and the Taoist, however, there was no further need for male attendants and Chia Yun resumed his tree-planting. Though Hsiao-hung did not want to drop the matter, neither did she want to arouse the suspicions of others by questioning the young man. She was wondering what to do when a voice called through her window:

"Are you there, sister?"

Peeping out she saw that it was Chia-hui, another maid who belonged to the same court. She asked her in. Chia-hui promptly entered and took a seat on the bed.

"I'm in luck!" she crowed. "I was washing clothes in the court just now when Pao-yu decided to send some tea to Miss Lin, and Hsi-jen gave me the errand. As it happened, the old lady had just sent Miss Lin some money which she was sharing out among the maids. When she saw me she gave me two handfuls of cash — how much it is I don't know. Will you look after it for me?"

She unwrapped her handkerchief and poured out the coins, which Hsiao-hung counted for her: "Five, ten, fifteen . . ." and then put away.

"How have you been feeling recently?" continued Chia-hui. "Take my advice and go home for a couple of days. Get a doctor to see you and prescribe some medicine, and that should set you right."

"What an idea!" countered Hsiao-hung. "I'm perfectly all right. Why should I go home?"

"I know what, then. Miss Lin's so delicate, she's always taking medicine. Ask *her* for some. That would do just as well."

"Nonsense. You don't take medicine at random like that."

"Well, you can't go on like this. All your appetite's gone — what's to become of you?"

"What does it matter? The sooner I die the better."

"How can you say such things?"

"You don't understand how I feel."

Chia-hui nodded thoughtfully.

"Well, I don't blame you," she said. "Things *are* difficult here. Just take yesterday, for example. The old lady said everyone worked so hard while Pao-yu was ill that, now he's better and all the vows have been paid, each one would be rewarded according to grade. I don't mind if the young ones like myself are left out, but why should *you* be left out? It isn't fair. I wouldn't have begrudged Hsi-jen ten times as much either — she deserves it. After all, to be honest, which of us can compare with her? Look how careful and conscientious she always is. And even if she weren't, she couldn't be passed over. What annoys me is having people like Ching-wen and Yi-hsien counted as top grade and boosted up just because their parents are senior servants here. Don't you call it maddening?"

"It's hardly worth being angry with them," retorted Hsiao-hung. "The proverb says 'Even the longest feast must break up at last.' Who's going to stay here for life? A few more years and we'll all go our different ways. When that time comes who will worry about anyone else?"

These words brought tears to Chia-hui's eyes, but not wanting to cry for no reason she forced a smile.

"That's true, of course," she agreed. "Yet only yesterday Pao-yu was talking about how he's going to rearrange the rooms and the clothes he means to have made, as if we had hundreds of years to put up with here."

Hsiao-hung laughed sarcastically. Before she could say any more in came a little maid who had not yet let her hair grow, to deliver two sheets of paper and some patterns.

"Here are two patterns for you to trace," she said, tossing them at Hsiao-hung.

"Who are they from?" called Hsiao-hung as the child scampered off. "Can't you finish what you have to say before running away? Have you steamed wheatcakes waiting which may get cold?"

"They're from Yi-hsien," cried the little girl through the window, then quickly galloped away.

Hsiao-hung crossly threw the patterns aside and rummaged in her drawer for a brush, but could not find any with a pointed tip.

"Where did I put that new brush the other day?" she muttered. "I can't remember. . . . Oh, of course, Ying-erh borrowed it the evening before last." She turned to Chia-hui. "Do you mind fetching it for me?"

"Fetch it yourself. Hsi-jen is waiting for me to lift some cases for her."

"If she were, could you stay here chatting? You only say she's waiting because I asked you a favour, you little beast!"

Hsiao-hung set out from Happy Red Court to Pao-chai's apartments, but stopped at Seeping Fragrance Pavilion when she caught sight of Pao-yu's old nurse, Nanny Li.

"Where are you off to, Mrs. Li?" she greeted her with a smile. "What brings you here?"

The old woman halted and clapped her hands.

"Tell me, why has he taken such a fancy to this tree-planter Yun or Yu, whatever his name is? Nothing would serve but that I go and fetch the fellow. When word of this gets to the Master, there'll be trouble."

"But do you have to give in to all his whims, nanny?"

"What else can I do?"

Hsiao-hung smiled.

"If that young man has any sense, he won't come."

"He's not crazy. Why shouldn't he?"

"Well, if he does come, you ought to bring him in with you. Not leave him to go blundering round on his own."

"Have I time to wait for him? I just gave him the message. I'll send one of the girls or matrons to show him the way." She hobbled off on her stick.

Instead of fetching the brush, Hsiao-hung stood there lost in thought till a maid came up and asked what she was doing. It was Chui-erh, and Hsiao-hung inquired where she was going.

"To fetch Master Yun," cried Chui-erh, running off.

Hsiao-hung had just reached the gate of Wasp-Waist Bridge by the time Chui-erh returned, leading Chia Yun. He cast a sidelong glance at Hsiao-hung, who stole a glance at him too under cover of talking to Chui-erh. When their eyes met she blushed and turned abruptly away, going on to Alpinia Park.

Chia Yun followed Chui-erh by winding paths to Happy Red Court. She went in first to announce him, then ushered him in. The young man had time to scrutinize the courtyard. There were a few scattered artificial rocks with plantains growing between, and two storks were preening their feathers under a pine. In the gallery surrounding the courtyard hung cages of every description containing all manner of rare exotic birds. The five-frame apartment before him had lattice-work carved with ingenious designs, while above its door hung a tablet inscribed with the words: Happy Red and Delightful Green.

"So that's why it's called Happy Red Court," he thought. "The name comes from that inscription."

He heard a laugh from behind one gauze-covered window and someone cried, "Come on in. Imagine my forgetting you for two or three months!"

Recognizing Pao-yu's voice Chia Yun hurried in. He was dazzled by the glittering gold and emerald and the elegance of all the furnishings, but could see no sign of Pao-yu. Turning to the left he noticed a large mirror from behind which emerged two girls in their mid-teens, of about the same build and height, who invited him into the inner room. Assenting without venturing to look at them, he stepped into a chamber screened with green gauze. On a small inlaid lacquer bed there with red curtains embroidered in gold lay Pao-yu, informally dressed, in his slippers. At sight of the visitor he threw down the book in his hand and stood up, smiling. Chia Yun advanced to fall upon one knee, and was offered a chair opposite his host.

"After I saw you that month and invited you to my study," remarked Pao-yu, "a whole lot of things happened to make it slip my mind."

"That was my misfortune," replied Chia Yun with a smile. "And then you fell ill, uncle. Have you recovered completely?"

"Yes, thank you. I heard you were quite worn out after all those days' hard work."

"That's just as it should be. Your recovery, uncle, is a blessing to our whole family."

A maid had come in to offer him tea, and while talking with Pao-yu he glanced surreptitiously at her. Slim with an oval face, she was dressed in a silver-red jacket, black satin sleeveless jacket and pleated white silk damask skirt. Having been in the mansion all through Pao-yu's illness, Chia Yun remembered most of the people of any importance there and knew that this was no other than Hsi-jen, who enjoyed a special status in Happy Red Court. As Pao-yu was sitting there while she served tea, Chia Yun rose to his feet with a smile.

"How can I trouble you to pour tea for me, sister?" he protested. "Don't treat me as a guest in my uncle's rooms. Let me pour the tea myself."

"Sit down, sit down," said Pao-yu. "Why stand on ceremony with the maids?"

"I mustn't forget my manners before the sisters in your apartments, uncle."

He sat down to sip tea while Pao-yu chatted idly with him, telling him which families had the best actors, the finest gardens, the prettiest maids, the most sumptuous feasts, and the best collections of curios. Chia Yun did his best to respond in the same vein. But when he noticed that his host looked tired, he rose to take his leave and was not pressed to stay.

"Drop in any time you're free," said Pao-yu, before telling Chui-erh to see the visitor out.

As no one else was about outside Happy Red Court, Chia Yun slowed down to chat with the maid, asking her age, her name and her father's trade. How long had she been working for Pao-yu? How much did she earn a month? How many other girls worked there? She answered each question in turn readily enough.

"That girl who spoke to you on our way in," he said, "isn't she called Hsiao-hung?"

Chui-erh laughed.

"That's right. Why do you ask?"

"She said something to you about a handkerchief. As it happens, I've picked one up."

At this Chui-erh smiled.

"She's asked me several times whether I've seen her handkerchief. As if I had time to bother about such things! She asked me again today and promised to give me something if I found it. I'm not making this up — you heard her for yourself in front of Alpinia Park. If you've found it, sir, do give it to me and we'll see what thanks I get."

The fact is that the month before when supervising the planting of trees, Chia Yun had picked up a silk handkerchief in the Garden. He knew it must have been dropped by one of the girls there, but not knowing which had not ventured to take any action. When Hsiao-hung questioned Chui-erh about it, he was delighted to learn that it was Hsiao-hung's. And now that Chui-erh gave him this opening, he had his plan ready worked out. He took a handkerchief of his own from his sleeve, and handed it her with a smile.

"All right, here you are," he told her. "But mind you let me know what reward you get. No cheating!"

Chui-erh readily took the handkerchief on these conditions and, having seen Chia Yun out, went off to look for Hsiao-hung.

But let us return to Pao-yu, who felt so lackadaisical after Chia Yun left that he curled up as if for a nap. Hsi-jen seated herself on the edge of his bed and nudged him.

"You mustn't fall asleep again," she said. "If you're feeling bored, why not go out for a stroll?"

"I would." Pao-yu took her hand. "But I can't bear to leave you."

"Get up, quick!" she answered laughingly, pulling him up.

"But where shall I go? I'm thoroughly fed up."

"You'll feel better once you're out. If you just stay moping here, you'll only get more fed up."

Pao-yu listlessly took her advice and pottered out. After playing for a while with the birds in the gallery, he strolled beside the River of Seeping Fragrance to have a look at the goldfish. As he did so, two fawns came bolting from the hillside opposite, and he was wondering what could have frightened them when he saw Chia Lan give chase, a small bow in his hand. Seeing Pao-yu ahead of him, the boy stopped short.

"So you're at home, uncle," he said cheerfully. "I thought you'd gone out."

"What mischief are you up to now?" asked Pao-yu. "Why shoot at those harmless creatures?"

"I've finished my lessons and I've nothing to do. I thought I'd practise archery."

"I suppose you won't stop," said Pao-yu, "till you've knocked out your teeth."

His feet carried him on then to the gate of a courtyard. Bamboos dense as phoenix plumage there made a rustling music. And the board above the gate bore the inscription:

Bamboo Lodge. Strolling in he found the bamboo portière down. Not a voice could be heard. As he approached the window a subtle fragrance drifted through the green gauze. He pressed his face against the gauze and heard a long faint sigh, followed by the words:

Day after day a drowsy dream of love.[1]

Pao-yu felt his heart strangely stirred. And looking more closely, he could make out Tai-yu, who was stretching herself on her bed.

He laughed.

"Why 'Day after day a drowsy dream of love'?" he called, then raising the portière walked in.

Blushing to think she had given herself away, Tai-yu hid her face with her sleeve and turned towards the wall, pretending to be asleep. As Pao-yu went up to her to turn her over, her nurse and two other old women followed him in.

"Your cousin's asleep, sir. We shall ask you in when she wakes up."

Tai-yu promptly turned over and sat up with a laugh.

"Who's asleep?"

The three old women smiled.

"Our mistake, miss."

They left after calling Tzu-chuan to attend to her young mistress.

"What do you mean by coming in when people are asleep?" Tai-yu challenged Pao-yu with a smile as, sitting on the bed, she smoothed her hair.

The sight of her soft flushed cheeks, and her starry eyes now faintly misted over, enraptured Pao-yu. He sank smiling into a chair.

"What was that you were saying just now?"

"I didn't say anything."

"Yes, you did. I heard you."

Tzu-chuan appeared at this point.

---

[1] This line and the two quoted later by Pao-yu come from *The Western Chamber*.

"Tzu-chuan," said Pao-yu, "pour a cup of that good tea of yours for me, will you?"

"What good tea have we got?" she retorted. "If you want good tea, better wait till Hsi-jen comes."

"Pay no attention to him," said Tai-yu. "First go and get me some water."

Tzu-chuan laughed.

"He's a guest, so of course I must get him tea before I fetch you water."

As she left to do this Pao-yu exclaimed, "Good girl!

> Should I share the bridal curtains with your
> sweet mistress,
> How could I give you the task of preparing
> the bed?"

At once Tai-yu's face clouded over.

"What's that you said?" she demanded.

"I didn't say anything, did I?" Pao-yu chuckled.

Tai-yu began to cry.

"So this is your latest diversion," she sobbed. "All the dirty talk you hear outside, you repeat to me; and any disgusting books you read, you quote to make fun of me. A laughing-stock for you gentlemen, that's what I've become!"

Scrambling off the bed she walked away in tears. Pao-yu followed her in alarm.

"Dear cousin, it was very wrong of me, but please don't tell!" he begged. "May it blister my mouth and rot my tongue if I dare say such things again."

Just then Hsi-jen came in.

"Quick," she said. "Come back and change. The master wants you."

This summons fell on his ears like a clap of thunder. For-getting all else he rushed back to change, and hurried out of the Garden. Pei-ming was waiting for him at the inner gate.

"Do you know why my father wants me?" asked Pao-yu.

"Hurry up, sir," said the page. "At any rate you'll have to go. You'll find out why when you get there."

He hustled his master off.

They passed the main hall, Pao-yu with a sinking heart, when a bellow of laughter sounded just round the corner. Out sprang Hsueh Pan, clapping his hands.

"If I hadn't said your father wanted you, you'd never have come so quickly," he declared.

Pei-ming, laughing too, fell on his knees.

It took some moments for Pao-yu to realize he had been tricked.

Hsueh Pan bowed in apology, raising clasped hands.

"Don't blame this young rascal," he said. "I put him up to it."

Pao-yu had no alternative but to smile.

"I don't mind your fooling me," he said, "but why pretend to be my father? Shall I go and ask your mother what she thinks of your conduct?"

"My dear cousin, I was in such a hurry to see you that I forgot that taboo. Another day you can get even with me by pretending that *my* father wants to see *me*."

"You wretch!" exclaimed Pao-yu. "You deserve to drop dead." He rounded on Pei-ming. "What are you still kneeling there for, you treacherous dog?"

The page promptly kowtowed and got up.

"I wouldn't have disturbed you," Hsueh Pan explained, "but the third of the fifth month will be my birthday. And Cheng Jih-hsing the curio dealer managed — goodness only knows where — to get hold of a fresh, crisp lotus root this thick and this long, a huge melon this size, a fresh sturgeon this long and a whopping great Siamese pig smoked with fragrant cedar which came as tribute from Siam. They must have been hard to come by, such presents, eh? The fish and the pig are just expensive rarities, but heaven knows how they managed to grow a lotus-root and melon of that size. I gave some at once to my mother, then sent portions to your old lady and your parents; but I've still quite a bit left. To hog it all myself might bring me bad luck; and after thinking it over I decided you were the only one fit to share it. So I came over specially to invite you. Luckily a singing-boy has just turned up too. Why don't we make a day of it together?"

By now they had reached his study where they found Chan Kuang, Cheng Jih-hsing, Hu Ssu-lai and Shan Pin-jen as well as the singing-boy. When greetings had been exchanged and tea drunk, Hsueh Pan ordered the feast to be served. At once his pages bustled about to lay the table, and when all was finally ready the party took their seats.

Pao-yu saw that the melon and lotus-root were quite phenomenal.

"I haven't yet sent you over a birthday present, but here I am enjoying myself at your expense," he remarked with a smile.

"That's right," said Hsueh Pan. "What are you planning to send me?"

"I haven't anything really. The money, clothes, food and stuff like that in my place aren't mine to give. The only thing I could give you of my *own* would be a scroll of my calligraphy or painting."

"Talking of painting," put in Hsueh Pan with a grin, "reminds me of an erotic picture I saw in someone's house the other day. Really superb it was. I didn't read all the inscriptions carefully, just noticed the artist's name: Keng Huang. The picture was marvellous."

Pao-yu was puzzled. He knew the work of many calligraphers and painters past and present, but had never heard of an artist called Keng Huang. After a little thought he burst out laughing. He called for a brush and wrote two characters on the palm of his left hand.

"Are you sure the name was Keng Huang?" he asked Hsueh Pan.

"Of course."

Pao-yu held out his hand.

"It wasn't these two characters? They're not very different."

When they saw he had written Tang Yin,[1] they declared,

---

[1] The Chinese characters for Keng Huang (庚黄) and Tang Yin (唐寅) look somewhat alike. For Tang Yin see Note 2 on p. 28.

laughing, "That must be it. Mr. Hsueh's eyes may have been blurred at the time."

Hsueh Pan grinned sheepishly.

"Who cares whether the fellow's name means 'sweet-silver' or 'nut-silver'?"[1] he spluttered in his embarrassment.

Just then "Mr. Feng" was announced by one of the servants. Pao-yu realized this must be Feng Tzu-ying, the son of Feng Tang, General of Divine Valour. All urged that he be asked in. And before the words were out of their mouths Feng Tzu-ying strode, chatting and laughing, into the room. They rose to offer him a seat.

"Fine!" Feng chuckled. "You don't go out, just enjoy yourselves at home."

Both Hsueh Pan and Pao-yu smiled.

"We haven't seen you for some time," they said. "Is your father well?"

"Very well, thank you. But my mother recently contracted a chill and has been out of sorts for two days."

Hsueh Pan noticed some bruises on his face.

"Been fighting again?" he asked. "Who left his mark on your face?"

"Ever since I beat up Colonel Chiu's son I've made a point of keeping my temper. No more fist-fights for me. This happened the other day out hunting on Iron-Net Mountain, when my falcon caught me on the cheek with its wing."

"When was that?" asked Pao-yu.

"We left on the twenty-eighth of the third month and only got back the day before yesterday."

"No wonder I didn't see you when I called on Shen on the third, or was it the fourth. I meant to ask where you were but I forgot. Did you go alone on this trip or with your father?"

"With my father, of course. I couldn't get out of it. Do you think me crazy enough to prefer roughing it to drinking

---

[1] Hsueh Pan does not know the Ming artist Tang Yin's name, so he makes the mistake of calling him "sweet-silver," which reads like "Tang Yin" in Chinese.

with you and listening to songs? This time, though, something lucky turned up in my bad luck."

As he had now finished his tea, Hsueh Pan and the others asked him to join them at the table and take his time telling them just what had happened. But instead Feng rose to leave.

"You must excuse me. Really I should drink a few cups with you, but I've some very urgent business today to report to my father."

Hsueh Pan, Pao-yu and the others would not hear of this and laid hands on him to keep him.

"Don't be ridiculous. You ought to know me better," he protested. "I really can't stay. But if you insist, get me a big cup and I'll drain two cups with you."

They had to agree to this. Hsueh Pan took the pot, Pao-yu held the cup, and they poured two large cupfuls which Feng Tzu-ying stood up and drained in a single breath.

"Do tell us before you leave what's your good luck in a stretch of bad," urged Pao-yu.

Feng Tzu-ying only laughed.

"I can't go into the details today. But I promise to invite you all to a special party when we can have a good talk. I've a favour to ask you too." Raising his clasped hands to say goodbye he started off.

"You're just whetting our curiosity," objected Hsueh Pan. "When is this party to be? Tell us now so as not to leave us in suspense."

"In ten days at the latest, maybe eight."

Then Feng Tzu-ying went out, mounted his horse and rode off. The others returned from seeing him off to drink some more before the party dispersed.

When Pao-yu went back to the Garden, Hsi-jen was still worrying about the summons from his father, not knowing whether it meant trouble or the reverse. Seeing that Pao-yu was tipsy, she asked him what had happened and he told her in detail.

"We were waiting here on tenterhooks while you had a good time," she said reproachfully. "You might at least have sent word."

"I meant to, but when Feng turned up I forgot."

Just then Pao-chai came in.

"So you've been treated to those delicacies of ours," she teased.

"Surely you and your family must have tasted them before us, cousin," he countered.

Pao-chai shook her head.

"Yesterday my brother did urge me to try them, but I didn't. I told him to keep them for others. I know it's not in my stars to deserve such dainties."

A maid brought her some tea as she spoke, and while she drank it they chatted. But no more of this.

Tai-yu too had been worried on Pao-yu's behalf when she heard that he had not come back all day after being sent for by his father. After dinner she learned of his return and decided to find out from him what had happened. As she strolled over she saw Pao-chai going into Happy Red Court before her. But noticing some unusually beautiful water-fowl of various species unknown to her splashing about in the pool by Seeping Fragrance Bridge, she stopped for a while to admire their brilliant colours. By the time she reached Happy Red Court the gate was closed and she was obliged to knock.

It so happened that Ching-wen was in a bad humour, having just quarrelled with Pi-hen, and at Pao-chai's arrival she transferred her anger to the visitor. She was grumbling in the courtyard:

"She keeps coming here and sitting around for no reason, keeping us up till the third watch at night."

Now this fresh knocking on the gate only incensed her further.

"They've all gone to bed," she cried, not troubling to ask who it was. "Come back tomorrow."

Tai-yu knew the maids' ways and the tricks they played on each other. Assuming that the girl in the courtyard had failed to recognize her voice and taken her for another maid, she called out again more loudly.

"It's me. Open the gate!"

Still Ching-wen did not recognize her voice.

"I don't care who you are," she said crossly. "Master Pao's given orders that no one's to be admitted."

Rooted indignantly to the spot and tempted to let fly at her, Tai-yu reflected, "Although my aunt's house is a second home to me, I'm after all an outsider here. With both my parents dead, I've no one to turn to except this family. It would be foolish to start a real rumpus."

As she thought thus, tears ran down her cheeks. She was wondering whether or not to go back when the sound of talk and laughter inside — she distinguished the voices of Pao-yu and Pao-chai — upset her even more. She thought back then to the events of the morning.

"Pao-yu must be angry with me, thinking I told on him," she reflected. "But I never did! You ought to investigate before flying into a temper like this. You can shut me out today, but shall we not see each other still tomorrow?"

The more she thought, the more distressed she felt. Oblivious of the cold dew on the green moss and the chill wind on the path, standing under the blossom by the corner of the wall she gave way to sobs. And the sound of this beauty's weeping — for Tai-yu was the loveliest creature ever seen — made the birds fly away from their roosts on the willows and flowering trees, unable to bear her distress.

Truly:

> The hearts of the flowers were broken,
> The birds were woken from their senseless
> dreams.

The reason is told in these lines:

> Peerless the beauty and talent of this girl
> Wrapped in scent from embroidered curtains
> come alone;

Before her first sob dies away
Flowers strew the ground, the affrighted birds
    have flown.

As Tai-yu was sobbing to herself the gate creaked open. If
you want to know who came out, read the next chapter.

CHAPTER 27

Pao-chai Chases a Butterfly to
Dripping Emerald Pavilion
Tai-yu Weeps over Fallen Blossom
by the Tomb of Flowers

As Tai-yu was weeping, the gate creaked open and out came Pao-chai escorted by Pao-yu, Hsi-jen and other maids. Tai-yu was tempted to accost Pao-yu, but not wanting to embarrass him in public she stepped aside until Pao-chai had left and the others had gone in, when she came back and shed more tears before the closed gate. Then she went back in low spirits to her room and prepared listlessly for bed.

Tzu-chuan and Hsueh-yen knew their young mistress' ways. She would often sit moodily frowning or sighing over nothing or, for no apparent reason, would give way to long spells of weeping. At first they had tried to comfort her, imagining that she missed her parents and home or that someone had been unkind; but as time went by and they found this was her habit they paid little further attention. So tonight they withdrew to bed, leaving her to brood by herself.

Tai-yu leaned against her bed-rail, clasping her knees. Her eyes were brimming with tears. There she stayed motionless as a statue, not lying down until after the second watch.

The next day was the twenty-sixth of the fourth month, the Festival of Grain in Ear. It was the time-honoured custom on this day to offer all manner of gifts and a farewell feast to the God of Flowers, for this festival was said to mark the beginning of summer when all the blossom had withered and the God of Flowers had to resign his throne and be seen off. As this custom is most faithfully observed by women, all the inmates of Grand View Garden rose early that day. The girls used flowers and osiers to weave small sedan-chairs and horses, or made pennants and flags of silk and gauze which they tied with gay ribbons to every tree and flower, turning the whole Garden into a blaze of colour. They decked themselves out so prettily, too, as to put the very flowers and birds to shame. But time forbids us to dwell on that splendid scene.

Now Pao-chai, the three Chia girls, Li Wan and Hsi-feng were enjoying themselves in the Garden with Hsi-feng's little daughter as well as Hsiang-ling and the other maids. Only one person was missing, and that was Tai-yu.

"Why isn't Cousin Lin here?" asked Ying-chun. "Surely the lazy creature isn't still sleeping?"

"I'll go and rouse her," volunteered Pao-chai. "The rest of you wait here and I'll soon bring her."

She set off instantly for Bamboo Lodge.

On the way she met the twelve young actresses headed by Wen-kuan, who greeted her and chatted for a while. Then Pao-chai told them how to find the others and, having explained her own errand, followed the winding path towards Tai-yu's quarters. As she approached Bamboo Lodge she saw Pao-yu enter the courtyard. That made her pause and lower her head in thought.

"Pao-yu and Tai-yu grew up under one roof," she reflected. "They're so free and easy together, they don't care how they tease each other or show their feelings. And Tai-yu's rather jealous and petty-minded. If I follow Pao-yu in, he may not like it and she may resent it. I'd better go back."

She had started back to rejoin the other girls when a pair of jade-coloured butterflies the size of a circular fan appeared before her. They fluttered up and down most bewitchingly in the breeze. What fun it would be to catch them! Pao-chai drew her fan from her sleeve and ran after them over the grass. Flitting now high now low, this way and that, the butterflies led her through the flowers and willows all the way to the water's brink. By the time she neared Dripping Emerald Pavilion, panting and perspiring from all her exertions, she decided to give up the pursuit and go back. But just then she heard muffled voices from the pavilion.

Now this pavilion, which stood out in the middle of the pool, was surrounded on four sides by covered corridors with balustrades and connected with the banks by zigzag bridges. It had papered latticed windows on all four sides. Pao-chai stopped outside it to catch what was being said.

"Look at this handkerchief. If it's the one you lost, you can have it. If not, I'll take it back to Master Yun."

"Of course it's mine. Let me have it."

"What thanks am I going to get? You don't expect me to do this for nothing, do you?"

"Don't worry. I promised you something, I won't cheat you."

"I should hope not, after I've brought it back to you. But how are you going to thank the man who found it?"

"Don't be silly. He's a young gentleman. It's only right he should return what he finds. How could I reward him?"

"If you don't, what am I to say to him? Besides, he told me repeatedly he wouldn't let me give you this unless you offered him some reward."

A short silence followed.

"All right," came the answer at last. "Give him this from me to thank him. But swear you won't let on to a soul."

"If I do, may a boil break out in my mouth and may I die a miserable death!"

Then a note of alarm was sounded.

"Goodness! We've been so busy talking, what if someone's eavesdropping outside? We'd better open the windows. Then if people see us they'll assume we're just chatting. And if anyone comes near we'll see her and can change the subject."

Pao-chai could hardly believe her ears.

"No wonder they say wicked people have always been cunning!" she thought. "How they're going to blush when they open the window and see me! One of them sounded like that sly, conceited Hsiao-hung who works for Pao-yu. She's a strange crafty creature if ever I saw one. 'Desperation drives men to rebel and a dog to jump over a wall.' If she thinks I know her secret there may be trouble, and that would be awkward for me.   Well, it's too late to hide now.   I must try to avoid suspicion by throwing them off the scent. . . ."

That same instant she heard the thud of a window opening. At once she ran forward as noisily as she could, calling out laughingly:

"Where are you hiding, Tai-yu?"

Hsiao-hung and Chui-erh, who had just opened the window, were staggered to see her before them.

"Where have you hidden Miss Lin?" Pao-chai asked them merrily.

"Miss Lin? We haven't seen her," Chui-erh answered.

"Just now, from the other bank, I saw her crouching here dabbling in the water.   I meant to take her by surprise but she spotted me coming and dashed off to the east.   And now she's disappeared.   Are you sure she's not hiding in there?"

She deliberately went in and made a search before going on.

"She must have popped into some cave in the rocks," she muttered.   "If a snake bites her, serve her right."

With that she went off, laughing up her sleeve at the way she had foxed them and wondering what they were thinking.

Hsiao-hung, in fact, had been quite taken in.   As soon as Pao-chai was safely out of earshot she caught Chui-erh by the arm.

"Heaven help us!" she whispered.   "If Miss Lin was here she must have overheard us."

Chui-erh said nothing, and a long pause followed.

"What shall we do?" asked Hsiao-hung.

"What if she *did* hear?   This is none of her business."

"It wouldn't have been so bad Miss Hsueh overhearing. But Miss Lin's narrow-minded and likes to make cutting remarks.   If she heard, and gives us away, what shall we do?"

A stop was put to this discussion by the arrival of Wen-kuan with Hsiang-ling, Ssu-chi and Tai-shu.   The two girls chatted with them as if nothing had happened until Hsiao-hung saw Hsi-feng beckoning from the slope.   Leaving the other girls, she ran over to her.

"Can I do anything for Your Ladyship?" she asked, smiling sweetly.

Hsi-feng had a close look at her and was favourably impressed by her neat good looks and pleasant way of talking.

"I didn't bring my maids with me today," she said. "But now I've remembered something I want done. Do you think you could deliver a message correctly?"

Hsiao-hung smiled.

"Just give me your instructions, madam. If I don't get the message right and hold up your business, you can punish me."

"Tell me, which of the young ladies do you work for? Then I can explain where you are if she asks for you."

"I'm attached to Master Pao's apartments."

Hsi-feng chuckled.

"I see. That accounts for it. All right, if he asks, I'll let him know where you are. Now go to my house and tell your sister Ping-erh that she'll find a packet containing a hundred and sixty taels of silver under the stand of the *Ju*-ware plate on the table in the outer room. That's for the embroiderers. When Chang Tsai's wife comes, she's to weigh it in her presence and let her take it. And there's another thing. I want you to bring me the pouch which is by the pillow on the bed in the inner room."

Hsiao-hung went off to carry out these orders. She returned presently to find that Hsi-feng had vanished. But Ssu-chi had just emerged from a cave and stopped to fasten her skirt. Hsiao-hung approached her.

"Know where the Second Mistress has gone?" she asked.

"I didn't notice."

Hsiao-hung looked around and went to ask Tan-chun and Pao-chai, who were watching the fish not far off.

"You'll find her with Madam Li Wan, I think," Tan-chun told her.

Hsiao-hung promptly set off to Paddy-Sweet Cottage, but on the way met Ching-wen and half a dozen other maids.

"Still prancing about!" exclaimed Ching-wen as soon as she set eyes on her. "You haven't watered the flowers, fed the birds or lit the tea-stove in our courtyard, yet you gad about outside."

"Yesterday Master Pao said the flowers needn't be watered today — once every other day would do," Hsiao-hung retorted. "I fed the birds while *you* were still asleep."

"And what about the tea-stove?" demanded Pi-hen.

"It's not *my* turn today, so don't ask me whether there's any tea or not."

"Just listen to the way she talks," jeered Yi-hsien. "You'd all better keep quiet and let her fool about."

"Who says I was fooling about?" snapped Hsiao-hung. "I've been on an errand for the Second Mistress."

With that she showed them the pouch to silence them, and they parted company.

"No wonder!" Ching-wen snorted as they walked on. "Now that she's climbed to a higher branch of the tree, she won't pay any more attention to us. Our lady may have thrown her a word or two, without even knowing her name, and she's already eaten up with pride. What's so marvellous about running a little errand? We shall see if anything comes of it or not. If she's all that clever she'd better clear out of this Garden and stay perched on the top of the tree."

Hsiao-hung could hardly have it out with her. Swallowing her resentment she went on and found Hsi-feng, sure enough, chatting in Li Wan's apartment. She stepped forward to make her report.

"Sister Ping-erh said, madam, that as soon as Your Ladyship left she put away the money; and when Chang Tsai's wife came for it, she weighed it in her presence and gave it to her." She handed the pouch to Hsi-feng and continued. "Sister Ping-erh asked me to tell Your Ladyship: Just now Lai Wang came to ask for your instructions before setting out to the mansion where you sent him, and she sent him off after explaining Your Ladyship's wishes."

"How did she explain my wishes?" Hsi-feng smiled.

"She said, 'Our lady sends her compliments to Her Ladyship. Our Second Master is away from home now, so Her

Ladyship shouldn't worry over a couple of days' delay. When the Fifth Mistress is better, our lady will come with her to see Her Ladyship. The Fifth Mistress sent a servant the other day to report that our lady's sister-in-law had inquired after Her Ladyship in a letter, and hoped her sister-in-law here would oblige her with two longevity pills. If Her Ladyship has any to spare, please send them to our lady, and the next person to go that way will deliver them to her sister-in-law."

"Mercy on us!" cut in Li Wan with a laugh. "I've lost track of all these ladies and mistresses."

"I don't blame you." Hsi-feng smiled. "There are five families involved." She turned to Hsiao-hung. "You're a good child and deliver messages clearly, not like some who mince their words or buzz like mosquitoes. You know," she turned to Li Wan, "my dear sister-in-law, I can't stand talking to most of the maids, apart from the few in my service. They don't know it, but I find it quite maddening the way they pad out a sentence and then break it down into several, the way they mince, drawl and stutter. Our Ping-erh used to be as bad as the rest. I asked her: Does a pretty girl have to buzz like a mosquito? And after a few scoldings she improved."

Li Wan laughed.

"Not everyone is a termagant like you."

"But I like this girl," Hsi-feng continued. "Admittedly, her two messages weren't long, but she spoke to the point." She smiled at Hsiao-hung. "You must come and work for me. I'll make you my adopted daughter and see that you turn out all right."

Hsiao-hung burst out laughing.

"What's so funny?" demanded Hsi-feng. "Do you think, because I'm not much older than you, I'm too young to be your mother? If so, you're crazy. Just ask around. There are plenty of people twice your age eager to call me mother — if only I'd let them. I'm doing you an honour."

"That wasn't why I laughed," replied Hsiao-hung. "I laughed because Your Ladyship has got my generation wrong. My *mother's* Your Ladyship's adopted daughter, yet now you talk of me as a daughter too."

"Who's your mother?"

"Don't you know her?" put in Li Wan with a smile. "This child is Lin Chih-hsiao's daughter."

"You don't say so!" exclaimed Hsi-feng in surprise. "Why, you can't get a word out of Lin Chih-hsiao and his wife, not even if you stick an awl into them. I've always said they were a well-matched couple, deaf mutes the pair of them. Who could have believed they'd produce such a clever daughter? How old are you?"

"Seventeen."

Next she was asked her name.

"I was first called Hung-yu," she answered. "But because of the '*yu*' in Master Pao's name they call me Hsiao-hung now."

Hsi-feng frowned and tossed her head.

"Disgusting! You'd think there was something special about '*yu*,' the way everybody wants that name. So in that case you can work for me. You know, sister-in-law, I told her mother, 'Lai Ta's wife has her hands full, and anyway she's no idea who's who in this household. You choose a couple of good maids for me.' And she promised that's what she'd do. But instead, she sends this daughter of hers somewhere else. Did she think the girl would have a bad time with me?"

"How suspicious you are," teased Li Wan. "This child was already here by then. How can you blame her mother?"

"In that case, I'll tell Pao-yu to ask for someone else and send this girl to me — if she's willing, that is."

Hsiao-hung smiled.

"Willing? As if that were for us to say! But if only I could work for Your Ladyship, I'd learn some manners and get more experience."

As she said this a maid came from Lady Wang to summon Hsi-feng, who took her leave of Li Wan. And Hsiao-hung went back to Happy Red Court, where we leave her.

Let us return to Tai-yu, who had risen late after a sleepless night. When she heard that the other girls were farewelling the

God of Flowers in the Garden, for fear of being laughed at for laziness she made haste to dress and go out. She was crossing the courtyard when Pao-yu came in.

"Dear cousin, did you tell on me yesterday?" he greeted her laughingly. "You had me worrying the whole night long."

Tai-yu turned away from him to Tzu-chuan.

"When you've tidied the rooms, close the screen windows," she instructed. "As soon as the big swallows come back, you can let down the curtains. Hold them in place by moving the lions against them. And cover the censer once the incense is lit."

As she said this, she walked on.

Pao-yu attributed this cold behaviour to the lines he had quoted at noon the previous day, having no idea of the incident in the evening. He bowed and raised his clasped hands in salute, but Tai-yu simply ignored him, walking straight off to find the other girls.

Pao-yu was puzzled.

"Surely what happened yesterday can't account for this?" he thought. "And I came back too late in the evening to see her again, so how else can I have offended her?"

With these reflections, he trailed after her.

Tai-yu joined Pao-chai and Tan-chun, who were both watching the storks dancing, and the three girls were chatting together when Pao-yu arrived.

"How are you, brother?" asked Tan-chun. "It's three whole days since last I saw you."

"How are you, sister?" he rejoined. "The other day I was asking our elder sister-in-law about you."

"Come over here. I want to talk to you."

The pair of them strolled aside under a pomegranate tree away from the other two.

"Has father sent for you these last few days?" asked Tan-chun.

Pao-yu smiled.

"No, he hasn't."

"Oh, I thought someone told me he sent for you yesterday."

"That someone must have misheard. He didn't."

Tan-chun chuckled.

"These last few months I've saved a dozen strings of cash. I want you to take them. Next time you go out you can buy me some good calligraphy and paintings, or some amusing toys."

"In my strolls through the squares and temple markets inside and outside the city," Pao-yu told her, "I haven't seen anything novel or really well made. Nothing but curios of gold, jade, bronze or porcelain, which would be out of place here. Or things like silk textiles, food and clothing."

"That's not what I mean. No, but things like you bought me last time: little willow baskets, incense-boxes carved out of bamboo roots, and tiny clay stoves. They were so sweet, I just loved them! But then other people fell in love with them too and grabbed them as if they were treasures."

Pao-yu laughed.

"If that's what you want, those things are dirt cheap. Just give five hundred cash to the pages and they'll fetch you two cartloads."

"Those fellows have no taste. Please choose some things which are simple without being vulgar, and genuine instead of artificial. Do get me a whole lot more, and I'll make you another pair of slippers. I'll put even more work into them than last time. How's that?"

"That reminds me." Pao-yu grinned. "I was wearing your slippers one day when I met father. He asked me disapprovingly who'd made them. It wouldn't have done to tell him it was you, sister; so I said they were a present from Aunt Wang on my last birthday. There wasn't much he could say to that, but after an awful silence he commented, 'What a waste of time and energy and good silk.' When I told Hsi-jen she said: 'Never mind that, but the concubine Chao's been complaining bitterly, "Her own younger brother Huan's shoes and socks are in holes yet she doesn't care. Instead she embroiders slippers for Pao-yu." '"

Tan-chun frowned.

"Did you ever hear such nonsense?" she fumed. "Is it *my* job to make shoes? Doesn't Huan have his fair share of clothes, shoes and socks, not to mention a whole roomful of maids and servants? What has *she* got to complain of? Who's she trying to impress? If I make a pair of slippers in my spare time, I can give them to any brother I choose and no one has any right to interfere. She's crazy, carrying on like that."

Pao-yu nodded and smiled.

"Still, it's natural, you know, for her to see things rather differently."

This only enraged Tan-chun more. She tossed her head.

"Now *you're* talking nonsense too. Of course she sees things differently with that sly, low, dirty mind of hers. Who cares what *she* thinks? I don't owe any duty to anyone except our parents. If my sisters, brothers and cousins are nice to me, I'll be nice to them too, regardless of which is the child of a wife or the child of a concubine. Properly speaking, I shouldn't say such things, but really that woman's the limit!

"Let me tell you another ridiculous thing too. Two days after I gave you that money to buy knick-knacks, she complained to me she was hard up. I paid no attention, of course. But after my maids left the room, she started scolding me for giving my savings to you instead of to Huan. I didn't know whether to laugh or lose my temper. So I left her and went to Her Ladyship."

But now Pao-chai called to them laughingly: "Haven't you talked long enough? It's clear you're brother and sister, the way you leave other people out in the cold to discuss your private affairs. Aren't we allowed to hear a single word?"

They smiled at that and joined her.

Meanwhile Tai-yu had disappeared, and Pao-yu knew she was avoiding him. He decided to wait a couple of days for the storm to blow over before approaching her again. Then, lowering his head, he noticed that the ground was strewn with balsam and pomegranate petals.

"She's too angry even to gather up the blossom," he sighed. "I'll take these over and try to speak to her tomorrow."

At this point Pao-chai urged them to take a stroll.

"I'll join you later," he said.

As soon as the other two had gone, he gathered up the fallen flowers in the skirt of his gown and made his way over a small hill, across a stream and through an orchard towards the mound where Tai-yu had buried the peach-blossom. Just before rounding the hill by the flowers' grave he caught the sound of sobs on the other side. Someone was lamenting and weeping there in a heart-rending fashion.

"Some maid's been badly treated and come here to cry," he thought. "I wonder which of them it is."

He halted to listen. And this is what he heard:

> As blossoms fade and fly across the sky,
> Who pities the faded red, the scent that has been?
> Softly the gossamer floats over spring pavilions,
> Gently the willow fluff wafts to the embroidered screen.
>
> A girl in her chamber mourns the passing of spring,
> No relief from anxiety her poor heart knows;
> Hoe in hand she steps through her portal,
> Loath to tread on the blossom as she comes and goes.
>
> Willows and elms, fresh and verdant,
> Care not if peach and plum blossom drift away;
> Next year the peach and plum will bloom again,
> But her chamber may stand empty on that day.
>
> By the third month the scented nests are built,
> But the swallows on the beam are heartless all;
> Next year, though once again you may peck the buds,
> From the beam of an empty room your nest will fall.
>
> Each year for three hundred and sixty days
> The cutting wind and biting frost contend.
> How long can beauty flower fresh and fair?
> In a single day wind can whirl it to its end.
>
> Fallen, the brightest blooms are hard to find;
> With aching heart their grave-digger comes now
> Alone, her hoe in hand, her secret tears
> Falling like drops of blood on each bare bough.
>
> Dusk falls and the cuckoo is silent;
> Her hoe brought back, the lodge is locked and still;
> A green lamp lights the wall as sleep enfolds her,
> Cold rain pelts the casement and her quilt is chill.
>
> What causes my two-fold anguish?
> Love for spring and resentment of spring;

For suddenly it comes and suddenly goes,
Its arrival unheralded, noiseless its departing.

Last night from the courtyard floated a sad song —
Was it the soul of blossom, the soul of birds?
Hard to detain, the soul of blossom or birds,
For blossoms have no assurance, birds no words.

I long to take wing and fly
With the flowers to earth's uttermost bound;
And yet at earth's uttermost bound
Where can a fragrant burial mound be found?

Better shroud the fair petals in silk
With clean earth for their outer attire;
For pure you came and pure shall go,
Not sinking into some foul ditch or mire.

Now you are dead I come to bury you;
None has divined the day when I shall die;
Men laugh at my folly in burying fallen flowers,
But who will bury me when dead I lie?

See, when spring draws to a close and flowers fall,
This is the season when beauty must ebb and fade;
The day that spring takes wing and beauty fades
Who will care for the fallen blossom or dead maid?

Pao-yu, listening, was overwhelmed with grief. To know more of this, read the next chapter.

CHAPTER 28

Chiang Yu-han Gives a New Friend
a Scarlet Perfumed Sash
Pao-chai Bashfully Shows Her Red Bracelet
Scented with Musk

As we saw, Tai-yu held Pao-yu to blame for her exclusion by Ching-wen the previous night. As today happened to be the occasion for feasting the God of Flowers, her pent-up resentment merged with her grief at the transience of spring, and as she buried the fading petals she could not help weeping over her own fate and composing a lament.

Pao-yu listened from the slope. At first he just nodded in sympathy, until she came to the lines:

> Men laugh at my folly in burying fallen flowers,
> But who will bury me when dead I lie?...
> The day that spring takes wing and beauty fades
> Who will care for the fallen blossom or dead maid?

At this point he flung himself wretchedly down on the ground, scattering his load of fallen flowers, heart-broken to think that Tai-yu's loveliness and beauty must one day vanish away. And it followed that the same fate awaited Pao-chai, Hsiang-ling, Hsi-jen and all the rest. When at last they were all gone, what would become of him? And if he had no idea where he would be by then, what would become of this place and all the flowers and willows in the Garden and who would take them over? One reflection led to another until, after repeated ruminations, he wished he were some insensible, stupid object, able to escape all earthy entanglements and be free from such wretchedness despite the —

> Shadows of blossom all around,
> Birdsong on every side.

Tai-yu, giving way to her own grief, heard weeping now on the slope.

"Everyone laughs at me for being foolish. Is there someone else equally foolish?" she asked herself.

Then, looking up, she saw Pao-yu.

"So that's who it is." She snorted. "That heartless, wretched. . . ."

But the moment the words "wretched" escaped her she covered her mouth and moved quickly away with a long sigh.

When Pao-yu recovered sufficiently to look up she had gone, obviously to avoid him. Getting up rather sheepishly, he dusted off his clothes and walked down the hill to make his way back again to Happy Red Court. Catching sight of Tai-yu ahead, he overtook her.

"Do stop!" he begged. "I know you won't look at me, but let me just say *one* word. After that we can part company for good."

Tai-yu glanced round and would have ignored him, but was curious to hear this "*one* word," thinking there must be something in it. She came to a halt.

"Out with it."

Pao-yu smiled.

"Would you listen if I said two words?" he asked.

At once she walked away.

Pao-yu, close behind her, sighed.

"Why are things so different now from in the past?"

Against her will she stopped once more and turned her head.

"What do you mean by 'now' and 'the past'?"

Pao-yu heaved another sigh.

"Wasn't I your playmate when you first came?" he demanded. "Anything that pleased me was yours, cousin, for the asking. If I knew you fancied a favourite dish of mine, I put it away in a clean place till you came. We ate at the same table and slept on the same bed. I took care that the maids did nothing to upset you; for I thought cousins growing up together as such good friends should be kinder to each other than anyone else. I never expected you to grow so proud that now you have no use for me while you're so fond of outsiders like Pao-chai and Hsi-feng. You ignore me or cut me for three or four days at a time. I've no brothers or sisters of my own — only two by a different mother, as well you know. So I'm an only child like you, and I thought that would make for an affinity between us. But apparently it was no use my hoping for that. There's nobody I can tell how unhappy I am." With that, he broke down again.

This appeal and his obvious wretchedness melted her heart. But though shedding tears of sympathy, she kept her head lowered and made no reply.

This encouraged Pao-yu to go on.

"I know my own faults. But however bad I may be, I'd never dare do anything to hurt you. If I do something the least bit wrong, you can tick me off, warn me, scold me or even strike me, and I won't mind. But when you just ignore me and I can't tell why, I'm at my wits' end and don't know what to do. If I die now I can only become a 'ghost hounded to death,' and not even the masses of the best bonzes and Taoists will be able to save my soul. I can only be born again if you'll tell me what's wrong."

By now Tai-yu's resentment over the previous evening was completely forgotten.

"Then why did you tell your maids not to open the gate when I called last night?" she asked.

"Whatever do you mean?" he cried in amazement. "If I did such a thing, may I die on the spot."

"Hush! Don't talk about dying so early in the morning. Did you or didn't you? There's no need to swear."

"I honestly knew nothing about your coming. Pao-chai did drop in for a chat, but she didn't stay long."

Tai-yu thought this over.

"Yes," she said more cheerfully, "I suppose your maids felt too lazy to stir and that made them answer rudely."

"That's it, for sure. I shall find out who it was when I get back and give them a good scolding."

"Those maids of yours deserve one, although of course that's not for me to say. It doesn't matter their offending *me*, but think what trouble there'll be if next time they offend your precious Pao-chai!"

She compressed her lips to smile, and Pao-yu did not know whether to grind his teeth or laugh.

They were summoned now to a meal and went over to his mother's apartment where, on seeing Tai-yu, Lady Wang asked:

"Has Doctor Pao's medicine done you any good, child?"

"Not much," the girl answered. "The old lady wants me to try Doctor Wang's medicine."

"You don't know, madam," said Pao-yu, "Cousin Lin suffers from an inherited weakness and has such a delicate constitution that she can't stand the least little chill. All she needs is a couple of doses to clear this up. Some pills would be best for her."

"The other day the doctor recommended some pills," said his mother. "I can't quite recall the name."

"I can guess," said Pao-yu. "Just ginseng tonic pills."

"That wasn't it."

"Eight-treasure-leonurus pills then? Left restorative? Right restorative? Or, failing that, six-flavour-digitalis pills?"

"No, it wasn't any of those. All I can remember are the words 'guardian angel.'"

Pao-yu clapped his hands and laughed.

"I've never heard of guardian-angel pills. If there are guardian-angel pills there must be bodhisattva powders too."

Everyone in the room burst out laughing.

Trying to repress a smile Pao-chai suggested: "Were they heavenly-king-fortifying-the-heart pills?"

"That's it," said Lady Wang. "How muddle-headed I've grown."

"You're not muddle-headed, madam," her son assured her. "Those angels and bodhisattvas have muddled you."

"That's enough from you," she scolded. "It's time your father gave you another beating."

"My father wouldn't beat me for that."

"Since we know the name we'll send out tomorrow to buy some."

"Those remedies are useless," protested Pao-yu. "If you'll give me three hundred and sixty taels of silver, I'll make up some pills for my cousin and I guarantee she'll be cured before they're all taken."

"Have some sense! What pills could be so expensive?"

Pao-yu chuckled.

"It's true. This is a unique prescription. I won't go into all the strange ingredients now, but one's the afterbirth of a first-born child, another's man-shaped ginseng roots with leaves on them — these alone would cost more than three hundred and sixty taels. Then there's polygonum the size of a tortoise, pachyma from the root of a thousand-year-old pine, and other things of the same sort. These are nothing unusual, just ordinary herbs; but the chief ingredient would give you a shock. Cousin Hsueh Pan pestered me for more than a year to give him this prescription. Even then, it took him more than two years and about a thousand taels of silver to have it made up. If you don't believe me, madam, ask Cousin Pao-chai."

Pao-chai raised a protesting hand, smiling.

"I know nothing and never heard a word about it. So don't refer auntie to me."

"After all she's a good girl," said Lady Wang. "Pao-chai wouldn't tell a lie."

Pao-yu turned where he was standing and clapped his hands.

"What I said is in fact true. Yet you accuse me of lying."

Whirling back he caught sight of Tai-yu, who was seated behind Pao-chai, laughingly drawing one finger across her cheek to shame him.

Hsi-feng had been supervising the laying of the tables in the inner room but now she came out to join in the discussion.

"Pao-yu isn't fibbing," she declared. "It's true. The other day Hsueh Pan came to me for some pearls. 'What for?' I wanted to know.

"He said, 'For a prescription.' And he grumbled, 'If I'd known all the trouble involved, I'd have left it alone.'

"I asked, 'What prescription is it?'

"He said, 'One of Pao-yu's.'

"I hadn't time to listen to all the ingredients he listed. Then he said, 'I could have bought some pearls, but pearls for this medicine must have been worn on the head. That's why I've come to you. If you haven't any loose ones, let me take the pearls from one of your trinkets and I'll find you some good ones later to replace them.'

"So I had to give him a couple of my pearl trinkets. He wanted three feet of red gauze from the Palace too. Said he meant to grind the pearls into a fine powder to be mixed with other powdered ingredients."

Pao-yu had punctuated Hsi-feng's speech with cries of "Buddha be praised! The sun shines at last in this room." As soon as she had finished he put in:

"This is actually only a makeshift, madam. The real prescription calls for pearls and gems worn by wealthy ladies of old from ancient tombs. But we can hardly go and dig up graves, can we? So we have to make do with pearls worn by living people."

"Amida Buddha!" cried Lady Wang. "The idea! Even if there are pearls in old tombs, how can you dig them up and disturb the bones of people dead for all those hundreds of years? No medicine made that way could be any good."

Pao-yu appealed to Tai-yu.

"You heard what's been said. Would my Cousin Hsi-feng back me up if I were lying?" Although facing Tai-yu, he glanced at Pao-chai as he spoke.

Tai-yu caught Lady Wang's arm.

"Just listen to him, auntie. When Pao-chai won't back up his fib, he appeals to me."

"Yes, Pao-yu is good at bullying you," said Lady Wang.

"You don't know the reason, madam." Pao-yu grinned. "Even when Cousin Pao-chai lived with her family she didn't know her brother's doings; so she knows even less now that she's in the Garden. But just now Cousin Tai-yu, sitting at the back, drew a finger across her cheek to shame me because she thought I was fibbing."

A maid came in then to summon Pao-yu and Tai-yu to dinner with the Lady Dowager. Without a word to Pao-yu, Tai-yu rose and started leading the maid away.

"Won't you wait for Master Pao?" asked the maid.

"He doesn't want anything to eat," replied Tai-yu. "Come on, let's go. I'm going." She walked out.

"I'll eat here with you, madam," said Pao-yu.

"No, no," objected Lady Wang. "This is one of my meatless days, so run along and have a proper meal."

"I'll have vegetarian food with you." He sent the maid away and took a seat at the table.

His mother told Pao-chai and the other girls to go ahead with their own meal and ignore him.

"You'd better go," Pao-chai urged him. "Even if you don't want anything to eat you should keep Tai-yu company, she's not feeling happy."

"Never mind her," he answered. "She'll be all right presently."

But as soon as the meal was over he called for tea to rinse his mouth, suspecting that his grandmother might be worried by his absence, and worried himself about Tai-yu.

Tan-chun and Hsi-chun smiled.

"Why are you always in such a hurry, brother?" they teased. "Even rushing through your meals and tea."

"Let him finish quickly and join Cousin Lin," said Pao-chai. "Why should he fool around here?"

Pao-yu gulped down his tea then and left, making straight for the west court. On the way he found Hsi-feng standing in the gateway of her compound and picking her teeth with an earpick as she watched a dozen pages move some flower-pots.

"You've turned up just at the right time," she called to him with a smile. "Come on in. Come in and write a few words for me."

Pao-yu had no option but to follow her in.

Once inside Hsi-feng called for a brush, inkstone and paper and started dictating to him:

"Forty rolls of red flowered satin; forty rolls of satin with serpent designs; a hundred rolls of Imperial gauze of different colours; four gold necklaces."

"What *is* all this?" asked Pao-yu. "It sounds neither like an account nor a list of presents. How am I to write it?"

"Just put it down. So long as I know what it means that'll do."

Pao-yu did as he was told. And when he had finished she put the list away.

"There's something else I want, if you're agreeable," she then said with a smile. "I'd like that maid called Hung-yu in your place to come and work for me. I'll find you a few others instead later. All right?"

"My place is swarming with people," said Pao-yu. "Take any of them you like. You don't have to ask."

"In that case, I'll send someone to fetch her."

"Do."

He was starting to leave when Hsi-feng called him back, saying that she had something else to tell him.

"The old lady is waiting for me," he demurred. "You can tell me when I come back."

By the time he reached the Lady Dowager's quarters they had finished their meal there.

"Well," his grandmother asked, "what good things did your mother give you to eat?"

"Nothing special, but I had one bowl of rice more than usual. Where's Cousin Lin?"

"In the inner room."

Pao-yu went in and saw a maid blowing at the charcoal in an iron. Two others were chalking patterns on the *kang* where Tai-yu, bending over, was cutting out some material. He walked forward with a smile.

"Why, what are you doing?" he asked. "Stooping like that just after a meal will bring your headache back."

Tai-yu paid no attention but went on with her work.

"That corner of the silk is still rather crumpled," one of, the maids remarked. "Better iron it again."

"Never mind it." Tai-yu put down her scissors. "It'll be all right presently."

Pao-yu was digesting this snub when Pao-chai, Tan-chun and the others arrived to chat with the old lady. Soon Pao-chai stepped into the inner room and asked Tai-yu what she was doing, then watched her at work.

"How clever you're getting," she commented, "even able to cut out clothes."

"This is just another specious way of fooling people," retorted Tai-yu.

Pao-chai smiled.

"Let me tell you something funny," she volunteered. "Cousin Pao's annoyed with me because I denied knowing anything about that medicine."

"Never mind him. He'll be all right presently."

Pao-yu told Pao-chai, "The old lady wants to play cards and there aren't enough people. Won't you take a hand?"

Again Pao-chai smiled.

"Of course, that's what I came for."

As she went out Tai-yu called after her, "You had better leave. There's a tiger here who might eat you."

She went on with her cutting and ignored Pao-yu, who suggested with a conciliatory smile: "Why don't you take a stroll before doing any more?"

Tai-yu remained silent.

"Who told her to do this?" he asked the maids.

"Whoever it was," said Tai-yu, "it's none of Master Pao's business."

Before he could say any more a servant came in to announce that someone was waiting outside to see him. As he hurried out Tai-yu called after him:

"Buddha be praised! I hope I'm dead before you come back."

Outside he found Pei-ming, who told him that Feng Tzu-ying had invited him over. Remembering what had been said the previous day, Pao-yu sent for his outdoor clothes and wait-ed for them in the library.

Pei-ming went to the second gate, where he waited until an old woman appeared.

"Master Pao is in the library waiting for his outdoor clothes," he announced. "Do you mind going in to tell them?"

"You farting fool!" she cried. "Master Pao lives in the Garden now and so do all his attendants. Why bring the mes-sage *here*?"

"Of course." Pei-ming laughed. "How idiotic of me!"

He hurried to the inner gate on the east and got one of the lads playing ball by the paved passageway to run in with the message. The youngster came back after a while with a bundle which Pei-ming carried to the library.

Pao-yu, having changed, called for his horse and set off with only four pages: Pei-ming, Chu-yao, Shuang-jui and Shuang-shou. When they reached Feng Tzu-ying's gate and were an-nounced, Feng came out to welcome them. Hsueh Pan had already been there for some time with a number of singing-boys, Chiang Yu-han, an actor who played female roles, and Yun-erh, a courtesan from Brocade Fragrance Court. The in-troductions were made and tea was served.

Raising his cup Pao-yu smiled at their host.

"Your remark the other day about good fortune and bad has been on my mind ever since," he said. "So as soon as your summons arrived I hurried over."

"How trusting you all are." Feng Tzu-ying chuckled. "That was just an excuse to get you over here, for otherwise I was afraid you might decline. Fancy your taking it so seriously."

Amid laughter wine was brought in and they took seats in due order. Feng made one of the boy singers pour the wine and asked Yun-erh to their table to toast the guests. After three cups Hsueh Pan grew rowdy and seized her hand.

"Sing a nice new song for me," he begged, "and I'll drink a whole jarful of wine. How about it?"

"Yun-erh had no choice but to take her *pipa* and sing:

> Two lovers have I,
> From both I'm loath to part,
> For while I think of one
> The other's in my heart.
> Both have so many charms
> They're hard to list;
> Last night by the rose trellis
> Was our tryst.
> One came to make love, one to spy;
> Caught in the act was I
> And, challenged by the two of them,
> Could think of no reply!

This sung, she said, "All right, now drink a jar."

"That wasn't worth a whole jar," protested Hsueh Pan. "Let's hear something better."

"Listen," put in Pao-yu. "If you drink so fast, you'll soon be drunk and we shan't have any fun. Suppose I empty a goblet first and we play a new game of forfeits? Anyone who doesn't do as I say will have to drain ten goblets in succession and leave the table to wait on the others."

When they all agreed to this, he picked up a goblet and drained it.

"Now," he said, "you must all make four lines about a girl's sorrow, her worry, her joy and her delight, explaining the reason for each. Then you must drink a cup of wine, sing a new popular song, and recite either a line from an old poem or couplet, or a saying from the *Four Books* or the *Five Classics* connected with some object on the table."

Before he had finished Hsueh Pan was on his feet protesting.

"I'm not doing that. Count me out. You just want to make fun of me."

Yun-erh stood up to push him back on to his seat.

"What are you afraid of?" she teased. "Don't you drink every day? Aren't you even up to me? I'm going to join in. If you do all right, well and good; if not, it won't kill you to drink a few cups. Or would you rather refuse and have to drink ten goblets and wait on the rest of us?"

All clapped their approval and Hsueh Pan had to subside. Pao-yu began:

"The girl's sorrow: Youth is passing but she remains single.

"The girl's worry: Her husband leaves home to make his fortune.

"The girl's joy: Her good looks in the mirror in the morning.

"The girl's delight: Swinging in a light spring gown."

All cried "Good!" except Hsueh Pan, who shook his head.

"No good," he growled. "He ought to pay a forfeit."

"Why?" asked the others.

"Because I didn't understand a word."

Yun-erh gave him a pinch.

"Be quiet and think out your lines. If you don't, *you'll* be the one to pay a forfeit."

She accompanied Pao-yu on the *pipa* as he sang:

> Like drops of blood fall endless tears of longing,
> By painted pavilion grow willows and flowers untold;
> Sleepless at night when wind and rain lash gauze
>   windows,
> She cannot forget her sorrows new and old;
> Choking on rice like jade and wine like gold,
> She turns from her wan reflection in the glass;
> Nothing can smooth away her frown,
> It seems that the long night will never pass;
> Like the shadow of peaks, her grief is never gone;
> Like the green stream it flows for ever on.

The only one not to applaud this song was Hsueh Pan.

"You were off beat," he objected.

Pao-yu drained his cup and picked up a slice of pear from the table.

" 'Rain buffets the pear blossom and the door is closed,' " he quoted.

It was now Feng Tzu-ying's turn. He started off:

"The girl's sorrow: Her husband falls mortally ill.

"The girl's worry: Her boudoir in the tower is blown down.

"The girl's joy: Twin sons at her first confinement.

"The girl's delight: Catching crickets on the sly in the garden."

Next, raising his cup, he sang:

> You can bill and you can coo,
> Be an imp of mischief too,
> But a fairy? No, not you,

> As my word you doubt.
> Ask around and you'll find out
> I love you, yes, I do!

Then, having drunk up, he picked up a piece of chicken.

" 'A cock crows at the moon by the rustic inn,' " was his quotation.

Yun-erh's turn came next and she began:

"The girl's sorrow: Will she find a husband to support her?"

Hsueh Pan sighed.

"Why child," he said, "with Master Hsueh here, what have you to worry about?"

"Don't muddle her," cried the others. "Don't muddle her."

Yun-erh went on:

"The girl's worry: Will the bawd always beat and scold her?"

Hsueh Pan cut in, "The other day when I saw that bawd of yours, I told her not to beat you."

"If you interrupt again," the others warned him, "you'll have to drink ten cups."

At once he slapped his own cheek.

"You've been warned. Not another word now!"

Yun-erh continued:

"The girl's joy: Her lover cannot bear to go home.

"The girl's delight: The pipes hushed, she plays a stringed instrument."

Then she sang:

> On the third of the third moon blooms the cardamom;
> Fain to creep into it an insect is come;
> Failing to enter it clings
> To the petals and there it swings.
> Dear heart, if I don't let you in,
> Your chances are thin!

She drained her cup and picked up a peach saying, " 'The peach trees are in blossom.' "

It was now Hsueh Pan's turn.

"All right," he said. "Here goes. The girl's sorrow...."

A long pause followed.

"What is she sad about?" Feng Tzu-ying prompted him. "Go on."

Hsueh Pan's eyes bulged, he was so frantic.

"The girl's sorrow. . . ."

He cleared his throat twice and persevered:

"The girl's sorrow: She marries a queer."

A roar of laughter went up.

"What's so funny?" he demanded. "Is that wrong? Wouldn't a girl be sad if the man she married insisted on being a bugger?"

Doubled up with laughter they gasped, "Quite right. Hurry up and go on."

His eyes bulging again he proceeded, "The girl's worry. . . ." Once more his voice trailed away.

"Well, what's the worry?"

"The girl's worry: A big gorilla springs out of her boudoir."

Roaring with laughter they cried, "Make him pay the forfeit. The last could just pass but this is impossible."

However, before they could fill the goblet Pao-yu put in, "As long as he rhymes it, that's good enough."

"If the man in charge passes it," blustered Hsueh Pan, "why should you lot kick up such a fuss?"

The others gave way.

"The next two lines are more difficult," said Yun-erh. "Suppose I do them for you?"

"Nonsense. You think I've nothing better coming? Listen. 'The girl's joy: Rising late after her wedding night.'"

"How poetic he's growing!" they exclaimed.

"The girl's delight: A good fuck."

All turned away crying, "For shame! Hurry up with your song."

Then he sang:

A mosquito buzzes, hum-hum.

"What sort of song do you call this?" they demanded.

He went on:

Two flies drone, buzz-buzz.

"That's enough. Shut up!" they cried.

"All right, if you don't want it. That's a new song called *Hum-hum*. If you can't be bothered to listen and want me to stop, you must let me off the drinking."

"We'll let you off. You're just holding up other people."

Then Chiang Yu-han took over.

"The girl's sorrow: Her husband leaves, never to return.

"The girl's worry: She has no money to buy pomade.

"The girl's joy: The wick forms two heads like a double flower.[1]

"The girl's delight: Husband and wife in harmony."

Next he sang:

> So many charms has Heaven given you,
> You seem a goddess come down from the blue;
> And blooming youth, life's springtide,
> Is just the time to mate the lovebirds true.
> The watch-tower drum is beating now,
> The Milky Way gleams high above;
> Make haste to trim the silver lamp
> And draw the bridal curtains on our love.

This sung, he raised his cup and said, "I know very few poems, but luckily I remember a line of a couplet I read yesterday which happens to fit an object on the table."

Having drained his cup he picked up a sprig of fragrant osmanthus and quoted:

" 'When the fragrance of flowers assails men we know the day is warm.' "

Everyone passed this, and so the game ended. But Hsueh Pan leapt to his feet.

"You've gone too far!" he shouted. "You must pay a forfeit. How can you mention a treasure that isn't here?"

Chiang Yu-han was puzzled.

"What treasure?"

"Don't try to deny it. Repeat that line again."

The actor complied.

"Isn't Hsi-jen a treasure?" demanded Hsueh Pan. "If you don't believe me, ask him." He pointed at Pao-yu.

---

[1] This was interpreted as a sign of a husband's return.

In some embarrassment Pao-yu stood up.

"How many cups should we fine you, cousin, for this?" he asked.

"All right. I'll pay the penalty."

Hsueh Pan picked up his cup and tossed it off.

Feng Tzu-ying and Chiang Yu-han asked for an explanation; and when Yun-erh told them who Hsi-jen was, the actor rose to his feet to apologize.

"You're not to blame," said the others. "You didn't know."

Presently Pao-yu left the room to relieve himself, and Chiang Yu-han followed him out to apologize once more in the corridor. Pao-yu was much taken by his charming appearance. Clasping his hand tightly he said:

"When you've time, do come and see me. By the way, I've something to ask you. In your honourable company there's an actor called Chi-kuan who's known all over the country, but I've never had a chance to see him."

Chiang Yu-han smiled.

"That's my professional name."

Pao-yu stamped one foot in delight.

"What luck!" he cried. "You certainly live up to your reputation. How can I mark this first meeting?"

After a second's thought he drew the fan from his sleeve, unfastened the jade pendant on it and gave this to the actor.

"Please accept this trifle as a mark of my friendship."

"What have I done to deserve this?" Chi-kuan smiled. "All right, I've something unusual here which I only put on for the first time this morning. It's still quite new. A small token of my devotion."

He raised his gown to undo the scarlet sash round his trousers and handed it to Pao-yu.

"This was part of the tribute from the Queen of Chien-hsiang," he explained. "Worn in summer, it will perfume your skin and stop you from perspiring. I was given it by the Prince of Peiching yesterday, and I put it on for the first time this morning. I wouldn't dream of giving it to anybody else. Would you mind letting me have your own in exchange, sir?"

Pao-yu took the scarlet sash with the greatest of pleasure, then untied his own pale green one and handed it to the actor. They were both fastening their new sashes when they heard a loud shout.

"Caught in the act!"

It was Hsueh Pan, who bounded over to seize them.

"What are you up to?" he cried. "Leaving your wine and slipping away from the feast! Come on, let's see what you've got there."

When they told him "Nothing," he refused to believe them. Not until Feng Tzu-ying came out did he let them go. Then they went back to their seats and drank until the evening, when the party broke up.

On Pao-yu's return to the Garden he took off his outer garments to drink tea and Hsi-jen, noticing that his fan-pendant was missing, asked what had become of it.

"I must have lost it out riding," said Pao-yu.

But when he went to bed and she saw the blood-red sash round his waist, she knew more or less what had happened.

"Now that you've got a better sash, will you return mine?" she asked.

Only then did he remember that the green sash belonged to Hsi-jen and he should never have given it away. He was sorry but could hardly explain to her what had happened.

"I'll get you another," he promised.

"I know what you've been up to again." She nodded and sighed. "You've no right to give my things to those low creatures. You should know better."

She let it go at that and went to bed too, afraid to provoke him after he had been drinking.

As soon as she woke the next morning, Pao-yu confronted her with a smile.

"You wouldn't know if a thief came in the night," he said. "Look at your pants."

Hsi-jen looked down and saw that the sash he had worn the previous day was now round her own waist. Aware that he had changed it during the night, she immediately took it off.

"I'm not interested in such trash. Take it away."

He pleaded with her until she consented to wear it. But as soon as he left the room she took it off, threw it into an empty case and put on another. Pao-yu did not notice this on his return.

"Did anything happen yesterday?" he asked.

"Madam Lien sent over for Hsiao-hung. The girl wanted to wait for your return but I didn't think that necessary, so I took it upon myself to send her away."

"Quite right. I knew. There was no need for her to wait."

"And yesterday the Imperial Consort sent the eunuch Hsia here with a hundred and twenty taels to be spent on masses, theatricals and sacrifices on the first three days of the month at Ethereal Abbey. She wants Lord Chen to take all the gentlemen there to burn incense and worship Buddha. She also sent over presents for the Dragon-Boat Festival."

Hsi-jen told a young maid to fetch his gifts: two fine Palace fans, two strings of red beads scented with musk, two lengths of phoenix-tail silk, and a bamboo mat woven in a lotus pattern.

Pao-yu, delighted with these things, asked if the others had received the same gifts.

"The old lady had an extra sandalwood *Ju-yi* sceptre and agate pillow. Lord Cheng, Lady Wang and Madam Hsueh each had an extra sandalwood sceptre. You got the same as Miss Hsueh, while Miss Lin and the three other young ladies were given fans and beads, nothing else. Madam Li Wan and Madam Hsi-feng each had two rolls of gauze, two rolls of silk, two aromatic pouches and two pills from the Palace."

"How can that be?" asked Pao-yu. "Why did Miss Hsueh get the same as me and not Miss Lin? There must be some mistake."

"Impossible. Each share was labelled when they were brought yesterday. Yours went to the old lady's apartments, and when I fetched it she said you must go to the Palace at the fifth watch tomorrow to express your thanks."

"Yes, of course."

He called for Tzu-hsiao.

"Take these things to Miss Lin," he instructed her. "Tell her this is what I got yesterday and she can keep anything she fancies."

The maid did as she was told, coming back to report, "Miss Lin says she received presents too; she wants you to keep yours."

He had the things put away then and washed his face before setting off to pay his respects to his grandmother. Meeting Tai-yu on the way, he hurried up to her with a smile.

"Why didn't you pick any of my things, as I asked?"

Tai-yu had forgotten her earlier grievance in her preoccupation with this new incident.

"I'm not cut out for such good fortune," she said. "I can't compare with Cousin Pao-chai and her gold and jade. I'm just as common as any plant or tree."

Pao-yu caught this innuendo.

"Other people may talk about gold and jade," he protested, "but if such an idea ever crossed my mind, may Heaven and Earth destroy me! May I never again be reborn in human form!"

Tai-yu knew from this how hurt he felt.

"What nonsense," she scoffed. "Why make such oaths for no reason? Who cares about your gold and jade anyway?"

"It's hard to tell you all that's in my heart, but you'll understand some day. You're the closest person in the world to me after my grandmother and my own parents. I swear there's no one else."

"There's no need to swear. I know I have a place in your heart. But whenever you see *her*, you forget all about me."

"That's your imagination. I'm not like that."

"Why did you appeal to me when Pao-chai refused to back up your fib yesterday? If I'd refused, goodness knows what you'd have done."

Seeing Pao-chai approaching just then, they moved on. And pretending not to have seen them — although she had — she walked on with lowered head to chat with Lady Wang before going on to the Lady Dowager's apartments. She found Pao-yu already there.

Now ever since her mother had told Lady Wang about the gold locket given to Pao-chai by a monk and his prediction that she would only marry a man with jade, Pao-chai had been rather distant to Pao-yu. Yuan-chun's gift of identical presents to them the previous day had made her even more sensitive on this score. Fortunately Pao-yu was so wrapped up in Tai-yu, so utterly engrossed in her, that he paid no attention to this coincidence.

Without warning now he asked Pao-chai to let him have a look at the red bead bracelet scented with musk on her left wrist. She had no alternative but to take it off. She was so plump, however, that this was by no means easy. And while he stood admiring her soft white arm it occurred to him: If she were Tai-yu, I might have a chance to stroke her arm. Too bad for me that it's *hers*!

Suddenly remembering the talk about gold and jade, he looked at Pao-chai more closely. Her face seemed a silver disc, her eyes were lustrous and almond-shaped, her lips red without rouge, her eyebrows dark without being pencilled. She was charming in quite a different way from Tai-yu. He was so fascinated that when she pulled off the bracelet and offered it to him, he did not even take it.

Embarrassed by the way he was staring, Pao-chai put the bracelet down and turned to go. She saw Tai-yu then in the doorway, biting her handkerchief with a mocking smile.

"Why are you standing there in a draught?" asked Pao-chai. "You know how easily you catch cold."

"I was indoors until I heard a strange bird-cry. When I came out to look, it was only a silly goose."

"Where is this silly goose? I'd like to see it."

"As soon as I came out it flapped away."

With these words she flicked Pao-yu's face with her handkerchief, catching him right on the eyes. He uttered an exclamation of surprise.

To know what came of this, read the next chapter.

CHAPTER 29

Favourites of Fortune Pray for Better Fortune
An Absurd, Loving Girl Falls Deeper in Love

Pao-yu was so absorbed by his thoughts that when Tai-yu flicked his eyes with her handkerchief, he gave a sudden start.

"Who's that?" he exclaimed.

She shook her head laughingly.

"Sorry, a slip of the hand. Cousin Pao-chai wanted to see the silly goose, and while pointing it out to her I hit you by mistake."

Pao-yu rubbed his eyes and bit back the retort which was on the tip of his tongue.

Then Hsi-feng arrived and, alluding in the course of conversation to the Taoist mass to be held at Ethereal Abbey on the first of the next month, she urged the young people to go there to watch the operas.

"It's too hot for me," objected Pao-chai. "Besides, there aren't any operas I haven't seen. I'm not going."

"It's cool there with tall buildings on either side," countered Hsi-feng. "If we're going I shall send servants a few days in advance to clear out the Taoist priests and clean the place up, then screen it off and close it to the general public. It will be rather pleasant then. I've already told Lady Wang. If *you* won't go I mean to go alone. Things have been so boring recently; besides, even when we have shows at home, I can't watch them in comfort."

When the Lady Dowager heard of this she said, "In that case, I'll go along with you."

"If our Old Ancestress is going as well," cried Hsi-feng, "so much the better — only I shan't be free to enjoy myself."

"I'll sit in the main balcony and you can watch from one of the side ones, will that suit you? Then you won't have to dance attendance on me."

"See how our Old Ancestress dotes on me!" Hsi-feng quipped.

"You must go, and your mother too," said the Lady Dowager to Pao-chai. "If you stayed at home you'd only sleep the whole day long."

Then Pao-chai had to agree.

The old lady sent a maid to invite Aunt Hsueh and to notify Lady Wang on the way that she meant to take the girls. Lady Wang had already excused herself on the grounds that she was unwell and expecting word from Yuan-chun. She received this message with a smile and the comment:

"What good spirits she's in. Go and tell them in the Garden that any of the young ladies who would like an outing may accompany the old lady on the first."

Those most excited by this news were the young maids who normally had no chance to cross the threshold, all of whom longed to go: If their mistresses were disinclined to stir they tried in every way to persuade them, to such effect that Li Wan and the rest all agreed to the trip. This pleased the Lady Dowager even more. Meanwhile servants had been sent to make everything ready.

When the first of the fifth month arrived, the road before the Jung Mansion was thronged with carriages, sedan-chairs, attendants and horses. As this mass had been paid for by the Imperial Consort and the Lady Dowager was going in person to offer incense, and as moreover it was just before the Double Fifth Festival, all the preparations were on a more lavish scale than usual.

Presently the ladies of the house emerged. The old lady's large sedan-chair had eight bearers; those of Li Wan, Hsi-feng and Aunt Hsueh, four apiece. The carriage shared by Pao-chai and Tai-yu was gay with a green awning, pearl-tassels and designs of the Eight Precious Things; that shared by the three Chia girls had crimson wheels and an ornamented covering.

Behind them followed the Lady Dowager's maids Yuan-yang, Ying-wu, Hu-po and Chen-chu; Tai-yu's maids Tzu-chuan, Hsueh-yen and Chun-hsien; Pao-chai's maids Ying-erh and Wen-hsing; Ying-chun's maids Ssu-chi and Hsiu-chu; Tan-chun's maids Tai-shu and Tsui-mo; Hsi-chun's maids Ju-hua and Tsai-ping; and Aunt Hsueh's maids Tung-hsi and Tung-kuei.

They were also accompanied by Hsiang-ling and her maid Chen-erh; Li Wan's maids Su-yun and Pi-yueh; Hsi-feng's maids Ping-erh, Feng-erh and Hsiao-hung; and Lady Wang's maids Chin-chuan and Tsai-yun, who because they wanted to go were attending on Hsi-feng today.

Ta-chieh and her wet-nurse rode in another carriage with other maids.

In addition there were two other maids and some old nurses from the different apartments, as well as some stewards' wives. The whole street was nearly hidden from sight by all their conveyances. Even after the Lady Dowager's sedan-chair had gone a considerable distance, these attendants were still mounting their carriages at the gate, where a babel of voices was heard:

"I don't want *you* in with me."

"Look out! You're sitting on my lady's things."

"Don't tread on my flowers!"

"You've gone and broken my fan."

There was no end to their noisy talk and laughter. Chou Jui's wife went back and forth to remonstrate:

"Now, girls, don't make such laughing-stocks of yourselves out in the street."

She had to repeat this several times to make them quiet down, by which time the front part of the retinue had reached the abbey gate. And as Pao-yu rode up on horseback before the Lady Dowager's sedan-chair, spectators lined the street.

As they neared the abbey gate, they heard the peal of bells and the roll of drums. Abbot Chang in his robes of office, holding a tablet, was waiting with his priests by the roadside to welcome them. The Lady Dowager's sedan-chair had just been borne through the gate when, at sight of the clay images of gods guarding the temple gate, those of two messenger gods — one with eyes able to see a thousand *li*, the other with ears able to catch each breath of rumour — together with local tutelary gods, she ordered her bearers to halt. Chia Chen and the young men of the family advanced to receive her. And Hsi-feng, knowing that Yuan-yang and the others were too far behind to help the old lady alight, got down from her own chair to do this. As she did so, an acolyte of twelve or thirteen, holding a case of scissors for cutting the candle-wicks, came darting out to see the fun and ran full tilt into her. She boxed his ears so hard that he pitched to the ground.

"Look out where you're going, little bastard!" she swore.

Too frightened to pick up his scissors, the boy scrambled to his feet to run outdoors. Just then Pao-chai and the other girls were dismounting from their carriages, escorted by a multitude of matrons and stewards' wives. At sight of the little fugitive, the attendants shouted:

"Catch him! Beat him!"

"What's happened?" asked the Lady Dowager.

Chia Chen hurried over to make inquiries, while Hsi-feng gave the old lady her arm.

"It's an acolyte who trims the wicks," she explained. "He didn't get out of the way in time and was rushing wildly about."

"Bring him here. Don't frighten him," the Lady Dowager ordered. "Children of humble families are well sheltered by their parents, they have never seen anything so grand before. It would be too bad to frighten him out of his wits — his father and mother would never get over it." She told Chia Chen, "Go and bring him gently here."

Chia Chen had to drag the boy over. His scissors now in one hand, trembling from head to foot, he fell on his knees. The old lady made Chia Chen help him up.

"Don't be afraid," she said. "How old are you?"

But he was speechless with fright.

"Poor little thing!" she exclaimed, then turned to Chia Chen. "Take him away, Chen, and give him some cash to buy sweetmeats. Don't let anyone bully him."

Chia Chen assented and led the boy away, while the Lady Dowager moved on with her train to see the different shrines.

The pages outside had just observed them enter the third gate when out came Chia Chen with the acolyte and ordered them to take him away, give him a few hundred cash and not illtreat him. Several servants promptly came forward and led him off.

Standing on the steps Chia Chen demanded, "Where is the steward?"

All the pages shouted in unison, "Steward!"

At once Lin Chih-hsiao came running over, holding on his cap with one hand.

"Although this is a large place," Chia Chen told him, "there are more people here than we expected. Keep those you need in this courtyard, send those you don't need to the other, and post some boys at the two main gates and side gates ready to carry out orders and run errands. You know, don't you, that all the ladies have come today, so not a single outsider must be allowed in."

"Yes, sir. Right, sir. Very good, sir," agreed Lin Chih-hsiao hastily.

"You may go. Wait! Why isn't Jung here?"

While he was still speaking Chia Jung hurried out from the bell-tower, buttoning his clothes.

"Look at him," sneered Chia Chen. "While I swelter here he finds somewhere to cool off."

He ordered the servants to spit at him, and one of the pages spat in Chia Jung's face.

"Ask him what he means by it," ordered Chia Chen.

So the page asked Chia Jung, "If His Lordship can stand the heat, why should you go to cool off?"

Chia Jung, his arms at his sides, dared not utter a word.

This had struck fear into Chia Yun, Chia Chin and Chia Ping; and even Chia Huang, Chia Pien and Chia Yuan promptly put on their caps and one by one edged forward from the shade at the foot of the wall.

"What are you standing there for?" Chia Chen snapped at his son. "Hurry up and gallop home to tell your mother and wife that the old lady and all the young ladies are here. They should come at once and wait on them."

Chia Jung ran off shouting repeatedly for a horse. He grumbled: "Why was this not thought of before? Now I'm the one to take the brunt." Then he swore at a page, "Are your hands tied that you can't bring me a horse?"

He would have sent a page in his place, if not for fear this might be discovered later. As it was, he had to ride back to town himself.

But to return to Chia Chen. As he was turning back to the hall he found Chang the Taoist standing beside him.

"In view of my special position I ought to attend the ladies inside," the priest observed with a smile. "But it's such a hot day, with so many young ladies here too, that I don't like to presume without your permission. I'd better wait here in case the old lady may want me to show her round."

Chia Chen knew that though this Taoist had been the Duke of Jungkuo's substitute,[1] later he had been made Chief Warder of the Taoist Script, with the title "Saint of the Great Illusion" verbally conferred by the previous Emperor, and now being Keeper of the Taoist Seal and entitled "Man of Final Truth" by the Emperor he was addressed as "Immortal" by nobles and officials alike. It would not do to slight him. Besides, during his frequent visits to the two mansions he had already made the acquaintance of all the ladies there, both young and old.

So Chia Chen responded with a smile, "What sort of talk is this among friends? Stop it at once or I shall pull out your beard. Come along in with me."

Laughing heartily the Taoist followed him in.

---

[1] By this superstitious practice rich people used to pay poor families' sons to be priests or monks in their stead in order to ward off evil.

Chia Chen found the Lady Dowager and with a bow informed her: "Grandfather Chang has come to pay his respects."

"Bring him here," she rejoined at once.

Chia Chen led in the priest, chortling.

"Buddha of Infinite Longevity!" he exclaimed. "I hope the Old Ancestress has been enjoying good fortune, long life, health and peace, and that all the ladies and young ladies have been happy too. I haven't called on you to pay my respects, but Your Ladyship looks in better health than ever."

"And are you well, Old Immortal?" she responded with a smile.

"Thanks to my share in your good fortune, yes. I keep feeling concerned about your grandson, though. How has he been keeping all this time? Not long ago, on the twenty-sixth of last month, we celebrated the birthday of the Prince who Shades the Sky. As few people would be coming and everything was quite clean, I sent to invite Master Pao to come; but they told me he wasn't at home."

"It's true, he wasn't."

The old lady called for her grandson.

Pao-yu, just back from the privy, hurriedly stepped forward to say, "How do you do, Grandad Chang?"

The priest took him in his arms and asked after his health.

"Yes," he remarked to the Lady Dowager, "he looks as if he's putting on weight now."

"He may look all right but he's really delicate. And his father is ruining his health, the way he keeps the boy poring over his books."

"I've seen some of his calligraphy and poems in different places recently. They're so remarkably good I can't understand why His Lordship should still complain he's idle. I'd say he's doing all right." Then, with a sigh, the old Taoist observed, "To me, with his face and figure, his bearing and way of talking, Master Pao seems the image of the old duke." Tears welled from his eyes as he spoke.

The old lady was painfully affected too.

"You're right," she agreed. "Of all my sons and grandsons, Pao-yu is the only one who takes after his grandfather."

The priest then remarked to Chia Chen, "Of course, sir, your generation were born too late to see the duke. I don't suppose even Lord Sheh and Lord Cheng remember too well what he looked like." He burst out laughing again before turning back to the Lady Dowager. "The other day in a certain family I saw a young lady of fifteen, a pretty girl. It seems to me time to arrange a match for the young master. And that young lady would do, as far as looks, intelligence and family go. But not knowing how Your Ladyship feels, I didn't like to do anything rash. I can go and broach the subject if Your Ladyship gives the word."

"A bonze told us this boy isn't fated to marry too early," she replied. "So we'll wait until he's older to settle things. But by all means keep your eyes open. Riches and rank are immaterial. Only if you find a girl pretty enough, come and let us know. Even if the family's poor it doesn't matter, we can always let them have a few taels of silver. But good looks and a sweet disposition are hard to find."

At this point Hsi-feng joined in with a smile: "Grandfather Chang, you still haven't brought our daughter her new talisman, yet you had the nerve to send round the other day to ask for yellow satin. And I didn't like to make you lose face by not giving it."

Chang the Taoist roared with laughter.

"My eyes are so dim, I didn't notice you, madam, and haven't thanked you. The talisman was ready long ago and I was meaning to send it, but when Her Highness ordered this mass to be held I forgot. It's still before the image of Buddha. I'll go and get it."

He hurried off to the main hall, returning presently with a talisman on a tray covered with a red silk sutra wrapper with a dragon design. As Ta-chieh's nurse took this from him, he held out his arms for the child.

"Why didn't you bring it in your hands?" Hsi-feng wanted to know. "Why use a tray?"

"My hands are too dirty, madam. A tray seemed cleaner."

"You gave me quite a turn when you brought in that tray," she teased. "I didn't know you had the talisman on it, I thought you'd come to ask for donations."

This set the whole party laughing. Even Chia Chen could not suppress a smile.

"What a monkey you are!" cried the Lady Dowager turning to Hsi-feng. "Aren't you afraid of going to the Tongue-Cutting Hell?"

"I've done him no harm," she countered. "Why is he always warning me that unless I do more good deeds I shan't live long?"

Chang the Taoist chuckled.

"I brought the tray for two reasons," he explained. *"Not* to collect donations, but to borrow Master Pao's jade to show my Taoist friends and disciples."

"If that's the case," said the Lady Dowager, "there's no reason why an old man like you should run around. Take Pao-yu out to show it to them all, then send him back. Wouldn't that save trouble?"

"No, Your Ladyship doesn't understand. I may be more than eighty, but thanks to your shared good fortune I'm hale and hearty; and there are so many of them out there that the place stinks. Master Pao, not being used to this heat, might be over-powered by the stench. And that would be too bad."

Accordingly the old lady told Pao-yu to take off his Jade of Spiritual Understanding and put it on the tray. Chang the Taoist laid it reverently on the silk and carried the tray respectfully out with both hands.

For their part, the Lady Dowager and her party went on strolling round the temple. They were climbing to the upper storey of one building when Chia Chen reported that Grandad Chang had brought back the jade. As he spoke, Chang appeared with the tray.

"Everyone felt most obliged to me for the chance to see Master Pao's jade, which they think most wonderful," he declared. "They've nothing else worth offering, so they've sent these Taoist amulets as tokens of their respect. If Master Pao thinks they're nothing special, he can keep them as toys or give them away, just as he pleases."

The Lady Dowager saw in the tray several dozen amulets of gold and jade engraved with the inscriptions "May All Your Wishes Come True" and "Eternal Peace." Each was studded with pearls or jewels and finely carved.

"This won't do," she expostulated. "How can priests afford such things? It's quite uncalled for. We can't possibly accept them."

"These are just a small token of their esteem. I couldn't stop them," he said. "If Your Ladyship won't accept them, they'll think you look down on me and don't consider me as your protégé."

So she had to tell a maid to take the gifts.

"Since Grandad Chang won't let us refuse, and these things are no use to me, madam," said Pao-yu, "why not let my pages carry them out with me now to distribute them to the poor?"

"That's a good idea," agreed his grandmother.

But Chang the Taoist immediately objected, "That's a charitable thought, Master Pao; but even if these things are of little value, some of them are well made. They'd be wasted on beggars, who'd have no use for them. If you want to help the poor, why not give them money instead?"

"All right," said Pao-yu. "We'll keep them and distribute some alms this evening."

Thereupon the priest withdrew, while the Lady Dowager and her party went upstairs to sit in the main balcony, Hsi-feng and her companions occupying that to the east. The maids, in the west balcony, took turns waiting on their mistresses.

Presently Chia Chen came to report that lots had been drawn before the shrine for the operas, and the first was to be *The White Serpent*.

"What's the story?" asked the old lady.

"It's about the First Emperor of Han who killed a serpent, then founded the dynasty. The second is *Every Son a High Minister*."[1]

"So that's the second?" The Lady Dowager nodded, smiling. "Well, if this is the wish of the gods, what must be must be. And what's the third?"

"The Dream of the Southern Tributary State."[2]

At this she made no comment. Chia Chen withdrew to prepare the written prayers, burn incense and order the actors to start. But no more of this.

Pao-yu, seated next to his grandmother upstairs, told one of the maids to bring him the tray of gifts. Having put on his own jade again he rummaged through his presents, showing them one by one to the old lady. Her eye was struck by a gold unicorn decorated with turquoise enamel, which she picked up.

"I'm sure I've seen something like this on one of the girls," she remarked.

"Cousin Hsiang-yun has one like that, only a little smaller," Pao-chai told her.

"So that's it!" exclaimed the Lady Dowager.

"All this time she's been staying with us, how come I've never noticed it?" asked Pao-yu.

"Cousin Pao-chai's observant," chuckled Tan-chun. "She never forgets anything either."

"She's not so observant about other things," remarked Tai-yu cuttingly. "But she's *most* observant about other people's trinkets."

Pao-chai turned away and pretended not to have heard.

As soon as Pao-yu knew that Hsiang-yun had a unicorn too, he picked this one up and slipped it into his pocket. Then, afraid people might see through him, he glanced surreptitiously round. The only one paying any attention was Tai-yu, who was nodding at him with a look of speculation in her eyes. Embarrassed by this, he took the unicorn out again and showed it to her.

---

[1] A story about Kuo Tzu-yi of the Tang Dynasty.

[2] Based on a Tang story in which a scholar had a dream of great wealth and splendour; then he woke up and found it was just an empty dream.

"This is rather fun," he said with a smile. "I'll keep it for you till we get home, then put it on a cord for you to wear."

Tai-yu tossed her head.

"I don't fancy it."

"If you really don't, in that case I'll keep it for myself." He put it away again.

Before he could say more, Madam Yu and Jung's second wife — Chia Chen's wife and daughter-in-law — arrived to pay their respects.

"You shouldn't have come," protested the old lady. "I'm just out for a little jaunt."

The next second it was announced that messengers had come from General Feng. For as soon as Feng Tzu-ying heard that the Chia family were celebrating a mass in the abbey he had prepared gifts of pigs, sheep, incense, candles and sweetmeats and had them sent along. The moment Hsi-feng knew this she hurried over to the main balcony.

"Aiya!" she exclaimed, clapping her hands. "I wasn't prepared for this. We just looked on this as an outing, but they've sent offerings under the impression that we're making a serious sacrifice of it. It's all our old lady's fault. Now I shall have to prepare some tips."

That same instant up came two stewards' wives from the Feng family. And before they had left more presents arrived from Vice-Minister Chao, to be followed in quick succession by gifts from all their relatives and friends who had heard that the ladies of the Chia family were holding a service in the abbey.

The Lady Dowager began to regret the whole expedition.

"This isn't a regular sacrifice," she said. "We just came out for fun, but we've put them to all this trouble."

So after watching only one performance she went home that same afternoon and refused to go back the next day.

"Why not go the whole hog?" Hsi-feng reasoned. "Since we've already put everybody out, we may as well amuse ourselves again today."

But Pao-yu had been sulking ever since Chang the Taoist broached the subject of his marriage to his grandmother. He was still fulminating against the priest and puzzling other people by muttering: "I never want to set eyes on him again." As for Tai-yu, she had been suffering since her return from a touch of the sun. For these reasons the old lady remained adamant. When Hsi-feng saw that she would not go, she took some others back with her to the abbey.

Pao-yu was so worried on Tai-yu's account that he would not touch his food and kept going over to find out how she was. Tai-yu, for her part, was worried about him.

"Why don't you go and see the shows?" she asked. "Why should you stay at home?"

The Taoist's officiousness still rankled with Pao-yu, and when Tai-yu said this he thought: "I could forgive others for not understanding me, but now even *she* is making fun of me." So his resentment increased a hundredfold. He wouldn't have flared up had it been anyone else, but Tai-yu's behaving this way was a different matter. His face clouded over.

"All right, all right," he said sullenly. "We've known each other all these years in vain."

"I know that too." She laughed sarcastically. "I'm not like those others who own things which make them a good match for you."

He went up to her then and demanded to her face, "Does this mean you really want to invoke Heaven and Earth to destroy me?" Before she could fathom his meaning he went on, "Yesterday I took an oath because of this, and today you provoke me again. If Heaven and Earth destroy me, what good will it do you?"

Tai-yu remembered their previous conversation and realized she had blundered. She was conscience-stricken and frantic.

"If I wish you harm, may Heaven and Earth destroy me too," she sobbed. "Why take on like this? I know. When Chang the Taoist spoke of your marriage yesterday, you were afraid he might prevent the match of your choice. And now you're working your temper off on me."

Now Pao-yu had always been deplorably eccentric. Since childhood, moreover, he had been intimate with Tai-yu, finding her a kindred spirit. Thus now that he knew a little more and had read some improper books, he felt none of the fine girls he had seen in the families of relatives and friends fit to hold a candle to her. He had long since set his heart on having her, but could not admit as much. So whether happy or angry, he used every means to test her secretly.

And Tai-yu, being rather eccentric too, would disguise her feelings to test him in return.

Thus each concealed his or her real sentiments to sound the other out. The proverb says, "When false meets false, the truth will out." So inevitably, in the process, they kept quarrelling over trifles.

So now Pao-yu was reflecting, "I can forgive *others* not understanding me, but *you* ought to know you're the only one I care for. Yet instead of comforting me you only taunt me. It's obviously no use my thinking of you every minute of the day — you've no place for me in your heart." To tell her this, however, was beyond him.

As for Tai-yu, she was reflecting, "I know I've a place in your heart. Naturally you don't take that vicious talk about gold matching jade seriously, but think of me seriously instead. Even if I raise the subject, you should take it perfectly calmly to show that it means nothing to you, that the one you really care for is me. Why get so worked up at the mention of gold and jade? This shows you're thinking about them all the time. You're afraid I suspect this when I mention them, so you put on a show of being worked up — just to fool me."

In fact, to start with their two hearts were one, but each of them was so hyper-sensitive that their longing to be close ended in estrangement.

Now Pao-yu was telling himself, "Nothing else matters to me so long as you're happy. Then I'd gladly die for you this very instant. Whether you know this or not, you can at least feel that in my heart you're close to me and not distant."

Tai-yu meanwhile was thinking, "Just take good care of yourself. When you're happy, I'm happy too. Why should you be upset because of me? You should know that if you're upset, so am I. It means you won't let me be close to you and want me to keep at a distance."

So their mutual concern for each other resulted in their estrangement. But as it is hard to describe all their secret thoughts, we shall have to content ourselves with recording their actions.

Those words "the match of your choice" infuriated Pao-yu. Too choked with rage to speak, he tore the jade from his neck and dashed it to the floor.

"You rubbishy thing!" he cried, gnashing his teeth. "I'll smash you to pieces and have done with it."

The jade was so hard, however, that no damage was done. So he looked around for something with which to smash it.

Tai-yu was already weeping.

"Why destroy that dumb object?" she sobbed. "Better destroy me instead."

Tzu-chuan and Hsueh-yen dashed in to stop this quarrel. Seeing Pao-yu hammering at the jade they tried to snatch it away from him but failed. And since this was more serious than usual they had to send for Hsi-jen, who hurried in and managed to rescue the stone.

Pao-yu smiled bitterly.

"I can smash what's mine, can't I? What business is it of yours?"

Hsi-jen had never before seen him so livid with rage, his whole face contorted.

"Because you have words with your cousin is no reason to smash this up," she said coaxingly, taking his hand. "Suppose you broke it, think how bad she'd feel."

This touched Tai-yu's heart, yet it only made her more wretched to think that Pao-yu had less consideration for her than Hsi-jen. She sobbed even more bitterly, so distraught that she threw up the herbal medicine she had just taken. Tzu-chuan hastily brought her a handkerchief which soon was completely soaked through. Hsueh-yen meanwhile massaged her back.

"No matter how angry you are, miss, do think of your health!" Tzu-chuan urged. "You were feeling a little better after the medicine; it's this tiff with Master Pao that's made you retch. If you fall ill, how upset Master Pao will be."

This touched Pao-yu's heart, yet also struck him as proof that Tai-yu had less consideration for him than Tzu-chuan. But now Tai-yu's cheeks were flushed and swollen. Weeping and choking, her face streaked with tears and sweat, she looked most fearfully frail. The sight filled him with compunction.

"I should never have argued with her and got her into this state," he scolded himself. "I can't even suffer instead of her." He, too, shed tears.

Hsi-jen's heart ached to see how bitterly both of them were weeping. She felt Pao-yu's hands. They were icy cold. She wanted to urge him not to cry, but feared that bottling up his resentment would be bad for him; on the other hand, comforting him might seem like slighting Tai-yu. Thinking that tears might calm them all, she wept in sympathy.

Tzu-chuan, who had cleaned up and was gently fanning Tai-yu, was so affected by the sight of the three of them weeping in silence that she had to put a handkerchief to her own eyes.

So all four of them wept in silence until Hsi-jen, forcing a smile, said to Pao-yu:

"Just because of the tassel on your jade, if not for any other reason, you shouldn't quarrel with Miss Lin."

At this Tai-yu forgot her nausea and rushed over to snatch the jade, seizing a pair of scissors to cut off the tassel. Hsi-jen and Tzu-chuan intervened too late to save it.

"All my work for nothing," sobbed Tai-yu. "He doesn't care for it. He can get someone else to make him a better one."

Hsi-jen hastily took the jade from her.

"Why do that?" she protested. "It's *my* fault. I should have held my tongue."

"Go ahead and cut it up," Pao-yu urged Tai-yu. "I shan't wear it anyway, so it doesn't matter."

During this commotion, some old nurses had bustled off without their knowing to inform the Lady Dowager and Lady Wang. For having heard Tai-yu crying and vomiting and Pao-yu threatening to smash his jade, they did not want to be held responsible should any serious trouble come of it. Their flurried, earnest report so alarmed the old lady and Lady Wang that both came to the Garden to see what dreadful thing had happened. Hsi-jen was frantic and blamed Tzu-chuan for disturbing their mistresses, while Tzu-chuan held Hsi-jen to blame.

When the Lady Dowager and Lady Wang found both the young people quiet and were told there was nothing amiss, they vented their anger on their two chief maids.

"Why don't you look after them properly?" they scolded. "Can't you *do* something when they start quarrelling?"

The two maids had to listen meekly to a long lecture, and peace was only restored when the old lady took Pao-yu away.

The next day, the third of the month, was Hsueh Pan's birthday, and the whole Chia family was invited to a feast and theatricals. Pao-yu had not seen Tai-yu since he offended her and was feeling too remorseful and depressed to enjoy any show. He pleaded illness, therefore, as an excuse not to go.

Tai-yu was not seriously ill, simply suffering from the heat. When she heard of Pao-yu's refusal to go she thought, "He has a weakness for feasts and theatricals. If he's staying away today, it must either be because yesterday's business still rankles or because he knows *I'm* not going. I should never have cut that tassel off his jade. I'm sure he won't wear it again now unless I make him another." So she felt thoroughly conscience-stricken too.

The Lady Dowager had hoped they would stop sulking and make it up while watching operas together. When both refused to go she grew quite frantic.

"What sins have I committed in a past existence to be plagued with two such troublesome children?" she lamented. "Not a day goes by without something to worry about. How true the proverb is that 'Enemies and lovers are destined to meet.' Once I've closed my eyes and breathed my last, they can quarrel and storm as much as they like. What the eye doesn't see the heart doesn't grieve for. But I'm not at my last gasp just yet." With that she wept too.

When word of this reached Pao-yu and Tai-yu, neither of whom had heard that proverb before, they felt as if a great light had dawned on them. With lowered heads they pondered its meaning and could not hold back their tears. True, they were still apart: one weeping to the breeze in Bamboo Lodge, the other sighing to the moon in Happy Red Court. But although apart, at heart they were as one.

Hsi-jen scolded Pao-yu, "It's entirely your fault. You used to blame boys who quarrelled with their sisters, or husbands who disputed with their wives, for being too stupid to understand girls' hearts. Yet now you're being just as bad yourself. The day after tomorrow, the fifth, is the festival. If you two go on looking daggers at each other that will make the old lady even angrier and no one will have any peace. Do get over your temper and apologize! Let bygones be bygones. Wouldn't that be better for both sides?"

Whether Pao-yu took her advice or not you may read in the next chapter.

CHAPTER 30

Pao-chai Uses a Fan to Make an Insinuation
Ling-kuan Writes on the Ground and
a Foolish Young Man Is Touched

Tai-yu for her part was also remorseful after her quarrel with Pao-yu, but could think of no pretext to go and make it up. So she spent all day and night in a state of depression, feeling as if bereft. Tzu-chuan, who guessed how she felt, tried to reason with her.

"The fact is you were too hasty the other day, miss," she said. "*We* should know Pao-yu if no one else does. After all, it's not the first time there's been a rumpus over that jade."

"So you side with the others and blame me," snapped Tai-yu. "In what way was I hasty?"

"Why did you cut off the tassel for no reason? That put you more in the wrong than Master Pao. I know how devoted he is to you, miss. All this comes of your touchiness and the way you twist his words."

Before Tai-yu could retort they heard someone calling at the outer gate.

"It's Pao-yu's voice." Tzu-chuan smiled. "He must be coming to apologize."

"Don't let him in."

"That wouldn't be right, miss. It's a scorching day. We don't want him to get sunstroke."

She went and opened the gate, ushering Pao-yu in with a smile.

"I thought you'd never cross this threshold of ours again," she remarked. "But here you are."

"You take things far too seriously." He chuckled. "Why shouldn't I come? Even if I were dead, my ghost would haunt you a hundred times a day. Tell me, is my cousin better?"

"In her health, yes. Not in her feelings."

"I know what's the trouble with her."

He went in and found Tai-yu indulging in a fresh fit of weeping on her bed, so much had his arrival touched her.

Walking cheerfully up to her bedside he asked, "Are you feeling a little better?"

When she simply wiped her tears without answering, he sat down on the edge of the bed.

"I know you're not really angry with me," he told her. "But if I stayed away others might think we'd quarrelled again and come to act as peacemakers, as if the two of us were strangers. So beat me or scold me as much as you like but for pity's sake don't ignore me, dear cousin, sweet cousin!"

Tai-yu had in fact determined to ignore him, but this speech proving that she was dearer to him than anyone else, and all the endearments he now poured out, made her break down again.

"You needn't flatter me," she sobbed. "I shall never dare be friends with you again. Behave as if I'd gone."

"Where would you go?" Pao-yu laughed.

"Home."

"I'd go with you."

"What if I should die?"

"I'd become a monk."

"What a thing to say!" She frowned sternly. "Why talk such nonsense? Think of all the sisters and girl cousins you have. Do you have so many lives that you can become a monk every time one of them dies? Wait and see what the others say when I tell them this."

Pao-yu could have kicked himself for this fresh blunder. Flushing red he hung his head without a word, thankful that no one else was in the room. Too angry to speak, she fixed him with furious eyes until his cheeks were burning. Then, clenching her teeth, she stabbed with one finger at his forehead. "You. . . ."

But this exclamation ended in a sigh as she took out her handkerchief and wiped her tears.

Pao-yu's heart was very full and he was ashamed of speaking so foolishly. When she struck him then sighed and wept without a word, he too was reduced to tears. He started to wipe them with his sleeve, having forgotten to bring a handkerchief, and Tai-yu noticed through her own tears that he was wearing a new lilac blue linen gown. While dabbing at her own eyes she turned and took a silk handkerchief from her pillow, tossed him this in silence and covered her face again.

Pao-yu took the handkerchief and wiped his tears, then stepped forward to clasp her hand.

"You're breaking my heart with your weeping," he declared. "Come, let's go and see the old lady."

"Take your hands off me!" She pulled away. "You're not a child any more, yet you still carry on in this shameless way. Can't you behave yourself?"

She was interrupted by the cry "Thank goodness!"

The two of them started, then turned to see Hsi-feng sweeping gaily in.

"The old lady's fulminating against Heaven and Earth," she informed them. "She insisted I come to see if you'd made it up. I told her, 'No need, they'll be friends again in less than three days.' But she scolded me for being too lazy to stir, so I had to come. Well, what did I say? I can't see what you two have to quarrel about. Friends one day, squabbling the next, you're worse than children. *Now* you're holding hands and crying, but yesterday you were like fighting cocks. Come along with me, quick, to your grandmother to set the old lady's mind at rest."

She caught hold of Tai-yu meaning to lead her away. Tai-yu turned to call her maids but not one was there.

"What do you want *them* for?" asked Hsi-feng. "*I'll* look after you."

With that she pulled her out. And Pao-yu followed them out of the Garden to the Lady Dowager's quarters.

"I said don't worry, they'll make it up themselves," announced Hsi-feng cheerfully. "Our Old Ancestress didn't believe me, and insisted I go along as peacemaker. I found they'd already asked each other's forgiveness, and were clinging together like an eagle sinking its talons into a hawk. They didn't need any help."

This set the whole room laughing. Pao-chai was also there. Tai-yu said nothing but took a seat by the Lady Dowager.

To make conversation Pao-yu told Pao-chai: "I *would* have to be out of sorts on your brother's birthday; that's why I haven't sent any present over or even gone to offer congratulations. If he doesn't know I'm unwell, he may think I couldn't be bothered and be offended. Do explain to him, will you, cousin?"

"You're over-punctilious," said Pao-chai. "We wouldn't dare put you to any trouble even if you wished to go, much less so when you're unwell. As cousins you're always seeing so much of each other, you've no call to behave like strangers."

"So long as you understand and will overlook it." He added, "But why aren't *you* watching the operas, cousin?"

"I feel the heat. After watching two pieces I couldn't stand it any longer. But as the guests hadn't left, I had to pretend to be feeling unwell in order to slip away."

This sounded to Pao-yu like a reflection on him. In his embarrassment he said with a sheepish smile:

"No wonder they compare you to Lady Yang, you're both 'plump and sensitive to the heat.' "[1]

Pao-chai was so enraged by this remark that she could have flown into a temper, but she restrained herself. This quip rankled so much, however, that she reddened and laughed sarcastically.

---

[1] Lady Yang, favourite of Emperor Ming-huang of the Tang Dynasty, was supposed to be rather plump.

"If I'm so like Lady Yang," she retorted, "it's too bad I've no brother or cousin able to be another Yang Kuo-chung."[1]

She was interrupted by one of the young maids, Tien-erh, who had mislaid her fan.

"You must have hidden it, miss," she said playfully. "Do let me have it back."

"Behave yourself!" cried Pao-chai sharply, wagging one finger at her. "Have *I* ever played such tricks with you, that you should suspect me? You should ask the other young ladies who are always joking with you."

This rebuff frightened Tien-erh away.

Pao-yu knew he had made another gaffe, in public too. Even more embarrassed than earlier on with Tai-yu, he turned away to talk to the others.

Tai-yu had been delighted to hear him make fun of Pao-chai. She would, indeed, have joined in if not for Pao-chai's retort regarding the fan. She decided, as it was, to change the subject.

"What were the two operas you saw, cousin?" she asked.

Tai-yu's enjoyment of her discomfiture at Pao-yu's remark had not escaped Pao-chai, who smiled at this question.

"One was that piece," she answered, "in which Li Kuei abuses Sung Chiang and then apologizes."[2]

Pao-yu laughed.

"Why, cousin," he cried, "surely you're sufficiently well versed in ancient and modern literature to know the title of that opera. Why do you have to describe it? It's called *Abject Apologies*."

"*Abject Apologies*, is it?" retorted Pao-chai. "*You* two are the ones well versed in ancient and modern literature, so of course you know all about 'abject apologies' — that's something quite beyond *me*."

---

[1] Lady Yang's cousin who through nepotism became prime minister. Corrupt and lawless, he was put to death by the Imperial Guards during the Tang general An Lu-shan's rebellion.

[2] From the novel *Shui Hu*. Li Kuei was a peasant rebel. Sung Chiang, the leader of the outlaws, was a capitulationist.

As both Pao-yu and Tai-yu were conscience-stricken, they immediately blushed. And Hsi-feng, although she did not understand such allusions, could guess from their expressions what was afoot.

"Who's been eating ginger in such hot weather?" she asked.

The others were mystified.

"No one's been eating ginger."

Hsi-feng put both hands to her cheeks with a show of astonishment.

"In that case, why are some people so red in the face?"

This embarrassed Pao-yu and Tai-yu even more. And when Pao-chai saw Pao-yu so out of countenance, she simply smiled and let the matter drop. So did the others, who had not caught on to this exchange between the four of them.

Presently Pao-chai and Hsi-feng left. Then Tai-yu turned with a smile to Pao-yu.

"Now you've come up against someone with a sharper tongue than mine. Not everyone's as simple and tongue-tied as *I* am, so easy to tease."

Pao-yu was already put out by Pao-chai's annoyance, and this fresh provocation added to his ill humour. But not wanting to annoy Tai-yu too, he kept his temper and sulkily left the room.

It was now mid-summer. The days were so long that after lunch masters and servants alike were exhausted. His hands behind his back, Pao-yu strolled through the grounds and did not hear a sound. From the Lady Dowager's quarters he wandered west through the passage hall to Hsi-feng's compound; but the gate there was closed and he knew he had better not call as she usually took a nap after lunch in the summer. So he sauntered through a side gate to his mother's apartments, where some maids were dozing with needlework in their hands while Lady Wang slept on a couch in the inner room. Chin-chuan, sitting by her to massage her legs, was nodding drowsily too.

Pao-yu tiptoed up to her and flicked one of her earrings, whereupon she opened her eyes.

"You sleepy-head!" he whispered.

She pouted, smiled and motioned him away, then closed her eyes again; but Pao-yu was reluctant to leave her. He stole a glance at his mother. Her eyes were closed. Then he took a peppermint pastille from his pouch and slipped it between Chin-chuan's lips. She accepted it without opening her eyes. At that Pao-yu pressed closer and took her hand.

"I'll ask your mistress for you tomorrow," he said softly. "Then we can be together."

Chin-chuan made no reply.

"Or rather I'll ask her as soon as she wakes."

The girl opened her eyes then and pushed him away.

"What's the hurry? 'A gold pin may fall into the well, but if it's yours it remains yours.' Can't you understand that proverb? I'll tell you something amusing to do. Go to the small east courtyard and see what your brother Huan and Tsai-yun are up to."

"I don't care what they're up to. It's *you* I'm interested in."

At this point Lady Wang sat up and slapped Chin-chuan's face.

"Shameless slut!" she scolded. "It's low creatures like you who lead the young masters astray."

Pao-yu had vanished like smoke as soon as his mother sat up. Chin-chuan's cheek was tingling but she dared say nothing and the other maids, hearing their mistress's voice, hurried in.

"Yu-chuan!" ordered Lady Wang. "Go and tell your mother to come at once and take your sister away."

At these words Chin-chuan fell on her knees and burst into tears.

"I shan't let it happen again, madam," she cried. "Whip me, scold me or punish me as you please, but for pity's sake don't send me away! I've been with Your Ladyship more than ten years. If you dismiss me now, how can I look anyone in the face again?"

Lady Wang was generally speaking too good-natured and easy-going to beat the maids; but the shameless way in which Chin-chuan had behaved was the one thing she could not abide.

That was why, flaring up, she had slapped and cursed her. Although the maid pleaded hard she refused to keep her, and her mother, old Mrs. Pai, had to take her away. So Chin-chuan went home in disgrace.

Meanwhile Pao-yu had scuttled back to Grand View Garden. The sun was high in the sky, trees cast ample shade and the air was full of the shrilling of cicadas, but no human voice could be heard. However, as he approached a trellis of roses, he heard sobbing and stopped in his surprise to listen. Yes, there was someone on the other side of the trellis. As it was now the fifth month, the roses were in full bloom. Peeping through the lattice-work, he saw a girl crouching below the flowers and weeping all alone as she scratched the ground with a hairpin.

"Can this be another absurd maid come to bury flowers like Tai-yu?" he wondered in some amusement. "If so, she's 'Tung Shih imitating Hsi Shih,'[1] which isn't original but rather tiresome."

He was on the point of calling out to the girl, "It's no use your trying to copy Miss Lin!" when he realized she was not one of the maids but looked like one of the twelve actresses, although he could not remember which role she played. He grimaced then hastily covered his mouth.

"It's a good thing I held my tongue," he told himself. "I've already annoyed Tai-yu and hurt Pao-chai's feelings by my tactlessness. It would be still more senseless to offend any of these girls."

With these reflections, he felt put out at not being able to identify the girl and he studied her more closely. With her finely arched eyebrows and limpid eyes, her delicate features, slender waist and graceful movements, she bore a striking resemblance to Tai-yu. He stood staring, unable to tear himself away. And now he observed that instead of using her hairpin to bury flowers she was writing something with it on the ground.

---

[1] Hsi Shih was a famous beauty in the ancient Kingdom of Yueh. Tung Shih was an ugly girl who tried to imitate her ways.

Pao-yu followed the pin with his eyes as it moved up and down. He counted the strokes — vertical, horizontal, dotted and curved — there were seventeen in all. Then he traced them in the same order on his palm and discovered that this was the character *chiang* for "rose."

"She must be trying to write a poem," he thought, "and these flowers have suggested the idea for a couple of lines. For fear of forgetting it, she's tracing the character while she thinks it out. Yes, that may be it. Let me see what else she writes."

He went on watching as the girl went on writing, but she merely repeated the same character.

Lost in thought, the girl by the trellis traced one *chiang* after another until she had written several dozen, while Pao-yu watched raptly from the other side, following the movements of the pin with his eyes.

"She must have some secret anxiety preying on her mind to carry on like this," he reflected. "Yet she looks too delicate to stand much anxiety. I wish I could share her troubles."

Mid-summer weather is unpredictable: a passing cloud may bring rain. Now a cool breeze sprang up and there was a sudden shower. Seeing that water dripped off the girl's head and in no time had wet her gauze clothes, he thought: It's raining. She's too frail to stand such a downpour. Impulsively he called out:

"Do stop writing! Look, you're getting drenched."

The girl raised her head with a start at hearing this shout from the other side of the trellis. As Pao-yu was finely-featured and as the thick foliage screened all but the top of his face, she took him for a maid.

"Thanks, sister," she said with a smile. "You don't seem to have much shelter out there yourself either."

Pao-yu uttered an exclamation of dismay as it came home to him how cold he was. Looking down he saw that his clothes were wet through.

"Bother it!" he cried.

He set off at a run then towards Happy Red Court, still worrying over the girl out in the rain.

Now as this was the eve of the Double Fifth Festival, the twelve young actresses had been given a holiday and were amusing themselves in different parts of the Garden. Pao-kuan who played young scholars and Yu-kuan who played young ladies were enjoying themselves in Happy Red Court with Hsi-jen, when it came on to rain. They stopped up the drain to make water collect in the yard and caught some water-fowl — green-headed ducks, speckled mallards and mandarin ducks. Having tied their wings they let these loose in the yard, after which they bolted the gate.

While they stood on the verandah enjoying the fun, Pao-yu arrived back only to find the gate closed. The girls were laughing too much to hear his knock, so that he shouted and pounded for a long time before they finally heard. And of course they were not expecting him back at this time.

"Who's that at the gate?" asked Hsi-jen. "Who'll go and see?"

"It's I!" cried Pao-yu.

"Sounds like Miss Pao-chai," said Sheh-yueh.

"Nonsense!" exclaimed Ching-wen. "Miss Pao-chai wouldn't come at this hour."

"I'll peep through a crack," offered Hsi-jen, "to see if it's somebody we should let in. If it's not, we'll let whoever it is get a soaking."

She went along the covered corridor to the gate and discovered Pao-yu there, drenched as a drowned cock. Torn between concern and amusement she hastily opened the gate, then doubled up with laughter, clapping her hands.

"How were we to know you were back?" she spluttered. "Where have you been, running about in such a downpour?"

Pao-yu, in a foul temper, had decided to punish whoever opened the gate. Without waiting to see who it was, and assuming that this was one of the younger girls, he kicked Hsi-jen so hard in the side that she let out a cry.

"You low creatures!" he stormed. "I treat you so well that you've lost all sense of respect. Now you dare make fun of me!"

At this point he lowered his head and heard Hsi-jen's cry. He realized then what a blunder he had made.

"Oh, is it you?" He smiled apologetically. "Where did I kick you?"

Hsi-jen had never had so much as a harsh word from Pao-yu. Now that he had lost his temper and kicked her — in public too — she felt overwhelmed with shame, resentment and pain. But sure that he hadn't done this deliberately, she did her best to control herself.

"It's all right," she answered. "Go in and change your clothes."

Once inside he said contritely, "This is the first time in my life I've lashed out in a temper — and it had to be at *you*."

Still wincing she helped him out of his wet clothes.

"I'm your number one maid," she answered jokingly, "so I should have first share of everything big or small, good or bad. I just hope you won't make a habit of kicking people."

"I didn't mean to do it."

"I'm not saying you did. Usually it's the younger ones who go to the gate. They're all so spoilt that nobody can stand them, and they're not afraid of anyone either. It would have served them right if you'd kicked one of them to frighten them. Today I'm to blame for not letting them open the gate."

By now the rain had stopped. Both Pao-kuan and Yu-kuan had left. What with the pain in her side and her vexation, Hsi-jen ate nothing that evening. And when she undressed to have her bath she was frightened by the bruise, the size of a bowl, below her ribs, but could hardly remark on it. The pain continued after she was in bed and made her groan in her sleep.

Though Pao-yu had not kicked her deliberately, Hsi-jen's obvious discomfort disturbed him. And hearing her cry out during the night he realized how badly he must have hurt her. He slipped out of bed, took the lamp, and went over to have a look. Just as he reached her bedside she coughed, then brought up some phlegm and opened her eyes with a gasp.

"What are you doing?" she asked in surprise when she saw him.

"You were groaning in your sleep. I must have hurt you badly. Let me have a look."

"I feel dizzy and there's a bitter-sweet taste in my throat. Throw the light on the floor, will you?"

Pao-yu did as she asked and saw that she had coughed blood. "How dreadful!" he exclaimed.

Hsi-jen's heart failed her at the sight of the blood.

But to know what followed, you must read the next chapter.

CHAPTER 31

A Torn Fan Wins a Smile from a Maid
A Pair of Unicorns Suggest a Match

When Hsi-jen saw the blood on the floor her heart failed her, for she had often heard tell: Spitting blood while young means an early death or infirmity for life. So her dreams of future honour and splendour had gone up in smoke! She could not help shedding tears. Pao-yu's heart ached too.

"How are you feeling?" he asked.

She forced a smile.

"All right."

He would have called someone at once to heat Shaohsing wine and fetch pills compounded with goat's blood, but Hsi-jen restrained him.

"If you make such a fuss that people come flocking in,' they'll blame me for getting above myself," she explained. "At present not a soul knows, but to noise it abroad would be damaging for us both. Just send a boy tomorrow to ask Doctor Wang for some medicine, and that will set me right. Far better keep the whole business quiet."

Since this made sense Pao-yu had to agree. He fetched tea for Hsi-jen to rinse her mouth and, knowing how worried he was, she lay there quietly letting him wait on her, for otherwise he would have roused the others.

Next day, at the crack of dawn, Pao-yu scrambled into his clothes. Not stopping to wash or comb his hair, he went off to find Wang Chi-jen whom he plied with questions. When the doctor heard what had happened, he assured him it was simply a contusion and prescribed some pills, giving directions as to their use which Pao-yu carried out on his return to the Garden. But no more of this.

This was the day of the Double Fifth Festival. The doors were hung with mugwort and rushes, everyone wore tiger-charms, and Lady Wang gave a family feast at midday to which Aunt Hsueh and her daughter were invited.

Pao-yu noticed that Pao-chai was cold-shouldering him because of what had happened the previous day. His own low spirits were ascribed by his mother to embarrassment over yesterday's episode with Chin-chuan, and therefore she deliberately ignored him. Tai-yu, for her part, assumed that his dejection was the result of having offended Pao-chai, and that displeased her too. As for Hsi-feng, she had heard the evening before from Lady Wang about Pao-yu and Chin-chuan, and in deference to her aunt's displeasure was not her usual cheerful, laughing self, making the atmosphere even more constrained. As Ying-chun and the other Chia girls were affected by the general lack of spirits, the company soon dispersed.

Now Tai-yu naturally preferred solitude to society. She reasoned, "Coming together can only be followed by parting. The more pleasure people find in parties, the more lonely and unhappy they must feel when the parties break up. So better not forgather in the first place. The same is true of flowers: they delight people when in bloom, but it's so heart-rending to see them fade that it would be better if they never blossomed." For this reason she grieved over what others enjoyed.

Pao-yu, on the other hand, wished that parties need never break up, flowers never fade; and although he could neither stop a feast from ending nor flowers from withering, he grieved every time this happened.

So whereas Tai-yu did not care when the feasters parted in low spirits today, Pao-yu went back to his room feeling so gloomy that he did nothing but sigh. When Ching-wen, who was helping him change, dropped his fan and broke it he sighed:

"How stupid you are! What's to become of you when in future you have a home of your own? Surely you can't go on being so careless then."

"How bad-tempered you've grown lately," she retorted with a snigger. "Always throwing your weight about. The other day you even beat Hsi-jen, and now you're picking on me. You can kick or beat us as much as you like, of course, but what's so dreadful about dropping a fan? Plenty of glass vases and agate bowls have been smashed before without your flaring up. It seems pointless to make such a fuss over a fan. If you're fed up with us, you can send us packing and get some better attendants. But why not part company in a peaceful, friendly way?"

"Don't worry," he cried, fairly trembling with rage. "We shall part sooner or later."

Hsi-jen, who had overheard them, now hurried in.

"Why take on again for no reason?" she asked Pao-yu. "Didn't I tell you, the moment my back's turned there's trouble."

"If you're so clever," sneered Ching-wen, "you should have come earlier to prevent this tantrum. You're the one who's looked after him since ancient times — I never did. It's because you're so *good* at it that you got kicked right under your heart yesterday. Heaven knows what punishment is waiting tomorrow for *me*, unfit as I am to wait on him."

Annoyance and mortification tempted Hsi-jen to make a sharp retort. She only controlled herself because Pao-yu was already livid with rage.

"Run along and amuse yourself outside, good sister," she said, pushing Ching-wen away. *"We're* the ones to blame."

This "we," obviously meaning Pao-yu and herself, made Ching-wen even more jealous.

"I don't know what you mean by 'we,'" she cried with a scornful laugh. "Don't make me blush for you. What you're up to on the sly is no secret to me. The fact of the matter is, you've not even earned the grade of a concubine yet, so you're no better than I am. How can you talk of '*we*'?"

Hsi-jen flushed crimson over her indiscretion.

"If the rest of you are so jealous," raged Pao-yu, "I'll raise her status just to spite you."

Hsi-jen caught him by the hand to restrain him.

"Why argue with a silly girl? You're usually broad-minded enough to overlook plenty of worse things than this. What's got into you today?"

"I'm too silly to be up to talking to you," snorted Ching-wen.

"Are you quarrelling with me, miss, or with Master Pao? If I annoy you just tell me, instead of squabbling with him. If Master Pao annoys you, don't make such a row that everybody hears. I came in to try to smooth things over and save everybody's face, but then you set on *me*. Which of us are you mad at, him or me? What's the idea, lashing out in all directions? Well, I'll say no more. It's up to you now."

With that she walked away.

"There was no need to fly into such a temper," said Pao-yu to Ching-wen. "I know what's on your mind. I'll tell the mistress you've reached the age to be sent home. How about that?"

"Why should I go home?" Tears of distress welled up in Ching-wen's eyes. "How can you trump up an excuse to get rid of me just because you've taken a dislike to me?"

"I've never been through such a scene before. You're obviously set on going. So I'd better ask my mother to send you away."

He was starting out when Hsi-jen barred the way.

"Where are you off to?" she asked.

"To tell my mother."

"What nonsense!" She smiled at him coaxingly. "How can you have the heart to shame her so? Even if she really wanted to leave, you should wait until she's cooled down and then mention it to the mistress casually. If you rush over now as if this were something urgent, Her Ladyship's bound to start imagining things."

"Not her. I'll just tell her that she insists on leaving."

"When did I insist on leaving?" sobbed Ching-wen. "You fly into a rage, then put words into my mouth. All right, go and report it. But I'll dash out my brains sooner than leave this house."

"That's strange!" he fumed. "If you won't go, what's all this fuss about? I can't stand these rows. Far simpler if you left."

He was so set on telling his mother that Hsi-jen saw no way to stop him. She fell on her knees to plead. This was the signal for Pi-hen, Chiu-wen and Sheh-yueh, who had been listening with bated breath outside, to rush in and kneel down beside her.

Pao-yu pulled Hsi-jen to her feet, sank with a sigh on to his bed, and sent the other girls out.

"What am I to *do*?" he demanded. "I've worn my heart out, yet nobody cares."

He wept and Hsi-jen shed tears in sympathy. Ching-wen beside them was trying to speak through her sobs when Tai-yu's arrival made her slip away.

"What's all this crying during the festival?" asked Tai-yu mockingly. "Are you fighting for sticky rice dumplings?"

The two of them laughed.

"Since *you* won't tell me I'll find out from *her*." Tai-yu patted Hsi-jen's shoulder. "What's happened, dear sister-in-law? I suppose you two have been squabbling again. Tell me what's wrong and I'll act as peacemaker."

"You're joking, miss." Hsi-jen pushed her away. "Don't talk such nonsense to us servant-girls."

"You may call yourself a servant-girl, but I regard you as my sister-in-law."

"Why give her another name for people to jeer at?" protested Pao-yu. "There's enough gossip already without *your* joining in."

"You don't know how I feel, miss," said Hsi-jen. "I'll never have any peace until I can die and be done with it!"

"I can't say what *others* would do if you died." Tai-yu smiled. "I'd die first of crying."

"I'd become a monk if you died," Pao-yu declared.

"Do be quiet," cried Hsi-jen. "That's no way to talk."

Tai-yu held out two fingers with a smile.

"That's twice, so far, you've become a monk. I must keep track of how many times you do it."

Pao-yu knew she was referring to their conversation the other day, and with a smile he let the matter drop.

Soon after that Tai-yu left and Pao-yu received an invitation from Hsueh Pan, which he could hardly decline, to a drinking party. He was unable to leave before the end. Dusk had fallen by the time he came back, slightly tipsy, and as he lurched into his courtyard he noticed someone lying on a couch there. Assuming that it was Hsi-jen, he sat down beside her and nudged her.

"Has the pain stopped?" he asked.

The figure on the couch sat up.

"Why are you back to plague me again?" she demanded.

It was not Hsi-jen but Ching-wen. He made her sit beside him.

"You're growing more and more spoilt," he teased. "When you dropped that fan and I just said a couple of words, you launched into such a tirade. I don't mind your scolding *me*, but was it right to drag Hsi-jen into it too when she meant so well?"

"It's so hot, keep your hands to yourself," countered Ching-wen. "What would people think if they saw? I'm not fit to be sitting here with you anyway."

"Then why were you sleeping here?" he asked with a grin. She giggled.

"It was all right before you came, but not now that you're here. Get up and let me have my bath. I'll call Hsi-jen and Sheh-yueh — they've already had theirs."

"After all the wine I've drunk I need a bath too. If you've not had yours, fill the tub and we'll bath together."

Ching-wen waved this proposal aside with a laugh.

"Not I. I wouldn't dare. I remember what happened that time Pi-hen helped you bath. Two or three hours it took and we couldn't go in — heaven knows what you were up to. When you'd finished and we had a look, the floor right up to the legs of the bed was all over water — even the bed mat was sopping.

Goodness knows what sort of bath you had! It kept us laughing for days. I haven't the time to mop up after you, and see no need for you to bath with me. Besides, it's so cool now I don't think you ought to have a bath; I'll just get you a basin of water to wash your face and comb your hair. Yuan-yang brought in a lot of fruit not long ago which is being chilled in that crystal bowl. I'll tell them to bring it for you."

"In that case, you mustn't bath either. Just wash your hands and bring the fruit."

Ching-wen laughed.

"If I'm so careless that I even break fans, how can I fetch fruit? If I broke a plate too, I'd never hear the end of it."

"You can if you want. Such things are meant to be used. You may like one thing, I another. People's tastes differ. For instance, fans are meant for fanning; but if I choose to break one for fun, what's wrong with that? But we shouldn't break things to work off a fit of temper. It's the same with cups or plates which are for serving things in. If you smash them because you like the sound, all right. Just don't work off your temper on them. That's what's called caring for things."

"If that's so, get me a fan to tear up. I love ripping things apart."

With a smile he handed her his own. Sure enough, she ripped it in two, then tore it to pieces.

Pao-yu chuckled.

"Well done! Try and make a bigger noise."

Just then along came Sheh-yueh.

"What a wicked waste!" she cried. "Stop it."

Pao-yu's answer was to snatch her fan from her and give it to Ching-wen, who promptly tore it up and joined in his loud laughter.

"What's the idea?" demanded Sheh-yueh. "Spoiling my fan — is that your idea of fun?"

"Just pick another from the fan case," Pao-yu told her. "What's so wonderful about a fan?"

"You'd better bring the case out here then and let her tear the whole lot up."

"You bring it." Pao-yu chuckled.

"I won't do anything of the sort. She's not broken her wrist, let *her* fetch it."

"I'm tired." Ching-wen lay back laughing. "I'll tear up some more tomorrow."

"You know the ancient saying," put in Pao-yu. " 'A thousand pieces of gold can hardly purchase a smile.' And what are a few fans worth?"

He called for Hsi-jen, who came out having just changed into clean clothes and got little Chia-hui to clear away the broken fans. Then they sat outside for a while enjoying the cool.

At noon the next day Lady Wang and the girls were gathered in the Lady Dowager's room when the arrival of Shih Hsiang-yun was announced. She entered the courtyard presently with a troop of maids and nurses, to be greeted by her cousins at the foot of the steps. As the girls had not seen each other for a month they naturally had a most affectionate reunion, after which Hsiang-yun went in to pay her respects to the others.

"It's hot," said the Lady Dowager. "Do take off your outer garments."

As Hsiang-yun did so Lady Wang remarked, "What a lot you're wearing, child."

"My second aunt made me," she replied. "*I* didn't want to put on so much."

"If you only knew, aunt, she loves dressing up in other people's clothes," said Pao-chai with a smile. "During her visit here in the third or fourth month last year, she put on Cousin Pao's gown and boots, as well as his chaplet, and stood behind that chair. At a casual glance she looked so like him — except for two extra earrings — that the old lady was quite taken in.

" 'Pao-yu, come here,' she cried. 'Don't let the dust from the lantern tassels over your head get in your eyes.'

"The little wretch just smiled and didn't stir. Then we all burst out laughing and the old lady had to laugh too.

" 'Well, you look even better dressed up as a boy,' she said."

"You don't know the half of it," put in Tai-yu. "The year before last she was fetched in the first month, and she'd only been here a couple of days when it started to snow. I believe my grandmother and aunt had just come back from bowing to the ancestral portraits, and the old lady's new red woollen cape was lying there. Cousin Shih put it on without anyone noticing, tying it at the waist with a handkerchief because it was too big and long for her. Then she went with the maids to the back yard to make a snow-man and fell flat on her face by the drain, covering herself with mud."

At the recollection of this everybody laughed.

"Nanny Chou," asked Pao-chai, "does your young lady still get up to pranks like that?"

Hsiang-yun's nanny only smiled.

"I don't mind her pranks," said Ying-chun. "But she chatters too much for me. Even in her sleep she rattles away, laughing and chattering. All the nonsense she talks — I don't know where she gets it from!"

"I expect she's better now," remarked Lady Wang. "The other day a match was proposed for her, and she'll soon be going to live with her mother-in-law. Then she'll have to change her ways."

"Are you staying here or going back today?" asked the Lady Dowager.

"Your Ladyship hasn't seen all the clothes we've brought," replied Nanny Chou with a smile. "Oh yes, we mean to stay for a couple of days."

"Isn't Cousin Pao at home?" Hsiang-yun now asked.

"Cousin Pao's the only one she thinks of." Pao-chai laughed. "It's because they're both fond of pranks. That shows she hasn't changed her mischievous ways."

"You're getting too big to go on calling each other by your pet names," said the Lady Dowager.

Just then Pao-yu walked in.

"So Cousin Yun's here!" he exclaimed. "Why didn't you come last time we sent to invite you?"

"The old lady said you must stop that," Lady Wang told him. "But there you go using pet names again."

Tai-yu told Hsiang-yun, "He has something nice for you."

"Something nice for me?"

"Don't believe her." Pao-yu laughed. "How tall you've grown in the short time you've been away."

"And how is Sister Hsi-jen?" she asked him.

"Very well, thank you."

"I've brought her a little present."

With that she produced a handkerchief tied in a knot.

"What is it?" he asked. "Why didn't you bring her a couple of red cornelian rings like those you sent over the other day?"

"What do you think these are?" Hsiang-yun unwrapped the handkerchief with a smile, disclosing four more rings of the same sort.

"Look at the girl!" cried Tai-yu. "Why didn't you give the servant these to bring too, when you sent those rings to us? Wouldn't that have been simpler? Now you turn up with more yourself. I thought it was something different, but it's only the same again. How silly you are!"

"Silly yourself!" Hsiang-yun smiled. "Let me explain and the rest of you shall judge which of us is silly. I sent those rings to you by the page you'd dispatched. The messenger needn't say a word, once you saw the rings you'd know that they were for the young ladies. Whereas if I'd sent some for the maids as well, I'd have had to tell him which was for which. If he'd been intelligent, all right; but if he'd been stupid he couldn't have remembered the names and would have mixed everything up, including *your* rings. A matron who knew the maids would have managed all right, but that day it happened to be a page who couldn't possibly be told the maids' names. So wasn't it simpler for me to bring them here myself?"

She put the four rings down.

"One for Hsi-jen, one for Yuan-yang, one for Chin-chuan, one for Ping-erh," she announced. "Could a page have remembered the four of them so clearly?"

Everyone laughed.

"Now she's cleared the matter up."

"Still such a talker!" cried Pao-yu. "She's never at a loss."

"Even if *she* couldn't talk, her golden unicorn could."

With this thrust Tai-yu rose and left the room.

Luckily her remark had been heard only by Pao-yu and Pao-chai. When the latter smiled Pao-yu had to smile too, conscience-stricken as he was. And seeing him smile, Pao-chai went off hurriedly to join Tai-yu.

"Have some tea and rest," the Lady Dowager urged Hsiang-yun. "Then you can go and see your sisters-in-law and stroll with your cousins in the Garden where it's cool."

Hsiang-yun did as she was told. After a short rest she wrapped up three of the rings and, accompanied by her nurses and maids, called on Hsi-feng and chatted for a while with her before going on to visit Li Wan in the Garden. And after a little conversation there she set off to see Hsi-jen in Happy Red Court.

"You needn't all come with me," she told her nurses and maids. "Go and see your friends and relatives. It'll be enough if I have Tsui-lu."

So the others went off, leaving just the two of them.

"Why isn't the lotus in bloom yet?" asked Tsui-lu.

"It isn't time yet."

"Their lotus is like that in our pool — it has double flowers."

"Theirs isn't as good as ours."

"Look, they have a pomegranate-tree over there, miss, with four or five branches trained together, one above the other. That can't have been easy to grow."

"Plants are like human beings," said Hsiang-yun. "When they're filled with vital force they grow well."

"I don't believe it." Tsui-lu shook her head. "If human beings and plants are alike, why haven't I seen a man with one head growing on top of another?"

Hsiang-yun had to smile at this.

"Can't you ever keep quiet?" she scolded. "How can I explain this to you? All things between heaven and earth are born from the dual principles *yin* and *yang*. So whether good or bad, weird or wonderful, everything that comes into being depends on the favourable or unfavourable influence of these two forces. This is true of even the rarest, strangest things."

"Do you mean to say everything's been a *yin* or a *yang* ever since Creation and the beginning of time?"

"What nonsense you do talk, you stupid thing." Hsiang-yun couldn't help laughing. "How could there be so many *yins* and *yangs*? *Yin* and *yang* are one. Where one ends, the other begins. It's not that after a *yang* is exhausted a *yin* comes into being, or the other way round."

"I find this *terribly* muddling," complained Tsui-lu. "What *are yin* and *yang*? Have they no shape or form, miss? Do just tell me what they look like."

"They're simply natural forces, but whatever they enter assumes a form. Heaven is *yang* and the earth *yin*, for instance. Water is *yin*, fire *yang*; the sun is *yang*, the moon *yin*."

"I see." Tsui-lu's face lit up. "Now I understand. No wonder people call the sun the 'great *yang*' and fortune-tellers call the moon the 'great *yin* star.' This explains it."

"Buddha be praised. So you've caught on at last."

"It's all very well for these big things to have *yin* and *yang*, but what about mosquitoes, fleas and midges? What about flowers and grass, or bricks and tiles? Do they have *yin* and *yang* too?"

"Of course they do. That leaf, for instance, has its *yin* and *yang*. The side facing the light is *yang*, the side underneath *yin*."

"So that's how it is." Tsui-lu nodded. "I see. But which is *yang* and which *yin* in these fans we're holding?"

"The front is *yang* and the back *yin*."

After nodding again Tsui-lu lowered her head to think up some more questions, and her eye fell on the golden unicorn which her young mistress was wearing as a pendant.

"Does this have *yin* and *yang* too, miss?" she asked.

"Of couse it has. The male of all beasts and birds is *yang* and the female *yin*."

"Is it male or female then?"

"Not even I know that."

"Never mind. If all other things have *yin* and *yang*, why don't human beings?"

"Get away, you low creature!" Hsiang-yun spat in disgust. "You're going too far."

"Why don't you tell me, miss? I know anyway, so don't think you can hide it from me."

"What do you know?" Hsiang-yun giggled.

"You're *yang*, miss, and I'm *yin*."

Hsiang-yun put her handkerchief to her mouth and burst out laughing.

"I get the point," insisted Tsui-lu. "Why should you find it so funny?"

"Quite right, quite right."

"People say that masters are *yang* and slaves are *yin*. Do you think I don't know an important rule like that?"

"You know all about it," replied Hsiang-yun with a smile.

By now they had reached the rose trellis.

"Look, what's that thing glittering like gold?" exclaimed Hsiang-yun. "Has someone dropped a trinket here?"

Tsui-lu quickly picked up the object and closed her fingers round it.

"Now we'll see which is *yang* and which *yin*," she cried with a laugh.

With that she took Hsiang-yun's unicorn to examine it. But asked to show what she had in her hand, she refused to let go of it.

"I can't let you see this treasure, miss," she teased. "I wonder where it comes from. How very odd! I've never seen anyone here with such a thing."

"Let me have a look."

At last Tsui-lu held out her hand.

"There you are."

Hsiang-yun saw it was a splendid gold unicorn, even bigger and handsomer than the one she wore. As she reached out for it and held it on her palm, a strange fancy crossed her mind. And just at that moment they were joined by Pao-yu.

"What are you doing here in the sun?" he asked. "Why don't you go and see Hsi-jen?"

"We're on our way there," replied Hsiang-yun, hiding the unicorn. "Let's go together."

They went on to Happy Red Court, where Hsi-jen was leaning on the balustrade at the foot of the steps in the breeze. She made haste to greet Hsiang-yun and led her inside to sit down, asking what she had been doing since last they met.

"You should have come earlier," remarked Pao-yu. "I've got something nice which I've been keeping for you." He rummaged in his pockets for a while. "Aiya!" Then turning to Hsi-jen he asked, "Did you put that thing away?"

"What thing?"

"That unicorn I got the other day."

"You've been carrying it on you all the time, why ask *me*?"

"I've lost it." He clapped his hands. "Where can I find it?"

He was about to go off in search of it. Hsiang-yun guessed that he was referring to her find.

"When did *you* get hold of a unicorn?" she asked.

"Only the other day, and I didn't come by it easily either. I can't think when I lost it. How stupid of me."

Hsiang-yun laughed.

"It's lucky it's just a toy, yet see what a state you're in!" With that she unclenched her fingers. "Look, is this it?"

Pao-yu was overjoyed to see she had it. If you want to know what happened next, read on.

CHAPTER 32

An Avowal Leaves Pao-yu Bemused
Disgrace Drives Chin-chuan to Suicide

Pao-yu was overjoyed to see the gold unicorn.

"Thank you!" He reached out for it, laughing. "Where did you find it?"

"It's lucky it was only this." Hsiang-yun smiled. "Will you let it go at that if you lose your official seal in future?"

"Losing an official seal is nothing." He grinned. "But I deserve death for losing this."

Meanwhile Hsi-jen had poured out tea which she offered to Hsiang-yun.

"Miss Shih, I heard the other day that you're engaged now," she remarked with a smile.

Hsiang-yun blushed and said nothing, simply sipping her tea.

"So coy!" cried the maid. "Remember what you told me one evening some ten years ago when we were staying in the alcove on the west side? You weren't coy then; why be so bashful now?"

"The things you say!" Hsiang-yun expostulated. "How friendly we were then! But after my mother died and I went home they sent you here to wait on Second Brother, and now when I come you're no longer the same to me."

"Well, I never!" Hsi-jen protested. "In those days I was 'sister' and 'dear sister' to you when you wanted me to comb your hair, wash your face and dance attendance on you. Now you've grown up, you've put on the airs of a young lady. If *you* stand on your dignity, how dare *I* take liberties?"

"Amida Buddha! That's not fair," cried Hsiang-yun. "May I drop dead if I ever give myself airs. Look how hot it is today, yet as soon as I arrive I hurry straight over to see you. If you don't believe me, ask Tsui-lu. At home I'm always saying how much I miss you."

"Can't you take a joke?" Hsi-jen and Pao-yu remonstrated. "You still flare up so easily."

"You won't admit how provoking you are, yet scold me for flaring up."

As Hsiang-yun said this she unwrapped her handkerchief from which she took a ring and passed it to Hsi-jen, who was loud in her thanks.

"Actually, I was given one of those you sent your cousins," she remarked. "And now you've brought me one yourself — a sure sign that you hadn't forgotten me. It's not the rings I value, it's the thought that counts."

"Who gave you one?" asked Hsiang-yun.

"Miss Pao-chai."

"I thought it was Miss Lin. So it was Pao-chai." Hsiang-yun sighed. "At home every day I often think that of all my cousins Pao-chai is the best. What a pity we aren't real sisters! If we were, it wouldn't be so bad being an orphan." Her eyes were brimming with tears.

"All right, all right," cried Pao-yu. "No more of this."

"What's wrong?" demanded Hsiang-yun. "I know what's worrying you. You're afraid your Cousin Lin may hear and be cross with me for singing Pao-chai's praises — right?"

"Miss Yun!" Hsi-jen burst out laughing. "The older you grow the more outspoken you get."

Pao-yu chuckled.

"I always say you girls are hard to talk with. And this proves it."

"Don't make me sick, dear cousin, speaking like that. You can keep your end up with us, but what happens when you cross swords with Tai-yu?"

"That's enough," interposed Hsi-jen. "I've a favour to ask you."

"What is it?" inquired Hsiang-yun.

"I've started on a pair of slippers but haven't been able to finish them because I've been poorly for the last couple of days. Have you time to do them for me?"

"Well, well," exclaimed Hsiang-yun. "This house is full of clever girls, to say nothing of sewing-women and tailors. Why pick on me? How can anyone who's asked possibly refuse?"

"Are you so dense?" parried Hsi-jen with a smile. "Don't you know that none of the needlework for *our* apartments is done by sewing-women?"

Realizing that the shoes were for Pao-yu, Hsiang-yun chuckled.

"In that case I'll do it — but on one condition. I'll make slippers for *you*, not for anybody else."

"There you go again," protested Hsi-jen. "Who am I to ask you to make slippers for me? The fact is they're not mine, but don't ask whose they are. At any rate I'd take it kindly of you."

"Of course, I've done plenty of sewing for you in the past. But you'll understand why I can't do it this time."

"Indeed, I *don't* understand."

Hsiang-yun laughed sarcastically.

"I heard the fan-sheath I made the other day was taken to compare with someone else's, and in a tantrum that someone cut it to pieces. I know all about it, so don't try to fool me. Am I your slave to be given tasks like this?"

Pao-yu cut in with a disarming smile, "I didn't know that sheath was your work."

"He honestly didn't know," Hsi-jen assured her. "I told him that recently there was a girl outside who did wonderful embroidery, and suggested trying her out with a fan-sheath. He took me at my word, then showed it off right and left. For some reason it upset Miss Lin again and she snipped it in two. When he came back to ask for another like it, and I told him you'd made it, he was ever so sorry."

"Stranger and stranger!" cried Hsiang-yun. "Why should Miss Lin be angry? If she can snip, ask *her* to make another."

"Out of the question," said Hsi-jen. "Even as it is, the old lady's afraid of her overtiring herself and the doctor has prescribed her a good rest. Who'd dream of troubling her with needlework? Last year it took her a whole year to finish one scented pouch. And this year I've not yet seen needle or thread in her hands."

As they were talking a servant came to announce: "Mr. Chia of Prosperity Street has called. The master wants the young gentleman to go and see him."

Knowing that it was Chia Yu-tsun, Pao-yu was most reluctant to go, but Hsi-jen lost no time in fetching his formal clothes. As he pulled on his boots he grumbled:

"Surely it's enough if my father keeps him company. Why must he see *me* each time?"

Fanning herself, Hsiang-yun replied with a smile, "It must be because uncle thinks you're a good host. Otherwise he wouldn't send for you."

"It's not my father's idea. It's that fellow who asks for me each single time."

" 'When the host is cultured, guests frequent his house,' " quoted Hsiang-yun. "He likes seeing you, surely, because he can learn something from you."

"Don't call me cultured," begged Pao-yu. "I'm the most vulgar of the vulgar herd, and I've no desire at all to mix with such people."

"You haven't changed one bit," sighed Hsiang-yun. "But now you're growing up. Even if you don't want to study and sit for the examinations, you should at least associate with officials and learn something about the world and administration. That'll help you to manage your own affairs in future and make some friends. What other young gentleman spends all his time, the way you do, playing about with us girls?"

"Please go and call on some of your other cousins, young lady," he retorted. "People with worldly wisdom like yours will be polluted here."

"Don't say such things to him, miss," Hsi-jen interposed. "Last time Miss Pao-chai gave him the same advice he just snorted and walked away without any regard for her feelings. In the middle of what she was saying he marched off. She flushed crimson and hardly knew whether to go on or not. Thank goodness it was Miss Pao-chai and not Miss Lin — *she'd* have made a fearful scene, weeping and sobbing. But there you are, it's true that nobody can help admiring Miss Pao-chai. She just blushed and went away. *I* felt very bad, sure she must be offended; but later she behaved as if nothing had happened. She's really good natured and tolerant. *He's* the one, believe it or not, who has since kept his distance. If you sulked and ignored Miss Lin like that," she asked Pao-yu, "how many apologies would you have to make her?"

"Has Miss Lin ever talked such disgusting nonsense?" demanded Pao-yu. "If she had, I'd have stopped having anything to do with her long ago."

Hsi-jen and Hsiang-yun nodded and laughed.

"So nonsense is the name for it."

Now Tai-yu had discovered Hsiang-yun's whereabouts and knew that Pao-yu had hurried back, no doubt to talk about the gold unicorns. That set her thinking. In most of the romances Pao-yu had recently acquired, a young scholar and beautiful girl came together and fell in love thanks to love-birds, phoenixes, jade rings, gold pendants, silk handkerchiefs, embroidered girdles or other baubles of the sort. So Pao-yu's possession of a gold unicorn like Hsiang-yun's might lead to a romance between them. She slipped over to see what was happening and judge of their feelings for each other, arriving just as Hsiang-yun was speaking of worldly affairs, and in time to hear Pao-yu answer, "Miss Lin never talks such disgusting nonsense. If she did, I'd have stopped having anything to do with her."

This surprised and delighted Tai-yu but also distressed and grieved her. She was delighted to know she had not misjudged him, for he had now proved just as understanding as she had always thought. Surprised that he had been so indiscreet as to acknowledge his preference for her openly. Distressed because their mutual understanding ought to preclude all talk about gold matching jade, or she instead of Pao-chai should have the gold locket to match his jade amulet. Grieved because her parents had died, and although his preference was so clear there was no one to propose the match for her. Besides, she had recently been suffering from dizzy spells which the doctor had warned might end in consumption, as she was so weak and frail. Dear as she and Pao-yu were to each other, she might not have long to live. And what use was their affinity if she were fated to die? These thoughts sent tears coursing down her cheeks. And therefore instead of entering she turned away, wiping her tears.

Pao-yu hurried out after changing his clothes to see Tai-yu walking slowly ahead, apparently wiping her tears. He overtook her.

"Where are you going, cousin?" he asked with a smile. "What, crying again? Who's offended you this time?"

Tai-yu turned and saw who it was.

"I'm all right." She gave a wan smile. "I wasn't crying."

"Don't fib — your eyes are still wet."

He raised his hand instinctively to wipe away her tears. At once she recoiled a few steps.

"Are you crazy? Can't you keep your hands to yourself?"

"I did it without thinking." Pao-yu laughed. "I was dead to all around me."

"No one will care when *you're* dead, but what about the gold locket and unicorn you'll have to leave behind?"

This remark made Pao-yu frantic.

"How can you talk like that! Are you trying to put me under a curse, or set on annoying me?"

Reminded of what had happened the previous day, Tai-yu regretted her thoughtlessness.

"Don't get so excited," she begged. "Why work yourself up over a slip of the tongue? The veins on your forehead are all swollen with anger, and what a sweat you're in!"

So saying, she too stepped forward without thinking and reached out her hand to wipe his perspiring face. Pao-yu fixed his eyes on her.

After a while he said gently, "You mustn't worry."

Tai-yu gazed at him in silence.

"Worry?" she repeated at last. "I don't understand. What do you mean?"

"Don't you really understand?" He sighed. "Could it be that since I've known you all my feelings for you have been wrong? If I can't even enter into *your* feelings, then you're quite right to be angry with me all the time."

"I really don't understand what you mean by telling me not to worry."

"Dear cousin, don't tease." Pao-yu nodded and sighed. "If you really don't understand, all my devotion's been wasted and even your feeling for me has been thrown away. You ruin your health by worrying so much. If you'd take things less to heart, your illness wouldn't be getting worse every day."

These words struck Tai-yu like a thunderbolt. As she turned them over in her mind, they seemed closer to her innermost thoughts than if wrung from her own heart. There were a thousand things she longed to say, yet she could not utter a word. She just stared at him in silence. As Pao-yu was in similar case, he too stared at her without a word. So they stood transfixed for some time. Then Tai-yu gave a choking cough and tears rolled down her cheeks. She was turning to go when Pao-yu caught hold of her.

"Dear cousin, wait. Just let me say one word."

She dried her tears with one hand, repulsing him with the other.

"What more is there to say? I understand."

She hurried off without one look behind, while he just stood there like a man in a trance.

Now Pao-yu in his haste had forgotten his fan, and as Hsi-jen ran after him with it she caught sight of Tai-yu face to face with him. As soon as Tai-yu left, the maid walked up to Pao-yu, still standing there as if rooted to the ground.

"You forgot your fan," she said. "Luckily I noticed it. And here it is."

Too bemused still to know who was speaking, he seized her hands.

"Dear cousin, I never ventured before to bare my heart to you," he declared. "Now that I've summoned up courage to speak, I'll die content. I was making myself ill on account of you, but I dared not tell anyone and hid my feelings. I shan't recover till you're better too, I can't forget you even in my dreams."

"Merciful Buddha, save me!" cried Hsi-jen in consternation. Shaking him she asked, "What sort of talk is this? Has some evil spirit taken possession of you? Go quickly!"

When Pao-yu came to himself and saw Hsi-jen there, blushing all over his face he snatched the fan and ran off without a word.

As the maid watched him go it dawned on her that his avowal had been meant for Tai-yu, in which case it must surely lead to trouble and scandal. That would be truly fearful. She wondered how best to avert such a dreadful calamity.

She was still lost in thought when Pao-chai appeared.

"Why are you standing here dreaming?" asked Pao-chai. "This sun is scorching."

"Two sparrows were fighting over there," improvised Hsi-jen hastily. "It was so amusing that I stayed to watch."

"Where has Cousin Pao rushed off to all dressed up? I saw him passing and thought of stopping him; but because nowadays he often talks so wildly, I decided not to call out."

"The master sent for him."

"Aiya! On such a sweltering day. What for? Could it be that something's made him angry and he's sent for Cousin Pao to lecture him?"

"It's nothing like that," replied Hsi-jen with a laugh. "I think a guest wants to see him."

"A guest with no sense." Pao-chai appeared amused. "Why gad about in such hot weather instead of staying indoors and keeping cool?"

"Why indeed?"

"And what was Hsiang-yun doing in your compound?"

"She just dropped in for a chat. You know that pair of shoes I started the other day? I've asked her to finish them for me."

Pao-chai glanced around to make sure no one was about.

"How could someone with your good sense suddenly be so inconsiderate?" she asked. "Piecing together what I've seen and heard recently, I guess Yun's a nobody at home. To save expense, her people no longer employ sewing-women but make practically everything they need themselves. That's why, during her last few visits, she's confided to me when nobody was about that she gets quite tired out at home. And when I asked about their daily life, her eyes filled with tears and she made some evasive answer. So I gather she's having a hard time of it because she lost her parents so early on. I can't help feeling sorry for her."

"That's it, that's it." Hsi-jen clapped her hands. "No wonder when I asked her last month to make ten butterfly-knots, it took her so long to send them.

" 'I've stitched them just anyhow,' she told me. 'I hope they'll do. If you want better ones, wait until I come to stay with you.'

"After what you've said, miss, I realize she couldn't very well refuse but she probably has to work late into the night at home. How stupid of me! If I'd known, I wouldn't have asked her."

"Last time she did tell me she has to work till midnight at home, and if she does the least bit of work for other people the ladies of the house don't like it."

"But we have such a stubborn, wayward young master he won't let the sewing-women make any of his things, big or small, and I haven't the time for it all."

"Never mind him. Just get the other girls to do it, and tell him you did it yourself."

"There's no fooling him. He'd know at once. No, I shall just have to slave away myself."

"Wait a bit." Pao-chai smiled. "Suppose *I* help you?"

"Will you really? What luck for me." Hsi-jen beamed. "I'll bring the shoes over this evening."

While she was speaking an old maid-servant came panting up to them.

"Just imagine!" she gasped. "That girl Chin-chuan, for no reason at all, has drowned herself in the well."

Hsi-jen gave a start.

"Which Chin-chuan?"

"How many Chin-chuans are there? The girl who worked for the mistress, of course. The other day, we don't know why, she was dismissed. She wept and sobbed at home but no one took any notice, till they found she'd disappeared. Just now one of the water-carriers was drawing water from that well in the southeast corner when he discovered a corpse. He fetched people to get it out, and it was Chin-chuan. Her family's trying frantically to bring her round, but of course it's too late."

"This is rather odd!" exclaimed Pao-chai.

Hsi-jen nodded and sighed, and the thought of her friendship with Chin-chuan made tears run down her cheeks. She went back to Happy Red Court while Pao-chai hurried off to condole with Lady Wang.

All was strangely quiet in Lady Wang's apartments, where she sat in the inner chamber shedding tears all by herself. Not wanting to mention the maid's suicide, Pao-chai sat by her aunt in silence until asked where she had come from.

"From the Garden," was her reply.

"Did you see your Cousin Pao?"

"Yes, I saw him just now going out in formal clothes, but I don't know where he's gone."

Lady Wang nodded tearfully.

"Did you hear this extraordinary business about Chin-chuan suddenly drowning herself in the well?"

"Why should she do a thing like that for no reason? It's very strange."

"The other day she broke something of mine, and in a fit of anger I struck her and sent her away. I was meaning to punish her for a couple of days and then to have her fetched back. I'd no idea she'd fly into such a passion she'd jump into the well. This is all my fault."

"You feel that way, auntie, because you're so kind-hearted. But I can't believe she drowned herself in a tantrum. She was playing by the well, more likely, and fell in. After being rather confined in your rooms she'd want to play around once she left, stands to reason. How could she work herself into such a passion? If she did, that was very foolish. She doesn't deserve any pity."

Lady Wang nodded.

"But even if you're right," she sighed, "I still feel bad about it."

"Don't take it so much to heart, auntie. If you feel bad about it, just give them a few extra taels of silver for her burial and you'll be doing all a kind mistress could."

"Just now I gave her mother fifty taels. I wanted to give them two sets of your cousins' new clothes to lay her out in as well; but according to Hsi-feng the only ones ready are two new sets for your Cousin Lin's birthday. She's such a sensitive child, so delicate too, that wouldn't she think it unlucky to have the clothes made for her birthday made over to a dead girl? So I've told the tailors to make two new sets as fast as they can. If it had been any other maid, I'd have felt a few taels of silver would be enough; but Chin-chuan was with me for some time and was just like a daughter to me." As she was speaking she could not help shedding more tears.

"There's no need to hurry the tailors," said Pao-chai. "The other day I had two sets made. I can easily fetch them for her. That would save lots of trouble. When she was alive she wore my old clothes and they were a perfect fit."

"But aren't you afraid it may bring bad luck?"

Pao-chai smiled.

"Don't worry, auntie. I'm not superstitious."

She rose to go, and Lady Wang sent two maids along with her.

When Pao-chai returned with the clothes a little later she found Pao-yu sitting in tears beside his mother. Lady Wang had been scolding him, but at Pao-chai's entrance she stopped. The girl was shrewd enough to guess pretty well what had happened. She handed over the clothes to Lady Wang, who sent for Chin-chuan's mother and gave them to her.

What happened next is related in the following chapter.

CHAPTER 33

A Jealous Younger Brother Tells Tales
A Worthless Son Receives
a Fearful Flogging

Lady Wang, having summoned Chin-chuan's mother and given her some trinkets, issued orders then and there for monks to be called in to say masses for the dead girl. Then the mother kowtowed her thanks and left the house.

Now Pao-yu, on his return from seeing Yu-tsun, had been cut to the heart by the news that her disgrace had driven Chin-chuan to suicide. He had nothing to say in reply to his mother's scolding, but Pao-chai's arrival gave him a chance to slip out. He wandered aimlessly along, his hands behind his back, hanging his head and sighing, until he found himself by the front hall. He was skirting the door-screen when as ill luck would have it he bumped full tilt into someone who shouted to him to stop.

Pao-yu started and, looking up, saw to his dismay that it was no other than his father. He had to stand aside respectfully, gasping with fright.

"Why are you moping like this?" demanded Chia Cheng. "It took you a long time to come out when Yu-tsun asked for you; and when you did come, you had nothing spirited or cheerful to say but looked quite down in the mouth, the picture of gloom. And now you're sighing again. What have *you* to moan about? Is anything wrong? Why are you carrying on in this way?"

Pao-yu normally had a ready tongue, but now he was so distressed by Chin-chuan's death that he wished he could follow her straight to the other world. He heard not a word his father said but just stood there in a daze. His stupefied silence — so unlike Pao-yu — exasperated Chia Cheng, who had not to begin with been angry. Before he could say more, however, an officer from the household of Prince Chungshun was announced.

Somewhat taken aback Chia Cheng wondered what this meant, for in general they had no dealings with this prince. He ordered the man to be shown in at once and, hurrying to meet him, found that it was the chief steward of the prince's household. He hastily offered him a seat in the reception hall and tea was served.

The chief steward did not beat about the bush.

"Excuse the presumption of this intrusion," he said. "I come at the order of the prince to request a favour. If you, my lord, will grant it, His Highness will remember your kindness and I shall be infinitely indebted to you."

More mystified than ever, Chia Cheng rose to his feet with a smile.

"What instructions have you for me, sir, from the prince?" he asked. "I beg to be enlightened so that I may do my best to carry them out."

The chief steward gave a faint smile.

"There is no need for you, my lord, to do more than say one word," he answered. "There is in our palace an actor by the name of Chi-kuan, who plays female roles. He had never previously given any trouble, but several days ago he disappeared. After searching the city for him without success, we instituted careful inquiries. We are told by eight out of every ten persons questioned that he has recently been on the closest terms with your esteemed son who was born with jade in his mouth. Of course, we could not seize him from your honourable mansion as if it were an ordinary household. So we reported the matter to His Highness, who says he would rather lose a hundred other actors than Chi-kuan, for this clever well-behaved lad is such a favourite with our master's father that he cannot do without him. I beg you, therefore, to ask your noble son to send Chi-kuan back, in compliance with the prince's earnest request and to save me from wearing myself out in a fruitless search."

He concluded this speech with a bow.

Alarmed and scandalized, Chia Cheng summoned Pao-yu, who hurried in without knowing why he was wanted.

"You scoundrel!" thundered his father. "Not content with shirking your studies at home, you commit such wicked crimes outside! Chi-kuan is in the service of Prince Chungshun; how dare a wretch like you lure him away and bring calamity on me?"

Pao-yu on hearing this was consternated.

"I know nothing about it," he cried. "I've never even heard the name Chi-kuan, let alone lured him away."

He burst into tears.

Before Chia Cheng could speak again the chief steward said with a sardonic smile:

"It is useless to keep it a secret, sir. Tell us whether he is hiding here or where else he has gone. A prompt avowal will save us trouble and win you our gratitude."

Still Pao-yu denied any knowledge of the matter.

"You may have been misinformed, I'm afraid," he muttered.

The steward gave a scornful laugh.

"Why deny it when we have proof? What good can it do you to force me to speak out before your noble father? If you never heard of this actor, how is it that you wear his red sash round your waist?"

Pao-yu was thunderstruck and stood aghast. "How did they find out?" he wondered. "If they've even found out such secrets, it's not much use trying to keep the rest from them. Better send him off before he does any more blabbing."

So he said, "If you know so much, sir, how is it you are ignorant of something as important as his purchase of property? I am told that twenty *li* to the east of the city, in a place called Sandalwood Castle, he has bought a house and a few *mu* of land. I should think he might possibly be there."

The chief steward's face brightened.

"He must be there if you say so. I shall go and investigate. If we find him, well and good. If not, we shall come back for further enlightenment."

He took a hasty leave.

Chia Cheng's eyes were nearly bursting from his head with rage. As he followed the chief steward out, he turned to order Pao-yu:

"Stay where you are. I shall deal with you presently."

He escorted the steward all the way to the gate, and was just starting back when he saw Chia Huan racing past with a few pages. In his fury he ordered his own pages to beat them.

The sight of his father paralysed Huan with fright. He pulled up short, hanging his head.

"What are you rushing about for?" demanded Chia Cheng. "Where are all the people supposed to look after you? Have they gone off to amuse themselves while you run wild?"

As he shouted for the servants who accompanied Huan to school, the boy saw a chance to divert his father's anger.

"I wasn't running to begin with," he said. "Not until I passed the well where that maid drowned herself. Her head's swollen up like this, and her body's all bloated from soaking in the water. It was such a horrible sight that I ran away as fast as ever I could."

Chia Cheng was astounded.

"What maid here had any reason to throw herself into a well?" he wondered. "Such a thing has never happened before in this house. Since the time of our ancestors we have always treated our subordinates well. Of late, though, I've neglected household affairs and those in charge must have abused their power, resulting in this calamitous suicide. If word of this gets out, it will disgrace our ancestors' good name."

He called for Chia Lien, Lai Ta and Lai Hsing.

Some pages were going to fetch them when Huan stepped forward and caught hold of his father's gown, then fell on his knees.

"Don't be angry, sir!" he begged. "No one knows about this except those in my lady's apartment. I heard my mother say. . . ."

He stopped and looked around, and Chia Cheng understood. At a glance from him the servants on both sides withdrew.

"My mother told me," Huan went on in a whisper, "that the other day Brother Pao-yu grabbed hold of Chin-chuan in my lady's room and tried to rape her. When she wouldn't let him, he beat her. That's why she drowned herself in a fit of passion."

Before he had finished Chia Cheng was livid with fury.

"Fetch Pao-yu! Quick!" he roared.

He strode to his study fuming, "If anybody tries to stop me *this* time, I'll make over to him my official insignia and property and let him serve Pao-yu! How can I escape blame? I'll shave off these few remaining hairs and retire to a monastery, there to atone for disgracing my ancestors by begetting such a monster."

His secretaries and attendants bit their lips or fingers in dismay and hastily withdrew as they heard him raging at Pao-yu again. Then Chia Cheng, panting hard, his cheeks wet with tears, sat stiffly erect in his chair.

"Bring Pao-yu in!" he bellowed. "Fetch the heavy rod! Tie him up! Close all the doors. Anyone who sends word to the inner apartments will be killed on the spot."

The servants had to obey. Some pages went to fetch Pao-yu.

Pao-yu knew he was in for trouble when ordered by his father to wait, but he had no idea of the tale Huan had since told. He paced helplessly up and down the hall, wishing someone would carry the news to the inner apartments; but it so happened that nobody was about — even Pei-ming had disappeared. As he was looking round anxiously, an old nanny finally appeared. He seized on her as if she were a treasure.

"Go in quick!" he cried. "Tell them the master's going to beat me. Do hurry! This is urgent!"

He was too terrified to speak distinctly and the old woman, being hard of hearing, mistook the word "urgent" for "drowning."

"She chose drowning herself," she told him soothingly. "What does it matter to you?"

Her deafness made Pao-yu frantic.

"Go and get my page to come," he begged.

"It's over now. Over and done with. And the mistress has given them clothes and silver too. Don't fret."

Pao-yu was stamping his foot in desperation when his father's servants arrived and he had perforce to go with them.

Chia Cheng's eyes blazed at the sight of him. He did not even ask his son what he meant by playing about outside and exchanging gifts with actors, or by neglecting his studies at home and attempting to rape his mother's maid.

"Gag him!" he roared. "Beat him to death!"

The attendants dared not disobey. They thrust Pao-yu down on a bench and gave him a dozen strokes with the heavy rod. His father, thinking these strokes too light, kicked aside the man with the rod and snatched it up himself. With clenched teeth he rained down dozens of vicious blows until his secretaries, foreseeing serious consequences, stepped forward to intervene. But Chia Cheng refused to listen.

"Ask *him* if such conduct as his can be pardoned," he cried. "You're the ones who've been spoiling him. When it comes to this do you still intercede for him? Will you still persist when he commits regicide or parricide?"

Realizing from this tirade that their master was quite beside himself with rage, they hurried away, feeling constrained to send word to the inner apartments. Lady Wang dared not tell her mother-in-law at once. Having dressed in haste she ran towards the study, regardless of who was about, while menservants and secretaries fled out of her way in confusion.

His wife's arrival roused Chia Cheng to still greater fury and he belaboured his son yet more mercilessly. The two servants holding Pao-yu instantly withdrew, but the boy was already incapable of moving. Before his father could beat him any further, Lady Wang seized the rod with both hands.

"This is the end!" roared Chia Cheng. "You're determined to be the death of me today."

"I know Pao-yu deserves a beating," sobbed Lady Wang. "But you mustn't wear yourself out, sir. It's a sweltering day and the old lady isn't well. Killing Pao-yu is a small matter, but should anything happen to the old lady that would be serious."

"Spare me this talk." Chia Cheng gave a scornful laugh. "I've already proved an unfilial son by begetting this degenerate. When I discipline him all of you protect him. I'd better strangle him now to avoid further trouble."

With that he called for a rope. Lady Wang hastily threw her arms around him.

"You're right to chastise your son, sir, but have pity on your wife!" she cried. "I'm getting on for fifty and this wretch is my only son. If you insist on making an example of him, how dare I dissuade you? But if you kill him today, it means you want *me* to die too. If strangle him you must, take this rope and strangle me first, then strangle him. Mother and son, we won't dare hold it against you, and at least I shall have some support in the nether world."

She threw herself down on Pao-yu and gave way to a storm of weeping.

Chia Cheng heaved a long sigh and sat down, his tears falling like rain. Lady Wang, clasping Pao-yu in her arms, saw that his face was white, his breathing weak, and his green linen underclothes were soaked with blood. When she undid them she cried out in distress at the sight of his buttocks and legs beaten black and blue, with every inch bruised or bleeding.

"Ah, my poor child!" she wailed.

As she wept for her "poor child" she remembered her first son and called Chia Chu's name.

"If you were still living," she sobbed, "I shouldn't care if a hundred others died."

Lady Wang's departure had roused the inner apartments, and she had been joined by Li Wan and Hsi-feng as well as Ying-chun and Tan-chun. Chia Chu's name did not affect the others so much, but it reduced his widow to sobs. And the chorus of lamentation made Chia Cheng weep more bitterly himself.

In the middle of this commotion a maid suddenly announced, "The old lady is coming!"

And they heard her quavering voice outside the window, "Kill me first and then kill him. That will be a clean sweep."

Chia Cheng rose in dismay and distress to greet his mother, who entered on a maid's arm, gasping for breath. At once he stepped forward to bow respectfully.

"Why should you vex yourself, mother, and come over on such a hot day? If you have any instructions, just send for your son."

The Lady Dowager halted to catch her breath.

"Were you addressing me?" she demanded sternly. "Yes, I have some instructions. The pity is I've borne no filial son to whom I can speak."

Appalled by this rebuke, Chia Cheng fell on his knees, tears in his eyes.

"If your son disciplines *his* son, it is for the honour of our ancestors," he pleaded. "How can I bear your reproaches?"

The Lady Dowager spat in disgust.

"So you can't bear one word from me, eh? Then how does Pao-yu bear your lethal rod? You talk of disciplining your son for the honour of your ancestors, but how did *your* father discipline you in the past?"

Her eyes filled with tears.

"Don't grieve, mother," he begged. "I was wrong to lose my temper. I shall never beat him again."

The old lady snorted.

"You needn't try to work off your rage on me. It's not for me to stop you beating your son. I suppose you're tired of us all, and we'd better leave now to save trouble all round."

She ordered the servants to prepare sedan-chairs and horses, telling them, "Your mistress and Pao-yu are going back to Nanking with me this instant."

The attendants had to make a show of complying with her orders. Then the Lady Dowager turned to her daughter-in-law.

"Don't cry," she urged Lady Wang. "Pao-yu's still a child now and you love him; but when he grows up and becomes a high official he may not have any consideration for his mother

either. Better not be too fond of him now if you want to avoid heartache later."

When Chia Cheng heard this he knocked his head on the floor.

"What place is there for me on earth, mother," he wailed, "if you reproach me like this?"

The Lady Dowager smiled sarcastically.

"You're making it clear that there's no place for *me*, and yet *you* start complaining. We are simply going away to save you trouble and leave you free to beat anyone you please."

She ordered attendants to pack up at once and make ready for the journey, while Chia Cheng kowtowed and earnestly begged her forgiveness.

But while storming at her son the old lady was worried about her grandson, and now she hurried over to look at the boy. She was further pained and enraged by the severity of his flogging today. Clasping him to her she wept bitterly. Lady Wang and Hsi-feng were hard put to it to soothe her. Then some of the maids who had assembled there took Pao-yu's arms, meaning to help him out.

"Stupid creatures!" scolded Hsi-feng. "Have you no eyes? He's in no state to walk. Go and fetch that wicker couch."

They hastily did as they were told. Pao-yu was laid on the couch and carried to the old lady's room accompanied by his grandmother and mother. As the Lady Dowager was still incensed Chia Cheng dared not withdraw but followed them, aware from a glance at Pao-yu that this time he had flogged him too severely. He turned to his wife, who was now lamenting even more bitterly.

"My child, my darling!" she wailed. "Why didn't you die as a baby in Chu's place? Then your father wouldn't be so angry, and all my trouble wouldn't have been in vain. If anything happens to you now I shall be left all alone, with no one to depend on in my old age!"

These lamentations interspersed with reproaches against her "worthless son" dismayed Chia Cheng and made him repent that he had beaten Pao-yu so mercilessly. But when he tried to mollify his mother she rounded on him with tears in her eyes.

"Why don't you leave us? What are you hanging around for? Won't you be satisfied until you've made sure that he dies?"

Then Chia Cheng was forced to withdraw.

By now Aunt Hsueh, Pao-chai, Hsiang-ling, Hsi-jen and Hsiang-yun had gathered there too. Hsi-jen was simmering with indignation which she could not express outright. And since Pao-yu was surrounded by people, some giving him water to drink, some fanning him, there seemed nothing for her to do. She therefore slipped out and went to the inner gate, where she told some pages to go and fetch Pei-ming.

"There was no sign of trouble earlier on. How did this start?" she asked him. "And why didn't you come to report it earlier?"

"It just happened that I wasn't there," explained Pei-ming frantically. "I only heard about it half-way through the beating. At once I asked people how the trouble had started. It was over the business of Chi-kuan and Sister Chin-chuan."

"How did the master come to hear about it?"

"In the case of Chi-kuan, it looks as if Master Hsueh Pan was behind it. Having no other way to vent his jealous spite, he got somebody from outside to come and tell His Lordship — then the fat was in the fire. As for Chin-chuan, it was young Master Huan who blabbed. Or so His Lordship's men told me."

Both stories seemed likely and Hsi-jen was convinced. She went back to find everyone ministering to Pao-yu. When there was no more to be done for him, the Lady Dowager ordered them to carry him carefully back to his own room. All lent a hand to convey him to Happy Red Court, where they laid him on his own bed. And after some further bustle the others gradually dispersed, leaving Hsi-jen able at last to wait on him hand and foot.

The next chapter tells how Pao-yu answered her questions.

CHAPTER 34

Moved by Affection, Pao-yu Moves His Cousin
A Wrong Report Makes Pao-chai Wrong Her Brother

As soon as the others had left, Hsi-jen sat down by Pao-yu's side and with tears in her eyes asked the reason for this fearful beating.

"Oh, nothing special. What's the use of asking?" Pao-yu sighed. "The lower part of my body hurts terribly. Do see how serious the damage is."

Hsi-jen gently set about removing his underwear, but the least movement made him grit his teeth and groan so much that she stopped. Only after three or four attempts did she succeed in undressing him. Then she clenched her teeth at the sight of his thighs, all black and purple with weals four fingers wide.

"Heavens! How could he be so cruel?" she exclaimed. "But, you know, this would never have happened if you'd paid the least attention to my advice. Well, it's lucky no bones are broken. What if you'd been maimed for life?"

Just then Pao-chai was announced. As there was no time to clothe Pao-yu again, Hsi-jen threw a lined gauze coverlet over him as Pao-chai walked in, a pill in one hand.

"Dissolve this drug in wine this evening and apply it as a salve," she told Hsi-jen. "That will draw the heat and poison from the bruise and help to cure him."

Having handed her the pill, she asked, "Is he any better?"

Pao-yu gratefully assured her that he was and asked her to take a seat. Seeing he was now able to open his eyes and talk, Pao-chai nodded in relief.

"If you'd listened to our advice, this wouldn't have happened," she sighed. "Now you've not only upset the old lady and your mother; when the rest of us see you like this, our hearts ache too...."

She broke off abruptly, regretting her indiscretion, and hung her head with a blush.

She had spoken with such intimate, tender concern, although attempting to hide her deep emotion, and she looked so indescribably charming in her bashful confusion as she hid her blushing face and fingered her sash, that Pao-yu completely forgot his pain in his elation. "I just get given a few strokes," he thought, "and they show such sweet distress and sympathy. How good and kind they are! How admirable! If I were to meet with some accident and die, they'd surely be quite overcome with grief. But it would be worth dying, even with nothing to show for my life, provided I'd won their hearts. Indeed, it would be silly if I wasn't a happy and contented ghost."

His thoughts were interrupted by a question Pao-chai put to Hsi-jen: "What's the reason for this sudden row and beating?"

Hsi-jen passed on what Pei-ming had said, and this was Pao-yu's first inkling of Chia Huan's tale-telling. But when Hsueh Pan's name came up he was afraid Pao-chai would be upset.

"Cousin Hsueh would never do such a thing!" he interposed quickly. "Stop making such wild guesses."

Pao-chai understood why he had silenced Hsi-jen. "How tactful and cautious you are in spite of your pain after such a dreadful beating," she thought. "If you can be so considerate of *our* feelings, why not pay equal attention to important matters outside? For then your father would be pleased, and you wouldn't get into hot water like this. You cut Hsi-jen short for fear of hurting me, but do you suppose I don't know my brother's wild, lawless ways? If such a rumpus was raised that time because of Chin Chung, much worse things are possible now."

After these reflections she turned to Hsi-jen with a smile.

"Why pin the blame on this person or that?" she said. "I think the master was angry because Cousin Pao doesn't behave well and keeps bad company. Even if my brother did let fall some careless remark about Cousin Pao, he can't have meant to make trouble. For after all, in the first place, it was the truth; in the second, he's the type who can't be bothered to gossip. You're used to Cousin Pao who's so considerate. You haven't met my brother, who fears neither Heaven nor Earth and blurts out whatever happens to be in his mind."

Pao-yu's interruption when she spoke of Hsueh Pan had made Hsi-jen realize that her tactlessness must have embarrassed Pao-chai, whose last remarks abashed her even more. As for Pao-yu, he could see that while saying what was right and proper Pao-chai was also trying to put him at his ease. He felt even more touched. But before he could speak again she rose to leave.

"I'll come back tomorrow to see how you are," she assured him. "Have a good rest. I've given Hsi-jen something to make you a salve tonight, and that should help."

With that she left, and Hsi-jen escorted her out of the courtyard.

"Thank you, miss, for taking so much trouble," she said. "When Master Pao's better he'll come himself to thank you."

Pao-chai turned and smiled.

"There's nothing to thank *me* for. Just persuade him to rest properly and not let his imagination run away with him. We don't want the old lady and the mistress and everyone disturbed. For if word of it reached the master's ears, even if he did nothing for the time being, there'd be trouble later on."

So saying, she went off. With a warm sense of gratitude to her, Hsi-jen returned to Pao-yu. Finding him in a dreamy, drowsy state, she went to the other room to tidy herself.

Although Pao-yu lay as still as he could, his buttocks were smarting as if scorched by fire, pricked by needles, or cut by knives. The slightest movement wrung a groan from him. Dusk was falling, Hsi-jen had gone, and he dismissed the other maids saying that he would call if he wanted anything.

Dozing off, he dreamed that Chi-kuan had come to tell of his capture by Prince Chungshun's steward; after which Chinchuan appeared, in tears, to explain why she had thrown herself into the well. Half sleeping and half waking, he paid only scant attention. But then he felt himself shaken and caught the faint sound of sobbing. He opened his eyes with a start to see Tai-yu. Suspecting at first that this was another dream, he propped himself up to look at her more closely. Her eyes were swollen, her face was bathed in tears: it was Tai-yu beyond a doubt. He would have gazed at her longer, but the pain in his legs was so unbearable that he fell back with a groan.

"You shouldn't have come," he said. "Though the sun's set, the ground is still hot. Walking here and back may make you unwell again. I'm not in any pain after my beating, just putting on an act to fool them so that word of it will get out to my father. I'm shamming actually. Don't you worry about me."

Tai-yu was not crying aloud. She swallowed her tears in silence till she felt as if she would choke. She had a thousand replies to make to Pao-yu, but not one word could she utter. At long last she sobbed:

"Never do such things again."

"Don't you worry," replied Pao-yu with a long sigh. "Please don't talk this way. I would die happily for people like them, and I'm still alive."

At this point some maids in the courtyard announced Hsi-feng's arrival. Tai-yu at once stood up.

"I'll go out the back way and drop in again later," she said.

Pao-yu caught her hand protesting, "That's a strange thing to do. Why should you be afraid of her?"

Tai-yu stamped one foot in desperation.

"Look at my eyes," she whispered. "She'd make fun of me if she saw."

At once he released her and she slipped past his bed and out through the back court just as Hsi-feng came in from the front.

"Are you better?" she asked Pao-yu. "If you fancy any-thing to eat, send someone to my place for it."

Aunt Hsueh called next. And then the Lady Dowager sent maids to inquire after the invalid. When it was time to light the lamps, Pao-yu swallowed two mouthfuls of soup and soon dozed off. Then came some of the older maid-servants, the wives of Chou Jui, Wu Lung-teng and Cheng Hao-shih, who were in the habit of calling and had dropped in after hearing of today's trouble. Hsi-jen hurried out to greet them with a smile.

"You're a second too late, aunties," she whispered. "Master Pao has just gone to sleep."

She offered them tea in the outer room and after sitting quietly for a while they left, having asked her to let Pao-yu know that they had called.

As Hsi-jen was coming back from seeing them off, one of Lady Wang's women accosted her with the message that her mistress wanted to see one of Master Pao's maids. Hsi-jen came to a quick decision. Turning softly she told Ching-wen, Sheh-yueh, Tan-yun and Chiu-wen:

"The mistress has sent for one of us. You see to things here. I'll be back presently."

She went with the other woman out of the Garden to Lady Wang's apartments, where she found her fanning herself with a palm-leaf fan on the couch.

"Why didn't you send one of the others?" asked Pao-yu's mother. "Who'll look after him in your absence?"

"Master Pao's sound asleep now, and the other girls know how to look after him," Hsi-jen answered confidently. "Please don't worry, madam. I thought perhaps you had some in-structions which one of the others might not understand, and that might hold things up."

"I've no special instructions. I just wanted to know how he is now."

"Miss Pao-chai brought us a salve, and after I applied it he seemed better. At first the pain kept him awake, but now he's sleeping soundly. It shows he's on the mend."

"Did he eat anything?"

"Only two mouthfuls of the soup the old lady sent. He complained he was parched and asked for some sour plum juice. But I thought to myself: Sour things are astringent, and when he was beaten and couldn't cry out some choleric humours must have rushed to his viscera; plum juice might affect them, bringing on a serious illness, and that would never do. Finally I talked him out of it and gave him some candied rose petals instead. He only ate half a bowl, though, then found it cloying and insipid."

"Why didn't you send and let me know before?" cried Lady Wang. "The other day I was sent a couple of bottles of scented flower juice and meant to give them to him, but thought he might waste them. If he finds rose petals cloying, take him these. One tea-spoon in a bowl of water is delicious." She told Tsai-yun, "Fetch those bottles of juice which were brought the other day."

"Two bottles will be plenty," Hsi-jen assured her. "More would be wasted. We can always come and ask for more when it's finished."

Tsai-yun went off on this errand, returning presently with two bottles which she handed to Hsi-jen. They were tiny glass bottles barely three inches high, with silver caps which screwed on, and yellow labels. On one was written "Pure Osmanthus Juice," on the other "Pure Rose Juice."

"What luxury objects!" Hsi-jen laughed. "Such small bottles can't hold much."

"They're for the Imperial use," explained Lady Wang. "Don't you see the yellow label? Mind you keep them carefully for him. Don't waste any of the juice."

Hsi-jen assented and was about to leave when Lady Wang told her to wait.

"There's something else I want to ask you," she said.

Having made sure that no one else was about she continued, "There's talk that the master beat Pao-yu because of some tale Huan told. Did you hear that? If you did, just tell me what it was. I won't make a rumpus about it. No one will know that it was you who told me."

"No, I didn't hear that," replied Hsi-jen. "I heard it was because Master Pao kept an actor from some prince's mansion, and they came to ask His Lordship to send him back."

Lady Wang shook her head.

"That was *one* reason, but there was another too."

"If there's anything else I really don't know it," rejoined Hsi-jen. She added, "May I make so bold, now that I'm here, to suggest something, madam? . . ."

She broke off at this point.

"Go on."

With a sly smile she went on, "I hope Your Ladyship won't think it presumptuous."

"Of course not. What is it?"

"Actually, Master Pao *does* need to be taught a lesson. If His Lordship doesn't discipline him, there's no knowing what may happen in future."

On hearing this, Lady Wang clapped her hands together, exclaiming "Gracious Buddha!" Then although so eager to hear more, she confided, "Dear child, I'm glad you are so understanding — that's exactly how I feel. Of course I know the importance of discipline. I haven't forgotten how strict I was with Master Chu. But there's a reason for my indulgence now. I'm getting on for fifty, and I've only the one son left; besides, he's rather delicate and the old lady dotes on him. If I were too strict so that something happened to him, or if the old lady were upset, the whole household would be turned upside down and that would be even worse. *That's* why he's been spoiled. I'm always scolding him, pleading with him, getting angry with him or crying over him, but after a short improvement back he slips. He'll never mend his ways unless he's made to smart. Yet if he's badly injured, I'll have no one to depend on in the future."

With this she burst into tears. And Hsi-jen, seeing her distress, wept in sympathy.

"He's your son, madam, of course you take this to heart. Even those of us who wait on him would be happy if everyone could keep out of trouble. If things go on like this we'll have no peace either. Not a day goes by but I reason with Master Pao, yet it has no effect. It's not *his* fault if people of that sort make up to him, and he loses patience when we reason with him. Since you've brought this up, madam, I'd like to ask your advice about something that's been worrying me for a long time. I've never raised it before for fear you might misunderstand. In that case, not only would I be wasting my breath but taking an outrageous liberty."

Lady Wang realized there was something behind this.

"Just say what's on your mind, my child," she urged. "I've heard nothing but good of you recently from everyone. I assumed it was just because you looked after Pao-yu well and were pleasant to everybody. Such thoughtfulness in little things is good. That's why I treated you like one of the old nurses. Now I see you have principles too and your views coincide with mine. Just say whatever's on your mind, but don't let it go any further."

"It's nothing else, only that I was hoping Your Ladyship might arrange for Master Pao to move out of the Garden."

Lady Wang was shocked. She caught hold of Hsi-jen's hand.

"Has Pao-yu been up to anything improper?"

"No, no, madam. Don't misunderstand me. Nothing of that sort. But in my humble opinion, now that he and the young ladies are no longer children and, what's more, Miss Lin and Miss Pao aren't members of the family, cousins of different sexes should live apart. When they spend all their time together every day, it's not convenient for them and we can't help worrying. Besides, it doesn't look good to people outside. As the proverb has it: Best be prepared for the worst. A lot of foolishness is quite innocent, but suspicious people always think the worst. Better make sure in advance that there's no trouble.

"*You* know, madam, what Master Pao is like and how he enjoys amusing himself with us girls. If no precautions are taken and he does something the least bit foolish — no matter whether it's true or not — there's bound to be talk. Low-class people *will* gossip. When they're well disposed, they laud you to the skies; when they're not, they talk as if you were worse than a beast. If people speak well of him, that's as it should be. If a single slighting remark is passed, not only shall we deserve a thousand deaths — that's not important — but his reputation will be ruined for life and how will you answer for it to His Lordship? Another proverb says: A gentleman should show providence. Better guard against this now. You're naturally too busy, madam, to think of these things, and they might not occur to us either. But if they do and we fail to mention it, that would be very remiss. Lately this has been preying on my mind day and night, but I couldn't mention it to anyone else. Only my lamp at night knew how I worried!"

Lady Wang felt thunderstruck on hearing this, borne out as it was by the case of Chin-chuan. The more she thought, the more grateful she felt to Hsi-jen.

"What a wise child you are to see so far!" she exclaimed. "Of course I've given some thought to this myself, but lately I've had too much else on my mind. Now you've reminded me. I'm glad you're so concerned for our reputation. I really had no idea what a good girl you are! All right, you may go now. Leave everything to me. But I tell you this: after what you've said today, I mean to entrust Pao-yu to you. You must look after him and keep him safe. That way, you'll be safeguarding *me* as well, and I shan't forget our obligation to you."

Hsi-jen hastily assented and withdrew. Back in Happy Red Court, she found Pao-yu had just woken up. When she told him about the juice he was delighted. He asked to taste some and pronounced it delicious.

Because Pao-yu had Tai-yu on his mind he was eager to send someone over to her, but for fear of Hsi-jen he had to resort to a trick. He dispatched Hsi-jen to Pao-chai to borrow some books, and as soon as she had left called for Ching-wen.

"Go and see what Miss Lin is doing," he said. "If she asks after me, tell her I'm better."

"I can't just go there without any excuse. Is there no message that you want to send?"

"Not that I can think of."

"Give me something to take then, or ask to borrow something. Otherwise what am I going to say when I see her?"

After a little thought Pao-yu picked up two handkerchiefs and tossed them to her.

"All right, tell her I sent you to give her these."

"This is even odder!" cried Ching-wen. "What would she want two old handkerchiefs for? She'll flare up again and say you're teasing her."

"Don't worry. She'll understand."

So Ching-wen took his gift to Bamboo Lodge, where she found Chun-chien hanging some handkerchiefs to dry on the balustrade.

Chun-chien held up a warning finger.

"She's gone to bed."

Ching-wen slipped into the dark room where the lamps were not yet lit. Tai-yu, lying on the bed, asked who it was.

"It's me, Ching-wen."

"What do you want?"

"Master Pao has sent you some handkerchiefs, miss."

Why should he send me handkerchiefs? Tai-yu wondered.

"Who gave these to him?" she asked. "I suppose they're specially fine ones. Tell him to keep them for someone else, I don't need them for the time being."

"They're not new," replied Ching-wen giggling. "He's often used them."

Tai-yu was even more mystified at this, but some careful thought cleared up the riddle for her.

"Leave them then," she said quickly. "You may go."

So Ching-wen put down the handkerchiefs and left, puzzling her head all the way back over this gift.

Meanwhile Tai-yu, touched by the meaning of this gift, was lost in reverie. Pleased as she was by Pao-yu's insight and sympathy, it was sad to think that all her concern for him might come to nothing. This unexpected present of two used handkerchiefs was rather laughable if it were not for the fact that she understood the thought behind it; yet it was scandalous that he should send and she accept a secret gift. And it made her ashamed of her habit of crying so much. As she mused in this way, her heart was very full, her mind in a turmoil. Having ordered the lamps to be lit, without any thought of the possible consequences she ground some ink on the inkstone, dipped her brush in it and quickly wrote these lines on the handkerchiefs:

> Vain are all these idle tears,
> Tears shed secretly — for whom?
> Your kind gift of a foot of gauze
> Only deepens my gloom.
>
> By stealth I shed pearly tears,
> Idle tears the livelong day;
> Hard to wipe them from sleeve and pillow,
> Then suffer the stains to stay.
>
> No silk thread can string these pearls;
> Dim now the tear-stains of those bygone years;
> A thousand bamboos grow before my window —
> Is each dappled and stained with tears?[1]

She would have written more but her whole body was afire, her face burning. Going to the mirror-stand she removed its silk cover and saw that her flushed cheeks were redder than peach blossom, but failed to realize that this was the first symptom of consumption. She went to bed with the handkerchiefs clasped in her hands and lost herself in dreams.

To return to Hsi-jen and her errand to Pao-chai, when she found that Pao-chai was not in the Garden but had gone to her mother's house, she went back empty-handed. And Pao-chai did not return till the second watch.

---

[1] Referring to a kind of bamboo with dark spots. According to a Chinese legend, after King Shun died, his two wives mourned for him and their tears made dark spots on the bamboo.

The fact is that Pao-chai's knowledge of her brother had led her to suspect that he was behind the visit of the prince's chief steward, and Hsi-jen's report confirmed her suspicion. Hsi-jen of course had this on hearsay from Pei-ming, who had simply been guessing, not having any proof. But she now was sure of his guilt. The joke was that for all Hsueh Pan's bad reputation he was not to blame this time, and yet everyone condemned him out of hand.

Coming home today after carousing outside, Hsueh Pan went in to greet his mother and found Pao-chai with her. After they had exchanged a few words he remarked:

"I hear Cousin Pao got a whacking. What for?"

Aunt Hsueh was already upset on this score.

"You trouble-maker," she snapped back, gnashing her teeth, "this is all *your* doing. And you have the impudence to ask!"

Hsueh Pan was genuinely taken aback.

"What trouble have I made?" he asked.

"Still playing the innocent? Everyone knows you were the one who told. Do you still deny it?"

"If everyone said I'd killed a man, would you believe it?"

"Even your sister knows it was you. Would she make up something against you?"

"Do keep your voices down!" put in Pao-chai quickly. "It will all be cleared up by and by." She turned to her brother. "Whether you told or not, it's over and done with. Don't let's quibble or make a mountain out of a molehill. Take my advice, though, and stop fooling around outside. Just mind your own business. You waste all your time with those rowdies and you're too careless. If nothing happens, well and good. But if trouble starts everyone is bound to suspect you, whether you caused it or not. Why, even *I* would suspect you, let alone others."

Blunt, outspoken Hsueh Pan could not stand such insinuations. Pao-chai's warning against fooling about outside and his mother's charge that his careless talk had caused Pao-yu's flogging made him stamp with rage and swear he must clear himself.

"Who's been shifting the blame on to me?" he fumed. "I'll smash the scoundrel's teeth. It's obvious that to make up to Pao-yu they're using me as a whipping-boy. Is Pao-yu the king of heaven? Whenever his father whacks him the whole household's bound to be upside down for days. After my uncle caned him for misbehaving last time, it somehow came to the old lady's ears that Cousin Chen was behind it and she summoned him to give him a big dressing-down. This time they're picking on *me*. Well, I'm not afraid. I'll go and kill Pao-yu then pay with my life — make a clean sweep!"

He seized the door bar and started rushing out. In desperation his mother dragged him back.

"You'll be the death of me, you monster," she scolded. "Off to pick a fight, are you? Better kill me first."

Hsueh Pan's eyes nearly started from his head in fury.

"What's all this nonsense!" he bellowed. "You won't let me go, yet pin this thing on me for no reason at all. As long as Pao-yu lives, I shall always be his whipping-boy. We'd better all die and be done with it."

"Do have patience," urged Pao-chai, stepping quickly forward. "Mother's so upset, yet instead of soothing her you raise this rumpus. When people — especially your own mother — advise you, it's for your own good. You shouldn't fly into a temper."

"So *you're* nagging again, are you?" he roared. "You're the one who started this."

"You only blame me for nagging, never blame your own thoughtlessness."

"Instead of blaming my thoughtlessness, why don't you blame Pao-yu for looking for trouble outside? Let's take just one example — that recent business of Chi-kuan. I've met Chi-kuan a dozen times without his making up to me once; but the very first time Pao-yu met him, before he even knew his name, Chi-kuan gave him his girdle. That was my fault too, I suppose?"

"There you go again," cried his mother and sister frantically. "That's *why* he got beaten. This *shows* you're the one who told."

"You want me to burst with anger," growled Hsueh Pan. "It's not being wrongly accused that enrages me, it's this fearful fuss you make over Pao-yu."

"Who's making a fuss?" retorted Pao-chai. "You started it by arming yourself and threatening to fight. Now you accuse *us* of fussing."

As all her arguments were so reasonable and even harder to refute than his mother's, Hsueh Pan cast about for some way to silence her in order to have his say. And being in a towering rage, he did not trouble to weigh his words carefully.

"It's no use flying into a huff with me, my dear sister," he sneered. "I can see into your heart. Mother's told me about your gold locket which has to be matched with jade. Naturally you looked round carefully, and now that you find Pao-yu has that rubbishy thing you're bound to take his side."

Pao-chai was speechless at first with indignation. Then catching hold of her mother she sobbed:

"Do you hear what he's saying, mother?"

At this Hsueh Pan knew he had gone too far and sullenly retired to his own room.

Though trembling with rage, Aunt Hsueh tried to comfort her daughter.

"You know that monster always talks nonsense," she said. "Tomorrow I'll tell him to apologize."

Bitterly wronged as Pao-chai felt, she could not make a scene for fear of upsetting her mother. So with tears in her eyes she took her leave and went back to her own apartment to cry all night.

The next morning she rose early and, without troubling to make a careful toilet, simply straightened her clothes and set off to see her mother again. On the way she happened to meet Tai-yu standing alone under the shade of some blossom and was asked where she was going. Pao-chai, not stopping, said she was on her way home. Tai-yu saw that she looked in low spirits, quite unlike her usual self, and had been crying.

She called mischievously after her, "Cousin, look after your health! Even if you fill two vats with tears that won't cure his welts."

To know how Pao-chai replied you must read the next chapter.

CHAPTER 35

Yu-chuan Tastes Some Lotus-Leaf Broth
Ying-erh Skilfully Makes a Plum-Blossom Net

Pao-chai heard Tai-yu's taunt but walked past without turning her head, so anxious was she to see her mother and brother. Tai-yu, standing in the shade of the blossom, went on staring into the distance towards Happy Red Court. She saw Li Wan, Ying-chun, Tan-chun, Hsi-chun and their maids pay short calls and leave again, but there was no sign of Hsi-feng.

"Why hasn't she called to see Pao-yu?" she wondered. "Even if she's busy, you'd think she'd put in an appearance to please the Lady Dowager and Lady Wang. There must be some reason why she hasn't come."

But just then, raising her head, she caught sight of a gaily dressed group proceeding in that direction. Looking more closely she could recognize the Lady Dowager on Hsi-feng's arm, then Lady Hsing and Lady Wang, with the concubine Chou and some maids bringing up the rear. Together they entered the court. Tai-yu nodded and tears ran down her cheeks as she reflected wistfully how good it was to have parents. A little later she saw Pao-chai enter with Aunt Hsueh, and then Tzu-chuan came up suddenly behind her.

"Do go and take your medicine, miss, before the boiled water gets cold," she urged.

"Must you always be hurrying me?" protested Tai-yu. "Whether I take it or not is none of your business."

"You shouldn't stop taking medicine just because your cough's beginning to be better. Although it's the fifth month and the weather's warm, you still ought to be careful. You've been standing here in the damp since first thing this morning. It's time to go back now and rest."

Tai-yu realized then that she was indeed rather tired, and after some hesitation she walked slowly back to Bamboo Lodge on her maid's arm. As they entered the courtyard, the chequered shade cast by bamboos on the moss reminded her of those lines in *The Western Chamber*:

> Who walks in this secluded spot,
> Where dew glimmers white on dark moss?

"Fate was unkind to Tsui Ying-ying," she told herself with a sigh. "But at least she had a widowed mother and a younger brother, whereas poor Tai-yu has nobody at all. The ancients said: All beauties are ill-fated. But I'm no beauty. Why should my fate be so cruel?"

She was walking on lost in thought when the parrot in the covered walk swooped down to squawk at her.

"You pest!" she cried, giving a start. "Smothering my hair with dust."

Flying back to its perch the parrot screeched, "Raise the curtain, Hsueh-yen. The young lady's here."

She stopped, her hand on the perch, to ask whether the parrot's bird-seed and water had been changed. The bird gave a wheeze much like one of Tai-yu's deep sighs. Then it rattled off the lines:

> "Men laugh at my folly in burying fallen flowers,
> But who will bury me when dead I lie?
> See, when spring draws to a close and flowers fall,
> This is the season when beauty must ebb and fade;
> The day that spring takes wing and beauty fades
> Who will care for the fallen blossom or dead maid?"

The two girls burst out laughing.

"Those are lines you often recite, miss," giggled Tzu-chuan. "Fancy him getting them by heart!"

Tai-yu made her take the perch down and hang it on a hook outside the moon window, then went inside and sat down by the window to take her medicine. The room was flooded with a dim green light, its tables and couches cool in the green shade cast by bamboos through the gauze netting. To while away the time she played with the parrot from inside, teasing it and teaching it some of her favourite poems.

But let us return to Pao-chai who reached home to find her mother doing her hair.

"What are you doing here so early in the morning?" asked Aunt Hsueh.

"I came to see how you were, mother. Did he come back after I left yesterday or make any more trouble?"

Pao-chai sat down beside her mother and burst into tears.

"There, child, don't take it so to heart," urged her mother, weeping too. "I'll teach the monster a lesson. If anything were to happen to you, on whom could I rely?"

Overhearing this, Hsueh Pan hurried in.

"Forgive me this once, there's a good sister," he begged, making Pao-chai several bows from left and right. "I had a few drinks yesterday so I stayed out late, then on my way back I knocked into a friend; and that made me arrive home so drunk I've no idea what nonsense I may have talked. I don't blame you for being angry."

Pao-chai, who had been hiding her face to weep, looked up at this with a smile.

"Don't put on that act!" She spat in disgust. "I know what a nuisance you find us. You're trying to make us leave you so that you can do as you please."

"How can you say such a thing, sister, not leaving me a leg to stand on? It's not like you to be so suspicious and unkind."

"You accuse her of being unkind," put in his mother. "Was it kind what you said last night? Really you must have lost your senses."

"Don't be angry, mother, and don't you worry, sister. I promise not to drink or fool about with those fellows any more, how's that?"

Pao-chai smiled.

"At last you're showing some sense."

"If you can stick to that, why, dragons can lay eggs," scoffed his mother.

"If you catch me fooling around with them again, sister, you can spit in my face and call me a beast, not a man. I don't want to be such a trial to you both all the time. Vexing mother is bad enough; if I worry my sister too I'm less than human. Instead of being a filial son and good brother now that father's gone, I'm only upsetting you both. I'm really worse than a brute!"

While talking, tears gushed from his eyes. Since their mother showed fresh signs of distress at this, Pao-chai forced herself to interpose.

"You've already made trouble enough without reducing mother to tears again."

Hsueh Pan dabbed quickly at his eyes and grinned.

"When did I reduce her to tears? All right, that's enough. Forget it. I'll get Hsiang-ling to pour you a cup of tea."

"I don't want any, thank you. As soon as mother's ready we're going to the Garden."

"Let me have a look at your necklace. Shouldn't it be gilded again?"

"No need. It's still a bright gold."

"You ought to make yourself some new clothes too. Just let me know what colours and patterns you fancy."

"I haven't yet worn all the clothes I have. Why make new ones?"

By now Aunt Hsueh had changed, and she led her daughter into the Garden while Hsueh Pan went out.

When Aunt Hsueh and Pao-chai reached Happy Red Court to inquire after Pao-yu, they knew from the throng of maids and nurses on the verandah that the Lady Dowager and others must be there. Having gone in and exchanged greetings with all the ladies, Aunt Hsueh asked Pao-yu if he were any better. He sat up on his couch to answer:

"Yes, thank you, auntie. I'm sorry to have put you and my cousin to such trouble."

She hastily made him lie down again.

"If there's anything you want," she said, "just let me know."

"Thank you, I will," he replied gaily.

"What would you like to eat?" his mother asked. "I can have it sent over later."

"I'm not really hungry, but I'd like some of that broth you once had made with small lotus leaves and lotus seeds."

"Just listen to him!" Hsi-feng laughed. "You may not have expensive tastes, but you're certainly choosy to want something like that."

"Have it made! Have it made!" the Lady Dowager ordered.

"Don't be in such a hurry, Old Ancestress," cried Hsi-feng. "I must try to remember where the moulds are."

She sent an old servant to fetch them from the head cook, and after a while the woman came back to report:

"The cook says those four moulds were returned, madam." Hsi-feng thought this over.

"Well, I can't remember to whom I sent them," she remarked. "They're in the tea pantry most likely."

She sent to ask the steward in charge, but he did not have them either. Finally the steward in charge of the gold and silver plate had them sent over.

Aunt Hsueh took the casket containing the four silver moulds and examined them curiously. More than a foot long and about one inch across, they were inset with more than thirty delicately fashioned shapes no larger than peas — chrysanthemum, plum-blossom, lotus flower, caltrop and the like.

"Your house is really the last word in refinement," she exclaimed to the old lady and her sister. "So many shapes just for one bowl of soup! I wouldn't have known what these were for if I hadn't been told."

Hsi-feng interrupted with a smile, "Why, auntie, the cooks preparing the Royal Feast last year thought this up, flavouring the dough shapes with fresh lotus leaves; but what really counts is the quality of the soup. It isn't anything special after all. Indeed, what family would often have such a soup! We did try it, though, when we first got the moulds; and he's suddenly remembered it today." She passed the casket to a maid with the order, "Tell the kitchen to kill a few chickens at once and make enough well-seasoned soup for a dozen people."

"Why so much?" asked Lady Wang.

"For a good reason." Hsi-feng smiled. "This is something we seldom have, and now that Cousin Pao has asked for it it would be a pity just to make some for him and none for the old lady and Aunt Hsueh. We may as well *all* have some while we're about it — then even I can taste this novelty."

"You monkey!" exclaimed the Lady Dowager. "Treating people at public expense."

"That's all right," countered Hsi-feng quickly amid general laughter. "I can afford this little treat." She turned to the maid. "Tell them in the kitchen to do their best and charge it to my account."

As the maid left on this errand Pao-chai said playfully, "In the few years I've been here, careful observation has led me to the conclusion that, however clever Cousin Hsi-feng may be, she's no match for the old lady."

"I'm old and slow-witted now, child," said the Lady Dowager. "But at Hsi-feng's age I outshone her. Still, even if she's not up to me she's way ahead of your aunt. Your aunt, poor thing, has no more to say for herself than a block of wood and can't show herself to advantage to her elders. They can't help liking Hsi-feng for her clever tongue."

Pao-yu chuckled.

"Does that mean you don't like people who don't talk much?"

"Oh, they have their merits too, just as those with smooth tongues have faults. It's better not to have too much to say for yourself."

"Quite so." Pao-yu laughed. "My sister-in-law never talks much, yet you treat her just as well as Cousin Hsi-feng. If you merely liked good talkers, the only ones of these girls you could fancy would be Hsi-feng and Tai-yu."

"Talking about the girls," observed the old lady, "I'm not saying this as a compliment to Aunt Hsueh, but the truth is that none of our four girls can stand comparison with Pao-chai."

"You're partial, madam," disclaimed Aunt Hsueh with a smile.

"But it's true," put in Lady Wang. "The old lady's often told me privately how good Pao-chai is."

Pao-yu, angling for compliments for Tai-yu, had not expected his grandmother to praise Pao-chai instead. He glanced at the latter with a smile, but she had turned away to talk to Hsi-jen.

At this point lunch was announced and the Lady Dowager rose. Having told Pao-yu to rest well and charged the maids to take good care of him, she took Hsi-feng's arm and urged Aunt Hsueh to lead the way. As they left, she asked if the soup was ready or not, and what Aunt Hsueh and the others fancied to eat.

"If there's anything special, just tell me," she said. "I know how to make this minx Hsi-feng get it for us."

"How you love to tease her, madam," replied Aunt Hsueh. "She's always offering you good things, but of course you don't eat very much."

"Don't say that, auntie," countered Hsi-feng. "If our Old Ancestress didn't think human flesh rancid, she'd have eaten me long ago."

That set the whole company laughing. Even Pao-yu joined in from his bed.

"What a terrible tongue Madam Lien has!" Hsi-jen commented with a smile.

He reached out to make her sit beside him.

"You must be tired after standing so long."

"How forgetful I am!" she exclaimed. "Do ask Miss Pao-chai before she leaves the courtyard to send Ying-erh over to make a few nets for us."

"I'm glad you reminded me."

Pao-yu sat up and called to Pao-chai through the window, "Will you send Ying-erh over after your meal, cousin? I want her to make me some nets if she has time."

"Of course," promised Pao-chai, turning back. "I'll send her presently."

The others who had not understood this exchange stopped to ask Pao-chai what was wanted. When she had explained the Lady Dowager said:

"That's a good child. Send her to do as he asks. If you need more hands I have plenty of girls sitting idle. You can send for any of them."

"We can manage without Ying-erh," Aunt Hsueh and Pao-chai assured her. "She's nothing to do every day and needs something to keep her out of mischief."

As they walked on they were greeted by Hsiang-yun, Ping-erh and Hsiang-ling, who had been picking balsam by some rocks and now left the Garden with them.

Lady Wang urged her mother-in-law to have a rest in her room, as she feared she must be tired. As the old lady's legs were aching she agreed. Maids were sent on ahead to see that all was ready; and because the concubine Chao had excused herself on the grounds of an indisposition, there was only the concubine Chou to help the serving-women and maids raise the portière and set out the back-rests and cushions. The Lady Dowager entered on Hsi-feng's arm and sat down with Aunt Hsueh in the places of honour. Pao-chai and Hsiang-yun took two lower seats. Lady Wang brought tea herself to her mother-in-law while Li Wan served Aunt Hsueh.

"Leave serving to the young people," said the Lady Dowager to Lady Wang. "You sit down and chat with us."

Seating herself on a stool, Lady Wang told Hsi-feng to have the old lady's meal brought there with some extra portions. Hsi-feng withdrew and told Lady Wang's serving-women to pass the order on to those of the Lady Dowager and ask her maids to hurry over, while Lady Wang instructed another serving-woman to fetch the young ladies. This took some time, and only Tan-chun and Hsi-chun appeared eventually; for Ying-chun had no appetite that day, and no one thought anything of Tai-yu's absence as she never ate more than one meal out of two.

Soon the food arrived and the table was laid.

"Our Old Ancestress and Aunt Hsueh mustn't stand on ceremony but do as I say," declared Hsi-feng, approaching them with a bundle of ivory chopsticks wrapped in a handkerchief.

"This is how we do things," the old lady told Aunt Hsueh, who acquiesced cheerfully.

Hsi-feng placed four pairs of chopsticks before the Lady Dowager, Aunt Hsueh, Pao-chai and Hsiang-yun, while Lady Wang and Li Wan superintended the serving of the dishes. Then Hsi-feng called for clean bowls and chose dishes for Pao-yu.

After the lotus broth arrived and the old lady had inspected it, Lady Wang commissioned Yu-chuan who was standing behind her to take Pao-yu his meal.

"She can't carry all this single-handed," remarked Hsi-feng.

Just then, as it happened, Ying-erh and Hsi-erh arrived. Pao-chai knew that they had eaten already.

"Master Pao wants you to make some nets for him," she told Ying-erh. "You'd better go with Yu-chuan."

As the two maids left on this errand Ying-erh asked, "How are we to carry this hot soup all that way?"

"Don't worry." Yu-chuan smiled. "Leave it to me."

She made an old nurse put the broth and dishes in a hamper and carry this behind them while they walked empty-handed to Happy Red Court. There Yu-chuan took over the hamper and the two girls went in. Hsi-jen, Sheh-yueh and Chiu-wen, who were amusing Pao-yu, stood up to greet them.

"How did you two happen to arrive together?" they asked, taking the hamper.

Yu-chuan promptly sat herself down on a chair, but Ying-erh would not presume to sit although Hsi-jen hastily fetched a foot-stool for her.

Pao-yu was delighted by Ying-erh's arrival but distressed and embarrassed by the sight of Yu-chuan, who reminded him of her elder sister Chin-chuan. For this reason he addressed himself exclusively to her. This made Hsi-jen afraid that Ying-erh might feel slighted, and since she refused to be seated she took her to the outer room for some tea and a chat.

Meanwhile Sheh-yueh and the others had fetched Pao-yu's bowl and chopsticks, but instead of starting his lunch he asked Yu-chuan:

"How is your mother?"

Scowling and refusing to look at him, for a long time she did not answer. Then she snapped out:

"All right."

Silence followed this snub. Then Pao-yu tried again.

"Who asked you to bring me my lunch?"

"The madams and the ladies, naturally."

Well aware that Chin-chuan's death was behind Yu-chuan's displeasure, Pao-yu cast about for some means to placate her. Not wanting to humble himself in front of the others, he dismissed them on various pretexts and then put himself out to be pleasant. And tempted though Yu-chuan was to cold-shoulder him, she could not but be mollified by the amiable way in which he put up with all her rudeness. It was her turn to feel embarrassed.

"Do pass me the broth to taste, dear sister," he begged when he saw her face begin to brighten.

"I've never fed anyone. Wait till the others come back."

"I don't want you to feed me but I can't get out of bed," he said coaxingly. "If you'll just pass me the bowl, you can report back so much the sooner and have your own meal. I mustn't keep you here starving. If you can't be bothered to move I'll have to fetch the bowl myself, however much it hurts."

He struggled to get out of bed and could not suppress a groan. At that Yu-chuan no longer had the heart to refuse.

"Lie down," she said, leaving her seat. "What a sight you are, suffering for the sins committed in your previous incarnations."

With a giggle she passed him the bowl.

"If you must be angry, dear sister, be angry here," advised Pao-yu amiably. "Try to keep your temper in front of the old lady and the mistress. If you carry on like this with them, you'll get another scolding."

"Drink your soup, go on. I'm not taken in by that sweet talk."

She made him drink a couple of mouthfuls, but Pao-yu pretended not to like the flavour and left the rest untouched.

"Gracious Buddha!" she exclaimed. "You're hard to please."

"It's got no taste at all. If you don't believe me, try it."

Rising to his bait, Yu-chuan took a sip. At once he cried with a laugh:

"Now it must taste delicious!"

Realizing that she had been tricked she said, "First you don't like it, now you say it's delicious. Well, I shan't let you have any more."

Though he smiled and pleaded she was adamant. She called the others to come to serve him his meal. As the maids came back they heard the unexpected announcement that two nannies sent by Second Master Fu had called to pay their respects.

Pao-yu knew that they came from the house of the sub-prefect Fu Shih, one of his father's former pupils who had prospered thanks to his connection with the celebrated Chia family. Chia Cheng treated him better than his other pupils, and Fu Shih was for ever sending servants over. Now Pao-yu disliked foolish old nurses as much as hulking men-servants, but today he asked these two in for the reason that Fu Shih's younger sister Chiu-fang was said to be remarkably talented and good-looking; and although he had never seen her, his admiration for such a fine girl made him feel it would be slighting her not to admit them. So he promptly invited them in.

Fu Shih, being an upstart, wanted to consolidate his own position by marrying his pretty, gifted sister into some rich and noble family. Indeed, his requirements were so strict that she was still not engaged yet at twenty-three; for no proposals had come from the rich and great, who looked down on his poverty and humble origin. Naturally, then, Fu Shih had his own reason for ingratiating himself with the Chia house.

The two nurses sent today happened to be exceptionally stupid. When invited in they paid their respects to Pao-yu, and Yu-chuan stopped teasing him to listen, bowl in hand, to the conversation. Pao-yu went on eating as he talked while both he and Yu-chuan kept their eyes on the two visitors. When he reached out suddenly for the bowl and upset it, splashing soup over his hand, Yu-chuan started although not hurt herself and gave a cry:

"What are you doing?"

As the other maids rushed forward to take the bowl, Pao-yu oblivious of his own pain cried:

"Where did you scald yourself, Yu-chuan? Does it hurt?"

Everyone laughed at that.

"You're the one who got scalded, not me," she pointed out.

Only then did he realize that his own hand was smarting.

No time was lost in mopping up the spilt soup. Pao-yu stopped eating, rinsed his fingers and sipped some tea while exchanging a few more remarks with the two nurses, who then took their leave and were seen off to the bridge by Ching-wen and some other girls.

As soon as they were alone, the old women started talking as they ambled along.

One of them said with a laugh, "No wonder Pao-yu's called a handsome fool. Handsome is as handsome does, and anyone can see he's a bit touched. He scalds his own hand and asks someone else if it hurts — what could be more stupid than that?"

"The last time I came here," the other rejoined, "I heard several of those girls say he's downright cracked. He got drenched himself in the rain and advised someone else to take shelter. Don't you call that soft? When there's no one about he laughs and cries to himself. When he sees a swallow he talks to the swallow, when he sees a fish in the stream he talks to the fish. He sighs or mumbles to the moon and stars, and has so little spirit he even puts up with the tantrums of those pert girls. When he's in a saving mood he treasures the least scrap of thread, but at other times he doesn't mind squandering millions."

Chatting like this they left the Garden and after taking leave of the others went home.

To revert to Hsi-jen, as soon as these visitors had left she brought Ying-erh in and asked Pao-yu what sort of net he wanted.

"I was so busy talking I forgot you," he told Ying-erh with an apologetic smile. "I want to trouble you to make me some nets."

"Nets for what?"

"Never mind about that. Make a few of each kind."

"Good gracious!" Ying-erh clapped her hands and laughed. "That would take ten years and more."

"You've nothing to do anyway, dear sister, so do make them for me."

"You're asking the impossible," protested Hsi-jen with a smile. "Let her first do a couple of the kind you need most."

"And which are those?" asked Ying-erh. "Nets to hold fans, scented pouches, or sashes?"

"Yes," said Pao-yu. "One for a sash would be nice."

"For what colour sash?" asked Ying-erh.

"Scarlet," said Pao-yu.

"A black or slate-blue net would make a good contrast, then."

"What would match a light green one?"

"That would go well with peach-pink."

"All right. Do me one also in peach-pink and another in leek-green."

"What design would you like?"

"How many do you know?"

" 'Incense-stick,' 'ladder,' 'lozenge,' 'double squares,' 'chains,' 'plum-blossom' and 'willow-catkins.' "

"What was that pattern you worked for Miss Tan-chun the other day?"

"That was 'clustered plum-blossom.' "

"That would do nicely," Pao-yu said. At the same time he asked Hsi-jen to fetch the thread.

Then a nurse called through the window: "Your lunch is ready, misses!"

"Go and have lunch," said Pao-yu, "and come back as soon as you can."

"How can we go when we've a visitor here?" asked Hsi-jen with a smile.

"Nonsense," declared Ying-erh, sorting out the thread. "Run along."

Then Hsi-jen and all but two of the youngest girls left. Pao-yu chatted with Ying-erh as he watched her work.

"How old are you?" he asked.

"Sixteen," she replied, her fingers busy netting the thread.

"What's your family name?"

"Huang."

Pao-yu smiled.

"Then you're aptly named, because you really are a golden oriole."[1]

"My name used to be Chin-ying, but my young lady found that awkward and just called me Ying-erh instead. Now everyone's got into the way of it."

"Cousin Pao-chai is very fond of you," he remarked. "When she marries she's sure to take you along with her."

Ying-erh smiled at this and said nothing.

Pao-yu went on, "I often tell Hsi-jen he'll be a lucky man, whoever gets the pair of you, mistress and maid."

To this she replied, "I don't think you quite realize that our young lady, apart from her good looks, has some wonderful qualities which you won't find in anyone else in the world."

Pao-yu was enchanted by Ying-erh's charming manner and the sweet, innocent way she spoke of her mistress.

"What wonderful qualities?" he asked. "Do tell me, dear sister."

"If I do, you mustn't let her know."

"Of course not."

Just then a voice outside asked, "Why are you so quiet?"

---

[1] "Huang" means "yellow" and "ying" means "oriole."

Looking round they saw that it was Pao-chai herself. Pao-yu hastily offered her a seat, and having sat down she asked Ying-erh what kind of net she was making. Examining the net, which was only half done, she remarked:

"This isn't very interesting. Why not make a net for his jade?"

"Of course, cousin!" Pao-yu clapped his hands in approval. "I'd forgotten that. But what colour would be best?"

"Nothing too nondescript would do," said Pao-chai. "But crimson would clash, yellow wouldn't stand out well enough, and black would be too drab. I suggest you get some golden thread and plait it with black-beaded thread to make a net. *That* would look handsome."

Pao-yu was so delighted with this idea that he immediately called for Hsi-jen to fetch the gold thread. She happened to come in at that moment with two dishes.

"This is odd," she told him. "Her Ladyship has just sent me these two dishes."

"There must be such a lot of dishes today that she has sent these for all you girls."

"No, they said these were specially for me, and I needn't go over to kowtow my thanks. This seems very strange."

"If they're for you, then eat them," put in Pao-chai with a smile. "Don't look so puzzled."

"But such a thing has never happened before. I feel rather embarrassed."

"What's there to be embarrassed about?" Pao-chai smiled significantly. "Some day more embarrassing things than this will happen to you."

Hsi-jen sensed something behind these words, knowing that Pao-chai was not one to make cutting remarks. Recalling Lady Wang's hint the previous day, she dropped the subject and simply showed Pao-yu the dishes before withdrawing again with the assurance:

"I'll fetch the thread as soon as I've washed my hands."

After lunch, having rinsed her hands, she brought the gold thread to Ying-erh and found that Pao-chai had been summoned by her brother and left. While Pao-yu watched Ying-erh at work, Lady Hsing sent two maids with two varieties of fruit for him and the message:

"If you're fit enough to walk, Her Ladyship hopes you'll go over tomorrow to have a little distraction. She's longing to see you."

"If I'm able I'll certainly come and pay my respects," he answered. "I'm already feeling much better. Please tell her not to worry."

He made the girls sit down and told Chiu-wen to take half the fruit to Miss Lin. She was just leaving to do this when they heard Tai-yu's voice outside, and Pao-yu lost no time in inviting her in.

To know what followed, read on.

CHAPTER 36

A Dream During the Embroidering of Mandarin
Ducks in Red Rue Studio Foretells the Future
Pao-yu Learns in Pear Fragrance Court
that Each Has His Share of Love

The Lady Dowager went back from Lady Wang's rooms to her own quarters very pleased by Pao-yu's steady recovery. To forestall any further summons from his father, she sent for Chia Cheng's chief page and gave him these orders:

"Next time your master wants Pao-yu to meet or entertain guests, you can tell him without reporting it to me that I've forbidden the boy to set foot outside the second gate until after the eighth month. For one thing, it will be several months before he can walk again after that terrible beating. For another, just now his stars are unpropitious, and he mustn't meet any outsiders while sacrifices are being made to the stars."

When the page had assented and left, Nanny Li and Hsi-jen were summoned and instructed to tell Pao-yu this to reassure him.

Pao-yu had an inveterate dislike of entertaining literati or men in general. He hated putting on ceremonial dress to pay calls, return visits or offer congratulations or condolences. Delighted by his grandmother's decision, he not only stopped seeing most relatives and friends but even grew lax about asking after the health of his seniors each morning and evening. After paying his respects early in the morning to his grandmother and mother he spent the rest of the day amusing himself in the Garden, often glad to idle away his time by offering his services to the maids. When Pao-chai or any of the others advised against this it only angered him.

"Imagine a pure, innocent girl joining the ranks of time-servers and place-seekers, who set such store by reputation!" he would fume. "This is all the fault of the ancients who had nothing better to do than coin maxims and codes to control stupid, uncouth men. It's too bad that in our time even those in refined ladies' chambers have been contaminated. This is an offence against Heaven and Earth which endowed them with the finest qualities."

Going further in his anger against the ancients, he burned all the Confucian classics in his possession except the *Four Books*. His wild ways discouraged people from talking to him about serious matters. And the only person he really admired was Tai-yu, precisely because she alone had never urged him to seek an official career or fame for himself.

But now let us return to Hsi-feng. After Chin-chuan's death several servants suddenly started bringing her gifts and coming to pay their respects or flatter her. She became at a loss to account for the stream of presents sent her. One evening, when no one else was about, she remarked to Ping-erh:

"These families never had much to do with me before. Why are they making up to me now like this?"

"Isn't it obvious, madam?" Ping-erh smiled. "I fancy their daughters are working for Lady Wang. Her four chief maids get one tael of silver a month, the others only a few hundred cash apiece. Now that Chin-chuan's dead they're all hoping to land this cushy one-tael job."

"Of course." Hsi-feng laughed. "Good for you. There's no satisfying some people. They've squeezed enough and no hard work ever comes their way. You'd think they'd be contented with getting their daughters off their hands, but no, they want something better. Well, it's not often they spend their money on me. Since they're doing this of their own free will I'll accept whatever they bring, but it won't make any difference to my decision."

So she waited until enough gifts had been sent before taking the matter up with Lady Wang.

Her chance came at noon one day when Aunt Hsueh, Pao-chai and Tai-yu were eating water-melons in Lady Wang's apartments.

"Since Yu-chuan's sister died you've been one maid short, madam," observed Hsi-feng. "If there's any girl you fancy, just tell me, and next month we can issue her allowance."

Lady Wang thought this over.

"I don't see why we must have a fixed number of maids," she said. "I've all I need, why not let it go at that?"

"What you say makes good sense, of course, madam," answered Hsi-feng. "This just happens to be the tradition. If even the concubines have two maids apiece, why shouldn't you have your full quota? It's only saving one tael in any case."

"Very well," said Lady Wang on second thoughts. "You can issue the allowance but don't assign me another maid. We'll give this tael to Yu-chuan. Chin-chuan waited on me all that time before coming to such a sad end, it's only fair this double pay should go to her sister."

Hsi-feng turned to look at Yu-chuan.

"Congratulations!" she called with a smile.

Then Yu-chuan stepped forward to kowtow her thanks.

"That reminds me," said Lady Wang. "How much are the concubines Chao and Chou allowed a month?"

"The regular two taels each. Concubine Chao gets another two for Huan, making four taels and an extra four strings of cash."

"Are they paid in full every month?"

"Of course they are," declared Hsi-feng in surprise.

"The other day I seem to have heard someone complaining that she was one string short. Why was that?"

Hsi-feng replied readily, "The allowance for the concubines' maids used to be one string a month, but last year the gentlemen in the treasury decided to reduce it by half — to five hundred cash for each. As each of them has two maids, that makes one string less. They can't complain this was *my* doing. I'd like to give them the usual amount; but since the gentlemen cut it, how can I make good the cut? I'm only the intermediary,

I've no say in the matter. I merely hand out what I'm given. Several times in fact I've suggested restoring their original pay, only to be told, 'This is the quota.' I can't do more. At least I pay them on the dot each month, whereas in the past those people in the treasury always kept them waiting. They were never paid so regularly before."

A short silence followed.

Then Lady Wang asked again, "How many of the old lady's maids get one tael?"

"Eight before, now seven. The other one is Hsi-jen."

"That's right. Pao-yu has no maids in the one-tael class, but Hsi-jen's still counted as in the old lady's service."

"Yes, Hsi-jen still belongs to the old lady and is simply on loan to Cousin Pao, so her money comes out of the allowance for the old lady's maids. It would certainly be wrong to reduce Hsi-jen's one-tael allowance because she's waiting on Pao-yu, unless we gave the old lady another maid. And in that case, if Hsi-jen's pay isn't cut Cousin Huan ought to have a maid with the same pay as well, to be fair. As for Ching-wen, Shehyueh and the other five of them, they get one string of cash apiece, while the eight younger girls like Chia-hui get half a string. This is all according to the old lady's instructions, so it's no use anyone cutting up rough about it."

"Just listen to her," cried Aunt Hsueh with a laugh. "She rattles on like walnuts tipped out of a cart. But how clearly and fairly she puts everything."

"Did I say anything wrong, aunt?" asked Hsi-feng.

"Of course not. But you'd save breath by speaking slower."

Suppressing a smile, Hsi-feng waited for further instructions. Lady Wang thought for a while.

"Now," she announced, "you must choose the old lady a good maid in Hsi-jen's place and stop Hsi-jen's pay, but give her two taels and one string of cash from the twenty taels *I* get every month. In future she's to have the same treatment as Concubine Chao, only her share is to come from *my* allowance, not from the general fund."

Having agreed to this, Hsi-feng nudged Aunt Hsueh.

"Did you hear that, aunt?" she asked. "What did I tell you?"

"This should have been done long ago," was Aunt Hsueh's comment. "Quite apart from the girl's looks, where would you find another with such ladylike manners, so polite and yet so firm and principled? She really is a treasure."

"You don't know half her fine qualities." There were tears in Lady Wang's eyes. "She's ten times as good as my Pao-yu. I ask no better luck for him than to have her looking after him all his life."

"In that case," suggested Hsi-feng, "why not go through the usual ceremonies and make her his concubine openly?"

"No, that wouldn't do. For one thing, they're both too young. For another, his father would never agree. Besides, when he behaves wildly, so long as Hsi-jen's his maid he listens to her; but if she were made his concubine now she wouldn't dare remonstrate strongly. Better let things stand as they are for a few more years."

After Lady Wang had finished, as she had no further instructions Hsi-feng withdrew. As soon as she reached the corridor she found some stewards' wives waiting for her there.

"What business has kept you so long today, madam?" they asked her gaily. "You must be feeling the heat."

Hsi-feng tucked up her sleeves and stood on the doorstep.

"It's pleasant here with the through draught, I'll cool off a bit before going on," she remarked. "It's not my fault if I've been a long time. Her Ladyship has been raking up ancient history, and I had to answer her questions one by one."

With a grim smile she added, "Well, from today on, I mean to show how ruthless I can be, and I don't care if they complain to Her Ladyship either. Rot those stupid, foul-mouthed bitches! They'll come to no good end. How puffed up they are with their own consequence! But they'll lose the lot, and sooner than they think. Blaming *us*, indeed, because their maids' pay is cut. Who do they think they are? Do *they* deserve maids?"

Still pouring out abuse, she went off to select a new maid for the Lady Dowager.

Meanwhile Lady Wang and the others had finished their melons, and after some further talk the party broke up, the girls returning to the Garden. Tai-yu, on the grounds that she must have a bath, turned down a suggestion by Pao-chai to call on Hsi-chun. And after the two girls had parted, Pao-chai walked on alone to Happy Red Court, hoping that a chat with Pao-yu would overcome the drowsiness induced by the mid-day heat.

To her surprise, his courtyard was utterly quiet. Even the two storks were sleeping under the plantain. Walking along the verandah into the outer room, she found his maids sprawled on their beds having a nap. She passed the curio cabinet into Pao-yu's room and discovered him sleeping too. Hsi-jen seated by him was sewing, a white whisk beside her.

Pao-chai tiptoed up to her.

"You're overdoing it, surely!" she said with a soft laugh. "You've no flies or mosquitoes here, so why the whisk?"

Hsi-jen raised her head in surprise, then hastily put down her work and rose to her feet.

"So it's you, miss," she whispered. "You gave me quite a start. We've no flies or mosquitoes, I know. But there's a kind of midge, so small you can hardly see it, which can get through the gauze and bite anyone who's sleeping. It's like being stung by an ant."

"That's true. You've not much open space behind the house, but you've fragrant flowers all around and this room is scented too. These insects which live on the pollen of flowers are attracted to anything fragrant."

While saying this Pao-chai had been examining the work in Hsi-jen's hand. It was a white silk stomacher lined with red, which she was embroidering with mandarin ducks at play among some lotus. The lotus flowers were pink, the leaves green, and the ducks a medley of colours.

"How charming!" exclaimed Pao-chai. "Whose is it, to be worth so much effort?"

Hsi-jen motioned with her lips towards the bed.

"Isn't he too big to wear such things?" asked Pao-chai.

Hsi-jen smiled.

"That's what *he* thinks. So to tempt him, I make them specially handsome. In this heat he's careless about covering himself; but if I get him to wear one of these it doesn't matter if he kicks off his bedding at night. If you think I've put a lot of work into this, you should see the one he has on."

"It's a good thing you have the patience."

"My neck aches from bending over so long today. Do you mind sitting here for a minute, miss, while I take a turn outside?"

With that Hsi-jen left the room.

Pao-chai was so interested in the stomacher that she sat down without thinking in Hsi-jen's place, unable to resist picking up the needle and going on embroidering the charming design.

Meanwhile Tai-yu had run into Hsiang-yun and suggested they go together to congratulate Hsi-jen. When they found the courtyard so quiet Hsiang-yun walked towards the servants' quarters in search of Hsi-jen, but Tai-yu peeped through the gauze of Pao-yu's window. She saw him lying fast asleep in a pink linen shirt while Pao-chai sat next to him sewing, a whisk beside her. Seeing this Tai-yu ducked out of sight and clapped one hand over her mouth to stifle her giggles, beckoning Hsiang-yun with the other hand. Her cousin ran over to see what was so amusing. She too was tempted to laugh, but restrained herself at the thought of how good Pao-chai had always been to her.

"Come on," she said, dragging Tai-yu away before she could make any cutting remarks. "I remember now, Hsi-jen said she was going to the pool at noon to wash some clothes. Let's go and look for her there."

Tai-yu saw through this ruse and snorted, but let Hsiang-yun lead her away.

Pao-chai inside had embroidered two or three petals when Pao-yu started calling out in his sleep:

"Who believes what those bonzes and Taoists say? A match between gold and jade? Nonsense! Between wood and stone more likely, I'd say."

Pao-chai was stunned by this when Hsi-jen returned.

"Still not awake?" the maid asked.

Pao-chai simply shook her head.

"I just met Miss Lin and Miss Shih. Did they come in?"

"No, I didn't see them. Hadn't they something to tell you?"

"Some nonsense," Hsi-jen said. "They were just having one of their jokes."

"They weren't joking this time, I assure you." Pao-chai smiled. "I was just going to tell you myself when you hurried off."

She was interrupted by one of Hsi-feng's maids who arrived with a summons for Hsi-jen.

"There you are!" Pao-chai chuckled.

Then Hsi-jen woke two of the other girls and left Happy Red Court with Pao-chai, going on alone to Hsi-feng's quarters. There she was indeed informed of her promotion and told to go and kowtow to Lady Wang, but not to trouble the Lady Dowager. Hsi-jen was quite overwhelmed.

On her hasty return from thanking Lady Wang, Pao-yu was awake and asked where she had been. She gave an evasive answer. Only that night when they were alone did she tell him the truth, at which he was overjoyed.

"I don't see you going home now," he gloated. "After your last visit home you tried to frighten me with heartless talk, saying your brother meant to redeem you and you'd no future here. *Now* we'll see who dares fetch you away."

"You've no call to talk like that." She gave an ironic smile. "From now on I belong to Her Ladyship. I can leave without so much as a word to you, just by getting permission from her."

"Well, suppose I behaved so badly that you got leave from her and left, people hearing of it would put the blame on me. Wouldn't you feel bad about that?"

Hsi-jen laughed.

"Why should I? If you turn bandit, should I have to go along with you? Anyhow, there is always death as a way out. All of us must die in the end, even if we live to be a hundred. Once I've breathed my last and can't see or hear any more, I'll be through with you, won't I?"

Pao-yu hastily put his hand over her mouth.

"All right, all right. Don't say such things."

Hsi-jen knew all his foibles. Whereas hypocritical compliments disgusted him, true sentiments of this kind distressed him too. Regretting her tactlessness she hastily turned to subjects more to his taste: the spring breeze and autumn moon; powder and rouge; and, finally, the good qualities of girls. When this led inadvertently to talk of girls' dying, she hastily broke off.

Pao-yu had been joining in with the greatest of pleasure, and when she stopped he responded cheerfully:

"All men must die. The thing is to die for good reasons. Those vulgar sods believe that ministers who die for remonstrating with the Emperor and generals who die in battle win immortal fame as fine, upright men — but wouldn't it be better if they didn't die? After all, there has to be a despot on the throne before ministers can remonstrate; but they court death in their eagerness to make a name, with a complete disregard for their sovereign. In the same way, there has to be a war before generals can die in battle; so they fight recklessly and try to win glory by dying, with no thought of the country's welfare. That's why I say these aren't worthy deaths."

"Loyal ministers and good generals only die when it's necessary," countered Hsi-jen.

"If a foolhardy general has no idea of strategy and gets killed through incompetence, is that *necessary*? Civil officials are even worse. They learn by heart a few passages from books and if the government has the slightest fault they remonstrate at random, in the hope of winning fame as loyal men. If they court death in a fit of temper, is that necessary too? They should know that the sovereign receives his mandate from Heaven. Heaven wouldn't entrust such an onerous task to anyone but a benevolent sage. So, you see, they die to win a reputation, not for the sake of noble principles.

"In my own case, if I had any luck I should die now with all of you around me; still better if your tears for me were to become a great stream and float my corpse away to some quiet spot deserted even by crows or any other birds, to vanish with the wind, never again to be born as a human being. *That's* how I should like to die."

To cut short such wild talk Hsi-jen said she was tired and gave up answering him. Then Pao-yu closed his own eyes and went to sleep. Nor did he revert to the subject the next day.

That day, bored with the Garden, Pao-yu recalled some songs in *The Peony Pavilion* and read through the libretto twice. Still not satisfied, he decided to look for Ling-kuan who played the part of young ladies and was said to be the best singer among the twelve young actresses in Pear Fragrance Court. So he went out through the side gate in search of her. Pao-kuan and Yu-kuan, whom he found in the courtyard there, greeted him pleasantly and invited him in.

"Where is Ling-kuan?" he asked.

"In her room," they told him.

He hurried in and found her lying alone on her bed, and she did not move when she saw him. Used as he was to playing about with girls, he imagined Ling-kuan would respond like all the others; so he sat down beside her and with a coaxing smile begged her to get up and sing for him the passage describing the visit to the garden.

To his surprise she sat up and moved away.

"I've strained my voice," she said gravely. "I didn't even sing the last time Her Imperial Highness sent for us."

Now that she had sat up, Pao-yu saw she was the girl who had written *chiang* at the foot of the rose trellis. Never before had he been snubbed like this. His cheeks burning, he left the room. And when Pao-kuan and the others asked what the matter was, he told them.

"Just wait a bit till Master Chiang comes," advised Pao-kuan. "If *he* asks her to sing, she will."

"Where is he?" asked Pao-yu, rather puzzled by this.

"He's just gone out. Ling-kuan must have taken a fancy to something and he's out trying to procure it for her."

Pao-yu waited, mystified, until Chia Chiang arrived with a bird-cage containing a bird and a miniature stage. He strode in cheerfully, eager to see Ling-kuan, but halted at sight of his uncle.

"What sort of bird is that," inquired Pao-yu, "able to hold a flag in its beak and walk round the stage?"

"It's a jade-crested oriole," Chia Chiang told him.

"How much did you give for it?"

"One tael, eighty cents."

Urging Pao-yu to sit a while, he went in to see Ling-kuan. By now Pao-yu no longer wanted to hear her sing but was curious to know her relationship to Chia Chiang, who had walked in gaily calling out:

"Get up and look at this!"

"What is it?" Ling-kuan raised herself on one elbow.

"I've brought you a bird to stop you feeling so bored. Let me show you how to put it through its tricks."

Holding out a few seeds, he coaxed the bird to pick up a mask and flag and strut round the stage. All the other girls laughed, exclaiming "How amusing!", but Ling-kuan gave a couple of snorts and lay down again in disgust.

"Like it?" Chia Chiang asked with a smile.

"It's bad enough your family cooping *us* up here to learn that old trash," she retorted. "And now you get a *bird* to do the same. You've obviously bought it to make fun of us, yet you ask whether I like it."

Chia Chiang was disconcerted and swore that he had never meant to hurt her.

"What a fool I am!" he cried. "I gave a couple of taels for this in the hope that it would amuse you, never dreaming that you'd feel this way about it. All right, I'll set it free — to make you feel better."

With that he let the bird out and smashed the cage.

"That bird may not be human," said Ling-kuan, "but it has a mother bird in its nest. How heartless you are, bringing it here to play with. I coughed blood twice today, and Her Ladyship said that a doctor should be sent to examine me. But *you* — you bring this here to make fun of me. How unlucky I am, ill, with no one to care for me."

She started sobbing again.

"I spoke to the doctor last night," Chia Chiang replied hastily. "He said it was nothing serious and he'd come to examine you again after you'd taken a dose or two of the medicine prescribed. I'd no idea you'd coughed blood again. I'll go and get him at once."

He started off, but Ling-kuan called him back.

"The sun's scorching just now," she said. "If you go off in a huff to fetch him, I won't see him."

So the young man had to remain where he was.

Meanwhile Pao-yu was lost in wonder as the significance of all those *chiangs* written on the ground dawned on him. And feeling superfluous there he took his leave. Chia Chiang being too absorbed in Ling-kuan to notice, it was left to the other girls to see him out.

Turning this discovery over in his mind, Pao-yu walked back in a daze to Happy Red Court where he found Tai-yu sitting and talking to Hsi-jen. Pao-yu went straight up to Hsi-jen.

"What I said last night was wrong," he told her with a sigh. "No wonder my father complains that I'm 'benighted.' It was wrong to say you'd all weep over my death. Now I know not *all* your tears would be for me — everyone will have his share."

Hsi-jen had forgotten those words spoken lightly the previous evening, and was surprised when he brought them up again.

"You really are crazy," she told him teasingly.

Pao-yu made no reply. Convinced now that all love was predestined, each having his allotted share, he was wondering wistfully who would shed tears for him when he was gone. But we need not attempt to guess all his inmost thoughts.

When Tai-yu saw the distracted state he was in she refrained from asking any questions, knowing that he must have been affected by something somewhere.

"I've just come from auntie," she told him. "Tomorrow is Aunt Hsueh's birthday, and auntie wants to know whether you'll go over or not. You'd better send someone to tell her."

"I didn't even go on my uncle's birthday," he said. "What if I were to meet someone there tomorrow? I'd rather steer clear of both birthdays. Besides, it's too hot for ceremonial dress. I'm sure Aunt Hsueh won't mind if I don't show up."

"The idea!" exclaimed Hsi-jen. "She's on quite a different footing from His Lordship. You live close by, and she's a relative. If you don't go, she'll wonder why. If it's the heat you're afraid of, why not go first thing to kowtow and come back again after a cup of tea. Wouldn't that look better?"

Before Pao-yu could answer, Tai-yu teased, "You should go anyway for the sake of the one who kept away the mosquitoes."

"What's this about mosquitoes?" he demanded.

Hsi-jen explained how Pao-chai had sat with him during his siesta the previous day, when there was nobody to wait on him.

"That's too bad," he cried. "How rude of me to sleep all through her visit. Well then, I must go tomorrow."

Just then Hsiang-yun appeared in formal dress. Her family had sent for her and she had come to say goodbye. At once they rose and asked her to be seated, but she could not stay and they had to see her out. Although her eyes were brimming with tears, she dared not complain in front of her family servants; but Pao-chai's arrival presently increased her reluctance to leave.

Pao-chai knew that if the servants reported this on their return to her aunt, Hsiang-yun might suffer for it. Accordingly she urged her to make a start. They saw her to the second gate, and Pao-yu would have gone further but Hsiang-yun stopped him. She turned back, however, and beckoned him to her side.

"If the old lady forgets me," she whispered, "do remind her to send someone to fetch me back."

Pao-yu promised to do this for her.

They followed her with their eyes while she went to her carriage, and then retraced their steps. If you want to know what happened next, read on.

CHAPTER 37

Begonia Club Takes Form One Day in the Studio of Autumn Freshness
Themes for Poems on Chrysanthemums Are Prepared One Evening in Alpinia Park

Chia Cheng, having been appointed this year an Examiner of Provincial Education, chose the twentieth of the eighth month to start his journey. On that day, after paying his respects to the ancestral shrines and to the Lady Dowager, he was seen off by Pao-yu and other young men of the family all the way to the Pavilion of Parting. But his doings outside need not concern us here.

His father's departure left Pao-yu free to do as he pleased in the Garden, and he frittered away whole months in idleness. He was feeling listless one day when Tsui-mo brought him a letter on fancy note-paper.

"I'm glad you've come," said Pao-yu. "I'd quite forgotten, I meant to go and see Third Sister. Is she better?"

"Yes, she's stopped taking medicine today," replied Tsui-mo. "It was only a slight chill."

Pao-yu unfolded the letter then and read:

Tan-chun greets her Second Brother.

The other night the moon was clear after the rain, and it seemed such a rare chance to enjoy the moonlight that I stayed up until midnight strolling under the trees. As a result, I caught a chill in the dew. You took the trouble to come in person and cheer me up yesterday, then sent your maids with gifts of fresh lichees and Yen Chen-ching's[1] calligraphy. I was extremely touched by your kind concern.

As I was resting quietly today it occurred to me that the ancients, even when pursuing fame and struggling for profit, kept a small hill or stream to which they could retire; and there, with a

---

[1] A famous Tang calligrapher.

few friends from far or near, they amused themselves in their cups by organizing poetry clubs or literary forums. The fame of those impromptu gatherings has come down through the centuries.

Though I myself have no talent I am lucky enough to live with others among rocks and fountains, and I admire the polished verses of Pao-chai and Tai-yu. It would be a pity not to invite poetizers to a feast in a cool courtyard and a moonlit pavilion or to make poems and drink in Apricot Tavern by Peach Stream. Why should the genius of the Lotus Society[1] be confined to men? Why should girls be excluded from cultured gatherings like those in the Eastern Hills?[2]

If you will condescend to come, I shall sweep the path clear of blossoms to wait for you.

Respectfully written.

Pao-yu clapped his hands delightedly.

"How high-brow Third Sister's become!" he chuckled. "I'll go now and discuss this with her."

He set off at once with Tsui-mo at his heels, and had just reached Seeping Fragrance Pavilion when the serving-woman on duty at the back gate of the Garden appeared with a letter. Catching sight of Pao-yu she approached him and announced:

"Master Yun sends his respects. He is waiting at the back gate and told me to give you this."

Pao-yu opened the letter and read:

Your unworthy child Chia Yun sends his respectful greetings and wishes his noble father boundless health and happiness.

Since I had the good fortune to become your adopted son, I have been longing day and night to please you but found no way to show my filial piety. Recently I was entrusted with the purchase of flowers, and thanks to your great influence I have been able to make the acquaintance of many gardeners and visit many celebrated gardens. I discovered a rare species of white begonia and after considerable difficulty have succeeded in acquiring just two pots. If you consider me as your own son, please keep these flowers to enjoy.

As the weather is so hot I will not presume to intrude, for fear of disturbing the young ladies in the Garden.

I kowtow with humble respect, wishing you good health.

Having read this Pao-yu asked with a smile, "Did he come all alone?"

---

[1] Monk Hui-yuan of the Tsin Dynasty organized this society in Lushan.
[2] The Tsin Dynasty landlord-official Hsieh An used to organize cultured gatherings in his country retreat.

"Just with two pots of flowers," said the old woman.

"Go and tell him I've read his letter and appreciate his thoughtfulness. You can put the flowers in my room."

With that he went with Tsui-mo to the Studio of Autumn Freshness where Pao-chai, Tai-yu, Ying-chun and Hsi-chun were assembled.

"Here comes another!" they cried, laughing, as he entered.

"Not so vulgar, was it, that sudden idea of mine?" asked Tan-chun gleefully. "I wrote a few invitations to see what would happen, and you all turn up in force."

"We should have started a club like this long ago," observed Pao-yu.

"Start one if you like, but don't count *me* in," said Tai-yu. "I'm not up to it."

"If you're not, who is?" countered Ying-chun with a smile.

"This is a serious business," declared Pao-yu. "We should encourage each other, not back out out of politeness. Let's all give our ideas for general discussion. What suggestions have you, Cousin Pao-chai? And Cousin Tai-yu?"

"What's the hurry?" asked Pao-chai. "We're not all here yet."

Before she had finished speaking Li Wan walked in.

"How very refined!" she cried, laughing. "If you're going to start a poetry club, I'll volunteer to preside. I had this very idea last spring, but on second thoughts decided it would only be asking for trouble as I can't write poetry myself. So I dropped the idea and forgot it. Now that Third Sister's so keen, I'll help you get this going."

"If you're set on starting a poetry club," said Tai-yu, "we must all be poets. And first, to be less conventional, we must stop calling each other 'sister,' 'cousin,' 'sister-in-law' and so forth."

"Quite right," agreed Li Wan. "Let's choose some elegant pen-names. I'll be The Old Peasant of Sweet Paddy. No one else can have that name."

"I'll be Master of Autumn Freshness," cried Tan-chun,

"There's something unreal and awkward about 'master' and 'scholar,'" objected Pao-yu. "With all these *wu-tung* trees and plantains here, why not use them in your name?"

"Yes, I know what. I like plantains best, so I'll call myself The Stranger Under the Plantain."

The others approved this as more original.

Only Tai-yu teased, "Drag her off, quick! Stew some slices of her flesh to go with our wine." When the others looked mystified she explained with a smile, "Didn't an ancient say, 'The deer was covered with the plantain'? If she calls herself The Stranger Under the Plantain, she must be a deer. Let's hurry up and cook this venison."

Amid general laughter Tan-chun cried, "Just you wait! You're very clever at making fun of people, but I've got the right name for you, a perfect name." She turned to the rest. "The wives of King Shun[1] shed so many tears on bamboos that thereafter their stems became speckled, and now the speckled bamboo is called by their name. Well, she lives in Bamboo Lodge and she's always crying. When one day she pines for a husband, I'm sure the bamboos there will grow speckled too. I propose we call her Queen of the Bamboos."

The rest applauded while Tai-yu lowered her head, reduced to silence.

"I've thought of a good name for Cousin Pao-chai," volunteered Li Wan. "A short one too."

"What is it?" asked Hsi-chun and Ying-chun.

"I'm entitling her Lady of the Alpinia. How's that?"

"An excellent title," said Tan-chun.

"How about *me*?" asked Pao-yu. "Think of one for me too."

"You've already got one." Pao-chai chuckled. "Much Ado About Nothing is just the name for you."

"Why not keep your old title of Prince of the Crimson Cavern?" suggested Li Wan.

Pao-yu smiled sheepishly.

---

[1] A legendary sage king who was said to have died in the course of an inspection tour.

"Don't bring up the silly things I did as a child."

"You've already got plenty of pen-names," said Tan-chun. "What do you want a new one for? We can just call you by any name we feel like."

"I've got one for you," offered Pao-chai. "It's vulgar, but it suits you to the ground. The two hardest things to come by are riches and nobility, and the third is leisure. Few people enjoy more than one of these, but you have all three. So you should be called The Rich and Noble Idler."

"That's too good for me." Pao-yu grinned. "But just as you please."

"What about Second Cousin and Fourth Cousin?" asked Li Wan.

"We're no good at writing poetry so we shan't need pen-names," rejoined Ying-chun.

"Even so, you'd each better have one," urged Tan-chun.

"As Ying-chun lives on Purple Caltrop Isle, let her be Mistress of Caltrop Isle," suggested Pao-chai. "And Hsi-chun in the Pavilion of Scented Lotus could be Mistress of Lotus Pavilion."

"Very good," said Li Wan. "Now as I'm the eldest you must all listen to me. I'm sure you'll agree to my proposal. We seven are starting this club; but as Second Cousin, Fourth Cousin and I are no poetesses you must leave us out when it comes to writing, and we'll each take charge of something."

"We've already got titles." Tan-chun giggled. "But we might just as well not have them, the way you're still talking. We must decide on forfeits for mistakes like that from now on."

"Wait till we've set up the club before laying down rules," said Li Wan. "My apartments are the largest, let's meet there. Though I can't versify, if you poets don't object to my vulgar company I'll act as hostess and in that way acquire some culture too. But if you elect me as warden, I shan't be able to manage on my own. We must have as our deputy-wardens the scholars of Caltrop Isle and Lotus Pavilion, one to set the theme and rhymes, the other as copyist and supervisor. We won't make a ruling that we three are *not* to write — when the subject and rhyme are easy we may have a go — but you four definitely *must* write. That's my proposal. If you don't accept it, I must withdraw from this illustrious company."

As Ying-chun and Hsi-chun had no liking for versifying and no chance of outdoing Pao-chai or Tai-yu, they willingly agreed to this arrangement which suited them down to the ground. The others, seeing their relief, acquiesced understandingly without pressing them.

"All right then," said Tan-chun cheerfully. "Seems funny to me, though. This was *my* brain-wave, but you three end up in charge."

"Now that's settled," put in Pao-yu, "let's go to Paddy-Sweet Cottage."

"Don't be in such a hurry," objected Li Wan. "We're still in the planning stage. Wait till I invite you."

"At least we should agree on how often to meet," urged Pao-chai.

"If we meet too often we won't enjoy it," predicted Tan-chun. "Let's limit it to two or three times a month."

Pao-chai nodded.

"Twice a month is enough. We'll fix dates and meet regardless of wind or rain. If anyone likes to invite people to her place or the usual place for another gathering on some other day, well and good. Wouldn't that be more flexible and greater fun?"

They all approved this idea.

"As this was *my* suggestion," said Tan-chun, "you must let me play hostess first. That's only fair."

"Very well then," agreed Li Wan. "You can call the first meeting tomorrow."

"Why not today? There's no time like the present. You set the subject, Caltrop Isle can fix the rhymes, and Lotus Pavilion can supervise."

"I don't think the subject and rhymes should be decided by one person," Ying-chun demurred. "Drawing lots would be fairer."

"On my way here," remarked Li Wan, "I saw them carrying in two pots of white begonia which looked simply lovely. Why not write on the begonia?"

"Without having seen them?" protested Ying-chun. "How can we?"

"It's only white begonia," countered Pao-chai. "There's no need to look at it first. The ancients wrote to manifest their own temperaments and feelings. If they'd only written about things they'd seen, we wouldn't have so many poems today."

"In that case let me settle the rhymes," said Ying-chun.

She took a volume of poetry from the bookcase and opened it at random at a *lu-shih* with seven-character lines. Having held this out for all to see, she told them to use the same metre. Then putting the book away she turned to a little maid.

"Say any word that comes into your head."

The maid, standing by the door, said, "*Men* (door)."

"Very well, that rhyme belongs to the thirteenth section of the rhyme system," announced Ying-chun. "And that word must come in the first line."

Next she asked for the box of rhyme cards, pulled out the thirteenth drawer and told the maid to pick four cards at random. These proved to be *pen* (pot), *hun* (spirit), *hen* (stain) and *hun* (dim).

" 'Pot' and 'door' aren't easy to fit in," was Pao-yu's comment.

Tai-shu prepared four lots of paper and writing-brushes, and all quietened down to think. All but Tai-yu, who went on fondling the *wu-tung* trees, looking at the autumn scene or joking with the maids. Ying-chun had a stick of Sweet-Dream Incense lit. Being only three inches long and no thicker than a lampwick, this burnt quickly. The poems had to be finished before it burnt out, on pain of a penalty.

Tan-chun was the first to finish. She wrote out her poem, made one or two corrections, and handed the paper to Ying-chun.

"Are you ready, Lady of the Alpinia?" she asked Pao-chai.

"Yes, mine's done, but it's no good," replied Pao-chai.

Pao-yu, his hands behind his back, was pacing up and down the corridor.

"Hear that?" he said to Tai-yu. "They've finished theirs."

"Don't worry about me," she answered.

Then he saw that Pao-chai had copied out her poem.

"Good gracious!" he exclaimed. "There's only one inch of the incense left, but all I've done is four lines." He turned to Tai-yu. "The incense is nearly burnt out. Do stop squatting on the damp ground."

Tai-yu paid no attention.

"I can't help you now," he said. "I must write mine out, however bad it is." With that he walked to the desk.

"We're going to look at the poems now," announced Li Wan. "Anyone who doesn't hand his in by the time we finish reading the others will have to pay a forfeit."

"The Old Peasant of Sweet Paddy may not write well herself," remarked Pao-yu, "but she's a good judge and absolutely impartial. We'll all stand by your verdict."

The rest agreed. First they looked at Tan-chun's paper.

> Chill the sunset grass in front of the closed door,
> Thick the green moss the rain-drenched pot below;
> Her spirit's purity surpasses jade,
> Her gentle form is ravishing as snow.
> A faint ethereal loveliness is hers,
> Her shadow at midnight chequers the moon's light.
> Do not fly from me, chaste goddess;
> Abide with me as fall the shades of night.

After admiring this they read Pao-chai's poem:

> For the sake of the flowers the door is closed by day
> As I go to water the pots with moss overgrown;
> Immaculate its shadow on autumn steps,
> Pure as snow and ice its spirit by dewy stone.
> Only true whiteness dazzles with its brightness;
> Can so much sadness leave a flawless jade?
> Its purity rewards the god of autumn,
> Speechless and chaste it stays as sunbeams fade.

Li Wan remarked with a smile, "Trust the Lady of the Alpinia!"

Then they turned to Pao-yu's poem:

> Autumn blooms cast chequered shadows by the door,
> Seven nodes of snowy flowers in pots arrayed,
> Like Lady Yang's shade, fresh from the bath, ice-pure,
> Or Hsi Shih's mournful spirit fair as jade.
> No morning breeze can scatter this infinite sadness,
> And the rain adds fresh tear-stains at night;
> Leaning by painted balustrade it seems sensate
> As pounding of clothes and fluting put dusk to flight.

When all had read this, Pao-yu expressed his own preference for Tan-chun's verse, but Li Wan insisted that Pao-chai's was more distinguished. She then asked Tai-yu for her poem.

"Have you all finished?" cried Tai-yu.

At once she took up her brush and dashed off eight lines which she tossed over to them. Li Wan and the others read:

> Half-rolled the bamboo blind, half-closed the door;
> Crushed ice serves as mould for jade pots.

"How do you do it?" exclaimed Pao-yu in admiration before reading on.

> Some whiteness from the pear-blossom is stolen,
> Some of its spirit winter-plum allots.

"Splendid!" cried the others. "She's really original."

They read on:

> The goddess of the moon sews a white gown,
> The maid's weeping in autumn chamber never ends;
> Silently, shyly, with never a word of complaint,
> She reclines in the autumn breeze as night descends.

"This is the best!" cried the young people.

"It's certainly the most charming and unusual," said Li Wan. "But our Lady Alpinia's has deeper significance and real substance."

"Quite right," put in Tan-chun. "The Queen of Bamboos should come second."

"And the Happy Red Prince last," said Li Wan. "Agreed?"

"Mine was no good, that's quite fair," said Pao-yu with a smile. "But you should reconsider which is the better, Lady Alpinia's or Queen Bamboo's."

"I'm the arbiter," insisted Li Wan. "You've no say in the matter. Any more argument will be penalized."

So Pao-yu said no more.

"I've decided that from now on we should meet on the second and sixteenth of each month," continued Li Wan. "And you'll have to accept the subjects and rhymes I choose. You can have extra meetings on other days if you like — I don't care if you meet every day. But mind you come to my place on the second and sixteenth."

"We must choose a name for this club," declared Pao-yu.

"Nothing too common," said Tan-chun. "Nothing too new-fangled either. As we happened to start with poems on begonia, why not call it Begonia Club? Even if this sounds a little commonplace, as it's based on fact that doesn't matter."

After some further discussion and some refreshments they parted, some going back to their own rooms, others calling on the Lady Dowager and Lady Wang. But no more of this.

Now Hsi-jen had wondered what Pao-yu was up to when he hurried off with Tsui-mo after reading the note. When two women from the back gate brought in two pots of begonia some time later, she asked where these were from and was told what had happened. Hsi-jen made them put the plants down and take seats in the servants' room while she went inside, weighed out sixty cents of silver and fetched another three hundred cash which she handed to the two women.

"This silver is for the boys who brought the flowers," she explained. "And the cash is for you to buy drinks."

The two women stood up, beaming, to thank her profusely and make a show of declining; but on Hsi-jen's insistence they accepted the tip.

"Are there any pages on duty outside the back gate?" she asked them.

"Yes, there are four of them there every day," they answered. "If there's anything you want done, miss, we can tell them."

"There's nothing *I* want," answered Hsi-jen, smiling. "But Master Pao wanted to send something today to Miss Shih in the house of the young marquis. It's lucky you came. When you go out, please tell those boys at the back gate to hire a carriage. As soon as it arrives you can come here to get the money. Don't let them knock around in the front."

When the women had left to see to this, Hsi-jen went back inside to look for a plate on which to put the gifts for Hsiang-yun; but the plate she wanted was missing from the carved cabinet. Turning round, she saw Ching-wen, Chiu-wen and Sheh-yueh busy with their needlework.

"What's become of that white agate plate with spiral designs?" she asked them.

The girls looked at each other but could not remember.

"It was used to send lichees to Miss Tan-chun," said Ching-wen after some thought. "They've not sent it back yet."

"There are plenty of everyday dishes you could have used. Why choose that particular one?" Hsi-jen inquired.

"Just what I said. But *he* insisted that plate looked best with the fresh lichees. And when I took it over, Miss Tan-chun liked it so much she told me to leave the fruit on it; so I didn't bring it back. Look, that pair of vases from the top shelf hasn't come back either."

"Speaking of those vases reminds me of something funny," put in Chiu-wen. "When our Master Pao takes it into his head to be filial, he really goes the whole hog. When he saw the fragrant osmanthus in bloom in the Garden he picked two sprays for himself, but all of a sudden he thought better of it. He said, 'These flowers have just bloomed in our own garden, I shouldn't be the first to enjoy them.' He promptly took down those two vases, filled them with water and put the sprays in himself, then having them carried over, he went personally to deliver one to his grandmother, another to his mother.

"This sudden filial piety on his part brought good luck to his messenger too. *I* happened to be the one who went that day, and the old lady was as pleased as pleased could be. She told everyone:

" 'What a good grandson Pao-yu is after all, even sending me flowers like this! Yet other people blame me for spoiling him.'

"You know how little the old lady usually has to say to me. I've never been a favourite of hers. But that day she told them to give me a few strings of cash, saying I was a 'poor, delicate little thing.' What an unexpected stroke of luck! A few strings of cash mayn't be much, but it was a rare honour.

"Then I went to Her Ladyship's place just as she was looking through some cases with Madam Lien and the concubines Chao and Chou, sorting out the bright clothes she'd worn in her young days to give away. When I went in she stopped looking at the clothes to admire the flowers. And to please her Madam Lien started praising Pao-yu for being such a considerate, filial son — she came out with two cartloads of compliments. Her Ladyship felt that in front of everyone she had gained credit because of him, and this should silence those who had gossiped about him. She was so delighted that she gave me two gowns on the spot. Clothes are nothing special either — we're given new ones at any rate every year — but this was a great mark of favour."

"Bah, you're easily pleased," scoffed Ching-wen. "She gives others the best and you the cast-offs, yet you feel you have big face."

"Cast-offs or not, it was kind of Her Ladyship."

"If I'd been you I wouldn't have taken them," retorted Ching-wen. "Anyone else's cast-offs I wouldn't mind; but why should someone in these rooms be superior to the rest of us? If *she* got the good clothes and I the cast-offs, I'd refuse them. Even at the risk of offending the mistress, I wouldn't put up with that."

"Who here got the good ones?" demanded Chiu-wen quickly. "I was ill for a few days at home, I didn't know. Do be a dear and tell me."

"If I tell you, will you return those gowns to the mistress?"

"Don't be silly. I just think it would be fun to know. Even if Her Ladyship gave me the dog's left-overs, I'd think it kind of her. I don't worry about other people's business."

The other girls laughed.

"You've hit the nail on the head. They were given to this foreign-species, spotted lap-dog of ours."[1]

"May all your tongues rot!" parried Hsi-jen with a smile. "Never miss a chance to make fun of me, do you? You'll one by one come to a bad end."

"So it was *you*, sister," said Chiu-wen. "I'd no idea. I do apologize."

"Stop fooling," urged Hsi-jen. "I wish one of you would bring that plate back."

"Those vases should be fetched back too," said Sheh-yueh. "It'd be all right in the old lady's place, but all sorts of people go to Her Ladyship's rooms. The rest don't matter, but if Concubine Chao and that lot saw things from here they'd try some mean trick to break them, and the mistress wouldn't pay too much attention. We'd better fetch them back before it's too late."

Ching-wen, hearing this, put down her needlework.

"All right, I'll go and get them," she volunteered.

"I'll go while you fetch the plate," offered Chiu-wen.

"No, it's *my* turn," insisted Ching-wen, laughing. "Are you going to take all the good errands and leave none for me?"

"Chiu-wen only got clothes that once," teased Sheh-yueh. "How can you expect to find them looking through clothes again today? That would be too much of a coincidence."

Ching-wen snorted.

"Even if I don't see any clothes, maybe the mistress will think me so trustworthy that she gives me two taels of silver a month from her own allowance too. Who knows?" She laughed. "Don't try to fool me. I know all about it."

With that she ran off, and Chiu-wen also left to fetch the plate from Tan-chun's apartments.

When the plate had been brought, Hsi-jen prepared the gifts then called for Nanny Sung who was attached to their compound.

---

[1] Hsi-jen's family name "Hua" could mean "flower" or "spotted."

"Get yourself spruced up and put on your outdoor things," she said. "I want you to take some presents to Miss Shih."

"Just give the things and message to me," said the nurse. "I'll get ready and go at once."

Hsi-jen picked up two small woven bamboo hampers. The first she opened contained fresh caltrops and euryale seeds; the second, powdered chestnut cake sweetened with osmanthus.

"These are fresh from our Garden," she explained. "Master Pao wants Miss Shih to try them. And the other day she admired this agate plate, so she must keep it. Then here, in this silk wrapper, is the needlework she asked me to do. I hope she won't find it too clumsy. Send her our respects and the young master's greetings."

"Has Master Pao any other messages?" asked the nurse. "Will you go and find out, miss, in case you've forgotten something."

"Did you see him with Miss Tan-chun?" Hsi-jen asked Chiu-wen.

"Yes, they were discussing starting some sort of poetry club and all busy writing poems. I shouldn't think he has any message. She needn't wait."

As Nanny Sung took the things and prepared to leave, Hsi-jen told her to go by the back gate where the boys had a carriage waiting. So the nurse left.

When Pao-yu came back, the first thing he did was to admire the begonia; then, going inside, he told Hsi-jen about the poetry club. She in turn reported how she had sent Nanny Sung with the gifts to Hsiang-yun. He clapped his hands at this.

"How could we forget her?" he cried. "I *felt* there was something missing, but couldn't think what it was. I'm so glad you mentioned her. I meant to invite her. Our poetry club will be no fun without her."

"It's not all that important — just a way to pass the time," rejoined Hsi-jen. "She's not as free as the rest of you and has no say at home. If you tell her she'll want to come, but she may not be able; and if she can't she'll be terribly disappointed. You'll only be upsetting her."

"That's all right," said Pao-yu. "I shall ask my grandmother to send and fetch her."

Just then Nanny Sung came back to report on her errand. Having expressed Hsiang-yun's thanks for the gift she told Hsi-jen, "Miss Shih asked what Master Pao was doing. When I told her, 'Writing poems with the young ladies and starting a poetry club,' she was most disappointed you hadn't let her know. Quite a state she was in!"

This made Pao-yu go straight to the Lady Dowager to insist that Hsiang-yun should be fetched at once. When the old lady told him that it was too late and she should be invited first thing the next day, he had to accept this reply and returned dejectedly to his own rooms.

Early the next morning he went back to urge his grandmother to send for Hsiang-yun, and did not relax until she finally arrived in the afternoon. After greeting her he lost no time in explaining the whole business to her. He was about to show her their poems when Li Wan and the others stopped him.

"Don't show her yet," said Li Wan. "Give her the rhymes. We'll fine her for coming late by making her write a poem in the same metre first. If it's good, we'll welcome her to join the club, if not, she'll have to stand treat first and then we'll think it over."

"You forgot to ask me; it's *I* who should fine you people," said Hsiang-yun laughingly. "All right, show me the rhymes. I'm no good, but I don't mind making a fool of myself. Just let me join the club and I'll willingly sweep the ground and burn incense for you."

"How could we forget her yesterday?" cried the others, delighted to find her so full of fun.

They quickly told her the rhymes. Hsiang-yun was too excited to give careful thought to her poems or to polish them. While chatting with the rest she made up some lines and casually wrote them out.

"I've done two verses using the same rhyme sequence," she said. "I don't suppose they're much good, they're just made to order."

She handed over her poems for their inspection.

"Our four poems exhausted the subject, we couldn't have written another," they commented. "Yet here you come up with *two*. How can you have so much to say, unless you're repeating us?"

As they said this they read the poems:

> A fairy flew down last night to the capital
> And planted in a pot these flowers of rare jade,
> Like the goddess of frost who loves the cold,
> But not the wandering spirit of some chaste maid.
> Whence comes this snow on a dull autumn day?
> A night's rain stains its loveliness;
> But poets will never tire of singing it,
> That it may not pass the day in loneliness.

The others all applauded this, then went on to read the next.

> Steps through alpinia lead to an ivy-clad gate;
> Fit place, the wall's corner, for this pot set apart;
> Love of purity makes the flower hold aloof,
> Grief for the autumn breaks its owner's heart;
> Wind dries the tears on jade candles,
> Crystal screens break up its shadow cast by the moon.
> I long to tell the moon goddess its secret,
> But in the corridor night fades too soon.

The others exclaimed in delight after each line.

"See what a good idea it was to write poems on the begonia," they said. "How right we were to start our Begonia Club."

"Tomorrow let me pay my penalty by standing treat and calling the first meeting. All right?" proposed Hsiang-yun.

"Perfect!" they cried.

Then they asked her opinion of the poems written the previous day.

That evening Pao-chai invited Hsiang-yun to stay with her, and by lamplight Hsiang-yun outlined her plans for entertaining the others and setting subjects for poems. But Pao-chai thought all her proposals unsuitable.

"Since you've called a meeting, you're the hostess," she pointed out. "Although it's just fun, you must make proper provision. Do the thing cheaply but give no grounds for complaints; then everyone can have a good time.

"You're not in charge at home, and the few strings of cash you get each month hardly cover your own expenses; yet you took this on yourself quite needlessly. When your aunt hears of it she's bound to scold you. Why, your whole allowance isn't enough to stand treat. Are you going home to ask for more? Or will you ask them here for money?"

This set Hsiang-yun worrying.

"Actually, I have an idea," continued Pao-chai. "One of the assistants in our pawnshop has a farm which produces fine crabs, and the other day he sent us several catties. Most of the people here, from the old lady down to those in the Garden, are very partial to crabs. Only the other day aunt talked of inviting the old lady to the Garden to enjoy the fragrant osmanthus and eat some crabs; but she's been too busy to ask her. So don't mention the poetry club but just issue a general invitation, and after the older people have left we can write all the poems we please.

"I'll get my brother to send us a few crates of the biggest crabs with some vats of good wine from our shop, in addition to which we'll prepare four or five tables of other refreshments. That's easily done and we'll all have a good time."

Hsiang-yun was extremely grateful.

"You've thought it all out!" she exclaimed admiringly.

"I'm only thinking of *you*," replied Pao-chai. "You mustn't be touchy or imagine I look down on you, because this is between friends. If you've no objection, I'll tell them to go ahead."

"My dear cousin, you're being touchy instead if you talk like that," said Hsiang-yun. "However scatter-brained I may be, I know when someone's being good to me. At least I've *that* much sense. If I didn't look on you as my own elder sister, I wouldn't have confided to you last time all the troubles I have at home."

Accordingly Pao-chai ordered a serving-woman, "Go and ask my brother to get us several crates of big crabs like those we had the other day. Tomorrow after lunch we're inviting the old lady and my aunt to see the fragrant osmanthus in the Garden. Tell him to be sure not to forget, as I've already issued the invitations."

The old woman went off to do as she was told.

Then Pao-chai advised Hsiang-yun, "The themes for verses shouldn't be too outlandish. You can see that the poets of old times didn't go in for far-fetched subjects or freakish rhymes. Such things don't make for good poems and seem rather low-class. Of course, poetry shouldn't be stereotyped, but we mustn't overdo the emphasis on originality either. So long as our ideas are fresh, the language can't be vulgar. In any case, writing poetry isn't important. *Our* main jobs are spinning and sewing. If we've time to spare, the proper thing for us is to read a few chapters of some improving book."

Hsiang-yun, having agreed to this, suggested, "As we wrote poems on the begonia yesterday, I wonder if we could write about the chrysanthemum this time?"

"Yes, the chrysanthemum is suitable for autumn. The only objection is that too many poems have been written about it in the past."

"That's what I feel. We could hardly avoid plagiarism."

Pao-chai thought this over.

"I know," she said presently. "We'll lay stress not on the chrysanthemum but on the people looking at it, and set themes about their *reactions* to the flower. In this way we shall have tributes to the chrysanthemum as well as descriptions of feeling. This hasn't been done before and can't be too stereotyped. In fact, this combination will have freshness and distinction."

"A good idea," agreed Hsiang-yun. "But how will you introduce the feeling? Give me an example."

After a moment's thought Pao-chai replied, "*A Dream of Chrysanthemums* for instance."

"Of course. I've got one too. How about *The Chrysanthemum's Shadow?*"

"Can do, although of course it's been used before. If we have a fair number of themes we can include it. I've thought of another."

"Go on!"

"*Questioning the Chrysanthemum.*"

"Splendid!" Hsiang-yun clapped one hand on the table. "I know. How d'you like *Seeking Out the Chrysanthemum?*"

"Good. We may as well think of ten themes and write them out."

They ground ink and dipped in the brush. Hsiang-yun wrote the themes out at Pao-chai's dictation, and in no time at all they had ten. After reading them through Hsiang-yun said:

"Ten doesn't make a set. Let's have twelve while we're about it, like those albums of calligraphy and painting."

So Pao-chai thought up two more, making twelve in all.

"In this case, let's arrange them in the right order," she said.

"Better still!" cried Hsiang-yun. "We shall have a chrysanthemum album."

"We'll start with *Thinking of the Chrysanthemum.* After thinking of it we seek it out; so number two will be *Visiting the Chrysanthemum.* After finding it we plant it; so the third will be *Planting the Chrysanthemum.* After it has been planted and flowers, we face it and enjoy it; so four is *Facing the Chrysanthemum.* To enjoy it further we pick it to put in a vase; so five is *Displaying the Chrysanthemum.* But to bring out its splendour once it is displayed we must write poems about it; so six is *Writing About the Chrysanthemum.* And as a verse must be accompanied by a painting, number seven is *Painting the Chrysanthemum.* Even though we've been to so much trouble over it, we shan't know all its rare qualities unless we ask questions; so eight is *Questioning the Chrysanthemum.* If the flower seems able to understand, we are so thrilled that we want to get closer to it; hence nine is *Wearing the Chrysanthemum.*

"This exhausts all that men can do but, as there still remain certain aspects of the flower which can be described, ten and eleven are *The Chrysanthemum's Shadow* and *A Dream of*

Chrysanthemums. And we end with *The Withered Chrysanthemum* to sum up all the emotions expressed before. In this way we shall cover all the fine sights and occupations of autumn."

Hsiang-yun copied out the themes again in this order and read them through once more.

"What rhymes shall we decide on?" she asked next.

"In general I'm against a hard-and-fast rhyme pattern," replied Pao-chai. "Why should fine lines be restricted by fixed rhymes? Let's not follow that petty rule but simply set themes. We want everyone to write some fine lines for pleasure, not to make it hard for them."

"I quite agree. In this way we should write better. But there are only five of us. Will each of us have to write on all twelve of these subjects?"

"No, that would be asking too much. We'll just copy out these themes and stipulate that the seven-character *lu-shih* form is to be used. We'll put the notice on the wall tomorrow, and people can choose whichever theme they like. If anyone's able to write on all twelve, well and good; but it's all right, too, not to do any. The winner will be the one who writes best and fastest. Once all twelve are done, those who haven't finished must stop and submit to the penalty."

Hsiang-yun agreed to this and, their plans made, the two girls put out the light and went to bed.

If you want to know what followed, read the next chapter.

CHAPTER 38

The Queen of Bamboos Wins First Place
with Her Poems on Chrysanthemums
The Lady of the Alpinia Writes a Satire
upon Crabs

Having laid their plans Pao-chai and Hsiang-yun slept, and the next morning the latter invited the Lady Dowager and others over to enjoy the fragrant osmanthus.

"What a delightful, refined idea," said the old lady. "We should take advantage of such an invitation."

At noon she took Lady Wang and Hsi-feng to invite Aunt Hsueh to accompany them to the Garden, and asked:

"Which would be the best spot?"

"It's up to you to choose, madam," said Lady Wang.

"Preparations have been made in Lotus Fragrance Anchorage," put in Hsi-feng. "The two fragrant osmanthus trees at the foot of the slope there are in full bloom, the water flowing past is green and clear, and you get a fine view from the pavilion in midstream. It's refreshing to look at water."

The Lady Dowager approved and led the way to Lotus Fragrance Anchorage.

This pavilion, built in the middle of the lake, had windows on all four sides, twisting corridors on left and right leading to both shores and, behind, a winding bamboo bridge connecting it with the bank. As they stepped on to this, Hsi-feng moved forward quickly to take the old lady's arm.

"Just step out boldly, Old Ancestress," she cried. "This bamboo bridge always creaks — it doesn't matter."

Upon reaching the pavilion they saw on the balcony two bamboo tables, one laid with cups, chopsticks and wine pots, the other with a tea-service. Beside them a few maids were fanning two stoves: one to brew tea, the other to heat wine.

"Tea — splendid! This is just the place for it," remarked the Lady Dowager. "Everything here is so clean."

Hsiang-yun said with a smile, "Cousin Pao-chai helped prepare this."

"Yes, I always say she's most provident, that child, and thinks of everything."

As the old lady made this observation, she noticed two inscriptions inlaid in mother-of-pearl on the black lacquer tablets hanging on the pillars. She asked someone to read them to her. Hsiang-yun complied:

> Magnolia oars shatter the reflections of lotus;
> Caltrops and lotus-root scent the bamboo bridge.

The Lady Dowager glanced up again at the inscription on the board above her head, then turned to Aunt Hsueh.

"When I was young we had a pavilion like this too at home," she said. "It was called Pillowed Iridescence or something of the sort. I was no bigger than these girls at that time and I used to play with my sisters there every day. Once I slipped and fell into the water and nearly drowned! They managed to pull me out, but a wooden bolt had gashed my head. That's how I got this dent the size of a finger-tip on my temple here. They were all afraid I was done for after that ducking and chill, but I recovered."

Before anyone else could comment Hsi-feng quipped, "If you hadn't, who'd be enjoying all this good fortune today? Obviously our Old Ancestress was destined from birth to good luck and a long life: that's why the gods dented her head — to hold her good luck! The God of Longevity originally had a dent in his head too, but it was so stuffed with good fortune it swelled up instead into a bump."

Before she had finished, the Lady Dowager and all the others were quite limp from laughing.

"This monkey's so dreadfully spoilt, she even makes fun of me," declared the old lady. "I ought to tear out that glib tongue of yours."

"We'll presently be eating crabs," said Hsi-feng. "I was afraid you might have indigestion if I didn't first make you laugh. If you're in good spirits it doesn't matter eating a little more."

"I'll make you stay with me day and night to keep me laughing," threatened the Lady Dowager. "I won't let you go home."

"It's because you're so fond of her, madam, that she's so spoilt," interposed Lady Wang. "And by talking like that you'll make her even worse."

"I like her as she is." The old lady chuckled. "Besides, she never really oversteps the mark. When we've no visitors we *should* joke and chat, so long as the young people don't break the main rules of propriety. Why should we expect them to behave like angels?"

Now that everyone was in the pavilion tea was served, after which Hsi-feng set the tables. The one at the head was for the Lady Dowager, Aunt Hsueh, Pao-chai, Tai-yu and Pao-yu; that on the east for Hsiang-yun, Lady Wang, Ying-chun, Tan-chun and Hsi-chun; and the small one near the door on the west for Li Wan and Hsi-feng. The seats at this were unoccupied, however, as they were waiting on the tables of the Lady Dowager and Lady Wang.

"Don't bring too many crabs," Hsi-feng told the maids. "Fetch us ten and keep the rest in the steamer, to be brought in as we need them."

Having called for water to wash her hands, she stood by the old lady and shelled a crab, offering the meat to Aunt Hsueh. But the latter declined it.

"Please don't trouble," she said. "I prefer to do it myself."

So Hsi-feng gave this crab to the Lady Dowager, the second to Pao-yu. She then sent for piping hot wine and ordered some young maids to fetch powdered green beans scented with chrysanthemum leaves and fragrant osmanthus, for use when they washed their hands.

Hsiang-yun, after eating one crab with her guests, left her seat to help the others and also went outside to give instructions that two dishes of crabs should be sent to the concubines Chao and Chou.

"You're not used to entertaining," said Hsi-feng coming over to her. "Go back and eat while I look after your guests for you. I'll eat after they've left."

But Hsiang-yun, declining this offer, had two more tables placed on the balcony for Yuan-yang, Hu-po, Tsai-hsia, Tsai-yun and Ping-erh.

"Since you're seeing to things here, madam," said Yuan-yang to Hsi-feng, "we may as well go and eat."

"Yes, go along, all of you. Leave everything to me."

At that Hsiang-yun went back to her seat and, after Hsi-feng and Li Wan had eaten a few hurried mouthfuls as a matter of form, Hsi-feng left the table again to do the honours. Presently she stepped out on to the balcony where the maids were enjoying the crabs. At her approach they rose and Yuan-yang asked:

"Why have you come out here, madam? Do let us enjoy our crabs in peace!"

"This little bitch has become quite impossible!" cried Hsi-feng laughing. "Instead of thanking me for doing your job, you're complaining. Hurry up and pour me some wine."

Smiling, Yuan-yang made haste to fill a cup and hold it to her lips. Hsi-feng tossed it off. Then Hu-po and Tsai-hsia poured two more cups and held them to her lips, and she drank them too. By this time Ping-erh had ready a shellful of yellow crab meat.

"Add plenty of ginger and vinegar," said Hsi-feng. And when this was eaten she told them, "Sit down and go on with your meal. I'm leaving you."

"How shameless!" Yuan-yang tittered. "Cadging from *us*."

"You'd better behave," warned Hsi-feng. "You know your Master Lien is in love with you and means to ask the old lady to let him have you as his concubine."

"Bah!" Yuan-yang spat out. "What a way for a lady to talk! I'm going to smear your face with my dirty hands to get even."

She stood up as if to carry out her threat.

"Let me off this time, good sister!" pleaded Hsi-feng.

"If Yuan-yang becomes a concubine, Ping-erh will make things hot for her." Hu-po giggled. "Just look at her. She's drunk a whole saucer of vinegar with less than two crabs — that's soured her."

Ping-erh had just scooped out the yellow flesh of a crab, and at this gibe she aimed it at Hu-po's face, laughing.

"You foul-mouthed bitch!" she swore.

Hu-po giggled and dodged so that Ping-erh, stumbling forward, smeared Hsi-feng's cheek with the crab flesh. Hsi-feng, still joking with Yuan-yang, cried out with a start which made everyone burst out laughing. Unable to help joining in herself, she cursed:

"Damn slut! Have you no eyes that you smear anyone?"

Ping-erh hastily wiped Hsi-feng's face and went to fetch water.

"Gracious Buddha!" cried Yuan-yang. "This is just retribution."

"What's happened?" called the Lady Dowager. "What are you laughing at? Let us into the joke."

Yuan-yang and the others, still shaking with mirth, called back loudly, "Madam Lien came here to steal our crabs. Then Ping-erh flared up and smeared her face with yellow crab meat. Now mistress and maid are scrapping."

Amid general laughter the Lady Dowager said, "Do take pity on the poor thing and give her some of the smaller legs and innards."

Yuan-yang cheerfully assented and cried loudly, "The table is covered with legs. Just help yourself, madam."

Then Hsi-feng, having washed her face, went back to wait on the Lady Dowager.

Tai-yu, the only one afraid to eat much, had contented herself with a little meat from the pincers, after which she left the table.

As soon as the old lady had had enough they all left their places to wash their hands, then strolled off to look at the flowers, play with the water or watch the fish.

"It's windy here, and you've just been eating crab, madam," said Lady Wang presently to her mother-in-law. "You'd better go back and rest. If you've enjoyed this you can come again tomorrow."

"Very well," replied the Lady Dowager. "I didn't want to spoil your fun by leaving; but since you suggest it, let's go." She turned to Hsiang-yun. "Don't let your cousins Pao-yu and Tai-yu eat too much." When Hsiang-yun agreed, she advised her and Pao-chai, "You two had better not eat too much either. Crabs are delicious but not very wholesome. If you overeat you'll have a stomach-ache."

Having assented and seen her out of the Garden, they returned and ordered the tables to be cleared and reset.

"There's no need for that," Pao-yu objected. "It's time to write poems now. Just put the wine and dishes on the big round table in the middle there. You needn't assign seats either. We can help ourselves and sit wherever we please. Wouldn't that be more comfortable?"

"An excellent idea," Pao-chai approved.

"That's all very well," said Hsiang-yun, "but we mustn't forget the others."

She had another table set and more hot crabs brought for Hsi-jen, Tzu-chuan, Ssu-chi, Tai-shu, Ju-hua, Ying-erh and Tsui-mo. Two rugs were spread at the foot of the slope under the fragrant osmanthus trees for the serving-women and the younger maids, who were urged to eat and drink as much as they liked and not to come unless called.

Then Hsiang-yun pinned the themes on one wall. And the others crowding round to look exclaimed:

"How original! But this isn't going to be easy."

She explained why they had chosen no definite rhymes.

"Quite right too," approved Pao-yu. "I don't like hard-and-fast rhyme schemes either."

As Tai-yu did not want much wine or crab, she sent her maid for an embroidered cushion and sat by the balustrade angling for fish. Pao-chai played for a while with a spray of fragrant osmanthus, then leaned out of the window to toss some petals into the water so that the fish would come and nibble at them. Hsiang-yun roused herself from a brown study to urge Hsi-jen's party and the maids at the foot of the slope to eat their fill. Tan-chun, Li Wan and Hsi-chun stood in the shade of the willows watching the waterfowl, while Ying-chun, standing apart in the shade of the blossom, threaded jasmine flowers with a needle.

Pao-yu first watched Tai-yu fishing, then went over to make a few remarks to Pao-chai, after which he joined Hsi-jen and the rest and sipped some wine with them while Hsi-jen prepared a shellful of meat for him.

At this point Tai-yu, laying down her rod, walked over to the table. She picked up a tarnished silver pot with a plum-blossom design and chose a tiny red soapstone cup shaped like a palm leaf. To the maid who hurried forward to pour her a drink she said:

"Go on with your meal. Let me pour my own wine, that's more fun."

By now she had poured half a cup and could see it was yellow wine.

"After eating a bit of crab I've slight indigestion," she said. "What I really want is a mouthful of hot spirits."

"There's some here," said Pao-yu promptly. He told the maids to heat a pot of spirits in which acacia flowers had been steeped.

After just one sip Tai-yu put the cup down. Pao-chai, coming over just then, picked up another cup and drank a mouthful before wetting her brush and ticking off the first title on the wall *Thinking of the Chrysanthemum,* beside which she wrote "Alpinia."

"Dear cousin," put in Pao-yu hastily. "I've got four lines already for the second. Do leave that one for me."

"I've only just taken one, yet what a fluster you're in!" replied Pao-chai mockingly.

Tai-yu silently took the brush from her and ticked off the eighth subject, *Questioning the Chrysanthemum,* as well as the eleventh, *A Dream of Chrysanthemums,* writing "Bamboo" beside them. Pao-yu, the next to take the brush, ticked off the second title *Visiting the Chrysanthemum* and wrote "Red" by it.

Tan-chun, strolling over now to look, remarked, "If no one's doing *Wearing the Chrysanthemum*, I'll try that." She wagged a finger teasingly at Pao-yu. "It's just been announced that no allusions to the inner chambers are allowed, so be careful!"

Meanwhile Hsiang-yun had come over to tick off numbers four and five, *Facing the Chrysanthemum* and *Displaying the Chrysanthemum*, next to which she wrote her name.

"You should have a pen-name too," Tan-chun objected.

"Though we've still a few pavilions and lodges at home, I'm not living there now," replied Hsiang-yun. "And there's no point in using a borrowed name."

Pao-chai countered, "Just now the old lady said your house has a water pavilion called Pillowed Iridescence. That's yours all right. Even though it's in other hands now, you're after all its old mistress."

"That's right," approved the rest.

Before Hsiang-yun could make any move, Pao-yu blotted out her name and wrote up "Iridescence" in its place.

Then, in less time than it takes for a meal, the twelve poems were finished, written out and handed to Ying-chun, who copied them out on a fresh sheet of coloured Hsueh Tao stationery,[1] adding the pen-name of the author to each. Li Wan and the others read them.

THINKING OF THE CHRYSANTHEMUM

I gaze around in the west wind, sick at heart;
A sad season this of red smartweed and white reeds;
No sign is there of autumn by the bare fence round
    my plot,
Yet I dream of attenuated blooms in the frost.
My heart follows the wild geese back to the distant
    south,
Sitting lonely at dusk I hear pounding of washing
    blocks.
Who will pity me pining away for the yellow flowers?
On the Double Ninth Festival they will reappear.
                    The Lady of the Alpinia

---

[1] Hsueh Tao, a Tang Dynasty poetess, made beautiful stationery.

VISITING THE CHRYSANTHEMUM

Seize the chance to ramble out on a clear frosty day
Rather than linger over wine or tea.
Who has planted this flower before the frost under
the moonlight?
Whence springs this autumn glory by balustrade and
fence?
Waxed sandals patter, come gaily from far away,
In soaring spirits he chants endless poems;
If the yellow bloom will take pity on the poet,
Let it welcome him with a string of cash hung from
his cane.

The Happy Red Prince

PLANTING CHRYSANTHEMUMS

With my hoe I moved them from their bed in autumn
To plant them by the fence before my court;
An unexpected rain last night revived them,
How good to see them flower in this morning's frost.
I chant a thousand poems to this autumn splendour
And drunk with wine toast its cold fragrance,
Seal its roots with mud and water it with spring water
To keep it free from dust by the three paths to the
house of the recluse.

The Happy Red Prince

FACING THE CHRYSANTHEMUM

Brought from another plot, more precious than gold,
One clump is pale, one dark;
Sitting bareheaded by the lonely fence,
In the cold clean scent I hug my knees and chant.
None, surely, in the world as proud as you;
I alone, it seems, know your worth.
We should make the most of autumn, gone so soon,
And facing you I treasure every moment.

Old Friend of Pillowed Iridescence

DISPLAYING THE CHRYSANTHEMUM

Music and wine gladly accompany
Chrysanthemum adorning a desk with style.
By the seat dewy fragrance as if from the garden path;
Tossing my book aside I face a spray of autumn.
Fresh dreams penetrate the curtain in clear frost,
Sunset in chill garden recalls a former visit.
You too disdain the world, for we share the same
taste,
Not lingering by breezy spring's peach and plum
blossom.

Old Friend of Pillowed Iridescence

WRITING ABOUT THE CHRYSANTHEMUM

Day and night the imp of poetry assails men;
Skirting the fence, leaning on the rock, they start
    chanting;
With the tip of the brush, by the rime, they write
    fine lines,
Or facing the moon croon their sweet melodies.
We may fill a page with sorrow and self-pity,
But who can put into words what autumn means?
Ever since Tao Yuan-ming of old passed judgement
This flower's worth has been sung through the
    centuries.

The Queen of Bamboos

PAINTING THE CHRYSANTHEMUM

Painting for pleasure after writing verses
One brushes on the reds and blues at random;
A thousand ink-dots form the leaves,
Traces of frost stain the clustering flowers;
Dark and light their shadows overlap in the breeze,
Under one's hand autumn exhales its fragrance.
Don't think these flowers are picked by the east
    fence,
They are fixed to the screen for the Double Ninth
    Festival.

The Lady of the Alpinia

QUESTIONING THE CHRYSANTHEMUM

My questions about autumn none can answer,
Musing alone I stroll to the eastern fence.
Proud recluse, with what hermit are you taking
    refuge?
All flowers must bloom, what makes you bloom
    so late?
So lonely in dewy gardens and frosty courts,
When swans fly off, crickets chirp, does your heart
    ache?
Say not there is none in the world worth talking to;
Since you understand, why don't we chat awhile?

The Queen of Bamboos

WEARING THE CHRYSANTHEMUM

Busy every day planting by the fence, picking
    for vases,
Not to adorn himself before the mirror,
The young lord of Changan is infatuated with flowers,
Just as the poet of Pengtse[1] was crazy for wine.

---

[1] Tao Chien or Tao Yuan-ming, famous Tsin Dynasty poet.

His short hair is wet with cold dew from the path,
His coarse cap stained with autumn frost and
fragrance;
This eccentric recluse is scorned by the men of today,
But let them clap their hands and jeer by the roadside.

The Stranger Under the Plantain

THE CHRYSANTHEMUM'S SHADOW

The teeming, diverse shades of autumn splendour
Quietly loiter about the mountain path;
The few lamps inside windows far or near cast their
shadows,
Chequered patterns of moonlight filtered through
wicker fence.
The soul of cold fragrance should dwell in these
reflections,
Empty even in dreams the frost tracery of their spirit;
Tread softly and take good care of this dark
sweetness,
For who can discern it in his drunken eyes?

Old Friend of Pillowed Iridescence

A DREAM OF CHRYSANTHEMUMS

A refreshing sleep by the fence while autumn mellows
And clouds and moonlight mingle hazily;
No need to envy Chuang Tzu his butterfly dream;
Recalling old friends, let me seek out Tao Yuan-ming.
In sleep the vision recedes with the flight of swans,
Aroused with a start we resent the chirp of crickets;
Awake, to whom can I describe my grief,
The infinite melancholy of cold mist and withered
grass?

The Queen of Bamboos

THE WITHERED CHRYSANTHEMUM

Slowly drooping below congealed dew and heavy frost
Just after a feast in its honour on the Day of Light
Snow,
The pale golden petals still retain some fragrance,
But the marred green leaves are withering on the stem.
Crickets chirp sadly under denuded boughs,
Wild geese wing slowly through far-flung frosty
clouds;
Next year in autumn we shall meet again,
No need to sorrow over this brief parting.

The Stranger Under the Plantain

As they read each poem they praised it, heaping compliments
on each other.

"Let me try to pass fair judgement now," said Li Wan with a smile. "On the whole each poem has striking lines but, speaking impartially, I rank *Writing About the Chrysanthemum* first, *Questioning the Chrysanthemum* second, and *A Dream of Chrysanthemums* third; for all three show originality in the theme, ideas and style. The Queen of Bamboos will have to be given first place. Next in order of merit come *Wearing the Chrysanthemum, Facing the Chrysanthemum, Displaying the Chrysanthemum, Painting the Chrysanthemum* and *Thinking of the Chrysanthemum.*"

Pao-yu clapped his hands in delight at this, exclaiming, "Absolutely right. Very fair."

"Mine didn't amount to much," Tai-yu observed. "They're rather contrived."

"But aptly so," rejoined Li Wan. "Not stiff and overloaded."

"To my mind," continued Tai-yu, "the best line of all is 'Sunset in chill garden recalls a former visit' which presents such a strong contrast. And 'Tossing my book aside I face a spray of autumn' is perfect, leaving nothing more to be said about displaying chrysanthemums, so that she had to revert to the time before the flower was plucked and put in the vase. Very penetrating, very subtle."

"Quite so. Still, your line about 'sweet melodies' is even better," countered Li Wan.

Tan-chun put in, "And what about the Lady of the Alpinia? 'No sign is there of autumn' and 'yet in dream I see' bring out the idea of nostalgia so vividly."

Pao-chai smiled and replied, "Your 'short hair wet with cold dew' and 'coarse cap stained with fragrance' do full justice to the subject too."

Hsiang-yun remarked gaily, "Questions like 'With what hermit are you taking refuge?' and 'What makes you bloom so late?' are bound to stump the flower."

Li Wan retorted, "I daresay your sitting bareheaded and hugging your knees while you chant, refusing to leave, would get on the flower's nerves too — if it had any."

At that there was general laughter.

"I'm last again," said Pao-yu cheerfully. "But surely my 'Who has planted this flower?' 'Whence springs this autumn glory?', 'waxed sandals come from far away,' and 'chants endless poems' describe visiting the chrysanthemum all right? And don't 'rain last night' and 'this morning's frost' describe the planting? It's just that they're not up to such images as 'facing the moon croon their sweet melodies,' 'In the cold clean scent I hug my knees and chant,' 'short hair,' 'coarse cap,' 'pale gold,' 'the marred green leaves are withering,' 'no sign is there of autumn' and 'seen in dreams.'" He added, "Tomorrow when I've time, I mean to write on all twelve themes."

"Your verses aren't bad," Li Wan told him. "They're not as distinctive as the others though."

After some further discussion of the poems they called for more hot crabs and sat round the big table to eat.

"Now that we're enjoying the fragrant osmanthus and eating crabs, we should write verses about this too," said Pao-yu presently. "I've already made one. Who else is game?"

With that he hastily washed his hands and wrote out his poem for the others.

EATING CRABS

How fine to eat crabs in the cool shade of osmanthus;
Gaily we pile on ginger, splash vinegar on each part;
A true gourmand should also have wine;
But this creature scuttling sidewise has no heart.
In our greed we forget how hard it is to digest,
Our fingers washed, the reek of its oil will remain;
The crab's sole function is to please men's palate,
And Su Tung-po[1] laughed because its whole life it's
    busy in vain.

"If you call that a poem," scoffed Tai-yu, "I can write you a hundred."

"No, you've exhausted your talent, you can't write any more. All you can do is to disparage other people."

Instead of answering and without stopping to think, she picked up the brush and promptly wrote a verse:

---

[1] Su Shih, Sung Dynasty poet.

Girt even in death with iron armour and long spears,
On the plate, delicious, it's sat,
Its pincers packed with meat like tender jade,
Its shell bulging with red, tasty fat.
How I love those eight succulent legs —
But who'll urge me to drink a thousand cups till
    my grief is overcome?
Let us toast this dainty at our feast today
When breeze ruffles fragrant osmanthus and frost
    gathers on chrysanthemum.

Pao-yu reading this was loud in his praise, but Tai-yu tore
it up and told the maids to burn it.

"Mine isn't as good as yours, so I'm burning it," she told
him with a smile. "Yours is fine. Better than your chrysanthemum poems. You should keep it to show other people."

"I've made a feeble attempt too," Pao-chai put in with a
laugh. "It's not much good, but I'll write it out to amuse you."

She did so and they read:

We sit, cups raised, in the shade of osmanthus and
    Wu-tung;
Mouths watering, for the Double Ninth we pine;
It crawls sidewise because the ways of the world
    are crooked,
And, white and yellow, harbours a dark design.

They all exclaimed at this point in admiration.

"That's the style!" cried Pao-yu. "My verse will have to
be burned too."

Then they read on:

Wine won't purge the smell without chrysanthemums,
And ginger is needed dyspepsia to prevent;
What can it do now, fallen into the cauldron?
On the moonlit bank all that remains is the millet's
    scent.

"It takes real talent to get deep significance into such a small
subject as eating crabs," the others commented. "But as a
satire, this is rather hard on the world!"

They were interrupted by Ping-erh's return to the Garden.
To know what her business was, you must read the next chapter.

CHAPTER 39

An Old Village Woman Tells
Tall Stories
A Romantic Youth Insists on
Following Them Up

On Ping-erh's return she was asked, "What's your mistress doing? Why hasn't she come back?"

"She's too busy," replied Ping-erh, smiling. "As she didn't get a chance to eat properly and can't come, she's sent me to ask whether there are any crabs left. If so, I'm to take a few back for her to eat."

"There are plenty left," Hsiang-yun assured her.

She promptly ordered ten of the largest crabs to be brought.

"Mostly female ones if you please!" added Ping-erh.

They tried to make her take a seat, but she refused.

"We insist!" cried Li Wan laughingly.

She forced her on to the seat beside her own, filled a cup with wine and held it to her lips. But after one hurried sip Ping-erh rose to go.

"Oh no, you don't," said Li Wan. "I can see the only one who counts for you is Hsi-feng. You won't listen to what *I* say."

She ordered some matrons to deliver the hamper of crabs and tell Hsi-feng that she was keeping Ping-erh there.

Presently a matron returned with the empty hamper.

"Madam Lien says you and the young ladies mustn't laugh at her greediness, madam," she reported. "In this hamper are some caltrop cakes and chicken-fat rolls sent by Aunt Wang for you, madam, and the young ladies." She then turned to Ping-erh. "She says she knew, once she sent you here, you'd stay to amuse yourself; but you mustn't drink too much."

"And what if I do?" retorted Ping-erh, as she went on helping herself to wine and crab.

"Such a lovely girl!" cried Li Wan, taking her arm. "What a pity she's fated to wait on other people. Anyone not in the know would take you for the mistress of the house."

Ping-erh, eating and drinking with Pao-chai and Hsiangyun, turned her head to protest with a smile, "Don't tickle me, madam."

"My, what are these hard things?" asked Li Wan.

"Keys," was the answer.

"Why, what valuables are you afraid of people stealing that you carry these keys about on you? It's as I always say: When Monk Tripitaka[1] was searching for Buddhist scriptures, a white horse turned up to carry him; when Liu Chih-yuan[2] was fighting for the empire, a melon spirit appeared to give him armour. In the same way, Hsi-feng has you. You're her master-key. What does she want these keys for?"

Ping-erh laughed.

"Now you're making fun of me in your cups, madam."

"It's true all the same," said Pao-chai. "When we've nothing to do but gossip, we always agree that each single one of you girls is one in a hundred. And the wonderful thing is that each one of you has her own good qualities."

"Providence orders all things, great and small," chimed in Li Wan. "For instance, what would the old lady do without Yuan-yang? Nobody else, not even Lady Wang, dares contradict the old lady; but when Yuan-yang does, the old lady listens to her. Nobody else can remember all the clothes and trinkets the old lady has, but Yuan-yang remembers. If not for her being in charge, goodness knows how many things would have been swindled out of them. Even so, the girl's broad-minded and instead of throwing her weight about she often puts in a good word for others."

---

[1] Monk Hsuan Tsang of the Tang Dynasty.
[2] King of the Later Han in the Five Dynasties Period.

"Only yesterday," remarked Hsi-chun with a smile, "the old lady was saying she's better than any of us."

"She's really fine," agreed Ping-erh. "We others can't compare with her."

"Tsai-hsia in my mother's apartments is an honest girl too," put in Pao-yu.

"Yes, she appears simple," said Tan-chun, "yet she's smart. Her Ladyship is as unworldly as a Buddha, but if she overlooks anything Tsai-hsia sees to it for her. She keeps an eye on everything down to the least details of our father's affairs at home and outside. So if her mistress forgets anything she quietly reminds her."

"True enough," said Li Wan. She pointed at Pao-yu. "And think what would happen in *this* young gentleman's rooms, if not for Hsi-jen's good judgement. As for Hsi-feng, why, even if she had the strength of the Conqueror of Chu who could lift a tripod weighing a thousand catties, how could she handle everything without Ping-erh here?"

"Four of us came with our mistress at the time of her marriage," said Ping-erh. "But the others have either died or gone, so that now I'm the only one left."

"So much the better for you as well as for Hsi-feng," commented Li Wan. "When your Master Chu was alive we had two maids too, and I'm not the jealous type, am I? But they bickered so much every day that after his death I married them both off while they were still young. If there'd been just one worth keeping, I'd have someone to help me now." Tears ran down her cheeks.

"Why let this upset you?" said the others. "You're better off without them."

So saying they washed their hands and went to pay their respects to the Lady Dowager and Lady Wang. While the other maids swept the pavilion and cleared away the cups and dishes, Hsi-jen took Ping-erh back with her to her room. And once seated there she asked her:

"Why has no one received the allowance for this month yet?"

"It'll be coming in a couple of days," Ping-erh whispered. "My mistress got this month's allowance some time ago but has loaned it out. She'll distribute it as soon as she's collected the interest. But mind you don't pass this on."

"I can't believe she's short of money. Why should she put herself to all that trouble?"

Ping-erh smiled.

"These last few years she's been lending out this money for the monthly allowances together with her own. The interest she gets on these loans comes to more than a thousand taels of silver a year."

"So the two of you, mistress and maid, have been using our money to get interest and kept us waiting like regular fools!" said Hsi-jen with a smile.

"There you go again, talking in that heartless way! You're not short, are you?"

"No, I'm not. *I've* nothing to spend money on, but I need a reserve for him."

"If you need money urgently, I still have a few taels you can be going on with. I'll deduct it later from your allowance."

"I don't need any at the moment, but if we run out I'll send somebody to fetch it."

Ping-erh, having agreed to this, left the Garden and returned to her own quarters.

Hsi-feng was out when she got back. But seated in her room, accompanied by the wives of Chang Tsai and Chou Jui, were Granny Liu and Pan-erh who had called before to ask for help. A few maids were emptying on to the floor some sacks of dates, pumpkins and other farm produce. They stood up when Ping-erh came in.

Granny Liu, who knew Ping-erh's status from her last visit, scrambled off the *kang* to greet her.

"All at home send their compliments," she said. "We'd have come before this to pay our respects to the mistress and to you, miss, but we've been very busy on the farm. This year we managed to get in a couple of piculs more of grain and a good crop of pumpkins, fruit and vegetables. These here are our first pickings. We didn't like to sell them but kept the best for you to taste. You young ladies must be tired of the delicacies you eat every day, and you may care to try our country fare. This is just our poor way of showing our gratitude."

Ping-erh thanked her for her trouble and asked her to take a seat. Having sat down herself she urged Mrs. Chang and Mrs. Chou to be seated too, then told a maid to bring tea.

"You're rather flushed today, miss," remarked the stewards' wives. "Why, even your eyes are red."

"I know," replied Ping-erh. "I really can't drink, but Madam Li Wan and the young ladies simply forced me. I had to swallow one or two cups, which made my face red."

"I wouldn't mind a drink myself, but nobody treats me," joked Mrs. Chang. "Next time you get an invitation, miss, I hope you'll take me along."

Everybody laughed.

"I saw those crabs this morning," remarked Mrs. Chou. "I reckon two or three of them must weigh a catty. Three big crates like those must have weighed nearly eighty catties." She added, "Still, I don't suppose there were enough for everyone, high and low."

"Of course not," said Ping-erh. "Only people of some consequence had a couple. Of the others, some were lucky and some weren't."

"Crabs that size cost five silver cents a catty this year," put in Granny Liu. "That's fifty cents for ten catties. Five times fifty makes two taels fifty; three times five makes fifteen. Together with the wine and eatables, that adds up to more than twenty taels of silver. Gracious Buddha! That's enough to keep us country folk for a whole year."

"Have you seen our mistress yet?" Ping-erh asked her.

"Yes," replied Granny Liu. "She told us to wait." Looking out of the window at the sky she added, "It's getting late. We ought to be going. If we found the city gate closed we'd be in a fine fix."

"True," said Mrs. Chou. "I'll go and see what she's doing."

She went out and reappeared after some time, beaming.

"Luck must be with you today, granny," she announced. "The two ladies have taken quite a fancy to you."

Ping-erh and the others asked her what she meant.

"Madam Lien was with the old lady," replied Mrs. Chou. "I told her quietly, 'Granny Liu wants to leave, so as to reach the city gate before it's closed.' She said, 'She's come all that way with a load of things; let her spend the night here and go back tomorrow.' Doesn't that show she's taken a fancy to you?

"That's not all either. The old lady happened to overhear us and asked, 'Who's this Granny Liu?' When that was explained by Madam Lien she said, 'I've been wanting to have a chat with some experienced old soul. Ask her over to see me.' Who could have imagined such a stroke of luck?"

She urged Granny Liu to go at once to the Lady Dowager.

"I'm not fit to be seen," objected Granny Liu. "Good sister, just tell her I've left."

"Go on, don't worry about that," said Ping-erh. "Our old lady is goodness itself to the old and needy. She's not haughty and high-handed like some people. If you're shy, Mrs. Chou and I can come with you."

So she and Chou Jui's wife set out with Granny Liu for the Lady Dowager's quarters.

When the pages on duty at the inner gate saw Ping-erh, they all stood at attention. Then two of them ran over to her, calling out a respectful greeting.

"Now what is it?" she asked.

"It's late, miss," said one boy, smiling. "My mother's ill and wants me to go for a doctor. Can I have a few hours off, please?"

"A fine lot you are," cried Ping-erh. "Ganging up to ask for leave in turn every day, and not reporting to the mistress either but pestering me instead. After Chu-erh went the other day, Master Lien happened to call for him; and when he wasn't to be found I was blamed for giving him leave. Now *you're* trying it on."

"It's quite true that his mother is ill," Mrs. Chou confirmed. "Do let him go, miss."

"Come back early tomorrow then," stipulated Ping-erh. "And listen, I've an errand for you, so don't wait till the sun bakes your behind before coming back. And take a message for me on your way to Lai Wang. Tell him from the mistress that if he doesn't bring in the rest of that interest tomorrow, she doesn't want it — he can keep it for himself."

The boy assented and made off in high spirits.

Ping-erh and the two others proceeded then to the Lady Dowager's apartments where all the girls from the Garden were assembled. Granny Liu had no idea who all these beauties decked out with pearls and emeralds could be; but she saw an old lady on a couch with a pretty silk-clad girl massaging her legs while Hsi-feng stood chatting to her. Concluding that this was the Lady Dowager, the old woman stepped forward, smiling, and curtseyed to her.

"Greetings, Goddess of Long Life!" she cried.

The Lady Dowager raised herself to greet her in return and ordered Mrs. Chou to fetch a chair for her. Pan-erh, of course, was still too shy to pay his respects.

"How old are you, venerable kinswoman?" asked the Lady Dowager.

Granny Liu rose to answer, "Seventy-five."

"So old, yet so hale and hearty! Why, you're older than I am by several years. If I live to your age, I doubt whether I shall be so spry."

"We're born to put up with hardships, madam, and you to enjoy good fortune," replied Granny Liu with a smile. "If we were all like you, who'd do the farming?"

"And your eyes and teeth, are they still good?"

"I can't complain. But this year one of my back teeth on the left side has come loose."

"I'm old and useless now," rejoined the Lady Dowager. "My sight's failing, I'm hard of hearing, and my memory's going. I can't even remember all our old relatives. When they call I don't see them for fear they'll laugh at me, I've become so helpless. All I can do is eat pap, sleep, or amuse myself for a while with these grandchildren when I'm bored."

Granny Liu smiled.

"That's your good fortune, madam. We couldn't manage it even if we wanted to."

"Good fortune? I'm nothing but a useless old thing."

Everyone laughed at that.

"Just now Hsi-feng told me you've brought us a lot of pumpkins and vegetables," the Lady Dowager went on. "I've asked to have them cooked at once. I've been longing for some freshly picked things of this kind. Those we buy outside aren't as good as yours, straight from the fields."

"This is rough country fare but at least it's fresh," Granny Liu answered. "We'd rather eat meat and fish ourselves, only we can't afford it."

"Now that we relatives have met, you mustn't leave with nothing to show for your visit. If you don't dislike our place, do stay for a couple of days. We have a garden too with fruit in it. Tomorrow you must try some and take some home, to show you've visited your relatives here."

Hsi-feng also pressed Granny Liu to stay, seeing what a liking the old lady had taken to her.

"Though our place here isn't as large as your farm we have a couple of empty rooms," she said. "Do stay for a day or two, and tell our old lady some of your village news and stories."

"You're not to make fun of her, you baggage," warned the Lady Dowager. "She's an honest village woman, how can she stand up to your teasing?"

She told the maids to offer Pan-erh some fruit, but with so many people about the boy dared not eat. So she ordered them to give him some cash and sent him off to play with the pages outside. Then Granny Liu, after sipping a cup of tea, regaled the Lady Dowager with some village gossip which quite delighted her.

Granny Liu was still holding forth when Hsi-feng told a maid to invite her to dinner, and the Lady Dowager sent her some of her own dishes. Knowing how pleased the old lady was with her, Hsi-feng sent Granny Liu back again after her meal; and Yuan-yang deputed an old nurse to take her to have a bath while she picked a simple change of clothing for her. Granny Liu, who was having the time of her life, changed quickly. Then, seated in front of the Lady Dowager's couch, she found some more gossip to tell her. Pao-yu and the girls were there too and never having heard such talk before they found it more diverting than the ballads of blind folk-singers.

Now Granny Liu though a countrywoman was no fool. Besides, being old and experienced she could see how delighted the old lady was and how eagerly the young people were listening. So when she ran out of gossip she drew on her imagination.

"In our village we grow grain and vegetables year in, year out," she said. "Spring, summer, autumn and winter, in wind and rain, what time have we to sit idle? We just knock off for a rest each day in the fields, and I can assure you we see all kinds of queer doings.

"Last winter, for example, the snow fell for several days on end and piled up on the ground three or four feet deep. I got up early one day and hadn't yet left the house when I heard a noise from the woodpile. I peeped through the window, thinking it must be someone filching our firewood. But it wasn't anybody from our village."

"I suppose it was some passer-by who felt cold," put in the Lady Dowager. "Seeing fuel ready at hand he took some to make a fire. That might well be."

"It wasn't a passer-by either," Granny Liu chortled. "That's what was so strange. Who d'you think it was, my lady? A slip of a girl of seventeen or eighteen, pretty as a picture, with hair as glossy as oil, wearing a red tunic and a white silk skirt. . . ."

Just then a sudden commotion broke out outside.

"It's not serious," someone shouted. "Don't alarm the old lady."

At once they asked what had happened. A maid explained that a fire had broken out in the stables in the south court, but there was no danger as it was now under control.

The Lady Dowager, being very easily frightened, got up quickly and made them help her out to the verandah. At sight of flames in the southeast part of the grounds she invoked Buddha in her terror, then ordered incense to be burned to the God of Fire. Lady Wang and the others hurried over to the Lady Dowager's apartments to comfort her.

"It'll soon be put out," they assured her. "Do go back inside, madam."

But the old lady waited till all the flames had died down before leading the whole company indoors again. At once Pao-yu asked Granny Liu:

"Why was that girl taking firewood when the snow lay so deep? Did she catch cold?"

"It was this talk about firewood that *caused* the fire," put in his grandmother. "Yet you still keep on asking about it. Don't mention it any more. Let's talk about something else."

Much against his will Pao-yu had to drop the subject, and Granny Liu thought up another tale.

"To the east of our village," she said, "there lives an old woman who's over ninety this year. She fasts and prays to Buddha every day. And would you believe it, this so moved the Goddess of Mercy that she appeared to her one night in a dream. 'You were fated to have no descendants,' she said. 'But I've told the Jade Emperor how devout you are, and he's going to give you a grandson.'

"The fact is, this old woman had only one son. This son, too, had just the one son; but they only managed to bring him up to the age of seventeen or eighteen when he died, nearly breaking their hearts. In due time, sure enough, another son was born to them. He's just fourteen now, as plump and white as a snowball and the sharpest lad you ever set eyes on. This shows, doesn't it, that there really *are* gods and spirits?"

This story was just the kind that appealed to the Lady Dowager and Lady Wang, hence even the latter listened with close attention. Pao-yu, however, was still trying to imagine what could have become of the girl who took the firewood, when he was addressed by Tan-chun.

"Yesterday Hsiang-yun treated us," she said. "When we go back let's talk over our next meeting and how to ask her back. Suppose we invite the old lady to come and look at the chrysanthemums?"

"The old lady says she means to give a party herself in return for Hsiang-yun's, and we'll be invited too," replied Pao-yu. "So we'd better wait till after that."

"If we wait until it's cold, though, the old lady may not like it."

"Why not? She enjoys rain and snow. Better wait for the first fall of snow and then ask her to a snow party. We'll have more fun ourselves too, writing poems in the snow."

"Writing poems in the snow?" put in Tai-yu mockingly. "I don't think that would be half as much fun as building a wood-pile and having a camp-fire in the snow."

Pao-chai and the others laughed, while Pao-yu flashed a glance at Tai-yu but said nothing.

As soon as the party broke up, he quietly took Granny Liu aside to ask her who the girl in her story was. This forced the old woman to improvise again.

"In the fields just north of our village there stands a small shrine," she said. "It wasn't built for any god or Buddha, but there was once a gentleman. . . ." She stopped to think of a name.

"Never mind," said Pao-yu. "Names don't matter, just tell me the story."

"This gentleman had no son, only one daughter called Ming-yu," continued Granny Liu. "She could read and write and was her parents' most precious treasure, but when she reached the age of seventeen the poor girl fell ill and died. . . ."

Pao-yu stamped his foot and sighed.

"What happened afterwards?" he asked.

"Her parents were so heartbroken that they built this shrine, had an effigy made of the girl, and kept someone there to burn incense and keep the lamp burning. That was many years ago. Those people are dead now, the temple is in ruins, and a spirit has taken possession of the effigy."

"It's not that a spirit's taken possession of it," he retorted quickly. "The rule is that people of this kind are immortal."

"You don't say! Gracious Buddha! If you hadn't told me, I'd have sworn it was magic. She often takes human form to roam about through the villages, farmsteads and highways, and it was *she* who took that firewood. In our village they're talking of smashing up this image and razing the shrine to the ground."

"Don't let them do that!" urged Pao-yu hastily. "It would be a great sin to destroy that shrine."

"I'm glad you told me, sir," said Granny Liu. "When I go back tomorrow I'll stop them."

"My grandmother and my mother are both charitable people. In fact, our whole family, old and young, like to do good deeds and give alms; and they take the greatest delight in building temples and having images made. So tomorrow I'll draw up a subscription notice to collect donations for you. When enough contributions have come in, you can take charge of repairing the shrine and restoring the image, and every month I'll give you money for incense. Wouldn't that be a good thing?"

"If you do that I'll have a few cash to spend too, all thanks to this young lady!"

Pao-yu then asked her the name of the district and village, how far it was there and back, and just where the shrine stood. She made up answers at random but he believed her, and on his return to his room he spent the whole night thinking the matter over.

The next morning, as soon as it was light, he sent Ming-yen with several hundred cash to find the place described by Granny Liu and bring him back a clear report so that he could make further plans.

Pao-yu waited hour after hour for Ming-yen's return, as frantic as an ant on a hot pan. He waited and waited till sunset, when his page came back looking very pleased with himself.

"Did you find it?" demanded Pao-yu eagerly.

"You must have got it wrong, Master Pao. You led me a
fine dance," replied Ming-yen, smiling. "It's not where you
said, and the name's different too. So it took me a whole day
to track it down. Then I found a tumbledown temple in the
fields to the north*east*."

Pao-yu beamed with joy.

"Granny Liu's old," he said. "Her memory probably plays
tricks with her. Well, what did you find? Go on!"

"The temple gate faces south all right, and the place is
tumbling down. I was fed up with hunting for it, and as soon
as I saw it I said to myself, 'At last!' I marched straight in.
One look at the image, though, made me take to my heels —
it's so fearfully lifelike!"

"She can take human form, so naturally she looks lifelike,"
replied Pao-yu cheerfully.

"But it isn't a girl." Ming-yen clapped his hands together.
"It's blue-faced and red-haired — the God of Plague!"

"You useless fool," swore Pao-yu in disgust. "You can't
handle the least little job."

"I don't know what books you've been reading, Master Pao,
or what nonsensical talk you've been swallowing, to send me
on a wild-goose chase of this sort. And now you say I'm
useless."

"Don't get so worked up," rejoined Pao-yu soothingly. "You
must try again some other day when you've time. If she was
having me on, of course there's no such place; but if there is,
you'll be doing a good deed and you can be sure I'll reward
you handsomely."

Just then a page from the inner gate announced, "Some girls
from the old lady's apartments are waiting for you, Master Pao,
at the inner gate."

If you want to know what this meant, read the next chapter.

CHAPTER 40

The Lady Dowager Feasts Again
in Grand View Garden
Yuan-yang Presides over
a Drinking Game

Pao-yu hurried over at this summons and found Hu-po by the screen.

"Come quickly," she urged him. "The old lady's waiting for you."

He went to the Lady Dowager's apartments, where she was discussing with Lady Wang and the girls how to repay Hsiang-yun's hospitality.

"I've a suggestion," said Pao-yu. "As we're not inviting outsiders, there's no need for too many dishes; let's just have a few we like. There's no need for tables either; each of us can have a teapoy with a couple of dishes we fancy, as well as a ten-compartment box of titbits and a winepot apiece. Wouldn't that be more original?"

The Lady Dowager approved. She sent instructions to the kitchen to prepare their favourite dainties the next day and put them in separate boxes, and to serve breakfast in the Garden too. By the time this was settled the lamps were lit, and they retired for the night.

The next morning, as luck would have it, the weather was fine. Li Wan rose at daybreak to supervise the matrons and maids as they swept up fallen leaves, dusted tables and chairs, and prepared the tea-services and wine vessels. While she was doing this, Feng-erh arrived with Granny Liu and Pan-erh.

"How busy you are, madam!" remarked Granny Liu.

"I knew you wouldn't be able to leave yesterday," replied Li Wan with a smile. "Yet you were in such a hurry to get away."

"The old lady made me stay to enjoy myself for a day," chuckled Granny Liu.

Feng-erh produced a bunch of keys and announced, "Madam Lien says there may not be enough teapoys out: we'd better unlock the attic in the tower and fetch some down to use for a day. She wanted to see to it herself, but she's talking with Lady Wang. So do you mind opening the attic, madam, and having the things brought out?"

Li Wan made Su-yun take the keys, and sent one of the matrons to fetch a few page boys from the inner gate. Standing with raised head at the foot of Grand View Pavilion, she ordered them to go up and open the Tower of Variegated Splendour and carry down the teapoys one by one. Pages, matrons and maids set to work then to bring down more than twenty, while Li Wan warned:

"Careful! Steady on! You're not being chased by ghosts. Mind you don't bump them."

Then she turned to ask Granny Liu, "Would you care to go up too and have a look?"

The old woman needed no pressing but promptly pulled Pan-erh up the stairs with her. She found the attic chock-a-block with screens, tables, chairs, ornamental lanterns large and small, and other similar objects. Although ignorant of the function of most of them, she was dazzled by their gay colours and fine workmanship.

"Gracious Buddha!" she exclaimed.

When she withdrew the door was locked and everyone came down.

Then it occurred to Li Wan that the old lady might feel disposed to go boating. So on her instructions they unlocked the door once more and brought down oars, punt-poles and awnings. Pages were also sent to the boatwomen to order two barges from the boathouse.

In the middle of this bustle, along came the Lady Dowager with a whole company of people.

"How bright and early you are, madam!" cried Li Wan hurrying to meet her. "I didn't think you'd have finished your toilet yet. I'd just picked some chrysanthemums to send you."

Pi-yueh held out a large emerald plate in the form of a lotus leaf, on which were chrysanthemums of different kinds. The Lady Dowager selected a red one and pinned it in her hair. Then, turning, she caught sight of Granny Liu.

"Come here and take a few flowers to wear!" she called with a smile.

While the words were still on her lips, Hsi-feng pulled Granny Liu forward.

"Let me make you beautiful, granny!" she cried.

Seizing all the flowers on the plate, she stuck them this way and that in the old woman's hair, reducing everyone present to helpless laughter.

"I don't know what meritorious deed my head's done to deserve this good fortune," cackled Granny Liu. "What a dash I'm cutting today!"

"Why don't you pull them out and throw them in her face?" gasped the others. "She's got you up to look a real old vampire."

"I'm old now, but when I was young I was flighty too and fond of flowers," chuckled Granny Liu. "So it's right I should be an old flibbertigibbet today."

While laughing and chatting they had come to Seeping Fragrance Pavilion. Maids spread a large brocade cushion they had brought on the railing of the balcony. The Lady Dowager, seating herself there with her back against a pillar, made Granny Liu sit beside her.

"Well, what do you think of this garden?" she inquired.

"Gracious Buddha!" ejaculated Granny Liu. "We country folk come to town before New Year to buy pictures to stick up; and when we're at a loose end we often say, 'If only we could take a stroll in these pictures!' We always reckoned the places shown were too good to be true, but coming to this garden today I can see it's ten times better than any painting.

I wish someone would paint me a picture of it to show the folk at home. Then I'd die content."

The Lady Dowager pointed to Hsi-chun. "See this young grand-daughter of mine?" she asked. "She can paint. Shall I get her to do a painting for you tomorrow?"

This offer so delighted Granny Liu that she hurried over to take Hsi-chun's hand.

"Why, miss! So young and pretty, yet so clever too — you must be a goddess come down to the earth."

After a short rest the Lady Dowager started showing Granny Liu round, going first to Bamboo Lodge. Inside its gate, a narrow pebbled path flanked with bamboos met their gaze. The ground on either side of it was carpeted with dark moss. Granny Liu left the path for the others, walking on the verge herself.

"Come up here, granny," urged Hu-po taking her arm. "That moss is slippery."

"That's all right, I'm used to it," said the old woman. "Just go ahead, young ladies. Take care not to get your embroidered slippers dirty."

Intent on talking, she slipped and fell with a thud, at which the whole company clapped their hands and laughed.

"You wretches!" scolded the Lady Dowager. "Help her up. Don't just stand there laughing."

"That was to punish me for boasting," chuckled Granny Liu as she scrambled to her feet.

"Did you strain your back?" asked the Lady Dowager. "Let one of the maids pummel it."

"I'm not so finicky. Hardly a day goes by without my falling. How could I get someone to pummel my back each time?"

Tzu-chuan had the bamboo portière raised ready for them. The Lady Dowager and others went in and took seats, after which Tai-yu with her own hands brought her grandmother a covered bowl of tea on a small tray.

"No tea for *us*," said Lady Wang. "Don't trouble to pour any more."

Then Tai-yu told a maid to fetch her favourite chair from the window for Lady Wang. Granny Liu, meanwhile, was struck by the brushes and inkstones on the desk by the window and the bookcase piled with books.

"This must be the young master's study," she said.

The Lady Dowager smiled and pointed at Tai-yu.

"This is my grand-daughter's room."

Granny Liu looked intently at Tai-yu.

"This isn't like a young lady's chamber," she remarked. "But it's far better than the best study."

"Where *is* Pao-yu?" asked the Lady Dowager.

"Boating on the lake," the maids told her.

"Who ordered boats?"

"I did," replied Li Wan hastily. "As we were fetching things from the attic just now, it occurred to me you might feel inclined for a turn on the lake, madam."

Before the old lady could answer, Aunt Hsueh was announced. And even as they rose to their feet she came in. When they had resumed their seats she remarked:

"You must be in good spirits, madam, to have come here so early."

"Only a minute ago I was saying all late-comers must be fined," the Lady Dowager chuckled. "I'd no idea the offender would be you."

They chatted for a while. Then the Lady Dowager noticed that the gauze on the window had faded.

"This gauze is pretty when new," she remarked to Lady Wang, "but it soon loses its vivid emerald colour. Anyway, as there are no peach or apricot trees in this courtyard and the bamboos are green themselves, green gauze is out of place here. We used to have window gauze in four or five colours, I remember. Tomorrow we shall have to change this for her."

"When I opened the storeroom yesterday," put in Hsi-feng, "I saw several rolls of pink cicada-wing gauze in one of the chests. There are several different designs — sprays of blossom, floating clouds and bats, butterflies and flowers — the colours so vivid and the gauze so soft, I've never seen anything like it. I took out two rolls, thinking they'd make good coverlets."

"Bah!" the Lady Dowager snorted. "Everybody says there's nothing you haven't seen or done, but you don't even know what this gauze is. You must stop bragging in future."

"However knowledgeable she may be, she can't compare with you, madam," said Aunt Hsueh. "Do enlighten her and let us hear as well."

"Yes, good Ancestress, do enlighten me," begged Hsi-feng smiling.

Then the Lady Dowager told them all, "That gauze is older than any of you. No wonder she mistook it for cicada-wing gauze. As a matter of fact, the two are so alike that those not in the know always mix them up. Its proper name is soft-mist silk."

"What a charming name," cried Hsi-feng. "I've seen hundreds of kinds of silk, but never heard of this one."

"How long have *you* lived?" retorted the old lady. "How many rarities have you seen? What have *you* to brag about? This soft-mist silk comes in four colours only: light blue, russet, pine-green and pink. Used for bed-curtains or window gauze, from a distance it looks like smoke or mist — that's how it got its name. The pink's also called rosy-cloud gauze. Even the Imperial gauze used in the Palace today isn't so soft and fine."

"I'm not surprised Hsi-feng hadn't seen it before," interposed Aunt Hsueh. "I'd never even heard of it either."

By now a roll had been fetched on Hsi-feng's instructions.

"That's it!" exclaimed the Lady Dowager. "We used it first just for windows, then found it was good for quilts and bed-curtains too. You must get some more out tomorrow and screen the windows here with some of the pink."

Hsi-feng promised to attend to this while the whole party admired the material. As for Granny Liu, her eyes were nearly popping out of her head.

"Gracious Buddha!" she gasped. "We couldn't afford to make *clothes* of this. It seems a shame to use it for windows."

"Clothes of this don't look well," said the Lady Dowager.

Hsi-feng promptly showed them the lapel of the red gauze tunic she was wearing, saying, "Look at this tunic of mine."

"Very nice too," said the Lady Dowager and Aunt Hsueh.
"This is made nowadays for the Palace. Still, it can't compare
with the other."

"You mean to say this shoddy stuff is made for the Imperial
use?" exclaimed Hsi-feng. "Why, it's not even up to the gauze
made for officials."

"We must see if there's any more of the blue," said the Lady
Dowager. "If there is, give a couple of rolls to Granny Liu
to make a bed-curtain. What's left can be matched with some
lining and made into lined sleeveless jackets for the maids.
Don't leave it there to be spoiled by the damp."

Hsi-feng agreed, and had the stuff put away. Then the Lady
Dowager rose to her feet.

"Let's stroll on," she suggested. "Why should we stay
cooped up here?"

Invoking Buddha again, Granny Liu remarked: "Everyone
says 'The great live in great houses.' When I saw your room
yesterday, madam, it was a grand sight with all those big cases,
big wardrobes, big tables and big bed. The wardrobes alone
are bigger and higher than one of our whole *rooms*. No wonder you keep that ladder in the back yard. I couldn't think
at first what it was for, as you don't sun things on the roof.
Then I saw it must be for opening the tops of wardrobes to
take things out or put them in, for without a ladder how could
you get up? But this small room is even better furnished than
that big one, with all these fine things — whatever they're
called — in it. The more I see of it, the less I want to leave."

"I'll show you better places than this," promised Hsi-feng.

Upon leaving Bamboo Lodge they saw a punting party out
on the lake.

"Since they've got the boats ready, we may as well go
aboard," suggested the Lady Dowager.

They were on their way to Purple Caltrop Isle and Smartweed Bank when they met several matrons carrying multi-
coloured lacquered hampers inlaid with gilt designs. Hsi-feng
at once asked Lady Wang where they should breakfast.

"Wherever the old lady chooses," was the reply.

The Lady Dowager, hearing this, called over her shoulder to Hsi-feng, "Your third cousin's place is pleasant. Take some people there to get it ready while we go by boat."

Then Hsi-feng turned back with Li Wan, Tan-chun, Yuan-yang and Hu-po, accompanied by the attendants with the food. Having taken a short cut to the Studio of Autumn Freshness, they arranged the tables in Morning Emerald Hall.

Yuan-yang remarked with a chuckle, "We often say that when the gentlemen feast outside they've someone who can raise a laugh to entertain them. Today we've a female entertainer too."

Li Wan was too good-natured to catch on, but Hsi-feng knew that Granny Liu was meant.

"Yes, she should be good for some laughs today," she agreed.

Then the two of them began to lay their plans.

"You're up to no good," protested Li Wan, smiling. "As bad as children. Mind the old lady doesn't scold you!"

"You won't be involved. Just leave the old lady to me," Yuan-yang giggled.

As they were talking the rest of the party arrived. They sat where they pleased and were first served tea by the maids. Then Hsi-feng placed before each the ebony chopsticks inlaid with silver which she had brought wrapped in a cambric napkin.

"Bring that small cedar table over here," directed the Lady Dowager. "I want our kinswoman to sit next to me."

As her order was carried out Hsi-feng cast Yuan-yang a meaning glance, and the maid led Granny Liu aside to give her some whispered instructions.

"This is the custom of our house," she concluded. "If you disregard it people will laugh at you."

When all was ready they took seats at the tables. All but Aunt Hsueh who, having breakfasted already, did not eat anything but sat on one side sipping tea. The old lady had Pao-yu, Hsiang-yun, Tai-yu and Pao-chai at her table; Lady Wang had Ying-chun, Tan-chun and Hsi-chun; while Granny Liu sat at the table next to the Lady Dowager's.

Usually Yuan-yang left the younger maids to wait on the old lady during meals, holding ready her rinse bowl, whisk and handkerchief. Today, however, she held the whisk herself and the other maids kept out of the way, realizing that she meant to bait Granny Liu.

Yuan-yang, standing there, now whispered to the old woman, "Don't forget!"

"Don't worry, miss," was the answer.

Having taken her seat Granny Liu picked up the chopsticks, but found them too awkward to manage. For Hsi-feng and Yuan-yang had decided to give her an old-fashioned pair of square-edged ivory chopsticks inlaid with gold.

"Why, these prongs are heavier than our iron shovels," the old woman complained. "How can I handle them?"

As everyone laughed, a matron brought in a box and stood holding it while a maid removed the cover, revealing two bowls. Li Wan put one on the Lady Dowager's table and Hsi-feng set the other, containing pigeon's eggs, before Granny Liu. The Lady Dowager urged her to make a start.

Granny Liu stood up then and declaimed at the top of her voice:

> "Old woman Liu, I vow,
> Eats more than any cow,
> And down she settles now
> To gobble an enormous sow."

Then she dried up abruptly, puffing out her cheeks and staring down at her bowl.

The others had been staggered at first but now everyone, high and low, started roaring with laughter. Hsiang-yun shook so uncontrollably that she sputtered out the rice she had in her mouth, while Tai-yu nearly choked and collapsed over the table gasping, "Mercy!" Pao-yu fell convulsively into his grandmother's arms and she chuckled as she hugged him to her crying, "My precious!" Lady Wang wagged one finger at Hsi-feng but was laughing too much to speak. Aunt Hsueh, too, exploded in such mirth that she sprayed tea all over Tan-chun's skirt, making her upset her bowl over Ying-chun, while Hsi-chun left her seat and begged her nurse to rub her stomach for her.

As for the maids, some doubled up in hysterics, others sneaked outside to squat down in a fit of giggles, yet others controlled themselves sufficiently to fetch clean clothes for their young mistresses.

Hsi-feng and Yuan-yang, the only ones with straight faces, urged Granny Liu to eat. But when she picked up the chopsticks she still found them unwieldy.

"Even your hens here are refined," she remarked, "laying such tiny, dainty eggs as these. Well, let me fuck one of them."

This caused a fresh outburst of laughter. The Lady Dowager laughed so much that tears streamed from her eyes and Hu-po had to pat her on the back.

"That wretch Hsi-feng's up to her tricks again," she gasped. "Don't believe a word she says."

Granny Liu was still admiring the dainty eggs and saying she wanted to "fuck" one, when Hsi-feng told her merrily:

"They cost one tael of silver each. Better try one while they're hot."

The old woman reached out with her chopsticks but failed to secure an egg. After chasing them round the bowl for a time she finally succeeded in catching one; but as she craned forward to eat it, the egg slipped and fell to the floor. She hastily put down her chopsticks and stooped to retrieve it. However, a maid had already picked it up.

"A tael of silver!" Granny Liu sighed. "And gone without a sound."

The others had long since stopped eating to watch her antics.

"This isn't a formal banquet. Who gave her those chopsticks?" demanded the Lady Dowager. "This is all the doing of that minx Hsi-feng. Get her another pair."

It was, indeed, not the maids but Hsi-feng and Yuan-yang who had brought the ivory chopsticks. Now these were removed, an ebony pair inlaid with silver taking their place.

"After the gold comes the silver," observed Granny Liu. "They're not as handy, though, as the ones we use."

"If there's poison in the dish," Hsi-feng explained, "the silver will show it."

"Poison! If this food is poison, ours is pure arsenic. But I'm going to finish the lot, even if it kills me."

The Lady Dowager found her so amusing as she munched away with relish that she passed her some of her own dishes, at the same time instructing an old nurse to help Pan-erh to everything that was going.

When presently the meal ended, the Lady Dowager and some of the others adjourned to Tan-chun's bedroom for a chat while the tables were cleared and another laid for Li Wan and Hsi-feng.

Granny Liu watching this said, "Leaving everything else aside, what I like best is the way things are done in your household. No wonder they say, 'Good manners come from great households.'"

"You mustn't take offence," responded Hsi-feng quickly. "We were only having fun just now."

Yuan-yang promptly stepped forward too.

"Don't be cross, granny," she begged with a smile. "Please accept my apologies."

"What a thing to say, miss!" Granny Liu laughed. "We were trying to amuse the old lady, why should I be cross? When you tipped me off, I knew it was all in fun. If I'd been annoyed I would have kept my mouth shut."

Yuan-yang then scolded the maids for not serving granny with tea.

"That sister-in-law there brought me some just now," put in Granny Liu hastily. "No more, thank you. You ought to have your own breakfast now, miss."

"Come and eat with us," said Hsi-feng to Yuan-yang, making her sit down at their table. "That'll save another commotion later on."

So Yuan-yang sat down with them and the matrons brought an extra bowl and chopsticks. The three of them finished so soon that Granny Liu commented with a smile:

"It's a marvel to me what small appetites you have. No wonder a gust of wind can blow you over."

"What's happened to all the left-overs?" asked Yuan-yang.

"Nothing's been done with them yet," replied the matrons. "They're still waiting here to be shared out."

"There's more than enough for the people here," said Yuan-yang. "Choose two dishes for Ping-erh and send them round to Madam Lien's quarters."

"She's eaten already," put in Hsi-feng. "There's no need."

"If she doesn't eat them your cat can have them," said Yuan-yang.

A matron promptly chose two dishes and took them off in a hamper.

"Where's Su-yun?" Yuan-yang asked next.

"They'll all eat here together," said Li Wan. "Why single her out?"

"That's all right then," replied Yuan-yang.

"Hsi-jen's not here," Hsi-feng reminded her. "You might send her a couple of dishes."

Yuan-yang saw that this was done, then asked the matrons whether the boxes of titbits to go with the wine were ready yet or not. On being told that this would probably still take some time, she sent them off to expedite matters.

Hsi-feng and the others now joined the rest of the party who were chatting in Tan-chun's room. This was really three rooms in one, as Tan-chun liked plenty of space. On the big rosewood marble-topped desk in the centre were piles of albums by noted calligraphers, several dozen good inkstones and an array of jars and other containers holding a regular forest of brushes. On one side a *Ju*-ware vase the size of a peck measure was filled with chrysanthemums white as crystal balls. In the middle of the west wall hung a large painting by Mi Fei, *Mist and Rain*, flanked by a couplet in Yen Chen-ching's[1] calligraphy:

> Indolent fellow among mist and clouds,
> Rustic life amidst rocks and springs.

---

[1] See Notes 1 on pp. 28 and 532.

On another table was a large tripod. To its left, on a red sandalwood stand, a big dish of *Kuan*-ware porcelain was heaped with several dozen handsome golden Buddha's-hands. To its right, suspended on a lacquer frame, was a white jade musical stone with a small hammer next to it. Pan-erh, over the worst of his shyness now, was reaching out for the hammer to strike the jade when one of the maids quickly stopped him. Then he wanted a Buddha's-hand to eat. Tan-chun gave him one explaining that it was to play with, not to eat.

At the east end of the room stood a large bed, its leek-green gauze curtain embroidered on both sides with flowers and insects. Pan-erh ran over to have a look.

"Here's a cricket!" he exclaimed. "Here's a locust!"

Granny Liu promptly gave him a slap.

"Little wretch!" she scolded. "Pawing everything with your dirty hands. If you're allowed in to look, don't raise such a rumpus."

At this Pan-erh set up a howl and the others had to intercede to soothe him. Meanwhile the Lady Dowager had been looking through the window gauze at the back yard.

"That *wu-tung* tree under the eaves looks well," she remarked. "It's not sturdy enough though."

Just then a gust of wind carried them the strains of distant music.

"Who's having a wedding?" she asked. "We must be quite near the street here."

"Not near enough to hear sounds from the street," replied Lady Wang. "It's those child-actresses of ours rehearsing their music."

"If they're rehearsing, let's get them to do it here. It'll be a little outing for them and we'll have fun too."

Hsi-feng promptly sent for the actresses and gave orders for tables to be brought and a red carpet spread.

"No, let's use that lake pavilion by Lotus Fragrance Anchorage," proposed the Lady Dowager. "Music sounds better on the water. And we can drink in the Tower of Variegated Splendour which is roomy and within easy hearing distance."

All approved this idea.

Then with a smile to Aunt Hsueh the old lady said, "Let's go. These girls don't really welcome visitors for fear their rooms may be dirtied. We mustn't impose on them. So let's go boating and then have a few drinks."

As everyone rose to leave Tan-chun protested, "What a thing to say! We only wish you'd come more often."

"Yes, my third grand-daughter's good that way," said the old lady. "It's Tai-yu and Pao-yu who are so pernickety. On our way back, when we're tipsy, we must go there just to annoy them."

They trooped out, laughing, and soon reached Watercress Isle where some boatwomen from Soochow had punted two pyrus-wood boats. Into one of these they helped the Lady Dowager, Lady Wang, Aunt Hsueh, Granny Liu, Yuan-yang and Yu-chuan. Li Wan followed them and so did Hsi-feng, who took her stand in the prow meaning to punt.

"It's not as easy as it looks!" warned the Lady Dowager from the cabin. "We're not on the river, it's true, but it's fairly deep here. So don't try, and come inside at once."

"It's quite safe," cried Hsi-feng. "Don't worry, Old Ancestress."

She pushed off with a shove for the middle of the lake, but when the small overloaded boat started rocking she thrust the pole into the hands of a boatwoman and hastily squatted down.

Ying-chun and the other girls followed in the second boat with Pao-yu, while the rest of the attendants walked along the bank.

"How disgusting those withered lotus leaves look," remarked Pao-yu. "Why not get people to pull them out?"

"What time has there been for that?" countered Pao-chai with a smile. "We've been out here enjoying ourselves every day recently."

CHAPTER 40   593

Tai-yu put in, "I don't like Li Shang-yin's[1] verses except for that single line:

> 'Leave the withered lotus to hear the patter of rain.'

But now you two don't want to leave them."

"That's a good line," agreed Pao-yu. "All right, we won't have them pulled out."

They had now reached Reed Creek by Flowery Harbour. In the shade here chill penetrated their very bones, while their awareness of autumn was heightened by the withered grass and caltrops on both sides. The Lady Dowager fixed her eyes on the airy lodge on the bank.

"Isn't that where Pao-chai lives?" she asked.

They told her it was.

At once she ordered the boats to go alongside and, climbing the stone steps to Alpinia Park, they were greeted by a strange fragrance. The advance of autumn had deepened the green of the rare plants and creepers there, from each of which hung charming clusters of berries like coral beads. The room which they now entered was spotless as a snow cave, with hardly an ornament in the whole place. The desk was bare except for a rough crackleware vase with some chrysanthemums in it, two sets of books and a tea-service. The blue gauze bed-curtains and bedding were also of the simplest.

"What a goose this child is!" cried the Lady Dowager. "Why not ask your aunt for some knick-knacks? It didn't occur to me, I just didn't think. Of course you left all your own things at home."

Having told Yuan-yang to be sure to fetch some curios, she called Hsi-feng to task.

"Why didn't you send over some pretty things for your cousin? How very stingy!"

"She wouldn't have them," explained Lady Wang and Hsi-feng. "She returned all the ones we sent."

"She doesn't care for such things at home either," put in Aunt Hsueh.

---

[1] A Tang Dynasty poet.

"This will never do." The old lady shook her head. "She may have simple tastes, but this wouldn't look well if relatives were to call. Besides, it'll bring bad luck for girls, this austerity. Why, in that case we old women ought to live in stables! You've all heard those descriptions in ballads and operas of the elegance of young ladies' boudoirs. Maybe these girls of ours can't compare with those young ladies, but they shouldn't go to the other extreme either. When we've knick-knacks ready at hand why not display them? Of course, if your tastes are simple you can have less.

"I used to have a flair for decorating rooms, but now that I'm old I haven't the energy. These girls should learn how to fix up their rooms too. The only trouble is if you've a vulgar taste, for then you'll make even handsome things look frightful; but I wouldn't call our girls vulgar. Now let me fit out this room for you, and I promise it'll be in quiet yet excellent taste. I've a couple of nice things which I've managed to keep by not allowing Pao-yu to set eyes on them — if he had, they'd have disappeared."

She called Yuan-yang over and ordered, "Fetch that miniature rock garden, that little gauze screen and the dark steatite tripod. Those three things will do nicely for the desk. And fetch those white silk bed-curtains with the ink painting and calligraphy in place of these."

"Very good, madam," said Yuan-yang. "But those things are in some cases in the east attic. They may take a little finding. Suppose I get them tomorrow?"

"Tomorrow or the day after, it doesn't matter. Don't forget, that's all."

After sitting a little longer they went on to the Tower of Variegated Splendour, where Wen-kuan and the other young actresses paid their respects and asked which tunes they should play.

"Just choose a few you want to rehearse," replied the Lady Dowager.

Thereupon the actresses withdrew to Lotus Fragrance Anchorage.

By now Hsi-feng and her helpers had everything in perfect order. There were two couches on the north side, left and right, spread with brocade cushions and velvet coverlets. In front of each couch stood two carved lacquer teapoys of different shapes with pyrus-blossom, plum-blossom, lotus and sunflower designs, some square, some round, one of which held an incense-burner, a vase and a box of various sweetmeats. The other was empty, ready for their favourite dishes. These two couches with four teapoys were for the Lady Dowager and Aunt Hsueh. Then there were a chair and two teapoys for Lady Wang, while the others had one chair and teapoy apiece. Granny Liu's seat was on the east; below it was that of Lady Wang.

On the west sat Hsiang-yun, Pao-chai, Tai-yu, Ying-chun, Tan-chun and Hsi-chun in that order with, last of all, Pao-yu. Li Wan and Hsi-feng had seats outside the inner screen, within the third row of balustrades. The designs on the comfit-boxes matched those of the teapoys. Everyone also had a tarnished silver wine-pot with engraved designs and a variegated cloisonné cup.

As soon as the party was seated the Lady Dowager proposed, "Let's begin with a few cups of wine. It would be fun to play a drinking game."

"I know you're good at drinking games, madam," chuckled Aunt Hsueh. "But how can *we* play them? If you just want to get us drunk, let's simply drink a few cups more apiece."

"How modest you are today!" retorted the Lady Dowager. "Do you find me too old for this company?"

"I'm not being modest. I'm afraid of getting laughed at for giving the wrong answer."

"Even if we can't answer," interposed Lady Wang, "it only means drinking an extra cup. And anyone feeling tipsy can go and lie down. No one will laugh at us."

"Very well then," Aunt Hsueh agreed. "But you must start off with a cup, madam."

"Of course."

The Lady Dowager drained her cup.

Hsi-feng stepped forward to propose, "If we're to have a game, let Yuan-yang take charge."

The whole party agreed, knowing that it was always Yuan-yang who made the rules for the old lady's drinking games. So Hsi-feng made her join them.

"If you're joining in, there's no reason why you should stand," said Lady Wang. She then ordered a young maid to fetch a chair and put it by Hsi-feng's or Li Wan's table.

After making a show of declining, Yuan-yang took the seat with thanks and drank a cup, after which she announced:

"Drinking rules are as strict as martial law. Now that I'm in charge I'll be no respecter of persons — anybody who disobeys me must pay a forfeit."

The others smiled and Lady Wang said, "Of course. Hurry up and tell us the rules."

But before Yuan-yang could speak Granny Liu left her seat, waving one hand in protest.

"Don't make fun of me like this. I'm leaving," she declared.

"That won't do," chuckled the others.

Yuan-yang ordered some maids to drag Granny Liu back to her table. They did so, giggling, while she pleaded to be let off.

"Anybody who speaks out of turn again will be made to drink a whole pot of wine," warned Yuan-yang.

At this the old woman held her peace.

"I shall use three dominoes," announced Yuan-yang. "We'll start with the old lady and go round in turn, ending with Granny Liu. For example, I'll take a set of three dominoes and read out what's on each of the three in turn, ending with the name of the set. You must say either a line of classical poetry, a proverb or an adage after each; and they must rhyme. A cup of wine is the forfeit for any mistake."

Laughingly they all approved and begged her to start.

"Here's a set," said Yuan-yang. "On the left is the 'sky.'"

"The sky is blue on high," responded the Lady Dowager.

"Bravo!" applauded the others.

"In the centre's a 'five and six,'" Yuan-yang continued.

"Six bridges with the scent of plum admix."

"The last piece is 'six and one.' "

"From fleecy clouds rises a round red sun."

"Together they make a 'ghost distraught.' "

"By his leg the ghost-catcher he's caught."

While the whole party laughed and cheered, the Lady Dowager tossed off a cup of wine.

Then Yuan-yang resumed, "Here's another set. The one on the left is a 'double five.' "

Aunt Hsueh responded: "Plum blossom dances when soft winds arrive."

"A 'double five' again here on the right."

"In the tenth month plum blossom scents the height."

"In the middle 'two and five' make seven."

"The Weaving Maid and Cowherd[1] meet in Heaven."

"The whole: O'er the Five Peaks the young god wends his way."

"Immortal joys are barred to mortal clay."

All applauded Aunt Hsueh's performance and she drank a cup.

"Here's another set," said Yuan-yang. "On the left 'two aces' combine."

Hsiang-yun capped this: "The sun and moon on earth and heaven shine."

Yuan-yang continued, "On the right 'double aces' are found."

"The idle flowers fall, noiseless, to the ground."

"In the middle, a 'four and a one.' "

"Red apricot leans on clouds beside the sun."

"Together: The cherries ripen nine times in all."

"Birds in the Palace orchard make them fall."

Her turn finished, Hsiang-yun drained her cup.

"Next one," said Yuan-yang. "On the left is a 'double three.' "

Pao-chai responded, "Pairs of swallows chirp merrily."

---

[1] Names of constellations in Chinese astronomy. According to Chinese folklore, the Weaving Maid and the Cowherd were lovers.

"Another 'double three' upon the right."

"The wind-trailed weeds seem belts of malachite."

"In the middle, 'three and six' make nine."

"Three hills across the azure sky incline."

"Together: A lonely boat moored by a chain."

"The wind and waves bring sorrow in their train."

In conclusion Pao-chai drank her wine.

Yuan-yang resumed, "The sign of 'heaven' on the left."

Tai-yu answered, "A fair season, a season bereft."[1]

Pao-chai turned to dart her a glance, but for fear of a penalty Tai-yu ignored her.

Yuan-yang continued, "In the middle a 'screen' finely wrought."

"No maid a message to the gauze window has brought."[2]

"That leaves only eight, by 'two and six' shown."

"Together they pay homage at the jade throne."

"Combined: A basket in which to gather posies."

"On her fairy wand she carries peonies."

Having finished her turn Tai-yu took a sip of wine.

Yuan-yang went on, "On the left, 'four and five' make nine."

Ying-chun responded, "The peach blossom is heavy with rain."

"Fine her! Fine her!" cried the others. "That doesn't rhyme. Besides, why peach blossom?"

Ying-chun smiled and took a sip. The fact is that Hsi-feng and Yuan-yang were so eager to hear Granny Liu make a fool of herself that they had urged the others to give wrong answers, so that all were fined. When it came to Lady Wang's turn, Yuan-yang answered for her. Then it was Granny Liu's turn.

"We country folk sometimes get together and play this when we've nothing better to do," said the old woman. "Mind you, our answers aren't so fine-sounding as yours. Still, I suppose I must try."

---

[1] A line from the Ming drama *The Peony Pavilion*.

[2] A line from the Yuan drama *The Western Chamber*.

"It's easy," they assured her. "Just go ahead, it doesn't matter."

Smiling, Yuan-yang announced, "On the left, 'four and four' make a man."

Granny Liu thought this over, then suggested, "A farmer?"

The company roared with laughter.

"Good," the Lady Dowager encouraged her. "That's the style."

"We country people can only talk about the things we know," said Granny Liu, laughing herself. "You mustn't make fun of me."

Yuan-yang continued, " 'Three and four,' green and red, in the centre."

"A big fire burns the hairy caterpillar."

The others chortled, "That's right. Go on in your own way."

Yuan-yang said, "On the right a really fine 'double ace.' "

"A turnip and head of garlic in one place."

Giggles broke out again.

Yuan-yang went on, "They make up 'flowers' in all."

Gesturing with both hands Granny Liu responded, "And a huge pumpkin forms when the flowers fall."

The others were shaking with laughter when they heard a commotion outside. What had happened will be told in the next chapter.

图书在版编目(CIP)数据

红楼梦 第一卷:英文/(清)曹雪芹,(清)高鹗著.
北京:外文出版社,1995
ISBN 7 - 119 - 01643 - 1

Ⅰ.红… Ⅱ.①曹…②高… Ⅲ.古典小说:章回小说:长篇小说
—中国—古代—英文 Ⅳ.I242.4

中国版本图书馆 CIP 数据核字 (95) 第 08461 号

红楼梦

(一)

曹雪芹 高 鹗 著

杨宪益 戴乃迭 译

*

©外文出版社
外文出版社出版
(中国北京百万庄路 24 号)
邮政编码 100037
北京外文印刷厂印刷
中国国际图书贸易总公司发行
(中国北京车公庄西路 35 号)
北京邮政信箱第 399 号 邮政编码 100044
1978 年(28 开)第一版
1995 年第一版三次印刷
(英)
ISBN 7 - 119 - 01643 - 1 /I·329(外)
10 - E - 1424SA